*To Matt,*
*The whole story!*

# Coach For A Nation
## The Life and Times of
## KNUTE ROCKNE

*Go IRISH!*

## Jim Lefebvre *Jim Lefebvre*

Author of the award-winning
*Loyal Sons: The Story of The Four Horsemen
and Notre Dame Football's 1924 Champions*

Great Day Press
Minneapolis

# Coach For A Nation
## The Life and Times of Knute Rockne

For More Information Contact:
Info@CoachForANation.com


Printed and bound in the United States
Using Soy Based Inks and Recycled Paper (10% PCW)
By Worzalla Publishing Co.
www.worzalla.com

Softcover Printing—December 2014

ISBN-13: 978-0-9818841-4-1

Library of Congress Control Number: 2013947422

Photographs courtesy of University of Notre Dame Archives
Cover design by Phil Velikan


Coach For A Nation is Distributed by:

Cardinal Publishers Group
2402 N. Shadeland Ave., Suite A
Indianapolis, IN 46219
800-296-0481
www.cardinalpub.com

# Table Of Contents

1.   Saying Goodbye ........................................................... 1
2.   Beginnings ................................................................... 11
3.   Chicago Beckons ........................................................ 27
4.   A Dazzling White City................................................ 39
5.   Football Comes West ................................................. 50
6.   A Family's Life ............................................................ 63
7.   Two-Fold Education ................................................... 76
8.   Making His Move........................................................ 88
9.   A 22-Year-Old Freshman............................................ 102
10.  Establishing Roots...................................................... 116
11.  Reaching the Big Stage .............................................. 131
12.  No Looking Back .........................................................147
13.  Becoming A Coach .....................................................161
14.  The World, The Nation, The University ..................... 180
15.  Star Power................................................................... 192
16.  A Year Unlike Any Other............................................. 209
17.  Back To The Old Days................................................. 225
18.  New Era Begins........................................................... 244
19.  Birth of a Backfield..................................................... 262
20.  Football Machine ........................................................ 279
21.  Defending the Faith.................................................... 296
22.  Outlined Against ........................................................ 312
23.  Run For The Roses ..................................................... 329
24.  After the Horsemen..................................................... 353
25.  Traveling Man ............................................................. 373
26.  High Flying.................................................................. 385
27.  The Decade Roars On.................................................. 398
28.  Rockne's Ramblers ..................................................... 414
29.  Perfection Again ......................................................... 428
30.  The Final Ride ............................................................. 443
     Epilogue......................................................................459
     Appendices .................................................................464
     Acknowledgements .....................................................479
     Bibliography ...............................................................481
     Notes ..........................................................................485
     Index............................................................................495

*For all coaches and teachers
with a passion for improving
the lives of our young people*

# Preface

Rockne.

There was a time in America, in the first third of the 20th century, when the name was a household word. It meant excellence in athletics, true enough, but it meant something more—an effervescent joy for living, a quick wit and an eager grin. An optimistic view of life, seeing the best in the next fellow, and moving forward. Always moving forward.

Knute Kenneth Rockne lived an extraordinary life, growing from an immigrant child to scale the heights of fame in a nation bursting with innovation, excitement, and advancements. He marveled at the technology of the Columbian World Exposition in his new hometown of Chicago. From there, he discovered the unbridled joy of competition through organized sports, first track and field and then football.

To Rockne, sports were always a means to an end, not an end in themselves. They were a way of testing one's self, and of measuring self-improvement, discipline, and dedication. They offered an opportunity to work in cooperation with others, honoring their strengths, while competing against opponents, and valuing the challenge they presented. A student of the ancient cultures, he subscribed to the Greeks' athletic ideal—the harmony of mind and body, the melding of the physical and spiritual, and the view of physical fitness as a civic duty, a contribution to the fabric of the larger society. The Greeks valued fluid motion over sheer muscle, often performed exercise to music, and found artistic style in athletics—all themes that resonated with Rockne.

It wasn't enough to feel and understand this ideal. It had to be shared, it had to be taught to others. And so we find Rockne the adventurer, continually walking through fear or doubt, to meet new people, places, and experiences. It was said of Rockne by fellow Scandinavian and poet Carl Sandburg, "The pure Norse strain made it inevitable for Rockne to push outward whenever he was conscious of a limit." A 22-year-old Protestant without a high school diploma heading off to the Catholic stronghold, the University of Notre Dame? It was just another challenge for Rockne. He mirrored the indomitable spirit of Father Edward Sorin, who in 1842 viewed a desolate spot in rural northern Indiana and proclaimed he would there build a great university. Rockne, who eventually converted to Catholicism, did more to animate millions of Catholic immigrants to a sense of pride and possibility, it could be argued, than anyone of his era.

As a football coach, Rockne's success was unprecedented. He posted a winning percentage that has stood atop college football for decades. He helped usher in a new game, one that rewarded quickness, precision, and deception over brute force and "mass play." But he didn't claim to have invented anything. He always gave credit to his college coach, Jesse Harper, who he said brought the game from Amos Alonzo Stagg at the University of Chicago, who in turn brought it from its true origins, under Walter Camp at Yale. What Rockne did was perfect the process, and market the result. His relationships with the newspapermen, his willingness to take his team from coast to coast, his writings and coaching schools all helped create a near-mythic connection to fans and friends everywhere.

Rockne squeezed as much life out of every 24 hours as was humanly possible. When illness laid him low, he said, "I'm not built for an invalid's routine. If you clip the wild duck's wings, he pines away and dies. I, too, must fly until I fall."

Here is the story of how he did it.

# 1

## Saying Goodbye

Holy Saturday, April 4, 1931 dawned breezy and overcast in South Bend, Indiana. About a mile east of downtown, in a growing neighborhood of handsome homes, a classic looking Tudor house on East Wayne Street seemed to have a mountain of flowers growing on its west wall. A pair of uniformed officers stood sentinel as day broke. Inside, in the comfortable sitting room framed by rich woodwork, a coffin held the remains of the home's owner, Knute Kenneth Rockne. The day before, in a chilly, drizzling rain on Good Friday, thousands of people streamed past the home, walking slowly but steadily while admiring the many hundreds of floral arrangements piled alongside the house, their ribbons floating in a gentle breeze. Every few minutes, two or three or more people would exit a vehicle, approach the house, and enter. Friends, players Rockne had played alongside and coached in his 21 football seasons at the University of Notre Dame, members of the sporting world. In the sitting room, four Notre Dame men stood straight as soldiers behind the casket, an honor guard of silent respect.

Elsewhere about the room, standing nearly as still, were men like Hunk Anderson, the coach's assistant and confidante, and Adam Walsh, strapping captain of the 1924 national football champions. They greeted visitors mostly with a firm handshake and a solemn gaze, the lump in their throats too great to allow words to pass. Strong men, big men, wanting to cry, but holding back tears. Their feelings for this man who was their mentor, their idol, and their friend remained held inside as they quietly greeted well-wishers. The room, like the yard outside, was overfilled with floral wreaths. On the wall, overlooking the closed casket, was a beautiful oil portrait of the coach, who had turned 43 exactly one month earlier. Now, four days after his death in a plane crash amid the Flint Hills of eastern Kansas, he was back in the comfortable home he shared with his wife Bonnie and their four children. They had lived there just a little more than a year, the perfect refuge from the many demands on his schedule.

For the Rocknes, the past four days had unfolded like a bizarre dream, one which had no ending. The two oldest sons, Bill, 14, and Knute Jr., 11, had just missed seeing their father. Their train back from spring vacation in Florida to Kansas City, where they attended the Pembroke School, was delayed, and their father departed on what became his final flight. On Wednesday, they boarded a train in Kansas City, which carried their father's casket, accompanied by Dr. Mike Nigro, the coach's long-time friend from his days as an undergraduate at Notre Dame, and Coach H.H. Francis, the boys' athletic director at Pembroke. Throughout the journey, some of Rockne's friends stood alongside the gray metallic box, holding the casket as the train rocked along. Doc Nigro had not left his friend's body since it had been brought from the crash site near Bazaar, Kansas to the funeral home in nearby Cottonwood Falls. The traveling party increased in size when four men from South Bend joined it—assistant coaches Hunk Anderson and Jack Chevigny; Father Michael Mulcaire, vice president of Notre Dame and chairman of the faculty athletic board; and Howard "Cap" Edwards, long one of Rockne's closest associates.

The train continued on the Santa Fe route, reaching a large, respectful crowd in Chicago on Wednesday evening. The body was transferred to a New York Central train leaving for South Bend at 9:15 p.m. At Michigan City and Gary, as was the case with every station since leaving Kansas, crowds jammed the platform trying to get a glimpse of the casket. In South Bend, a crowd gathered at the Union station shortly after 10:00 p.m., an hour before the train was due. In minutes, hundreds packed the waiting room; parking spots had been filled for blocks in every direction. So many times over the past two decades, crowds similar to this had filled one or the other of South Bend's stations, waiting eagerly to greet and cheer a Notre Dame football team returning from another glorious victory or, in a few cases, a valiant attempt in defeat. This time, the growing mass of humanity was different. Any talking was done in hushed tones. A tension permeated the crowd. Notre Dame students, especially, bore faces filled with sadness, having little to say to one another, still in shock.

Just after 11 p.m., a railway employee announced the approach of the train from Chicago. The murmuring of voices stopped, and the throng in the interior of the station pushed toward the corridor leading to the track stairways. But only a small group was permitted on the platform. They included Mayor W. R. Hinkle and city council members; Frank Hering, president of the Notre Dame Alumni Association; A. R. Erskine, president of the Studebaker Corporation and chairman of the Notre Dame board of lay trustees; Adam Walsh; Frank Coughlin; and the Reverend Charles L. O'Donnell, C.S.C., president of the university. As the train eased to a stop, Father O'Donnell stepped forward to the baggage car and gazed in silence at the casket carrying Notre Dame's beloved coach. Scores of Notre Dame football men and other students formed a cordon around the car as the casket was lowered and placed in a hearse, headed for the McGann Funeral Home on North Michigan Street. The crowd of friends, neighbors, intimate associates, and adoring fans had a hard time believing what they were seeing. Even as the casket was carried from the train, their focus was on a man they thought would live forever just as they had always known him—active, animated, with a mind always looking forward, always on the move.

The next evening, Thursday, April 2, another train from Chicago carried the other major players in this drama. Bonnie Rockne and her two younger children, Mary Jeanne and Jack, had traveled from Miami, where Knute had left them just a few days earlier. There, Mrs. Martha Rockne, the coach's mother, and three of his sisters, all residents of Chicago, joined them. They traveled to South Bend accompanied by Father John O'Hara, long-time university official and friend of the coach, who had been such an integral part of that triumphant 1924 year. Arriving in South Bend, the group went directly to the Rockne home on East Wayne.

For three days, tributes flowed from around the world of athletics, politics, and business—by telegram, statements to the press, and editorials in newspapers. Said Cornell football coach Gil Dobie, "With his passing, football loses its most powerful advocate." Chick Meehan, president of the American Football Coaches Association of whom Rockne was a charter member, noted, "Knute Rockne was the finest character and greatest leader football ever knew." And Stanford's Glenn "Pop" Warner, who had matched wits with Rockne in the 1925 Rose Bowl classic added, "He will be greatly missed everywhere." Northwestern's Dick Hanley, another coaching comrade, summed up Rockne's impact on the sport. "Knute Rockne's death is the greatest loss athletics ever has suffered. Rockne took football to the public…Rockne and the spirit of Rockne popularized the sport. Teams which opposed Notre Dame's great eleven of 1929 observed that spirit of Rockne, whose boys, when their tutor was unable to direct them personally on account of illness, went out and fought to their limit to show their affection and loyalty for their great leader. We learned to know Rockne personally and to appreciate the spirit of fair play, magnanimity, and generosity of sportsmanship which typified him."

King Haakon of Norway cabled the Norwegian consul, Olaf Bernts, in Chicago, delegating him to attend services as the official representative of the crown of Norway. It was said the king had planned to bestow the symbol of Norwegian Knighthood on the coach in the coming months. Studebaker's Erskine, who had only recently made Rockne his company's vice president for sales promotion, hailed the coach as "a great citizen who brought fame to South Bend…but at least we have the inspiration of his work and his example." Indiana Governor Harry Leslie said, "The name of Knute Rockne is synonymous with clean sportsmanship and virile manhood." Ring Lardner, who went from a simple boyhood in nearby Niles, Michigan to fame as a New York writer, said, "The whole country will miss him." The humblest of citizens joined the chorus of those grieving. A railroad switchman, who in his own small way idolized the Rock of Notre Dame, sent his heartfelt tribute scrawled in pencil. At churches in South Bend and across the nation, young and old prayed for the repose of Rockne's soul.

On Friday afternoon, Bonnie Rockne walked over the slopes of Highland Cemetery, selecting the exact plot where her husband would be buried. Accompanying her were Knute's mother; Jesse Harper, Rockne's coach at Notre Dame from 1913; George Keogan, the university's basketball coach; and Dr. Nigro, always available for wise counsel and support. Headed to South Bend from all points on the compass were classmates and former players of Rockne's, along with many of the leaders of athletics. "It is a gloomy homecoming for hundreds of former players and coaches who have come here to tender tribute to their old master," one report noted. "The lighter thought is missing in conversation and old friends who have not seen each other for years exchange glances in silence." Members of Notre Dame's class of 1914—Rockne's class—were chosen to serve as an honor guard. Close friends Joe Byrne and Walter Clements. Johnny Plant, a fellow trackman from Chicago who had been so instrumental in convincing Rockne to attend Notre Dame, and fellow football standouts Al Feeney, Ray Eichenlaub, Freeman Fitzgerald, Mal Elward, Ralph Lathrop, Fred Gushurst, and Bunny Larkin. And of course, Rockne's great friend and passing mate, Gus Dorais.

They and so many others came to pay their respects, visiting East Wayne Street on Good Friday. Coach Harper, and Jimmy Phelan, Charlie Bachman, and Skip Madigan, now nationally famous coaches themselves. Norman Barry, known in Chicago for coaching championship teams in high school and pro ball while launching a successful law career. Roger Kiley, Eddie Anderson, Chet Wynne, Art Parisien, Paul Castner—all heroes of former years, back to honor the coach who taught them how to be men. And also arriving were the four backs whom Rockne called, of all his stars, the closest to his heart—Jim Crowley, Elmer Layden, Harry Stuhldreher, and Don Miller, the famous Four Horsemen. The more recent stars, Frank Carideo, Marchy Schwartz, Moon Mullins, and many others took turns standing silent vigil over the coffin in two-hour shifts.

Some 140 men were named honorary pallbearers. These included Rockne's friend Tom Hickey, his next-door neighbor for several years on St. Vincent Street, and several other South Bend residents, among them O. A. Clark, Mike Calnon, Paul Hoffman, George Hull, and Bernard Voll. There were fellow coaches who came from all points on the map, much the way Rockne had ventured out to meet them in their locations. The list included Howard Jones of Southern Cal, Wally Steffen of Carnegie Tech, Bill Alexander of Georgia Tech, Paul Schissler of Oregon State College,

D. X. Bible of Nebraska. Jesse Harper and Doc Meanwell, of course, along with Major John Griffith, commissioner of the Big Ten. Other dignitaries included New York Mayor Jimmy Walker. A team of newspaper men, including Warren Brown, Jimmy Corcoran, Harvey Woodruff, and Frank Wallace. The "old guard" men, Warren Cartier and Frank Hering. And long-time friends Jay Wyatt, Leo Ward, and Byron Kanaley.

Bonnie Rockne, it was reported, "deeply wounded and crushed by the tragedy, came home bravely and faced the task of laying her famous husband to rest, with striking courage. Her only desires were for simplicity and to do the things 'Rock' would have liked. He was a national figure, but she brushed aside all suggestions of an elaborate ceremony. She wanted him at home, his boys with him, and then to take him to his grave with quiet dignity. It was a contrast in restfulness compared with his own rushing, busy life." Shortly after noon on Holy Saturday, lines of automobiles picked up the out-of-town guests from South Bend hotels and ferried them to East Wayne Street. There, the greatest collection of Notre Dame football stars ever assembled milled about, sprinkled with representatives of numerous other universities and communities that had hosted Rockne in his extensive travels, and several of the newspapermen who so enjoyed his repartee.

The clouds had broken and sunlight illuminated the tremendous display of flowers alongside the Rockne home. The air now felt soft, with the harshness of winter gone. Life in the trees and in the soil was poised to bloom. On a day of such terrible sadness, the promise of new life seemed to envelop the scene. Inside the Rockne home, Bonnie Rockne led her four children into the sitting room to bid their father farewell. She stroked the sides of the casket and kissed the crucifix fastened to the top. Billy, Knute Jr., Jeanne, and Jackie did the same. Outside, the honorary pallbearers began to form in ranks six deep along the sidewalk. The whispering died away, until the only sounds were the scuffling of someone's shoes, or the rustling of branches in the young birch trees in the Rockne's yard. At the appointed moment, the door of the Rockne home swung open, and six leading members of the 1930 national championship Fighting Irish—Frank Carideo, Marchy Schwartz, Moon Mullins, Marty Brill, Tom Conley, and Tommy Yarr—all fighting back tears, respectfully carried the coffin of their late coach, draped in the blue and gold of a Notre Dame football blanket. They lovingly transported it down the steps, along the sidewalk, and into a waiting hearse. A moment later, Bonnie Rockne came from the home, aided by Jack Chevigny and Doc Nigro. She trembled, the black mourning veil only partially hiding her tears. Then, sensing the great crowd gathered, she straightened up, and walked swiftly to the waiting car.

In minutes, the afternoon sun glistened like a long, shiny ribbon on the tops of more than 100 automobiles that rolled in a procession toward the Notre Dame campus. More than a mile long, the line of cars stretched behind an escort of sputtering motorcycles, carrying South Bend city police in blue and Indiana State Police in olive. Tens of thousands of onlookers, many local but many others who had traveled to South Bend for the historic occasion, lined the route. Shops, businesses, and offices in South Bend and Mishawaka were closed to allow citizens to view the proceedings. With the new football stadium, Rockne's home for just one season, visible just off to the east, the procession rolled up Notre Dame Avenue, with its twin flanks of trees pointing the way to the center of campus. A bell in the single spire of Sacred Heart Church tolled as the cortege approached. The cars swept past the golden-domed Main Building and swung in front of Sacred Heart. At the end of the procession of vehicles, the hearse bearing Rockne pulled up, and again his pallbearers swung into action. The tolling bell and the voices of radio announcers quietly describing the scene were the only sounds as Rockne's casket was carried into the church.

At the door of the church, Bishop John Francis Noll, leader of the Fort Wayne diocese, and Father Michael Mulcaire, vice president of the university, met the casket, while the Moreau Choir filled the church with the sounds of *Miserere*, 50 voices "swelling and receding with all the cadences of an organ." With room for only 1,400 in the church, several thousand mourners gathered outside. Loudspeakers set up on the porch of the Administration Building carried the sounds of the chants and the voices of the services to the crowd. And as the Columbia Broadcasting Company had obtained permission to transmit the services, the final goodbye was broadcast around the world.

There would be no funeral Mass; a ritual not celebrated by the Catholic Church on Holy Saturday. The highlight of the service would be the sermon presented by university president Father O'Donnell. He began by reciting Psalm 133 and a line of scripture that says, "Blessed are the dead who die in the Lord." His voice trembled with emotion at times, clearly shaken by the loss of his friend. Among his words:

> In this holy week of Christ's passion and death there has occurred a tragic event which accounts for our presence here today. Knute Rockne is dead. And who was he? Ask the President of the United States, who dispatched a personal message of tribute to his memory and comfort to his bereaved family. Ask the King of Norway, who sends a special delegation as his personal representative to this solemn service. Ask the several State legislatures, now sitting, that have passed resolutions of sympathy and condolence. Ask the university senates, the civic bodies and societies without number; ask the bishops, the clergy, the religious orders, that have sent assurances of sympathy and prayers; ask the thousands of newspaper men, whose labor of love in his memory has stirred a reading public of 125,000,000 Americans; ask men and women from every walk of life; ask the children, the boys of America, ask any and all of these, who was this man whose death has struck the nation with dismay and has everywhere bowed heads in grief?
>
> Was he perhaps a martyr who died for some great cause, a patriot who laid down his life for his country, a statesman, a soldier, an admiral of the fleet, some heaven-born artist, an inventor, a captain of industry or finance? No, he was Knute Rockne, director of athletics and football coach at Notre Dame. He was a man of the people, a husband and father, a citizen of South Bend, Indiana. Yet, had he been any one of these personages that have been mentioned, the tributes of admiration and affection, which he has received, could not be more universal or more sincere.
>
> How is this fact to be accounted for? What was the secret of his irresistible appeal to all sorts and conditions of men? Who shall pluck out the heart of his mystery and lay bare the inner source of the power he had? When we say simply, he was

a great American, we shall go far towards satisfying many, for all of us recognize and love the attributes of the true American character. When we say that he was an inspirer of young men in the direction of high ideals that were conspicuously exemplified in his own life, we have covered much that unquestionably was true of him. When we link his name with the intrinsic chivalry and romance of a great college game, which he, perhaps, more than any other one man, has made finer and cleaner in itself and larger in its popular appeal, here, too, we touch upon a vital point....

I think, supremely he loved his neighbor, his fellow man, with a genuine, deep love. In an age that has stamped itself as the era of the 'go-getter'—a horrible word for what is all too often a ruthless thing—he was a 'go-giver'....

It is fitting he should be brought here to his beloved Notre Dame and that his body should rest a little while in this church where the light of Faith broke upon his happy soul, where the waters of Baptism were poured on his brow, where he made his first confession, received his first Holy Communion, and was confirmed by the same consecrated hand that today is raised in blessing above his coffin. He might have gone to any university in the land and been gladly received and forever cherished there. But he chose Our Lady's school, Notre Dame. He honored her in his life as a student, he honored her in the monogram he earned and wore, he honored her in the principles he inculcated and the ideals he set up in the lives of the young men under his care. He was her own true son.

O'Donnell's voice cracked with emotion, and his words slowed, as if he didn't want to finish. But the final blessing came. "Eternal rest grant upon him, O Lord, and let perpetual light shine upon him. May his soul and the souls of all the faithful departed through the mercy of God rest in peace. Amen."

Two hours before dusk set upon the area, the procession started again, headed to Highland Cemetery. The line of cars stretched longer than before, with thousands on the sidewalks straining for a look at the cortege. For blocks, hundreds of cars were parked, their passengers flocking through the cemetery toward the Council Oak. There, centuries before, the great meetings of LaSalle and Tonti with the Potawatomi took place; the Jesuits Allouez and Marquette also likely engaged in councils at this spot. Now, just a stone's throw away, a modern-day explorer was about to be laid to rest. An area was roped off from the eager crowds, and a great wall of floral tributes adorned the spot. Large Notre Dame monograms of gold and blue blooms provided a colorful background. Workers from the Chicago Post Office sent a special display, remembering Rockne's years as an employee there. As the six young men brought the casket to its final resting spot, dozens of other friends, former players, and coaches gathered around the grave. Bonnie followed the casket, supported by Jack Chevigny and Dr. Nigro as she stood at the edge of the grave. Nearby were his mother, all four of his sisters, and closest friends.

Father O'Donnell stepped to the edge of the grave, sprinkled the casket with holy water, and spoke the final prayers, with murmured responses from those assembled. In just a few minutes the simple service was finished. Bonnie turned from the grave, just as an airplane roared overhead, outlined against the approaching dusk. The bronze casket was slowly lowered into the ground, as the crowd turned to leave. But two men looked down into the grave, until the casket finally rested in place. Jack Cannon and John Law, two of the greatest of Rockne's men, would stay, watching, maybe still not believing it all was real, till the last moment. Two of the toughest men on the gridiron it had been Rockne's privilege to coach. And now, both stood there, tears streaming down their faces. They still couldn't believe it. Knute Rockne was gone.

# 2
## Beginnings

In southwestern Norway, about 50 kilometers inland from the sea, sits the area of Vossegangen. Its snow-capped mountains, fertile valleys, dense forests, verdant fields, shimmering lakes, and swift-flowing rivers create an outdoor wonderland. At the center is the village of Voss, anchored by a stone church built in 1277, and the nearby Finnesloftet, a wooden guildhall that also dates to the 13th century. It is said that none other than King Olav, who would become St. Olaf, converted residents of Voss to Christianity. In the late 19th century, the 5,000 Voss residents were intimately connected to the land, working to extract what it could offer in terms of sustenance. The land also provided recreation in countless ways—hiking, swimming, and boating in the summer; skiing, skating, sledding, and otherwise enjoying the snow and ice of the long winter. It was here in the late-winter chill of March 4, 1888 that Knute Rokne was born. He was the second child of Lars Knutson Rokne and Martha Gjermo Rokne, joining sister Anna, four years older. The family rejoiced over the addition of healthy Knute (whose name they pronounced Ka-nute). Lars could not hide his pleasure over being blessed with a son who could someday take over the family business.

The Roknes of Voss had sunk down deep roots in the area—for gen-

11

erations they had operated farms in the valleys outside the village proper—but their hard work and ingenuity could not be contained. Young
Knute's great-grandfather, Knute L. Rokne, in addition to farming, exhibited a fine skill for repair work and became a blacksmith tending to the
equipment of neighboring farmers. He was said to be the first smith in
the region to build a wheeled vehicle, a simple horse-drawn carriage that
replaced earlier vehicles which used wooden runners, which were functional over snow but cumbersome on hard ground. Little Knute's grandfather and namesake Knute Knutson Rokne, operated both the farm and
blacksmith shop until 1852, when he moved his family into town, and
concentrated on serving the area as a machinist, blacksmith, and hardware merchant. He carried the vehicle work a step further by constructing
buggies and wagons, which featured seats. By the early 1880s Lars Rokne,
young Knute's father, had taken over the work as machinist and blacksmith while his father focused on hardware sales. Over the next few years
Lars enlarged the machine shop and began to craft an even greater variety
of carriages, including the "kariol," a highly functional vehicle that could
carry a load of hay, crops, or a variety of other materials. He was also the
first to use steel springs, creating a much safer, more comfortable ride.

Lars' skills in crafting carriages caught the attention of Kaiser Wilhelm II, who frequently traveled to Voss' resorts to enjoy the refreshing air and ambience. Marveling at the quality workmanship, the Kaiser
ordered a Rokne carriage. Another vehicle won a prize at the Great Fair
in Liverpool. And it was carriage-building that brought Lars, and eventually his family, to the New World. In 1891, Lars was invited to display
his wares at the great world's fair being planned in Chicago—the 1893
Columbian Exposition. In October 1891, the 33-year-old Lars set off on
the trip of his life, for America, leaving behind Anna, 7, Knute, then 3
and-a-half, and infant Martha, 15 months, under the care of their mother.
Before leaving, Lars gifted his son with a pair of rubber boots imported
from the United States. They allowed the youngster to explore in ever
broadening circles, and one day, so the family lore tells, it landed him on
an ice floe that broke off and floated him well off the shore in a lake that
stretched for miles. Townspeople gathered to mount a rescue, with one
of the villagers able to snatch him off the floating ice and back to safety.
So it was with the tyke, who took to all forms of locomotion—skating,

sledding, skiing, swimming, and scampering—whenever and wherever he could. From the youngest age, he exhibited a never-ending energy to see, to experience, to go somewhere. Perhaps harking to the particular Norse strain, the same deep-seated desire for discovery and adventure that sent the early Vikings on their battles in Ireland, or Leif Erikson on his way to the New World, or Lars Rokne to Chicago, Knute was destined to move beyond the borders of a small village.

When Lars Rokne left Norway, he was following a well-worn path from Voss to America. For several decades, Voss residents had been among the swelling crowds lured to a new life across the ocean. The religious oppression, famine, and abject poverty that propelled those from other countries to immigrate were largely not found in Norway; rather, it was the specter of living—and farming—in wide-open spaces near large numbers of potential customers that drove a steady stream of Norwegians to America. From 1870 to 1890, a total of more than 270,000 Norwegians crossed the Atlantic, mostly to settle in the rich farming country of Wisconsin, Minnesota, and North Dakota. People from Voss found one particular locale in Wisconsin much to their liking. In 1839, three men from Voss set out from LaSalle County, Illinois, walking 150 miles north to Milwaukee, then another 80 miles west toward Madison, until they reached the Koshkonong Prairie in eastern Dane County. Nils Gilderhus, Nils Bolstad, and their guide, Odd J. Himle, were in search for land on which to homestead. Upon their arrival on Koshkonong, they wrote that they found a wilderness featuring a "luxuriant growth of grass, and a great profusion and variety of beautiful flowers, displaying the colors of ten thousand rainbows painted not by the hand of man."

The area offered abundant hardwood timber and marsh hay and excellent fishing in nearby creeks and lakes. Each man selected 40 acres, along with another 40 for a friend, Magne Bystolen. With winter's approach they walked back to LaSalle County by way of Milwaukee. Early in the spring of 1840, Gilderhus, Bolstad, Bystolen, and Andrew Finno started for Koshkonong driving wagons drawn by oxen. They arrived on the prairie at the end of April and took possession of their land. Their vivid descriptions of Koshkonong Prairie lured many of their countrymen in the ensuing years. The Koshkonong settlement grew to one of the greatest concentrations of Norwegians in North America. It also provided the country with politicians and inventors. Knute Nelson, who emigrated from Voss in 1850, settled near Albion, Wisconsin. A Civil War veteran, he studied law and was admitted to the Wisconsin bar in 1867. He served as a member of the Wisconsin assembly (1868-1869) before moving to Alexandria, Minnesota in 1871. He became a member of the University of Minnesota's Board of Regents before being elected as a Republican member of the U.S. Congress from 1882 through 1888. He was elected Governor of Minnesota in 1892 and 1894, after which he resigned to successfully run for the United States Senate in 1895. Ole Evinrude emigrated with his family in 1892 from Vestre Toten, Norway and settled near Cambridge, Wisconsin. Evinrude moved to Madison, where he worked in machinery stores and studied engineering on his own. He became a machinist and worked at various tool firms in Milwaukee, Pittsburgh, and Chicago before inventing the first practical and reliable outboard motor in 1907.

The significant numbers of Norwegians, the men from Voss, and Lars Rokne himself, were all part of the greatest wave of immigration in American history. Between 1880 and 1920, more than 25 million immigrants arrived on American shores—an influx that was distinctive in its size, its demographics, and its impact upon American culture and society. More than 80 percent of the arrivals after 1890 were so-called "new immigrants," natives of Southern and Eastern Europe, culturally and ethnically perceived to be different from the Germans and Britons who had embodied the bulk of the immigration into the United States in earlier periods. Italians, Poles, Slavs, and Jews—ethnic groups rarely encountered en masse earlier in American history—arrived in large numbers. Major cities, especially New York and Chicago, proved particularly attractive to the new arrivals because of available jobs, their location as major transportation hubs, and the presence of compatriots who could help the immigrants adjust. According to census records of 1910, about three quarters of the population of New York, Chicago, Detroit, Cleveland, and Boston consisted of immigrants and their children.

Castle Garden, an island off the southwest tip of Manhattan, served as the first examining and processing center for immigrants from 1855 through 1890. The Immigration Act of 1882 pushed immigration into federal jurisdiction, and by 1890 the government appropriated $75,000 to build the first federal immigration station on Ellis Island. While the new immigration station was under construction, the Barge Office on the Battery on the tip of Manhattan was used for immigration processing. On January 1, 1892, the first Ellis Island Immigration Station was officially opened and a "rosy-cheeked Irish girl," Annie Moore, age 15, from County Cork became the first to pass through. She came with her two younger brothers to join their parents in New York City. That first day, three large ships waited to land, and 700 immigrants passed through Ellis Island. By year's end, the number stood at 450,000.

Before arriving at Ellis Island, medical inspectors boarded incoming ships in a quarantine area of New York Harbor to examine everyone but U.S. citizens aboard. Passengers were inspected for possible contagious diseases such as cholera, plague, smallpox, typhoid fever, yellow fever, scarlet fever, measles, and diphtheria. Once released from the quarantine area, the ship docked and steerage passengers poured across the pier to a waiting area. Each wore a nametag with the individual's manifest number written in large figures. The immigrants were then assembled into groups of 30, according to manifest numbers, and they were packed on the top decks of barges while their baggage was piled on the lower decks. When they finally landed on Ellis Island, with the ground still swaying like waves beneath their feet and the shrill shouts of a dozen different languages assaulting their ears, they met their first American, a nameless interpreter, who spoke on average six languages.

Medical examiners inspected everything from an immigrant's hair to their hands. Chalk was used to mark an "X" (bad shoulder) or a "B" (back problems). Any "marking" would result in further examinations. Eye examiners looked for symptoms of trachoma, a bacterial disease whose discovery meant certain deportation. Sick children age 12 or older were sent back to Europe alone and were released in the port from which they had come. Parents were required to accompany children younger than 12. There were many tearful scenes as families with a sick child decided who would go and who would stay. Ultimately, about 20 percent of those arriving at Ellis Island were detained for medical treatment or a legal hearing; the rest were free to go after only a few hours. Approximately two percent of the immigrants seeking refuge in America would fail to be admitted. Most of the new arrivals labored in tedious and difficult jobs in industrial America: building and maintaining railroads out West, coal mining in Pennsylvania, meatpacking in Chicago, and garment-making in New York City. They had exchanged accustomed lifestyles for an unfamiliar, often harsh, existence in an American society that was itself undergoing rapid change. Immigration, technology, and an industrial revolution transformed the United States from a largely rural to a much more urban country that saw the number of city dwellers skyrocket from 9.9 million to 54.1 million. Life for many of the millions of urban-based immigrants was often a combination of hope for a better life along with daily struggles against grinding poverty. Situations varied, but to enter the immigrant districts of an American metropolis was to enter a physical world that was often distinguished by filth, foul air, congestion, and dilapidated or inferior housing.

Lars Rokne and his fellow Norwegian immigrants were overwhelmingly Lutheran, and had little to fear that their religion would be in any way problematic in their new country. Such was not always the case for those of other faiths, especially Catholics. The massive waves of immigration—particularly among the Irish—drastically altered the face of Catholicism in the United States. Between 1820 and 1860, the Irish constituted more than one third of all immigrants to the United States. It was the cataclysmic potato famine of 1845 to 1851 that initiated the greatest departure. From the beginning of the famine until 1860, about 1.7 million Irish left Ireland for the United States. The famine Irish were not the Protestant, relatively well-to-do immigrants who had assimilated seamlessly into American society for nearly a century. A warm welcome did not await the new Irish immigrants, who were largely poor, unskilled, unfamiliar with urban life, and Catholic. Instead, they faced intense discrimination including attacks on convents and Catholic schools.

Irish immigration helped to build a Catholic Church of more than three million members by 1860, and the 1880s influx of Italians, Poles, and other Eastern Europeans further swelled the ranks of Catholics in the United States. By the end of the 19th century, Americans took stock of where they were and assessed all the changes that had taken place. There were more railroads, more factories, more cities, and yes, more Catholics. The accommodation of immigrants became the central theme of Catholic life in the United States and thus the church that developed was not a monolithic institution. Rather, it was a mix of various cultures with the gospel being spoken in more than 20 languages. Although the pews now contained Catholics of multiple origins, often in the popular mind, the word "Catholic" meant Irish. One reason was that by the 1900s, more than 60 percent of U.S. bishops were either born in Ireland or of Irish heritage. It was no accident that Catholic churches became landmarks in cities—they were powerful symbols of faith and identity proclaimed in a visible way that Catholic immigrants were creating a place for themselves in America. The neighborhood Catholic Church was not just a place of worship; it was the focal point of a whole community, a whole way of life. Religious sisters taught immigrant children English in Catholic schools; priests tried to protect political interests and shield the newly arrived from a sometimes hostile Protestant environment; and the local church held religious festivals and social events designed to keep ties to the "old country."

Not unlike other immigrant populations, Catholic newcomers found themselves clustered in large American industrial cities working at low-wage jobs. The reality for many included the fear of temporary joblessness or an unexpected medical expense that could destroy even the most carefully crafted budget and push a worker's family from the edge into the depths of poverty. Such living conditions deeply shaped one second-generation Irish priest, Father John A. Ryan, who became one of the most noted Catholic social activists at the turn of the 20th century. Father Ryan, born in 1869 to Irish immigrants, grew up in Minnesota and was deeply affected by the attempts of St. Paul Archbishop John Ireland to acculturate the Roman Catholic Church to America without compromising its essential beliefs and structures. Ryan never forgot his first reading of Pope Leo XIII's *Rerum Novarum* ("Of New Things"), the 1891 encyclical that would transform the landscape of Catholic social doctrine for decades to come. When he read those words, Ryan was a seminarian studying for the priesthood. The encyclical emphasized government's obligation to ensure the dignity of the worker in the industrial world. The pope's letter gave Ryan the tools he needed to bring his Catholicism to bear on his economic ideas. Ordained in 1898, Ryan attended Catholic University in Washington, D.C., and his doctoral dissertation, published in 1906, "A Living Wage," propelled him onto the stage as a leader for social reform. *A Living Wage* sought to quantify how much an average family needed to survive. Ryan advocated a legal minimum wage when there was none; indeed, he drafted the legislation for Minnesota, which, though slightly modified from his original version, became law in 1914. He pushed for federal legislation on a range of basic employee rights, from the right to unionize to unemployment insurance. In 1919, he authored the Bishops' Program for Social Reconstruction, which advocated for these measures as well as for public housing and regulation of public utility rates.

Catholic education—whether for its priests or growing immigrant population—was a critical component of the American Catholic Church. Parish schools continued to thrive and the establishment of Catholic universities continued as the population moved west. Catholic secondary schools such as St. Louis University (1818), Loras College (1839), Loyola of Chicago (1870) and the University of Detroit (1877) were welcoming the children of immigrants to their campuses. And on a patch of land in the middle of nowhere in Northern Indiana, the Holy Cross Congregation, led by Father Edward Sorin, founded the University of Notre Dame du Lac in 1842. Before Sorin died in 1893, Notre Dame was on its way to establishing itself as a national leader in Catholic education.

European Catholic missionary priests had been prominent in United States history since the discovery of the New World. By the mid-1800s, the Northwest Territories were swelling with immigration from the eastern states. Catholic churches were few and priests were even scarcer. Vincennes, Indiana Bishop Celestin Guynemer de la Hailandiere, whose diocese included the entire state of Indiana, wrote to the Reverend Basil Moreau seeking help. In response Moreau, the head of the Congregation of the Holy Cross (Congregiazione di Santa Croce), a Catholic religious order based in France, sent six Holy Cross brothers and the Reverend Edward Sorin. The group stayed in Vincennes for a year before Sorin accepted an invitation to establish a school in St. Joseph County in the northern reaches of the Indiana diocese. Reverend Stephen Badin, the first Catholic priest ordained in the United States, had purchased the land and left it in trust to the Bishop of Vincennes for anyone who would found a school on the site.

Sorin and the others arrived in South Bend, Indiana on November 26, 1842 with a single-minded focus: to create a Catholic stronghold on the western frontier of an expanding United States. The Holy Cross order— and Moreau in particular—envisioned a religious group whose primary task was to convert people to the Catholic faith, preach the gospel to them, and provide Christian education to the youth. For the next half century, Sorin would preside either directly or indirectly over the University of Notre Dame du Lac. The trek from Vincennes took 11 days, and when Sorin reached South Bend he spent his first night at the home of Alex Coquillard, a businessman who had begun his career as a fur trader with John Jacob Astor's American Fur Company. After a brief rest, Sorin asked to be escorted to Badin's tract of land two miles away. Sorin later wrote: "Everything was frozen over. Yet it all seemed so beautiful. The lake especially, with its broad carpet of dazzling white snow, quite naturally reminded us of the spotless beauty of our august Lady whose name it bears…We went to the very end of the lake, and, like children, came back fascinated with the marvelous beauties of our new home." The sweeping snow blocked the fact that there were actually two lakes on the site. Badin and Sorin remained true to their objective of forging in America an institutional Catholicism based on the European model, which included permanent locations for schools, colleges, orphanages, and hospitals. Sorin acknowledged the deep missionary roots of the land on which he planned to expand his dream of an educational establishment when in a letter in 1843 to a fellow companion he said:

> The site of Notre Dame du Lac is perhaps the first locality in the West that was visited by missionaries and moreover had missionaries in residence. It is at least certain, the bishop tells me, that Pere Marquette was here in 1669 and that he resided here until his death in 1675, when Pere Allouez replaced him. The latter had already worked among the Potawatomi and the Miami since 1669. It is astonishing how many memories crowds around this parcel of land.

Our Lady's University began with two students in that snow-filled 1842 and slowly expanded as Sorin reached out to the missions surrounding him. By the spring of 1844 the collegiate Main Building was practically finished; the school had been granted a state charter as a university; and crops were being planted on newly cleared land. Father Sorin's vision was clearly taking shape as he described it in a letter to Father Moreau shortly after arriving:

> Will you permit me, dear Father, to share with you a preoccupation which gives me no rest? Briefly, it is this: Notre Dame du Lac was given to us by the bishop only on condition that we establish here a college at the earliest opportunity. As there is no other school within more than a hundred miles, this college cannot fail to succeed.... Before long, it will develop on a large scale.... It will be one of the most powerful means for good in this country. Finally, dear Father, you cannot help see that this new branch of your family is destined to grow under the protection of Our Lady of the Lake and of St. Joseph. At least, that is my deep conviction. Time will tell if I am wrong.

Sorin was a complex individual described as forceful, ambitious, and as someone who refused to entertain the possibility of failure. His belief that God and the Virgin Mary had summoned him to America to accomplish great work was so deep that no obstacle could confound him. He never doubted that good would come from all things. This demeanor served him well in his continued work for curriculum expansion and financial support during the university's formative days. An example of his skilled diplomacy came shortly after he became a naturalized citizen in 1850. Sorin sought to establish a post office within the Notre Dame campus and the appointment of himself as postmaster. When his original request was denied, he turned to Kentucky Senator Henry Clay to help move through governmental bureaucracy. Sorin's great negotiating skills were honed through countless engagements with his superiors in the New World and those back in France as he continually maneuvered to sidestep obstacles that stood in the way of his vision for Notre Dame. Sorin sent a letter complimenting Clay on his "just, wise and moderate views" expressed in Clay's speech delivered on the senate floor on February 5 and 6 as part of the celebrated Compromise of 1850 between free and slave states. Clay, flattered by Sorin's letter, intervened and Sorin received his reward as the Notre Dame post office opened in 1851.

Sorin never wavered in his belief that a divine hand guided his work, even during the darkest and most trying events that would hit his beloved university. His self-confidence drove the development of the school even as he faced struggles with his superiors, his staff, a fire that destroyed parts of the university in 1849, and a typhus epidemic in 1854 that killed several of his closest confidants. Sorin, the great visionary, pushed forward with building a university staff, increasing the student body, assuming the role of Superior General of the Congregation of the Holy Cross in 1868, expanding on-site buildings, and working closely with the Holy Cross nuns to establish nearby St. Mary's College. By the 1870s, Notre Dame included a School of Manual Labor; a residence school for young lads, the so-called "minims," who were taught basic "letters and numbers;" and a boarding school that could house 250 college-level students.

Sorin could look with great pride as Father William Corby assumed his second tenure as university president in 1877. As Holy Cross Superior General, Sorin prepared for another trans-Atlantic voyage in April 1879, making his way first to Montreal before his scheduled departure from New York when word reached him of a disaster back at Notre Dame that tested even the strength of this stalwart.

A day off from classes had the young lads playing outdoors in their recreational yard next to the Main Building. It was the minims who were the first to sound the alarm "College on fire!" as they saw smoke curling up from the roof of the Main Building on April 23, 1879 at 11 a.m. Three hours later, the six-story building, which housed classrooms, refectories, dormitories, the college library, offices, and professors' rooms, was a burnt- out shell filled with smoldering piles of rubble. Four other structures to the northeast of the Main Building—the infirmary, the small music hall, the minims' gymnasium, and an elder hostel had also gone up in flames. Miraculously, no fatalities were recorded. It mattered little that no official cause of the fire was ever determined. Some suggested that students, in defiance of rules, were smoking in a fifth-floor dormitory room. Another conjecture was that a live ember blown from the steam plant's chimney had ignited refuse on the Main Building's roof. The one theory with the most merit centered on the fact that workmen, applying new coal-tar to the roof, had left behind enough combustible material for a stray spark, or even the heat of the April sun to ignite it. The fire began less than a half hour after the workers left.

Malfunctioning water tanks on campus and a lack of fire-fighting capacity made the blaze impossible to stop. When word reached South Bend, the volunteer firemen were fetched from their shops and forges. They harnessed horses to their steam-driving fire engine and hastened toward the campus. But they were too late, as the Main Building had largely vanished within 60 minutes. Father Corby would later write to the South Bend community with his grateful acknowledgement for their assistance. "In a particular manner are our thanks due to the press of the city and to the leading business men, for sympathy and aid, offered personally or by letter, but still more to the fire department for its generous and effective help in bringing the fire engine, which saved at least three important buildings for us. We do not dare to mention any names where we are indebted to so very many, but we desire all to know that we are most grateful to all our generous friends." On the afternoon of the fire, Corby assembled the entire Notre Dame community into Sacred Heart Church, which miraculously escaped the fire. He announced all classes were suspended for the remainder of the year, but he boldly proclaimed that rebuilding would begin immediately and the institution would reconvene as scheduled on the first Tuesday in September. Corby dispatched university librarian Professor James Edwards on the evening train bound for Canada to inform Sorin. The two returned to Notre Dame on April 27. Law school professor Timothy Howard later recalled the scene as Sorin walked amidst the ruins.

> ...Those who followed were confounded by his attitude. Instead of bending, he stiffened. He signaled all of them to go into the church with him. I was present when Father Sorin, after looking over the destruction of his life's work, stood at the altar steps and spoke to the community what I have always felt to be the most sublime words I have ever listened to. There was absolute faith, confidence, resolution in his very look and pose. 'If it were

ALL gone, I would not give up' were his words in closing. The effect was electric. It was the crowning moment of his life. A sad company had gone into the church that day. They were all simple Christian heroes as they came out. There was never more a shadow of doubt as to the future of Notre Dame.

Clearing away the debris began at once, Sorin, age 66, provided the "hands-on" presence needed to keep morale high. A report in the *Scholastic* described Sorin as being able to "wheel off a load of bricks with great grace and dignity." Just as quickly, Sorin began a nationwide competition to find an architect for the rebuilding and by May 14 had chosen Chicago architect Willoughby J. Edbrooke. Sorin's determination to complete the building before September was evident in his letter to Corby in May:

> The final adoption of a plan for the rebuilding of Notre Dame, being in its results the most important act ever accomplished by the Congregation here or anywhere, it is our duty to consider… the magnitude of the undertaking, the brief time allowed for it, and the scarcity of materials, if not of hands, required for its accomplishment by the given date…I confess I feel very uneasy…two and a half million bricks are to be laid; at 2,000 a day for each, it will take 50 masons to lay 2,5000,000 in a month… which is certainly not one-half of the whole job. I see nothing else feasible but to give out the entire building to three reliable head men, each bringing in his own crew…I would telegraph Mr. Edbrooke to get a proposal for three reliable men.

Nothing would dampen his belief in raising the money to finance the reconstruction, as he claimed "St. Joseph is our treasurer" and various Notre Dame constituencies sprang into action. Now national alumni responded generously, especially among a large contingent centered in Chicago. And the South Bend community proudly did its part. Alexis Coquillard, whose surname evoked the pioneer days of 40 years before and who had been one of the original students in the college, promptly contributed $500 and at a public rally urged his fellow townspeople to follow suit. He pointed to Notre Dame's importance to the local economy. "Every merchant, mechanic, clothinghouse, boot-and-shore store, dry goods store, grocery, lumberman, and miller can testify" to that fact he proclaimed.

Classes resumed in September as Corby had promised, although the number of students fell. Work continued on the Main Building through the fall and winter; the Luigi Gregori interior murals came much later. For Sorin, however, the adornment that mattered most, the golden dome and the statue of the Virgin Mary atop it, was finally accomplished in 1882. It was the original 2,000-pound statue that had sealed the college's fiery fate in 1879, collapsing in on the building. But Sorin remained determined that the new statue would be grander, more striking, and more beautiful for the new Notre Dame, which was to be superior to the old. Sorin knew exactly the model he wanted for the statue. He contacted Chicago artist Giovanni Meli, who fashioned the 16-foot high, 4,400-pound icon in a matter of months to resemble the statue of the Virgin that stood on an obelisk on the edge of the Piazza di Spagna in Rome. The statue remained on the front porch of the Main Building until the dome was finished. Although Sorin's colleagues urged their superior general to finish the dome with gold paint, Sorin would have none of it. He insisted upon genuine gold leaf to top the structure. Sorin was so pleased with the progress made since the fire that by the end of October he had rescheduled his trans-Atlantic journey. Upon his return in 1880, the rebuilding was nearing completion so that it caused him to comment: "This is a grand sight, we hear it repeated by every visitor, even from the first opening of Notre Dame Avenue a mile and a quarter from the College. But the beauty of the scenery increases as you come nearer to the building."

Despite nagging aches and pains that persisted for the university founder, he continued to oversee and advise on the expansion of Notre Dame du Lac and its growing reputation as a significant religious and intellectual center. To help celebrate the success, Sorin and Father Thomas Walsh inaugurated the annual conferral of the Laetare Medal in 1881, awarded by the university to a distinguished American Catholic lay person. The first recipient was the historian John Gilmary Shea, a former Jesuit considered the "father of American Catholic history." As Sorin's golden jubilee approached in 1888, plans were made to honor the man who had devoted his life to expanding Catholic faith and education in the New World. The celebration would be divided into two parts. The first was to be held May 26 and 27 and was restricted to the immediate

Notre Dame and St. Mary's family of religious, faculty, and students. The public celebration, in which the consecration of the new buildings would also occur, was slated for August 15, the feast of the Assumption of the Blessed Virgin Mary.

The May celebration included entertainment at Washington Hall, featuring music, poems, and addresses. Sorin rose to the stage to speak to those in attendance and offered formal thanks: "...What intensifies still more my gratitude...is the selection by God himself of the rich field where I was to labor; oh, how often it has filled my soul with joy! Allow me to declare...honestly that I claim but a very small fraction of the merits you assign me but justly return it all to the Blessed Virgin herself, and to the devotedness of my modest and faithful co-laborers in the field already promising such an abundant harvest for the advance of science and the salvation of immortal souls." As dusk fell, a horse-drawn carriage transported Sorin and Corby from the Main Building to cheers of students and "multicolored skyrockets" that burst above. The next day after celebrating Mass, Sorin departed the church to bless the cornerstone of the building that would soon bear his name—Sorin Hall.

The August celebration featured Baltimore Cardinal James Gibbons as Mass celebrant and St. Paul, Minnesota Archbishop John Ireland as homilist. A master orator, Ireland acknowledged all that the aging Notre Dame founder had accomplished: "Fifty years of ceaseless, brave work in God's kingdom...you never tired, though the burden was heavy. You never faltered through trials crossed upon you and the shadow of defeat often darkened the sky above you. We might in some measure tell what you have accomplished. What you have endured to bring your labors to completion we could not tell. God knows all, and he will repay." Ireland concluded with the basic themes that had marked Sorin's life: "From the moment he landed on our shores he ceased to be a foreigner. At once he was an American, heart and soul....He understood and appreciated our liberal institutions. There was in his heart no lingering fondness for old regimes or worn-out legitimism...Fifty years hence, what will the Church in America be? Let us live and work as Father Sorin has lived and work and all will be well."

Early in 1893, Sorin suffered the first in a series of internal hemorrhages and his health continued to fail. Sorin was confined to his bed by the time classes started in September. The feast day of St. Edward's on October 13 had always been a cause of celebration on campus. This year, however Sorin needed help to be brought to the porch of the presbytery to wave to a small delegation of faculty and students. By October 31, the university's founder was dead. On a cold November day, much like when he first arrived at Notre Dame in 1842, Sorin was laid to rest in the cemetery on campus. As Sorin's life came to a close, it was hard to ignore the accomplishments at Notre Dame under his stewardship. It paralleled the growth and maturing of the American Catholic Church, which too was evolving as more immigrants were arriving in the United States.

# 3
# Chicago Beckons

The Chicago that awaited Lars Rokne in October 1891 pulsated with excitement and activity in anticipation of hosting the World's Fair in 1893. Lars was among hundreds of craftsmen, inventors, and entrepreneurs from nations far and near who descended on Chicago and tinkered with the versions of their masterpieces that they intended to show at the Fair. Fortunately for Lars and other Scandinavians, there was a logical place in which to settle. The Logan Square area of northwest Chicago had one of the most populous concentrations of Norwegians anywhere in the United States. In the 1830s and 1840s, pioneer Norwegians squatted on land along the Chicago River, near where it empties into Lake Michigan. It was a close-knit community of some 500 residents, living in the most primitive structures. The building of railroads, factories, and warehouses soon overtook the settlement. The Norwegians moved to the west and north, settling west of the North Branch of the Chicago River along Milwaukee Avenue. The upwardly mobile among the settlement found their way to the north and the desirable Wicker Park neighborhood. In the 1880s, Norwegians again pushed further to the west—the Logan Square and Humboldt Park area—as more recent immigrants, including Italians, Poles, and Russian Jews, replaced the Scandinavians in the crowded, dirty areas closer to the river. The area was undergoing rapid development, though it still retained vestiges of its earlier years as an unnamed part of mostly rural Jefferson Township.

In 1836 a 24-year-old schoolteacher from upstate New York named Martin Kimbell looked for land on which to stake a claim. Legend holds he passed on a parcel at Dearborn and Lakes streets, describing it as "a damned mudhole," and instead found 160 acres five miles to the northwest on which to start his hay farm. It had been Potawatomi territory before the tribe had sold its land. The surrounding land was often impassably wet, so it was a boon when the state legislature ordered a survey for a road to run northwest from Chicago, consolidating a confusing series of old Indian trails. Eventually, the Northwest Plank Road, featuring three-inch oak boards, ran from Chicago 23 miles out to Wheeling. In 1850, Jefferson Township was formed, and over the decades several scattered settlements sprouted up here and there. The township's borders were Devon Avenue on the north, Harlem Avenue on the west, Western Avenue on the east, and North Avenue on the south.

The Logan Square area grew quickly in the years following Chicago's Great Fire of 1871. Builder-constructed, moderately priced large frame houses immediately appeared, especially in the Maplewood neighborhood, south and west of the Chicago & North Western Railroad's new Maplewood station at Diversey Avenue and along Milwaukee Avenue. The elevated train line was built to the Milwaukee Avenue station in 1890, accelerating the building of new homes nearby. Before long, the city paved the grand boulevards of the area—Logan, Kedzie, and Humboldt—along Logan and Palmer Squares, and they planted thousands of trees Before long, large graystone single-family homes and two- and three-flats lined the boulevards, while simple frame houses filled the side streets. Lars Rokne boarded in the home of a fellow Norwegian immigrant in this area when he first arrived.

Lars and the other Norwegian immigrants of his time had the advantage of moving into an established cultural and ethnic colony, with Norwegian-run shops and social organizations nearby. The newspaper *Skandinaven*, founded in Chicago in 1866, in time became the largest Norwegian-language journal in the world—no newspaper in Norway even

came close. Norwegians' strong Lutheran identity was evident throughout the area, with numerous Lutheran churches dotting the landscape.
Their role went well beyond providing Norwegian-language services; they
served as a key social hub for immigrants. Immigrants also found established healthcare systems, including the Norwegian-American Hospital and the Norwegian Lutheran Deaconess Home and Hospital. By the
1890s, second-generation Norwegians found opportunities in the healing
professions. The Woman's Hospital Medical College offered a unique opportunity for women, such as Helga Ruud, its first nursing graduate in
1889. In the building trades, architects and engineers were increasingly
Scandinavian. Norwegian-born Thomas Pihlfeldt became Chicago's chief
bridge engineer, and eventually supervised the construction of more than
50 bridges in the city.


It was only natural that Chicago would honor the 400th anniversary of
Christopher Columbus and his journey to the New World with the 1893
World's Columbian Exposition. From the days when Pere Jacques Marquette and Louis Joliet pulled their canoes from the river in September
1673 looking for the Mississippi River to the founding of Fort Dearborn
in 1795 until the rebuilding after the Great Chicago Fire of 1871, Chicago
was a city that continually beckoned explorers and adventurers. Before the
Fire, Chicago had built its reputation as the country's premier western city.
The opening of the Illinois and Michigan Canal (1848) and the founding
of the Illinois Central (1851) and the Michigan Southern and Michigan
Central railroads (1852) transformed the city from frontier boomtown to
a nexus between the manufacturing East and the agricultural West. Chicago's boosters were correct when they argued that, the fire notwithstanding; its future was never in doubt. The city was not an isolated metropolis
that accidentally appeared out of nowhere; rather it was a critical piece in
an interdependent system that was defined by an ever-increasing flow of
people, money, goods, and information.

From 1837 to 1871, considered the first period of development, the
city grew to be the dominant commercial center of the Midwest, surpass-
ing Cincinnati, St. Louis, and New Orleans to become the major city of
the entire region and the greatest grain and lumber mart in the country.

The Great Chicago Fire created the second developmental period that culminated with the World's Columbian Exposition. A city that sat in ruins two decades earlier celebrated a great triumph as people flocked to Chicago for the World's Fair to embrace a metropolis ready to shape the future and the next century.

Fires were a common occurrence in Chicago, and there were several in the week before October 7, 1871. The Great Fire, however, driven by a strong wind out of the southwest, was unprecedented as it took dead aim on the center of the city. It divided unpredictably into separate parts by hurling out flaming brands on the superheated draft it generated, leaping the South Branch of the Chicago River. One observer noted that the fire was like a snowstorm, only the flakes were red instead of white. By 1:30 a.m. the fire reached the Court House tower, from which the watchman barely escaped. When city officials realized that the building was doomed, they released the prisoners from the basement jail just before the great Court House bell, which had been sounding the alarm, plummeted through the collapsing tower. Fascinated as well as fearful, people tried to gain the best vantage and flee for their lives with what little they could salvage, creating havoc in the streets and wild crowding on the bridges crossing the river.

Husbands and wives, parents and children, were separated. It seemed as if the ground itself was on fire, which in fact it was, since the streets, sidewalks, and bridges were made of wood. In the 30 hours the fire raged, it left a corridor of ruin more than four miles long and almost a mile wide. Property worth $190 million was destroyed—73 miles of streets and 17,450 buildings—and almost 100,000 persons were left homeless. Florenz Ziegfeld Sr., a Chicago immigrant who was the headmaster at the Chicago Musical Academy, found himself one of many who raced to Lake Michigan for salvation from the flames. In the first hours he tried in vain to save his pianos, but eventually scooped up his wife and his two young sons, Florenz Jr. and Carl, and made it through the holocaust. Eventually the Ziegfelds would be part of the multitudes that rebuilt Chicago and their new residence on West Adams Street would be part of the new structure and order.

The county coroner estimated nearly 300 died, although only 120 bodies were recovered. An accurate count was impossible because people fell from bridges into the river and their bodies were never found. Many more were literally annihilated, "leaving no trace of a life or a death." Frederick Law Olmsted, sent by the *Nation* to observe the damage, reported: "Very sensible men have declared that they were fully impressed at such a time with the conviction that it was the burning of the world." On that same day, more than 1,100 people were killed in and around Peshtigo, Wisconsin, as a tornado of flames tore through the Wisconsin forest toward the city. The fire was fed by shavings and other debris left in piles by lumbermen cutting timber for buildings in Chicago that simultaneously burned like tinder. The *Chicago Tribune* reappeared two days after the fire with an editorial declaring, "Chicago Shall Rise Again." The newspaper's editor and part-owner Joseph Medill was elected mayor in November 1873. He led the city's reconstruction, which began almost immediately. Chicago businessmen were determined to make it the safest city in the world. The poor and their shanties would be removed from the larger and more modern downtown area, and the latest technology, which included fireproof materials such as brick, stone, marble, and limestone, would be used for construction. When architects John Wellborn Root, Daniel Burnham, and Louis Henry Sullivan assessed the city's reconstruction a year later, they noted a city excited about expressing itself through new buildings, as if the new architecture was a Christian metaphor of rebirth and resurrection and redemption could be achieved in the buildings that quickly rose above scenes of the recent devastation.

In the interval between the Great Fire and the World's Fair, the era of reconstruction had given way to a Gilded Age. It was a time characterized by frantic industrial growth, mass immigration, and class violence as evidenced by Chicago's 1886 Haymarket Square bombing. Labor unrest in Chicago had been brewing since the 1870s and culminated in the Haymarket Riot of May 4, 1886. Police clashed violently with militant anarchists and labor movement protesters. Seven policemen and several protesters were killed, leading to murder convictions for seven radicals, four of whom were executed.

Immigration and the industrial revolution also helped power Chicago's population boom to more than half a million by 1880. Post-fire resettlement led to the development of outlying neighborhoods and the first commuter suburbs, which appeared like beads strung along the radiating railroad lines. Meatpacking and railroads were two industries that fueled the growth. After the Civil War Chicago became the country's largest meatpacking center and the acknowledged headquarters of the industry. Philip Armour built large plants west of the stockyards, developed ice-cooled rooms so they could pack year-round, and introduced steam hoists to elevate carcasses and an overhead assembly line to move them. Gustavus Swift, who came to Chicago to ship cattle, developed a way to send fresh-chilled beef in ice-cooled railroad cars all the way to the East Coast. By 1900 this dressed beef trade was as important as pork packing, and mechanical refrigeration increased the efficiency of both pork and beef operations. Moreover, Chicago packers were preserving meat in tin cans, manufacturing an inexpensive butter substitute called oleomargarine, and, with the help of chemists, turning previously discarded parts of the animals into glue, fertilizer, glycerin, ammonia, and gelatin.

Railroad development in Chicago provided a two-prong approach to life in the 1870s and 1880s. On one hand train travel brought the "morning time of luxury long distance train travel." Dining cars served the "best ham what am" from the Chicago packing houses on tables set with Belgian linen and fine English China. By 1887 daily service from New York City began from Penn Station in the "most elegantly appointed passenger trains." The trip took 25 hours to cover the 900 miles. The fare, including the sleeping berth was $28. The bright green coaches of The Limited belonged to the Pullman Palace Car Company, organized after the Civil War by the former Chicago building raiser George Mortimer Pullman. However, for those working the rails, life presented itself in continued labor organizing and strikes for better wages and living conditions. By the 1880s, operating workers had achieved a high degree of union organization and maintained some job security. Chicago, home to several rail unions, was at the center of several important rail strikes, most notably the Pullman Strike of 1894, in which neighborhood residents in city and suburbs aided members of the American Railway Union (ARU) in their unsuccessful boycott of Pullman cars. It was during that 19-day confrontation between labor and management that Eugene V. Debs, labor activist and president of the ARU, was hopeful that a peaceful, non-violent strike could produce fruitful efforts. However, after a federal injunction to end the strike was ignored, President Grover Cleveland sent the U.S. Army to Chicago over the protests of Governor John Altgeld. The arrival of federal troops was enough to break the strike. Debs was jailed for his role in the strike for "mail obstruction," as Pullman cars were an integral part of trains carrying the U.S. mail.

To live in the big city of Chicago as the 19th century was entering its final stages was to be in "the great stream of life," which oozed daily contrasts from every artery. While young immigrant women and girls scraped for jobs as domestics in private homes and hotels, Potter Palmer made his fashionable hotel a caucusing center for the Democratic Party's national convention and the arcade of the Palmer House was the largest, the busiest, and the most lavishly appointed. At the same time that fortunes were amassed by a few, the daily drudgery of hundreds of thousands led reformer Jane Addams to set out from Rockford, Illinois to open Hull House, her settlement house in a Chicago immigrant slum in 1889. Theodore Dreiser, looking back on his youth in Chicago in the1880s wrote of a city "seething with energy and excitement, an unequaled place to watch a new world...in the making."

By 1893, Chicago was the city of Marshall Field, Philip Danforth Armour, and George Mortimer Pullman—the Chicago Trinity as the newspapers called them. The department store magnate, the meatpacking giant, and the railroad tycoon each helped to carve a part of the city and its heritage. Chicago residents of the day included social and political reformer Florence Kelley, attorney Clarence Darrow, Norwegian immigrant and economist Thorstein Veblen, and Ida B. Wells, a young African American insurgent who moved to Chicago in 1893 to mobilize a national crusade against lynching and racial segregation. It was also a time of intellectual birth for the city as it made its mark to becoming a major urban area. In 1890, the American Baptist Education Society and oil magnate John D. Rockefeller founded the University of Chicago on land donated by Marshall Field. The university was deemed the "most important event in shaping the outlook and the expectations of American higher education." Rockefeller described his donation as the best investment he ever made and an impressive list of nine former college or seminary presidents formed the first staff when classes began in October 1892—all drawn to Chicago by the idea of creating a community of great scholars. The faculty also included Amos Alonzo Stagg, associate professor of physical culture.

It was no accident that Lars Rokne was among the hundreds of thousands who came to this city of dreamers and doers. His sharp mind and his aptitude for mechanics had him always on the lookout for building more advanced means of transportation. He may well have been content serving the needs of Voss-area farmers for the rest of his life. Yet, something greater beckoned. It was a chance to meet and mingle with other inventors from distant shores, and see how their mind-power and skilled hands were moving the world's residents. And it was no accident that all this happened in a place that had come so far just 20 years after it was a devastated shell of a city. The two decades since the Great Chicago Fire of 1871 had brought extensive rebuilding, new residents by the thousands, and a sense of prosperity and possibility. It was against this complex and energizing backdrop of immigrant migration, labor unrest, and the enormously complicated rituals of daily life that Chicago undertook one of the most astonishing feats of its day: serving host to the World's Columbian Exposition, better known as the Chicago's World Fair.

Queen Victoria opened the first true world's fair in Hyde Park, London on May 1, 1851. It was the first attempt to put structure around the great changes that had elapsed from the Industrial Revolution, and the fair's success quickly caught the imagination of the rest of the world. In the ensuing decades, New York, Paris, Vienna, Philadelphia, Sydney, and Melbourne would all host a world's fair. National pride meant as much about making an impressive showing abroad as the holding of a successful fair in one's own country. That was true of American cities, which developed rivalries in bidding to host a world's fair. American world fairs also placed a greater emphasis than European cities on popular entertainment features. This was due in part to the growing mass consumer trend of the time. Yes, Americans wanted to be informed, but they also wanted to be entertained. American fairs were as much about show as they were about tell.

At the closing of the 19th century, America was undergoing a transformation from rural to urban setting. Midwestern cities such as Milwaukee, Chicago, Detroit, and Cleveland had doubled, if not tripled, their populations between 1876 and 1890. And nowhere did the contrasts of the emerging urban centers seem more pronounced than in Chicago, the wonder city of the Midwest. In the years following the Great Fire, several townships voted for city annexation, which offered better services, such as improved water supply, sewerage, and fire and police protection. The largest single annexation followed an election on June 29, 1889 when Chicago gained 125 square miles and 225,000 people. It became the largest city in the United States in area and passed Philadelphia to become second in population behind New York, with just more than one million by 1890. The population growth was due in part to the physical expansion of the city through new developments in mass transportation (cable cars, elevated railways and electric streetcars). Between 1876 and the turn of the 20th century, Chicago earned the title of "the most radical of American cities." The awareness of the social, economic, and ethnic disparities challenged Chicago's leaders to channel efforts into elevating the city as one known for its libraries, museums, and educational institutions. The city's industrial and financial giants were besieged with requests for philanthropic support and even Philip Armour, who insisted that he had absolutely no other interest but making money, found himself creating the Armour Institute in 1893.

The success of the 1876 Philadelphia centennial World's Fair introduced Americans to the concept of the world's fair as an appropriate institution for expressing national self-awareness. By the end of the fair's Philadelphia run, talk began of an American sponsorship for a world's fair to celebrate Columbus' discovery of the New World. Chicago support to host the fair was slow in gathering, but the entry of Cincinnati and St. Louis into the competition mobilized Chicago's newspapers to more strongly editorialize for hosting the event. By 1888, Chicago's civic and political clubs had adopted resolutions to host the fair, and Chicago papers engaged in hearty debate as to whether New York, St. Louis, or Chicago was best suited to be host city. The *Chicago Tribune* stated, "Chicago was the embodiment of American progress and spirit while New York was America's Liverpool" and that "St. Louis has no right to ask for the fair till it has been more thoroughly Chicagoized." It was during this vigorous and often vocal competition that Charles A. Dana, editor of the *New York Sun*, dubbed Chicago "that windy city."

A Chicago lobbyists and citizen's committee was formed in the summer of 1889 to head the city's campaign. P.T. Barnum advised the committee to "make it the greatest show on earth—greater than my own show if you can." The "who's who" list advocating for Chicago included: Marshall Field, George Pullman, Potter Palmer, Philip Armour, Charles T. Yerkes, financier and developer of Chicago's mass-transit system; Ferdinand W. Peck, businessman and philanthropist, best known for financing Chicago's Auditorium Building; Charles L. Hutchinson, who helped to found the Art Institute of Chicago in 1882; Cyrus J. McCormick, Jr., son of the founder of the McCormick Harvesting Machine Company; Joseph Medill, publisher of the *Chicago Tribune* and former mayor; Edward T. Jeffrey, president of the Illinois Central Railroad; and Lyman J. Gage, one of the city's leading bankers.

In December 1889 the debate shifted from the editorial pages to the halls of Congress. Four cities remained in the running: Washington, D.C., New York, Chicago, and St. Louis. Special Congressional committees began considering city applications in January 1890. After heated debate, Chicago, on the eighth roll call of the full House of Representatives, received 157 votes, three more than necessary to win. What swung the vote was Chicago's reputation as a convention center, unrivaled rail connections, its proven capacity for carrying through on big municipal projects, and its pledge of an additional $4 million. The Chicago fair delegation immediately responded by pledging an additional $10 million to guarantee the selection and on April 28, 1890 President Benjamin Harrison signed "An Act to Provide for the Celebration of the 400th Anniversary of the Discovery of America by Christopher Columbus, by holding an International Exhibition of Arts, Industries, Manufacturers and the Products of the Soil, Mine and Sea, in the City of Chicago, in the State of Illinois." The date was pushed back one year, from the actual anniversary of 1892 to 1893, to allow Chicago the time it would need to put on what its newspapers called a "jumbo" event.

Chicago now had to make good on its claim to be the best representative of the country to the rest of the world and to give a positive expression of the progress and unity of the American people. Although the original proclamation provided for an additional year, the time was short for Chicago to deliver. Frederick Law Olmsted, America's foremost landscape architect who had written of the Great Fire in 1873, now returned and was given responsibility for laying out the fairgrounds, which would occupy 630 acres in Jackson Park and the Midway Plaisance. The architecture of the buildings was under the direction of Daniel Burnham, Director of Works for the fair. Burnham had built some of Chicago's earliest skyscrapers of 10 stories and was known for his development of urban planning. The main site was bounded by Stony Island Avenue on the west, 67th Street on the south, Lake Michigan on the east, and 56th Street on the north. The Midway Plaisance, a narrow strip of land between 59th and 60th Streets, extended west from Stony Island to Cottage Grove Avenue. The Exposition was the first world's fair with a separate amusement area. The noisy and distracting attractions were concentrated on the Midway so as not to disturb the park-like atmosphere of the rest of the exposition.

Construction of the White City, the Exposition's Court of Honor, began in 1891 and before the Fair opened on May 1, 1893, more than 10,000 people a day paid an admission charge just to see the largest construction site in modern times. Most of the buildings of the White City were designed in the classical style of architecture and were clad in white stucco, which, in comparison to the tenements of Chicago, seemed illuminated. However, it was the expansion of Thomas Edison's 1879 achievement of not just an incandescent electric light, but also an electric lighting system that contained all the elements necessary to make the incandescent light practical, safe, and economical that gave the White City its "electrifying" appeal. The Exposition, and in particular, The White City, was to be more than just a show place of inventions. It was to help display the idea of an orderly society coming together as the industrial revolution was transforming the country from rural to city life. During the construction of the White City, Burnham would note: "Chicago, in common with other great cities, realizes that the time has come to bring order out of the chaos incident to rapid growth, and especially to the influx of many nationalities without common traditions or habits of life. Among the various instrumentalities designed to accomplish this results, a plan for a well-ordered and convenient city is seen to be indispensable."

The Court of Honor, which included more than half a dozen buildings, was not only a metaphor for a new Chicago, but it was a blueprint for the transformation to come. Burnham would later write: "The World's Fair of 1893 was the beginning in our day and in this country, of the orderly arrangement of extensive public grounds and building." He believed that more than the size of the White City buildings, visitors would grasp the powerful idea that the World's Columbian Exposition was not a grand-scale trade and agricultural show or a celebration of new machines, but a capital, the gateway to a new century and era. More than 12,000 workers laid railroad tracks that crisscrossed the site of the Exposition and more than 36,000 carloads of materials were delivered. A harsh winter in 1892 forced Burnham to drive his work crews to complete the mammoth task, but as the world arrived in May 1893, Chicago was ready. For Lars Rokne the wait was also over. After 18 months of paving the way, his family was ready to join him for the World's Fair and for the new life that waited.

# 4

# A Dazzling White City

Martha Gjermo Rokne descended from a long line of Norwegians accomplished in education, science, and medicine. Hers was a world of cultivation, culture, and ideas. Now, in the spring of 1893, the 34-year-old mother of three was hearing a new call. Her husband Lars, after 18 months in Chicago working and preparing for the World's Fair, had sent the fare for the rest of his family to join him on his American adventure. For Martha, there would be long, tearful goodbyes to relatives and friends in Voss, with uncertainty whether they would see one another again.

In early May, all the necessary arrangements had been made. Martha ventured first to Bergen with her three children—Anna, 9, Knute, 5, and young Martha, just shy of 3. In Bergen, there was a delay as the boat was being repaired. Little Knute, curious as ever, could not sit still, and instead wandered off to explore some of the sights of the historic town. It was but a brief foray, but certainly enough to concern the young mother. It would not be the last time Knute's curiosity and rambunctiousness got the better of him. After the connector trip from Bergen, the ultimate journey across the Atlantic began at Christiansand on the southern tip of Norway, aboard the SS *Moravia*, part of the Hamburg America Line. The steamer, built a decade earlier at Glasgow by A. & J. Inglis, was christened as the Bengore Head for the Ulster Steamship Co. before she was bought by Hamburg America. At 361 feet by 41 feet, she could reach 12 knots while carrying nearly 800 passengers and cargo. On this trip, the *Moravia* carried 775 passengers, including 380 Swedes who boarded at Gothenborg and 220 Danes. The Roknes were among 150 Norwegians aboard—young Knute was passenger No. 599. From May 14 until arrival in New York on May 29, similar to millions of other immigrants, the 775 endured crowding, noise, rough seas, seasickness, and monotony—but arrived safely without incident.

That was not always the case on immigrant ships, including the *Moravia*. Just nine months earlier, shortly after the start of a voyage from Hamburg, Germany, a young boy in steerage began experiencing severe diarrhea. That alone wasn't unusual, as illness among immigrant children traveling in steerage on ocean crossings was common. But within a day, the boy suffered increasingly severe convulsions, became rigid, and died. Within hours, a 9-month-old girl met the same fate. Their bodies were sewn into weighted gunnysacks and lowered into the Atlantic. Five more children soon died, and others filled the ship's hospital, sick with diarrhea, cramps, and cold chills. Their skin began to blacken from their illness. By the time the *Moravia* nudged into its New York dock late on the night of August 30, 1892, after its 10-day journey, 22 of its 358 passengers had been buried at sea, victims of Asiatic cholera. Those aboard the ship didn't know that cholera had broken out in Hamburg in the days after the *Moravia* left port. A panic erupted on both sides of the Atlantic. The U.S. Consul ordered the steamship lines to fumigate the baggage of all incoming passengers with sulphur fumes for no less than six hours. In New York, the *Moravia* was quarantined to Hoffman Island, where passengers were bathed and their clothing fumigated. After that, they remained in quarantine while doctors waited to see if cholera would develop.

For Martha Rokne in May 1893, her greatest fear as the Moravia approached New York harbor was keeping track of her three young children. So she bound them to her waist with strong ribbons. Knute would later comment, "How my mother ever managed that tedious voyage which I still recall with qualms; how she guided us through the intricacies of entry, knowing nothing of English, and took us into the heart of a new, strange and bewildering country without mishap—how…she achieved the first step in our Americanization unaided by anybody, is one of the millions of minor miracles that are…the stuff and fabric of America." The first object every pair of eyes spotted was the Statue of Liberty. As the ship neared Ellis Island, it was possible to look north into Lower Manhattan and see the golden dome atop the New York World Building, the city's greatest skyscraper at 309 feet tall. Built just three years earlier, it housed Joseph Pulitzer's *New York World* newspaper and anchored a district soon renowned as Newspaper Row. Ellis Island was both a symbol and reality in the story of immigration. For those who had come to America's shores, Ellis Island was the last stop on the excursion from the old country and the first step into the new.

For the Rokne family, the journey continued to Chicago via train, where Lars greeted his family and brought them to the Logan Square flat he had rented. Now, the family's focus—similar to that of countless others—was the epic event unfolding seven miles to the southeast.


The World's Columbian Exposition, after years of planning, numerous setbacks, delays, and controversies, opened to the public on May 1, 1893. Over the course of the next six months, more than 27 million people—14 million from outside of the United States—would pass through its gates, venture amid the pavilions, and enjoy the Midway. It was the greatest tourist attraction the nation had known. American families mortgaged their farms and houses, borrowed money on their life insurance, or trimmed their Christmas budgets to save up for a summer week in Chicago. On opening day, a parade of 23 shiny black carriages bearing dignitaries set out from the Lexington Hotel on Michigan Avenue toward Jackson Park. President Grover Cleveland rode in one, and the Duke of Veragua, a direct descendent of Columbus, in another. The final carriage was reserved for Mayor Carter Harrison, who received hearty cheers from the gathered crowds. Behind the entourage came an estimated 200,000 people on foot and horseback, in all manner of carriages and other vehicles, and on streetcars. Thousands of others arrived via "cattle cars"—the bright yellow cars of the Illinois Central, designed to carry maximum numbers of people to the fair. Once at the gate, adults paid 50 cents admission, those under 12 paid 25 cents, and children under 6 were admitted free.

Greeting the fairgoers was the colossal Statue of the Republic, Daniel Chester French's sculpture of a 65-foot high "golden lady" welcoming immigrants to her shores. It overlooked a large pool facing the Court of Honor, the fair's signature buildings. Water was a main theme of the grounds, as the pool, along with numerous canals and lagoons, symbolized Columbus' journey to the New World. A nod to Norwegian pride in claiming discovery of the New World went to Magnus Andersen, who sailed a full-sized replica of a Viking ship across the ocean for the fair. Andersen recalled, "As I thought this over more closely, I found the idea more and more attractive. That Leif Eriksson had been in America before Columbus had been clearly proved but was not commonly known either in America or elsewhere, not even Norway." The replica was decorated with a silk banner embroidered with ravens. The ship was christened *The Raven,* but the American popular press quickly named it *The Viking. The Viking* sailed from Bergen, Norway in spring and reached Newfoundland four weeks later. The crew, uncertain how the ship would handle on the open seas, found it had exceeded all expectations. "We noted with admiration the ship's graceful movements," Andersen wrote. From Newfoundland, *The Viking* headed south to New York, and then sailed into the Great Lakes. Mayor Harrison boarded and took command for the last leg of the voyage, arriving at Jackson Park on Wednesday, July 12, 1893. *The Viking* moored at Jackson Park for the remainder of the fair.

Footsore sightseers could climb aboard a "swift and silent" electric launch or flag down a smaller battery-run boat and head to the next spot on their guidebook agenda. The railroad that circled the grounds was the first in America to operate heavy, high-speed trains by electricity. And it ran on an elevated track—posing no danger to pedestrians. At the Captive Balloon Park, visitors boarded a large hydrogen balloon for a birds-eye view of the fair, while tethered to the ground below. In nearly 200 buildings on the 600-acre site, tens of thousands of exhibitors from hundreds of nations exhibited their wares. Products from Shredded Wheat cereal to Juicy Fruit gum to Pabst beer—known after the Fair as Pabst Blue Ribbon—were first presented to the public at the Fair. There was a 22,000-pound block of cheese in the Wisconsin Pavilion; a chocolate Venus di

Milo; and a scaled-down version of the Statue of Liberty carved from a block of salt. Philadelphia sent the Liberty Bell, as well as two replicas: one made of rolled oats, another of oranges.

Fairgoers who stayed on the grounds into the evening received an unforgettable display of the splendors of electricity in the nighttime illumination of every building and walkway. Visitors were amazed to see the sheer volume of electric lamps producing day-like conditions. Light bathed the Court of Honor, which was described as being "etched in fire against the blackness of the night." The streetscape became a futuristic vision, as thousands of street lamps turned night into day and made it possible to safely navigate the grounds after sundown. It was electricity-producing light, on the grandest scale ever attempted. Huge searchlights, the largest ever manufactured, lit the grounds and nearby neighborhoods and could be seen some sixty miles distant.

Technological advances, agricultural and mechanical devices, and cultural flourishes all dominated the Fair's pavilions. But spreading to the west, at a right angle to the White City, the mile-long Midway Plaisance attracted countless fairgoers with its relatively low-brow entertainment. The first such district attempted at a world's fair, the Midway was marked with sideshow barkers, "kooch dancers" who performed exotic routines, and, camped just outside the Midway, Buffalo Bill's Wild West show. Flo Ziegfeld, Jr., son of the Fair's musical director, had been captivated by Buffalo Bill's show a decade earlier when it played Chicago. The younger Ziegfeld was fascinated by the Midway and its attractions. Headliners. Attention grabbers. Something to puzzle the crowd. The ideas stuck with Ziegfeld, himself not a musician, who set out for New York City shortly after the Fair closed. But it was George Washington Gale Ferris' big steel wheel on the Midway Plaisance that rivaled nighttime illumination as the fair's most wondrous sight.

On March 18, 1893 the 89,320-pound axle, forged in Pittsburgh by the Bethlehem Iron Company, arrived in Chicago. It was 45.5 feet long, 33 inches in diameter. Four and one-half feet from each end it carried two 16-foot diameter cast-iron spiders weighing 53,031 pounds. On March 20 the placing of the first tower post was completed; eventually the immense axle assembly was hoisted to the top of the 140-foot high towers and placed neatly in its sturdy pillow blocks. The cars were 24 feet long,

13 feet wide, and 10 feet high, and weighed 26,000 pounds. Each car carried fancy twisted wire chairs for 38 of the 60 passengers. The five large plate glass windows on each side were fitted with heavy screens and the doors at each end were provided with secure locks. Conductors rode in each car to answer patrons' questions or, if necessary, to calm their fears. Due to the complexity of its construction, the Ferris Wheel was not ready for the Fair's opening in May. But on June 21 the Iowa State Band struck up "America" and to the cheers of the assembled thousands the Great Wheel slowly and majestically revolved, towering above them in its magnificence. A trip consisted of one revolution, during which six stops were made for loading, followed by one nine-minute, nonstop revolution. On a clear day, patrons could see the Fairgrounds, the city, and state as well as miles out onto Lake Michigan and the surrounding states of Wisconsin, Indiana, and Michigan. Large incandescent light bulbs were mounted on the wheel, and its dazzling sight made the Ferris Wheel as much of an attraction as the unprecedented view it offered.

Transportation and movement were central themes at the Columbian Exposition. Whether a triumph of up-to-the-minute technology such as the Ferris Wheel or the latest in "hot air" balloon development, the Fair acknowledged what transportation meant to the American people. It was more than simply minimizing distance. Transportation meant movement, which was the embodiment of the American dream. The Transportation Building, designed by architect Louis Sullivan and built at a cost of more than $1 million, offered visitors a view of everything from pack mules and horse-drawn carriages to bicycles and boats. Most exciting to Fair goers were the rows of massive American-built steam locomotives that towered over everything else in the hall. Beginning at the north and occupying nearly the entire center of the annex was the exhibit prepared by the Baltimore & Ohio Railway Co. known as "The Railways of the World." To the south was a display of two trains of Pullman palace cars. Following that exhibit were passenger cars, various forms of freight, street, and tram cars, and an exceedingly large variety of locomotives representing all but two of every locomotive building establishment in the United States.

By 1893 railroads were the premier transportation system in the country. In the early part of the century, basic routes were carved out by a handful of companies such as the New York Central, the Baltimore and

Ohio, and the Pennsylvania. A railway's presence or absence caused major cities to rise or fall. Philadelphia's founders invested heavily in the Pennsylvania Railroad to ward off competition from New York City, who already had heavily invested in the building of the New York Central with Cornelius Vanderbilt at the helm. Railroads developed so quickly that by 1850 the Pennsylvania Railroad, eventually headed by J. Pierpont Morgan, employed more people than any other industry or company in the state. In addition to jobs, railroads offered wider markets for business. By the start of the Civil War, 30,000 miles of track crisscrossed the country.

President Abraham Lincoln signed the Pacific Railroad Act of 1862, which provided for the Transcontinental railroad and its feeder lines to be built by private entrepreneurs, with the government providing generous endowments to encourage private investment. Thus, railroads opened up the West to settlement after the Civil War as pioneers rode the rails into the wilderness and built new towns. Omaha, Tulsa, Wichita, and Denver all experienced population booms overnight. Whether hauling freight or passengers, by the 1880s the United States consisted of a honeycomb of more than 163,000 miles in operational, intersecting lines. Steel rails replaced iron and electric locomotives took over for steam. And at each juncture along the way stood train agents who helped to plan passenger trips, sell tickets, and sometimes operate the telegraph office. By the time the World's Fair opened in Chicago, the New York Central's Empire State Express had exceeded 100 miles per hour on its runs to Chicago. As for comfort, Pullman cars of the day rivaled the finest hotels for the level of service and creature comforts provided. Railroads offered convenience, taking travelers across the continent in less than a week, while "down branch" lines could transport passengers to the most remote Appalachian hamlet in a matter of days.

Strolling to the annex and other transportation classifications brought fairgoers to the display of "Vehicles and Methods of Transportation on Common Roads." Included were "spring vehicles of every kind; carriages, buggies, spring and express wagons, trade wagons for meat, bakery, and milk." A major exhibitor, the Studebaker Bros. Mfg. Co., of South Bend, Indiana and Chicago displayed "wagons and carts, pleasure carriages, and light pleasure vehicles." The catalogue described the Studebaker showings as "Fine carriages of every description, from the light speeding wagon to the massive four-in-hand coach, including many styles not produced by other manufacturers. Fine harnesses, both light and heavy, and everything for the perfect equipment of rider and driver." The international exhibitors included the Norwegian contingent of vehicles, vessels, boats—marine, lake, and river transportation. Exhibitor 6 in Department H from Vossevangen, Norway was Rokne, K., showing in Exhibit 513 his "Kariol" and in Exhibit 517 his "Sleigh." Lars Rokne, as a solo craftsman, stood in stark contrast to a major manufacturer such as Studebaker.

H&C (named for brothers Henry and Clem) Studebaker was established on February 16, 1852 as a wagon-making business. After supplying wagons to the United States government for its fight in the 1838 Mormon Wars in Utah, the brothers turned to carriage making around 1860. Word of their fine workmanship spread quickly and soon the White House ordered a Studebaker carriage. It was a Studebaker carriage that drove President Abraham Lincoln and his wife Mary to Ford's Theater in April 1865. By 1878 the company exhibited its wagons at the Paris Exposition and won a silver medal for excellence. The British Parliament put its stamp of approval on the Studebaker brand when a number of their wagons were used in the Boer War in South Africa in 1880. An official British report claimed: "Wagons were imported from the United States, and these proved to be superior to any other make, either of Cape or English manufacture." The company's craftsmanship continued to grow in prestige as well in the United States as Presidents Ulysses S. Grant and Rutherford B. Hayes used Studebaker carriages. So successful was the Studebaker carriage-making business that by 1877 it claimed to be the largest manufacturer of vehicles in the world. To celebrate the good fortune, Clem was able to begin construction on Tippecanoe Place for his new South Bend residence. It was a veritable castle built of limestone complete with lawns and luxurious gardens that was completed in 1889. The Studebaker brothers also expanded into the Chicago real estate market and counted among their friends Cyrus McCormick, Philip Armour, and Marshall Field.

The sights and sounds of the World's Fair mesmerized a young Knute Rockne, who later recalled its "glittering palaces" and "amazing crowds." Fair food made an impression on the five-year-old, as he enjoyed pop-corn, pink lemonade, and that most American of fare—the hot dog. His memories of attending the Fair include once again wandering away from his family, this time to romp with a group of American Indian children on a mock "reservation." The tow-headed Norwegian lad felt perfectly at home with black-haired natives, donning a feather headdress and wielding a wooden toy tomahawk. His rollicking adventure ended when he was finally found by Fair police and returned to his worried parents.

The Columbian Exposition made an impression on fairgoers of all ages. The White City so amazed one visitor, children's writer Frank Baum; it was the inspiration for the Emerald City of Oz for his book *The Wonderful Wizard of Oz*, published in May 1900. The Japanese temple on the fair's wooded island mesmerized a young rising architect with Adler & Sullivan, the firm that designed the Transportation Building. Frank Lloyd Wright would later use its style elements in some of his "Prairie" residential projects. Thirty-year-old Henry Ford, then chief engineer with the Edison Illuminating Company, saw an internal combustion engine at the fair that fueled his dreams about the possibility of designing a horseless carriage. Ford returned to Detroit more committed than ever in his quest to develop a gasoline-driven automobile. Three years later, he debuted his first quadracycle. A pair of young bicycle makers from Dayton, Ohio named Wilbur and Orville Wright came away inspired by the technology they witnessed, especially in the transportation building. They apparently did not attend the Aeronautical Congress, featuring an opening address by Octave Chanute, the French-born railway engineer and aviation pioneer. The Congress' focus was primarily hot-air ballooning, yet Chanute may have been looking forward to the development of the heavier-than-air flying machine when he said, "It is well to recognize from the beginning that we have met here for a conference upon an unusual subject, one in which commercial success is not yet to be discerned, and in which the general public, not knowing of the progress really accomplished, had little interest, and still less confidence."

Among the thousands of constructions workers for the Fair was one Elias Disney, a native Canadian who had already traveled the continent widely in search of employment. His journeys took him to California with his father in 1878 in search of gold. Later he worked on his father's Kansas farm, labored in a railroad machine shop alongside co-worker Walter

Chrysler, helped build the Union Pacific railroad through Colorado, played fiddle professionally in Denver, and worked as a postman in Kissimmee, Florida. When his third son was born during the Fair, Elias wanted to name him Columbus in honor of the Exposition. His wife preferred Roy. Eight years later, the couple, residing not far from the Rocknes, welcomed their youngest son and named him Walter Elias (Walt) Disney.

For millions of visitors the electrical illuminations of the Fair were a source of wonder and excitement about the possibilities of lighting America's farms and cities. Whether they saw the Fair firsthand or experienced it through postcards or accounts in newspapers and magazines, most Americans regarded the World's Columbian Exposition as a cultural touchstone and remembered it the rest of their lives. George Ade, American writer and newspaper columnist, noted: "The world's greatest achievement of the departing century was pulled off in Chicago. The Columbian Exposition was the most stupendous, interesting, and significant show ever spread out for the public." Henry Demarest Lloyd, the prominent journalist, political activist, and leading citizen of Winnetka, Illinois said the Fair had shown Americans "the possibilities of social beauty, utility, and harmony of which they had not been able even to dream. No such vision could otherwise have entered into the prosaic drudgery of their lives, and it will be felt in their development into the third and fourth generation." The Exposition led President Harrison to declare October 12 a national holiday in honor of Columbus. And every major fair going forward would feature a Midway and a Ferris Wheel.

One of the most stunning views from atop the Ferris Wheel looked over the major new cultural gems of Chicago. The newly constructed University of Chicago hugged the lakefront near the fairgrounds and the new Art Institute of Chicago occupied a prominent space just off the Loop. They helped to create a relocated cultural axis, a center for a new international Chicago, built at the eastern edge of the old city. There was little doubt that the university would chose William Rainey Harper to lead the development of an institution to rival the best of the East. Rainey, a Yale professor of Hebraic studies, was one of the country's leading academics and was famous for innovative programs with a populist appeal. From its inception, this new university was molded with a special modern concentration on the sciences. Harper was deliberate in his selection of

Henry Ives Cobb, a celebrated local architect, to design the university's building with Gothic spires. Along with the Art Institute and the Chicago Symphony Orchestra hall, the university bound the city's intellectual life to a definite space on the city grid. It was hoped that these institutions, encouraged by the fair and the White City, assured Chicago's consolidation of high learning and culture.

# 5

# Football Comes West

When a group of 25 Princeton University students made the short trip north to New Brunswick, New Jersey on November 6, 1869 to meet a similar number of men from Rutgers University in the first game of intercollegiate football, the contest more resembled a cross between soccer and rugby. Teammates ran interference ahead of the man who controlled the ball, and players were allowed to catch or swat the ball with their hands. The home team prevailed that day, putting six goals across while holding Princeton to four—including one inadvertently scored by a Rutgers player. The game was played on a meadow across the road from Westland Mansion, which would later serve as the retirement home of President Grover Cleveland. A week later the teams met for a rematch on the Princeton campus. During that week the Princeton players convinced several of their classmates to attend the game and let out with organized shouts in an attempt to unnerve the visitors—and so the first football cheers were born.

Princeton won the rematch and quickly took its place as one of the Big Three of football, along with Yale and Harvard. In the fall of 1873, Princeton, Rutgers, Yale, and Columbia met to codify the rules of the soccer-like game. Harvard refused to join in, and looked elsewhere for competition. In May 1874, a team from McGill University of Montreal visited the Cambridge campus and introduced a game featuring Canadian rugby rules, which allowed players to pick up the ball and run with it until stopped. Harvard immediately took to this version of football and in the next year converted Yale to the new style of play. A kick that crossed the goal line was still the only means of scoring, but advancement by running with the ball soon made the college forget about soccer. Versions of the new game, with local adornments, soon popped up in various locales. In 1883 a team from the University of Michigan came east to take on the established schools. It lost badly to Yale, but suffered only narrow defeats to Harvard and Wesleyan, and won at Stevens Tech. A fifth game, against Cornell, was proposed for the neutral site of Cleveland. It was nixed by the Cornell president, former Ann Arbor history professor Andrew White, with the unforgettable jibe, "I shall not permit thirty men to travel four hundred miles merely to agitate a bag of wind." But it was that bag of wind that soon had scores of colleges, and the people who supported them, in its thrall.

The most significant advancements in the first quarter-century of intercollegiate football sprang mostly from the inventive mind of Walter Chauncey Camp. Born to a family of educators in New Haven, Connecticut, Camp naturally matriculated at Yale, where he was a star running back for all or part of seven seasons (1876-1882). He also earned a bachelor's degree and advanced through medical school for three years. But it was the emerging game of football that was his undying avocation. He remained a graduate advisor to Yale teams for decades in a role once described as "Yale's unofficial, unpaid, unquestioned chief mentor and arbiter." His influence, though, would radiate far beyond the New Haven campus.

American football in the 1870s resembled a form of English rugby. After each scrum, a player was ruled downed and the ball would be placed between the two teams for the next scrimmage (which became scrum). Camp in 1880 proposed a change that gave possession of the ball to one side, which would execute a succession of planned movements. So was born the line of scrimmage, and a set of tries—or "downs"—in which the offensive team had to gain five yards to retain possession. That began a long line of contributions to the development of the game that earned

Camp the title of "the father of American football." In the ensuing years, Camp's influence on the game would continue unimpeded. He fashioned the modern scoring system, the center snap, the move to 11 players on a side (7 linemen and 4 backs), and a host of other rules modifications. As great as all that were his contributions as a promoter of the modern game, it was through his writing and selection of All-American teams, which continued until his death in 1925 that kept him in the national limelight. His many magazine articles dissected the emerging game, and helped a curious public better understand the nuances of the spectacle unfolding before them. As such, Camp played an essential role in football becoming a source of mass entertainment.

American football began as a game to be played, not necessarily watched. Men at some of the nation's elite colleges viewed it as an invigorating test of manhood. But within a brief ten-year span (1880-1890) football had become a great public spectacle with an immense following. It's not surprising that football's developmental years coincided with the golden age of print, an era when newspapers and periodicals abounded, and reached a larger and more varied audience than ever before. Pre-Civil War census data showed just more than 2,000 newspapers in circulation; by 1890 the number had expanded to more than 11,000. General interest weekly magazine readership also grew as Americans clamored for information. *Harpers, Collier's,* Frank Leslie's *Illustrated Weekly, Century,* the *Saturday Evening Post,* and The *Atlantic* boasted readership in the hundreds of thousands; the *Century* topping all with a circulation of 175,000 by the 1890s. And adjacent to articles on politics, culture, and art, the periodicals began to carry sporting news written by Walter Camp and Caspar Whitney, who collaborated with Camp in choosing the annual All-America football team.

Football's formative years were read within the cultural context of an era reshaping America. Thus, the football narrative was defined in a multitude of terms. Was it a mere pastime to be enjoyed as leisure time increased? Was it a sport for gentlemen? Or was football the epic Darwinian struggle framed within a game of rules and infringements? Was football a game of brutality or a game of manly virtues? Camp wanted it to be seen as a game of discipline, obedience, pluck, and tactical genius, which he felt mirrored the American corporate culture rising to new prominence. He held firmly to the belief that building a strong body was needed to match mental toughness. He looked at the giants of his day—James J. Hill, Cornelius Vanderbilt, Marshall Field. They had become strong by working outdoors: Hill worked in railroad construction camps, Vanderbilt hoisted sails, and Field grew up on a farm. "The sons and grandsons of men like these are now city born and bred. Body building toil has gone out of their lives," Camp said. He also believed a true sportsman was not a "good loser." He claimed, "A true sportsman is a good winner; a man who disdains all small and crooked tricks, but who spares no pains to achieve victory by all honorable means, including, a thorough preparation."

In the earliest years, football contests were barely noted outside the campuses involved. For bigger events, such as the Yale-Princeton Thanksgiving Day games, four or five paragraphs may appear in the New York dailies. But from these meager beginnings, the coverage of football games expanded through the 1880s. Before long, the major newspapers included almost daily reports on the development of the teams at the Big Four (Harvard, Yale, Princeton, and Penn). Slightly less attention was given to the second tier teams in the East (Cornell, Columbia, Brown, Lehigh, Lafayette, and Army).

No one was more aware of how athletic activities were evolving into an American spectacle than Joseph Pulitzer, a Hungarian immigrant whose life reflected the so-called American dream. Pulitzer arrived penniless in 1864 and by 1883 he towered over a newspaper empire with his purchase of the *New York World*. In New York City, four out of five residents were either foreign-born or children of foreign-born parents. Pulitzer understood the desire of these new residents for information on political, social, and recreational activities. Pulitzer, who kept the daily price of the *World* at two cents, doubled circulation in the first three months of ownership. Circulation stood at 250,000 in 1887, making it the nation's largest paper. Pulitzer soon found himself engaged in a newspaper war with William Randolph Hearst as they battle for readership in what was known as "golden age" of journalism.

Hearst, the son of a wealthy U.S. Senator (George Hearst of California) and celebrated Washington socialite, stepped out of his parents' shadow in 1895 with the purchase of the *New York Morning Journal*. A youthful Hearst, who attended Harvard, witnessed the meteoric rise of Pulitzer and came prepared to take on Pulitzer and New York with a sensationalized and self-promoted "yellow journalism" never before undertaken. Pulitzer's life was a complete contrast. He left Hamburg, Germany in 1864 as a contracted enlistee substitute for a Civil War draftee. Upon arrival in Boston, Pulitzer jumped ship and headed for New York City. He eventually worked his way to St. Louis where in 1878, at age 31, he emerged after several shrewd business dealings as the owner of the *St. Louis Post-Dispatch,* and a rising figure on the journalistic scene. In 1883 he and his wife left for New York to board a ship on a doctor-ordered European vacation. However, instead of boarding the steamer, he met with financier Jay Gould and negotiated the purchase of the New York World.

As college football began to emerge from a college-campus-only experience to an event of public interest, the two newspaper magnates realized the potential readership gains to be made with increased reporting and features on athletic competition. Horse racing, prizefighting, baseball, and football went from paragraph-length coverage in the daily papers to multi-paged features drawing on the full range of the papers' personnel and resources. Before Pulitzer bought the *New York World* in 1893, illustration was an "occasional novelty" in newspapers. As soon as he assumed ownership of the *World,* Pulitzer made illustrations a significant part of daily journalism. He developed Sunday supplements that included separate sections for comics, women's features, and a weekly "magazine." By 1895, Pulitzer found himself engaged with his nemesis in a battle to describe the football match of the year.

The greatest rivalry in the new game of American football matched Princeton and Yale in 1895, and interest had reached fever pitch by Thanksgiving Day as the two were scheduled to play at New York's Manhattan Field. All the papers sent correspondents. Hearst sent something more—Richard Harding Davis, the most dashing figure in Victorian New York, who was rumored to be the model for the Gibson Boy, the debonair counterpart to the new American Girls in Charles Dana Gibson's magazine illustrations. By age 31, Davis had published fiction in *Scribner's*, developed a popular newspaper column, and served as managing editor of

*Harper's Weekly.* Hearst hired him to cover Princeton-Yale at the princely fee of $500 for the single piece. Davis, an ardent sports fan, had covered prizefights and football. His name was a guaranteed draw, a sure way to distinguish the *Journal's* report of what would be a well-covered event. To get his money's worth, Hearst paraded the story over two pages, including the whole of a Sunday front, and ran the author's byline almost an inch high in print. The text was accompanied by depictions of the action, the crowd, the coaches, and a bird's eye view of Manhattan Field. Two highly detailed charts followed the ball through each half of the game. A former Yale coach offered a technical assessment of the action, and the famous boxer James Corbett weighed in with his thoughts. Among Davis' most striking prose was his reaction to the crowd of 40,000 packed into Manhattan Field. Mass audiences were clearly as new to sport as they were to newspapers:

> It was like a great crater of living people, and those who were on a level with the players saw the blue sky above them as a man sees it from the bottom of a well. A circle a half of a mile in circumference, and composed of people rising one above the other as high as a three-story house, is a very remarkable sight, and when half of these people leap suddenly to their feet and wave blue flags and yell, and then sink back as the many they have been cheering is tackled and thrown, and the other half jump in the their turn and wave orange and black flags, the effect is something which cannot be duplicated in this country.

Davis' account of the Yale-Princeton football match during Hearst's first month in New York sold out the edition. And it marked a significant moment in coverage of the sport—the crowds themselves were now part of the story. Readers who hadn't attended the game could envision what happened as if they had been there. It fueled interest in the sport as nothing else could have. From coast to coast, colleges jumped on the growing phenomenon created by football. And Yale University, where so many of the game's roots had taken hold, played a major role in spreading its popularity. Yale men fanned out to college and schools far and near, teaching the game that Walter Camp codified. None of Camp's protégés had as large an impact as did Amos Alonzo Stagg.

In the early 1890s, as the preparations for the World's Columbian Exposition were being made, so too was the planning underway for an institution that would serve as a beacon to the city, region, and world—the University of Chicago. The idea began in New York City, where John D. Rockefeller, one of the nation's wealthiest and most ambitious philanthropists, dreamed of founding a new kind of university: rigorous in academics, yet open to educate and serve the masses of Americans who would soon be seeking higher education. Unlike Harvard, Yale, Princeton, and their like, Rockefeller's university would not be tethered to generations from the same families, educated at the same eastern prep schools. He would seek to educate men and women in body, mind, and spirit, bringing together top minds in a diverse range of fields to leads the various departments of study. Rockefeller's plans coalesced around his relationship with a prolific young educator and minister, William Rainey Harper. Born to a small-town Ohio grocer in 1856, Harper made such quick work of his schoolwork that he entered the hometown Muskingum College at the age of 10. A linguistic prodigy, he gave a commencement address in Hebrew at the age of 14. Even after some time working in his father's store, to allow his body to catch up with his mind, Harper was just 17 when he entered graduate studies at Yale in 1873. He joined the faculty of the Baptist Union Theological Seminary of Chicago in 1878 as a Hebrew instructor. A dedicated academic, Harper disagreed with the established practice of essentially closing down for the summer, and he soon developed a system of some 30 summer schools nationwide, focusing on Hebrew and other ancient languages.

Harper's superlative work caught the attention of Rockefeller, a leading trustee of the Chicago seminary, who pleaded with Harper to stay when the young professor was offered a chair in Semitic languages created specifically for him at Yale in 1886. At the same time he moved to Yale, Harper was hired as chief of education at the up and coming Chautauqua Assembly in upstate New York. The ultimate summer session, Chautauqua lasted 60 days and featured 300 lectures by a faculty of 100 educators and civic leaders to some 2,000 students. Harper's charge included traveling the United States recruiting instructors. He was able to display his skills in identifying and attracting scholars and others capable of delivering outstanding lectures. By the next year, Rockefeller and

Harper were envisioning together their major new university, and Harper was successful in shifting Rockefeller's focus to Chicago. There, outside of the long shadow of the traditional Eastern prestige universities, was the opportunity to create something truly unique. Their initial teaching staff in 1892 would include nine former college or seminary presidents, as well as prominent academicians such as Thorstein Veblen, a Norwegian immigrant and leading economist of his day, and John Dewey, an American psychologist, philosopher, educator, and political activist.

There was another important hire for the founding of the University of Chicago: Amos Alonzo Stagg, who was named Associate Professor of the Department of Physical Culture and Athletics. Physical education thus became part of the academic mission of the university, the first time in the history of American higher education that such a tenured appointment was made. The physical education requirement was significant: three quarters of work per year in a student's first two years, then two quarters each of the final two years. Classes met for four and a half hours per week, and students received physical examinations to help determine their coursework in physical education. There was another component to Stagg's hiring: overseeing intercollegiate athletics. And these responsibilities, essentially as a tenured coach, would soon come to far outweigh his work as a professor of "physical culture."

As mercurial as was Harper's rise through academia, Stagg's course was slowed by family hardship. Stagg was the fifth of eight children born in West Orange, New Jersey; his father, a cobbler and general laborer, supported the family. Lonzo, as he was called, often found his formal education interrupted by stints working with his father, and doing a variety of other jobs. He did not enter ninth grade until he was 18. An assistant principal at Orange High School was a Yale graduate and suggested Stagg may be interested in college work. But upon graduation in 1883, Stagg found his high school preparation inadequate to matriculate in New Haven. However, he was able to follow a friend, George Gill, for a year of post-graduate work at Phillips-Exeter Academy in New Hampshire. There, over a bitter winter, the 21-year-old Stagg slept in an unheated garret room, lived on 16 cents a day worth of soda crackers, stale bread, and milk, while studying Latin, Greek, and mathematics. His work ethic was strained to the limit, but he survived and made it to spring, when he could enjoy being outdoors, pitching for the Exeter baseball team.

Pitching was Stagg's greatest joy and success. It soon attracted the attention of colleges, and Dartmouth wrote all but assuring Stagg a spot on its varsity. But Dartmouth did not have a divinity school, so it was Yale where the 22-year-old Stagg arrived with $32 in hand in 1884. For the next six years, until a graduate student in 1890, he would pitch for the Yale varsity, compiling a 42-8 record against main rivals Harvard and Princeton alone. His pitching earned him wide praise, including this description in *The Young Man's Journal* in 1890: "Of America's young men none perhaps are more widely known than A. Alonzo Stagg, the robust Christian athlete of Yale College."

Stagg refused numerous offers to play professional baseball, instead professing a loyalty to his college, and a disdain for a game around which hangers-on would tempt athletes with gambling, alcohol and sinful ways; he would say "the whole tone of the game was smelly." While building his impressive resume on the pitching mound, Stagg had given scant attention to football during his undergraduate years. He failed to make Yale's 1884 team, and did not take up the sport again seriously until the fall of 1888, as a graduate student. It was that fall that the first two great figures in American football—Lonzo Stagg and Walter Chauncey Camp—first crossed paths in a significant way. Camp took over as Yale's first officially recognized head coach in the fall of 1888. That first squad not only included Stagg but also William (Pudge) Heffelfinger, the 6-foot-3, 206-pound lineman from Minneapolis who would become a three-time All-American—as chosen by Camp. The pair led a Bulldog squad that won all 13 games, outscoring its opposition by a combined 698 to 0. Yale faced Wesleyan three times (76-0, 46-0, and 105-0), Amherst twice (39-0 and 70-0), and Pennsylvania twice (34-0 and 58-0).

In 1889 Stagg spent his only year in Yale's divinity school, and it was his final year as a Yale athlete. This time Camp arranged a 17-game schedule, again meeting Wesleyan three times and playing two games each against Amherst, Williams, Cornell, and the Crescent Athletic Club. The competition provided some greater drama than 1888. A mid-season battle at Penn resulted in a 20-10 Yale win; a trip to Brooklyn to play Crescent was just a 5-0 triumph; and Yale came away from a pitched battle with Harvard, winning 6-0. Yale took a 16-0 record into the finale, against

Princeton in the city, but fell to the Tigers, 10-0—Yale's first loss since dropping a 6-5 decision to Princeton in 1885. Stagg's two-year record as a Yale player thus ended 29-1. Camp would coach Yale just three more seasons; he finished with a five-year record of 68-2. Along the way he sent some of the biggest names out across America to guide the newly standardized game. Included in 1900 was Dr. Henry L. Williams, who led the University of Minnesota for 22 years, producing some of that school's strongest teams. The list also comprised George Woodruff, who would guide Penn to its greatest period of success. And to the new University of Chicago, Amos Alonzo Stagg.

As football "missionaries," Williams and Stagg took the game as played by the "holy trinity" of Yale, Princeton, and Harvard and spread it westward. For Stagg, it was a natural extension of his actual missionary work. Upon graduation in 1888, Harper hired Stagg to be the director of the athletic program at the Chautauqua Assembly in upstate New York. From there, he gained a wider influence, ministering to evangelical youth for Dwight L. Moody's summer conferences, first in Massachusetts, then in Wisconsin.

At the newly opened International YMCA Training School in Springfield, Massachusetts, Stagg studied and taught alongside another young Christian, this one a Canadian from McGill University—James Naismith, who had invented an unusual new game involving a peach basket to keep athletes occupied indoors during the harsh New England winters. Stagg was sent out with a suitcase of "lantern slides" to promote the new school and speak to groups of young Christian athletes. The new college also fielded a football team—the Christians—and Stagg was put in charge. For two seasons (1890-1891) Stagg guided the team, gaining considerable praise for his ability to train young men in this relatively new pursuit. He also hinted at his future as a showman, guiding his team in a midnight game at Madison Square Garden—considered America's first indoor football game. Before he joined Harper in Chicago, Stagg made it known that he had been approached by both Yale and Penn to guide their football fortunes and had at least a conversation with Harvard about the same. Johns Hopkins University in Baltimore was also said to desire his services as director of physical culture. Stagg's letters to Harper quickly turned to the matter of salary, and the president promised to make the move worthwhile for the young athletic director.

It soon became apparent that the goals and motivations of William Rainey Harper and Amos Alonzo Stagg were in significant alignment—especially in regard to football. Harper would earn the moniker of "the P.T. Barnum of education," operating the University of Chicago, "The Greatest Show on Earth." This "born propagandist" would talk of promoting "physical culture" for the student body, but what set his juices flowing was the possibility of creating a big-time football program, in an era where there were precious few models to emulate. "The University of Chicago believes in football," Harper said. "We shall encourage it here." Stagg poured himself into intercollegiate athletics. He saw building successful teams as a way to encourage "strong college spirit" while adding that the men on such teams could act as Christian role models.

University of Chicago football began on the school's initial day of classes—October 1, 1892—when Stagg met with 300 students to select a "varsity yell." In his role as player-coach, he attracted enough eager students to form a team. They played an ad hoc schedule, with games against high school and other teams often set up just days in advance. They were able to schedule two games each against Illinois and Northwestern, going 1-2-1, but the highlight without a doubt was a trip to Toledo, Ohio to face Michigan, already the primary Western power. Chicago performed admirably, losing just 18-10, and in the process gained publicity for the new institution. The 1893 season brought the Maroons a home field when prosperous Chicago store owner Marshall Field donated land at the university's northern edge. The team thus began what became one of its hallmarks under Stagg: playing the vast majority of its games at home. The 1893 Chicago team made just one trip, and that only as far as Evanston for a 6-6 tie with Northwestern. It also began the cornerstone of Chicago's annual schedule, a home game against Michigan on Thanksgiving Day. Newspapers in Chicago hailed the game as an important breakthrough, a signature football event that could be the West's equivalent of the Yale-Harvard or Yale-Princeton affairs. Michigan fans arrived via special excursion trains, and President Harper sent invitations to many of Chicago's most prominent residents. Without an alumni base to rely on for support, the university created an almost overnight bond with the local citizens, especially those of the professional and business elite, many of whom had graduated from college themselves. Since no stands had yet been erected at Marshall Field, the well-heeled arrived in fine carriages to watch the action—and each other. Each team had as its mascot a huge turkey in school colors, strutting about and letting out "gobbles almost as loud and effective as the yells of the rival universities." The transformation of Chicago football from a vigorous, healthful activity for its students to a prime slice of entertainment and publicity for the college had been achieved within the space of two football seasons.

The turkey day extravaganza did not, however, mark the end of Chicago's season. Stagg reprised his earlier foray into Madison Square Garden by staging a pair of postseason games at the nearby indoor Tattersalls Arena on a field measuring a skimpy 65 by 30 yards. A December 16 match with Northwestern ended when a punted ball smashed an electric lamp, littering the field with glass fragments. More successful as an athletic exhibition was the game played on New Year's Day, 1894, against the team from the University of Notre Dame, resulting in an 8-0 Chicago victory. It was just the 12th game played in Notre Dame's football history, which had operated sporadically since its inaugural game in November 1887. Stagg had by this time developed a fellow instructor, Joseph A. Raycroft, as his replacement at quarterback, but after an injury to Raycroft, Stagg inserted himself back into the lineup for the Notre Dame game.

The establishment of the University of Chicago was the fulfillment of the dreams envisioned at the World's Fair in 1893; the cultural and educational foundations for a new city were established. By 1894 the city and the university became the shining light of the West. And on the athletic fields, Stagg planned a most ambitious campaign. After three preseason games against Chicago high schools, the Maroons went 9-5-1 through a 15-game regular season from September 12 through November 29, the Thanksgiving battle with Michigan. It was what followed the 1894 season that made the year most notable. Stagg had arranged for his team to make a splash unprecedented in American football: a 6,200-mile tour to the Pacific Coast and back to play a series of postseason games. There was no question as to its purposes: the opportunity to draw large crowds and profitable gates and advertise the University of Chicago far beyond its Midwestern home. Stagg arranged a pair of games against another relatively new institution, Leland Stanford Jr. University of Palo Alto, California. Negotiating for Leland Stanford was none other than Stagg's mentor at Yale, Walter Camp, who had left New Haven to become Stanford's first coach in 1892, and after a year's absence, was again coaching the new school. Also representing Stanford was the treasurer of its athletic association, student Herbert Hoover.

The Maroons experienced adventure before ever arriving in California. They had been given the use of a benefactor's private rail car. Their first look at it came upon their departure from Chicago, and Stagg later called it a condemned Pullman that "looked as though Sherman had marched through it." Sure enough, while crossing the Rockies, the coal stove ignited the woodwork, and the coach and his players fought the fire with axes and water, and then abandoned the wreck at Sacramento. The first game against Stanford was played Christmas Day at San Francisco. Like the train trip, it didn't go entirely smoothly.

As the players were leaving the field at halftime, a scuffle erupted between the referee and Chicago quarterback Frank Hering, with conflicting reports of who struck whom first. The game had to be finished with a substitute referee, and Chicago prevailed, 24-4. The teams met again four days later in Los Angeles in what might be called the first true college bowl game—two teams playing away from their respective campuses well after the regular season, primarily to attract a healthy profit and promote the institutions. The tour continued with a match against the Reliance Athletic Club on January 1, 1895, and the return trip included a 52-0 Chicago victory against the Salt Lake YMCA.

Camp, already a prolific football writer, was collecting a series of statements supporting football's role on college campuses, and received this one from Stagg: "Football has done a great deal toward arousing college spirit where little or none existed, so we feel it has been of special value in our university life." Inside of three years, Rockefeller's university had constructed a form of intercollegiate athletics that expanded on the form of its Eastern forbears and blazed a path that set up college football as a major source of entertainment, revenue, and school spirit.

# 6

# A Family's Life

In the aftermath of the World's Columbian Exposition, the White City entered the world's consciousness as a brilliant example of inspired design uplifting an urban area. Leaders of cities in the United States and abroad viewed the Chicago fair as an elegant template of what could be achieved in making urban areas functional and beautiful. They sought out Daniel Burnham, the Fair's Director of Works. He was asked to apply his model of urban planning to their cities. Soon San Francisco, Cleveland, and Washington, D.C. were using his expertise and vision. The City Beautiful movement grew out of the Chicago Fair. It promoted beauty and monumental grandeur not only for its own sake, but also to encourage moral and civic virtue among urban populations. In Chicago, leaders and citizens were left with great civic pride—a feeling that in Chicago, anything was possible. The planning for recently annexed areas combined effective land use and efficient transportation routes with open spaces, greenways, and ornamentation. Visitors to the Fair had been impressed with the grounds and with the continuous system of broad, tree-lined boulevards and spacious parks that ringed the city; they dubbed it the Emerald Necklace.

The Emerald Necklace had not been built haphazardly, but by forward-thinking planning. A quarter-century earlier, in 1869, the Illinois legislature had created the South, West, and North Park districts and detailed the location of the parks and connecting boulevards. Although much of the land was located outside of Chicago's city limits at the time, the system was designed to encourage and guide orderly expansion of the growing city. The South Park District commissioned the firm of Olmsted and Vaux, designers of Central Park in New York City, to design its park and boulevard system, which ultimately led to the creation of the Midway Plaisance, a pivotal space before and after the World's Fair.

In 1870 the West Park District commissioned the design of Douglas, Garfield, and Humboldt parks and the connecting boulevards. Each side of the resulting wide boulevards sported orderly lines of trees planted with impressive squares—including Logan Square—at the boulevard turning points. The parks were designed to provide recreational space and break up the formality of the boulevards, which were seen as promenades for carriage rides and leisurely walks. Gas lighting was installed along the boulevards and entrances to the parks. A street washer system was put in place to combat the dusty road conditions, to irrigate the medians, and to water the graveled streets to hold down dust. To ensure that the boulevards provided pleasure drives, speed limits were set at a maximum of eight miles per hour in 1871, and all vehicles "transporting merchandise, commercial goods, building materials, manure, soil, and other articles" were banned from the boulevards in 1873. Originally the boulevards served the wealthy, who built their mansions along the parkway. Soon, however, public phaetons (carriages) traveled along the boulevards to permit greater access to the parks by all citizens.

The northwest corner of the Emerald Necklace featured Humboldt Park, Logan Square, and Humboldt and Logan boulevards. As was the case with many immigrant neighborhoods, churches dominated the landscapes. Norwegian-American artist Anton Reihnoltzen created paintings for the Bethel Lutheran church on Humboldt Avenue. Within walking distance one could see the spires of the Logan Square Norwegian Baptist Church and the Kedzie Avenue Methodist Church. Norwegian pride was also evident in the founding of the Leif Erikson Monument Society in 1891, which capitalized on the preparation for the Colombian Exposition and its showcasing of the Norwegian explorer. The area anchored an attractive, orderly corner of the city that was appealing to both established and growing families—including one newly arrived from Voss, Norway.

After the fair, the Rockne family focused on assimilation into American life, starting with the spelling of its last name. Lars became Louis, young Knute added the middle name of Kenneth, and just a year after the family joined the father in Chicago, the first American-born family member, Louise, arrived in June 1894. Knute now had three sisters with whom to share his parents' time and attention. Louis began taking English language and civics classes in the evening, starting the route toward naturalization. Norwegian was still spoken frequently at home, but out in the world the Rocknes were becoming increasingly American. It was a constant tug-and-pull for those recently settled in the New World; one could not forget their heritage as they built new futures. Ties to the past helped many Norwegians in Chicago put a framework around the rapidly changing environment.

The Norwegian-American press held significant influence in the Chicago community and helped with the transition. These Norwegian-language papers expressed diverse agendas and addressed separate audiences but nonetheless promoted a sense of community. As early as June 1, 1866 *Skandinaven* published its first issue, which helped play a role in community-building. It printed news from immigrant churches, clubs, and societies and encouraged the process of Americanization among Norwegian and other Scandinavian immigrants. The papers served as civic educators and provided a political voice for those seeking election to public office.

By 1870 *Skandinaven* was publishing three times a week for its Chicago readers and followed soon with a daily. John Anderson took over sole ownership of the paper in 1878 and moved offices to an imposing building on Peoria Avenue in 1883. From his wood-paneled offices, Anderson advertised his papers to be "printers of all languages." He took advantage of the flood of immigrants arriving in Chicago beginning in the 1880s; they helped to swell subscription rolls and to secure a permanent prosperity for the firm. By 1892 the daily edition of *Skandinaven* printed more than 10,000 copies and it was read in nearly every Norwegian home. Readers, like the Rocknes, enjoyed the telling of immigrant experiences, which muted differences as well as encouraged the celebration of Norwegian heritage.

For Louis Rockne, assimilation and providing for his family eventually intersected. In America with large, established vehicle companies such as the Studebaker Brothers, his work on carriages was more of an avocation. He was rigorous in doing what was necessary to provide a comfortable life for his growing family. Within a short time, that meant moving his family of six into a sturdy brick home on North Rockwell. Built a decade earlier, it was well-located just a few blocks north of Logan Boulevard and nearby both church and school. And with the move came a shift in occupations. Louis would now pack his lunchbox and head to work as an engineer for Anderson's Norwegian-American newspaper enterprise. Anderson, also from Voss, had arrived in Chicago in 1846. He sold apples on the streets of Chicago and peddled newspapers to support his family. Anderson worked in the composing room of the *Chicago Tribune* where he learned that papers could be a profitable business venture as well as a communication tool. Anderson was more than happy to extend work to a fellow countryman from Voss who was a skilled craftsman. Louis Rockne would now put his talents to work ensuring the presses ran smoothly. One could ill-afford a press shutdown to slow the printing and distribution of papers sold in the city and packed on trains headed to Norwegian settlements in non-urban areas.

Louis was ever the craftsman and fine technician, no matter what his occupation. Any thoughts, however, that Knute might follow the same path were likely dashed early, after an incident with Knute and a sharp chisel-like tool. Knute accidently stepped on the device, causing it to flip in the air and gash his leg. His clumsiness with a hammer and nail led to an apt, but no doubt painful, nickname from his father: Klureneve, Norwegian for "all thumbs." Neither carpentry nor tinkering with machinery set Knute's young heart ablaze. Rather, it was adventure, striking out to see new places, meeting new fellows and experiencing what this amazing New World offered.

For as much as the great boulevards and the homes being built on and around them were defining the new city, there was still a patchwork of small former hay farms and other open spaces to investigate. Knute and his fellow explorers were continually organizing hikes, fishing expeditions, and jaunts that ventured out into what was still considered the nearby country. It was as if sunshine, fresh air, and open spaces were the required ingredients for a contented existence, and there was enough of each in young Knute's world to help build a great capacity for imagination, exploration, and self-expression. For it was in traveling from one place to another that a footrace among this group of lads might occur. And the challenge of keeping up or, on some days, setting the pace, brought a sense of exhilaration to young Knute. He also participated in many of the athletic events that were part of the Chicago-Norwegian community—perhaps none more prominent than *syttende mai*, which celebrated the Norwegian Constitution Day observed on May 17 each year. In addition to offering young lads the opportunity to race competitively, *syttende mai* featured colorful parades and folk festivals. Parade participants included the Norwegian Turner Society, the Norwegian Rifle Club, the Norwegian Athletic Club Sleipner, and the Norge Ski Club, which represented Norwegian prowess on snow and ice. "In this manner mother Norway's emigrated children ought to celebrate her proudest moment," proclaimed one issue of *Skandinaven*. Hakon Lehn, a machinist at *Skandinaven*, encouraged ski-lovers to form a society to promote the sport. In response to his call, 18 young, Norwegian-born men met at Peterson's Hall on California and North Avenues to form the club. By 1907 they were performing competitions at Fox River Grove in Cary, about 35 miles north of Chicago and at Shoot-the-Chutes Park in Chicago.

Over time, the Rockne neighborhood became a grand playground with all manner of games and sports tried out in season. The vacant lot the boys used one week might well become a building site the next, but the cavalcade of races and games simply found another temporary home nearby. An old clothesline could become the site of a pole vaulting or high jumping competition. The iron weight from an old kerosene chandelier provided the equipment for the shot-put. Any patch of ground less than rock-hard could be suitable for a hop, skip, and jump.

Halfway around the world in Athens, Greece the Olympic Games were revived in April 1896 after an absence of some 1,500 years. Pierre de Coubertin, a young French baron and historian, nearly single-handedly organized the games, which consisted largely of track and field events, along with some swimming, cycling, fencing, and rifle competition. A total of 285 athletes from 13 nations participated in the revival. The United States team consisted of 10 trackmen—four from Princeton and six from Boston—along with two riflemen and a swimmer. Robert Garrett, the Princeton track captain, paid the way for his teammates and himself. Along with the Boston tracksters, they made their way overseas via two lengthy boat excursions, followed by an all-night train ride, arriving just in time to compete at the Panathinaiko Stadium. An estimated 80,000 spectators jammed the stadium for the opening ceremonies on April 6 with the athletes, grouped by nation, in the infield. Crown Prince Constantine gave a welcoming speech, then his father, King George I, spoke: "I declare the opening of the first international Olympic Games in Athens. Long live the Nation. Long live the Greek people."

The Greek people were justifiably proud when Spyridon Louis, a previously little-known water carrier, became a national hero by winning the Games' feature event, the long-distance race from the village of Marathon over the historic road followed by the famous messenger centuries ago bearing the news of the defeat of the Persians. But Louis was the only home-country champion at the Games, as other Greek favorites were upstaged. Two such events were the shot-put and discus throw, in which Princeton's Garrett won gold. Garrett's discus throw of 29.15 meters defeated Paraskevopoulous, the Greek champ, by 19 centimeters.

Thomas Burke of the Boston Athletic Association gained great fame in Athens, winning the 100-meter race in 12.0 seconds and the 400-meter race in 54.2 seconds. In both events, Burke was the only competitor to use the "crouch start" which placed one knee on the ground. The technique caused confusion among track officials, but was ruled legal. Reports from Athens told about the crowds that viewed the Games from outside the massive stadium:

> The Stadium has no roof, and on each side of it rise hills from which a good view can be had. These hills were fairly black with spectators, thousands of whom were too poor to pay the small price of admission to the Stadium, but who were determined to see the revival of the ancient Greek festival. The sight was a remarkable one, and seldom have such interest and enthusiasm been displayed over any recent event in the Grecian capital.

And this about the overall scene: "In the evening the Acropolis and city were illuminated by myriads of electric and other lights. The scene was

beautiful and fairylike. Everywhere there was the greatest enthusiasm."
The World's Fair had showed cities and countries that transportation, architecture, and electricity had dimensions far beyond the simply functional. In similar fashion, the early Olympic Games illustrated that amateur
athletic competition, unsullied by gamblers or cheats, could be conducted
in an atmosphere of pomp, celebration, and cooperation among nations.
It was, simply, sports as spectacle. Amateur, from the Latin to mean to
love. The pure love of the sport. The splendor and ceremony of the
Athens Games—and those at the 1900 Paris Olympics—inspired young
athletes around the globe, including those displaying their athleticism in
the open lots of Northwest Chicago neighborhoods. A young lad might
touch his knee to the ground in preparing to sprint, a la Burke, toward
whatever finish line lay ahead. Another may picture himself as Garrett of
Princeton, straining to heave the shot, or iron weight as the case may be,
to a distance beyond that of the Greek favorite.

Outdoors, the boys fashioned whatever stick or pole they could find
into a baseball bat, until that rare day when someone showed up with
actual equipment. Mitts consisted of whatever padding they could cram
into a discarded work glove. Young Knute's mind gravitated to the pitching mound—one man in the center of all the action and attention. He
fashioned himself as a young Rube Waddell, star major league pitcher of
the century's first decade. Waddell won an impressive 193 major league
games in a career that included a brief stop in Chicago with the 1901 Or-
phans, who a year later would become known as the Cubs.

Knute loved the story—apocryphal or not—about how Rube came
upon baseball. Dressed like a scarecrow, the story goes, Rube drove a
team of mules and a wagon onto a crowded ballfield in Harrisburg, Pennsylvania and interrupted the game. After parking the wagon near one dug-
out, he proceeded to the mound and struck out 12 batters in a row. The
Rube was a favorite of kids, Rockne said, letting them into games for free,
"and we'd even follow him miles and miles in his eccentricities." Waddell,
who sometimes would leave his team during a game to follow passing
fire trucks to their destinations, would take an unauthorized leave from
the ball club. He may have shown up in Libertyville or some other town
and pitched for a local semi-pro outfit. The man was a great showman.
Once in a semi-pro game, he turned dramatically in the box, waved in all

the outfielders, sent them to the bench, and struck out every batter. Fans of opposing teams found they could easily distract him by holding up shiny objects, puppies, or other items which seemed to send him into a trance. Waddell's odd antics, sometimes fueled by alcohol, led to friction, as well as fisticuffs, with teammates and managers, and his career included numerous trades. He continued to rack up strikeouts and victories, and pitched 50 shutouts in his big-league career.

Rockne's other pitching hero was also an unusual fellow, but perhaps of a nobler bent. Mordecai Peter Centennial Brown was born on a farm in Nyesville in west-central Indiana in 1876 as the United States celebrated its 100th anniversary. As a youngster on the farm, he was pushing material into a feed chopper when he slipped and the machine's blades mangled his right hand. He lost most of his index finger and suffered damage to the others. A subsequent fall broke several finger bones, which were not reset properly, especially the middle finger, which would be crooked for life. Through countless hours of throwing rocks against the barn, he learned to grasp and throw a baseball effectively. In fact, his unorthodox grip caused greater spin on the ball, and he fashioned a nasty curveball. Known as Three-Finger Brown, he was the mainstay of the Cubs pitching staff for nearly a decade.

Without any involvement from adults, young Rockne and his pals kept a full slate of athletic competition going. As recalled by a friend, "Emissaries were sent to other neighborhoods challenging (them) to baseball and football games. Uniforms or no uniforms, race, creed, color or size of opponents—nothing made any difference. If your shirt were torn, play in your undershirt—this was the spirit." Rockne recalls "impromptu and sometimes violent" games involving his team, known as the "Swedes" but encompassing the various Scandinavian nationalities, against the "Irish." The games were played on a huge vacant corner lot on Wednesday and Saturday afternoons, under the watchful eye of an Irish cop remembered as "O'Goole." When the Irish lads were administering a licking to the Swedes, he gave his approval: "It's an elegant game, good for the youngsters." But if the Swedes had added some tough guys to the roster, perhaps even an Italian or two, and were getting the better of the Irish, the copper could be counted on to intervene and break up the battle, unpiling Swedes and proclaiming, "The game is altogether brutal and unfit for small boys."

The Swedes had little recourse except to petition the local precinct captain to assign a Scandinavian cop, if he had one, to the patrol.

For children in many times and locations, team sports were at least as much about belonging. Knute took pride in his role as an end on one neighborhood team, the Tricky Tigers—so named for a triple-pass trick play that would be pulled out on occasion to flummox the opponent as well as impress any onlookers. From an early age, the notion that football could be a theatrical event, and not merely a brutal slugfest, captured Knute's imagination. Knute and some of his neighborhood pals later graduated to the Barefoot Athletic Club, which was dominated by many of their former Irish opponents. It was a more organized level of the sport, and on one memorable fall Saturday, the Barefoots were taking on the Hamburg Athletic Club for the district championship on a large lot near South Side Park, home of the White Sox. Rockne recalled that "crowds lined the gridiron and broke into it as the game progressed," also noting that "the more pugnacious spectators slipped away every now and then for refreshments at nearby saloons."

At a critical point of the game Rockne's number was called for an end run. Using his only weapon, his sprinter's speed, he raced around end and past the Hamburg defense, with only open field ahead of him. His path to a deciding touchdown was clear—until Hamburg fans stepped out onto the field, threw him down, and made off with the ball. Something of a minor riot ensued and most participants made it home with evidence of the brawl in the form of busted lips and black eyes. That was a problem for Knute, as football was the one activity he enjoyed on a strictly undercover basis. A pair of patched moleskin football pants, his most prized possession, had to be smuggled in and out of the house. His parents, whom he said considered football "a system of modified massacre," saw the results of the Hamburg scrum on his face and put an end to any further footballing. As it was almost winter, he didn't think too much of it. Spring was right around the corner, and his family approved of baseball. The irony came when Knute found himself caught in the middle of an argument that developed during an extra-inning game, and a swung bat smashed his nose, creating the somewhat flattened effect going forward. He could joke during his athletic career about the football ban from his parents, while "he got this nose from baseball."

But to Louis and Martha, this was serious business. They came by their suspicions over football quite naturally. Through the 1890s and the first few years of the new century, headlines in the Chicago papers regularly read:

"Killed in the Tackle"

"Deaths from Football"

"Revolt Against Football"

"Death on the Gridiron"

"Bill to Stop Football"

On October 31, 1897 Richard Von Gammon, member of a prominent Rome, Georgia family and a freshman fullback for the University of Georgia, died from "concussion of the brain" suffered in a game against the University of Virginia. The next day, the Georgia team was disbanded and the season's remaining games canceled, as "Chancellor Boggs has announced that the game will be entirely stricken from the college's list of sports." Within a day, "a storm of public sentiment has swept over the entire state, demanding the immediate and absolute abolition of the brutal sport." Anti-football bills were introduced in the state legislature. Within a month a leading medical journal, *The Medical Record*, called for the abolition of football, stating:

> In view of the great number of serious accidents on the football field between college teams it is impossible any longer to view the game in the light of innocent recreative amusement with harmless and healthful athletics as its object…There is hardly a game played in which some one of the contestants is not more or less seriously hurt…If we wish to develop pluck, courage, endurance, and strength we can do so in more healthful and safer ways.

At the conclusion of the 1897 season it was reported that eight football players died from game action, "an appalling record (that) shows conclusively that something must be done regarding the playing of football if it is to continue." Several of the deaths occurred at the high school level, and a majority took place in Pennsylvania. Blame was laid on the University of Pennsylvania, which "uses the destructive guards-back mass play, which many experts say is in direct violation of the rules forbidding momentum plays." The play featured 10 men forming a "flying wedge" protecting the ball carrier inside the formation.

Fatalities and serious injuries had already caused the game to be banned at numerous colleges and schools, including ones as prominent as Georgetown College in Washington, D.C., where "students themselves (testified) that some of the injured ones were slugged and others were brutally kicked after they were down." At Hedding College, a Methodist school in downstate Abingdon, Illinois, president Evans prohibited the playing of football by the students, characterizing the game as brutal and unmanly and as a "blot on our civilization." In an editorial entitled "Regulating the Game of Football," the *Chicago Daily Tribune* as early as 1894 pointed out the effects of the college game on younger players: "Seeing that the students of colleges kick, maul and slug each other, the students of academies and high schools imitate them, and kick, maul and slug each other. No excuse can be made for this brutal game. It is ungentlemanly, ruffianly, cruel and disgusting as it is now conducted." One of Walter Camp's players at Yale in the early 1880s, Henry D. Twombly, laid most of the blame for the brutality of the game in the mid-1890s to "the time and attention of the Captain and coaches of a team are given to the perfecting of team interference at the expense of most of the other points of the game." He advocated opening up the game, to "do away with mass plays, the close, uninteresting shoving in the line, and the long waits for the recovery of injured men."

Against that backdrop, college and university officials and football coaches met in 1896 to address the issue and how best to safeguard the continuation of the sport amidst demands for increased safety. One area of change by the turn of the century included equipment. Shin guards, heavy shoes, leather shoulder pads and "head harnesses" all became standard issue. A.G. Spalding, a former baseball player, began a large athletic supply business offering much of the new required equipment. Rules changes became inevitable when the eastern Intercollegiate Football Rules Committee invited University of Chicago's Amos Alonzo Stagg to join them for discussions in 1898, and the move to create a more open and less violent game was underway. Stagg, more than anyone, envisioned a game in which an offense emphasizing quickness and cunning might counteract the older "mass play" in which brawn was the essential force.

Stagg foresaw the day when the forward pass would open up the game, noting in 1906, "I have been doing a good deal of experimenting with the forward pass, and I believe it is going to have quite an influence upon the game." By 1905, reforms and equipment changes had done little to change the perception of a violent game that needed curbing if not outright banishment.

Another survey in 1905 indicated 18 dead and 159 serious injuries from football. Within a context of progressive reforms sweeping the country, many looked at the reform of football the way Ida Tarbell and Lincoln Steffens approached John D. Rockefeller's monopolistic oil industry. President Theodore Roosevelt, caught between his belief in the character-building benefits of college football and a public clamor for reform, used a commencement address at Harvard in 1905 to denounce the excessive roughness and violence. It was only when Roosevelt realized that some academic institutions (Columbia and New York University) had abolished football and that others were considering it, did he tamper his reproach of the game. By October 9, 1905 Roosevelt called a football conference at the White House to discuss the matter. Present from the eastern big three were Walter Camp and John Owsley of Yale; Bill Reed and Edward Nichols of Harvard; and Princeton's John Fine and Arthur Hildebrand. Providing Roosevelt with power-broker assistance was Secretary of State Elihu Root, a Yale graduate. By nightfall, the six had agreed to abide by "in letter and spirit the rules of play." Camp released a draft of the agreement to the press, and the *New York Times* in an editorial on October 10 congratulated Roosevelt saying, "Having ended the war in the Far East (the Russo-Japanese war), ...grappled with the railroad rate question, today President Roosevelt took up another question of vital interest to the American people. He started a campaign for reform in football."

Further rules changes followed to meet the largest areas of criticism without lessening the attractiveness of the game. Most notable was the encouragement of the forward pass to open the game. By 1906 a Midwestern Intercollegiate Conference met to also discuss reforms regarding spectators (who would secure the most profitable site for games); coaching reforms (how best to deal with paid staff who were instructing only collegiate athletes and for only short durations of time); and player reform (player eligibility). For young Knute Rockne, amidst the subject of football's brutality, there was always one refuge: the pure athletics of track and field. There, on any vacant lot or backyard, an organized game, or even teammates, were not necessary. Instead, the competition was simplified— the object was one's personal best. It could be worked on at any time, with or without witnesses. It was the essence of challenging oneself, of dedication, perseverance, discipline, self-sacrifice. All in an effort to achieve the Olympic motto, proposed by Pierre de Coubertin on the creation of the International Olympic Committee in 1894: Citius, Altius, Fortius—Latin for "Faster, Higher, Stronger."

# 7

# Two-Fold Education

O f the millions who immigrated to the United States in the 19th century, many came penniless and entered the American work-force at the very bottom of the economic ladder. Some, like Lars Rokne, brought marketable skills and experience, which made the way forward easier in the new land. And a few were of such accomplishment that their lives had a tremendous effect on both sides of the Atlantic. Such is the story of Lorenz Brentano. Born in 1813 in Manheim, Baden in Germany, Brentano earned a law degree, practiced law, and was twice voted mayor of Manheim. He was elected to the Parliament at Frankfurt in 1848, and by the close of the session he was named leader of the Liberal party. In the German political upheaval of the times, Brentano was made president of the provisional government of Baden. In this role, he advanced the cause of trial by jury and equal rights for Jewish citizens of the district. When monarchists regained power, he was forced to flee to Switzerland and in 1849 immigrated to the United States. He published a German-language newspaper in Pottsville, Pennsylvania in 1850. Due to his paper's strong stand against slavery, an element of the citizenry burned the newspaper office and drove him from the area. He settled near Kalamazoo, Michigan, where he farmed for several years before acquiring an interest in another German-language paper, the Chicago-based Staats-Zeitung. Brentano moved to Chicago and was elected to the Illinois general assembly in 1863. He served on the Chicago Board of Education for seven years, five as its president. He was later made Consul to Dresden and was elected to a term as U.S. Congressman in 1876. In his later years, he wrote extensively for German papers and law journals, contrasting the American and European codes of criminal justice.

Judge Elliott Anthony hailed Brentano, after his death in 1891, as "a great public character, (who) first and last filled a large space in the world's history. He displayed a zeal in the cause of freedom and...uniting with his energy great sagacity and shrewdness, he became...a leader of men.... Possessed of an indomitable will and of the most transcendent industry, he was indefatigable and untiring, and never allowed anything to interfere with his literary pursuits or the discharge of his duties." It is little wonder that a year later, when the Chicago Board of Education began construction of nearly two dozen new schools, it decided to name one of them for Lorenz Brentano.

The new school, located at Linden and Maplewood avenues in the Logan Square neighborhood, was one of several new grammar schools Chicago desperately needed to educate an enrollment that was swelling annually due to the growth of the city via annexation and immigration. These structures, handsome three-story brick buildings, were each constructed at a cost of $70,000 and contained 16 rooms. The same year, at Potomac Avenue and Davis Street, Northwest Division High School, with 18 rooms plus an assembly hall, was built for $105,000. The Rockne children, and those who lived in the area, were the beneficiaries of a Board of Education intent on providing as strong a public education as possible to the thousands of new students. As Brentano School, Northwest Division High, and the other new schools opened on September 1, 1893, a total of 170,000 students were expected at nearly 300 Chicago schools. In previous years, not all prospective students could be accommodated, but as noted in the *Chicago Daily Tribune* in 1893, "it is probable this year, on account of the new school buildings, even taking into consideration the increase in population, none will be turned away."

A typical classroom might include between 40-50 students. Brentano listed a capacity of 972 students, about 60 per classroom. The strong turnout showed the eagerness of families to assimilate into mainstream American culture. The Chicago Board of Education decreed that there would be fewer German classes taught, and none at all in the primary grades by the 1893-94 school year. "There will be less singing, less paper pasting, less sewing, and less color work. Physical culture study has been greatly reduced."

It was clear the emphasis would be on the basic subjects, including reading, arithmetic, history, and civics. Less than three decades after a bloody Civil War nearly split the nation apart, every effort was being made to educate and unite students in a truly American curriculum. The school year ran nearly 10 months, with closing exercises in late June honoring 40 graduates at Brentano. As Brentano completed its first year, "a pleasing feature of the morning's exercises was the exhibition of dumbbell drill and Indian club swinging." Louis D. Pelham received the first Brentano School medal, and the prize for "best work in calisthenics" was awarded to Irving Quackenbush. Brentano quickly established a reputation for academic rigor and discipline, under Principal W. D. Smyser. By its third year of operation, 1894-95, it was among 33 Chicago schools selected as centers for college preparatory work. The Board of Education adopted a special college preparatory course and decided to begin as early as the seventh grade. It was noted, "the educational value of pointing the pupils toward a college course can hardly be overestimated because of the encouragement given to them to continue their education."

For all the advancements in school operation, there were also major challenges, some of a personal nature. Disputes in which parents confronted teachers or principals over an issue would occasionally devolve into physical combat. For instance, Principal Kletzing of Ravenswood School had reprimanded a student who, with a long and powerful bow, had shot out the eye of a fellow student. The miscreant's father came to school and assaulted Kletzing. In the spring of 1896, another parent, a Dr. Keaton, attacked Kletzing, who at 15 years in his position was a principal of far greater experience than most. Kletzing's fellow educators were outraged, and soon a headline read, "Teachers To Go Armed." It was reported, "many of the teachers and principals of the public schools have laid in a supply of firearms and cartridges for what they term 'brutes of the Keaton stripe.' Principal Smyser of the Brentano School openly declared he kept a gun ready for visitors who came to thrash him."

Enrolled at the Brentano School, young Knute Rockne showed early signs of excellence, owing to "his remarkable memory and zest for study." His marks were nearly perfect, and he showed an especially strong love of reading. He also displayed an inventive mind as applied to acquiring books in which he was interested. A rule in the Rockne family at the time allowed the purchase of any item as long as it was a gift for another family member. It is said that Knute gifted his sisters with books more than anything, and more often than not he became the first to read each one. His interests included history, geography, and exploration—the stories of figures in the past who reached beyond their origins and far outdistanced any perceived limitations.

As much as the Brentano School served as a bridge to assimilation for newly arrived immigrants in the neighborhood, the Rockne family's church kept the links to Norwegian culture intact. The family belonged to the Immanuel Norwegian Lutheran Church, which was founded in 1887, and had constructed a handsome, modern church building in 1890 at Maplewood Avenue and Cherry Place, about six blocks south of the Rockne home. Services were conducted in the Norwegian language, still spoken in the homes of many congregants. The church belonged to Hauge's Norwegian Evangelical Lutheran Synod in America, known as The Hauge Synod, named after Norwegian revivalist lay preacher Hans Nielsen Hauge.

The synod was considered "low church," placing a greater emphasis on personal faith than on formal worship. Hauge himself spent much of his life traversing Norway by foot, leading charismatic meetings, and his organization challenged the established way of the state church. He and his followers were persecuted; at his death at age 51, Hauge had spent nine years in prison. Hauge Synod pastors received their training at the Red Wing Seminary located in Red Wing, Minnesota, which operated until the Hauge Synod merged into the Norwegian Lutheran Church of America in 1917. Pastors serving the Rockne's congregation included Minnesota natives Reverend Julius A. Quello (1902-07) and Reverend John Nilson Walstead (1907-15). As an eighth-grader, Knute Rockne received confirmation instruction from Reverend Quello. On one occasion, when Knute and his friend and fellow confirmation candidate Tom Oyen were waiting for Pastor Quello to arrive, Knute took on a dare from another student, and "walked" on his hands along the church's picket fence. The others in the class were amazed as Rockne's arm strength and his daring; one false move could have resulted in some unpleasant injuries. But, as testament to Knute's growing confidence as an athlete, he performed the stunt flawlessly.

Although Knute's happiest moments were spent in the open fields and impromptu neighborhood playgrounds, home life had its own enjoyments. He could pester his sisters, and he quickly learned just how to get the desired reaction from each of them. For one, it simply took pointing at her and exclaiming, "Weep a little!" More often, though, he would hoist one of his younger sisters onto his shoulders for a quick trip around the house. School and play did not occupy all of the growing lad's time. Early on, he learned and liked the idea of earning cash with some honest labor. The clumsiness he may have shown around the home workshop disappeared when there was some pay to be earned. He assisted the school custodian in keeping the classrooms clean, and he became an expert window-washer, earning a penny-and-a-half per window.

During summer vacation, he could make 10 cents an hour weeding onions on a nearby vegetable farm. Later, during high school summer vacation, he headed north to Wisconsin and worked on a Lake Michigan ferry as well as in farm fields. School-year studies limited work activities to Saturday deliveries for department stores. Any track meet or football game scheduled for Saturday afternoons would require a quicker pace for completion of work-related activities.

Knute finished eighth grade shortly after turning 13. He was the youngest member of his class and one of the slightest built boys as he headed off to Northwest Division High. The academic promise he showed at Brentano disappeared, causing consternation for his parents. His grades were passing, but nowhere near the top of the class. Athletics—especially track and field—had become his nearly sole focus. Every available moment was spent honing his abilities as a sprinter, a half-miler, a long-jumper, a pole-vaulter, a shot-putter. If he could eat lunch in a minute, or not at all, it gave him extra time to work on track.

The young boys who had improvised track events in backyards and empty lots just a few years earlier were now growing into hearty young men, realizing new capabilities for speed and stamina. And they didn't need to look far to see where athletics could take them. The glorious competition that began in far-away Greece eight years earlier was now just one state away, as the first Olympic Games held in the United States took place in 1904 in St. Louis. In the discus, M. J. Sheridan of the Greater New York Irish Athletic Association beat his own world record by five feet, reaching 132 feet for a gold medal. But an even more notable result came in one of Knute's events, the half-mile, or 800-meter run. In what was called "the greatest race of the day and one of the most sensational of the entire meeting," James D. Lightbody of the Chicago Athletic Association lowered the Olympic record by five and two-fifths seconds, taking home gold with a time of 1:56, but he "ran the legs off the German representative, who collapsed at the finish." Imagine a young Rockne realizing that one of Chicago's own brought home glory.

For Knute and his mates, it was all about the race. They were mesmerized by speed, in all its forms. At nearby Garfield Park, they marveled at the balance, coordination, and control of the bicycle racers. After the World's Fair, bike racing became such a passion in the area that Chicagoans began building cycling tracks that attracted competitors from around the country. Garfield Park's half-mile loop track was designed especially for speed. It attracted some of the most well-known cyclists of the time, including Marshall W. "Major" Taylor, the first black athlete to be a member of an integrated professional sports team. When racist policies prevented Taylor from entering other Chicago races, including the popular Pullman race, he used the track at Garfield Park to set several world records. Ignaz Schwinn was one of the leading technical minds in the country drawn to the thriving bicycle-building world of the 1890s. Born in 1860 in Hardheim, Germany, Schwinn arrived in America in 1891 with his eyes set on the World's Fair and a desire to tap into the popularity of bicycles. An exhibitor at the World's Fair, Schwinn shared space with the carriage makers and train displays in the Exposition's Transportation Building. Schwinn, who lived not far from the Logan Square area, was part-founder of Arnold, Schwinn & Company.

Bicycling increased mobility for working classes and provided new means for young people to explore outside their neighborhood and meet, perhaps even court others from different areas and stations in life. Bicycle clubs tended to erase social distinctions, as it was common for the rich to enjoy a day's ride along with those from less privileged economic classes. Carter "Man of the People" Harrison, Jr. was elected mayor in 1899 partly on the strength of his campaigning to make better roads, which would greatly aid bicycling. By the 1890s more than 100 bicycle clubs existed in Chicago, with some estimates as high as 500 clubs. The Arnold, Schwinn & Company was one of dozens of bicycle manufacturers in Chicago. Others included Western Wheel Works, one of the largest bicycle makers in the nation; the Pope Mfg. Co; and Gormully & Jeffery, makers of the "high wheelers." By 1895 bicycles sold for less than $100—considered the barrier to break for a mass market, and projections called for 400,000 bicycles to be sold nationwide that year. On October 3, 1896, when Chicago's new cement oval bicycle track at Garfield Park was dedicated, an estimated crowd of 40,000 crammed the grounds for the inauguration, delighting in watching skilled cyclists battling banked turns with high-speed teams.

Bicycling may have been the rage, but football and track remained the athletic mainstays for Rockne the highschooler. Playing football took a backseat for Knute in his early high school years at Northwest Division. His small stature made making the high school team all but impossible. This was especially frustrating at a time, thanks largely to Coach Stagg's success, when the game was becoming bigger than ever in Chicago. Stagg's University of Chicago Maroons received extensive coverage in the city's numerous daily newspapers, and crowds made games at Marshall Field the place to be. And there were plenty of games for fans to see there. About 90 percent of Chicago's games were played at home before sizable crowds, the revenue from which usually made both teams financially content.

Typical was 1901, when the Maroons played 11 home games, plus a trip to Ann Arbor; and 1902, which featured 11 home games and the only "away" contest was a quick jaunt to whip the soldiers at Fort Sheridan 53-0. President Harper, ever cognizant of how the paying customers viewed the games, had suggested to Stagg as early as 1897 the addition of a "bulletin board" so that all fans could understand the progress of the game, giving birth to the scoreboard. Harper also asked, "Should there not be a band at the Michigan game Thanksgiving day?"

It was ironic that an away game cemented the Maroons as a major power and put Western football on the map. On October 29, 1898, Stagg's squad met the mighty University of Pennsylvania at Franklin Field in Philadelphia. Penn was considered the nation's top team, having won 64 of its previous 65 contests over four-plus seasons. Although the result was a 23-11 Penn victory, Chicago led at the half and impressed everyone with a style of play that featured quickness and deception over brute force. Walter Camp noted, "Stagg brought out of the West a decidedly advanced style of play." At season's end, Chicago star Clarence Hershberger became the first player from a school other than Eastern powers Yale, Princeton, Penn, Harvard, or Cornell to be placed on Camp's annual All-America team.

Stagg gained enormous fame while serving as head football coach and athletic director, a dual role that quickly became the norm at colleges and schools nationwide. Stagg's success ushered in the era of men who specialized in coaching as a profession; just as schoolmasters were becoming superintendents, football coaches became athletic directors. Stagg took great pride in his work, noting, "Our profession is one of the noblest and perhaps the most far reaching in building up the manhood of our country." His national stature increased when, in 1904, he became the first coach from outside the East to serve on the Intercollegiate Football Rules Committee.

Elite Eastern colleges excelled in football in the late 19th and early 20th century in large part because of the steady flow of students skilled in academics and athletics from the long-established prep schools of the region. In a similar way, Chicago's position as the largest and best-established city in the West provided the University of Chicago an excellent supply of college-ready football players. Football was sponsored early on by local high schools. The Cook County High School League formed in 1889, including English High, Englewood, North Division, Hyde Park, South Division, Calumet, Marshall, Austin, Lake, Lake View, University High, and Oak Park High. For young men of these schools, the University of Chicago and its highly visible, successful football program was the school of their dreams.

Still, in May of 1902, President Harper presented to the university's Board of Physical Culture and Athletics a series of seven resolutions he and Stagg had developed to support and formalize the recruitment of high school athletes. Among the proposals was to use nine prep schools in Illinois and Indiana which already had an affiliation with the University of Chicago both as official "feeder schools" and as destinations for Maroon athletes who wished to teach and coach when their playing days ended. Another proposal set up a similar system with the local public high schools. One far-reaching resolution called for "a system (to) be devised for obtaining information in regard to athletics in secondary schools." Subject to wide interpretation, it essentially allowed Stagg to set up a comprehensive card file on prospective Maroon players, including tracking correspondence between school and student.

The proposal also impacted track and suggested, "that interscholastic meets be held of the Academies and high schools in relationship to the University." Just eight days after all the proposals passed, the First Annual Interscholastic Track Meet was held at Marshall Field and brought together some 200 athletes from 40 schools, including individual state champions from high schools and prep academies in Illinois, Wisconsin, Iowa, and Michigan. Young stars from the Great Lakes State would have another option besides playing for Fielding Yost at Ann Arbor. Everything at the meet was designed to impress the youngsters. They could catch a glimpse of big-time college track as the Maroons hosted the University of California in a dual meet. The prospective Maroons were housed in fraternity houses and "entertained in great style" by leaders of athletics and student groups. Chicago coaches met personally with each attendee, and Maroon athletic alumni were on hand to sing the praises of their alma mater. The annual meet quickly became a major focus of University of Chicago recruiting and the event had nearly doubled in size by 1903 with the addition of track stars from Indiana, Ohio, Missouri, and Minnesota. By 1905, representatives of 75 schools, from as far away as Nebraska and Kentucky, made the meet.

Stagg also supervised a series of other track meets around Chicago, including some in which a half-miler named Rockne competed for glory. Rockne didn't recall ever actually meeting the great coach, unless perhaps, "under the stands when I dropped out of longer distance foot-races, as invariably occurred." But Stagg's reputation for guiding young men and his great interest in track and field as second only to football—and in some ways a necessary preparation for the gridiron—no doubt made an impression on young Rockne of Northwest Division High.

Coach Stagg played a role in an historic Chicago high school event the first week of December 1902, when he directed the Hyde Park High School football team through a grueling two-hour workout. Hyde Park was located just south of the university campus, and its star athletes were well known to Stagg and his fellow Maroon athletic leaders. This particular Hyde Park team, led by its stellar quarterback Walter Eckersall, had gained tremendous acclaim, hailed as "one of the best elevens which has represented a local school." In fact, only four local high schools had even agreed to play the juggernaut that season, and the combined score of those games was 231-0, Hyde Park. Typical was the game with Englewood, traditionally Hyde Park's strongest rival, which ended in a 57-0 rout.

Hyde Park was strong enough to take the field against two Western Conference college teams—Chicago and Wisconsin. Early in the season, the high school boys gave Stagg's Maroons a scare, "playing them off their feet," losing 6-5 only due to a missed kick after touchdown. And on October 4, Hyde Park held Phil King's Badgers to a 6-5 halftime lead before the Badgers performed as expected in the second half to win, 24-5. At season's end, after being proclaimed high school champions of the West, team officials, aided by school alumni, looked for an Eastern team to challenge for what was called the "national high school championship." They found an opponent in Brooklyn Polytechnic Prep, who despite two losses during the season was considered the New York champion when it defeated archrival Brooklyn High, 5-0, in their annual Thanksgiving Day battle contested before a crowd of more than 10,000.

Hyde Park alumni scrambled to put up $1,350 for a travel guarantee that would allow Poly Prep to send a team of 15 players aboard a special train and stay at the Chicago Beach hotel. Reports noted, "The expense attached makes it the most extensive high school venture yet undertaken." Gerald Parker, manager of the 1901 Hyde Park team, acted as manager of the championship game and telegraphed expense money to Brooklyn in time for the squad to leave New York Wednesday evening prior to the

Saturday game at Marshall Field. Not much was known about the Poly Prep team except that its coach, Oscar Aubut, was "a newspaper man, who has had every opportunity to see the latest in football tactics, and several of his defensive formations were a revelation to those who had not kept abreast of the game as played by the big eastern universities." Aubut was said to use some of Yale's formations and trick plays. For his part, Aubut feared his team's layoff after the Thanksgiving game would weaken his team's performance. On leaving New York, several hundred fellow students gave the team a raucous sendoff from the station. Numerous well-wishing telegrams awaited the team in Chicago. Arriving at Englewood Station over the Nickel Plate at 9 p.m. Friday, the squad was met by the Hyde Park team and students and driven to the hotel in tallyho carriages.

Preparations in Chicago included students from Hyde Park fanning out to the other Chicago high schools selling tickets. The game also attracted "the attention of those persons who usually confine their interest to the college games." One high school student who passed on purchasing a ducat was Northwest Division's Knute Rockne, who used his preferred method of attending a game—by crashing the gate. After Stagg worked the Hyde Park team in midweek practice, he said, "Brooklyn will have to play good football to beat that Hyde Park team. Those boys play well for a high school team. The team was pretty well coached before I took charge, and needed but little work." Game officials were three graduates of Eastern powers—Harvard, Dartmouth, and Yale—chosen in deference to the visitors. They called Eckersall and Poly Prep captain Mulvihill to the center of a mostly frozen Marshall Field as snow began to fall to start the contest. It was all but over in minutes. Hyde Park stopped Poly Prep's first thrust easily and scored two plays later when Sammy Ransum, its "colored star," ran 20 yards for a score. From that point, the Chicago papers noted, "touchdowns followed one another in monotonous succession." Eckersall accounted for three touchdowns, one on an 85-yard run. With Eckersall returning kicks for long yardage, calling plays, and kicking deep into Brooklyn territory, the host team was in complete control.

Mesmerized by the non-stop action, 14-year-old Knute Rockne marveled at the field general's performance. "With no more than four fundamental plays," Rockne recalled, "he worked so quickly and coolly that he made his offense bewildering. Eckersall's sharp staccato calling of signals; his keen handsome face and the smooth precision with which he drove and countered and drove again, handling his players with the rhythm of an orchestra leader—all this gave football a new meaning to me." Hyde Park led, 40-0, at the half, and continued the onslaught in the second half. Eckersall took a hard hit and left the game with a 99-0 lead. It finished 105-0, Hyde Park. Eighteen touchdowns and 15 kicks were made by the Western—now national—champs. As the game ended, a crowd gathered on the field and chanted Eckersall's name. Rockne tried for a closer glimpse of the great star, but "two or three thousand other youngsters were trying to do exactly the same thing, so I had to go home without a handshake—yet, for the first time in a young and fairly crowded life, I went home with a hero."

# 8

## Making His Move

B y 1904, Knute Rockne had finally worn down his parents' opposition to football. As a 16-year-old high school senior he tried out and made the Northwest Division High School team. The game, still played in a rather rudimentary fashion at several schools, had precious little quality coaching. At Northwest a pair of teachers, Mr. Peters and Mr. Ellis, volunteered to do what they could to teach the squad how to play the game. For Rockne, trying to play the end position, it meant learning some of game's finer points away from the high school practice field. That fall, a young Rockne probably enjoyed watching football as much as he did playing it. The biggest draw was, as always, the University of Chicago Maroons, now quarterbacked by the snappy field general, Walter Eckersall. Rockne recalls, "It was a favorite trick of the crowd I played with to hook into the Chicago University football field through the motor-car gates, guarded even less closely than the turnstiles." Once inside, Knute and his fellow gate-crashers marveled that they were watching football royalty they had only read about in the dailies—teams including Fielding Yost's Michigan eleven, the purple of Northwestern, and the vaunted Redskins from Haskell Institute. Rockne's focus was always on the flair of the Maroon quarterback.

Rockne, anxious to play for himself and show his ability, found the 1904 Cook County High School League still in its organizational infancy. The League divided teams into major and minor divisions based on the strength of the teams. Three schools—Hyde Park, Englewood, and North Division—had developed strong programs and annually were the class of the league. There was a significant drop off at the next level of first-division teams. Those included West Division, Oak Park, John Marshall, and Rockne's Northwest Division team. A number of schools, including West Division, Oak Park, Austin, English, and Wendell Phillips (formerly South Division), "have always been anxious to class with the minor league teams, as they can hardly compete with Englewood, North Division, and Hyde Park." In late September, as team managers were ready to gather and draw up a schedule, Wendell Phillips dropped out entirely. Later, John Marshall, West Division, and Northwest Division would follow suit, due to a dispute over new eligibility rules.

So Rockne's only season of high school football featured an abbreviated, ad hoc schedule. The Northwest Division gridders defeated John Marshall, tied a game with Crane High, and lost to the reserves of mighty North Division. Rockne recalls that Walter Steffen, North's talented quarterback, "joshed us from the sidelines." Also taking in the matchup from the sideline was Luther Pollard, a member of one of the first black families in the Rogers Park community. A post-season analysis said Pollard "stands in a place by himself, from the record he has made in the few games in which he has played." The strange season ended when the champion was declared by vote rather than on the field. The board had to resolve a dispute between North Division and Oak Park that resulted from a scheduling mix-up. On the day the teams were to meet, Oak Park claimed a forfeit, as North Division was nowhere to be seen. Captain Steffen and the Northsiders were 50 miles northwest in Rockford, Illinois, playing a previously scheduled game against Rockford High. The board presented a plan under which the championship could be settled on the field, with a rescheduled game in December. But Oak Park rejected the idea; its team had already dispersed and there was no chance of reuniting them.

The uncertainty and disorganization of the high school football season most likely contributed to Rockne and his track teammates' intense focus on improving their times and distances at the earliest opportunity. Enthused by the showing of the American athletes at September's Olympic Games in St. Louis, Rockne and the other tracksters anxiously prepared for the start of the indoor season. Track and field was, like football, a fairly disjointed activity. The high schoolers were essentially self-organized and self-coached. Participants came and went between high school teams and other, better-organized clubs. North's Steffen, for example, was expected to "run for the First Regiment in the indoor events, but will not be on the track for the school under the opening of the outdoor season." Rockne participated in both school and club track and field. While still at Northwest Division, he was asked to join the Chicago Athletic Association junior team, based on his strong showing for one of the lesser clubs in the area. He said his work as a half-miler "won me a small reputation." He broadened his versatility by spending more time with the pole vault, and gained some notice with a jump of 12 feet, 4 inches. The club affiliation meant more training, more meets, and more chances to achieve his personal best in both disciplines.

Trained in the Classics as part of his high school education and with a revival of the Olympic Games in Greece less than 10 years earlier, Rockne had begun to understand the importance of sport and recreation as part of culture. Rockne witnessed the intense work ethic displayed by the immigrant population, yet he was introduced to the Greek athletic ideal that recognized the social value of physical fitness. And of all the modern sports, track most symbolized the Greek value of physical fitness as a form of harmony of mind and body—both of which were required as an individual strived to reach the pinnacle of athletic success. Former classmates who had already achieved such success also provided Rockne and his track colleagues with inspiration. In 1901, Rockne's last year of grade school, the Northwest Division track team tied for fourth in the Illinois state meet. Ernest Quantrall placed second in the high jump, and Frederick Speik earned a slew of points with a second-place finish in the shotput and third place in the discus, hammer, and standing broad jump.

One fine spring day in 1905, the principal of Northwest Division walked through Humboldt Park, near the school, when he came upon

Rockne and his track mates earnestly involved in practicing their various events—sprinters exploding out of crouches and shot-putters emitting great groans as they powered weights across the horizon. Shouts of encouragement and joking showed the camaraderie of the group. It all would have been a scene to bring a proud smile to the face of a school administrator—except that classes were fully in session at the moment, and none of these fellows had anything close to an excuse for missing them. Gone was the noble embodiment of physical and mental abilities building the stronger man. Punishment was swift and severe: the track team was immediately disbanded, and each miscreant was given the opportunity to immediately enroll at another Chicago high school, to be chosen by the Northwest principal.

For Rockne, just turned 17 and only weeks away from barely earning his high school diploma, it brought to the surface an issue that had been simmering for some time. His father had earlier expressed his strong desire that Knute enroll at the University of Chicago. The Midway was where the up-and-comers in a variety of fields would find like-minded scholars, leading professors, and the opportunity to gain a high-caliber education. But as each half-mile run and series of pole vaults negated the time available to study his subjects, it had become more obvious to all that Knute would not have the academic credentials to attend Chicago. A father's dream for his son was gradually dying, and the expulsion from Northwest Division sealed the decision. It was time, Louis Rockne told his son, to go out and start earning a living. Employment for Knute in 1905 consisted of a handful odd jobs. However, he never lost track of the University of Chicago football and his hero Walter Eckersall. Rockne, like the rest of the city, was captivated by the Maroons Thanksgiving Day 1905 battle with Fielding Yost's Michigan squad at Marshall Field. The game was important to football followers everywhere for it would decide the championship of the West. Michigan was undefeated in four seasons and Chicago, led by All-American Eckersall, was undefeated. Walter Camp noted in his *Harper's Weekly* column that Chicago was "bending every energy toward at least stopping Michigan's conquering ways." More than 27,000 people viewed the contest, with additional fans watching from stands set up on the roofs of houses across the street.

The game was superbly played, and it became evident that the two evenly matched squads were headed for a scoreless tie. Only an error in human judgment, it seemed, could decide the game. That element entered the game when Michigan halfback Dennison Clark attempted to advance an Eckersall punt he fielded near the goal line late in the game. Instead, he veered backward and was carried into the end zone by two Chicago defenders. The resultant safety yielded the final score: Chicago 2, Michigan 0. The win propelled Chicago and Stagg onto the national scene and opened two decades of Chicago dominance of Midwestern football. The Michigan press was less than sympathetic to Clark's error with one paper saying "that Clark of Michigan defeated his own eleven." Another said it was a "lapse of brain work." Even Walter Camp described the play as "rank blunder." Clark went missing for days immediately following the game and reported that he was contemplating suicide: "I shall kill myself because I am in disgrace." It was a grim prognostication by the inconsolable Clark, who seven years later shot himself. In his note he expressed hope that his "final play" would somehow atone for his mistake against Chicago.

Knute spent most of 1906 working on a ferry, toiling on farm fields, and earning wages by doing a series of more odd jobs. Seeking something that was regular and paid better, he sat for the civil service examination for the Chicago Post Office. The exam required an essay, and Rockne wrote on "The Advisability of Our Having a Larger Navy Is Becoming Greater Since Japan Whipped Russia." Shortly after his 19th birthday, on March 21, 1907, the outdoor-loving Knute Rockne became a postal clerk working indoors in the stamper mailing division of the main Chicago Post Office at the salary of $50 per month. The work could be tough and gritty, handling bags of mail that averaged fifty pounds. His shift began at midnight and ended at 8:30 a.m., but he never missed a day. The model presented by his father, of doing whatever work was necessary day after day, served Knute well. After just a few months, on July 1, he was transferred to a dispatching job in the mailing division.

Those who worked with Knute at the Post Office recalled that it would take the average clerk six months or more to learn and memorize the volume of information about the departures and arrivals of various railways and countless stations needed to pass the periodic examinations. Knowing train departures was critical because of the Post Office's innovative technology of moving mail. By 1900, the Chicago Post Office had miles of just-laid underground tubes used to move the mail. Up to 600 letters were stuffed in canisters and whooshed off at an average speed of 35 miles per hour to waiting trains. Knute, they said, had such a keen mind and encyclopedic memory that he could wait until a few days before the exam, concentrate on studying, and pass easily. The score needed to continue in the position was 95; Knute usually scored closer to 100. Whether the route was from St. Louis or St. Paul, Pittsburgh or Pottstown, Rockne could reel off the correct departures and arrivals. For Rockne, it was more of a mental game.

"Most of the old-timers called me a fool to tackle a tough job (like dispatching)," Rockne once said. "But there was excellent memory training in it. Even now, I carry a map of Illinois and several eastern states in my mind, and know just what main lines, branch lines, and spur lines touch which territories. This has been a good investment in mental energy." Rockne completed his work assignments in much less than the allotted time, and he often used the leftover hours to improve his mind and body. "He was a deep thinker," said a co-worker. "He was always reading books. He even took a book to work with him to read whenever he got a chance." He also worked on sprinting, jumping, and footwork in a lengthy driveway that led into the Post Office, which served as the perfect straightaway for no less than 30 minutes of sprinting each shift.

The transportation revolution that took over mail delivery also dominated all forms of mechanical vehicles. By the turn of the century, electric trolleys had become a fixture throughout America. Their speed, and in some cases downright luxury compared with horsecars, fueled their wild popularity. Some trolleys featured solid mahogany door frames, exquisitely paneled maple ceilings, and carved panes along each seat, from which passengers looked through windows trimmed by curtains made of Russian leather and silk embroidery. One observer wrote that "trolley cars travel fast enough to produce a feeling of mental exhilaration, which is absent or scarcely felt by passengers in horsecars." In addition to carrying the mail, trolleys carried workers to their jobs and were available for hire on special occasions. Conductors wore uniforms befitting a high military standing, with double rows of brass buttons and highly festooned hats. The jobs were so respectable that trolley companies could demand that conductors abstain from smoking, drinking, swearing, and gambling. A conductor could be fired for just stepping into a saloon while in uniform.

In Chicago, the first coal-burning, steam-powered elevated railway was built in 1892 in part to take fairgoers to the Columbian Exposition. By 1895, the "El" was electrified and built out to serve Logan Square, Garfield Park, and Lake Street. The period also saw the arrival of an Englishman who would have a significant influence on Chicago transportation. Samuel Insull, born in London in 1859, emigrated at the age of 21 to become personal secretary to Thomas Edison. He was a founder, along with other pioneers of Edison's inventions, of the Edison General Electric Company. He rose to vice president of the company, but when he was passed over to become president, he headed west to lead the Chicago Edison Company. There, he devised a system for selling excess capacity from a new stream-electric turbine to electric streetcar companies at rates low enough that he soon owned a monopoly in the market.

Growing as fast as any mode of transportation was a new type of railway: the interurban. It featured closed cars heavier and faster than the open-sided trolleys. Indiana attorney and congressman Charles L. Henry introduced the interurban with a short line that linked Anderson and Alexandria, Indiana, expanded his operations, and eventually purchased the Indianapolis and Cincinnati Traction Company. Interurban lines were being built at a frantic pace. In Ohio alone, 144 electric railway companies were chartered from 1898 to 1901. Pickle and catsup magnate H.J. Heinz was an investor in the Winona Traction Company of Indiana, which built a line specifically to transport religious congregations to hear sermons by evangelist Billy Sunday at Winona Lake.

Indianapolis had 13 different lines radiating like spokes from its downtown. Even smaller cities had numerous lines, including Toledo's nine and Dayton's eight. South Bend boasted of three electric interurban lines. Overbuilding, an uncertain economy, and the rise of the automobile ultimately led to the demise of numerous interurban companies. Indiana's Henry would continue to battle the odds to try to make interurbans succeed, and boldly predicted, "The fad feature of automobile riding will gradually wear off and the time will soon be here when a very large part of the people will cease to think of automobile rides and the interurbans will carry their old time allotment of passengers."

Henry Ford's Model T proved Charles Henry's prediction a bit off base. The Model T was well on its way to becoming a "car for the people," as it symbolized freedom from the rigidity of train schedules. The first Model T was produced on August 12, 1908 and left the Piquette Plant in Detroit the following month. Ford proudly proclaimed that he offered his lightweight Model T in "any color you choose as long as it's black... and so low in price that no man making a good salary would be unable to buy one." It was inexpensive, lightweight, and durable. Boxy in its basic design, the car weighed 1200 pounds and was propelled by a 4-cylinder 20-horsepower engine that was crank started. The driver used three pedals—one for forward, one for reverse, and one for a brake. It initially sold for $850, and it literally transported Americans into the modern age. It represented the good life in America. This "universal car" spearheaded a new era of consumer prosperity, as the Model T appeared as the most common symbol of a new age of material comfort.

By 1910, nearly a half million motor vehicles were on American roads, 187,000 of them produced that year alone. In 1900 automobiling was a sport; by 1910 it had become a business.

It seemed to Rockne as if the rest of the world was in constant motion while he remained stationary in his job at Post Office. Whether hopping a trolley or purchasing a Model T, people were on the go. And nowhere was that more evident than with the development of another avenue of travel: the flying machine. Orville and Wilbur Wright, the Dayton-based bicycle-building brothers who were struck by the inventions displayed at the Columbian Exposition, were the first to answer the question as to whether controlled power flight in a heavier-than-air vehicle was possible.

On the frigid morning of December 17, 1903, along the Atlantic Ocean beach in Kitty Hawk, North Carolina, conditions were far from ideal, but the brothers were running out of time to experiment with flight as the harsh winter was descending quickly. By 10:30 a.m. everything was ready and the engine to their prototype was started. As it warmed up, Wilbur and Orville shared some final words and shook hands. A witness later recalled the scene, saying, "We couldn't help notice how they held onto each other's hand, sort of like they hated to let go; like two folks parting who weren't sure they'd ever see each other again."

Orville sat in the pilot's position as Wilbur steadied the "Flyer" at the right wing tip. At 10:35 a.m. the Flyer began to move slowly forward into the brisk wind. The speed over the ground was only 7-8 miles per hour, but as the Flyer jolted into flight, airspeed was close to 30 miles per hour with the wind. In the excitement, the brothers forgot to start their stopwatches to time how long the first flight had lasted. They later judged the time to be about 12 seconds. It had been a brief flight covering only a short distance, but a true flight nevertheless. It was a moment that forever changed the world.

Aeronautics and aviation were covered on the front pages of newspapers across the country. The *New York World* took on a full-time reporter to cover the air beat and other dailies followed suit. Popular magazines published articles about aviation firsts, competitions, and the parade of exciting advances. Millions read about the dramatic new "air ships" that moved in all three dimensions, like a bird. In 1909 an estimated one million New Yorkers witnessed Wilbur Wright fly past the Statue of Liberty, and Orville declared the dawn of a new era: the Age of Flight. In 1910, when Glenn Curtiss, the Wrights' great rival, flew 150 miles from Albany to New York City's Governor's Island to claim a $10,000 prize, the *New York Times* devoted six pages to the feat.

Curtiss began his aviation career in earnest as a member of the Aerial Experiment Association, a group that included inventor Alexander Graham Bell and U.S. Army Lieutenant Thomas Selfridge. Curtiss, a champion bicycle racer who had designed and built his own bikes, was supplying engines for hot air balloons at the time of the Wright Brothers' Kitty Hawk flight. Critical of Orville and Wilbur's need to experiment in private and without fanfare, Curtiss followed the Wright Brothers' achievement on March 12, 1908, when he was at the controls of the "Red Wing" and made the first public flight in America on the frozen surface of Keuka Lake, New York. Curtiss and The Red Wing remained aloft for 20 seconds, covering a distance of 318 feet, 11 inches, before the plane went down on one wing and crashed. Less than two years later in January 1910 Curtiss was the toast of the nation having earned the title of "world's greatest flier." He had just returned from Europe after winning the International Aviation Cup and was one of the top draws for an air show in Los Angeles that dominated front-page news from the *Billings Daily Gazette* to the *Nevada State Journal* to the *Indianapolis Star*.

Rockne read of aviation daredevils who grabbed headlines from the inception of flying. They pushed the safety and speed limits of this new invention, dazzled crowds, and garnered prize money that was almost unthinkable to the average wage earner. On Sunday, January 9, 1910, the first aviation meet in the United States took place at Aviation Field, just outside Los Angeles. The crowds gathered all day to witness the miracle of what was still called "the heavier-than-air flying machines." They boarded Pacific Electric trains and rode 15 miles to disembark and were ushered by 300 deputy sheriffs, many of whom were on horseback. They queued patiently to pay their $1 admission fee, clicked through the turnstiles, and then rushed to seek out the best vantage point. By day's end, Frenchman Louis Paulhan bested Curtiss that day and won more than $15,000 in prize money and set world's records for endurance and altitude.

Chicago native John Bevins Moisant was another daredevil willing to risk life and limb in pursuit of entertainment and to push the development of faster and safer airplanes. On August 17, 1910 he became the first aviator to cross the English Channel with a passenger, touching down in a field of oats six miles inland from the English coast. The colorful Moisant became one of America's top celebrities and aviators upon his return home. In an interview with the *New York Evening Sun* of October 13, 1910 he criticized those who saw no potential in the aircraft as a military weapon. "People talk of shooting at flying machines from the ground and warding off an attack in that way. We can travel seventy miles an hour, more than that soon, and can go up 5,000 feet or more. Can they hit us under those conditions?" Moisant also predicted that future generations of Americans "will use airplanes as we use automobiles." The increasing number of aviation events being scheduled that offered rich prizes of up to $10,000 intrigued Moisant. He soon formed a traveling show, the "Moisant International Aviators" (one of whom was the famous French pilot Roland Garros), and they began touring the United States, thrilling fans with aeronautical acrobatics. By 1911 Moisant was reputed to have brought in $500,000 for his feats, dazzling crowds across the country.


How frustrating was it for a young man with a creative mind to plod along at the Post Office while the rest of the nation became fascinated by air travel? Rockne could only wonder if aviation would ever touch his life. One way to dream and envision the future was to focus on other pursuits, prime among them athletics and leisure. Like millions of other Americans of the time, he enjoyed popular culture, including music and moving pictures. In the early years of the new century, that meant the nickelodeon. From Edison's invention of the Kinetoscope in 1893 to the craze of the nickelodeons at the turn of the 20th century to the "talkies" that came to dominate film by the end of the 1920s, the universal appeal of film and storytelling captivated the imaginations of immigrants and millionaires alike.

"I am experimenting upon an instrument which does for the eye what the phonograph does for the ear, which is the recording and reproduction of things in motion," said Thomas Edison in 1888. From the time Edison articulated his vision, technology and innovative genius fashioned an entertainment vehicle to be enjoyed by the masses. Edison's initial work drew heavily on the talents of William Kennedy L. Dickson, a member of Edison's experimental staff who was also a photographer. Edison provided the resources and the ideas, but Dickson provided most of the knowledge of photography that fueled their inventions. By 1892 Edison and Dickson invented a motion picture camera and a peephole-viewing device called the Kinetoscope. Although the Electric Building at the World's Columbian Exposition in Chicago in 1893 was filled with numerous wonders created by Edison, the public inauguration of the Kinetoscope was delayed until after the World's Fair had closed.

The following year Edison films were exhibited commercially; the first Kinetoscope Parlor opened on April 14, 1894 in New York City. A second followed in Chicago in May, and the final machines were shipped to San Francisco for a parlor that opened on June 1. Kinetoscope parlors opened across the country just as fast as the Edison Manufacturing Company could supply machines. The novelty of the Kinetoscope, however, wore off quickly as audiences were anxious to see "projected' movies. New devices and discoveries, including the "lantern slide," pushed film-makers to capture action and adventure on film. The advanced method of storytelling eventually led to the 1903 motion picture *The Great Train Robbery*, which was so popular that it continued to be shown for years after its first release, earning an estimated $2 million by 1908.

The nickelodeon era, which dominated the next phase of motion picture development, officially began on June 19, 1905 when vaudevillian Henry Davis' Pittsburgh theater attracted about 450 viewers over the course of the day. Soon thousands of nickelodeon theaters sprang up across the nation, earning their name from the nickel admission charged. These theaters, which projected films onto a screen, were accompanied by live piano playing, sing-along songs, or lectures, and the programs usually featured a series of short films lasting from 10 minutes to an hour each. Nickelodeons made the cinema accessible to mass audiences of blue-collar workers.

Nickelodeon operators changed pictures daily, and the demand for new films was so overwhelming that it created the "westward movement" of the film production and distribution industry from New York to Chicago. By June 1907 the Chicago-based trade magazine *Show World* proclaimed that "Chicago leads the world in the rental of moving picture films and in the general patronage of the motion view." Chicago was likely to have had more film theaters per capita than any other city in the United States, with nickelodeons oftentimes anchoring a neighborhood's business development. The insatiable appetite of the movie-going audiences also helped to push Chicago to the top of the list as the country's leading movie distributor. The "film exchanges" created a new niche in the industry, giving exhibitors access (through rentals) to a larger number of films than they could afford to purchase and allowing theaters to change their films frequently.

By 1907 there were more than 15 film exchanges operating in Chicago, and they controlled 80 percent of the film distribution market for the whole United States. William Selig added the next element—movie production, when in 1907, the Selig Polyscope Company built a production facility at Irving Park Road and Western Avenue that covered three acres and employed more than 200 people. Competition came from the

Essanay, founded by George Spoor and Gilbert Anderson, a noted actor who gained enormous popularity in hundreds of Western shorts, playing the first real cowboy hero, "Bronco Billy."

The Essanay studio, built in Uptown on Argyle Street in 1908, lured away a promising young actor named Charlie Chaplin for the unprecedented salary of $1,250 per week, with a bonus of $10,000 for merely signing with the company. The 14 films Chaplin made for the company, including *The Tramp*, were distinctly designated upon release as the "Essanay-Chaplin Brand." A 16-year-old Chicago native named Gloria Svensson visited Essanay in 1914 and asked to be an extra "just for the fun of it." A director was so impressed with the young beauty that he featured her in a short film *At the End of a Perfect Day*. Svensson renamed herself Swanson and soon joined Chaplin as they both ventured west to seek their fame among the orange groves of Hollywood.

For Knute Rockne, the routine of working at the Post Office brought rewards of regular income, a level of self-sufficiency, and predictability. His salary rose annually, taking him from $800 in 1908 to $900 in 1909 and the significant sum of $1,000 as of April 1, 1910. He was fairly prudent with money and was able to save a good deal of his salary; his mother acted as the banker. Being able to train for and compete in athletics brought some challenge and excitement to an otherwise mundane life as a postal worker. He caught the eye of the Illinois Athletic Club by running the half-mile first for the Irving Park Athletic Club, and then the Central YMCA. That provided Rockne with his first real coaching in track and field, from Martin Delaney and Michael "Dad" Butler. For a young man unable to connect with his own father over the pursuit of athletic accomplishment, Rockne enjoyed being under Dad Butler's watchful eye and reasoned guidance. He studied Dad's temperament, his ways of communicating with his athletes, and remembered how it all seemed to come so naturally for Dad.

In his earlier years, Rockne had competed for a number of smaller clubs. In May of 1905, for instance, he won the 440-yard dash in 59.02 seconds, running for the Lexington Athletic Club, sponsored by the Lexington Avenue Baptist Church, in a dual meet with the Reynolds class of Grace Church. He helped the Central YMCA intermediate team win the

Cook County YMCA championships in 1907, winning the shot-put with a heave of 37 feet, 11 ½ inches, while tying for third in the pole vault. Ironically, some of his feats occurred back at the school that sent him packing in 1905. Northwest Division was now known as Tuley High School, and Rockne was among "alumni" who competed as the "Tuley night school" against day students. In such an indoor meet in February 1909, Rockne's time of 27 and 4/5 seconds in the 220 tied the "gym record."

With the Illinois Athletic Club, Rockne was now competing with and against a higher class of athletes. He rubbed shoulders with such Olympic stars such as Ralph Rose, the 1904 gold medal shot putter; William Hogenson, the silver medal winning sprinter; and even the great Jim Lightbody, who also brought home gold in the 800-meters. But above all, Rockne enjoyed competing with fellows he had known for years, especially local stars John Devine and John Plant, both of whom ran for Tuley just after Rockne had attended when it was Northwest. Running for Tuley in the 1907 Illinois state championships, Devine finished second in the half-mile.

Participating in meets with the Illinois Athletic Club didn't preclude the occasional drop down in class. In early September 1910, Rockne revisited his roots with the Irving Park Athletic Association, taking part in its second annual meet on the grounds at Irving Park Boulevard and Springfield Avenue. It was his finest hour as a Chicago trackster. Rockne was the individual star, racking up 17 of the 30 points won by Cullom Athletic Club, which captured permanent possession of the James F. Clancy Cup by winning the meet for a second consecutive year. Showing his versatility, Rockne won three events: the 120-yard low hurdles in 16 and 4/5 seconds; the shot put at 38 feet, 5 inches; the running broad jump at 20 feet, 9 inches; and was second in the pole vault. For his achievement, Rockne was presented a cup donated by businessman George B. Westerstraat.

Those track victories seemed to signify something more than just excellence in running. It was as if the need to move on to another phase of his life could wait no longer.

# 9

# A 22-Year-Old Freshman

K nute Kenneth Rockne would quietly contemplate his future from time to time while working at the Chicago Post Office in 1910. Life as a civil servant mail dispatcher held limited possibilities. Occasionally, a vague plan would emerge that included saving a thousand dollars and then heading to Champaign to see what the University of Illinois could teach him.

A fellow Chicago track athlete, Avery Brundage, had found some success taking that path. Brundage had moved with his family to Chicago when he was five. By the time he was ready for high school, Brundage traveled seven miles by public transportation to attend Crane Tech, one of Northwest Division's rivals, where he earned a reputation as a high school track star. Brundage, similar to Rockne and his teammates, was a self-directed athlete. In Crane Tech's workshop, he fashioned the shot and hammer he would throw in competition. He graduated from Crane in 1905, just weeks after Rockne had been bounced from Northwest Division. Brundage headed to the University of Illinois directly after graduation, where he studied engineering, wrote for campus publications, and played a number of sports. He earned varsity spots in basketball and track, and as a senior in 1909, he helped Illinois upset Coach Stagg's Chicago Maroons for the Western Conference track championship. After graduation, Brundage went to work as a construction superintendent for Holabird and Roche, one of Chicago's leading architectural firms. In 1910, as a member of the Chicago Athletic Association, he finished third in the national all-around championships sponsored by the Amateur Athletic Union, and he set his sights on the 1912 Olympics in Stockholm.

Rockne couldn't help but envy his CAA teammate as he began to feel the tug of time. How long could he postpone entry to college before it became too unlikely to even attempt? The dream of attending Stagg's prestigious university had died, but a trek to Champaign still seemed possible. At a local meet Rockne struck up conversation with fellow tracksters John Plant and John Devine and inquired about their future plans. An emphatic response followed: they were both headed 90 miles east to give the University of Notre Dame a try. Rockne quickly decided to have some fun with them. "Who ever heard of Notre Dame?" he quipped. "They've never won a game in their lives."

Of course, he knew full well that, ever since baseball great Cap Anson picked up a bat as a Notre Dame prep schooler in 1866, the school had been attracting legions of Midwestern lads who wanted a vigorous athletic program to match the advancement of their education. Plus, the previous fall, Notre Dame's football team had traveled to Ferry Field in Ann Arbor and erased the taste of eight previous defeats by Michigan—five by shutout—in upsetting Yost's Wolverines 11-3. The winning score came when fullback Robert "Pete" Vaughan smashed through the Michigan line with such force that his head, or maybe shoulder, as the story went, broke the wooden goal post. But far more than athletics weighed on Rockne's mind. The practical questions dominated. Where could he more easily earn money? And which school would be lighter on expenses? Plant and Devine spoke up strongly on Notre Dame's behalf. Campus employment was plentiful and easy to obtain, they argued. And just a short distance from campus, the city of South Bend provided a modern hub of industry with opportunity everywhere. The cost of room and board also promised to be less than it was at Champaign.

The two Johns stoked Rockne's sense of tempting the unknown, and their sales pitch proved effective. Rockne agreed to accompany them east, rationalizing that trains ran in both directions. If he didn't like it, he could cut his losses and return home. That was a well-used justification for many young men of his generation, who might "try out" four or five colleges before settling at one they liked. And Notre Dame's admission requirements were not as stringent as those at the University of Chicago. From the time Father Sorin founded the school, the Holy Cross fathers had adopted a philosophy of accepting anyone who requested admission. Often, admission requirements went no further than the ability to pay and not necessarily in currency or coin; Father Sorin also cheerfully accepted livestock or the services of a tradesman or some other "in-kind" payment. Nor were admissions limited by religious preference. The school's mission and inspiration were indisputably Catholic, but from the beginning Father Sorin made it clear that would-be students of any religious persuasion were welcome. Rockne never forgot that a Protestant Norwegian was as welcome at Notre Dame as any Catholic immigrant from Chicago, Detroit, or St. Louis.

Rockne's sisters were elated at his decision. They advocated strongly over the past years that their brother continue his education. They were aware—as were many immigrant families—that through hard work and education, second generation immigrants, especially men, would be able to expand on the abundance of opportunities that appeared open to them in this new century and new country. And Notre Dame president Father John Cavanaugh, son of Irish immigrants, continued his pursuit of making Notre Dame the intellectual center of the west. He realized that more stringent academic standards would come, but in 1910, much like the rest of a national post-secondary educational system, the foundation for entrance standards was just being laid.

After a hasty goodbye to his family, Rockne was off with Plant and Devine to Notre Dame. If nothing else would be familiar there, at least he would know these two fellows who had become close friends. A battered suitcase and his savings of $1,000 were the only other possessions he took. On the train ride, he wondered what campus life would look like. Despite the non-Catholics who were welcome, would he still be self-conscious about being "a lone Norse Protestant?" Then there was the matter of his age: 22 years and six months, much older than most of the other freshmen. Early balding and his flattened nose made him look even more mature. On a campus of just 700 students—from the grade-school minims to prep school teenagers to young undergraduates and seminarians—how much would he stand out? And could he make the grades? That part of his doubt was quickly erased after arriving on campus when, not being the holder of a high school diploma, he was required to sit through an oral entrance exam for the Department of Pharmacy, his intended course of study. He impressed the proctors and took his spot in the Class of 1914.

The change from the hustle and bustle of city life in Chicago was obvious as soon as Rockne arrived in South Bend. Memories of Voss stirred in him as he saw the woods and farm fields that surrounded the campus proper, which consisted of only a handful of buildings—the golden-domed Main Building, Sacred Heart Church, Science Hall, Badin Hall, and Washington Hall. As it had since rebuilding after the fire in 1879, the Main Building housed much of the university, including classrooms, the refectory, and the infirmary. On the third floor of the east and west wings were Carroll Hall and Brownson Hall, true dormitories. Each man had a tiny space with a simple bunk, small desk, and chair. Privacy came in the form of hanged sheets, which created a small "room." Rockne took up his assigned space in Brownson and began his college days.

Another Chicagoan to arrive in 1910 was 12-year-old Norman Barry, who joined the grade-school division known as the minims, the school established by Father Edward Sorin on Notre Dame's campus. As committed as Sorin was to founding a Catholic university, so too was his pledge to provide educational opportunities for the youngest generation. Barry's father Chris had emigrated from Ireland's County Cork as a 22-year-old in 1892, and arrived in Chicago, where he began working in the stockyards. He steadily advanced through various jobs before becoming a livestock broker; his wife started teaching school so that they might provide Norman with a private education. There was little question as to where; Norman had cousins already attending Notre Dame's grammar school and prep school. One year, 68 out of the 110 minims were from Chicago.

Minims had their own vigorous athletic program, and occasionally, a Notre Dame varsity athlete might be available to coach them. Norman and his classmates might sometimes peek in on Notre Dame's varsity practicing at Cartier Field. Barry would often wonder, "Could I be out there with them some day?"

It didn't take long for Rockne to notice one of the main features of the campus: the enormous green known as Cartier Field. Created 12 years earlier when alumnus and lumber merchant Warren Cartier provided the planks to fence in the 10-acre site, as well as build a small grandstand and some bleachers, the athletic complex hummed with activity every day from mid-afternoon on. A 220-foot straightaway track was included. It was apparent Notre Dame, harkening back to the classical days of the ancient Greeks, embraced the concept of athletics as an integral part of education. Physical training was mandatory and fellows of seemingly all ages, from the grade-school minims to prep schoolers to college gents, all made Cartier their playground. Rockne would note, "Ancient Greece was a cradle of culture, and ancient Greece was a nation of athletes." It was easy to understand how Rockne, or most students at Notre Dame, would be expected to try out for their hall football team should they fail to make the varsity.

Top varsity players traditionally coached interhall teams, and the Brownson squad, with an enthusiastic Rockne a member, fell under the tutelage of starting left end Joe Collins, a senior from Boston. His 6-foot, 185-pound athletic frame made the 5-foot-8, 145-pound Rock feel as though the varsity suited up on another planet. But Knute's speed and acumen for his assignments impressed Collins so much that the hall coach recommended Rockne for a chance with the varsity. For the first time in his athletic career Rockne met a college football coach—Frank Chandler "Shorty" Longman. The Ann Arbor native was a star fullback on Michigan's "point-a-minute" teams of 1903 to 1905. It was written that Longman, a handsome and sturdy athlete, "hits the line like a stone shot from a catapult" and was "a great line plunger" and "a splendid blocker." After coaching at the University of Arkansas for two seasons and the College of Wooster for one, Longman arrived at Notre Dame in 1909 and fashioned a 7-0-1 season, including the great upset of his alma mater.

"Never on any football field was there so dismal a flop," Rockne recalled of his brief stint with the varsity. Longman inserted him as a fullback in a practice game for the backups against the regulars. Rockne recalled being unable to field a punt, and when called on to deliver one, "a 200-pound tackle smashed into me...for a 15-yard loss." He was quickly sent back to the Brownson Hall team. "I was a dud, a washout, not even good enough for the scrubs," was Rockne's over-dramatic self-assessment. It wasn't long after he arrived that Rockne found himself fighting a bout of self-pity. Fed up with his on-campus job of cleaning up "slop in the chemical lab" and wracked with homesickness, a tearful Rockne packed his suitcase and headed to the train station. But Devine, Plant, and Fred Steers, another track star, received word of his exit and intercepted him. They had to deliver their sales pitch once again, assuring Rockne he could stick it out and look forward to better days ahead. They turned the unusual freshman around, and back to campus he went to continue his try at college life.

Rockne's pals only had to remind him of why he chose Notre Dame in the first place—the likelihood of finding employment. In 1910, South Bend was thriving with successful businesses and plentiful jobs in a variety of industries. Just as his father before him had been drawn to Chicago, Knute was attracted to a city ripe with opportunities for entrepreneurs and dreamers. A decade into the new century, South Bend held a reputation as an up-and-coming area of the country with an exciting cultural scene and modern conveniences that included miles of paved streets and a city water system. The Central Union Telephone Company proudly announced with completion of its new switchboard that South Bend would "have the simplest and most efficient telephone system in the world that would serve as a model for telephone engineering of the future."

Approximately one quarter of South Bend's 54,000 residents worked in one of the nearly 140 factories; Studebaker Brothers Manufacturing Company held the premier position among them. By 1910 Studebaker was producing more than one million horse-drawn vehicles and related equipment. Its reputation for product quality and the existing plant facilities helped position the South Bend company to also produce just more than 4,000 motor vehicles. Studebaker was quickly becoming a global leader in a new transportation industry that was transforming society. Counted among the automobiles produced was the Studebaker-Garford Model B used to transport President William H. Taft in his travels around Washington, D.C. in 1908. Studebaker's competition for the new automotive market came from other local manufacturers, including the Diamond Automobile Co. and the Simplex Motor Car Co. in Mishawaka, South Bend's neighboring city.

City businesses that boasted the "world is our market" included the South Bend Watch Company, established in 1903. Their wares were sold in more than 14,000 retail jewelers in the United States. The Malleable Steel Range Company manufactured a complete line of ranges of every size, including coal and gas ranges, hotel ranges, steam tables, laundry stoves, boilers, and kitchen outfits. The company also created complimentary yearly cookbooks for the women in the local community. Other prominent local companies included the Singer Sewing Company, The Philadelphia chocolate and candy company, Coca-Cola Bottlers, the Muessel Brewing Company, and the Co-Operative Ice and Fuel Company, who harvested an ice crop each winter from the frozen lakes. The Oliver Chilled Plow Works, which covered 75 acres and occupied 45 acres of floor space, produced more than 500,000 plows annually. Branch offices stretched from Rochester, New York to Portland, Oregon.

The downtown Oliver Hotel, named for the company founder James Oliver, advertised as "the largest, most elegantly appointed hotel in Indiana." The Oliver Hotel's Grill Room offered their 50 cent "Special Business Men's Lunch." Other buffet-style eateries provided fast, cheap, informal lunches, and often liquor, beer, and cigars. William F. Martin's buffet sold Val. Blatz Exquisite Beer, and The Post Café and Buffet promised "splendid short order service" and a "businessman's lunch." South Bend Mayor Charles L. Goetz was the head of the Goetz Cigar Factory, founded in 1886. The company advertised its "steady and healthy growth" and boasted that its plant was among the most modern of its kind in the country, always open to the inspection of the smoking public. Cigar stands proudly displayed the "Mirella," for 10 cents, while the "Mirella, Jr." and the "Goetz No. 1" sold for a nickel.

The Studebaker Company also felt great civic pride toward its home city and in 1908 donated a new YMCA building to the city. In his letter from 1902 outlining the gift, John M. Studebaker wrote:

…Since the founding of the business of Studebaker Brothers Manufacturing Company, the Board desirous of carrying out the oft expressed wish of each of the five Studebaker Brothers that some day
this company should in this city of South Bend, where their business was founded and has grown to its present proportions, erect
some building which should be devoted to philanthropic purposes
and which should be in the nature of a memorial and thank you
offering; believing that a gift to the Young Men's Christian Association of a permanent home will best serve this purpose.

Fraternal societies, service organizations, and cultural clubs provided
community and business networking opportunities. The Elks, Eagles,
Masons, Odd Fellows, Owls, and Woodmen were the most prominent.
Ethnic, religious, and occupation-based societies, such as the Knights of
Columbus and the Grange, provided death benefits, funeral assistance,
and social support to its members. The Knife and Fork Club, founded in
1908 and headquartered in the Oliver Hotel, brought in military officers
and U.S. senators to lecture to "men from the factory-bench and the
trades sit(ting) side by the side of professional and businessmen." Topics
ranged from travelogues to lectures on racial issues and military history
to "Citizenship in the Making."

Orchestras traveled the country, stopping in South Bend to play the
Oliver or Studebaker theaters or one of a dozen other smaller places.
The upbeat sounds of ragtime bellowed from local venues. Theaters, including the Majestic and the Scenic, advertised "Continuous Vaudeville
Afternoons and Evenings." South Bend residents could walk downtown
or ride the streetcars to purchase supplies from a variety of merchants
offering shoppers the latest in grocery and clothing options. Fruit and
vegetable purchases came from Butzbach Fruit, and F.W. Mueller's supplied "everything in the grocery line." Stetson hats could be had at the
Ettinger-Steed-Johnson Co. or at Meyer Livingston Sons. Robertson's
Bros. Co., advertised that "The First News of the Styles Is Always Told in
Robertson's Ads." And Stephenson Underwear Mills promised any man,
regardless of his occupation, would feel well dressed in a closed-crotch
union suit. South Bend women shoppers were curious about the new
fashion designs that offered relief from the unnatural "S" figures pushed

and pulled with bustles and corsets. These were replaced with ankle-length dresses and skirts that accentuated a straight, natural figure. The waist was loosened, and the frills and flounces of the previous decade were gone. Fuller skirts for outdoor wear provided additional freedom. For women who made their clothes at home, the Butterick Quarterly promised the latest fashion patterns from Paris and New York.

Errand boys rode their bicycles making home deliveries of pharmaceutical orders and other products from places such as the Economical Drug Store. One such young delivery lad was John Boyer, a recent orphan from Stevens Point, Wisconsin, who was sent with his three sisters to South Bend. Six Boyer children had been orphaned in 1909 when their parents John and Mary died within months of each other. Their uncle Mike Krajeski, a saloonkeeper in Chicago and himself a father of two young boys, took young Henry Boyer under his wing. Unable to care for all of his dead sister's children, the uncle asked other Polish immigrant friends in South Bend to help care for the other youngsters. They joined a city brimming full of recent immigrants. By 1910 approximately one quarter of South Bend's residents had been born abroad. Immigrant neighborhoods and churches grew to accommodate those who had arrived from Germany, Hungary, Russia, Austria, Belgium, Sweden, Poland, and dozens of other countries. A 22-year-old Rockne would have found in South Bend a sort of "little Chicago" with its heavy immigrant influences.

Merchants were grateful for an eager young errand boy to help with deliveries, and millinery shop owners were happy to take in young Gladys, Winifred, and Helen Boyer to help with hat-making and shop upkeep. Easy access to the six railroads that serviced South Bend and the approximately 150 miles of interurban railways allowed an ever-watchful Krajeski to keep track of the well being of his nephew and nieces. It was upon his urging that young John enrolled as a minim at Notre Dame, where he would take his place with Norm Barry, who had arrived from Chicago. On rare occasions, the youngsters were permitted a summer trip to Springbrook Park, which featured candy treats and ice cream from The Philadelphia confectionary. The park was located about halfway between South Bend and Mishawaka on the northwest corner of the intersection at Lincoln Way East and South Ernsperger Street. One especially enchanting evening for young Gladys included a trip to the Studebaker mansion Tippecanoe to watch as newly installed electric lights emerged as dusk settled on the city.


By 1910, Reverend John William Cavanaugh was in the early stages of his tenure as president of Notre Dame and was tasked with moving the university into the 20th century. Enrollment would grow to nearly 1,000 students in the early years of the century's second decade. This still included all pupils in the elementary and preparatory schools and the School of Manual Labor. Staff was expanding with priests still serving as the majority of instructors. However, Cavanaugh realized as academic and professional specialties would continue to grow at Notre Dame that the hiring of qualified staff would mean reaching out past the ranks of the Holy Cross Congregation. He mulled over what expansion would mean to Father Sorin's vision of a Catholic university.

Cavanaugh was born in Leetonia, Ohio and schooled in Catholic education his entire life. Ordained in 1893, the year Sorin died, Cavanaugh served as superior of the Holy Cross Seminary before assuming the presidency in 1905. The role of lay faculty would remain an endless source of tension for Cavanaugh in his term as president. He oversaw constant contentious arguments from both sides as he weighed how best to balance the benefits of lay and priest faculty.

Cavanaugh believed Catholic education was more than an aggregation of buildings, books, and teachers. He believed an "authentic Catholic" education should provide instruction in the arts and sciences while ensuring that moral training and virtuous example would produce students who conducted their lives in superior fashion. He was keenly aware of the responsibility placed on Notre Dame by parents sending their young sons to be trained educationally and spiritually. Cavanaugh pushed for educational advancements within the university and also urged residential hall staff to watch over the morals of their youthful charges. While Cavanaugh contemplated the expansion of the university and how best to seek funds to do so, Junior Thomas A. Lahey welcomed the incoming class of 1910 with the following:

College life! How much that phrase suggests to the uninitiated!

How it glows with the light of promise in the imaginative mind of the new student. Alas, that so many of our universities should so soon dispel that golden ideal with their cold, training—camp methods of education. At Notre Dame it is not so. Here is found college life as the youth dreams of it, fellowship as the writer would revel in, and that added something which the boy forgets, but the man never–the influence of noble association. The school which must act as the tutor, the parent, and the preceptor of one thousand or more students during ten long months of the year must needs be a varied, a wonderful institution, and Notre Dame is all that.

Knute Rockne quickly felt "the influence of noble association," making fast friends with those who brought sharp minds and inquisitive natures to the study of the sciences. Fellow students like D. M. Nigro from Kansas City and Leo O'Donnell afforded Rockne stimulating conversation as well as competition and cooperation in the mastering of the sciences. The challenging study matter was just what Rockne needed, and his first-year academic success was astounding—all marks of 94 and above, including a 99 in Bacteriology. Other courses included Microscopy (98), Chemistry (97), Pharmacognosy (97), Physiology (94), Elements of Pharmacy (94) and Pharmacy Arithmetics (94). He also began to work under the direction of his future academic mentor, fellow immigrant Father Julius A. Nieuwland. The Holy Cross priest saw in Rockne a kindred spirit, a highly developed mind always curious about how things worked and what was over the next horizon. Nieuwland was born in Hansbeke, Belgium in 1878 and as a toddler emigrated with his family in 1880, joining a thriving Belgian community in South Bend and Mishawaka. Nieuwland studied Greek and Latin at Notre Dame, graduating in 1899, after which he began his studies for the priesthood. Ordained in 1903, Nieuwland attended graduate school at The Catholic University of America in Washington, D.C. where he studied botany and chemistry. He showed extraordinary promise as a research chemist; however, Notre Dame needed a botany instructor in 1904 when he returned to his alma mater. As a disciplined scholar, Nieuwland accepted the challenge. He poured himself into the study of local flora and fauna, and his extensive notes of the northern Indiana environment led Nieuwland to establish and become editor of the *American Midland Naturalist*. It has been reported that he often carried a pistol with him on his walks around the campus looking for specimens to collect. If a leaf were out of reach Nieuwland would just pull out his pistol and shoot it down.

Father Nieuwland spotted Rockne's aptitude for the sciences—a nearly encyclopedic memory, diligence in completing assignments, and curiosity about what might be discovered in the laboratory. Rockne's maturity impressed Nieuwland, and the priest-scientist identified the freshman as a prime prospect to work closely with on his research. It would be the start of a close relationship of equals. Not in terms of experience, of course. But Rockne's keen mind and questioning nature would prove to be a valuable complement to Nieuwland's work as Notre Dame's premier chemist.

The Notre Dame football season of 1910 was notable more for a game not played than for any of the six that were contested. In three engagements at Cartier Field, Longman's squad shut out Olivet (48-0), Butchel from Akron, Ohio (51-0), and Ohio Northern (47-0). The team traveled to Terre Haute to defeat Rose Poly, 41-3; suffered its only loss at Michigan Agricultural College in East Lansing, 17-0; and finished with a hard-fought 5-5 tie with Marquette in Milwaukee. On November 4, Notre Dame's gridders began their journey to Ann Arbor to defend their 1909 victory over the Wolverines in a game scheduled for Saturday, November 5. But they made it only six miles, to Niles, Michigan, when they were called back to campus. Michigan, based on accusations from football coach Fielding Yost, had just informed Notre Dame it was cancelling the game, questioning the eligibility of two Notre Dame stars from Oregon. From the *Scholastic*'s report:

> The trouble centered on our intention to play (Ralph) Dimmick and (George) Philbrook, Michigan claiming that both these men were ineligible because of the fact that they had played out their time as collegiate football players. A review of the athletic careers of both of these men shows that in 1904-05 they were preparatory students at Tullatin Academy and competed on teams there. The following year both men were students at Peason's Academy, an institution apart from Whitman College. In September 1907, they registered at

Whitman College, taking two freshman studies and three or four preparatory studies. Dimmick remained at Whitman until February 1908, and Philbrook until June of the same year. Whitman College is not named in the list of conference colleges issued in September 1907. Because of that it is only reasonable to presume these men as participating in preparatory athletics prior to their coming to Notre Dame. On these grounds we maintain that Philbrook and Dimmick are eligible and will continue to hold these grounds.

The *Scholastic* also reported Notre Dame had inquired as to whether the pair would be allowed to play as early as January 1911, when the game was arranged, and was assured by Michigan athletic director Philip Bartelme that "there would be no trouble on that score." There were also assertions made that Michigan players Clarke and Cole, who had played three years of competition at Oberlin, would be allowed in the game, thus seemingly clearing the way for Notre Dame's two Oregonians. However no such January game occurred, as both schools were unable to resolve the issues at hand.

The controversy underscored the very inexact nature of educational institutions' demarcations between prep school and college enrollment. And that made application of eligibility rules, such as they existed, extremely elastic. Even with the establishment of Intercollegiate Athletic Association of the United States in 1906, truly uniform, enforceable rules over eligibility in college football were still many years away. On a more basic note, there were observers who felt that Fielding Yost and Michigan were simply looking for an excuse to avoid the possibility of another upset defeat at the hands of the upstarts from South Bend.

For his part, Knute Rockne could observe all the charges and counter-charges with a certain amount of bemusement. His football togs were packed away for the season after the Brownson Hall team completed its interhall schedule. His confidence was fortified by his outstanding academic performance combined with the prospect of reuniting in training and competition in track with Plant and Devine as the Christmas break awaited. A strong bond was building between Rockne and his roommate Gus Dorais, who chuckled at Rockne's never-ending attempt to battle baldness. "Sometimes I think you took chemistry just to save your hair,"

Dorais told him. Rockne would borrow one concoction after another in an attempt to find the right mix. The odor from the mixes was overpowering in their room. He even slept on newspaper based on the suggestion that it might help grow hair. Soon, Rockne would turn his attention to his first athletic love—the indoor track season, which was scheduled to start when school resumed in January.

On January 21, 1911, Rockne proudly wore the Notre Dame colors in a triumphant return to one of his old Chicago haunts—the massive First Regiment track meet, where top competitors from across the region gathered. Already a factor on the Notre Dame varsity track, Rockne competed in the hurdles, quarter-mile, shot put, and pole vault. The championship of the meet came down to a battle between Rockne's former mates with the Illinois Athletic Club and his new squad at Notre Dame. In the quarter-mile, all three Notre Dame entrants were leading the field, with Bill Martin and Forrest Fletcher battling for first, Rockne slightly behind them. On the final lap, with a strong likelihood that Coach Bertrand Maris' sprinters would sweep all three spots, Martin and Fletcher collided and both were thrown badly off their stride. "Rochne in evading the spilled athletes lost his stride, but recovered sufficiently to take second place in the event." The mishap handed the meet's title to the IAC. Later, in the outdoor season, Rockne and his team played host to the IAC in a dual-meet rematch, this one won by the home team, with Rockne winning the pole vault at 10 feet, 6 inches.

The first year at Notre Dame was winding down and Rock's homesickness had eased. A successful track season matched continued accomplishments in the classroom. Stronger bonds were made with other students. The persistence Rockne showed in his four years of working at the Post Office was paying dividends—he faced and met challenges, one day at a time. He was doing the required work needed to move forward, whether in the classroom or on the athletic fields. The second-guessing on his decision-making was over. Notre Dame was now home.

# 10

## Establishing Roots

John L. "Jack" Marks, who made a name for himself as a backfield star at Dartmouth, took over as Notre Dame's coach in 1911. His style, as a refined, somewhat reserved Ivy Leaguer, presented a contrast with his predecessor Shorty Longman, who had decided to leave the football-coaching world. The difference worked its way into Rockne's description of the two men. He recalled Longman's locker-room oratory as dramatic and of questionable efficacy. Before a game against, say, Olivet College, Longman would stride into the locker room, "toss back his shock of black hair and burst into rhetoric, 'Boys, today is the day. The honor of the old school is at stake. Now or never, we must fight the battle of our lives. I don't want any man with a streak of yellow to move from this room. You've all got to be heroes…heroes, or I never want to see you again. Go out and conquer. It's the crisis of your lives!'"

The squad "conquered" Olivet, 48-0. A week later, as the players lounged in the locker room before its meeting with Buchtel, Longman entered and broke into a speech: "Boys, today is the day of days. The honor of the old school is at stake. The eyes of the world are on you. Go out and bleed for the old school, and if anybody has a yellow streak, let him…"

Bergman, said Rockne, turned to a teammate and asked, "What do you think of the act today?" Dorais answered, "Not so good. I thought he was better last week." Whether the home team was inspired or bored by the oratory, they prevailed, 51-0. Still, the 1911 Notre Dame team was inexperienced in several spots. Gone were key linemen, including the 1910 captain, right tackle Ralph Dimmick, along with guard John Stansfield and center Tom Foley. A slew of halfbacks, led by Walter Clinnen and Lee Mathews, and fullback Art Clippenger had moved on. One particularly weak position appeared to be left end, where Joe Collins and baseball star Cy Williams were also not returning.

The *Scholastic* welcomed a record number of students back to campus in September 1911, with an editorial looking askance at what it called the "school trotter: the young man who with every coming September heads to some other school until the next September comes around....who attempts to get an education...by making a circuit of colleges." It concluded by advising, "Those of us who expect to grow should get rooted." Among the changes greeting students upon their arrival that fall was the banishment of cigarettes, which the *Scholastic* noted was not a great imposition because of the relatively low number of students who smoked them. Recreation areas in the halls had been updated, and Walsh Hall was "busy with billiards tables and bowling alleys in use until the bell rings." The college's military battalion attracted more students than ever, and the start of the supper hour had been moved back to 6:15, "to give more time for concerts and military drill." The Sorin Hall rec room boasted a $100 piano, and it soon developed the nickname "The Notre Dame Conservatory of Rag-Time Music."

A pair of sophomores—Knute K. Rockne and Charles "Gus" Dorais—returned having survived their first year of college and its challenges and bouts of homesickness. Rockne began making a name for himself as a leading track man, and Dorais, despite his 5-foot-7, 145-pound size, had assumed the position as starting quarterback on the football team. They were roommates, friends, and teammates, and eagerly awaiting the start of football.

Dorais grew up in the town of Chippewa Falls in northwest Wisconsin, where the cold, swift-flowing waters of the Chippewa River fueled a number of industries, including brewing. In the spring of 1867, Jacob Leinenkugel and John Miller founded a brewery at Chippewa Falls, and a few years later Leinenkugel bought out Miller, consolidating control of the firm in his family. The Leinenkugel Brewery became a major employer in town, and its products were met with great satisfaction in the region. Dorais attended Chippewa Falls' Notre Dame High School through his junior year, where he made a name for himself as a talented football player. Father C.F. X. Goldsmith, a French missionary, founded the Church of Notre Dame in 1856. The oldest parish in the state, it operated the one-room high school.

Although school life held promise, Dorais' home life was difficult. His father had abandoned the family, and his mother Malvina was taking in laundry, working as a midwife, and doing other odd jobs to clothe and feed Gus, older sister Flora, and younger brother Joe. Gus transferred to the Chippewa Falls public high school for his senior year and quarterbacked the football team, garnering a fair amount of press coverage. Gus' goal was to earn a football scholarship to the University of Minnesota, which was quickly becoming a major power in the Western Conference. Dorais' small stature, however, caused the Gophers esteemed coach, Dr. Henry Williams, to pass on extending an offer. The rejection did not deter Gus, who was seeking the opportunity for a good education as well as the opportunity to play football. Through an acquaintance, he was put in touch with Coach Longman in South Bend. Longman was aware of the Dorais' financial situation and made a pitch for Gus and another possible student in a letter to university president Father John Cavanaugh.

Longman received a reply in a letter from Father Cavanaugh on March 22, 1910:

> My Dear Mr. Longman:
>
> I was glad to get your recent letter referring to the two men you have in mind. I hope you land Davidson. At your suggestion I have sent him a catalogue. I wish you would have Mr. Dorais write a letter to Mr. Francis McKeever, 806 Ashland Bl'k, Chicago, Ill., the contents of which should be a request for aid in getting through Notre Dame with an expression of a willingness

to be useful in any service the University may need him for. I hope you are well and trust that business is flourishing.

Very Sincerely yours,

Gus followed the instructions in Father Cavanaugh's letter and received the referenced assistance. Similar to Rockne, Dorais arrived at Notre Dame in the fall of 1910, and he soon felt the pangs of homesickness. It seemed he was not prepared for life away from home in a strange place, "so light, young and lonesome the day he reported for classes at Notre Dame." He packed his suitcase and decided to go home. A friend caught Dorais as he was boarding the streetcar for downtown and persuaded Dorais to return to campus. Gus didn't realize the favor his friend had extended him when he persuaded him to remain under the Golden Dome.

At Notre Dame, Dorais quickly established himself as a force on the football field. He exhibited a certain fearlessness, perhaps due to his diminutive size. He was speedy, quick-thinking, and sure of himself— all traits that Rockne and others immediately admired and emulated. Through the 1911 September workouts, new coach Marks patiently observed and analyzed the 40 candidates out for the team, and found what he believed would be adequate replacements for the departed stars. Al Feeney, a quick-witted sophomore from Indianapolis, would do just fine at center with his 5-foot-11, 190-pound frame. Another Indianan, Livingston's Paul Harvat, seemed able to man one of the guard spots. And 5-foot-9, 185-pound Luke Kelly, a senior from Boston, earned the right to take over both Dimmick's spot at tackle and his role as team captain. Kelly felt a burst of Irish-American pride the first week of the new school year, when Boston Mayor John Francis "Honey Fitz" Fitzgerald, a son of Irish immigrants, paid a visit to the campus, along with his wife Mary and daughter Rose Fitzgerald.

Alfred "Dutch" Bergman, who lettered as a freshman backup in 1910, led the new backfield starters. Bergman came from an athletic family in Peru, Indiana, 75 miles south of Notre Dame. His father Joseph operated a Peru bar and restaurant and organized local teams in baseball and other sports. Alfred was the second oldest of five children, with sisters Henrietta and Stella and younger brothers Arthur and Joseph. Across town, at an estate known as Westleigh Farms, another Peru family had a single child, born the same year as Stella Bergman. Samuel Fenwick Porter worked as a Peru druggist and his wife Kate was the daughter of James Omar "J. O." Cole, a coal and timber speculator known as "the richest man in Indiana." At age 14, J.O. Cole sent his grandson, Cole Porter, away to Worcester Academy in Massachusetts in the hope that he would eventually study law. Young Cole brought an upright piano with him and discovered that entertaining others with music helped him make friends among the academy's students. Cole Porter never strayed far from that model. Peru boasted of a history steeped in entertainment. Numerous circuses, such as Ringling Brothers, Hagenbeck-Wallace, and Buffalo Bill's Wild West Show, wintered at Peru's Circus Winter Quarters. There, crews repaired and painted circus wagons and gold-leafed their carvings. A thousand horses roamed the Winter Quarters' fields, and hundreds of exotic animals were housed and trained in numerous barns. Zebras and camels grazing on snow-covered ground were a common sight for passers-by and tourists. In 1892, the International Circus Hall of Fame was established on the grounds, and future circus clown Emmett Kelly was born in Peru in 1898.

Another Indiana town—Howe, 50 miles east of South Bend—produced the other starting halfback, Alvin "Heinie" Berger. In preseason workouts, the 6-foot Berger was described as "another surprise with 185 pounds of nerve and muscle." Backups were Joe Pliska from Chicago and Art Smith of Minneapolis. The job of fullback fell to a massive freshman from Columbus, Ohio, 6-foot, 205-pound Ray Eichenlaub. Coach Marks' charge to big "Ike" was simple: "Feeney and the others will make the holes. You tear through them." Eichenlaub-up-the-middle aside, Marks was not a great proponent of simple, smash-'em football. He introduced an early version of the shift, as it was used at Dartmouth.

Marks saw the value of speed over size. How else could he build an offense around a 5-foot-7, 145-pound quarterback? Or elevate a 5-foot-8, 165-pound sophomore—Knute Rockne—to starting left end? As the *Scholastic* of September 30 stated, "The marked improvement in Rockne's form over that of last season makes him one of the favorite candidates for an end." As the team entered its final week before the October 7 opener vs. Ohio Northern, it appeared that, with four exceptions, its lineup would "consist entirely of men who have yet to win their monograms in football with the gold and blue." Only Captain Kelly, quarterback Dorais, and returning lineman Philbrook and Oaas were back to man their positions. Torgus "Turk" Oaas was a rugged type from the lumber town of Merrill, Wisconsin, who stood 6-feet, 185 pounds. Notre Dame still showed an open date several weeks before the season started before John P. Murphy, manager of athletics, scheduled Ohio Northern. "With the short time at his disposal to fill this date, the manager deserves great credit," opined the *Scholastic*. Ohio Northern had twice visited Cartier Field, losing to the home team 58-4 in 1908 and 47-0 in 1910.

At noon on Friday, October 6, a general meeting of all the college men was held in Washington Hall with a goal of "perfecting the general rooters' organization." Faculty and students made speeches and practiced cheers, with manager of athletics Murphy speaking "enthusiastically of the spirit which the organization can awaken if properly pushed." The group, in planning its official debut for the home opener the next day, selected Rockne's close pal, half-miler John Devine, as head cheer leader, assisted by James Nolan. "No doubt Cartier field will be awake during the entire progress of today's game," said the *Scholastic*.

October 7 dawned bright and brisk on the Notre Dame campus, and spirits were high among the students and townspeople anxious to see what Coach Marks had assembled from such an inexperienced group. "The early practice proved that many of the recruits possessed speed and dodging ability, but the work of...all of the first year men was better by far than even the most ardent rooter had hoped to witness." One first-year player recalled a rather inauspicious start. On the first pass thrown his way, left end Rockne said, "I was so high-strung and tense that I met the ball with frozen fingers and dropped it—and at the same time learned that loose hands and relaxed fingers are the only effective tools for making the soft, non-resisting catch essential to a forward-pass receiver." It wasn't his only opportunity, though. On a later drive, "passes from Eichenlaub to Dorais and Dorais to Rockne worked perfectly, for a further gain of forty yards." On the game, the blue and gold had its way with Ohio Northern, with numerous long runs and successful passes making significant gains and "shift formations which netted more than the required distance... were of such frequent occurrences as to make the squad appear one of the best turned out in several years." Kicking and defense were also impressive; on one Eichenlaub punt to the opponents' 20-yard line, Rockne followed the ball and stopped Smith "as soon as he received the oval." For a 23-year-old making his college football debut, Rockne relished being part of a solid team effort.

The following week's visitor to Cartier Field, St. Viator College of Bourbonnais, Illinois, was no stranger to Coach Marks. He had coached the college the previous year, and spoke highly of the spirit displayed by his former pupils. But the coach showed no mercy to his former squad, letting Notre Dame loose for a 43-0 romp. "Dorais displayed more of his real ability at quarter both in carrying the ball and in the accuracy of his passes." Dutch Bergman ran for three touchdowns, and Eichenlaub's punting kept the visitors boxed in their own end. St. Viator's only appreciable advance came when Notre Dame was assessed a 50-yard penalty by referee Kittleman for side-line coaching.

On October 21, Butler from Indianapolis figured to provide stiffer competition in its invasion of Cartier for the first-ever meeting between the in-state rivals. The visitors were said to have a speedy group of backs ready to challenge Marks' men. But heavy rains inundated South Bend in the days leading up to the contest and continued through the game. Rockne was held out because of an injury, and he missed a game which saw numerous fumbles and miscues by both sides. "The ball was carried into the shadows of the goal posts several times, only to be lost on fumbles." In the final minute of the first half, Dutch Bergman fielded a punt at the Butler 35-yard-line and made "one of the few sensational sprints of the game." His touchdown and Dorais' kick gave Notre Dame a 6-0 lead. It took until the fourth quarter for the home team to break open the game with four more scores, to complete a 27-0 victory.

With a 3-0 start in which an inexperienced Notre Dame team was rounding into form and had outscored its opposition, 102-6, the campus mood would have naturally been one of celebration and excitement. But on Sunday, October 22, a telegram from Reverend Joseph Gallagher, president of Columbia University in Portland, Oregon, sent Notre Dame into shock. Ralph Dimmick, star tackle of the past three seasons and captain of last fall's team, who had graduated with a law degree just four months earlier, had died. He had been accidentally injured a few days earlier while playing football for the Multnomah Club of Portland. Dimmick, after graduating from Notre Dame, had returned to his native Oregon and was coaching the football team at Columbia. "It was hard to accept its full meaning," noted the *Scholastic* of the grim telegram. "And when the word was passed around among the students, there was a very noticeable gloom everywhere." Among those stunned was Knute Rockne, who had spent considerable time with Dimmick on the varsity track team the previous year, both working to perfect their shot-put techniques. It was the first such loss of a contemporary for the 23-year-old Rockne, and he was deeply saddened.

Of Dimmick, the *Scholastic* noted, "Among Notre Dame's great athletes, he has surely won deserved immortality." Yet, more than that, "he was high purposed, yet gentle in his ways. He was kindly and cheerful, and always a loyal son of the University." Dimmick had summarized his affection for the school, when he said at a social event his senior year: "Among the deepest inspirations of my life will be the thought that I have received my diploma from this grand old University." There was some consolation felt at Notre Dame when it was learned that Dimmick, prior to his death, was baptized into the Catholic Church by "one of the devoted sisters who nursed him." Dimmick was buried from Portland's St. Mary's Cathedral on Tuesday, October 24. At Notre Dame on Thursday, requiem high Mass was sung at Sacred Heart Church by the president for the repose of the soul of Ralph Dimmick. Columbia immediately discontinued its football schedule. And two former Notre Dame pals of Dimmick's, Dominic Callicrate and Bill Schmitt, turned in their football suits to the manager of the Multnomah Club team out of respect to their departed mate. Notre Dame's season was to go on, though, and the next visitor to Cartier Field was a replacement for a cancelled game. DePaul was originally scheduled to be the opponent on October 28, but a conflict in dates wiped the contest out, and another Chicago institution, Loyola, agreed to the place on Notre Dame's schedule.

The result: "The most severe drubbing handed a visiting team in years...one continual round of dashes up the field and down...affording Coach Marks an opportunity to judge the ability of the various candidates in action against strangers." When it was over, Notre Dame had scored 14 touchdowns and 10 goals-after for a total count of 80-0. All thirty Notre Dame men dressed for the game participated; a rejuvenated

Rockne started at left end and was spelled by McGinnis and McLaughlin. Dutch Bergman again stood out, scoring three touchdowns and barely missing a fourth when he fielded a kickoff and "sprinted through the crowded field" before being stopped at the Loyola 5-yard line. But it was Art Smith, the little-known backup to Heinie Berger at left half, who had a day to remember. Smith "earned a niche in the hall of fame" by scoring seven touchdowns. Smith's career day against Loyola did not earn him a spot on the travel squad five days later, however. On Thursday, November 2, 20 players, Coach Marks, Manager Murphy, and Coach Bert Maris, who was overseeing the physical condition of the players, left for Pittsburgh and "the first real contest of the season," against the University of Pittsburgh. The teams had battled once before, in 1909, when Notre Dame went east and eked out a 6-0 victory, which propelled it to a 7-0-1 season and acclaim as "Western champions." Pittsburgh would be eager for revenge—and a good showing—after suffering a 17-0 defeat to Carlisle Indian School and a 9-3 setback at Cornell.

A crowd of some 10,000 turned out at Forbes Field in Pittsburgh, with a strong showing of Notre Dame alumni and fans. "Their rooting made it hard to realize that the game was not being played on our own Cartier field." Back at Notre Dame, Rockne friend, trackman, and cheer leader John Devine was poised to call out the progress of the game to the student body assembled at Cartier, as he was to receive regular wire reports. Here it was, the first big-time game in a major league setting for Knute Rockne as a college football player. He and his 19 teammates ran onto the field and were "overawed by what looked like assembled millions." But he learned something valuable upon the kickoff. "The moment the ball went into play I had promptly forgotten that anybody was looking on," he said. His focus was on stopping his opposite number and carrying out his assignments with precision. Pitt threatened early, reaching the Notre Dame 13-yard line on one occasion, then the 2-yard line on its next drive. But both times, Rockne and company repelled the charge. Through the first half, the scoreboard read zeroes, and after rolling up 182 points the previous four Saturdays, Notre Dame was feeling a little flustered.

It was time for some trickery. For the start of the second half, Eichenlaub executed a perfect onside kick and Rockne scooped up the ball and took off toward the Pitt goal line. Using his sprinter's speed and the element of surprise, he raced into the clear. Notre Dame fans went wild with cheering as he crossed the Pitt goal line. For the first time, he had scored a touchdown for the varsity—in a crucial point of a hard-fought battle. One by one, his teammates joined him in the end zone to congratulate. But soon, confusion reigned. Referee F.D. Godcharles, a respected man from Lafayette College, waved his arms frantically. Notre Dame, he ruled, had begun the play before he formally opened the quarter with a whistle and was technically offside. The ball was returned to midfield, with a penalty instead of a touchdown. The teams continued to slug it out without a score. Later, as if dictated by the conditions, a Pitt touchdown was also called back due to an offside call.

A star for Pitt was its big, speedy right end Hube Wagner. His assigned role was to somehow corral the shifty Dorais, already acclaimed as one of the best open-field dodgers in football. The little signal-caller could change directions like a hummingbird, it seemed, leaving his larger pursuers grasping for air. But not Wagner. He devised a new method of tackling. Instead of the conventional method of diving for Dorais' legs, Wagner would sprint at him and attempt to corral him by the neck. It worked well enough to keep Notre Dame off the scoreboard. Captain Kelly, meanwhile, was the star for Coach Marks' fellows, continually thwarting the Pitt offense and blocking kicks. By the time twilight closed in on Forbes Field, both teams had resorted to a kicking game, "each seeming to realize the impossibility of overcoming the other by straight football."

After the scoreless tie, the weary Notre Dame warriors were "feted and feasted" by the school's Pittsburgh alumni, led by Ray Dashbach, with "characteristic hospitality and good cheer." There was nothing but glowing accounts of the treatment accorded the team by Notre Dame men of the area. A *Scholastic* editorial commented:

> All told, the Pittsburg game was highly successful. We should
> like to have won for our own sakes—for our own here and our
> own in Pittsburg. But we didn't lose, and that's something. Everything taken into consideration, indeed it is a very great deal.
> We hope the contest will continue to be an annual event. It will

serve to bind faster the chords of memory between us of today who are here and those of yesterday who are in Pittsburg. It will serve to prove that the University has the secret of binding to her those sons whom time and calling have scattered far and wide. It will serve to show the present generation how strong is the affection of the sons for the mother.

Notre Dame was learning the importance of playing games in distant locations, Pittsburgh being the furthest the team had yet traveled for a game. The Notre Dame family was putting down roots in cities and towns across the land. The next Saturday, November 11, it was back to Cartier Field for the final 1911 home game, against first-time opponent St. Bonaventure College of Olean, New York. Marks used the occasion to rest most of his regulars, including Rockne, after the rugged battle at Pittsburgh. Among those who took advantage of added playing time was Joe Pliska, who started at left half and scored three touchdowns, adding three goals after touchdown, in the 34-0 victory. The *Scholastic* reported, "The last opportunity to encourage the team drew forth some spirited cheering from the rooters' association. The Brownson brigade of amateur musicians furnished a surprise" performance at the game.

Notre Dame finished the season with two away games—Wabash and Marquette. The Wabash game was a rare Monday contest, on November 20, at the campus in Crawfordsville, Indiana, 140 miles south of South Bend. The contest was billed as the championship of Indiana. Wabash had opened the season with a 3-0 win at Purdue, its fifth straight victory over the Boilermakers, and second straight by a single drop kick against Purdue and its star, Elmer Oliphant. Wabash then played a scoreless tie against rival DePauw, and later defeated Earlham and Rose Poly. An 11-9 loss at Marquette gave the Little Giants a 3-1-1 mark heading into the Notre Dame game. Rockne and his mates threw off their blankets and breathed the cold November air as they took the field, fully aware of the possible stiff competition. On the home sideline stalked Wabash's determined coach, Jesse Harper, who had brought the team a long way in just his third year on the job. Exactly two years earlier, Harper and Wabash were thrashed, 38-0, by Notre Dame on Cartier Field, one of five games in which the Little Giants were shut out that season.

Jesse Claire Harper was born on December 10, 1883 on his parents' farm near East Paw Paw, Illinois in DeKalb County, about 75 miles west of Chicago. At the age of 10, a fire destroyed their barn, and the family moved west to Mason, Iowa, near Fort Dodge. There, his father resumed his work in farming and raising cattle. Baseball was a favorite sport in the family, with Jesse, his brothers Floyd and Frank, and their father taking their turn playing on town baseball teams. Education was also a priority, and when Jesse was 16, the family sent him to Morgan Park Academy, a boarding school affiliated with the University of Chicago. Upon graduation from Morgan Park, he entered the university in 1902.

Jesse Harper did not have the appearance of a great athlete, being somewhat slight and small in stature. He also suffered from rheumatism, which held back his athletic participation at times. At Chicago, it forced him to miss the 1903 and 1904 football seasons. He excelled at baseball, though, as a swift outfielder and, when needed, as catcher. He was also named captain of the Maroon team of 1905. In the fall of 1905, Harper saw his most significant football season, playing halfback and backing up the All-American Walter Eckersall. He played enough to earn a letter, but more importantly, he closely studied the ways of his coach, Amos Alonzo Stagg. Part of his fascination was with the technical aspects of game strategy, but at least as important was how Stagg chose his team, motivated his players, and guided their personal development. From that time, Harper developed a deep desire to enter the coaching profession, and when the opportunity to become football coach at Alma College in Michigan arose in 1906, he jumped at the chance. Two successful seasons there led to the Wabash job.

In 1910, Harper guided the Little Giants to a spectacular start—four straight shutout victories of Georgetown of Kentucky, Purdue, Butler, and St. Louis. But in the St. Louis game, tragedy struck. Ralph Lee "Sap" Wilson, freshman halfback for Wabash, was attempting to stop a St. Louis run when he "dodged the interference and dived for the runner. In diving, the right side of his head struck the Saint Louis player's knee. His skull was fractured in three places." The next day Wilson, a Crawfordsville boy, died in a St. Louis hospital. Gloom quickly spread across the campus and town, and the rest of the Wabash season was immediately canceled. Crawfordsville High also canceled its remaining games, as did a number of other nearby schools. At Butler in Indianapolis, the season went on minus the Wabash game, but several players quit the squad, vowing never to play the game again. In a cemetery in Crawfordsville, Wilson's gravestone was etched with his reported dying words: "Did Wabash Win?"

Harper's task in 1911 was to move the Little Giants beyond Wilson's death and concentrate on becoming the best possible team it could. The campus paper predicted success, noting, "The genius of Harper will probably fix things up alright." And so it appeared with the opening victory against Purdue. By the time the Little Giants hosted Notre Dame, they appeared ready to spring the upset. "The opening quarter furnished enough thrills to fill an ordinary game," noted one report, including an early Notre Dame interception, which set up a place kick attempt by Dorais, which sailed wide. A series of punts and fumbles created near-constant changes of possession, and on one, "Eichenlaub booted to Elgin, who was downed in his tracks, Rockne and Crowley striking him almost as soon as the ball." But from scrimmage, Wabash's nifty quarterback Skeet Lambert was able to gain enough to attempt a 30-yard drop kick, which put the Little Giants ahead, 3-0.

In the third quarter, Wabash threatened to gain a commanding lead when Lambert threw a perfectly executed pass to Howard for an apparent touchdown. But the officials stopped the game, measured the distance, and found that the pass had traveled just more than 20 yards beyond the line of scrimmage, and was therefore illegal. Wabash was penalized, and soon Notre Dame had the ball back. The Little Giants hung on to the 3-0 lead well into the fourth quarter, when on an exchange of kicks, Wabash lost ground "on account of the high wind." On a subsequent run, Lambert was injured and had to leave the game. His replacement Watt had to face "a series of smashing plunges" that advanced the ball from the Notre Dame 35 toward the Wabash goal line. Pliska lugged it to the 2-yard line, and Berger charged over for the winning touchdown. Dorais' kick-after made the final Notre Dame 6, Wabash 3. The Little Giants had come close to repeating their one previous victory over the blue and gold, a 5-0 shocker in 1905 at Cartier.

Ten days later, on a brilliant afternoon at Campus Field in Milwaukee, Notre Dame met Marquette in the schools' fourth consecutive Thanksgiving Day meeting, this one drawing "the largest crowd ever to witness a football game in Milwaukee." Walter Eckersall had a good view of the game as its field judge, and he wrote the game story that appeared in the Chicago *Daily Tribune*:

> Playing with fierceness and aggressiveness, which have charac-
> terized their games since they resumed football relations, Notre
> Dame and Marquette played a scoreless tie…When the final
> whistle blew there was little to choose between the two elevens.
> Although the game was bitterly fought, it was much cleaner than
> former contests."

Notre Dame had its best chance to score on a first-quarter drive in which a Dorais pass to Rockne brought the ball to the Marquette 5. On the next play, "over anxious to obtain the touchdown, the Varsity was guilty of holding and the penalty returned the ball to the 20-yard line." Dorais attempted a 25-yard drop kick, but missed. In the third quarter, Marquette had its best chance when Huegle appeared headed for a long gain, but fumbled the ball. When the final whistle blew, "both teams showed the effects of the hard struggle when they left the field, and coaches of both elevens were satisfied, although each had expected his team to win." With a final record of 6-0-2, Notre Dame had shown itself well in a season that relied on so many first-time regulars. Rockne felt he had the advantage of "not being too green when I broke into big football company. I was 23 and able to wear a lettered sweater without too much intoxication." Any added strain of playing varsity football didn't appear to affect Rockne's work in the classroom. He again posted spectacular marks, including a 94 in Pharmacognosy and 93s in Physiology, Inorganic Pharmacy, and Qualitative Analysis Chemistry.

Rockne's 1912 spring semester once again included a heavy schedule of track and field. In a dual meet against Northwestern, "the most pleas-ing showing…was made by Rockne in the pole vault. Our stocky vaulter broke the Cartier field record by going over the bar at 12 feet." John Plant won the half-mile in 2:08 2/5, Eichenlaub prevailed with a 40 feet, 9 and one-half inches shot put, and Rockne ran the opening leg on the winning relay team with Birder, Plant, and Bergman. In an early May dual meet with Vanderbilt, Notre Dame won the loving cup presented by South Bend dentist R. F. Lucas, with Rockne contributing a first place in the pole vault. Just days later, Rockne was summoned to the Main Building. His heart raced—what had he done, or been accused of? There was that time as a freshman when some sacramental wine had gone missing and he was wrongly suspected. But it couldn't be that. His grades were excellent, and he had comported himself well on the football field, on the track, and in social situations.

The answer soon came, when he was informed his father had died un-expectedly. At age 54, Lars Rokne, who never missed a day of work as Louis Rockne in the new world, providing a home and all necessities for his wife and five children, was gone. Knute packed his grip and got on the next train home to Chicago. This changes everything, he thought. Football… track…chemistry…pharmacy. All could be finished, he surmised. The family would need him to provide support.

# 11
## Reaching The Big Stage

When Pastor J.N. Walstead of Immanuel Norwegian Lutheran Church spoke words of consolation at Lars Rockne's funeral in May 1912, the family future appeared uncertain. Like many around them, the Rocknes' reliance on the father to keep the family comfortable and secure was nearly absolute, and his death was a great blow, both in psychological and material terms. There was no thought given to widow Martha Rockne, 53, finding work; her role as a mother of five would make employment outside the home almost impossible. Two teenagers—Louise, 17, and Florence, 13—were still in her charge. Her oldest daughter, Annie, had worked for several years as a machine operator, then a teacher, and was now married. Daughter Martha, 21, could offer what support she could from her work as a stenographer for a wholesale millinery downtown on Wabash Avenue. Amid the handshakes of comfort and support offered by friends and neighbors, Knute weighed the options in front of him. No matter which route his mind took, he always seemed to end up at the same spot: he would have to give up dreams of a college degree and a future as a pharmacist or possibly even a doctor, and return to Chicago support the family.

It was then the wisdom and unselfishness of his oldest sister prevailed. Annie would have none of this plan. "If you quit, all right," she said. "You may earn a living, but it will be as a mail dispatcher." The family would get by, they assured Knute. Louise could enter the workforce, following Martha's path as a stenographer. The four women could find more affordable quarters, which they did in short order, moving after 17 years on Rockwell Avenue to a smaller home on Wrightwood Avenue, just west of Logan Square. Knute, still two years from graduation, would continue to be self-sufficient, looking forward to the time he would earn enough money to send some financial support home.

For nearly two decades in Chicago, Knute had watched Lars build a solid life for his family in the New World while still keeping a foot in the nation of his heritage. Knute respected his father for his dedication to all things Norwegian, especially as Lars had taken his craftsman hands and turned them to work for a Norwegian-language publisher. But Knute realized his life's journey would be made strictly as an American. He dreamed of a future in which he might visit many of the locations he used to read on return addresses at the Post Office. His embrace of the United States, and all the possibilities it offered, animated his return to Notre Dame to complete his sophomore year the following month. Yet, as summer 1912 began, it was difficult for Rockne not to take a morsel of pride in his Scandinavian heritage.


Rockne, similar to the rest of the country, was mesmerized by the start of the 1912 Olympics in Stockholm, Sweden; it was the greatest sporting event ever hosted by a Scandinavian country. The United States track team led a strong American contingent ready to showcase its talent on a worldwide stage. Although the revival of the Greek games in 1896 had been met with great enthusiasm, the following three Olympiads had been less than spectacular. Financial concerns and sporting controversies had plagued the 1900 (Paris), 1904 (St. Louis), and 1908 (London) gatherings. For many, the 1912 Games represented a make or break scenario for the Olympics. King Gustav V opened the 1912 Games on July 6 with a record number 28 nations and 2,500 athletes participating. When the Red Star Line SS *Finland* set off from New York for Europe on June

14, the U.S. delegation was described as "America's athletic missionaries," charged with proving the growing prominence of the United States in the athletic arena to the rest of the world. "Never in my long life have I seen its equal," said former AAU president and founder James E. Sullivan, now the organization's secretary-treasurer and head of the American Olympic Committee of the American athletes.

The buzz of the 1912 American squad centered on native American Jim Thorpe, the renowned track star at Pennsylvania's Carlisle Indian School who dazzled the country with his athletic feats. Thorpe had recently competed in a pre-Olympic meet in New York City that drew crowds to see "an exhibition of jumping such as has not been seen in New York." In his only event at that meet, the high jump, Thorpe's winning jump of 6-feet, 5-inches bettered that of two athletes who would win medals for the event in Stockholm. But it was Thorpe's decision to compete in the two new Olympic events testing the all-around abilities of the track and field athletes—the decathlon of ten events, and pentathlon of five events—that so fascinated the country and the world.

The pentathlon, which began on the second day of the Games, was originally created by the Greeks to showcase "the complete man." The event was meant to "reconcile the irreconcilable: speed and resistance, dynamism and statism, strength and lightness, power and relaxation." The crowd anticipated a win by either a Swede or an Englishman. Thorpe, however, finished first in the running broad jump; placed a disappointing third in the javelin, an event he had taken up only two months before; dazzled the crowd with a first-place finish in the 200 meters; and easily won the discus. Seven contestants remained for the final event, the 1,500 meters. Avery Brundage, a heavy favorite to win, did not finish the race.

Pacing himself for the distance, Thorpe took the lead on the third lap and finished five seconds ahead of the second-place finisher to take the gold medal. In the three-day decathlon, which commenced several days after the pentathlon, Thorpe won the gold with a point total of 8,412.95 points out of a possible 10,000, a full 688 points ahead of silver medalist Hugo Wieslander of Sweden. The crowd roared its admiration at the medal ceremony, in which Thorpe received his second gold medal and challenge trophy presented by King Gustav V. Another trophy, reportedly made by Fabergé and given by Tsar Nicholas II of Russia, was also presented. A smiling King Gustav said to Thorpe, in English, "You, sir, are the most wonderful athlete in the world."

Former Notre Dame track standouts Forest Fletcher and George Philbrook were part of the American delegation; the 24-year-old Fletcher competing in the high jump and the long jump, and the 24-year-old Philbrook in the discus, shot put, and the decathlon. The 5-foot-11, 154-pound Fletcher from Lincoln County, Tennessee finished seventh in the standing high jump event and ninth in the standing long jump competition. Philbrook, a 6-2, 190-pound field event specialist from Sierra Valley, California finished fifth in the shot put, seventh in the discus and although at one point in second place to Thorpe in the decathlon, Philbrook failed to finish the grueling event.

In the fall of 1912, Knute Rockne had embraced the fervor over American politics that was part of campus activity at Notre Dame. He became treasurer of the Young Men's Woodrow Wilson Club and worked to fulfill the club's charter to "secure in all honorable means possible as many votes for Woody." The 1912 presidential election featured a collision between reformers, conservatives, and Teddy Roosevelt's new "Bull Moose" Party. Infighting within Roosevelt's Republican party left him unable to support President William Howard Taft, so Roosevelt took the more progressive plank of the Republican party, which called for women's suffrage, environmental conservation, child labor laws, economic reforms, and workers' compensation. He declared himself fit as a bull moose to run for president. The Democratic Party candidate was the rising new star, New Jersey Governor Woodrow Wilson. An intellectual who had served as president of Princeton University, Wilson held social and reformist ideas similar to Roosevelt. Eugene V. Debs occupied the fourth spot on the ballot, running for the third time as the Socialist Party candidate. Debs brought his magnetic eloquence to the campaign and drew larger crowds than ever.

Wilson would win the 1912 election with relative ease and set about creating his "New Freedom" administration. The most surprising outcome of the election was the showing of Debs. He more than doubled his vote total from four years earlier, gaining over 900,000 popular votes and six percent of the total. Observers believed his strong showing was due to neither major party addressing voters' longings for stronger measures to combat the growing power of big business. The political scene also felt the impact of the increasing presence of women in the workforce. The Rockne sisters were no different than many other women of their time who were branching out to take on new jobs. The feminization of school teaching advanced into secondary schools. More women became sales clerks and secretaries. Women college graduates already dominated the field of social work, and President Taft had appointed Julia Lathrop director of the newly established Federal Children's Bureau. Women's appearance and behavior was changing too. Magazines now showed women driving cars, and Isadora Duncan used her daring dancing to promote unencumbered approaches to art and life. The most conspicuous signs of change came with rising skirt lengths—which reached mid-calf—and short, bobbed hair, which was the rage by 1912. Smoking in public became acceptable, and some women, including Margaret Sanger, began advocating the use of birth control.

With changing roles it was only natural that there was an increase in the already existing cause for women's suffrage. The National Woman Suffrage Association petitioned Congress in 1906 for an amendment to the Constitution to abolish sex discrimination in voting. State legislatures in Washington, California, Arizona, Kansas, and Oregon added "equal suffrage" by 1912. In a 1910 article in the *Ladies Home Journal*, 50-year-old Jane Addams, reformer and founder of Hull House in Chicago, noted: "In closing, may I recapitulate that if woman would fulfill her traditional responsibility to her own children; if she would educate and protect from danger factory children who must find their recreation on the street; if she would bring the cultural forces to bear upon our materialistic civilization; and if she would do it all with the dignity and directness fitting one who carries on her immemorial duties, then she must bring herself to the use of the ballot—that latest implement for self-government. May we not fairly say that American women need this implement in order to preserve the home?"

Also gaining strength by 1912 was the long-standing battle against alcohol consumption in the United States. The roots of prohibition were deeply intertwined with the women's suffrage movement. By 1874 Frances Willard, a temperance reformer and women's suffragist, formed the Women's Christian Temperance Union. It perceived alcoholism as a cause and consequence of larger social problems, many of them directly impacting women. By 1895 it had morphed into the Anti-Saloon League. And by the early 20th century, the Anti-Saloon League cemented its relationship with some of America's Protestant denominations, mainly the Methodist Episcopal Church and the Southern Baptists. The churches used their pulpits to deliver political and moral messages that provided a grassroots network for distributing prohibition literature. Estimates of the number of churches supporting prohibition by the early 20th century were as high as 60,000.

Evangelist William "Billy" Sunday proved to be one of the most powerful prohibition voices of the era. Sunday, a former major league baseball outfielder, had a conversion experience in Chicago in 1888 when the strains of hymns from a nearby mission caught his ear. When he began attracting crowds larger than could be accommodated in the rural churches and town halls, Sunday began erecting tents from which he preached. It was estimated that Sunday preached to more than 300,000 during his evangelical career. Sunday viewed liquor as "God's worst enemy" and "hell's best friend." He once told a rally at the University of Michigan: "I will fight them till hell freezes over and then I'll buy a pair of skates and fight 'em on the ice."

The Notre Dame *Scholastic,* representing the views of young men on campus, took a definitive editorial stand on prohibition by 1912, warning against its legislation: "If prohibition as a movement to enforce temperance in the use of liquor, has been a failure, it seems that it has been such because it makes no effort to conciliate that very considerable portion of the population which believes in the use of intoxicants...If instead of putting so much energy into a hysterical and bombastic campaign to make the use of liquor illegal, these apostles of prohibition made a personal appeal to those who are addicted to alcohol, winning them over and not antagonizing them, the cause would be promoted more rapidly."

Change was in the air on college gridirons as well in the fall of 1912. New rules shortened the field to 100 yards; the offense now had four downs instead of three to gain 10 yards; and the value of a touchdown increased to six points. New powers were emerging. Minnesota, under Doc Williams, had won or shared the Western Conference title three years running. Each year the Gophers had scored decisive mid-season victories over Stagg's Chicago teams. This season, the showdown at Marshall Field was moved to the season finale November 23; the Chicago-Wisconsin game lost its key spot as the finale and was instead scheduled for early November.

In the East, Princeton had a new star—a smooth, skilled athlete named Hobart Amory Hare "Hobey" Baker. Born of an aristocratic Philadelphia family, he attended St. Paul's School, where he amazed onlookers with his moves on the hockey rink and led his squad, which was the equal of top collegiate teams on many occasions. Mirroring a certain Notre Dame footballer, his favorite recreation was said to be walking on his hands. Baker was the cornerstone of the Princeton football team; in a game dominated by kicking, he would attempt drop kicks from anywhere inside 45 yards. As safety, he might be called upon to field as many as 25 or 30 punts in a game.

To conclude the 1911 season, Baker successfully fielded an afternoon's worth of kicks with Yale's much larger ends bearing down on him. He helped Princeton to a 6-3 victory and the national championship, earning the admiration of all observers, one of whom wrote that he was "a man who could not have been spared," earning "a very high place in the admiration of the spectators." The Tigers anticipated the key battles of November, a visit to Harvard and the season-ender vs. archrival Yale. It was in the latter than Baker introduced his greatest contribution to football, his "most sensational variation on the conventional tactics for a safety man; no one who ever saw him use it would forget it. He would deliberately stand about five yards back of the place he calculated the ball would land; while the ball spiraled down the field and the end converged on him, he would stand like a matador, slowly flexing his legs up and down, and then take off on the dead run. He caught the ball at his stomach by wrapping both arms around it, forming a cradle with his elbows and hands, then either shot between the ends or cut outside." His punt return yardage would often exceed what Princeton gained from scrimmage.

The United States Military Academy at West Point also faced several monumental games, including home contests against Yale and Glenn

"Pop" Warner's mighty Carlisle Indian squad, along with the season-ending rivalry game at Philadelphia vs. Navy, winners of the two years' previous battles by 3-0 scores. Rutgers, Colgate, and Syracuse also figured to give the soldiers a battle. At Notre Dame, the schedule under second-year coach Marks looked much the same as the previous year. A trip to Pittsburgh was clearly the highlight, and the season-ending meeting with Marquette was to be played at White Sox Park. For the most part, though, Marks' focus was on developing a strong football team, more so than playing it in front of large crowds of paying spectators.

Prospects for the team appeared strong, with many returning stars, including captain Dorais at quarterback: "This little player has a head full of 'gray matter' and a foot with which he can punt from 45 to 50 yards. He is a good, conscientious worker, and we may be sure he will give the best that there is in him." At the ends, Rockne and Crowley were considered two of the best in the country. Crowley carried the responsibility of the vice captaincy. Rockne, it was said, "has improved to such an extent during the summer that there is no doubt of his performance at left end." In addition to varsity football and his role with the "Woody" society, Rockne found time for some coaching duties. "A large squad of Sorinites have donned the moleskins and are practicing diligently. The rigorous daily workouts are well calculated to put the team in perfect trim for the opening of the football season. Knute Rockne is coaching, and with the promising material at hand, should develop an excellent eleven."

Improvements at Cartier Field increased seating capacity, and all were eager to see what the blue and gold could do. The opener, against Marks' old squad from St. Viator, proved to be something of an embarrassment for the visitors. Albert "Red" Kelly—star halfback of the 1909 blue and gold, captain of Notre Dame's 1910 baseball team, and coach of the 1911 nine—returned to his former school after earning a law degree at Notre Dame, and brought his squad from Bourbonnais with high hopes, but little solid material. Three full elevens dressed for Notre Dame, though the starting left end didn't, as an old knee problem kept Rockne on the retired list. Most regulars also found their way to the bench. Rockne and his fellow starters watched their underlings rack up a 116-7 victory against a badly outmanned opponent. For the second straight year, a game against DePaul University was wiped off the slate, this time replaced by a visit from Adrian College from Michigan. Similar to the St. Viator game, it turned into little more than a scrimmage, with Notre Dame largely powered by its reserves romping, 74-7. It provided Rockne a punchline in future years. Adrian was such a thin squad that it had used up all its substitutes, and its coach asked whether Notre Dame would agree to Adrian sending men back into the game. Marks agreed, and returned to the sidelines. Some time later he saw a strange player on his bench.

"You're on the wrong bench," he said.

"I know it," replied the Adrian man. "I've been in that scrap four times already and they're not going to send me back if I can help it. I've had enough."

Later that afternoon, new track coach Frank Gormley conducted an interhall track meet at Cartier, open to all students. The call went out in hopes of drawing as many candidates for the spring varsity squad. The Stoeckley championship trophy "was won in a trot by Corby hall" with Rockne as the high point man. Showing few effects of the sore knee, Rockne won the 300-yard dash in 33 seconds and the shot-put at 39 feet, 10 inches, and finished second in the broad jump.

October 19 brought a distant visitor to campus. The football team from Morris Harvey College of Charleston, West Virginia made the trip to fill what had been an open date. It was considered the surprise of the season that Morris Harvey kept the score at 39-0 instead of the even greater margins of the previous two weeks. Eichenlaub sprinted 50 yards for the first Notre Dame touchdown, but after that, "only by fighting of the hardest kind were the additional tallies obtained." Morris Harvey made the 400-mile trek from Charleston, West Virginia to Notre Dame under the direction of its third-year head coach Andrew Kemper "Skeeter" Shelton, who was four months younger than Rockne. Born in Huntington, West Virginia, Shelton played quarterback at West Virginia University, but was most noted as a baseball infielder, setting a school record by belting three triples in a game against the University of Cincinnati. Shelton rode the minor league baseball circuit through Huntington, Wheeling, Youngstown, and Maysville, Kentucky, and coached football at Morris Harvey in the baseball off-season. The following Saturday, an overflow crowd watched Notre Dame claim the "championship of Indiana" with a 41-6 thrashing of Jesse Harper's Wabash Little Giants. The game bore little resemblance to the nail-biter the previous season at Crawfordsville. A top sports writer, W. Blaine Patton, described the scene this way:

> Bruised, bleeding, battered, and heartbroken, the scarlet wearers crept to the gymnasium to nurse their aching limbs in silence, while the joyous followers of the gold and blue prepared for a big bonfire and gave vent to their enthusiasm with a snake dance on Cartier Field. The familiar old, 'Yea, Wabash,' sounded so many times after victorious invasions, was conspicuous by its absence.

Although proud of his team's fight, Harper had to be impressed with the overall talent and drive of the home team. Then there was the atmosphere at Cartier Field, where not an empty seat was to be found in the bleachers, which now almost completely encircled the gridiron. The *Scholastic* observed, "For the first time in years, cheering has been placed on an organized footing….Mr. Joe Byrne deserves all possible credit for the way he maneuvered the yelling machine and drowned out the Wabashers. It was a real demonstration of what organization can do. Keep it up!" The *Scholastic* also praised football managers for reserving stands for alumni and others "appropriately separate" from the student rooters. Among the prominent alumni and others guests was the Hon. Charles W. Fairbanks, former vice president of the United States, who "was very enthusiastic over the form displayed by the Varsity." Visitors noted the dazzling brilliance of the Golden Dome, newly covered in gold leaf. "It is the supreme ornament of the university—a sight that gladdens and inspires."

Just as in 1911, there were now four lopsided wins in the books, with a trip to Pittsburgh looming. Notre Dame was determined to secure victory at Forbes Field this time. They didn't count on the condition that greeted them: bone-chilling cold, biting wind, and snow. In these conditions, every yard was a battle; numerous fumbles and penalties kept both sides bottled up all day. Even when Rockne was able to break free for a gain of 33 yards on a perfect pass from Dorais in the third quarter, penalties derailed the drive and forced another punt. In the end, it was a 25-yard drop kick by Dorais that gave Notre Dame a hard-fought, 3-0 victory. Several players made home visits after the Pittsburgh game, which left little time for sufficient practice and preparation in the short week before the team departed to play at St. Louis University the following Saturday. But any fears about Notre Dame's preparedness were unfounded. They came out against the Billikens, scored three touchdowns in the first quarter, and rolled to a 47-7 triumph. Fullback Eichenlaub was nearly unstoppable, ripping through the St. Louis defense for gains of 20 yards or more several times. Pliska went over for three scores, and Berger made the play of the game when he skirted the end, stiff-armed one defender, flattened another, and raced 85 yards for a score. Rockne, as was becoming customary, played a superlative game on defense.

A fluke in the schedule gave the varsity the next two Saturdays off. A November 16 game against Transylvania had been canceled; the next Saturday was the open date before the Thanksgiving game with Marquette. The game was originally set for Milwaukee but moved to Chicago when Charles Comiskey donated the use of his ballpark for the contest. Several Chicago Notre Dame alumni, including Joseph Farrell, Bill Draper, and Stewart Graham, were instrumental in promoting the game. The *Scholastic* praised Farrell for making "personal business sacrifices in order to quicken interest in the game."

Students who made the trip to Chicago were under the requirements spelled out in the weeks before the game: classes resumed Friday afternoon, and all were expected to be in attendance. Saturday morning classes would go on as usual. Fans entering Comiskey Park expecting to see anything resembling the scoreless tie of 1911 were shocked at what transpired before their eyes. Referee Walter Eckersall blew the whistle to start the game at 2:15 p.m. and within minutes, it was clear this was Notre Dame's day. Up and down the field raced the team's backs, and Marquette tacklers were left grasping at air. Eichenlaub alone accounted for four touchdowns. Pliska, Gushurst, Berger, Finnegan—each found the end zone in a game that finished 69-0.

Afterward, Coach Marks' charges looked at one another, hardly believing what they had accomplished. A team that had played Notre Dame to ties each of the last three years, one at 5-5 and the other two scoreless, had been thoroughly dominated on this day. It brought the final tally on the 1912 season to seven wins and no losses. Notre Dame had outscored the opposition, 389-27. And none of the points allowed had come with a game on the line; they were all consolation scores in games long since decided. It was that defensive prowess in which Knute Rockne took the most pride. Yes, he appreciated the well-designed and perfectly executed offensive play. But it was the challenge of continually shutting down the best the opponent had to offer that became a source of great focus in his play.

"With the exception of the championship year of 1909," the *Scholastic* exclaimed, "Notre Dame never has had reason to feel so proud over the gridiron efforts of her sons as during the past season…Recognition, long withheld, has been granted in a manner that stamps Notre Dame as one of the football leaders of the West. A foundation has been established in public opinion upon which future teams may build high and strong, secure in the knowledge that 1912 affords the basis for the highest efforts." The entire campus looked ahead optimistically, as the core group of players would remain intact, setting the stage to repeat the success of 1912. The *Scholastic*, however, made a crucial error in its review of Rockne's season, misidentifying him as a graduating player: "It is not easy to separate 'Rock' from Crowley, as this pair, we believe, made the best set of ends in the country. Both have been on the all-State teams two years running, and, what is hardest to say, both are seniors. Rockne is an ideal end for the style of play used this fall, and although handicapped by a sprained knee, he played in all the games and won enviable honors. His genial disposition and earnestness as a student have won him a legion of friends who will miss him next year."

Tuesday, December 10 was a day of great ceremony and celebration on the Notre Dame campus, as well as an important day in the life of 24-year-old junior Knute Rockne. President's Day meant no classes, and instead a gala day of festivities honoring the university president and, by extension, the very spirit and history of Notre Dame—"the best loved of our scholastic feast days (filling) Faculty and students with a spirit of glad rejoicing." A solemn high Mass, offered in thanksgiving for the blessings upon the university, its officers, and its noble work, opened the celebration. The faculty processed into the mass in academic robes, the upcoming graduating class in cap and gown, and undergraduates in military uniforms. After Mass, student speakers presented greetings to President Cavanaugh and assembled guests. At 9:30 the military companies fell into ranks in the gymnasium, forming a square with the university band and company buglers in its center. Father Cavanaugh and Captain Stogsdall inspected the troops, while students and visitors looks on from the gallery. Among the many guests on campus were Bishop Allerding of Fort Wayne; Hon. William P. O'Neil, Lieutenant Governor-elect; Judge Timothy Howard; J. M. Studebaker; J. D. Oliver; C.H. Fassett, editor of the *South Bend Tribune*; Mayor Charles Goetz of South Bend; and other clergy, prominent alumni, and local officials.

A 10:30 band concert in the rotunda of the Main Building provided a festive spirit prior to the noon banquet "of the Thanksgiving Day or Christmas type" served in the dining room. After the banquet the celebration moved to Washington Hall, where John T. Burns, president of the senior class, came forth from the wings in classic cap and gown to represent the students with a message of appreciation, respect, and affection for President Cavanaugh. "Rev. President...had you been content merely to follow the policies of the school as you found it, yours would have been a great work. But ever mindful of the accomplishments of those that had gone before you, you labored on and on, ever looking to the past, always building for the future, until under your guidance, Notre Dame has become the consummation of Sorin's ideal." Father Cavanaugh, as might be expected in such a setting, deflected praise from himself to his fellow priests and lay faculty. He added: "The spirit of union between faculty and students is a joy in the present and a happy augury for the future." President Cavanaugh also made a point of praising the football team for carrying heavy course loads while still earning averages generally from 85 to 90 percent. "He surprised us somewhat and delighted us a great deal more," said the *Scholastic*.

At 2 p.m., an overflow audience in Washington Hall saw the climatic closure to President's Day: the annual dramatic performance. Under the direction of drama professor Charlemagne Koehler, the play *David Garrick* presented a dramatic interpretation of Edmund Burke, James Boswell, and Dr. Samuel Johnson. In a long-standing tradition, Notre Dame students performed all roles, meaning that some men were asked to portray women. So it was that Knute Rockne had the role of Mrs. Smith. Said the *Scholastic*'s reviewer: "Mr. Rockne gave a sufficiently large presentation of Mrs. Smith; moreover, he did what many in a like position must surely have failed to do—held himself in wholesome restraint." That Rockne could pull off the role indicated his confidence and ease in relating with others in any number of settings. As he did in playing his beloved flute for the band and orchestra, he eagerly accepted an opportunity to participate in the play and broaden his horizon of experiences. He was doing what came naturally—being open to challenging himself in a variety of roles. The performance of *David Garrick* was delightfully successful, with a sustained standing ovation—and it wasn't the best reception Rockne received that day.

That evening, at the annual football post-season banquet at the Oliver Hotel, 14 men who just received their Notre Dame monograms, plus another five who were given honorable mention elected Rockne their captain for the 1913 season. Eichenlaub received the next largest number of votes, to become assistant captain. Any awkwardness between Rockne and his good friend Dorais, the 1912 captain, was well hidden. The vote wasn't so much a sign of any dissatisfaction with Dorais; the team gladly followed the lead of their diminutive field general and would continue to do so. Rather, it was a broadening of the leadership to include the left end who put his entire self into his play on the field. Coupled with a few mentions by selectors of All-American teams, it confirmed Rockne's upward trajectory on the football field.

In looking back on the just-completed season, Walter Eckersall, the former University of Chicago quarterback, now a referee and *Chicago Tribune* sports writer, stated that the Notre Dame team was the only one capable of disputing Wisconsin's 1912 title as champions of the West. Such high praise always brought great satisfaction on the campus in the spring of 1913. At Notre Dame, as at any of a number of schools fighting for football glory, it was important for the achievements to be properly recognized. It was even more crucial for a school that found itself shut out of playing the teams of the Western Conference. Perhaps it was due to accusations of eligibility irregularities noted by other conference schools. But there was no doubt a strain of anti-Catholicism that ran through the conference's decision-making. Not only would teams refuse to play Notre Dame, but also the conference remained steadfast in its rejection to admit Our Lady's University as a member. Notre Dame's 1908 application for entrance to the Western Conference was denied, and university vice president Father Thomas Crumley, chairman of the athletic board, wrote the battle had been "fought on theological rather than athletic grounds." By the end of 1913 the Notre Dame administration once again applied for membership into the Western Conference, but at its annual meeting Chicago and Minnesota led the charge to keep Notre Dame out. Many sportswriters as well as the student publication the *Dome* suggested the underlying reason:

> It is easy to understand why Northwestern and Indiana—teams that would end last in our interhall race—objected, but why Chicago and Minnesota, with the pretension to Western Championships demurred makes no sense...But the professional prejudices of the conference's 'Academic Men' as well as the growing anti-Catholicism of Midwestern state legislatures were more important factors. The N.D. administrators involved in this and previous applications to the conference, Father's Crumley and Walsh, attributed to their school's 'lack of success'...first of all to religious prejudice.

That put an added strain on the scheduling of quality opponents, which in turn caused a financial handicap that was difficult to overcome. For all the success under Jack Marks in 1911 and 1912, the business side of things looked bleak. Football operated at a net loss of $2,300 and $500 in the two seasons, and Father Cavanaugh, stressed with his own fundraising difficulties to expand the university's buildings and staff, couldn't understand why. If the team was winning games decisively and gaining headlines across a larger geographical area, why could it not also have some financial success? It was just such a conversation Cavanaugh had with a Notre Dame alumnus on a visit to Crawfordsville in late 1912 that led to a major change in the program. The alum sang the praises of Wabash coach Jesse Harper, noting that Harper believed in football paying for itself. That's what Cavanaugh wanted to hear. He knew that from a strictly football standpoint, Harper had proven himself a quality coach— his near-victory over Notre Dame in 1911 was a good reminder of that. In December 1912, seemingly days after high tributes to Jack Marks on a job well-done, Cavanaugh hired Jesse Harper to become Notre Dame's first truly full-time coach and athletic director. He would run the entire athletic operation and coach football, basketball, baseball, and track for an annual salary of $2,500.

Twenty-nine year old Harper, the protégé of Stagg who was Eckersall's backup quarterback for the huge Chicago-Michigan game on Thanksgiving Day 1905 was now fully in charge of Notre Dame athletics. Gone would be the days of allowing a student manager to be in charge of scheduling that often resulted in open dates and cancellations at the last minutes. Harper immediately began work on his 1913 schedule, writing a number of colleges across the country as to their availability. On December 18, 1912, he wrote the U.S. Military Academy at West Point. His timing could not have been better. Army had just received word that Yale was planning to cancel their long-standing series. The teams had played 20 straight seasons from 1893 to 1912, with Yale usually emerging as the winner. But Army defeated Yale in 1910 and 1911, and more opponents were looking askance at Army's eligibility practices; college football players could play for years at their original college, but once they received an appointment to West Point, the eligibility clock started again. That's how Elmer Oliphant, Purdue's All-American back, enjoyed a second career at Army from 1911 through 1913.

It was actually baseball that began the Notre Dame-Army athletic tradition. Notre Dame was well established as a baseball power, having sent dozens of its diamond stars on to the major league. In recent years, the Notre Dame baseball team included an Eastern swing on its schedule, a 10-game trip in 1912. The 1913 team made an eastern tour that included games at Catholic University in Washington, D.C., Navy, Pennsylvania, and a 3-0 defeat at West Point on May 24. And Army wasn't the only recipient of Harper's letters to answer the call. His efforts resulted in a schedule that featured not only Army, but also a visit from highly respected South Dakota; and trips to Penn State and a Thanksgiving battle with the University of Texas at Austin. Indeed, 1913 figured to be a memorable season for Notre Dame.

# 12

# No Looking Back

It was known as "the queen of American watering places." Cedar Point, a seven-mile spit of sand and rock jutting into Lake Erie near Sandusky, Ohio, went by many superlatives, including "America's most beautiful summer pleasure health resort" and "the finest bathing beach in the world." The centerpiece of the resort, its Grand Pavilion, opened in 1888 and hosted numerous activities, including dances and other social events in its huge upper level dance hall, called the "largest dancing pavilion on the Great Lakes." In the early 1900s the resort's owners installed a few rides and in 1902 constructed an early version of the roller coaster along the beach. Built by Fred Ingersoll, the famous Pittsburgh ride and park designer, The Racer featured 11 cars that traveled a figure-eight and rose to a height of 46 feet, providing mild thrills for just a nickel. Nearby, a pony track featured animals from Texas and the West Indies. And moving pictures were shown starting in 1900 on the Kinodrome and later in the nickelodeon. Hotels and cottages provided lodging for the growing number of guests visiting during the resort season, which lasted less than 100 days. Steamers from Cleveland, Detroit, Toledo, and other Great Lakes cities would deposit resort-goers by the hundreds.

Around the turn of the 20th century Cedar Point developed a tradition of hiring college students, including several from Notre Dame, for summer work. They worked as lifeguards, waiters, dishwashers, bathhouse attendants, and a host of other positions. Harry "Red" Miller, star of the 1909 Notre Dame football team, was a frequent Cedar Point worker and brought classmates and teammates from as far away as Oregon to spend their summers working at the resort. Sam "Rosey" Dolan, Glen Smith, and Ralph Dimmick all joined Miller there during their time at Notre Dame. Later, each of Miller's four football-playing brothers called Cedar Point home in between academic years at Notre Dame.

So when Knute Rockne and Gus Dorais decided to head to Cedar Point for the summer of 1913, they were simply joining a well-established tradition. They worked their way through the summer as restaurant checkers, night-watchmen, telephone operators, night clerks, lifeguards— whatever was available that might add up to a decent payday. "But we played our way on the beach with a football, practicing forward passing. There was nothing much else for two young fellows without much pocket-money to do," Rockne recalled. Over time, the daily practice brought perfected patterns and long passes thrown on an arc, landing in the receiver's outstretched arms. Rockne would run along the beach, and Dorais would throw, from all angles. "People who didn't know we were two college seniors making painstaking preparations for our final football season probably thought we were crazy," said Rockne.

Seven years earlier, in 1906, football rules were changed to allow the forward pass, and that season St. Louis University became the first team to build its offense around it. New St. Louis coach Eddie Cochems, a former star halfback at the University of Wisconsin who scored four touchdowns when the Badgers routed Notre Dame, 54-0, in 1900, was reunited with Bradbury Robinson, a quarterback transfer from Wisconsin the previous year. Robinson then began learning how to throw a spiral pass. To prepare for the first season under the new rules, Cochems convinced the university to allow him to take his team to a Jesuit sanctuary at Lake Beulah in southern Wisconsin to study and develop the forward pass. It was on the shores of a bucolic lake that the first forward pass system ever devised was born.

In the season opener on September 5, 1906, against Carroll College at Waukesha, Wisconsin, Robinson threw the first legal pass, which fell incomplete, giving the ball to Carroll under the rules at the time. Later, Robinson lofted the rugby-style ball to teammate Jack Schneider for a 20-yard touchdown, helping St. Louis to a 22-0 victory. St. Louis completed the 1906 season undefeated at 11–0 and led the nation in scoring, defeating its opponents by a combined 407-11. Included was a 31-0 whipping of Iowa in which St. Louis completed eight of 10 passes, four for touchdowns. In the ensuing years, many other teams incorporated passing into their attack, including giants like Stagg and Warner. Still, it was largely seen as a desperation move to be used when trailing in the game. And it took further rules changes in 1912 to eliminate some of the risk. Nobody, however, prepared to use the weapon in the manner of Dorais and Rockne.

At Cedar Point, the pair did more than fling footballs in their spare time. Cedar Point, similar to so many summer places, needed waitresses as well as waiters, and in their off hours, groups of young men and women could be seen in their bathing suits, cooling off in the refreshing waters of Lake Erie. One waitress, 21-year-old Bonnie Skiles of Kenton, Ohio, caught Rockne's eye. Demure, dark-haired, and like Rockne, rather shy, she remained his romantic interest during and after that summer. In Chicago or South Bend, John Devine, the half-miler, and his future wife Kitty Leeper would occasionally double-date with Rockne. Kitty recalled that Rockne "was so bashful and self-conscious that he would scarcely say a word all evening and hence rarely had a repeat date with the same girl." Bonnie was different, though, and Knute felt he had found someone special.

As a senior, as captain of the football team, and as an active participant in multiple activities, Knute Rockne was enjoying life on campus. His grades continued to show his ability to excel in a wide range of subjects. Reverend Nieuwland, Rockne's chemistry professor, described Rockne as the most remarkable student he ever knew. Rockne often audited classes other than his own to deepen his knowledge. Rockne had an uncanny knack for concentration, and he was an efficient multi-tasker. He could be in a dorm room or rec room with a handful of other fellows, talking football or politics, and follow the discussion in detail, even dropping in with a cogent remark, all the while studying his textbook subject without missing a beat. When studying by himself, his routine was to place a book on his desk and, after reading a while, pace back and forth rolling a pencil between the palms of his hands, memorizing what he had just read.

But student life was not all academics. He participated in the orchestra, being remembered more as an industrious performer rather than a virtuoso on the flute. He campaigned hard on campus for the dedication page of the 1914 *Dome*, the student yearbook, to go to his chief chemistry professor, Father Nieuwland. And his flair for the theatrical was never more on display than when he helped to form the Monogram Club Absurdities. This Follies-like annual stage farce of singing and dancing student-athletes would "bring the house down" as lumbering linemen would take to the stage in choreographed fashion. He gained a considerable reputation for his dramatic talents, playing a variety of roles in everything from impromptu vaudeville acts at a hall's smoker to campus-wide performances at Washington Hall. In several shows, Rockne displayed his versatility by portraying females, to wide acclaim from audiences. There were other adventures for fun, and sometimes profit.

A common campus activity was skiving—coming and going from one's hall outside of accepted curfew hours, by means of climbing in and out of non-official entrances. For nearly two years, Rockne and Dorais shared a room in Corby Hall that had a window near ground level; they rigged the screen so that it appeared closed during the day, but would easily swing open at night. There, they set up a "toll" system, collecting cash from late-comers seeking to avoid detection by the authorities. Rockne was also known to pick up a few dollars by traveling some distance from campus, to towns like Gary, Indiana, and appear in boxing matches, usually under the pseudonym Kid Williams. His "corner man" and "business manager" was fellow student Joe Gargan.

Above all, though, Rockne was a competitor. If there was a competition, over just about anything, he wanted in. Dozens of students—some straining their necks for a better view, others perched in trees—form a circle around two students fighting it out for the campus marbles championship, and in the center is one of the combatants: Knute Rockne. The dirt-floored gymnasium, in a quiet moment absent basketball or track, is being used for a tennis match, and there taking on an Asian student is

Rockne, fighting to win that tennis match as hard as he had fought in any football game.

Football workouts in late September confirmed what Coach Harper, Captain Rockne, and others had suspected—Notre Dame was ready for a big year. With the wily veteran Dorais ready to quarterback the squad for the fourth year, Eichenlaub anxious to mow down the opposition, Pliska and Berger primed to break loose from their halfback spot, the team was primed for success. The season began on the overcast afternoon of Saturday, October 4, as Rockne led his squad from the Fieldhouse out onto Cartier Field for the opener against Ohio Northern. Using a variety of passes, end runs, and line plunging, the home team rolled to an 87-0 victory; Eichenlaub crossed the goal line four times and Pliska three. The only drawback to the game, the *Scholastic* reported, was an injury to Rockne. About the middle of the second quarter, Rockne was tackled hard around the waist and suffered a damaged rib; however, he managed to stay in the game until the end of the half.

South Dakota, next up on the schedule, promised to provide a much stiffer test. In 1912, the Dakotans had defeated Minnesota, 10-0, and held Michigan to a 7-6 score. This year, they had opened the season with a 14-0 loss at Minnesota, with both scores coming on fumble recoveries. Upon their arrival in South Bend, the visitors were feted with a rally that "proved the greatest demonstration of pep" in years. "Nig" Kane called his rooters together in the big gym Friday evening and went through the cheers with them, followed by remarks from Coach Harper. Rockne represented his team at the coin toss before the kickoff, but his injury kept him out of the game, and South Dakota took immediate advantage. Within three minutes of the kickoff, the Coyotes tore through Notre Dame's line at will, and quarterback Gene Vidal led a drive downfield for a 7-0 lead. The rest of the afternoon belonged to the blue and gold, however; Dorais guided the team with a master hand and kicked two field goals, while Eichenlaub had several long gains. Notre Dame prevailed, 20-7, in a game that was as difficult as expected.

Next up was a meeting with Alma College of Michigan, where Coach Harper had begun his coaching career. In the final tuneup before the trip to West Point, the varsity whipped the visitors, 62-0. Noted the *Scholastic*: "One of the greatest pleasures of the game was the sight of Capt. Rockne at his old end position. Although his rib is still giving him some trouble, he did not give evidence of the fact in Saturday's playing, for he made flying tackles, carried the ball on line plunges, and grabbed forward passes in mid-air like he has always done when in the best of form."

In practice the following Wednesday, the final workout before heading east, the Notre Dame players began showing the fighting spirit Harper sought. Rockne was "working at top-notch speed in his old left end position, getting interference with the same ease that has made him such a factor on the defensive work of the team." Coach Harper said, "We are going for a victory, but of course I'm not going to make any forecast of the result. Chances seem about even, but with chances even, Notre Dame always wins. I consider this the hardest game on our schedule, and the men are going to fight a battle of their lives." In their final workout before leaving, the varsity took on the freshmen team posing as Army, and the frosh "were powerless before the confusing formations and quick attacks of the Varsity."

Shortly after noon on Thursday, October 30, 19 players boarded the train in downtown South Bend headed for West Point. The traveling roster included ends Rockne, Gushurst, Kelleher, and Nowers; tackles Jones, Lathrop, and Cook; guards Fitzgerald, Keefe, and King; centers Feeney and Voelkers; halfbacks Pliska, Berger, and Larkin; fullbacks Eichenlaub and Duggan; and quarterbacks Dorais and Finegan. They didn't need to be told this game would be the supreme test of their playing careers. They all knew the big names they would face: Army's strong line included two All-Americans—McEwen at center and Merrilot at end. Quarterback Vernon Pritchard was also outstanding. What they didn't know was whether the game mattered as much to Army as it did to Notre Dame. The Army already had victories over Rutgers, Colgate, Stevens Tech, and Tufts.

Nearly the entire Notre Dame student body saw the team off to the day coach that carried the squad to Buffalo—a dreary, all-day trip. But at the brief layover, someone snapped a photo of the team and their handful of fans, including George Hull and Mike Calnon, proprietors of "Hullie and Mike's," the well-known billiard hall in downtown South Bend. The looks on the players' faces gave an appearance of excitement and adventure; for some, it was the longest train trip they had experienced. From Buffalo it was on to West Point. The men enjoyed the luxury of sleeping-car accommodation—regulars in lowers, substitutes in uppers. "There was no pampering," Rockne remembered. "We wanted none of it. We went out to play the Army like crusaders, believing that we represented not only our own school, but the whole, aspiring Middle West." West Point treated their first-time visitors with great hospitality. They were housed in Cullum Hall and given the freedom of the Officers Club. The Notre Dame men were impressed by the size of the academy's grounds and buildings. But there was one locale they especially wanted to see: the football field. There, they found an emerald paradise, smooth and well-marked, appealing to the eye. They quickly understood why Army rarely played anywhere else, save for the annual meeting with Navy on a neutral field. In a brief workout Friday afternoon, Harper's lads limbered up their legs by punting and their arms with long forward passes.

Though Army would have the familiarity and backing of its home supporters, Notre Dame was not without its own rooters. The Notre Dame Club of New York City chartered a train to West Point to lead Notre Dame yells and encourage the team. A respectable crowd of some 10,000 on a cold, raw November day gathered around the soldiers' field. The corps of cadets and most other spectators seemed ready to see the home team flex its muscles. And for the first few minutes, that's exactly what they did. Army outweighed the Notre Dame line by 10 or more pounds per man. Rockne noted that they "pushed us all over the place before we overcame the tingling realization that we were actually playing the Army. I recall Merrilot shouting: 'Let's lick these Hoosiers!'" Finally, after a series of plays that pounded the visitors' line, Notre Dame held. Dorais, in a huddle, said: "Let's open up." The Army guards and tackles, expecting line plunges, massed near the line of scrimmage. Instead, Dorais stepped neatly back and flipped the ball to an uncovered end or halfback. Rockne recalled the scene:

> Our attack had been well rehearsed. After one fierce scrimmage I emerged limping as if hurt. On the next three plays, Dorais threw three successful passes in a row to Pliska, our right halfback, for short gains. On each of those plays I limped down the field acting as if the thing farthest from my mind was to receive a forward pass. After the third play the Army halfback covering me figured I wasn't worth watching. Even as a decoy he figured

I was harmless. Finally, Dorais called my number, meaning that he was to throw a long forward pass to me as I ran down the field and out toward the sidelines. I started limping down the field and the Army halfback covering me almost yawned in my face, he was so bored. Suddenly, I put on full speed and left him standing there flat-footed. I raced across the Army goal line as Dorais whipped the ball and the grandstands roared at the completion of a forty-yard pass. Everybody seemed astonished. There had been no hurdling, no tackling, no plunging, no crushing of fiber and sinew. Just a long-distance touchdown by rapid transit. At the moment when I touched the ball, life for me was complete.

But the game was far from over. Army drove through the Notre Dame defense for two touchdowns in the next several minutes, taking a 13-7 lead. It was time for an answer. As *The New York Times* would recount: "Dorais hurled the ball far and straight for 25 yards and Rockne, on the dead run, grabbed the ball out of the air and was downed at midfield." Dorais then hit Pliska with a 35-yard gain and Army partisans "burst forth in a sincere cheer for the marvelous little quarterback." A moment later, Pliska ran for a score, putting Notre Dame ahead, 14-13, at the half. The game was hard-fought from beginning to end. In particular, Notre Dame's Freeman Fitzgerald and Army's great center John McEwan waged a heated battle. Between plays, the two exchanged pointed words, and as Notre Dame continued to dominate, Fitz lined up closer to McEwen on each play. Before one snap, he punched McEwan on the jaw, instantly yelling, "Hey, referee." Just at the moment the referee turned to look, McEwan smacked Fitzgerald in the nose, and was immediately ejected. Rockne's version of what happened next: "As captain of our team I had to stop and explain that both boys had been too boisterous and so the referee let them both stay in the game. From then on their decorum was more proper."

In the second half, Notre Dame had Army thoroughly confused. If the Cadets laid back in wait for the pass, Dorais would send Eichenlaub or another back pounding through the line for a nice gain. When they massed to stop the line rushes, Dorais instantly changed tactics, firing off a barrage of passes that kept the ball moving down the field. Two touchdowns by rushes, and another pass to Pliska, accounted for the final margin: 35-13. The small band of Notre Dame rooters cheered mightily as their warriors trotted off the field in victory. In addition to Hullie and Mike, others included young alumni such as Joe Byrne, last year's cheer leader; Pritchard, late of the track squad; and Dan McNichol, George Lynch, "Red" McConnell, and "Skeets" Walsh. They had just witnessed the seemingly impossible: Notre Dame had completed 14 passes of 17 attempts for 243 yards through the air—numbers impossible to fathom. What most amazed onlookers was the length of Dorais' passes. Many of the spirals traveled 35 to 40 yards in the air, into Rockne's or another receiver's arms.

Back in the South Bend, students and fans had gathered outside the *News-Times* offices awaiting returns. Details were spotty, with the 14-13 halftime lead posted for the longest time before the fourth-quarter scores were added. When it was final, the *South Bend Tribune* reported:

> Pandemonium broke loose among the students. With wild shrieks of delight they turned into Main Street and in a few moments 300 had gathered to celebrate the overwhelming victory. A snake dance was quickly formed and the men invaded Michigan Street winding from curb to curb and yelling like demons. At frequent intervals, Cheer Leader Nig Kane called a half and the varsity yells were given with a view to proclaiming the splendid achievement of the Notre Dame football machine. After the demonstration on Michigan Street, the crowd returned to the Oliver hotel, where, after cheering individual members of the team, the students dispersed.

Sunday's major newspapers reflected the magnitude of the victory, as many predicted the game would change how football would be played. "The Army folks from Gen. Leonard Wood down to the youngest substitute on the scrubs were shocked at the way the Army team was put to rout," noted the *New York Times*. "It took a so-called smaller college to come east and display an attack, versatile and dazzling, that may revolutionize the style of offensive play throughout this section of the country," predicted the *New York Evening Telegram*. The *New York Evening Sun* noted that the Notre Dame lads showed that "they could run circles around the fleet soldiers and that in the giving and receiving of forward passes, the

Army still has much to learn." And "only the whistle saved the Army team from a bigger defeat," noted the *New York World*. "It is the greatest exponent of new football in the country," exclaimed the *Chicago Evening Journal*. "Coach Harper undoubtedly has put together the best eleven which ever wore the Blue and Gold," assessed the *Chicago Daily News*. "The team is almost perfect in every detail of technical play, and in addition possessed two stars of the first magnitude in Eichenlaub and Dorais." Wrote Walter Eckersall in the *Chicago Tribune*:

> The Catholic team traveled to the Army stronghold and bewildered, cuffed and kicked the Army into submission, 35 to 13, a score that is not only decisive, but stamps the Notre Dame men as a team of unusual strength…In the open style of attack, Notre Dame's superiority was shown…It was a great triumph for Western football. Many critics have been condemning the forward pass as a happy-go-lucky play at best, one that will fail far oftener that it will succeed…Well, along comes Notre Dame to open the eyes of football lovers here….Nothing like that was ever seen in an Eastern game.

Rockne himself later observed: "Looking back over that match and its surprising revelation to Army players versed and skilled in the old-style game, it's no wonder that they could not solve the forward-pass problem in a single hour." Notre Dame's toughness and defense also gained admirers. "Notre Dame showed that when it had made up its mind to prevent further scoring the decision was irrevocable," stated the *New York Evening Sun*. "The Western linemen played hard and charged fast. Their tackling was unerring and deadly and they laid their men out all over the field." The *Scholastic* gleefully printed many of the reviews from the major papers and added its own take: "It is, we think, a great triumph of the new game over the old style of play; but it is rather a triumph of Notre Dame's style of the progressive, wide-open game over the rest of the country's conservative attack than a victory of the West over the East." Such an aerial attack "is superior for ground-gaining purposes; it is less dangerous to the players; and it makes a prettier game to view from the sidelines…It looks like we're a school for better football, and it is a pleasure to be recognized as such."

The Notre Dame party left West Point immediately after the game and reached Buffalo on Sunday morning. The players were given some time for rest and a visit to Niagara Falls. The trip continued, reaching a triumphant return to South Bend on Monday, November 3. "At South Bend, the whole town turned out," Rockne recalled. "Brass bands, red fire, speeches; as if we had repulsed and conquered an attack upon the West by the East." Dorais said that Captain Rockne was called upon to make a speech on behalf of the team, but his nervousness rendered it mostly inaudible. "The players themselves," said sports writer and Notre Dame alum Arch Ward, "had the most enjoyable trip of their lives."

But there was precious little time to savor the triumph, with a Friday afternoon game at Penn State looming. Monday afternoon brought a two-hour practice in which sore spots from the great win were worked out. The *South Bend Tribune* wrote: "Confirmed in his conviction of the worth of the forward pass by the demonstration in the east last week, Harper is coaching the men steadily at this play. It was the perfect handling of the ball over the heads of the husky Cadets that won the last game and the men are getting ready to pull a few new stunts along this line in Friday's contest." Harper took 20 players with him to Penn State, departing at 4:30 Wednesday afternoon. They arrived in State College on Thursday afternoon and had a brief drill on the home team's field. Dorais liked to practice drop kicks, and made a series of 30-yard kicks "almost at will." The team went through a short forward pass exercise, which caused Penn State fans to stir. An unusually large, animated crowd descended on State College for the battle, which would kick off Homecoming weekend festivities. Penn State Coach Bill Hollenback exhorted his troops by shouting, "Tear 'em to pieces and show the east and west that we have got a team!"

Much of the game featured strong running by both squads. In the second quarter, Dorais broke loose and scampered 40 yards for a touchdown, and Eichenlaub did likewise in the third. They were the first scores made against Penn State on its home field in five years. The home team closed to within 14-7, but that remained the final score, and Notre Dame's record climbed to 5-0. The team returned home to another joyous celebration—and the news that Wabash had asked to cancel the next week's game "because their team would not be a match for the Catholics." Harper instead focused on the possibility of a match with Nebraska. But with a long trip to Texas already on the slate, and the players' academic obligations always a concern, the Nebraska game would have to wait.

With the open date, there was time to recover from the whirlwind of the back-to-back eastern trips. Rockne reflected on how swiftly the season was flying by, and how soon his college football playing days would be over. The homesickness of freshman year seemed as though it was a lifetime ago. He greatly enjoyed the camaraderie of practice, the give-and-take and needling among good friends. "Dory." "Ike." "Heinie." There was a freshman, too, who impressed Rockne. Charlie Bachman, a guard from Chicago, seemed to have the right attitude, absorbing all he could of the game swirling around him. Harper gave his squad five days vacation while he made visits to Indiana University and met with Coach Stagg at Chicago. He also picked up a few fine points from other coaches, and upon his return, the *South Bend Tribune* wrote: "That Harper is going to put Notre Dame athletics on a higher plane seems certain, and though nothing definite has been arranged, it is probably that the gold and blue will be matched against opponents of the first class in the near future."

For now, it was a two-game Thanksgiving week trip to close out the season and Rockne's career. The squad left South Bend early on the morning of Friday, Nov. 21, to arrive in St. Louis on Saturday for a meeting with the Christian Brothers College, coached by Luke Kelly, star and captain of the 1911 blue and gold. With a heavy rain beating down on the players continuously, Notre Dame found itself scoreless deep into the second quarter. But Dorais came through with a 40-yard punt return for one score, Eichenlaub smashed through for another, and Dorais completed a long run for a third. Notre Dame won, 20-7. The team boarded the train with Austin, Texas its next destination. There, the Notre Dame squad had a friendly base of operations. St. Edward's College, a school also run by the Congregation of the Holy Cross, opened its campus and practice field to its northern brothers. For three days, Harper's men could recuperate from the battle of St. Louis and prepare to face a team, the Texas Longhorns, that claimed superiority in the southwest, having defeated Oklahoma and the Kansas Aggies in their previous two games. Overall, Coach Dave Allerdice's team was 7-0 on the season, and supremely confident.

The novelty of a strong northern eleven descending on Austin, and the unblemished records of the two teams, created tremendous interest in the game, and a large throng crowded Clarke Field on a warm, though sometimes rainy Thanksgiving Day. Notre Dame traveled with its own water, but at times the heat seemed like it would overwhelm them. On an early possession, Dorais faked a pass and ran 15 yards for a score. His kicking was also a factor, as he booted three field goals and two kicks after touchdown, for a total of 17 points. Notre Dame was never seriously challenged, throttling the Longhorns, 29-7. Rockne would tell of his final game as Notre Dame's captain:

> A giant hunchback tackle had been treating me rough when he was sent in as a sub toward the end of the first half. He left me with a limp so that in the rest between halves, I dreaded returning, getting myself set mentally, for thirty minutes of hell. I've played against many strong linemen; but never against one as strong. This man was a murderer. In that—to us—terrific heat, he smashed into me like a ton of animated ice. I was glad when the half ended.
>
> In the second half, a cool northerner blew in, and with the temperature comfortably reduced, everything was rosy. We scored two touchdowns and the game seemed in the bag. But the Texas coach returned the hunchback to the line, and the hunchback returned to me. He knocked my poor, sweating, ill-treated carcass sideways, backways and always. Suddenly I had an idea. Elward, my substitute at end, was just ten minutes short of the sixty minutes big-game play necessary to win a football monogram, emblem of team membership.
>
> I called to the coach: 'Send Elward in; he needs ten minutes for his monogram.'
>
> 'Darned nice of you,' said the coach as I hurried out of the game.
>
> 'If that hunchback does to Elward what he's done to me, he won't think I'm so nice!'

It was a self-deprecating way for Rockne to describe the close of his playing career. But his teammates, and all observers, made no mistake about his contributions to the team, as a leader, as a fearless defender, and as a ground-breaking, long-distance pass receiver. "Our brilliant pair of ends, Rockne and Gushurst, likewise gave noble account of themselves in their last fight for Notre Dame," the *Scholastic* summarized. When the 1913 All-America teams were named, Rockne received mention as a second or third-team pick on several elevens. The consensus first-team All-America ends were Army's Merrilat and Robert Hogsett of Dartmouth. At quarterback, selectors were nearly unanimous – Gus Dorais was first-team All-American, the strongest showing to date by a Notre Dame player. Harvard's Eddie Mahan and Charles Brickley were top picks at halfback and fullback, while Princeton's Hobey Baker, like Rockne, picked up some second and third-team honors.

Three years on the varsity. Twenty wins, no losses, two ties. The two longest and most consequential trips in the school's football history. And the friendship and respect of teammates, classmates, and friends of the university. It was hard not to reflect on what the journey meant; it had not been without its obstacles. From Voss, Norway to Chicago. The drudgery of his days at the Post Office. The homesickness of those early days on campus and the death of Lars. A lot of life had been packed into 25 years. Rockne had no regrets. It was the journey that lay ahead that most piqued his curiosity and sense of adventure.

# 13

## Becoming A Coach

The spring of 1914 presented Knute Rockne with another full schedule in his final semester as a Notre Dame student. There were more dramatic roles and an editor's position with The *Dome*. His studies included another full round of scientific courses. While awaiting conference of his Bachelor of Science degree in pharmacy, Rockne pondered his future. Would he continue his chemistry studies, or possibly become a pharmacist or a doctor? Whatever the decision, the task at hand remained working diligently at completing his final year of track. In early workouts, a freshman showed great promise in a number of events, including Rockne's old specialty, the shot-put. Charlie Bachman, the freshman from Chicago, burst onto the Notre Dame track scene with great energy and boundless potential. Rockne and Bachman had first met in 1911 at the Illinois Athletic Club handicap track meet at the 1st Regiment Armory in Chicago. Bachman was competing for Englewood High School, where he was also a football star in the Cook County High School League, competing against Hyde Park in the city's most intense gridiron rivalry. The pair reconnected in the fall of 1913, in Bachman's first weeks as a Notre Dame student. Similar to so many others, Bachman felt the pangs of homesickness, and he knew how easy it would be to hop a South Shore train back to Chicago. As a senior, one of Rockne's roles was to pick up the mail for his section of Corby Hall at the office of the hall rector, Father John Farley. Rockne couldn't help but read a postcard from Bachman's sister that implored him to "grow up and make up (your) mind to stay in school and get a college education."

In an instant, Rockne found himself transported to his freshman year, when his homesickness overwhelmed him. It was the insistence of his sisters that had kept Rockne at Notre Dame, so he decided to stop in Bachman's room for a talk. Rockne handed Bachman the postcard and asked Bachman to join him and Dorais in a little excursion that evening. A little-kept secret on campus was the loose screen in the storeroom that Rockne and Dorais could manipulate enough for fellow students—and themselves—to come and go at any hour, avoiding the 10 p.m. hall curfew. That evening, the three exited the dorm, with Rockne expertly putting the screen back in place. They headed about a mile south of campus to Steve Odyssey's saloon for a couple of beers. Then, sitting on empty beer cases in an open field, lit by a giant harvest moon, they talked. Rockne shared with Bachman how he felt in his first week at Notre Dame, how homesick he was, and how his grip was packed before he was intercepted by John Devine, John Plant, and Fred Steers and turned back to campus. The talk had the desired effect, and Bachman put off any travel to Chicago until the Christmas break.

Bachman felt privileged to be included in many conversations involving Rockne, Dorais, and other upperclassmen. They would gather in the room shared by Rockne and Dorais and talk about everything from football to religion to politics to current events and culture. "We gathered in that particular room because of Knute Rockne, who was the center of interest and good company," Bachman said. "He had a magnetic personality, a fine mind, a wonderful memory, a delightful sense of humor…and a tremendous desire to excel in anything he did." Rockne enjoyed his role as a mentor to Bachman. In track workouts, he would pass on little tips to the talented freshman. Then, on the first weekend of February, Bachman would follow Rockne's path in another sphere, making a triumphant return to the 1st Regiment Meet in Chicago. It was there Bachman won the shot-put with a heave of 44 feet, 7 inches. It was a throw that caused comparisons to Notre Dame Olympian George Philbrook. Rockne didn't place.

Turning 26 on his next birthday, Rockne was far from an old man. Yet there could be little argument that his best days as an athlete may have passed. Younger, faster, stronger men—like Charlie Bachman—were ready to take the mantle of excellence just as Rockne, Dorais, and others had in turn accepted it from those who came before them. But athletics had become such an important part of Knute Rockne; life without it was unimaginable. Rockne had gone from a football scrub to a star with national recognition on a Notre Dame team unlike any before it. The victories and exciting finishes in numerous track meets. Even the less-heralded moments—playing with Dorais for "Pop" Farley's Corby Hall baseball team; rowing for the junior class crew at commencement in 1913; even taking on the undisputed campus marbles champion—all brought a smile to Rockne's face. He had developed a keen appreciation of what it took to be a champion athlete: dedication, perseverance, and attention to detail. He knew the elements of a successful team, with each man understanding and accepting his role and doing his best to make the team reach its goals. Perhaps, he thought, there will be a chance to coach others.

Rockne didn't have to wait long for that opportunity. Long a tradition since football's inception, spring practice represented a chance to dust off the past and focus on the future. At Notre Dame, spring football practice became more formalized with the 1914 calendar and there was now a need for a coach to oversee it. With Jess Harper busy coaching the baseball team, the opportunity arose for Rockne to lead this initiative. Among his duties was equipment man, handing out uniforms to the prospects. And, one of his main tasks was to find a suitable replacement for himself at left end. One candidate was Bill Kelleher, a fiery native of Ireland and a backup from the 1913 team. During a scrimmage using the Notre Dame shift, Kelleher was playing the flexing right end position. On the team's "51 off-tackle play" Kelleher shifted out about one yard and his opposite number on defense, the veteran Ralph "Zipper" Lathrop, went with him, but well to his outside. Lathrop easily made the tackle, as Bill Kelleher was out of position.

"Bill, you've *got* to *block* the *tackle*," came Rockne's staccato voice, emphasizing key words. They tried the play again, and Kelleher shifted about one foot wider, but Lathrop lined up well to his outside, and again stopped the play.

"Bill, you've *got* to *block* the *tackle*," Rockne again exhorted. For a third time, the offense ran "51 off-tackle" with Kelleher still wider, and Lathrop again beating him.

"Bill, you've *got...*" Before Rockne could finish, Kelleher had his helmet off, handed it to Rockne and said, "Let me see you block him." Rockne eagerly accepted the challenge. For one play, the result was the same. Then, walking back to the huddle, Rockne asked the quarterback to send Eichenlaub, the big fullback, inside Lathrop. With Lathrop so far to the outside, the hole was now huge, and Ike went for a big gain.

"Bill," Rockne said, handing Kelleher back his headgear, "football is a game of wits and observation. You've got to use your head." He patted him on the back, sent him back to the right end position and spent the next 15 minutes working with him on each play. The challenge of seeing a deficiency, working to correct it, and turning it into a strength—the process had great appeal to Rockne. It mirrored his work in the chemistry laboratory, where there was continual trial and error, observation of the results, and adjustments made to achieve different, better outcomes.

Rockne could look in almost every direction around the country and see former Notre Dame stars making their mark as coaches. Frank "Shag" Shaugnessy, the 1904 football captain, coached Clemson University in 1907, then moved to Canada, where he was a minor league baseball manager. In 1912, he became the first full-time football coach at McGill University in Montreal. Several stars from the 1909 Notre Dame eleven that recorded the historic first victory over Michigan were now in the coaching ranks. Harry "Red" Miller, one of the brightest stars in that Michigan win, had just finished his fourth year as head coach at Creighton University in Omaha. Robert "Pete" Vaughan, who went on from Notre Dame to play more football at Princeton, was back in Indiana as football line coach and head basketball coach at Purdue. Lee Matthews, star end from that team, developed the football squad at St. Edward's College in Austin, Texas. His opposite number at end, Joe Collins, was coaching Heidelberg College in Tiffin, Ohio. Sam "Rosey" Dolan had already been head coach of the

Oregon Aggies for two seasons. And their quarterback, Don Hamilton, now led St. John's Military Academy in Delafield, Wisconsin. Two former Notre Dame athletes coached teams on Notre Dame's recent schedules: Albert "Red" Kelly, captain of the 1910 Notre Dame baseball team, now guided the gridders of St. Viator College; Luke Kelly, 1911 football captain, coached the Christian Brothers College in St. Louis. Further west, James Henry Bach ('07) took charge of athletics at Columbia College in Portland, Oregon, after Ralph Dimmick's death.

For Dorais and Rockne, playing one year under Jesse Harper showed them the possibilities that existed for employment from sports—from that of athletic director in control of various sports to coaching as many as was practical. It could add up to a reasonable salary, and it kept one on a college campus, if there was interest in further study. On one campus in Dubuque, Iowa, there was a need for someone to run athletics. The school had existed in fits and starts since Bishop Mathias Loras founded its predecessor, St. Raphael's Seminary in 1839. Father Samuel Mazzuchelli, a pioneer Italian Catholic missionary who brought the church to many areas of Illinois, Wisconsin, and Iowa, guided the first class of four seminarians. After periods of being known as St. Raphael's Academy and Mount St. Bernard's College and Seminary, the school closed during the Civil War. It later re-opened as St. Joseph's College, and started granting bachelor's degrees in 1895. Now, in the spring of 1914, newly renamed Dubuque College opened Loras Hall, the largest of the campus buildings, and the school prepared for another period of growth. It would offer a well-rounded athletic program aimed at attracting more students. Both Rockne and Dorais were candidates to take the job of athletic director.

Around the same time, Rockne pursued what sounded like a promising opportunity in St. Louis. He lined up a job coaching high school football, then presented his credentials to St. Louis University for admission into its medical school. He was ultimately rejected. School authorities told him they didn't think he'd be able to handle both medical school and coaching at the same time. The job situation quickly sorted itself out when Dorais accepted the Dubuque position and Rockne received an offer to remain at Notre Dame. He could become Harper's assistant in football, head track coach, and chemistry instructor in the preparatory school, for an annual salary of $1,000. Both men were pleased.

The pair that had made football headlines around the country was now parting ways. Though the time had passed quickly, they felt fortunate that the game of their youth provided an avenue for the future. Rockne would miss the banter and exchange of ideas; letters and an occasional wire would now be the basis of communication. For Dorais, the Dubuque job held some appeal as a chance to strike out on his own and be in charge of an athletic operation. For Rockne, it was a chance to work under Harper, the man who had learned from Stagg, who had taken the lessons from Walter Camp. Rockne relished the idea of following in the footsteps of these men who had crafted the sport with an eye toward building mind and body through the game. He may have missed out on the chance to attend Stagg's University, but now he had a chance to learn from someone who had.

Rockne was also glad to remain in South Bend where he had established deeper ties over the years. The thriving business community would also be an excellent city in which to bring a new bride and lay down family roots. Knute and Bonnie Skiles had maintained their long-distance relationship over the past year, and on July 15, 1914, in a simple ceremony at the parish rectory of Saints Peter and Paul in Sandusky, Ohio, Rev. William F. Murphy married them. The witnesses were Charles Dorais and Marie Balzarina, a friend of the bride. Several weeks before the wedding, Bonnie had come to Father Murphy to make arrangements for the ceremony. Later, Father Murphy would describe her as "a pious and devout young lady, without ostentation, modest in her ways and manners, capable of winning the hand and heart of the staid and judicious Rockne. Her womanly qualities were of a superior kind." Almost four years his younger, Bonnie enjoyed Knute's maturity, yet she saw a playful, kind, and gentle nature to the rugged exterior. She would later note how thankful she was to never have to wonder, as other women sometimes did about their husbands' kindness and thoughtfulness, because Rockne expressed it through word and action.

The happy couple headed back to South Bend, a trip much anticipated by Bonnie. The prosperous city, with its ample supply of stores, theaters, and industry, offered much more adventure than she had had in Ohio. The two began married life in a boarding house on St. Louis Boulevard, just south of the campus, and she looked forward to setting down roots of her own and raising a family. There was an aura of comfort that surrounded them in the shadow of the Golden Dome.

The fall of 1914 presented Rockne with his first challenge as assistant coach. He was bound to run into players who had been his teammates just a season earlier. With no established coaching style, would those former teammates recognize and accept his new authority? That question was answered quickly. It was Rockne's old friend Charlie Bachman, the lad Rockne had talked out of leaving for home in the fall of 1913, who presented the first test. One afternoon, Rockne spent a half hour with Bachman teaching his preferred blocking position—a low crouch and a quick, spread step. But Bachman had his own ideas, and disregarded the Rockne method. The young coach felt there was only one option.

"Come out of there, Bachman," Rockne yelled. "Go to the showers and turn in your suit. We don't need you anymore."

Everyone within earshot was shocked. A first-year assistant coach dismissing a strong varsity player? It was unheard of. But Harper backed up his assistant, and was prepared to hold firm. Bachman apologized, explaining that someone had told him that Rockne might have been a fine pass-catching end, but that his knowledge of blocking was limited. Emotions cooled, and Bachman returned to the squad, destined for an outstanding career. Recalled Rockne: "This example gave me the reputation of being a martinet—a reputation valuable to any coach provided he doesn't work too hard to keep it."

The assistant quickly developed a philosophy that boiled down to this: Lay down strict discipline in training and on the field of play, but combine it with genuine interest in all other relations with your players. Rockne found that humor, even sarcasm, could engender a good relationship with some players, though it depended on the individual. However, he had one steadfast rule: Never ridicule beginners. One smart remark at the wrong time could kill budding talent. It was a personal experience that had burned this maxim into his coaching. Back in 1911, proud to be taking the field for the first time as a member of the varsity, Rockne ran onto Cartier Field to clearly hear one wise guy from the stands yell, "Who's the homely Swede at end?" Rockne thought of himself as fairly thick-skinned regarding criticism, but this was a personal slap that stung. He never forgot its effect.

Coach Harper's persistent efforts to upgrade the football schedule created a slate of games in 1914 that surpassed any previous year. In addition to the second ever game at Army, Harper had arranged a season-ending trip to Syracuse. Games against the two most prominent football-playing Indian schools—Haskell Institute of Lawrence, Kansas and the Carlisle Indian Industrial School, coached by Glenn "Pop" Warner, were set, the latter to be held at Comiskey Park in Chicago. Certainly, the biggest date was the game set for October 17 in New Haven, Connecticut. For the first time, Notre Dame would be playing one of the Big Three of college football with its trip to meet mighty Yale. Yale, where the inimitable Walter Camp had created the game of modern American football that was now played throughout the country. Camp, for his part, was never bigger, as his newspaper columns, magazine features, books, and All-American selections had given him a huge following. Everyone wanted to know what the grand old man thought of this team, that player, or the latest big-name coach.

In the previous 14 seasons, each Yale head coach had led the team for a single season, with only one man, Howard Jones, serving more than once, coaching the Elis in 1909 and 1913. His 1913 squad finished an uncharacteristic 5-2-3. Between 1898 and 1912, one selection entity or another awarded Yale the national championship. The latest man to receive the call to coach Yale was Frank Hinkey, who had the distinction of being a four-time All-American end from 1891 through 1894. Hinkey was a fierce leader, often bordering on maniacal. It was said, "when he snarled and frothed at the mouth and a murderous glare appeared in his eyes, sunk deep in a face of deathly pallor, even his own teammates feared him."

Notre Dame opened at home with easy victories over Alma, 56-0, and Rose Poly, 102-0, giving the blue and gold a 16-game winning streak over three seasons on Cartier Field. Since Notre Dame last tasted defeat, against the Michigan Aggies in the 1901 campaign, it sported an overall mark of 24-0-3. The student body, the faculty, the townspeople of South Bend—all had become so used to winning that they anticipated Yale, especially coming off a subpar season, to become yet another victim. "Everybody," noted Rockne, "including myself, was suffering from a bad case of what we call fathead. That is, all except Jesse Harper. He pleaded and stormed like a lone voice in the wilderness, but all in vain." Said Harper before departing: "I believe Notre Dame has a possible chance of defeating Yale, although the odds are against us. We have been handicapped a great deal by injuries to our leading men....We have been further handicapped by not having strong enough opposition in our first few games of the season. From all reports, Yale has the best team it has had in years... and is using the open style of game very effectively." Just how open would come as a shock to Notre Dame. In its first three games—wins over Maine, Virginia, and Lehigh—Yale could play somewhat conservatively. There were rumors that Hinkey had a revolutionary attack planned for the later big games with Princeton and Harvard. But it was said that Yale alumni in the Midwest, inundated with reports of Notre Dame's strength, pressured the coach into using his "secret weapons" now, rather than keeping his powder dry for later games.

Harper, Rockne, and a squad of 23 men departed South Bend on the morning of Friday, October 16. The *Chicago Tribune* noted, "Never before in the history of the school was a team given a more rousing sendoff. Every student of the university was at the train and before it pulled out, yells were given for every player." The team sported a clean bill of health, with stars Eichenlaub and Bachman healed from recent injuries. Alfred "Dutch" Bergman faced the unenviable task of replacing Dorais at quarterback, but was handling the role well. Allen "Mal" Elward was in Rockne's left end spot, and Stan Cofall, a sophomore from Cleveland, had showed well in his first varsity action at halfback. The Notre Dame traveling party arrived in New Haven in the midst of a 24-hour drizzle that promised to make Yale Field a muddy mess and likely doom the success of an aerial strategy. Unable to use the field, Coach Harper directed practice in the Yale gymnasium while his assistant coach trekked to New York to purchase mud cleats for the players.

A short distance west of campus, the finishing touches were being put on the most fabulous of college football shrines: the newly-constructed Yale Bowl. Seating for more than 60,000 spectators, all directly encircling the field, would make it unlike any previous American sports venue. With a design proposed by 1871 Yale alum Charles A. Ferry, the stadium cost

$750,000—a sum that in 1914 very few schools could hope to raise. Once again, Yale proved itself the colossus of college football. And since it played nearly all of its games at home, save every other year trips to Harvard and Princeton, it could look forward to many big paydays from huge crowds in the new stadium. The game with Notre Dame would be one of the last few played at Yale Field before the opening of the Yale Bowl a month later in "The Game" against Harvard.

With 12,000 looking on at a soft Yale Field, both teams defied the conditions with some flashy play in the first half. Bergman, the "mere stripling of the field," gained on one run after another, varying the attack with an occasional pass completion. Yale's secret soon became evident. It was an offense patterned on the Canadian rugby system, under which two, three or all four backfield men may touch the ball on a given play: "When the man carrying the ball is about to be tackled, he will toss the pigskin to a running mate who is not in immediate danger of an opponent." The system of lateral passing opened up the game and created offensive variables that were almost unstoppable.

Shifty halfback Harry LeGore and his backfield mates made the field their personal playground, with the football flying in all directions and angles. Notre Dame stopped it a few times, though, with a timely interception or fumble recovery. Yale only scored once in the first half, after which Notre Dame quickly mounted a response in the closing minutes of the half. Eichenlaub returned the kickoff nearly 50 yards, and then he fired two "hair-raising and successful" forward passes over the line. The ball was on Yale's two-yard line when the whistle blew, ending the half with Yale ahead, 7-0.

In the third quarter the Elis continued their whirlwind of lateral passing and broke free for a couple of scores. Typically, running plays would include three to five laterals. On other plays, the last man to receive a lateral would then loft a forward pass, and the Notre Dame defense, now concentrating on the runners, would be susceptible to a big gain. Yale added another touchdown in the fourth quarter to take a 28-0 lead. But a certain spirit kept Notre Dame battling, and led to this description: "In spite of the fact that they were out-generaled and consequently outplayed, the fighting Irish met Yale at its own game and never, even when it was inevitable that defeat would be their portion, showed a sign of faltering.

Outplayed? Yes. Outfought? No." So this band of Notre Dame gridders, led by Harper and Rockne, earned the name that sang with descriptive lilt—the Fighting Irish. In the game's closing minutes, the fight was evident when Notre Dame again threatened to score. Bergman was hurt while rushing to Yale's 5-yard line. Young Stan Cofall rushed in to play quarterback before anyone realized he had already been substituted for that quarter. The penalty put the ball back out to the 15, and a final pass attempt went to the 2, before the final whistle blew. Notre Dame had ended both halves on Yale's 2-yard line, but couldn't score.

On the train ride back to South Bend, Rockne made an attempt to link the result to the players' attitude going out to New Haven. "I know what was wrong with you boys today," he sniffed. "You forgot to bring your scrapbooks with you. The Yale team didn't know how good you were!" Later, Rockne would observe that the loss was "the most valuable lesson Notre Dame has ever had in football. It taught us never to be cocksure. Modern football can be dated from that game, as we made vital use of every lesson we learned." When the Fighting Irish arrived back in South Bend on Sunday, they witnessed an amazing scene. More than 1,200 students greeted them "as hearty a reception as they would if it had succeeded in defeating Yale. Every player was given a lusty cheer as he alighted. Then they got in machines, and a snake dance, which was about three-quarters of a mile long, followed behind them."

The cheers finally subsided, though, and at Monday's practice, it was back to work. Eichenlaub had been allowed to stop at his home of Columbus, Ohio for some rest, and Bergman was out with his injury. The rest of the Irish backs received instruction in a new twist of offensive strategy that Harper had learned from Stagg at Chicago—the backfield shift. Stagg had begun experimenting with various shifts a decade earlier, and they had brought his Maroons success. In essence, shortly before the snap from the center, the four backs would shift from a standard T-formation to any of a number of other formations, such as a "box" with four corners. The snap could go to any of the four backs, creating tremendous versatility in the plays that could be run out of the formation. Ideally, all four backs would possess a variety of skills, as one individual might be called upon to provide interference on one play, and kick on the next. Dr. Henry Williams at Minnesota had also trained his team in the advantages of using the shift.

Harper and Rockne thus began that week to systemize the shift and make it Notre Dame's own. Its main features would be deception and quickness and eventually, a syncopation, which had the players moving right up until the instant the ball was snapped; some argued that they were actually in motion during the snap. Rockne would later write that Stagg deserved "credit for this revolution in football that gave us the shift—the dramatic equalizer between 'big' teams and 'little' teams. The shift…was new and spectacular and gave the un-technical football fan a chance to see something of the game besides mass huddles, flying wedges and stretcher-bearers." Notre Dame men, Harper and Rockne argued, would be well-suited for the mental challenge in adapting to the shift: "It gives the small man, the clever chap, the quick mover and quick thinker a chance to play the game on equal terms with the big, bruising fellow."

The backbone of the shift involved using brains, speed, and perfect execution to gamble for big yardage, rather than smashing into the line for a conventional gain of two or three yards, and plenty of bone-jarring collisions. Harper and Rockne were discarding the old "push and pull" system, in which both teams just slugged it out for one short gain, or loss, at a time. "If you want to play that kind of a game," Rockne noted, "you might just as well have a tug-of-war on the field and do away with intricate formations and signal calling." Coaching the shift, and all its many variations and possibilities, engaged Rockne's scientific and curious mind. As coach of Notre Dame's ends, he added another twist to the strategy, suggesting that while the backs shifted, the ends "flex" to take a different angle in blocking their opposite number. Together, it was an entirely new approach to the game. Notre Dame football would never be the same.

The Notre Dame defeat at Yale, and possible changes in strategy, dominated conversation around South Bend that week. Gradually over the years, and especially given the university's great success from 1911 to 1913, football cast a large shadow around town. Similar to numerous football hot spots around the Midwest, places such as Canton and Massillon, Ohio, and Green Bay, Wisconsin, a number of football teams took up play, representing athletic clubs, parks, and companies. Some star players were paid on a per-game basis; often, receipts depended on a wager the team would put up before playing, or by passing the hat during the game among whatever onlookers were present.

South Bend teams of the time included the Huebners, Muessels, Portage Park, Budweiser, Century Club, Szabos, Nationals, Shamrocks, Magyar House, and the River Parks. They scheduled games against one another on a haphazard basis, and faced nearby town teams from Mishawaka, Elkhart, or even Hammond. Into this loosely organized and constantly changing football realm stepped 26-year-old Knute Rockne. Yes, he had plenty of responsibilities at Notre Dame, assisting Harper, which included managing equipment, organizing the road trips, and acting as a "mother hen" to the players. He needed to keep the trackmen busy, as well. And there was the rigid schedule of instructing chemistry classes, overseeing lab work, and correcting assignments.

But if anyone could take on another assignment, it was Rockne. He didn't stop to contemplate the meaning of his station in life; he simply rolled up his sleeves and undertook the next task at hand. With a young bride, and the prospect of a family in the near future, any extra dollars beyond his Notre Dame salary would be greatly welcomed. So in the fall of 1914, he agreed to coach the football teams of the Muessel Brewing Company. A year earlier, Rockne stopped at Mussel's practices several times to observe and share some plays. Now, he was in charge. Beyond the dollars, coaching Muessel afforded Rockne a laboratory for trying out strategies and approaches. The more advanced of the brewery's two teams, Huebner's, laid claim to an Indiana state championship the previous year, and changed its name for the 1914 season to Silver Edge, one of Muessel's main beers. The second team, known as Muessel's, consisted of less advanced players.

Most of the South Bend independent teams played their games in open parks and playgrounds that might be available as needed. But the Silver Edge gained exclusive rights to use Springbrook Park, the only enclosed venue in town, which included the South Bend Fairgrounds and an amusement park. Scheduling games was a constant challenge; often, the opponent and day or time for a weekend game wasn't set until midweek. But at least the Silver Edges knew they'd be using Springbrook. Since it was enclosed, they could charge 50 cents to as much as two dollars admission. Other teams might try to put up temporary barricades—sometimes a line of automobiles—around old Baker Field on Washington Boulevard, or J.L. Oliver Field, to try to charge admission.

During the week, Rockne guided practice as best as it could fit into his schedule. There might be one practice in daylight per week, the rest around dusk or later. As an assistant, Rockne brought along Stan Cofall, the star sophomore running back for the Fighting Irish, who needed extra dollars to help pay for school. Rockne devoted most of his time to the Silver Edges, especially before their important games, and had Cofall oversee the Muesell practices. Rockne worked closely with the men who hired him, local businessmen and team managers John Smogor and Frank "Slicie" Niezgodski. The rosters of players reflected the ethnic makeup of South Bend, and included Johnny Klosinsky, Paster Sobieralski, Lodge Sokolowski, Lot Borkowski, and Tommy Grzegorek.

After returning from the Yale game, Rockne helped Harper install the shift at Notre Dame practice, then headed across town to work with the Silver Edge, which had a big contest the following Sunday to play at the vaunted Fort Wayne Friars. The local papers reported:

> Knute Rockne has been giving the Silver Edge squad some strenuous workouts this week, including drill in fancy plays he picked up at Yale. The Friars have been practicing an open game, but the Benders promise to go them one better with some bewildering Canadian rugby tactics behind the line of scrimmage. The Edges are improving every week under Rockne's tutelage, and look like the best independent bet in the state.

Cofall cut short the Muessel practices so the players could watch the strategy Rockne was installing with the Silver Edge—three or four lateral passes behind the line of scrimmage, followed by either a run or a pass, followed by another lateral. The approach worked, and the Silver Edge took down the Friars, 22-12. But the Friars quickly claimed that there were "ringers from Notre Dame" on the Silver Edge. It was a dilemma for the university. The Friars, after all, represented the heavily Catholic diocesan seat and had many influential Catholics among its fans. After a brief investigation, Notre Dame announced it was suspending five unnamed students. None were current varsity football players, though some had been out for football earlier that fall. Rockne himself was said to be "on the carpet" regarding the whole affair, but the fact that he was traveling to and from Sioux Falls for Notre Dame's game with South Dakota that weekend, and wasn't in Fort Wayne, "probably saved face for all concerned."

The Fighting Irish walloped South Dakota, 33-0, and downed Haskell, 20-7, in the final two home games. But in its return trip to Army, the magic of 1913 could not be duplicated. The Cadets simply had too much talent and were lying in wait for Notre Dame. Early on, Dutch Bergman fielded a punt when Army ends Bob Neyland and Lou Merillat hit Bergman immediately, high and low. The Cadets recovered the fumble and soon scored. Later, the All-American Merillat blocked a Cofall punt and recovered in the end zone for a 14-0 lead. So it went, with more stars emerging for the home team. Elmer "Ollie" Oliphant, the former Purdue All-American bruiser, came off the bench to hammer the Irish defense, and Omar Bradley spelled the regular centerman and made a number of key defensive plays. The two-loss Irish responded by pounding Carlisle, 48-6, at Comiskey and then traveling to Syracuse, where they blanked the Orange, 20-0 on Thanksgiving Day. Rockne's first season as assistant coach ended with a record of 6-2. Perhaps more significant than any victory, the season brought a wealth of new experiences that helped shape his coaching philosophy.


For the 1915 season, Harper secured a second trip to Texas on Thanksgiving Day, followed by a visit to Rice Institute just two days later. But his biggest achievement was booking an October 23 game at the king of the Midlands, the University of Nebraska. With Eichenlaub graduated, the primary cogs in the Irish backfield were Cofall, Bergman, and Bachman, the latter moved from his guard position. Another product of Portland, sophomore Jim Phelan, was poised to take over at quarterback. Two of Rock's 1913 linemates, Emmett Keefer and Freeman "Fitz" Fitzgerald, were still holding the guard positions. The new center was a 6-foot man from Grand Rapids, Michigan, Hugh O'Donnell.

Prior to facing Nebraska, the Irish opened with one-sided shutouts against Alma and Haskell. Rockne missed the Haskell game when Harper wired Nebraska coach Ewald O. "Jumbo" Stiehm to tell him that he was sending Rockne out to scout the October 9 game at Lincoln against the Kansas Aggies. Jumbo Stiehm, from Johnson Creek, Wisconsin, earned all-conference recognition as a center at Wisconsin in 1906, the first Badger so honored. After one year coaching Ripon College, he was hired as Nebraska's first full-time, year-round football coach in 1911. He crafted the Cornhuskers into a juggernaut, going 27-2-3 in his first four seasons. Since losing to Minnesota early in 1912 the Huskers had won 20 games and tied one entering the 1915 season. Despite his nickname, he preferred lighter, quicker players and devised a system of quick-striking running plays that proved hard to stop.

As 27-year-old Knute Rockne boarded the train in South Bend bound for Lincoln, for the first time he was traveling not as part of a team with a structured routine, but on his own. He was able to ply his natural curiosity about places and people, athletic strategy and psychology. He might strike up a conversation with a stranger in the club car, train station, or hotel lobby, and the other person, if he followed sports, was quite likely to have heard of Notre Dame and its end who helped beat Army. Rockne made friends easily, especially in athletic circles. He was full of questions about how football and track were conducted at the major universities. At Nebraska, he took notes of the Cornhuskers' tendencies as they trounced the Kansas Aggies, 31-0. Much of his attention centered on Guy Chamberlin, the Huskers' superb 6-foot-1, 200-pound standout halfback. As Chamberlin made gain after gain, Rockne noticed that he always stayed wide on his end runs, and never cut back in toward the middle. Further, Rockne noticed, the left-handed Chamberlin tended to lick his fingers before throwing a pass. If he left his fingers alone, you could bet on a run. Upon his return, Rockne, satisfied with his reconnaissance, reported these two facts to Harper.

The Fighting Irish made their initial trip to Nebraska and as was to become the tradition, the visitors arrived early on the day before the game and stayed at the Hotel Lincoln. The charge was $2.50 per room for two men, two beds, and a private bath. Harper requested fish and eggs for both lunch and dinner for his team on Friday, noting, "I hope you will be able to get us some nice fresh fish." In the first quarter, they took the lead when Cofall hit Bergman with a pass in the corner of the end zone. The kick failed, so Notre Dame led, 6-0. On the first play of the second quarter, though, Chamberlin went on one of his standard end runs. The Irish defenders all swung wide, overcommitting themselves with the knowledge Rockne's scouting report had brought. But to their surprise, Chamberlin cut inside, where he found smooth sailing for a 20-yard touchdown run. After the kick gave the locals a 7-6 lead, "the 8,000 spectators went wild. Hats were thrown into the air and on the field, and the game had to be delayed a few minutes until order was restored and the field cleared."

In the fourth quarter, with the score tied 13-13, Chamberlin again started out on an end run, having not groomed his fingers. But suddenly he stopped, whirled, and threw a long pass which set up Nebraska's winning touchdown. The Nebraska rooters again went wild and the cheering kept up for fully five minutes. It died down as Notre Dame charged back and Dutch Bergman went around right end for a touchdown. But the kick was missed, and the Irish left the field with a disappointing 20-19 loss. Perhaps the lesson that day was to never put too much stock into an opposing player's tendencies.

The Irish bounced back to edge South Dakota, 6-0, the following Saturday in the final home game of the season. Then it was on to West Point, where the Irish received a warm welcome in what was quickly becoming a cherished tradition. The strong bond that was developing between the two schools spoke of their similarities—a tradition of rigid discipline, which was marked by a Spartan lifestyle by students from the common class, many just a generation removed from the old country. The Cadets serenaded their guests "with Notre Dame songs that had been rehearsed all week by the Corps. The yell leader would mount the First Captain's table in the mess hall and direct a rousing welcome...meanwhile, the 'enemy' would be at the training table with the Army team." Friday evening, both teams' coaches and their assistants gathered at the Officers Club for a relaxed evening of conversation and cigars. Army head coach Charlie Daly, an old-school gentleman, and the rest of his staff made Harper and Rockne feel welcome. It was in this type of setting that the assistant reveled—hearty men discussing the game of football, what was happening at this college or that, who were the top players and rising coaches.

On the morning of the game, Rockne and some of his players were up early, inspecting the condition of the field. Marty Maher, a soldier who embodied "the long gray line" of Cadets greeted them. The native of Ireland had his eye on a group of soldiers removing hay, which had been spread on the field to protect it from rain. He spoke like a true son of Erin, with a lilting brogue. Rockne engaged him in conversation, which centered on Army's great star, Elmer Oliphant. Rockne asked Maher what he thought of the Army star.

"One o' th' finest," came the reply. "That lad is dynamite!"

"What did I tell you?" said Rockne, turning to his charges. "I only hope he blows up before the game. I don't want any of you getting killed."

O'Donnell entered game with a broken rib. Harry Tuthill, the trainer for Army, designed a specially padded shield for O'Donnell prior to the game. As the opposing centers lined up for the first play from scrimmage, John McEwan asked O'Donnell which side was injured. O'Donnell pointed, and through the game, McEwan never made contact with the injury. As if to balance this act of sportsmanship, McEwan focused his attention—and aggression—at leading Irish rusher "Dutch" Bergman. Every chance he had, McEwan gave Bergman an extra pounding. After a while, the rough play was evident to all. The beating McEwan was giving Bergman incensed Rockne. After a particularly nasty tackle near the Notre Dame bench, Rockne bolted onto the field to confront the Army center. Big Mac saw him coming and hollered: "Get the hell out of here. You're a coach now, and this is a fight among us players."

And what a fight it was, a grueling deadlock that called on every bit of strength the players could muster. Every time it appeared one team had a chance to break through, the opponent rose up to make a stop. Punt after punt drove deep into each other's territory. Late in the fourth quarter, Ollie Oliphant circled under a punt and called for a fair catch at the Notre Dame 47. "Let's see you kick one from here," kidded one of the Irish. Oliphant took him up on the challenge. The officials had to explain the situation to Notre Dame: Army could elect to attempt a field goal from here, and it would be a free kick. They had never seen this attempted. With a teammate holding the oval, Oliphant gauged the wind, spit on his hands, and approached the ball. With a mighty swing of his leg, he launched it goalward, the crowd shrieking. It hit the crossbar at dead center, bounced straight up, hit the bar again and fell back onto the field, short of success. The game remained scoreless.

Notre Dame had the ball with three minutes left. Cofall sprinted around end for a 27-yard gain. From near midfield, O'Donnell sent the ball straight back to Cofall as Bachman blocked the Army rusher. Cofall faded back, then launched the ball upfield, where Bergman made a spectacular leaping catch. He crossed the 30, made a head fake, and outraced Oliphant to the end zone. In just three plays, Notre Dame went from watching Oliphant's potentially game-winning kick to scoring the winning touchdown. At the final whistle, eleven Notre Dame men who had each played the entire game trudged off the field, to the congratulations of Rockne, Harper, and the Irish fans. Leading sports writer Ring Lardner wrote of Mexican bandits conducting raids across the Texas border: "It is said that President Wilson, in the event of a war with Mexico, will leave the Army at home and send Notre Dame to the front." The adulation of the Fighting Irish continued to spread. More newspapermen, and more prominent ones, were now updating their legions of readers with the feats of the "fighting Irish." When the season ended Thanksgiving week, with victories of 36-7 at Texas and 55-2 at Rice, Notre Dame's fame was spread even wider.

Rockne ended his year with some coaching of local pro teams, but his time and energy would soon be diverted to another area. On December 20, 1915, Rockne celebrated the birth of his first child, christened William Dorais Rockne. The gentle nature and kindness which Bonnie had so carefully noted during their courtship took on an even stronger hue. Bonnie recalled that despite the financial pressure, the weight of his role as Notre Dame instructor, and the time needed for coaching, Knute gladly helped daily with child-rearing and household chores.

The peace and tranquility for many, including the Rocknes, was on the verge of shattering.

# 14

# The World, The Nation, The University

T he possibility of the United States entering the war in Europe had been a contentious affair since the conflict began in August 1914 after Archduke Franz Ferdinand and his wife were assassinated in Sarajevo. President Woodrow Wilson's initial public calls for U.S. impartiality stemmed more from his fears of the conflicting emotions among many Americans whose origins were based in the warring nations rather than from some deep-seated opposition to the conflict. However, when a German submarine sank the British passenger liner *Lusitania* on May 15, 1915, the European battleground was no longer something happening "over there." The 1,198 people killed as the ship was within sight of the Irish coast included 128 Americans. Although war was not immediately declared, citizens were put into a war preparedness mode. The Preparedness Movement argued that the United States needed to immediately build up strong naval and land forces for defensive purposes; an unspoken assumption was that the United States would fight sooner or later. General Leonard Wood, ex-president Theodore Roosevelt and former secretaries of war Elihu Root and Henry Stimson were the driving forces behind the movement.

Although the Preparedness Movement focused on ground and naval forces, in Europe, a new type of warfare had taken to the skies. The shadow of war hastened aviation progress there, moving the industry beyond its rambunctious adolescence. Governments subsidized air manufacturers and poured funds into development and production. Only as the United States moved toward war did Washington finally press the aviation industry to set aside patent battles, close a series of cross-licensing agreements, and transform the manufacture of aircraft from small-scale custom work to a national operation capable of mass-producing airplanes. Congress jumpstarted the aviation industry on July 24, 1917 with a commitment of $640 million to its efforts. Domestic airline production shot up from 411 ships in 1916 to more than 14,000 in 1918.

In Germany, the name Fokker became synonymous with early aviation warfare. Rising to prominence as a builder of biplanes and triples used extensively by Germany in the war, Anthony Fokker made aerial combat possible by inventing a device to synchronize machine gunfire with propellers. A brilliant and opportunistic aviation businessman, Fokker's early success was due as much to good timing and marketing strategies as to engineering genius. His reluctance to invest in research and development led to his struggles with quality control throughout his career and played a role in the eventual decline of his aeronautical empire in later years. Rittmeister Manfred von Richthofen, better known as the Red Baron, flew more than 80 war missions in the premier German aircraft— Fokker's D.I design. Fokker claimed, "In official tests, the D.I proved to be the fastest and most efficient fighter available." Official records, however, offered a different view. Documents included a statement that indicated while from a distance the Fokker D.I looked good, a closer examination revealed flaws in both the design and workmanship.

The main cause was Fokker's apparent insistence on using the cheapest materials available regardless of their fitness for the task for which they were being bought. Fokker often disregarded adequate quality control of both components procured and his standard of workmanship in his production workshops. An examination of the records of virtually all of Fokker's wartime aircraft revealed that each went through a period when defects in either its manufacture or the materials used for its construction were exposed and later rectified at his expense. At one time, the use of his aircraft for combat was banned and he came close to being prosecuted on the grounds that he was both defrauding the German government and endangering the lives of German pilots.

When the November 1918 Armistice stopped all German aircraft production, Fokker was left with silent factories. He then smuggled his money out of Germany to Holland via boats and suitcases, established Dutch nationality, and began manufacturing Dutch aircraft. The U.S. Air Service, which had been impressed with some of Fokker's designs, sent officers to Holland to negotiate purchases of his new prototypes. This in turn led Fokker to make multiple trips to the United States and to eventually establish the Atlantic Aircraft Company, a subsidiary of his Dutch-based company, in New Jersey. Thus Fokker began to build aircraft in the United States, sidestepping American prejudice against the purchase of foreign aircraft for national airlines. He eventually established permanent residence in the United States in 1925. In 1926, he became an American citizen and established the Fokker Aircraft Corporation with headquarters in New York City, becoming an active participant in the expanding airplane manufacturing industry.


In 1915, the Preparedness Movement came to Notre Dame—a school that already had compulsory military training for most students. Specifically, cadet regiments had been formed and were present at Memorial Day observances that year when Secretary of the Navy Josephus Daniels was the honored guest of university president Father John Cavanaugh for the unveiling of a statue to honor former Notre Dame student John Henry Shillington, killed while on board the U.S.S. *Maine* in Havana Harbor in 1898. The regiments, led by the university band, marched in columns of platoons from the Grand Trunk Railway Station downtown to the Oliver Hotel to escort Father Cavanaugh and Secretary Daniels to campus for the ceremonies.

The cadets, along with other honored guests, boarded a train of seven interurban cars, which carried them to Notre Dame. Long lines of uniformed men snapped to attention as Secretary Daniels entered the Main Building. Daniels, in his speech, lauded the trained citizenry shown at the university as international apprehension loomed.

War or not, the never-ending need to raise money for building and faculty expansion nagged at Cavanaugh daily. Cavanaugh would often ponder as he took his evening walks around campus on how best to keep the intimate atmosphere of Our Lady's University intact as he continued to project it into a more prominent role within an evolving world environment. He would eventually oversee a reconstruction of Badin Hall, the closing of the School of Manual Labor in 1916, the beginning of summer school courses for graduate work, and the design and building of the university's new, free-standing library in 1917. Father Cavanaugh, an avid reader with an interest in everything intellectual, fought long battles with his provincial superiors to secure approval for the new library, which was the vision of Holy Cross Father Paul J. Foik, who had become head librarian in 1912.

Foik passionately believed a new library facility was necessary if Notre Dame was to survive and prosper as an institution of higher learning. He worked with Cavanaugh to convince former university president Father Andrew J. Morrissey that Notre Dame ought to have the "finest library in the whole state of Indiana and the finest Catholic library in the whole United States." It took Foik almost two years of constant agitation to gather the necessary approvals and appoint a library building committee with himself as chairman. The Lemonnier Library, named for Father August Lemonnier—third president of Notre Dame and nephew of founder Father Edward Sorin—was completed and dedicated as part of the university's Diamond Jubilee celebration on June 8, 1917.

The Diamond Jubilee proved to be a celebration of progress already made, with a list of dignitaries that included Apostolic Delegate, the Most Reverend John Bonzano; Baltimore Cardinal James Gibbons; Archbishop George W. Mundelein of Chicago, who preached the sermon at Mass; and the Most Reverend Edward Hanna, archbishop of San Francisco. Gray skies cleared by the afternoon, and tolling bells and resounding cheers greeted the motorcade that carried Gibbons and Admiral William Shepherd Benson, the Chief of Naval Operations and the 1917 Laetare Medalist. President Woodrow Wilson and Secretary of the Navy Josephus Daniels sent congratulatory letters to Father Cavanaugh on the selection of Benson for the award. At Mass, Archbishop Mundelein read a letter sent by His Holiness Pope Benedict XV in which the pope thanked the university and the Holy Cross Congregation for giving "the Church and the State so many sons eminently schooled in religion and learning." The letter continued:

> How gratifying this is to us, need hardly be expressed. In the midst of the trials of the present hour which press upon us, so heavily, the brightest ray of hope for the future lies in the special care that is being bestowed upon the education of youth. In this age when young men, to our great sorrow, are so drawn in evil by the allurements of vice and the insidious teachings of terror, it is, above all, by training youth to virtue that the life of nations is to be fashioned and directed in righteousness and truth.

After Mass, an enthusiastic crowd encompassed the large steps that led to the new library. Reverend Thomas Shahan, rector of the Catholic University in Washington, D.C., blessed the library, and Indiana Judge James Deery, President of the Ancient Order of Hibernians, presented Father Cavanaugh with a check for $1,000 and assured the Notre Dame president that "this is the first installment from the Hibernians and Ladies Auxiliary of Indiana for they hope some day to hail Notre Dame as the centre [sic] of Irish learning in the United States."

Father Cavanaugh also built on a foundation established by Father Sorin—strengthening ties with the South Bend community. The city built along the St. Joseph River continued to boom as an industrial center, anchored by the Studebaker Bros. Corporation. By 1915 Studebaker had continued its steady rise as a premier player in the automobile industry, as they were producing more than 45,000 vehicles annually. During the European war years, the company built horse-drawn wagons as well as tanker trucks, ambulances, and gun carriages.

By 1915, the Studebaker family had turned over business to Albert Russel Erskine, when he was named company president. Erskine led a dazzling expansion of the corporation in which Studebaker became one of the first automobile manufacturers to use wholesale and retail financing to stimulate sales. Erskine echoed Henry Ford in regard to labor relations, but Erskine's efforts were more progressive and far-reaching. By November 1, 1915, the eight-hour workday was instituted in Detroit and Walkerville, Ontario, two of Studebaker's plants. Profit-sharing plans, which included dividends on wages, vacations with pay, life insurance, pensions, and stock purchase provisions for all employees were instituted. Later, when the South Bend manufacturing plant was built in 1916, large employee dining rooms and cafeterias were included. Of the $8.2 million the company spent on new plants and facilities, 90 percent of it was spent in South Bend. Participation in athletics was also encouraged with Studebaker factory teams competing in hockey, indoor baseball, bowling, and basketball.

Erskine, a true business competitor, was known for his broad vision, his comprehensive knowledge, his practical sense, his just mind, and his generous heart. Born in Huntsville, Alabama on January 24, 1871, his family lost its fortune after the Civil War. Erskine made his way through multiple businesses from bookkeeping up to chief clerk, until reaching vice president and director of Underwood Typewriter Company in New York City, when a friend advised him that Studebaker was looking for new blood. He started at a salary of $20,000 per year in October 1911 and quickly endeared himself to the Studebaker family as a man poised to help the company move into the next generation of transportation.

He never shied away from his accomplishments, and he once bragged: "No other individual manufacturer, except Ford, can produce as many closed bodies as we can and no manufacturer can make them better, because we have experienced wood workers and trimming craftsmen who used to make Studebaker carriages."

Erskine engaged in multiple civic-minded endeavors. He served on the South Bend Planning Commission and was chairman of campaigns to raise building funds for the city hospitals, the YMCA, and Notre Dame. Father Cavanaugh was among the dignitaries who bestowed platitudes when Erskine was feted at the Oliver Hotel in 1919 as South Bend's premier citizen. By 1920 new Notre Dame President James Aloysius Burns sought Erskine's help with the university's fund-raising efforts, and by 1921, Erskine, a high school dropout, was named president of the university's Board of Trustees and chairman of the three-person finance committee.

Erskine was well connected with the leaders of corporate America and knowledgeable about corporate managerial practices, which was considered crucial as Notre Dame began expanding its educational, physical, and athletic boundaries that would require significant financial investment.

Rapid transformation and growth for the university came with another reality. Too much change too quickly left some Americans fearful and that fear helped to fuel the growth and revival of anti-immigration and anti-Catholic movements, embodied most notably by the Ku Klux Klan. Although Klan origins were deeply rooted in the post-Civil War South, the group's activities spread throughout the country as more and more "newcomers" to the shores arrived. William J. Simmons, the son of an Alabama farmer, became the Imperial Wizard of the newly resurrected "empire in white" in 1915, and he established new Klan headquarters in Atlanta. The Klan now had a wider program, adding white supremacy, intense anti-Catholicism, and an anti-Semitic platform that more closely resembled the Know-Nothing movement of the mid-19th century. As a result, Klan appeal spread rapidly throughout all parts of the country.

Around 1912, a 12-volume series of pamphlets called *The Fundamentalists* reached a receptive audience of American theologians. Fundamentalists wanted the Protestant Bible restored to its pre-Civil War place in American public schools. They denounced evolution and free interpretations of scripture. They rejected all forms of religious "modernism" and supported the temperance movement against the sale and consumption of liquor. America's eventual entry into the war in 1917 unleashed a militant patriotism that fed into religious fundamentalism. In the Klan's eyes, the nation needed to be defended against alien enemies, slackers, idlers, strike leaders, immoral women, and papists—and the Klan gladly accepted the challenge. One of the Klan's major allies included Bishop Alma Bridwell White, a former Methodist turned evangelical preacher from Denver who, after divorcing her husband, formed her own church—The Pillar of Fire—in 1917 with headquarters in New Jersey. The Klan supported her because of her viciously anti-Catholic magazine, *The Good Citizen,* which began publication in 1913. The *New York Times* called her the only woman bishop in the world and Bishop White called Catholics "toe kissers" and "wafer worshipers." Unless America fought Rome, "we shall be swept into paganism," she wrote.

To the Klan, the pope was a bigger threat than German Kaiser Wilhelm because the pope already had "foreign emissaries" operating in the United States in the form of parish priests. Klan propaganda claimed that every time a Catholic family had a newborn male child, the Knights of Columbus donated a rifle to the Catholic Church. Another circulating story said that steeples on Catholic churches were built so high so that they could rain gunfire down on Americans when the pope declared war against the Protestants. One rumor even suggested that the sewer system at Notre Dame was actually a gigantic arsenal filled with explosives and heavy artillery. Few Catholics, especially those in the Hoosier state, found these outlandish stories funny.

However, the reality was that Indiana provided a strong Klan base in the first half of the 20th century, with membership eventually reaching 400,000 by 1923. It was estimated that 30 percent of Indiana's white native-born male population were Klan members. Although a Union state during the Civil War, Indiana was settled from south to north by homesteaders from Kentucky, Tennessee, and the Carolinas. In the late 18th century, pioneers traveling through the northern part of the Indiana Territory found swamps and a prairie not fit for farming. Native Americans who objected to the pioneers' usurpation of their land frequently made life in the northern sections of the state dangerous. Therefore, settlers moved to Ohio or pushed westward to Illinois and beyond, or northward to Michigan. By the time of the Civil War, Indiana was a microcosm of the divided nation. From 1880 to the European war years, Indiana tripled its industrial base, yet retained an agricultural center that glorified rustic simplicity and pioneer Protestantism. It would become fertile soil for Klan membership.

The Klan may have been spreading anti-Catholic, anti-immigrant hatred throughout the country, but the reality was that Irish Catholic immigrants were providing the muscle and sweat to build post-industrial America. One particular area to which these Irish Catholics flocked was the copper mines of Butte, Montana. Long a mining boomtown, immigration to Butte had been increasing since the 1870s. The Copper King industrialists called for more manpower and immigrants flowed in from Ireland, England, Lebanon, Canada, Finland, Austria, Italy, China, and other places. It was said that the "no smoking" signs in the Butte mines were written in 16 languages. The Irish, however, felt a special connection to Butte. Beginning their immigration during the famine years of the 1840s, many came from the Beara Peninsula where they had mined before leaving for America. They arrived from Cork, Mayo, and Donegal. At a quarter of Butte's population, the Irish made up a higher percentage than they did in any other American city at the turn of the 20th century. Seventy-seven various families of Sullivans left Castletownbere, Cork and came to Butte. By 1908 Butte hosted 1,200 Sullivans.

In 1917, years of labor unrest and martial law had turned Butte into a powder keg waiting for a match. The beginning of the war in Europe and the insatiable appetite for copper to keep up with the demand for electricity had turned Butte into an industrial complex that rivaled the steel mills of Pittsburgh. As the mining companies fought for control of the copper industry, the larger operators expanded into railroads, logging, and other industries, pushing their smaller competitors out of business. Monopolies meant that corporations held increasing power over the families that lived in mining towns, and unions could do little to change the occupation's hazards.

On the night of June 8, 1917, a group of men descended to the 2,400-foot level of the Granite Mountain mine to inspect an electrical cable that had fallen loose while being strung by a crew on an earlier shift. When the cable fell, the workers from the earlier shift decided to leave it until the next day. The protective sheathing frayed as it fell against rocks and timbers. When Ernest Sullau, the assistant foreman, inspected the cable, he accidentally touched his hand-held carbide lamp to uncovered paraffin paper wrapping, and the cable caught fire. Sullau literally lit the fuse that would ignite the powder keg. The tragedy was compounded because the Granite Mountain was a well ventilated mine, allowing the flames and smoke to spread quickly. The fire and deadly smoke fanned through the shafts to connecting mines. The final toll stood at 168 men killed. When the mourning and grief subsided, miners demanded safer working conditions, but the mine owners refused. Butte became a violent place, with union halls blown up and miners jailed or even murdered. When a strike at one mine lasted for seven months, the miners were accused of treason during wartime and were eventually marched into the mines at gunpoint when federal troops were called in. However, labor strife within the mines remained a volatile issue throughout the end of the decade.

While Butte drew mainly Irish immigrants to its mines, another rich copper area became an ethnic stew, with Finns, Danes, Swedes, Norwegians, Croatians, Poles, Slovenes, Cornish, Irish, Germans, and Italians among its most prominent nationalities. The Keweenaw Peninsula, jutting into Lake Superior atop Michigan's Upper Peninsula, became known as Copper Country. It was the nation's leading producer of copper from 1850 until 1887, when it was exceeded by Butte. In its peak years, Michigan's Copper Country produced more than three quarters of the nation's copper, peaking at more than 95 percent in 1869. The most productive copper mines were located along a strip about two miles wide and 24 miles long, from the Champion mine on the southwest to the Ahmeek mine on the northeast, passing through the towns of Houghton, Hancock, Calumet, and Laurium. Between all the men needed to fill mining jobs and the associated industries that sprang up in the area, Copper Country became a mecca for immigrants who sought ready employment. Between 1890 and 1910, the population of Houghton County alone soared from 35,000 to more than 88,000. Combined with Keweenaw County and a part of adjoining Ontonagon County, the total population of Copper Country in 1910 exceeded 100,000 residents.

Finns represented the leading nationality among the mineworkers. The highly successful Calumet & Hecla Mining Company began to offer the greatest opportunities for employment both in the mine and in surrounding business. By 1880, in the mine's settlement area around the Village of Red Jacket, Finns made up approximately one in five residents. Finnish immigrants quickly established several ethnic institutions in Calumet, the community that emerged as their earliest *pesapaikka,* or "nesting place," in America. By 1880 Calumet's Finns supported a newspaper, two churches, a mutual aid society, a literary society, a printing company, a lending library, a land company and two mining companies. Finns also operated a general store, a watchmaker-shop, nine public saunas, and a saloon in Calumet.

In the early 20th century, copper companies began to consolidate. With very few exceptions, such as the Quincy Mine at Hancock, the mines in the Copper Country came under the control of two companies: the Calumet and Hecla Mining Company north of Portage Lake, and the Copper Range Company south of Portage Lake. The companies' relentless pressure to increase copper production had made life increasingly stressful for those who worked the mines. Intense efforts by the Western Federation of Miners (WFM) to unionize workers helped to create an atmosphere in the summer of 1913 that ultimately led to the Copper Mine Strike of 1913-1914. Outside labor leaders, including 83-year-old United Mine Worker organizer Mother Jones, arrived to rally support and organizing efforts. Many of her talks, as she rode from Hancock to Ahmeek and South Range, needed to be translated; the Finnish, Croatian, Italian, Hungarian, and Polish miners spoke little English. She praised strikers of 26 different languages for standing together as one. Adding to the tensions in the region was the presence of troops who had been brought in at the request of Governor Woodbridge Ferris.

The hot summer and even hotter tensions led to a stalemate by Christmas Eve 1913. The WFM helped to organize contributions to cheer the lives of miners and their families at the holiday. Baskets of food, including apples and bread; clothing, including mittens for the children; and bags of candy were readied for a gala celebration to be held at the Italian Hall on the afternoon of December 24. A steep stairway was the only way to the second floor, which hosted more than 500 children that day. What ensued that afternoon in the crowded hall, with the intense noise of conversation in multiple languages, has never been determined. Many reported that someone yelled, "fire," yet others said a Croatian miner asked for water in his native language. How close was the Croatian word *watra* to the English word fire when shouted over a noisy crowd? What followed was a mass panic for the downstairs, which had only one exit and one set of doors. The chaos and crush of bodies left 74 dead, 59 of them children. Cause of death for many was suffocation.

Mining families grieved, buried their dead, and remained on strike until April 1914 when intra-union struggles reached an impasse. When the WFM decided to cut strike benefits, it effectively ended the labor dispute. Company revenue loss was estimated at $4 million, while wage loss estimates stood at $1 million. By August, a depressed economy slowed productivity in the Upper Peninsula and copper prices fell again when war in Europe arrived. The Michigan strike proved to be a microcosm of America's industrial economy of the early 20th century. Anti-trust legislation aimed at breaking up monopolies, immigrant workers forming unions, and reformists pushing for laws to better protect workers would continue for years.

The Finns of the Copper Country, and to an extent the other nationalities, valued literacy and education as a central force of the entire population, not merely reserved for the elite. At Hancock, the Finns established Suomi College; their leadership of public education was widespread throughout the region. Coupled with the strong tax base created by the mining industry, public schools of the area were of the highest quality. At Calumet, for example, high school students started their day in the ornately adorned "homeroom" that seated hundreds of students. Many families of miners, and associated businesses, saw a future in which their children would use education to broaden their horizons and achieve a better life.

# 15

## Star Power

Like many of his fellow students, Robert Emmett Proctor worked his way through the University of Notre Dame in the first years of the 20th century. He waited on tables, held a variety of jobs for the New York Central Railroad, wrote as a correspondent for various newspapers, and served as one of the editors of The *Scholastic*. He earned his law degree in 1904 at the age of 21 and began a practice in his hometown of Elkhart, Indiana, just 20 miles east of campus. In 1908, at the age of 25, Proctor ran for and was elected to the Indiana State Senate, joining a wave of Democrats—such as new governor Thomas R. Marshall—who overtook seats long held by Republicans. In his two terms Proctor was a prominent leader, an adroit speaker, and one of the most active and effective advocates in the state senate. He was also a loyal son of Notre Dame and an active alumnus. Proctor had a particular interest in baseball; in 1910, he served as president of the short-lived Indiana-Michigan League, a Class D minor league with teams in Elkhart, Gary, and Ligonier, Indiana, and nearby Niles, Dowagiac, and Berrien Springs, Michigan. And, he guided a summer baseball team of Notre Dame students on a Midwestern barnstorming tour. It was an adventure for the Notre Dame students, living apart from the constraints of either home or campus. The tour sought out town teams wherever they might be, and when it hit Wisconsin, or northern Michigan, or the Upper Peninsula of Michigan, an added benefit was the relatively cooler weather.

During one stretch in the U.P., Proctor found his team shorthanded and worn down, and a string of losses followed. Before a series of games in the Keweenaw, Proctor negotiated to add a couple of local fellows—Paul Hogan and Wilbur "Dolly" Gray—to the Notre Dame squad. The duo from Calumet was just what Proctor's team needed, and the group continued its tour with a decent winning streak. Gray was subsequently offered a baseball scholarship to Notre Dame, which he accepted. It started a connection that would bring several Copper Country athletes to South Bend. Gray played on Notre Dame's outstanding varsity baseball team from 1910 to 1914, where he crossed paths with track and football athlete Knute Rockne. Gray received his Bachelor of Law degree, while Rockne attained his Bachelor of Science degree at commencement in June 1914. Gray remained in the area for several years, playing semi-pro baseball in Indiana before returning to work in Copper Country. The lure of the piney woods and the waters of nearby Lake Superior made a return home an easy choice. There was something about the Keweenaw that kept young men active and energized. They made the most of the long, cold winters with skiing, sledding, skating, and hockey. And when the snow and ice finally melted in spring, they were ready for all the games they could squeeze in before the weather turned again in the fall. With the population growing to eventually become the second most populous area in the state, after Detroit, there were young boys aplenty to compete in sports; the best were bound to be quite accomplished.


Antoine Gipp was born in Lutzrath, Prussia in 1820 and emigrated to the United States in 1848. He moved with his wife Agnes and two young children to Michigan in 1857, after he read about a copper find in the Upper Peninsula. Antoine went to work as a laborer for the Calumet & Hecla Consolidated Mining Company, and the family had three more children. They lived on a tract of land owned by the mining company in an area that would become the village of Laurium. In 1862, at age 42, Antoine enlisted in the Union Army and a year later saw action in the battle of

Gettysburg. During the battle of Spotsylvania, Pennsylvania, Gipp suffered a severely wounded right arm. Antoine and Agnes' son Matthew, born in 1854, went to work for the mining company as soon as he was able, joining the C&H payroll as a carpenter. In June of 1877 he married Isabella Taylor, an Irish immigrant whose family escaped the potato famine of the 1840s. Matthew and Isabella lived in a small home at 432 Hecla Street in Laurium, built by Antoine Gipp with Matthew's help. There, they raised eight children, four boys and four girls. The second youngest, son George, was born on February 18, 1895.

The young Gipp developed an independent streak—after all, how much attention could be lavished on the seventh child of a mining family? Growing up he spent many hours at the Calumet YMCA, where he learned to swim, play basketball, and shoot billiards. And whenever he could, he played baseball, often with boys much older than he was. "He just bubbled with enthusiasm," recalled one coach. "He'd chase four balls all day long if you'd let him, and never complain. He just wanted to play." Watching him for a minute with either bat or glove, it was said, was enough proof that he was a natural."

As a 13-year-old in 1908, Gipp won the annual Laurium foot race, creating such a sizable lead that he could rest for a while and wait for the field to approach the finish line, before bursting over in victory. In 1910, he was a starter on the Calumet High School basketball team that won 24 consecutive games. Calumet High School was a gem, with excellent facilities and a highly paid faculty, thanks to the success of the Calumet & Hecla Company. But, more often than not, Gipp was unable to participate on its athletic teams. Known for his quick wit, Gipp's sharp tongue or misguided pranks sometimes resulted in suspension or expulsion from school for disrupting classes or missing them altogether. During his senior year, Calumet principal E. J. Hall expelled him for the last time, reportedly for smoking in the hallway.

Gipp played YMCA basketball and semi-pro football, and excelled in baseball, playing for a variety of teams in and around Calumet. In football he displayed talent as a runner, passer, and defensive player. But it was baseball that really fueled his fire. In the summer of 1915, he helped lead a Laurium team to the championship of the Trolley League, one of the amateur circuits in Michigan. That led to a postseason game with the winner of another county league. With his team trailing by a run in the eighth-inning, Gipp smashed a towering two-run game-winning homer. It was said the ball was still ascending as it went over a coal pile beyond the center field fence. "It was the longest drive ever hit by anybody up here," said one observer. It was said after one game, Laurium manager Joe Swetish, was going through the club's lineup in answer to a question of how many extra-base hits each player had. When he reached Gipp, he said, "And we have a double and a round-tripper for the Gipper." Someone turned to Gipp and said, "Hey Gipper, Joe's a poet." And the name stuck.

However, Gipper, it seemed, had found that just about more than anything he preferred shooting pool and playing cards—for money. He had a gambler's mentality, always looking for the next chance to extract a few greenbacks from someone. He could sit down to a poker game with a group of miners and clean them out of their wages. Any game of chance was an opportunity for a payday. Gipp and a pal, Angelo Stappas, would paint a football white, and play what they called "ghostball." They would sneak onto the Calumet High field at night, with a group of Italian immigrants more familiar with soccer. Stappas and Gipp would stage a field-goal kicking contest, Stappas kicking a soccer ball and Gipp the "ghostball." Starting from the 15-yard line and moving out, they would trade attempts. Gipp would "go easy" in his early attempts, to keep the gamblers coughing up their money. But as they moved further away, his accuracy increased, and so did his winnings, which sometimes totaled $100 in a night.

By the summer of 1916, Gipp was spending much of his time at Jimmy O'Brien's Pool Room, just three blocks from his home on Hecla Street. To practice his pool-shooting, Gipp and his buddy Peter Giroux would sneak into the Elks club in Calumet after hours, with Peter's younger and much smaller brother Wilfred "Jazzy" Giroux sliding down a coal chute to get into the club and open the door for the others. With the C&H company increasingly flexing its muscles and labor tensions high in Laurium and Calumet, Gipp vowed he would not do what most men in town did: work for the company. He occasionally picked up jobs from Roehm Construction and on weekends worked as a waiter and chauffeur for The Michigan House, the area's leading hotel and restaurant. He would ferry visitors between the train station and The Michigan House. Dolly Gray, back in the Calumet area in the summer of 1916, ran into Gipp on the street and the conversation turned to Gray's experience at Notre Dame. Surely, Gray said, Gipp was an accomplished enough baseball player to earn a scholarship to the school. Further, with all the baseball stars Notre Dame had sent on to the major leagues, Gipp would have the opportunity to do the same.

"I'm too old to try school again," replied Gipp, now 21. "Besides, I don't have any money." It was true that, for all the money he won at billiards, cards or other pursuits, Gipp held on to precious little of it. For Gipp, it was the game, the challenge, that mattered more than the payoff. He spent and lent freely, and saving was a foreign concept. Another barrier to college was his lack of a high school diploma. But Gray, Hogan, and other friends convinced Gipp it could be done, and so he agreed to give college a try.

George Gipp arrived at Notre Dame in mid-September 1916 and passed examination for admission as a college freshman. He took up residence in Brownson Hall and very quickly found the basement recreation room in nearby Corby Hall. There, fellow students say, he would shoot pool by himself for an hour or two at a time. "It was nothing for him to run off upwards of 80 balls without a miss," said one. Gipp would focus on the cue and ball, saying little to anyone. Gipp, much like another older freshman who entered in 1910, felt uncomfortable, in part because of his age. On a letter to a friend back home, he wrote, "I got here alright and got away with a pretty good start....I'm in a mood tonight where I'd like to go straight up. I want to come and go as I please. Sometimes I wonder what I'm here for....Something makes me feel that I'm all wrong and will stay that way...I'd like to give up and quit right now, chuck everything and go anywhere." But Gipp, like Rockne, Bachman, and so many others before him, moved past his homesickness. He had a full course load of English, History, German, Political Science, and Biology. Although he attended classes, he showed little interest in their discussion.

Assistant coach Rockne had a habit of walking out to Cartier's practice field, taking in whatever impromptu games might be going on among students on his way. One early autumn day, on an otherwise nearly deserted field, he noticed a tall fellow in everyday clothes kicking a football to a young man in a football suit, a candidate for the freshman team. At first, it looked like nothing more than a football aspirant and a roommate or friend helping him prepare for practice. But the punting of the taller lad caught Rockne's eye. He had a certain grace, an ease of motion. He picked up the ball, perfectly timed its drop to the ground, and with an easy swing of the leg drop-kicked it 50 yards or more. Rockne stopped in his tracks and watched. For 10 minutes, this young man kicked with ease, placing each ball exactly where he intended, to give the freshman player valuable practice at fielding kicks.

When they finished, Rockne positioned himself to intercept the kicker. "What's your name?" the coach asked. "Gipp," came the reply. "George Gipp, from Laurium, Michigan."

"Played high school football there?" Rockne probed. "Nope," Gipp answered. "Don't particularly care for football. Baseball's my game." "What led you to come to Notre Dame?" Rockne continued. "Friends of mine are here," Gipp answered, though the man responsible for him being there, Dolly Gray, was back in Laurium.

Rockne issued his invitation. "Why don't you put on a football suit tomorrow, and come out with the freshmen scrubs. I think you'll make a football player." Over the next few weeks, Rockne's prediction looked quite solid. On the very first play of a practice game for the freshmen, Gipp burst through the line in his first carry in an organized setting. Every few days, Rockne would leave the varsity practice and check in on his find. He was amazed to see how readily Gipp, with little real football experience, had mastered the techniques used in running, passing and kicking.

The varsity, led by its captain, Rockne's brewing-team assistant coach Stan Cofall at left halfback, started the 1916 season looking unstoppable. The Irish hung a pair of 48-0 defeats on two Cleveland schools which would one day merge—Case Tech and Western Reserve, the later game being played at Cleveland. Next came a 26-0 victory over the Haskell Institute. The following week, Wabash was set to visit Cartier Field. Coach Harper came down with a severe cold, and removed himself from the assignment of coaching the game against his former squad, putting Rockne in full control and giving him his first taste of being at the helm.

Despite the absence of Harper, the varsity's preparation for the game went on pretty much as usual. Wabash had recovered from several sub-par years immediately following Harper's move to Notre Dame. The Little Giants went 7-0-1 in 1915 and started 1916 with easy wins against Rose Poly, Hanover, and Butler, though they also dropped a 28-7 decision at Purdue. In his pregame address to the team, Rockne became a man possessed, possibly by the spirit of Shorty Longman. He railed against the motives of the Little Giants. "Through an unrevealed source," as one Irish player described it, "Rockne had discovered that some sinister and diabolical influence at Wabash had marked Notre Dame for oblivion. He intimated that if every man including the cheerleaders gave all he had, we might through some perhaps providential intervention, possibly mitigate the smirch about to befall us." In a final, desperate exhortation, Rockne fairly screamed, "Now get out there and crucify 'em!" Whether inspired, scared, or just plain more talented, the Fighting Irish rolled to a 60-0 victory. Notre Dame was now 4-0, having outscored the opposition, 182-0, with the Army waiting.

The team had three days of practice scheduled before heading to West Point on Thursday, November 2. Rockne called Gipp from the freshman squad to try to copy the running style of Oliphant, the great back who again led the Army attack, and within the three days, Gipp was able to give an excellent imitation of the Army star. The next day, Gipp participated in his first football game for Notre Dame, as the freshmen took on St. Viator. Gipp entered the game in the second half, and made a long drop-kick to help the freshmen win, 10-7.

That same day, the varsity was on its way to West Point when Rockne and some of the players stepped off the day coach to breathe some fresh air at the Cleveland station. They heard some murmuring and learned that ex-President Teddy Roosevelt, now running for president on the Bull Moose Party ticket, was in a private car at the end of a nearby train. They gave him a cheer, were invited in, and spent the next several minutes talking football with the man who most people felt was responsible for saving the game. One of the Irish predicted to Roosevelt what Notre Dame would do to the Army the next day.

"That sounds bully, Coach," Roosevelt bellowed to Rockne.

"Yes, sir. Just plain bull, sir," a wan Rockne, who was supporting Woodrow Wilson in the 1916 presidential race, replied, trying to cover his player's brashness.

The next day at West Point, the team appeared headed toward another memorable day on Cullum Field. Through nearly three quarters they held Oliphant and Army in check, allowing just two field goals, and led, 10-6. Back on the dirt floor of the Notre Dame gymnasium, the student body was gathered to hear the game's progress. Tim Galvin, one of the school's top orators, read the updates as they arrived on the ticker. "The outlook for the soldiers was as dark as the shades which were fast enveloping the historic plains," described the *New York Sun*. "Then the Army hearkened back to that November day in 1913 when a team from Notre Dame came here and amazed and demoralized a cadet eleven….Suddenly the West Pointers opened up a far-flung forward-passing attack…the passing game succeeded even beyond the wildest expectations of the Army and its adherents." The Cadets completed nine of 12 passes, three of which were caught and turned into touchdowns by Gene Vidal, the speedy South Dakotan. Oliphant's kicking kept Notre Dame bottled up, and the Army ran away with a 30-10 victory.

The following week, as the varsity sought redemption on a trip to Sioux Falls to play South Dakota, the freshmen traveled to Kalamazoo for a game with Western Normal. Gipp, who had been named captain of the freshman squad, scored his first Notre Dame touchdown, and the game was tied, 7-7, with only minutes left. Gipp had accounted 174 of 216 total yards for the Irish. Time was running out and Notre Dame had the ball on its 38-yard line when quarterback Frank Thomas called for a punt, seemingly the only logical play.

"Why settle for a tie," Gipp protested. "Let me try a drop kick."

"Forget it, just punt the ball," Thomas ordered.

Gipp lined up as if to punt, and Western safety Walter Olsen dropped back to receive. Olsen had already fielded a couple of 50-yard punts by Gipp, so he was plenty deep. Gipp took the snap, and with ease let the ball drop perfectly straight to the ground. The instant it make contact with the earth, he connected with a mighty kick. The ball soared high and far, toward the Western goal. Irish end Dave Hayes sprinted downfield toward Olsen. He was shocked to see Olsen turn his back, looking skyward. The ball continued to sail as if in orbit. Hayes, in a state of confusion, asked, "What happened?"

"The sonofagun drop-kicked," came Olsen's reply.

The ball cleanly split the uprights, giving the Notre Dame freshmen a dramatic 10-7 victory. Nobody in the recorded history of football had ever drop-kicked a ball that far for three points. To assistant coach Rockne, who closely studied the strengths and weaknesses of each Notre Dame football player, Gipp represented an extraordinary, and unusual, talent. The game just seemed to come easy to him. He didn't appear to strain or even exert much energy. This was foreign to Rockne, who as an athlete had to fight mightily to extract every ounce of athleticism from his 5-foot-8, 165-pound frame. What could Gipp possibly do, Rockne wondered, if he were properly motivated? Certainly, the young coach figured, he could help the varsity avoid embarrassments such as the loss at Army.

Though Gipp's feat spread quickly in news accounts and conversations around the country, Gipp showed little emotion over his achievement. "Where another boy would be flushed in triumph," Rockne would note, "this youngster took congratulations calmly. Gipp had the superb personal policy of being indifferent to everything." Rockne invited Gipp to spend some time in practice with the varsity, and the player's only response was, "All right, if you think I can do any good." The varsity recovered from the Army loss to throttle South Dakota, 21-0. Buoyed by a rooting section of students in a university-organized trip to East Lansing, the Irish downed the Michigan Aggies, 14-0. Next up was a 46-0 thrashing of Alma. The *South Bend News-Times* described the game, saying, "Assistant Coach Rockne, who handled the Notre Dame team from the bench, sent in a team comprised entirely of substitutes at the start of the game and he allowed only four regulars to enter the contest at all."

The Irish had just a couple of days to prepare for their final game—the Thanksgiving Day battle with Nebraska at Lincoln. Harper again had to miss the game, as he was headed to Chicago for the Western Conference meetings, where he hoped to interest one of the league schools in a game for 1917. He succeeded in scheduling Wisconsin, the first game Notre Dame would play against a conference team since the 1909 victory at Michigan. With Rockne at the helm, the blue and gold ventured into the hostile territory of Lincoln, where anti-Catholic sentiment was growing and citizens' support of the Huskers was intense. The Irish seemed intent on not letting the game come down to a single kick, as had the first meeting a year earlier. With the campus essentially closed for the holiday, a large crowd of students gathered in front of Jimmie and Goat's cigar store to hear the returns of the game. When it was over, Notre Dame celebrated a 20-0 victory, sweet revenge for 1915, and "the crowd gathered in the center of the square and led by Andy McDonough cheered for half an hour." The final mark for the season stood at eight wins, all by shutout, along with the loss to Army. Notre Dame scored 293 total points to 30 for the opposition. The Harper-Rockne machine was on a roll.

Rockne's role was rapidly approaching more of a co-coach with Harper. Many news stories covering the Irish mentioned both equally. Harper gave his assistant great latitude in training the players and running long, challenging practices. Rockne took naturally to the work, demanding great effort from the players in repeating plays until they approached perfection. In his first several seasons as Harper's assistant, Rockne showed every sign of being capable of running his own program. Age was not a precluding factor—several former Notre Dame footballers were out in the field as head coaches immediately following their playing days. Harper, for his part, wrote to athletic leaders at not only Wabash but larger schools such as Kansas and Iowa State recommending his assistant for a head coaching job. "I think he has the making of the best coach of any young fellow I have ever known," Harper said in one of his letters. But no offer was made, and Rockne remained at Notre Dame with at a raise to $1,500 per year, and his work as head track coach and prep instructor in chemistry was factored into that salary. He was able to supplement his pay by continuing to coach semi-pro teams, and even on rare occasions play in a game. While wanting to provide as well as possible for Bonnie and young Billy, Rockne also just enjoyed the camaraderie he found in his athletic teams. As a coach, he was starting to feel special pride whenever one of "his boys" achieved a notable feat—especially if the odds had been against him in any way.

So, when the returning lettermen for 1917 elected quarterback Jim Phelan as their captain, it was a moment that warmed Rockne's heart. Phelan rose to prominence in the fall of 1914 as the quarterback of the St. Joseph interhall team. Going up against a much heavier Brownson team, Phelan kept the opponent at bay for three quarters with his superior kicking, all the while suffering from a broken collarbone. It became the stuff of legend in the annals of interhall football. On the varsity in 1915, Phelan stepped in where needed the most, replacing Dutch Bergman at left halfback. And in 1916, he shrugged off illness and injury to become a respected signal-caller. Phelan would operate with a significant addition to his 1917 backfield: second-year man George Gipp.

After the fall of 1916, Gipp returned home to enjoy a vacation, doing some hunting with buddy Angelo Stappas. Mostly, however, he played pool and poker, earning substantial winnings, which he promptly gave away, making it a bright holiday for those in need. When it came time to return to South Bend, he was again without funds, and another collection was taken to buy Gipp a train ticket. Back on campus, Gipp briefly tried his hand at basketball and track, and then he reported for baseball, which he still considered his primary sport. But his Notre Dame baseball career lasted just one game. In the late innings, he was instructed to bunt, and instead swung away, blasting a long home run. He is reported to have reasoned, "It's too hot to run the bases today." By the next day, he turned in his uniform and quit the team. The action was duly noted by baseball Coach Jess Harper, who pondered what Gipp's actions meant should he show up for football. Rockne, too, wondered how this seeming penchant to quit so easily would play out on the football field, where dogged effort was the order of the day. He hoped that Gipp, if he stayed at Notre Dame, would mature.

Forming next fall's team wasn't the primary concern, as the nation had finally formally entered the great war raging across the Atlantic. Woodrow Wilson had ridden to reelection in 1916 with the slogan, "He kept us out of war." However, when Germany announced its intentions to resume submarine warfare in the Atlantic in spring 1917, Wilson called Congress into a special session on April 2, 1917. He asked the special joint session to declare war on the German Empire. "We have no selfish ends to serve," he said. He claimed the war would "make the world safe for democracy" and later that it would be a "war to end war." On Good Friday, April 6, 1917, the U.S. Senate voted 82-6 for a war resolution. Included among the handful of no votes was Wisconsin Senator Robert M. LaFollette, who would later run for president on the newly formed Progressive Party in 1924. In the House, the declaration passed 373-50. Almost all of the opposition came from those representing districts in the West and the Midwest. By year's end, nearly 600 Notre Dame students were in the Armed Forces fighting overseas.

The Draft Act was signed into law in May 1917, which fueled anti-war sentiment among many Americans. The grinding horrors of the stalemate that developed along the Western Front in Belgium and France added to American resistance. Newspaper and magazine accounts, illustrated with battlefield photography, depicted the soldiers mired in trenches, confined by barbed wire and exploding shells. Terre Haute, Indiana native Eugene V. Debs, the fiery orator who had been arrested for his role in the Pullman Railroad Strike of 1888, ended his political retirement to oppose U.S. entry into the European conflict.

Eventually Debs would be jailed for violation of the Espionage and Sedition Acts, enacted in 1917-1918, for a speech he gave in Canton, Ohio on a hot June afternoon in 1918. He told the crowd: "They have always taught you that it is your patriotic duty to go to war and to have yourselves slaughtered at command…And here let me state a fact—and it cannot be repeated too often: the working class who fight the battles, the working class who make the sacrifices, the working class who shed the blood, the working class who furnish the corpses, the working class have never yet had a voice in declaring war."

War would come to Notre Dame, even though it was but one of many problems confronting Father Cavanaugh. Former president Father Andrew J. Morrissey, serving as Holy Cross provincial, had taken ill. Cavanaugh's trusted aid, Father Matthew Walsh, who had served as vice president since 1911, was one of eight Notre Dame priests to volunteer as chaplains for the war. The burden of decision-making was now almost exclusively on Cavanaugh's shoulders for both the school and the province. Added to that was the growing tensions between Ireland and Great Britain. A son of Irish immigrants, Cavanaugh was deeply saddened by the British response to the Easter Rising of 1916, in which the Irish volunteers, now explicitly declaring a republic, launched an insurrection whose aim was to end British rule and to found an Irish Republic. The rising, in which more than four hundred people died, was almost entirely confined to Dublin and was put down within a week. Cavanaugh remained hostile toward all things British even as the United States was aligning with Great

Britain over action in Europe.

But once war was declared, Cavanaugh threw his support behind the efforts and announced that any student enlisting and called up to serve during a term would receive full credit for that term. He described himself as a "red hot American through and through" and eventually consented to the establishment of a Student Army Training Corps (SATC) on campus in 1918 to make up for revenue loss as enrollment dropped by nearly a third during the 1917-18 school year. Nearly 700 soldier-students were assigned to Notre Dame with the SATC, many of whom were not Catholic and few of whom had been subjected to the sort of disciplined behavior expected of Notre Dame men. Cavanaugh found the money received offset by annoying disturbances. His bedroom was directly under one of the soldier-student dormitory areas, and Cavanaugh complained bitterly about the noise and carousing of the soldier-students.

Despite all the changes, it appeared as if football would continue in somewhat of a normal fashion—except for the fact that Rockne's star was missing in action. Gipp spent the summer of 1917 back in Laurium playing for the town team in the Trolley League. In early August, the *Daily Mining Gazette* published a list of 42 young men, including Gipp, who were to be inducted into the Army in September. But when a train departed for an Army installation in Battle Creek, Michigan, Gipp was not on board. He continued to play ball for Laurium and drove a dump truck for Roehm Construction. Classes and football practice began at Notre Dame, and the *South Bend Tribune* reported, "Both Harper and Rockne presume at this time that Gipp must be in the Army." Apparently, there had been no communication between the coaches and their presumed star player.

Gipp may have been playing semi-pro baseball while the fall term at Notre Dame began. One story had Rockne making a trip to Kenosha, Wisconsin to retrieve his missing star. "Gipp resisted Rockne's usual psychological devices and laughed off the coach's petulant sarcasm. Rockne dealt with Gipp by being completely straightforward. 'We need you in the backfield, George.'" To which Gipp was said to reply, "Since you put it that way, Rock, when does the next train leave?" However, Gipp didn't make it in time for the first two games—a 55-0 smashing of Kalamazoo and a scoreless tie at Wisconsin. Next up was Notre Dame's third trip to Nebraska, scheduled much earlier in the season this time, October

20. Gipp had little time to prepare, and the coaches did not start him; he played about half the game. Hugo Otopalik, a heavy Nebraska back, plunged over for the game's only score. In the third quarter, Gipp broke loose for a 30-yard run to the Nebraska 10. But Notre Dame was intercepted on the next play and never threatened again, losing 7-0.

Notre Dame clobbered South Dakota, 40-0, at Cartier Field the next week, with Gipp making several long runs. His defensive play stood out, though. The South Dakota center, Carl Hoy, said Gipp "would knock you down with a vicious tackle and then, after helping you up, apologize for hitting you so hard." Phelan was another star for the Irish, playing with the knowledge that he was scheduled to leave immediately after the game for his military deployment. Backup quarterback Joe Brandy led the Irish into their annual battle at West Point. In a defensive tussle, Army held a 2-0 lead late in the fourth quarter, but Brandy engineered a drive that crept to the Army 5. The soldiers, looking for Gipp to get the call, were caught off guard by a faking Brandy, who strolled into the end zone. Notre Dame won, 7-2.

The next week Notre Dame made its first trip to Sioux City, Iowa to face Morningside College. Morningside had rolled over three weak opponents by a count of 174-7, and the previous season had battled South Dakota to a scoreless tie and lost only 7-0 to Iowa A&M. Still, Notre Dame was a heavy favorite, and when Gipp circled right end on the first play from scrimmage, it looked like it could be the first of many scores. But before he could reach the end zone, Gipp was knocked out of bounds by two Morningside players and went crashing into a steel fence post that mysteriously had been temporarily erected for the game. Gipp winced in pain as he lay on the ground, his ankle broken. Horace Wulf, one of the players who hit him said, "I'm sorry, boy, I hope it isn't bad." To which Gipp replied, "Forget it, pal, you had to come in. It's all in the game." Gipp spent the next 11 days in Sioux City's St. Vincent Hospital. He missed Notre Dame's final two games—a 23-0 pasting of the Michigan Aggies, and a 3-0 thriller at Washington & Jefferson. When Gipp returned to South Bend, he promptly dropped out of school and headed home. In January, still limping, he went before the Draft Board in Laurium for a physical exam, and was given a six-month deferment.

Notre Dame celebrated a 6-1-1 season in which the Irish allowed just nine points—the touchdown in the loss to Nebraska, and the safety against Army. Rockne again received high praise for his coaching role. Increasingly, he had become the voice and face of the football team, acting as Harper's spokesman to the press in discussing the schedule and Notre Dame's chances in upcoming games. Rockne also kept a toe in the local semi-pro game, but had scaled back after the embarrassment of Notre Dame players on his Muessel team in 1914. For 1917, Rockne agreed to coach the Jolly Fellows Club; travel for Notre Dame games limited his time. He considered installing the Notre Dame shift with the JFC, but decided against it when he determined it would required too much time to teach and adjust. The team won nine and lost two, with one of the losses coming to the Pine Village team of Lafayette, Indiana, featuring former Irish stars Deak Jones and Gus Dorais. One report noted, "The South Bend line was strong on defense and held their men for downs a good many times. With Knute Rockne's coaching, they should improve wonderfully."

Michigan Agricultural College, a frequent foe of Notre Dame, had been so impressed by Rockne's coaching style that they offered him the position of head coach. Rockne gave a verbal commitment to go to East Lansing. But again, an unexpected turn developed before anything was formalized. Jesse Harper, who in five seasons had held the Notre Dame football coaching job longer than anyone before him and compiled a sterling record of 34-5-1, was leaving the profession to take over his family's farming and oil operation in Kansas. Harper's father-in-law, who operated the sprawling, 30,000-acre Ranch of the Alamos, had died suddenly, and the family needed stable leadership. Harper also felt uncertain about the future of college athletics; there was already some talk of cancelling the 1918 season due to the war effort. He was also weary of the pressure beginning to build—to schedule stronger teams and then to win those games. The time appeared right for Harper to try a new profession.

In early 1918, Harper announced that upon completion of the baseball season, he would leave Notre Dame. He lobbied hard for Rockne to be named coach. Initially, Father Cavanaugh wasn't sold. He had already received word from what he called "many well-known coaches" inquiring about replacing Harper. Notre Dame athletics had risen to a level of prominence to attract such candidates. In one of their meetings, Harper finally let Cavanaugh know that, a couple of years earlier, he promised Rockne when the time came for Harper to leave, the job would be Rockne's. "Well, Jess," responded the president, "if you promised it to him, we surely will have to offer him the job, won't we?"

Harper had done more for Notre Dame football than merely improve the schedule. He had recruited, trained, and ultimately groomed his successor—a man Harper was convinced could build further on a rock-solid coaching foundation that had been laid by Walter Camp, brought west by Amos Alonzo Stagg, and taught to Harper. The moment was now Rockne's. Shortly after his 30th birthday in early March, wife Bonnie pregnant with their second child, Knute Rockne signed a one-year contract for $5,000 to become Notre Dame's athletic director and head football coach. The Norse Protestant would now have control over an increasingly important segment of the campus of the Holy Cross fathers. The *Scholastic* had no doubt as to Rockne's readiness for the position. They remembered Rockne, the Notre Dame student, who knew first-hand the expectation of those who attended here. They had witnessed his football skill on display in multiple games of importance, and they had watched Rockne the track coach transfer his love of running and jumping to those who had never before participated in the sport:

> Rockne seems to have the ability to impart his knowledge of the game in such a way that the man he is instructing immediately grasps what he is being told…Rockne has been an unprecedented success thus far because he is an insidious student of human nature. He tries to understand thoroughly each man who he is instructing. He counts each athlete as his personal friend and his assistance does not stop when the athlete goes into civilian attire. He has been paid back a thousand times in increased effort for all the pains he has taken with his men.

It was almost impossible for Rockne to calculate just how his first effort to lead a football team would unfold, especially because duties as head track coach remained Rockne's focus in spring. The Notre Dame campus, as much as any, showed the effects of war. Enrollment was down as young men began serving the military. The impact on sporting teams was also unavoidable, and Rockne oversaw a decimated track squad.

All four runners on his champion two-mile relay team from 1917—Cy Kasper, Pete Noonan, Andy McDonough, and Ed Meehan—were now in the service; Lt. Meehan with Headquarters Company 137, Field Artillery at Camp Shelby. Coach Rockne put out an impassioned appeal to any student. Never one to shirk the opportunity to help train young men in running track, Rockne gladly accepted the call to help the prep school with its athletic endeavors.

On the varsity level, Rockne's work with the track team that season was perhaps his finest hour as a Notre Dame coach to date. He cobbled together a squad around four returning monogram men, attracting a number of interhall athletes and underclassmen, to make a respectable showing in meets with Illinois and Michigan and the always important Drake Relays. Without an individual standout performer or relay team, he knew motivation and adapting talent was crucial. Among Rockne's special gifts was the ability to connect with each man where he was in his development—be it in academics, athletics, or otherwise. Perhaps it was his relative maturity when entering the university at age 22, for Rockne was aware of the traits needed for success. Rockne could recognize and understand when a man struggled with a particular challenge; he seemed to have an innate sense of whether to cajole, needle, reprimand, or comfort the individual. Far beyond mere chalkboard strategy, Rockne understood a coach's job often entailed that of mentor, father, counselor, friend. The *Scholastic's* season review noted:

> Notre Dame may well feel proud of Coach Rockne, the man who made the track team what it was. With only two men of notable record to begin with at the opening of the season, he brought the best out of the material left him, and saved Notre Dame from utter rout on the cinder path. Coach Rockne is an inspiration to his men. He has an effective method all his own of training men. He succeeds because his men like him, and are always willing to break their necks for him.

# 16

## A Year Unlike Any Other

By early 1918, the Great War was impossible to ignore. Young American men by the hundreds of thousands answered the call to serve their country, either training at a U.S. base or fighting on the European front lines. Around the country, citizens were inundated with posters of a finger-pointing portrait of Uncle Sam proclaiming, "I Want You." Entertainment celebrities such as Hollywood's Douglas Fairbanks, starlet Mary Pickford, international opera star Enrico Caruso, and vaudevillian Al Jolson led coast-to-coast Liberty Loan rallies to help finance the war effort, aided by sports idols Ty Cobb and Babe Ruth. In South Bend, Liberty Loan parade participants included Coaches Rockne and Harper and the Knights of Columbus. Wherever held, these rallies drew large crowds; employees were even given time off to attend. Rockne watched the war unfold and affect his personal and professional life in a way he could not have envisioned even a year earlier. Married, and a father, the 30-year-old Rockne was not part of the front-line military effort; yet so many of friends and compatriots were.

His former passing-combo partner Gus Dorais had entered the Third Officers Training Camp at Fort Dodge, Iowa, where old pal Grover Malone was also stationed. Rupe Mills, the all-around athlete who had gone on to play first base for the Newark Feds, was in Officers Training at Camp McClellan in Alabama. Charlie Bachman, who had been coaching track and swimming and assisting with football at DePauw University, enlisted in the Navy and was sent to Great Lakes Training Station just north of Chicago. The Station sent out a publicity release, noting that Bachman "weight in the Navy at 205 pounds, and expected to put on a little more as soon as he gets going in the work. (His supervising ensign) has made Charlie the master-at-arms of his company—a bouncer in the Navy— and predicts that no trouble will start for a few days at least." Chet Grant, backup quarterback for the 1917 Irish, distinguished himself at the same position for the Camp Shelby team at Hattiesburg, Mississippi and quickly rose from private to a first lieutenant. Joe Gargan, Rockne's old corner man in boxing, was also a lieutenant, among several Notre Dame men who ate Christmas dinner in France. Joe Byrne, one of Rockne's closest friends, was now Sgt. Byrne, also headed to France. Joe Pliska, his old backfield mate, was in Officers Training at Fort Sheridan near Chicago.

Although the departure of friends brought its own sense of loss, the reality of young men dying was all too real for those at Our Lady's University. The first Notre Dame man killed in service to his country was Joseph Archer Smith, who died in an automobile accident while on duty at Camp Dodge. And it was not only the war effort that brought sadness. Students, and especially football and baseball players on campus, were stunned upon their returned from Christmas vacation in January 1918 to learn of the death of Tom Spalding and his cousin Mary Simms, a student at St. Mary's. Spalding, a popular student of "cheery disposition and quiet humor" and member of the football and baseball teams, was returning to his home in Springfield, Kentucky, and was traveling with Mary on the Louisville and Nashville Railroad, when he lost his life in a horrible train wreck in Shepherdsville, Kentucky, that killed more than 50 people on December 20. "Expressions of sorrow and regret on the lips of students returning to the University showed how warmly they loved him and how keenly they feel his loss," the *Scholastic* reported.

Rockne, the son of an immigrant, had learned at an early age that life brought triumph and defeat, sadness and joy. Yet his life was a testament to optimism for the future. His theatrical background provided just the spark needed to help lift campus spirits. Basil Stanley, a former player, was suffering from football injuries and needed financial assistance to cover daily living expenses. So Rockne organized a Stanley Benefit Vaudeville night on campus, featuring numerous athletes and other students. It raised more than $400 for the fund and provided a brief respite from the current world problems. Comedians, acrobats, singers, dancers—everyone did what they could, and "the performance was a scream from first to last." Rockne himself, ever the performer, took a turn in a sketch called "Boys Will Be Boys."

As the conflict intensified, the War Department used college campuses to recruit men for the air service. It sent press articles depicting the high level of man needed for flying, and the *Scholastic*, similar to most college publications, dutifully published them in prominent positions:

> College men are needed for the Air Service. There, of all places, they are best suited to serve. There they can use the education and the physique that their peculiar advantages have given them; there they can express their own individuality and be their own directing general…Warfare in the clouds has become as specialized in the last four months as that on land. It is fought in different strata by different planes….The one greatest of all places for real airmen is in the colleges. There indeed is the flower of the country, men who have received much, owe much.

By commencement in 1918, nearly 300 Notre Dame men who had been enrolled in the 1916-17 and 1917-18 school years had enlisted in the military; many alumni were also serving. The *Scholastic* helped tell their stories, publishing intact letters sent by former students back to priests and other professors at Notre Dame, under the heading "Letters from Camp." Former footballer Ray Miller was now Lieutenant-Adjutant of the 135th Machine Gun Battalion at Camp Shelby in Alabama. He wrote of his amazement when the camp's new chaplain reported to him:

> A few days ago…a tall man in the olive drab overcoat and barracks cap whom only at second glance I recognized as none other than Father Walsh, our vice president at old N.D. walked into the office to say: 'Here I am, your chaplain—where are you

going to put me?

Can you imagine me, who used to come shivering into Father Walsh's room for permission to 'go to the dentist'—in reality to go to the Orpheum—being now his superior officer? Can you imagine Father Walsh now coming to me for permission to go to town? Can you imagine Ray Miller, who 'subbed it' on the football team when 'Eich' was a whirlwind, now being the superior officer of the vice president of Notre Dame, with authority to give or refuse him 'per.'

Miller added this about the service of his fellow Fighting Irish: "I have come to the conclusion that it is the loyalty and patriotism Notre Dame instills into her students that has caused them to respond so numerously and so enthusiastically to the country's call."

Stan Cofall, the star back of the 1917 football squad, wrote from the 330 Battalion Light Tank Corps from Gettysburg, Pennsylvania: "Many times have I wished that I could be taken back four years so that I might live over again those four years at Notre Dame. Now we are engaged in something mighty serious; the thought of it rather takes the liveliness out of a fellow. Anyhow, we have that privilege of looking back to those happy days." And Joe Gargan sent back long, detailed letters describing the action on the front lines in France. Commanding a detail of six Americans and six Frenchmen crawling out well beyond their "wire" into no man's land at night, when it was impossible to distinguish anything in the darkness; encountering and "knocking off" Germans, finding out later that they had planned a raid on Gargan's location; trenches that were filled with "mud up to our knees" and thousands of rats "running in all directions and squealing frightfully."

Gargan, like many, wrote wistfully of the Notre Dame days, noting that "I long to be back again where I could go in and bounce a big nickel off the plate glass at Hullie and Mike's and, if there was a crowd around, ask for 'Naturals' and have them slip me a pack of 'Favorites.'"

But, as great a contrast as many made between the sylvan campus and the locales of the world's conflagration, there was also a special link between the discipline and development of young men at an institution committed to developing strong, intelligent men such as Notre Dame, and the service needed by the United States. Charles Call, one of the mainstays of Rockne's make-do track squads, penned an eloquent ode to the Notre Dame athlete-soldier a few weeks before his graduation:

This world war has proved a number of things but none more emphatically than that intercollegiate athletics, often as they have been questioned in time of peace, have made sinewy and adroit the arm of a nation hastening to the conflict of battle. Greater than that of any other group of athletes has been the service of the college-bred athlete since the United States entered this war last April. Not having learned to capitalize his skill or strength as his professional brethren, he was the first to rush to the colors when Uncle Sam assumed the gigantic task of warring with the Kaiser. In the pink of condition, just entering that decade in a young man's life when mind and muscle coordinate for the highest efficiency, he hurried to his biggest game. Taught many a time the value of a good beginning in any athletic event he got away with a flying start, and set the pace for the representatives of other bodies of men who followed after him.

As a corollary of the prominent part intercollegiate athletics in general have taken in this game of games, Notre Dame athletes have more than held their own with the competitors of their college days. Endowed physically better than most men, coached to do big things in a big way, accustomed to accomplish the thing they set out to do, the brawny Notre Dame men promptly packed away with the camphor balls their monograms and put on the khaki tendered them by Uncle Sam. Their fitness was soon recognized. The first officers' reserve camps were no sooner history than a large number of Notre Dame men were lieutenants. Brilliant service, and steady promotion have marked their careers thus far, but no one can but believe that these men habituated to fight hard till the whistle blows are just preparing for far greater work to come.

Military men have often commented upon the readiness and eagerness of the Notre Dame man for the difficult tasks in the service. They were not petted or privileged while in school; they ask no particular favors now. Used to discipline throughout their years in college, they find army regulations no great burden now. Fed on competition during their years at school, they welcome the chance to spar for position with their fellowmen in the army today. Above all they fight, fight with that relentlessness that asks no quarter and gives none, fight with that good old Celtic dash that made them the wonders of the athletic world, fight because they like to fight, fight because it is their duty to fight.

Go on, men of Notre Dame, Uncle Sam has greater honors in store for you.

From his study of ancient culture, Rockne knew that physical preparedness was more than simply an individual expression; the Greeks valued physical development as a civic duty, at least in part as it related to defending one's country. Rockne recognized a real Notre Dame man, a fully developed Notre Dame man—be he on the front lines in Europe, at a military training camp in some distant state, or still on the campus—had all the attributes of physical and mental toughness needed for any kind of skirmish, on a battlefield, gridiron, or cinder track. Athletics, the coach reasoned, could be used as a means to call out and develop a man's full potential.

Summer brought a mixture of emotions for Rockne. Bonnie, pregnant and anticipating an August delivery of their second child, understood Knute's need to fulfill his patriotic duties. She would miss his help with the daily household chores as well as watching the joy he exhibited playing with young Billy. For Rockne's military service tour, he would serve as director of athletics at Fort Sheridan, just north of Chicago. His task was to keep the servicemen in shape and physically ready for battle. It was an obvious setting for a man who had written his civil service exam on the topic of increased need for naval defense after the 1905 the Russo-Japanese war and who had also spent the last eight years strengthening the physical condition of America's youth.

The 1918 football schedule, announced in early spring, offered what appeared to be an appealing slate of games, even as war left an uncertainty to anything, including football. The high point would be the November 2 contest at West Point. The Irish would again travel to Nebraska, on October 19; host the Great Lakes Training Station team on November 9; and finish the season November 23 by renewing their rivalry with Purdue, which had been on hiatus since 1907 due to the Western Conference boycott of the Fighting Irish. Other key battles included Washington & Jefferson at home, and Michigan Agricultural at Lansing. Yet, he wondered just how the influence of war would impact the type of squad he would send out on the gridiron in his first year as head coach.

But there was precious little time to speculate; the war's impact continued to swirl around the young men of Notre Dame, and indeed, all citizens of the nation, as they hoped and prayed for a speedy resolution to the hostilities. The summer of 1918 saw one of Notre Dame's most promising athletes back home in Calumet, Michigan playing pool and high-stakes poker, and a little town-team baseball. George Gipp's ankle had healed, and he was starting to feel like himself again. With his military deferment expiring, life back at college held a certain appeal. But with a return trip to Notre Dame apparent, he wanted some familiar company. "Why don't you come down to Notre Dame and play football," Gipp suggested to his old pal, Fred "Ojay" Larson. "If we don't kill you by the time the season is over, then join the Army."

Larson agreed, and together, he, Gipp, and Dolly Gray approached another former Calumet high teammate, Heartley "Hunk" Anderson. They were armed with the current *Dome* yearbook, and when Anderson flipped through its pages, he noticed a large number of Roman collars.

"Is this place Catholic?" Hunk asked, knowing full well it was.

"Yep," replied Gipp. "Just remember—when in Rome, do as the Romans do."

Anderson protested that he wouldn't have the money to attend college, but Gipp assured him that Rockne would help him secure a campus job. Hunk's dad, William J. Anderson, was a Canadian native who worked his entire career for railroads. He had been a yardmaster in Ontario when he was transferred to Calumet to work as a brakeman. It was a chance to establish a home, and he took the job. The family had its financial hardships, as did many in the area. Every once in a while, the elder Anderson would bring home some discarded railroad ties he got from the section foreman. Father and son would cut them up, each on one end of a cross-cut saw; the wood provided heat for the simple frame house on Tamarack Hill, and for cooking all winter.

The thought of attending a prestigious college such as Notre Dame was beyond Hunk's imagination. He hoped some college was possible, especially after he was named to Michigan's all-state team as a senior at Calumet. His sister was enrolled at Marquette Normal, studying to become a teacher, and any financial assistance the parents could afford would first go to her. Hunk had doubts whether his father, a dedicated Mason whose family belonged to the Presbyterian Church in Calumet, would accept his son attending a Catholic university. But that worry appeared to be unfounded. "I don't care if you come back a priest," said his father. "Just get an education."

Gipp and Larson traveled to Notre Dame a few days before the semester began. Anderson was working in Houghton, chauffeuring for wealthy businessman Skif Sheldon, who owned a 12-cylinder Packard and a Pierce Arrow. Hunk had just finished a shift when a telegram arrived from Gipp. "Come on down, everything's OK—Gipp." Hunk let out a war hoop. He was on his way to college. When Anderson arrived at the Grand Trunk station in downtown South Bend, Gipp and Larson were waiting. Rockne, said Gipp, was finishing lunch at Hullie and Mike's, and would be by in a minute. When the coach appeared, Gipp said, "Coach, this is Hunk Anderson, the fellow I was telling you about." Rockne rolled his cigar to the side of his mouth and eyed Anderson carefully.

"What position do you play?" the coach inquired.

"Fullback?" came the response. "We don't need fullbacks. We need guards."

"Well, coach," Anderson said, thinking quickly. "You're looking at the best guard you'll ever see."

"I hope so," said Rockne. "Of course, if you have the natural ability that George says you have, we can teach you."

Rockne seemed pleased with the exchange, winked at Gipp and said, "See ya on campus."

Gipp and Larson helped Hunk with his huge trunk, wrestling it into a cab for the ride to campus. It was then Gipp offered Hunk this advice, which always stuck with Anderson: "Hunk, you may have a lot of friends here, but remember, they're after the same job. Anytime you have that uniform on and somebody is in front of you, knock 'em down on their fanny…and if they get up, knock 'em down again."

The heavy toll of the war weighed upon Father Cavanaugh as he addressed the student body in his sermon at the welcoming Mass for students and staff in September 1918. "Never before has the University taken up its work in such disturbed and bewildering conditions," he said. "Behold how are the times changed and out of joint. The University transformed into a barracks; the gentle masters become pedagogues of war; the University ideal no longer the scholar, but the soldier! No more do poets write their radiant dreams and apocalyptic visions in letters of fire and in words of measured music, but, like the deathless Joyce Kilmer, they dramatize them by shedding their blood on the battlefields of France." Cavanaugh blamed the war on the modernism that was creeping into Western Civilization as evident by the "paganism and irreligion rampant in the press, in litera- ture and in societies was nowhere so rampant as in the Universities. In a word, Christianity had ceased to be a vital force in the lives of millions of people, in nearly every country of Christendom. Then came this brutal, barbarous war, originating in the sins and lusts, the plottings and the tyr- annies of so called Christian men."

He cautioned the young men, as he had two days earlier in a general session, to avoid the temptations of misconduct, whether it be on the streetcars, in downtown South Bend, or about campus. Cavanaugh con- cluded by recounting the letter he had received from one Notre Dame man who said that every time he shot a bullet into the heart of an enemy he whispered a prayer for that soldier, "because there are no enemies after death."

The next day, students began their routine of studies and athletics— which now included the Student Army Training Corp, now firmly en- trenched on Notre Dame's campus. Some cynics called it "Safe At The College." Anderson's campus job, similar to those of other freshman ath- letes, consisted of serving in the mess hall and pushing carts full of food. The SATC training corps drilled its members in military tradition, science,

217

and tactics. It was a grueling routine; students rose at 5:30 a.m. and drilled for 90 minutes before breakfast. After a few sessions, with the start of football approaching, Gipp took his chances and dropped out of the program. Larson and Anderson continued on.

That September, Knute Rockne assumed his position as head football coach at Notre Dame, beginning fall workouts 11 days in advance of the opening game. If ever Rockne had allowed himself the luxury of thinking ahead to what the first days of head coaching would be like, surely what was playing out in front of him was not part of that dream. Camp, Stagg, Harper; had any of them really faced such a challenge? Now, there were no assistant coaches; Rockne would assume every role, including that of equipment manager, giving each man his suit. As trainer, Rockne would travel with a roll of tape and bottle of iodine in his pocket. Would there be sufficient time to train and develop the physical and mental conditioning of the young men in his charge, he wondered?

Without a line coach, Rockne was quick to develop Hunk Anderson's potential. Rockne came up to him to demonstrate how to execute a certain blocking technique. He then instructed Hunk to give it a try; Rockne would stand in as the opponent. Don't worry, Rockne advised; in fact, he told Anderson to go the drill at full speed. Hunk complied, and knocked Rockne onto his backside. The coach insisted Hunk do it five more times, and each play had the same result. A first-year player from the U.P. had won a starting guard position. A head coach demonstrated that developing a young player's skills and confidence was more important than the coach's physical comfort. The rosters—made thin by the war effort—consisted in large part of first-year men. Notre Dame joined other colleges in taking advantage of relaxed freshmen eligibility rules for campuses which hosted the SATC. As all the men were in the service of the military through SATC, it followed that all should be given equal standing to represent their school in varsity play. Among those newly arrived for Rockne's opening scrimmage on September 19 were a handful of first years who, by one account, "made themselves felt in the scrimmage and attracted Rockne's notice." They included yet another player from the Upper Peninsula, a lineman from Ironwood, Michigan, named Romanus "Peaches" Nadolney, and a back from Green Bay, Wisconsin by the name of Earl "Curly" Lambeau.

As if player shortages weren't enough to cause headaches for a new coach, scheduling woes soon surfaced. It was announced that the game with Washington & Jefferson was dropped, "owing to the government request to cancel all long trips." A possible replacement game might be scheduled with Camp Custer near Kalamazoo. The team was still allowed to make the trip to Cleveland for the September 28 opener with Case Tech, where Rockne fielded a team that was the greenest and lightest in anyone's memory at Notre Dame.

After Case took an early 6-0 lead, Gipp and Pete Bahan started to take control of the game. They drove the Irish deep into Case territory, where Lambeau crashed over the line to tie the game. In the third quarter, Gipp scored twice, and Notre Dame cruised to a 26-6 victory. "The team as a whole was ragged," Rockne said after the game. "Nevertheless, this team, despite its light weight has all the spirit and fight that any of the older and heavier teams had. The great asset of this year's team is its fighting spirit, which never lagged all during the game Saturday."

But any momentum from the opening victory was short-lived. By the first week of October, the football season was in turmoil. "Never before at Notre Dame have athletics been at such a standstill," one report noted. There were problems and delays getting Notre Dame students success-fully into the SATC. The transfer orders from each man's home draft board to the one in South Bend were so slow in arriving that "most of the fellows have to look on while a comparatively small number are assigned quarters and given military drill. They hang around the gymnasium and Corby hall in the hope of getting word from their home boards," reported the *News-Times*.

The football schedule was also disintegrating. In addition to Washington & Jefferson, the trip to West Point was now canceled, owing again to the government's request to cancel all games in which overnight travel was involved. The Nebraska game was still on the schedule; only one morning drill would be missed by those traveling, and Rockne arranged to replace that session by giving a two-hour presentation on the train, describing his summer experiences at Fort Sheridan. Later in the week, Kalamazoo College canceled its scheduled October 5 game at Notre Dame, as it was suffering similar delays in getting its men into the SATC. Rockne was now in a full scramble, hoping to find a military team to come to campus on

October 12. Years of preparation and diligent service as a student-athlete, captain, and assistant coach had put Rockne into the position of guiding Notre Dame's entire athletic operation. Now, just weeks into his tenure, it had become something of a nightmare. The specter of war and death overwhelmed any sense of play on campus. And there was more darkness to come.

Throughout 1918, a somber mood had overtaken the campus with the reports of the deaths of students and alumni in the Great War. In the fall, indications that the fighting might soon abate were reason for optimism. Yet the idea of celebration was short lived, as the impact of the nationwide epidemic of Spanish influenza reached the South Bend area by mid-October. It sometimes seemed as though one could not unwind the sorrow from the two events. As much as the agony of the war and the flu epidemic seemed linked, so too, was the cause and effect of one upon the other. In 1918, the Public Health Service had just begun to require state and local health departments to provide reports about diseases in their communities. The problem? Influenza wasn't a reportable disease. But in early March 1918, officials in Haskell County Kansas sent a worrisome report to the Public Health Service. Although these officials knew that influenza was not a reportable disease, they wanted the federal government to know that "18 cases of influenza of a severe type" had been reported there. During that time a young soldier named Dean Nilson came home to Haskell County from Camp Funston, part of the Fort Riley, Kansas military camp. Little did Nilson know that on March 4, 1918, a private at Funston—a cook—reported ill with influenza. Within three weeks more than 1,100 soldiers were sick enough to be hospitalized; 38 died. As Funston fed a constant stream of men to other American bases and to Europe, the killer virus began its trek around the world.

By October 1918, public gatherings in South Bend were banned for three weeks, schools were closed, and the influenza fatality lists were published daily in the *South Bend Tribune*. Before the epidemic slowed, more than 200 Notre Dame students would be afflicted; classes were canceled for days and at least nine students died. So serious was the epidemic at Notre Dame that Cavanaugh described its impact on the campus in a letter to a friend 10 months later as "the death of all human joy." South Bend was no different than other communities. Quarantines were imposed to prevent the spread of the disease. As the bodies mounted, funerals were held outdoors to protect mourners against the spread of the disease. The Great War claimed an estimated 16 million lives. The global influenza epidemic that began in 1918 killed an estimated 50 million people, approximately 650,000 in the United States.

Young John Boyer, the former bicycle delivery boy, South Bend resident, and student at Notre Dame, had his schooling interrupted when he registered for service in the Navy. He was stationed at the Great Lakes Naval Training Station in Chicago working as an orderly. He would later recount that when he reported for his shift, his sole task was to pull sheets over the bodies of the young boys who had died from the flu. It was an experience that would have profound impact on him. Upon his graduation from Notre Dame in 1920, Boyer would enter medical school in hopes of serving his fellow man.

On Thursday, October 10, Dr. Emil G. Freyermuth, head of the South Bend health department, ordered all churches, schools, theatres, and other public places of amusements closed, and prohibited public gatherings of any nature, including club meetings, lodge gatherings, and public dances effective midnight that night. In adjacent Mishawaka, it was reported that "any person to have a cold or cough or to be sick in any way, will not under any circumstances be allowed to congregate in any public place, moving picture shows, or schools. It is especially urged that any person who had a cold or any indication of influenza should remain at home." Almost daily, students and faculty at Notre Dame were being asked to pray for the repose of the soul of a victim of war or disease. LeGrande Hammond, who graduated with Rockne in 1913, died in Decatur, Michigan of influenza at age 27. Lt. George J. Ryan died in October of wounds received in France. Great sadness at the death of Carroll Hall resident Robert Corrigan was expressed after his death from pneumonia; Father Cavanaugh preached at the solemn requiem Mass. On campus, tamping down reports of influenza became a major endeavor. Father Cavanaugh took to the pages of the *Scholastic* with a letter to "check any wild rumors about sickness at the University." In it he said the deaths of two students at St. Joseph's Hospital on October 22 were not related to the illness of the 50 listed as sick on campus, whether those 50 were in the Infirmary, the Minims, or the SATC Hospital:

> At the present time there are just three very sick boys…we have had very little evidence of the presence of the so-called Spanish Influenza. This may be due to the fact that the Notre Dame boy, as a rule, is in exceptionally good shape physically…We have had four deaths this year out of a population of 1500 students. One was little "Bobbie" Corrigan. He was constitutionally weak and all of us knew he would never get through his youth. The others were Lester Burrill, William Conway and George Guilfoyle. Guilfoyle and Conway died this morning. They have been fighting a battle with pneumonia all week. I make this statement so as to prevent ignorance and malicious people from frightening the public needlessly and also, to clip the wings of sensation mongers.

Less than two weeks later, Father Cavanaugh was at his only sister's bedside in Leetonia, Ohio on November 5 as she succumbed to pneumonia. This came two days after the news of the death of Mary Farrell, wife of history Professor N.E. Farrell on November 3 at St. Joseph's Hospital of pneumonia. It was noted that influenza had set in days earlier.

The same Thursday that Dr. Freyermuth announced the closing of public buildings, Rockne released a revised football schedule that met the latest government requirements, which stated that no college teams could make any trips during October, and they could make no more than two trips in November. The Irish would host military teams from Municipal Pier October 19; Camp Custer, October 26; and Great Lakes, November 9. The Michigan Aggies would visit Cartier Field November 16, and away games were to be at Nebraska November 2 and Purdue November 23.

One report in the *South Bend News-Tribune* noted that the team "is getting better every day. Considering the disturbance of the daily schedule caused by the SATC and also the fact that Rockne has had a hard attack of grippe, which he is only now wearing off, wonders have been accomplished by him and the team." But that same week, the paper quoted

Rockne as wailing after a scrimmage: "They don't think. They don't think, and they can't learn signals." And, the paper noted, "old fans know what Rockne, of all coaches, thinks of a man who can't or won't think." Rockne and his men were greatly disappointed when the Municipal Pier game was canceled the week of the game, but vowed to go forward, determined to be in shape for the next opponent—whoever it might be. Eventually, the Camp Custer game would also fall to the travel restrictions, and the Nebraska game moved to Thanksgiving Day, November 28.

Rockne never ceased trying to secure opponents, and with just several days notice, he convinced Wabash College to agree to a game on November 2. At 5 a.m. that Saturday, a group of Fighting Irish boarded a train for Wabash, as the trip had to be completed within a single day. The game itself was no contest, Notre Dame winning 67-7. Gipp ran wild before taking himself out of the game for the second half. Meanwhile, signs were pointing to a possible end to the war. Headlines screamed, "Now Within Grasp of Allies Armies; Both Kaisers Ready to Go" and "German Army May Soon Hear Emperor Has Quit."

Next up was the game with Great Lakes Training Station. Rockne proclaimed that "the game will positively be played if they have to battle behind closed gates, although everything now indicates that the ban will be lifted and the public allowed to see this contest." Great Lakes would bring a team featuring several former college stars, including George Halas of Illinois, John "Paddy" Driscoll of Northwestern, Con Ecklund of Minnesota, and three familiar faces across the line—Notre Dame's own Charlie Bachman at center, and Emmet Keefe and "Deak" Jones at the guards. Before a large, boisterous crowd at Cartier Field, delighted to be watching football again and hopeful that the rumored end of the Great War was near, Gipp led the Irish on a long first-quarter drive and broke through off tackle for a touchdown. The lead held up until a 35-yard touchdown run by Driscoll in the third quarter. The game ended at 7-7, considered an excellent showing by Notre Dame against a more experienced, heavier eleven. "I am satisfied with the game," Rockne told reporters. "We went into the game like underdogs and gave them a good fight. The game shows we have as good a team as any in the west."

And the following Monday, November 11, thousands gathered in the streets of South Bend— as they did in city centers across the country—to celebrate the Armistice, making the downtown district "a living mass of laughing, singing, shouting noisemakers." A large gathering at Leeper Park enjoyed a huge bonfire, while bands played among the cheering crowd. All day long, impromptu parades of vehicles and pedestrians filled Main and Michigan streets, with celebrators waving flags and blowing horns and whistles. It would be the last mass gathering of 1918 in the area, as the Great Lakes game would be the final home football game of Notre Dame's abbreviated season. After the two games against military teams were canceled, Rockne attempted to convince the Michigan Aggies to visit Cartier Field, but to no avail. So he took his squad up to Lansing on November 16. In a hard-fought game played on a muddy field, the Irish fell, 13-7, with both Bahan and Gipp suffering injuries. Young Norman Barry took over in Gipp's spot, and one report called him "a lighter man, but wonderfully fast."

While Notre Dame prepared to visit Purdue the next Saturday, Rockne continued to try to set up another game for December 6, but again was unsuccessful. His squad went to Lafayette and whipped the Boilers, 26-6. Gipp led the way with 137 yards on 19 carries, his strongest game to date. Reports called him "a tower of strength in Notre Dame's offense, as he tore holes through the Purdue line." On a soft field in Lincoln on Thanksgiving Day, the Fighting Irish and Nebraska struggled to a scoreless tie. "Nebraska fought with the single idea of keeping the visitors from the home goal with the realization that the odds were against it. Nebraska on the whole was playing not so much to score as to keep the other team from scoring." Gipp and Barry did most of the ground-gaining for the Irish.

Mercifully, a football season, and an autumn unlike any other was finished. The Great War ended, the influenza pandemic tamed. For someone who was adept at flexibility and change, 1918 presented the first-year coach with challenges unlike anything he had expected. For now Knute Rockne would celebrate the health of his family and surviving the season; both were worth savoring.

# 17

## Back To The Old Days

I
n South Bend, 1919 began as a year of great optimism. Albert Erskine announced a bold plan in which his Studebaker plant would
add 7,000 employees. An issue of $15 million series gold notes would
allow "enormous strides toward greater production," or some 100,000 automobiles per year. He predicted that the city's population would increase
by 15,000 to 20,000 people. Although the city, like the rest of the nation,
mourned the death of former president and college football reformer
Teddy Roosevelt, the overall mood was upbeat. Notre Dame prepared for
a post-war bump in enrollment and looked forward to restoring a sense
of normalcy after the grim fall of 1918. The *Scholastic* of January 11, 1919
welcomed students back and hoped for new beginnings:

> Though classes have been going on since September, the aca-
> demic has been shared with the military, to the detriment, let
> us say mildly, of the former. The academic spirit is one of qui-
> etness, well-regulated leisure and tranquility, a spirit conducive
> to thought, to study, and to planning; the military gives quite
> another atmosphere, an atmosphere of action and of readiness

to drop the matter in hand and fall into ranks…But we are back once more to the old days; and we greet our old days with renewed resolution. We are better for having experienced other ways, and we know now something we did not realize before— the vast advantages which are ours. With the beginning of 1919, we start a new era in our school and in our lives."

The new era would move forward with a new university president, as that spring Father Cavanaugh announced his retirement. Many assumed vice president Matthew Walsh would be named to take over the top position. Instead, the university tapped 52-year-old Father James A. Burns. Modernization was coming to Notre Dame, and it would require changes in how the university related to important public entities upon which the institution was becoming more dependent.

James Aloysius Burns grew up in Michigan City, Indiana and began his schooling at age 15 at Notre Dame's School of Manual Labor as an apprentice printer, before enrolling in the university. He earned his college degree in 1888 when he entered the Holy Cross novitiate. He began teaching chemistry at Notre Dame in 1893, and in 1900, Father James Zahm made him superior of the Holy Cross house of studies in Washington, D.C. Burns used his time in the nation's capital wisely, earning a Ph.D. in 1906 from Catholic University, where he would teach for the next 13 years. He returned to Notre Dame to assume the presidency at the same time students returned in record numbers. Notre Dame maintained its tradition of never turning away an applicant, and the post-war surge saw enrollment spike to more than 1,200 students by 1920. The faculty stood at a record 165—including 60 laymen. Father Burns' top priorities included modernizing the campus, which in particular needed additional dormitories to house the nearly 600 students who were still living within the city of South Bend. He also believed Catholic colleges that shared facilities, faculty, and resources with secondary schools located on their campuses were prevented from achieving levels of academic performance comparable to other private and public colleges. So Burns began the process of closing the preparatory school, which had been a fixture of the campus since the days of Father Sorin. The last preparatory school class graduated in 1922.

Burns, the oldest, most academically qualified priest to serve to date as president of the university, argued that if Notre Dame was to grow and prosper it needed to provide the kind of expanded coursework that would continue to attract top students. He improved organizational efficiency by dividing the university into four distinct colleges: Arts and Letters, Science, Engineering, and Law. The ever-increasing student enrollment in professional courses forced Burns to hire more lay faculty. He would maneuver between the secular world needed to create an endowment to sustain Notre Dame among the elite universities while still adhering to rigorous religious operations. Burns weaved his way through the maze created by the Catholic Education Association that said Catholic schools and colleges should emphasize the religious and moral dimensions of their faith with a new post-war world of financial contributions, philanthropic foundations, and fundraising.

American soldiers who drank a pint of ale before sailing to fight the war to end all wars returned home in November 1918 to find prohibition awaiting ratification. The official push for the 18th Amendment, which would prohibit the sale and manufacture of alcoholic beverages, began in 1914 with the Hobson-Sheppard Resolution. Although it passed the House of Representatives with a 197-190 vote, it lacked the two-thirds majority to be enacted as a constitutional amendment. It was still considered a victory for the Anti-Saloon League because many dry congressmen were elected in 1914 with the League's influence, and a sense of near-victory filled the Washington, D.C. air. When the United States declared war on Germany in 1917, the League wasted little time in targeting the brewing industry as un-American and sympathetic to German causes. Nowhere was this more evident than in Milwaukee, Wisconsin, which had been settled heavily by German immigrants and German brewers such as August Pabst, Joseph Schlitz, Valentin Blatz, and Frederick Miller, whose son Fred would later captain the 1928 Notre Dame football team.

Prohibition advocates painted brewers as taking the bread out of the mouths of starving Europeans. Yale economist Irving Fisher, a prohibition supporter, issued a report entitled "Theory of Interest," in which he claimed the same amount of barley used in American breweries could instead yield 11 million loaves of bread a day. William Jennings Bryan, a former presidential candidate, a dry advocate, and Woodrow Wilson's Secretary of State until 1916 said: "How can we justify the making of any part of our breadstuffs into intoxicating liquor when men are crying out for bread?" In February 1918, former Wisconsin Lieutenant Governor and dry politician John Strange told the *Milwaukee Journal:* "We have German enemies in this country too. And the worst of all of our German enemies, the most treacherous, the most menacing, are Pabst, Schlitz, Blatz, and Miller."

Indiana Governor James P. Goodrich signed the Indiana prohibition act in January 1917, joining other "dry" states to prohibit alcohol sales even before ratification of the 18th Amendment. The Notre Dame *Scholastic* cautioned in its February 10 editorial, "With public sentiment indifferent to the enforcement of such a law, it is very likely to do more harm than good." On a campus with thirsty young men who occasionally found their way to downtown South Bend drinking establishments, the topic of prohibition proved lively throughout the spring of 1917. Animated debates on the topic continued until the term ended with students from other "wet" universities engaging the Notre Dame debate club. In South Bend, home to breweries and many thousands of residents who supported them, the many corner saloons and neighborhood beer halls would soon start calling themselves "soda fountains." In the back rooms of these establishments, it would be fairly easy to find something harder than soda water to imbibe. The city also had another type of dual-purpose gathering place: cigar stores, which almost all had back rooms loaded with billiard tables of all types—pool, pocket and three-cushion. It was also a place where one could place a wager on the day's major sporting events.

Golden D. "Goldie" Mann was known as the leading impresario of such joints, operating four of them at one time. Among the most popular spots was Jimmy and Goat's Place. Co-owner Eddie "Goat" Anderson, a colorful former ball-player, had reached the major leagues with the Pittsburgh Pirates in 1907. Another place was Hullie and Mike's, the city's most popular cigar store. George Hull and Mike Calnon met a few years earlier when Calnon ran a restaurant in the Sterling Building on Jefferson Boulevard, and Hull had his cigar store next door. Calnon's restaurant was a novelty known as a "three-center" because every item one could order at the counter—a sandwich, a slice of pie, a cup of coffee—cost exactly three cents. But for special occasions, Calnon could offer a heartier spread. His restaurant hosted the first official Notre Dame football banquet after the 1914 season, when steak, potatoes, bread, and coffee were served for 17 cents a plate. Hull and Calnon, such strong supporters of Notre Dame football that they were among the handful of souls accompanying the team to West Point in 1913, joined forces to create Hullie and Mike's at 112 South Michigan Street. Typical of other establishments, it featured a cigar counter, lunch counter, and dairy counter in front, with pool and card tables in the rear. It was a hit among Notre Dame students and followers right from the start, and a favorite lunch spot of Knute Rockne.

George Gipp enjoyed Hullie and Mike's as a relaxed place to shoot billiards, and his matches with Hull, an expert player, were legendary. They developed a friendship that went beyond billiards, and Gipp was a frequent dinner guest at George and Maude Hull's home on Vassar Avenue. There, the football star was so quiet and unassuming that other friends of the Hulls who dined there would say afterward, "That was Gipp?" Gipp had become increasingly well-known for his pool shooting when, in the winter of 1919, he faced his greatest challenger, a Chicago pool shark known as "the Greek." Frank Rydzewski, Gipp's teammate in 1917 who earned All-American mention, had left school and was back in Chicago, when he brought the Greek over to take on Gipp. Appearing relaxed and taking it easy, as if it were a friendly match with Hull, Gipp defeated the Greek, making winners—and friends—out of the many who bet on Gipp to do so. Although the gambling aspect happened largely out of public view, billiards was covered by the local press as it would any other sport. The papers ran updates on the city's first open three-cushion tournament that spring, which featured a team from Hullie and Mike's, led by Gipp, against the best players from the Oliver Hotel's pool room. Gipp won all his matches, leading his team to the championship, and became the undisputed city champ of pocket and three-cushion billiards.

Gipp, flush with winnings, rented a room on the second floor of the Oliver, where he eventually moved his belongings from Sorin Hall. He also started working in a variety of jobs for the hotel. Gipp used the room to host all-night poker games, where he matched wits with a regular lineup of the area's top players. He also began shooting billiards more frequently in the Oliver's poolroom. The Oliver's management had hoped the well-appointed room would be an added feature for those staying at the hotel, but instead it became a haven for local players. Gipp was winning at such a pace that he sometimes gave Hunk Anderson several hundred dollars at a time for safekeeping in Hunk's steel locker box. More often, he spent it on food, drink, or other forms of gambling such as dice, where his skills did not translate to winning. "He just didn't care much about money," Hunk said later. Gipp's appearances on campus became more rare as his billiards and poker activities intensified.

In the final days of the semester, Gipp was shaken by the sudden death of Leo Owens, 24, a Notre Dame student from Ogdensburg, New York, the same hometown as football teammate Joe Brandy. "Leo was a favorite with everyone who knew him," said the *Scholastic*. "Strong and athletic, a good student and a cheerful, happy companion...The smiling good humor of the 'Sarge' was contagious and made him a welcome figure in every student gathering." Owens died from septicemia furunculosis, the poisoning of the bloodstream via boils on the skin. Gipp knew his own tonsils were bad, yet did nothing about the condition—other than worry he could suffer the same fate as Owens.


Rockne was gearing up for the 1919 season both as coach and athletic director. The on-field team held great promise and as athletic director, he announced a solid nine-game schedule that included the resumption of the Army series in West Point, trips to Nebraska and Purdue, and a game against Indiana, the first time the state rivals would meet since 1908. Rockne also made his first major hire by bringing back his good friend Gus Dorais. Recently discharged from the army in December, Dorais gladly accepted Rockne's invitation to coach basketball, which was slated to start on January 14 against Purdue. Dorais had been stationed at Camp MacArthur near Waco and served as athletic officer, similar to the position Rockne held at Fort Sheridan. Dorais would also coach baseball in spring and assist Rockne with football duties in the fall, taking over as backfield coach.

In the autumn of 1919, men returned to campus who had missed one or two years of school—and football. Joe Brandy, Frank Coughlin, Cy De-

Gree, Fritz Slackford, Dave Hayes, Walter Miller, Slip Madigan, and Grover Malone were glad to be preparing for clashes that included footballs rather than live ammunition. Gipp and Hunk Anderson had another pal from Calumet with them at Notre Dame. Gipp had talked Percy Wilcox, a skilled hockey and basketball star in the North Country, to give Notre Dame a try. Rockne, as a personal favor to Gipp, arranged for Wilcox to get a campus job so he could attend school. Not as fortunate was the group's pal Ojay Larson. Financial difficulties at home had forced him to leave school. As Rockne's assistant, Dorais managed the backfield, which was brimming with talent. Bahan, coming off a strong summer playing baseball in Butte, Montana, took over at quarterback; Gipp and Bergman were proven performers at the halfback spots; and Slackford, backed up by Miller, were ready to go at fullback. On Rockne's line, first-year George Trafton was making an impression at center, where he alternated with Madigan. Hunk Anderson led the guards; Coughlin and DeGree were solid at tackle; and Eddie Anderson, a swift star from Mason City, Iowa, was primed for a big year at an end position.

In the opener, 5,000 came to Cartier Field to see Rockne's heralded squad take on a respectable eleven from Kalamazoo College. In pregame warm-ups, it was said Gipp brought two balls to the 50-yard line, drop-kicked the first ball over one of the goal posts, then turned and did the same over the other crossbar, eliciting a tremendous roar from the crowd. Rockne wanted to give his team a strict test, so he asked the officials to be vigilant in calling penalties. In the first quarter alone, Gipp had touchdown runs of 80 and 68 yards called back due to offsides. Rockne claimed his star stopped and said to the referee, "Next time give me one whistle to stop and two to keep going." It took until the third quarter for Notre Dame to score in a 14-0 victory. The following week, Mount Union College, the Ohio college champions of 1918, came to town. Gipp dominated early, with 123 yards on just 10 carries, and another 48 through the air. He left the game with Notre Dame leading, 27-7, on its way to a 60-7 romp. Said Rockne of his budding star:

> Some native principle of conserving energy fashioned his conduct against weak teams. In an important game, he never wavered, never flinched; he was striking energy every second. He

never spared himself. He'd take out an end for any other ball carrier even more quickly than they'd cut the man down for him. Gipp never hesitated; never held himself precious. Only against pushovers was he lazy and deliberate, reducing his effort to a minimum when an easy game was on ice. The high dramatic moments of the major battles found him daring, hard-hitting, almost vicious in his attack.

The season's first such major battle came October 18, when the Fighting Irish visited Nebraska, which held a 2-1-1 lead in the emerging rivalry. Despite the importance of the game, the team had left town uncharacteristically unnoticed by the students. On Wednesday, an overflow crowd jammed Washington Hall to greet Irish Republic President Eamon DeValera. DeValera arrived the night before and was feted at the Oliver Hotel. He spoke to an audience of more than 2,000 packed into a local high school and waved to throngs who lined a cavalcade through city. "This is the happiest day since I arrived in America," DeValera said.

By Friday night in downtown Lincoln, some 3,000 Nebraska students, alumni, and citizens paraded the streets "with torch, banner, and band" and ended with a rally at Notre Dame's hotel. There were songs, cheers and speeches hailing both teams. At one point, the crowd chanted, "We want Rockne! We want Rockne!" It was a humbling moment. Here was the young mentor, not yet 10 games into his career at Notre Dame's head coach, and his fame had already spread to such a level that crowds clamored to hear him speak. Coach Rockne stepped to the balcony and spoke briefly, congratulating the Nebraskans on their spirit and enthusiasm.

The next day, with 10,000 frenzied fans at cheering wildly, Notre Dame opened up with a trick play that Rockne designed and had his team practice to perfection. In taking the kickoff, Gipp swung wide as if to pick up blockers, then quickly lateraled to Bergman, who raced to the open side of the field. Hunk Anderson, seeing that only Nebraska's star Clarence Swanson had a shot at Bergman, broke out of the interference and hit the Husker star, clearing the way for Bergman to complete a 90-yard touchdown run. Gipp went on to complete several key passes, and his kicking kept Nebraska bottled up in a 14-9 Irish win. In the closing minutes, Gipp frustrated the Huskers by slowing the game down. William "Doc"

Lars Rokne traveled from the village of Voss, Norway (above) to the 1893 World's Columbian Exposition in Chicago.

The Ferris Wheel became one of the biggest attractions at the World's Fair, which drew millions of visitors to the dazzling "White City."

A family portrait of the Rockne family in Chicago, with Knute at back right.

(Right) Young Knute with his older sister Anna and his younger sister Martha.

A young Knute Rockne packed his schoolbooks to study at Brentano School in Chicago (left).

After the World's Fair, Lars Rokne worked as a press engineer at *Skandinaven* (office pictured below), which promoted its papers as "printed in all languages," including Norwegian.

Rockne would come to say that all football emanated from Yale's Walter Camp (right).

As a youngster, Rockne watched Amos Alonzo Stagg coach the University of Chicago football team (below). Stagg was a student of Walter Camp, who is credited as the father of American football.

Knute Rockne enjoying a game of tennis as a young lad (left).

Rockne as a 22-year-old freshman (right) ready to enter Notre Dame in 1910.

Rockne (front row, second from left) with fellow Notre Dame chemistry students, studying under Father Julius Nieuwland, CSC.

Rockne's love of track began at an early age and remained with him throughout his life. He is pictured with Chicago track star John Plant and teammate Ed Pritchard (left). Plant was instrumental in persuading Rockne to attend Notre Dame.

In addition to pole vaulting (right), Rockne ran the half mile and relay teams as well as shot-put.

Always actively involved with campus life, Rockne (center right) took on the reigning Notre Dame marbles champion.

Rockne (above, third from right) was a member of the school's crew team his junior year.

Rockne (top row, third from right) played baseball for the Corby Hall team. He often spent time relaxing with fellow students in the rec room of Corby Hall's basement (center front, below).

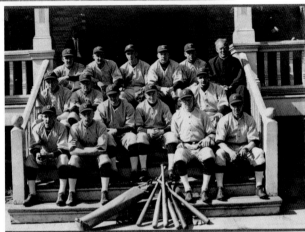

Rockne, leading the blocking, during a 1912 game vs. Marquette at Comiskey Park in Chicago.

Along with his good friend and teammate Gus Dorais, Rockne spent the summer of 1913 working at Cedar Point resort on Lake Erie (right).

1913 Notre Dame team captain Knute Rockne, at midfield for the coin toss before the game against South Dakota at Cartier Field (below).

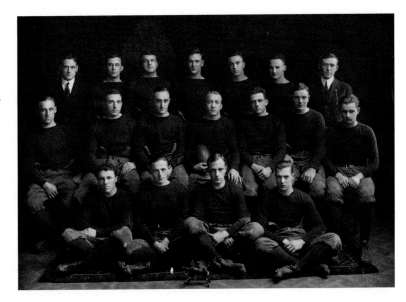

Rockne (center, holding football) served as captain of the 1913 football team.

Rockne (above, far right) played as the starting left end. Below, he leads the players onto the field for the 1913 season opener against Ohio Northern at Cartier Field.

History was made in 1913 when Rockne (above, top back row, second from right) and his teammates traveled to West Point to take on a vaunted Army team.

Rockne rambles downfield after catching a pass from quarterback and roommate Gus Dorais (above).

Coach Jesse Harper with Rockne. Harper, who played for Amos Alonzo Stagg at the University of Chicago, helped shape a more wide-open game of football. Rockne assisted Harper from 1914-1917.

Rockne's first year as Notre Dame head coach (1918) pictured with his team (back row, far left). The newly appointed coach faced unusual circumstances that initial year: a country at war and a nation battling an influenza epidemic. His star player George Gipp (right) would go on to garner national fame before his untimely death in 1920.

Rockne's 1914 Notre Dame graduation picture.

Rockne would also serve as head tra[ck] coach for nearly his entire tenure as he[ad] football coach at Notre Dame. Shown he[re] (below) coaching on the finer points of t[he] shot-put.

Rockne (front row, center) while serving his country as athletic director at Fort Sheridan, just north of Chicago in the summer of 1918, during the Great War.

Fans would pack Cartier Field in the 1920s to watch Notre Dame football.

The famous Four Horsemen of Notre Dame (left to right) Don Miller, Elmer Layden, Jim Crowley, and Harry Stuhldreher were famously named by sportswriter Grantland Rice after Notre Dame's win over Army on October 18, 1924. Shown below is action from the game played at the Polo Grounds in New York City.

The undefeated 1924 season was capped by a train odyssey that took the team from South Bend to Chicago (pictured top) and then on to Memphis, New Orleans, Houston, and Tucson before arriving in Los Angeles for the post-season game vs. Stanford (middle) in the Rose Bowl on January 1, 1925. The day after the thrilling 27-10 win, Rockne was feted at several events, including a meeting with silent screen idol Rudolph Valentino (left), the star of the movie *Four Horsemen of the Apocalypse*.

The legendary Notre Dame football coach embraced a philosophy that sought to bring out the best in individual players. Whether working with 1924 captain Adam Walsh (right) or collectively, Rockne prepared his charges for the next football battle and the challenges of life. His practices became well-attended by youngsters (shown above) anxious to learn whatever they could from Rockne.

(Top) The Notre Dame band salutes the school's coach. Coach Rockne was beloved by Notre Dame students and players throughout his 13-year coaching career at the school.

Knute Rockne married Bonnie Skiles (left) on July 15, 1914. Together they raised a family of four (below left to right): Billy, Mary Jeanne, Jack, and "Junior." By the mid-1920s, the family would often vacation in Florida, where they would enjoy the sun and surf of Miami.

Youngsters from all across the country enjoyed summers at Camp Rockne, near Winter, Wisconsin (right). The coach oversaw a day's swimming activity from the dock at the camp (above).

Rockne operated coaching schools with his friend, Wisconsin basketball coach Walter "Doc" Meanwell (left).

In Yankee Stadium with Lou Gehrig and Babe Ruth.

Rockne had close relationships with most of his fellow coaches, including Glenn "Pop" Warner (left). They often worked together at coaching schools across the country.

In 1923, Rockne taught the football course at the physical education summer school at Brigham Young University in Provo, Utah.

A favorite stop on Rockne's annual summer schedule of coaching schools was Corvallis, Oregon, home of Oregon Agricultural College. There he reunited with his Chicago track coach Michael "Dad" Butler (left) and football coach Paul Schissler.

Attending a banquet with Notre Dame President Father Charles O'Donnell and Studebaker's Albert Erskine (seated).

Personal secretary Ruth Faulkner, hired in 1925, proved a valuable addition to Rockne's staff.

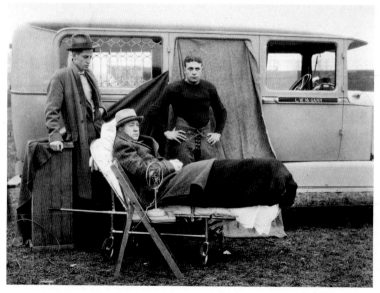

Phlebitis hampered Rockne's mobility in 1929.

Rockne, suffering from phlebitis, would coach from a wheelchair in 1929 (above), but by the time of the stadium dedication ceremonies on Friday night, October 10, 1930, Rockne was in good health and spoke to the crowd (below).

The new Notre Dame Stadium on October 11, 1930 in the dedication game against Navy (above). The outline of Cartier Field is visible just north of the stadium. Below, Coach Rockne speaks to the dedication crowd of more than 45,000.

Rockne remained close to nearly all of his players. Jack Elder, a star from 1929, stopped in to visit his old coach (above left). On November 11, 1930, just over a year after the stock market crash, Rockne entered a new field, opening a South Bend brokerage, a branch of the R. H. Gidson & Co. of Cincinnati (above right).

The Rockne plane crash, March 31, 1931.

Visitors came to pay their respects at the Rockne home before the funeral.

(Right) Pallbearers take the coach's body from his home. Notre Dame President Charles O'Donnell memorialized Rockne at the funeral service inside Sacred Heart Church on April 4, 1931 (below).

Thousands gathered outside Sacred Heart Church to listen to the live broadcast of the Rockne memorial services (above).

His widow and friends at the gravesite (right). Notre Dame students and athletes pay their respects (below).

Knute Kenneth Rockne
Born March 4, 1888
Died March 31, 1931

Head coach, 1918-1930
Record: 105-12-5
Winning percentage: .881

Spaulding, in his 14th season as head coach of the Western Normal Hill-toppers, brought a promising squad to South Bend on October 25, led by punishing fullback Sam "The Black Streak" Dunlap, one of the leading black players in the West. They were no match for Rockne's men, though, as Gipp scored twice early and the Irish rolled, 53-0. The resumption of the Indiana series was played in a quagmire at rain-drenched Washington Park in Indianapolis on November 1. Hunk Anderson made the game's first big play, blocking a punt to set up Notre Dame's first score. Gipp was everywhere, rushing and passing through the slop, and adding a drop-kick field goal in the 16-3 win.

The 5-0 record was the best Notre Dame had ever brought to a game on the Plains at West Point. But the Irish were hurting; Dutch Bergman was back on campus, nursing a knee twisted against Indiana, and Gipp and Degree had lesser injuries, but could play. Hunk Anderson, Clipper Smith, and Frank Coughlin were stout defending against the soldiers, but Army held a 9-6 lead late in the third quarter. Gipp rose to the occasion, hitting Eddie Anderson on the dead run with a perfect pass for 26 yards to the Army 7. Walter Miller drove over two plays later for the winning touchdown. "The Notre Dame timing is uncanny," said one observer, "and their new coach is obviously a master in the small details that spell the difference between success and failure in a play." Notre Dame's 12-9 victory featured 185 total yards by Gipp, including 115 on seven completed passes.

Back on campus, the Notre Dame student body celebrated by forming "columns of fours" in front of the campus post office, then marching toward South Bend. When the front of the column reached the Colfax Bridge, it broke into a long single line for a snake dance, then the entire group reassembled in front of the Oliver Hotel. Alfred Slaggert, head cheer leader, shouted cheers from the hotel balcony. The students then marched back to campus, where an immense bonfire was lit on an unused portion of Cartier Field. On Sunday, 20 men from each hall, plus a good share of day students, marched downtown to greet the team's train. A few minutes after 11 a.m., the train arrived to a tremendous cheer. Players were hustled into automobiles provided by George Hull and Goat Anderson and "followed to the Four Corners by Notre Dame enthusiasts."

George Gipp—perhaps uncomfortable with the adulation, perhaps just bored by the thought of another week's routine starting—vanished. He missed all classes and practices during the week as the team prepared for Michigan Agricultural College and didn't appear on campus until the eve of the game. An exasperated Rockne was tiring of his star's peccadillos. But what would be a suitable punishment? And would it have any effect on the mercurial star? Aggies coach Chester Brewer told his team Gipp would not play on Saturday; Brewster crediting the information as coming directly from Rockne. But Rockne, ever conflicted over how to handle his star, ended up suspending Gipp for just the first quarter. He entered the game and ran and passed Notre Dame to a 13-0 victory.

With a 7-0 mark and their star back in tow, Rockne's lads headed to Lafayette to meet Purdue. Gipp finished with 11 completed passes for 217 yards—numbers that were unheard of for the time. With the 33-13 victory, Notre Dame could again claim the Indiana college championship. And when Illinois upset Ohio State, 9-7, that afternoon, the Irish had a chance to add Western champs to their accolades. Notre Dame's undefeated season generated national attention, and Rockne was approached about meeting the University of Oregon, Pacific Coast co-champions, in a postseason game on Christmas Day. But Notre Dame faculty, who opposed postseason play, protested loudly and no game was ever scheduled.

Four days later, on Thanksgiving Day, Notre Dame closed out its season with a sluggish 14-6 victory over Morningside College in front of 10,000 fans at Sioux City. A driving snowstorm, stiff winds, and chilling temperatures made the afternoon uncomfortable for all involved. Midway through the third quarter, Gipp ambled over to the sideline and said, "I'm through for the day." "Like hell you are," Rockne snorted. He had just about had enough of his star's impudence. Not only that, but the game was still in doubt. What couldn't be denied was Gipp's excellence on the field. In Notre Dame's 9-0 season he totaled 729 yards on the ground, 727 through the air. And he was just as stellar on defense. Walter Eckersall and other Midwest writers included Gipp on their All-America teams, though Walter Camp and the major Eastern selectors still overlooked him. On December 14, 1919, the team was feted in a gala banquet at the Oliver Hotel, arranged by Rockne and Dorais and featuring plenty of "food, jokes, soloists, and songs." The team had a vote for its 1920 captain and

Gipp edged Frank Coughlin by a single vote.

Rockne breathed a sigh of relief upon season's end. The roller coaster ride of 1918 appeared to have stopped. The chaos, the unpredictability the sadness, and the horror of war and disease no longer impacted his personal and professional life. In reality, he thought, this was really his first season at the helm, and it had produced an undefeated season. Surely, 1920 would offer smooth sailing.

As the spring 1920 semester started, Gipp spent even more time on pool and late-night or all-night poker games. He started to look gaunt and pale, and his friends estimated he smoked two to three packs of cigarettes a day. Gipp would try to catch up on sleep during the day, and began to cut classes even more regularly than usual. One of his law professors said, "With a little application he could easily have been a summa cum laude graduate, and I feel he would have made a superb attorney." Gipp had also started a relationship with Iris Tripper, the daughter of a prominent attorney in Indianapolis. Gipp's frequent visits to Indianapolis, over the objections of Iris' father, added to the strain on his academic and athletic schedules. Gipp's name became a major source of discussion among school administrators. One faculty member, it was said, had spotted Gipp exiting the Tokio Dance Hall on Michigan Street, a dime-a-dance emporium that had been ruled strictly off-limits for Notre Dame students.

Within his first year, Father Burns faced his first test of authority. Burns was described as someone who set high standards of obedience and performance of himself and he expected it of others. On March 8, 1920, he summoned Gipp into his office to inform Gipp he had been expelled, effective immediately. Over the next few weeks, support for Gipp's reinstatement came from prominent local citizens, 86 of whom signed a petition that articulately argued for Gipp's return. Meanwhile, the star athlete received numerous offers to play football at other schools—from Fielding Yost at Michigan, Glenn "Pop" Warner, now at the University of Pittsburgh, and West Point, under the direction of its newly-appointed superintendent, Douglas MacArthur. Gipp, who also had two $4,000 offers to play baseball—for the Chicago Cubs and White Sox—laid low. He moved his possessions into his room at the Oliver, and picked up cash as the house billiards player at Hullie and Mike's. Father Burns once again found himself between the realities of his two worlds. On one hand, he was cognizant of the need to build and maintain excellent relationships with the South Bend business community; Burns was just building the foundation for raising Notre Dame endowment funds. On the other, he wanted to create a renowned educational institution that upheld academic and athletic standards. Burns reacted quickly to the petition and reinstated Gipp on April 29.

It did little to change the wayward star's behavior, however. Gipp appeared in two varsity baseball games before abruptly quitting the squad on May 21. He left the university shortly after that without taking any final examinations. He accepted an offer from Coach Bingo Brown at the University of Detroit to play football there in 1920. There would be no problem with eligibility, and Gipp could come and go as he liked, without restriction. When Gipp cleared out of the Oliver Hotel in early June, he didn't expect to ever return to South Bend. How much did a lovesick heart play in all of this behavior? Iris had stopped writing in response to Gipp's letters. He boarded a train to Indianapolis and met Iris at the Claypool Hotel. In the ensuing conversation, Gipp promised to return to Notre Dame and finish his law degree. He would do anything to win her love. She smiled her approval and agreed to marry him if he did as promised. The stress would continue to pile up for Rockne. In addition to Gipp's uncertain situation, center George Trafton had been expelled for playing in some professional games in Chicago after the 1919 season; Bernie Kirk, starting end, was in academic trouble and looking for another school; and several other players were considering a change of school. As fall practice started in September, Rockne was in a near panic when he found out Gipp was already practicing with the Detroit team.

Rockne, too, needed the support of the local business community. Studebaker's Erskine had recently purchased 100 season tickets, and having to explain that Gipp was no longer with the football team would be an unenviable task. Rockne sent assistant Dorais to Detroit to convince Gipp to return, and made it clear to Dorais that both of their jobs could be hanging in the balance. Rockne didn't specify what Dorais should say, and when Gus met with Gipp, he painted a rosy—and unauthorized— picture of what life would be back in South Bend for the star. Among

Dorais' sales points was the assertion that the Faculty Board in Control of Athletics had ruled Gipp eligible for 1920. In fact, while Gipp was en route from Laurium to South Bend, the Board met and declared both Gipp and Bahan ineligible on account of academic deficiencies. Over the next few days, though, Father Burns prevailed upon the Board to reverse itself, making Gipp eligible despite an academic record filled with holes. The reality of building a coalition with area businesses to expand and improve the university won out over athletic purity. Rockne had paid a price to ensure Gipp's return. Rockne dearly wanted to develop a team that could work together, support and respect one another, and improve as a unit. That would all be difficult on a team that included George Gipp. The star returned to live at the Oliver, skipped his classes, attended football practice only when the mood suited him, and acted as something of a co-coach. Was the price worth it? It was a question Rockne could not shake.

Just before heading to South Bend, Gipp and his friend Alger Train visited the Calumet office of Dr. A. C. Roche, who gave George advice he didn't want to hear: Gipp's tonsils, chronically infected for years, needed to be removed. Gipp ignored the doc, telling Alger he was afraid of "going under the knife." Back on campus, Gipp took a small room in the Sorin subway, signed up for several law classes, and reported to practice on Friday, October 1, the day before the season opener against Kalamazoo. Rockne was also starting the year without his trusted friend and assistant coach Gus Dorais, who had accepted a position as head coach at Gonzaga University in Spokane, Washington in May. Dorais was enticed by Gonzaga's promise to build a top-level football program as well as the offer to serve as head coach of the baseball and basketball teams. The university also promised to upgrade it athletic facilities, eventually building an 11,000-seat football stadium. In Dorais' place stood Walter Halas, from an athletic family in Chicago.

Ojay Larson, financial matters in order, was back and starting at center next to guard Hunk Anderson. Joe Brandy was now at quarterback, Norm Barry across from Gipp at right half, and Chet Wynne at fullback. Roger Kiley, a second-year man from Chicago was making his first start at Kirk's end position. A few minutes into the Kalamazoo game, with Notre Dame already in charge, Gipp found Kiley wide open and fired a perfect pass, which the jittery end dropped. "If a gate had been open I would have run to Chicago," Kiley said later, describing how open he was. The team huddled again, and Gipp said to Brandy, "Joe, call it again." This time, Kiley caught Gipp's pass, and he would go on to catch several more. Gipp then suggested Kiley join him early for extra practice the coming week, adding "we'll stand them on their heads." They did on this day, to the tune of 39-0.

The next week, the other team from Kalamazoo—Western Normal—came calling, and the result was almost identical, a 41-0 romp. Gipp racked up 123 yards rushing on just 14 carries, and had two touchdowns called back because of penalties. Heading to Lincoln, Rockne and his men knew the game with Nebraska could be the toughest test of the season. Early in the game, Wynne was struggling against the hard-charging Huskers, and Rockne was thinking of lifting him. Gipp spoke up for "Chetter," who went on to make several key plays. Another star was Norm Barry, who caught several Gipp aerials. In the fourth quarter, Notre Dame ahead just 9-7, Gipp hit Barry with a pass to the Huskers 20. On the next play, Gipp executed a perfect fake pass, then broke free and ran for the clinching touchdown. The 16-7 victory impressed all those who witnessed it. "The gameness of the visitors delighted the 10,000…who crowded the park," noted one report. Clarence Swanson, Huskers star, later said Gipp was the best passer, runner and kicker he had ever seen.

Next up was Valparaiso on October 23, coached by an up-and-coming favorite of Rockne's, George Keogan. The Minnesota native had already held several jobs coaching basketball, including Superior State Teachers College in Wisconsin, St. Louis University, and the College of St. Thomas in St. Paul, Minnesota. In football, he coached Allegheny College in Pennsylvania two years, and was in his second season at Valparaiso. A crowd of 8,000, the largest to date at Cartier Field, watched Rockne's stars take on a team that outweighed them. Imagine their surprise when Rockne started a group completely composed of second-stringers. The reserves held Valparaiso in check for a quarter and a half, after which the regulars gave Army scouts little to look at, using straight-ahead football to score a 28-3 victory.

The second unit quickly picked up the nickname "Shock Troops," after the military maneuver that sends in an initial, highly-mobile charge to penetrate through enemy defenses, drawing the first "shock" from the opposition. Rockne pioneered the innovation, and used it repeatedly from this point, explaining, "We know by experience that two football teams generally hit the hardest in the first quarter. The second team acts very much in the capacity of shock absorbers." The idea was to preserve the energy of the first team, and "save then from this bruising and unnecessary thumping...save them as much as possible from Saturday to Saturday." This was particularly important as Rockne began using smaller, quicker players. But at least as important was the psychological value; the opponent would expend great amounts of energy in the early going, only to then see the Notre Dame regulars come into the game—fresh, rested, and ready to give their all. There was also a strategic edge in having the regulars on the sidelines the first part of the game, studying the tendencies of the opposition. As to the Shock Troops name, Rockne said, "I don't care what you call them. We just like what happens." It was Rockne's ability to develop and draw the best out of 22 players—not just 11 as most other teams—that allowed the tactic to work.

The October 30 battle with Army was hailed as a monumental showdown between undefeated elevens. Army scouts at the Notre Dame-Nebraska game said they would consider the season "a glorious success" if the Cadets could defeat the Irish, regardless of the outcome of the Army-Navy game. With 10,000 looking on at the Plains, the teams traded first half scores, and the Cadets took a 17-14 lead into the locker room. Army's Walter French raced for 40 yards for one touchdown, going past a seemingly disinterested Gipp. Rockne wasn't pleased, and let his charges know it. He was just about finished with his oratory, when he spotted Gipp, leaning lazily up against a door, smoking a cigarette. The coach nearly became apoplectic. "What about you, Gipp?" Rockne snapped. "I don't suppose you have any interest in this game?"

"Look, Rock," Gipp retorted. "I got $400 bet on this game, and I'm not about to blow it." To his teammates, Gipp said, "You guys give me a little help and I'll beat this Army team." Gipp missed a field goal that would have tied it in the third quarter, but his consistent gains rushing, and passes to Kiley and Mohardt, kept the Irish charging. They started the fourth quarter on Army's 20, and Gipp drove them with three carries, then played the decoy as Mohardt crashed over the winning touchdown. The Irish later executed another brilliant drive, keyed by Gipp's pass to

Kiley and a spectacular trick play, which sent both backs to the flanks, allowing Wynne to thrust through the line for a touchdown. The Irish defense held for a 27-17 win that sent the eastern press into a tizzy.

"George Gipp is an All-American or there are no real All-Americans this season," said the *New York Herald Tribune*. "If anything can be done on a football field which Gipp didn't do yesterday, it is not discernible to the naked eye." Said the *New York Times*, "Gipp is a tireless worker and was as irrepressible a citizen as ever decorated an Eastern gridiron." A huge crowd greeted the victors upon their return to South Bend. Gipp shied away from the masses by slipping out of the train several cars to the rear. He approached the edge of the crowd, when he found Bonnie Rockne holding Junior, now a two-year-old toddler. Gipp relieved Bonnie in holding the youngster, and the two watched the proceedings, including a short speech by the coach.

A large crowd gathered again on Friday, November 5, the night before the Irish hosted Purdue in the school's first designated Homecoming game, and the Boilermakers' first visit to South Bend since 1901. The town was filled with alumni from all years and locales. The Notre Dame student body led a march to the Oliver Hotel, where they serenaded a huge crowd with cheers for both teams. Coach Scanlon, captain Birk and several other Purdue players spoke, then the attention turned to the Irish. The crowd chanted for "Gipp, Gipp, All-American halfback," but, not surprisingly, the star was nowhere to be found. He made his presence felt the next afternoon, before a record crowd of 12,000 at Cartier Field. He accounted for an amazing 257 total yards, including 129 rushing on 10 carries, Notre Dame hammered Purdue, 28-0, to boost its record to 6-0.

The following Friday morning, Rockne and his men boarded the train for Indianapolis and a game with Indiana, considered to be something of a breather on the schedule. In fact, the Irish were such prohibitive favorites over the Hoosiers, it was said Gipp had trouble finding anyone to bet, as he sauntered from one poolroom to another in downtown Indianapolis Friday night, trying to place a bet on his team. Gipp faced another setback on game day. Gipp helped his sister Dolly, in town to watch the game, settle in at the Claypool hotel. Afterward, he met Iris in the hotel's mezzanine area. To Gipp's shock, he stood and listened as Iris informed him she had married another man. Stunned, he walked away convinced she had been "making a damned fool of him." He was distraught as he prepared for the game.

Whether or not his performance was affected by the news, the game was a struggle for the Irish. With 14,000 fans packing Washington Park, the underdog Hoosiers played like madmen. Five-foot-eight, 158-pound Charles "Chick" Mathys, another star from Green Bay, Wisconsin, repeatedly dented the Irish line for gains. Mathys had played for Green Bay West, the arch-rival of Green Bay East star and ex-Notre Dame player Curly Lambeau. Indiana took a 10-0 lead into the fourth quarter. Since early in the second quarter, Gipp stood alongside Rockne on the sideline, draped in a blanket, shivering in the cold. Early in the second quarter, he had been tackled violently by two Hoosiers and suffered a badly separated shoulder. Nobody was sparking the Irish, and it looked like their 15-game winning streak was about to end. "We were a beaten team," Rockne would later say.

With only minutes to play, the Irish finally gained some momentum. Quarterback Brandy alternated giving the ball to Mohardt and Barry, and the two took turns charging through the inspired Hoosiers. They gained ground to the Indiana 7. On the sideline, Gipp, now with a heavily taped shoulder, came to Rockne and insisted on entering the game. Reluctantly, the coach consented. "He charged on the field," Rockne described, "and the stands rose to acclaim. Rarely have I seen a more thrilling sight than those stands, gaunt in dusk, banked thousands screaming the name of one man—Gipp!" Gipp smashed over tackle and was stopped cold. But on the next play, he barreled through the defense to score and then added the point to bring Notre Dame to within 10-7. Minutes later, the Irish again on the move, Gipp dropped back and took a snap from the Indiana 15. Everyone expected a drop kick that would tie the game. Instead, Gipp found Eddie Anderson with a perfect pass that Anderson took to the 1-yard line. On the next play, Ojay Larson cut down the Indiana center and Brandy snuck through for the winning touchdown. Indiana's last possession ended on a fumble recovered by Chet Wynne. The Irish kept their chances for a Western title alive, and the fans outside Hullie and Mike's were delirious in celebration as returns rolled in.

Saturday evening, back at the Claypool, Gipp, his arm in a sling, had dinner with Rockne. Mathys, the Indiana star, joined the pair for a long, friendly chat. The two stars complimented each other on their gutsy performances. Rockne was pleased with the victory, of course, but concerned about the condition of his battered halfback. On Sunday, while his teammates got off the train at South Bend, Gipp continued on to Chicago. He had agreed to help his former Irish mate Grover Malone, now coaching Loyola Academy, by showing the lads a few tricks in their practices. Tired and in pain from his shoulder, Gipp worked with the young football players, including showing them how to drop-kick, while a cold wind blew in from Lake Michigan. On the train ride back to South Bend, Gipp felt the first signs of a new cold taking hold. With his ailing tonsils, it was not an uncommon situation. Gipp stayed in bed in his Sorin room the rest of the week. On Friday Rockne came to visit him, just hours before the team would board the train for its game against Northwestern the next day. "Think you're up for the trip?" Rock asked.

"I suppose so," said Gipp.

"If you're not feeling up to par when we get there, I don't intend using you," Rockne said.

"That's jake with me," Gipp responded.

Notre Dame's Alumni Association designated the game as George Gipp Day. Fans filled more than two dozen train coaches from South Bend to Evanston Saturday morning. A huge crowd of 20,000 packed into the Northwestern field in excited anticipation of seeing the great back play one of his final games for the Irish. But when it was announced that Mohardt was the starter, the crowd groaned. The crowd, not knowing of Gipp's condition, thought Rockne was trying to be clever in resting his star, and they booed Rockne mercilessly, and chanted, "We want Gipp! We want Gipp!" Finally, Rockne could no longer ignore the chants, and he agreed to send Gipp into the game. He expected just a token appearance by the ailing star, but in an instant, Gipp was firing off passes and hit Eddie Anderson with a 35-yarder for a touchdown. Moments later, he unleashed a bomb that went 55 yards in the air to the Wildcat 15, where Barry caught in and walked into the end zone. The 70-yard play was a record-setter. In the closing minutes of the 33-7 romp, Gipp tried for more heroics. Obviously ailing, he caught a punt and gamely tried to elude tacklers. The two Northwestern ends had the punt covered, met Gipp at midfield, and in a remarkable show of sportsmanship, and the respect they had for Gipp, gingerly set him down on the turf.

By Monday evening, Gipp confided to Anderson: "Hunk, I feel terrible. My throat's cutting me up, and I have a high fever." The two of them pulled Rockne away from the speaker's table at a banquet to tell him how Gipp felt. Rockne agreed with Hunk that Gipp needed to be hospitalized, and he made the arrangements to have Gipp brought to St. Joseph's Hospital. When he was admitted Tuesday morning, November 23, his temperature was 104. He lay in a bed in a private room, while Notre Dame went to meet the Michigan Aggies on Thanksgiving Day, winning 25-0 to complete another perfect 9-0 season. But the crowd in Lansing was bitterly disappointed they weren't watching the Irish star.

Gipp's condition far overshadowed any football concerns. Daily reports filled newspapers from coast to coast. At one point, his condition improved as the fever dropped. Hope sprang that the worst was over. Then he was diagnosed with pneumonia. Chicago specialists arrived, and after numerous treatments, they announced they expected Gipp to recover. On November 30, Walter Camp's prestigious All-America team included Gipp's name, the highest honor for a college football player. The doctors and Rockne conferred and agreed it might lift Gipp's spirits if he was informed. Rockne and assistant Halas visited Gipp's room, where the coach informed him of the accomplishment.

"How does that make you feel," Rockne asked, "knowing that you're the first player in Notre Dame's history to receive the honor?" "Well, that's jake, Rock," came Gipp's whispered reply.

Through the first week of December, it was reported Gipp was in serious, but stable condition. Doctors thought if he could improve just a bit, he could get through this. But by Sunday, December 12, it was clear to doctors Gipp had suffered a relapse. On Monday, Gipp rallied a bit, before another turn for the worse. Father Pat Haggerty made four visits to Gipp's bedside that day. At one point that evening, Gipp motioned Rockne over to the bed; the coach leaned over, and the two had a brief conversation. Shortly after 2 a.m. on Tuesday, December 14, Gipp looked up and smiled at his mother and sister, then lapsed into a coma. Father O'Hara gave him the last rites of the Catholic Church. And moments later, the great and sometimes perplexing star was gone.

# 18

## New Era Begins

The snow began flying early in the morning of Wednesday, December 15, 1920 on the campus of Notre Dame. The bells of Sacred Heart Church sounded a somber welcome to those attending the 8:15 a.m. Requiem High Mass for the repose of the soul of George Gipp. At Notre Dame, separation from this earth—whether for an elderly member of the Congregation of the Holy Cross, a victim of war or influenza, or a football hero dying young—brought out the ritual best of the American Catholic Church. After the service, a solemn procession headed toward downtown South Bend. Led by a platoon of police officers, the football team walked in formation with the left halfback spot left vacant, followed by the Monogram Club and the rest of the 1,400 students, marching four abreast. Next came the hearse from McGann Funeral Home bearing Gipp's casket. Alongside were six of the saddest young men around. Norman Barry, Joe Brandy and Frank Coughlin lined on one side, and on the other, three students who followed Gipp's athletic path from Michigan's Upper Peninsula to Notre Dame—Hunk Anderson, Ojay Larson, and Percy Wilcox. Last, automobiles carried Gipp's family members. The six pallbearers would be the only representatives from Notre Dame to accompany Gipp back home.

At the South Bend New York Central station, where Rockne, Gipp, and so many other Fighting Irish heroes had begun numerous football journeys, the next train would bear Gipp's body through Chicago to be laid to rest back in the Upper Peninsula. A *South Bend Tribune* reporter described the scene:

> When the first of the escort reached the station, the lines separated and the students bared their heads to the snow as the body of their Gipper went on to its appointed end. Here, where Notre Dame could do no more for its wonder man, the procession waited. As the Chicago train arrived the crowd moved forward toward the casket, which was being prepared to enter the baggage car. A blanket of flowers on which the Notre Dame monogram was mounted, the last of the love of the Notre Dame student body, remained atop it, destined to accompany the body to its final resting place. Telephone poles, baggage trucks, and every point of vantage at the station were utilized as the casket was elevated to the door of the car. As though by an unspoken command a hat came off here and there, and in a flash the crowd was bareheaded. Silently, with almost defiant faces, the students gazed at the departing form of their idol.

In Chicago, a crowd estimated at several thousand braved the cold to pay their respects as Gipp's train pulled into the LaSalle Street station at 1 p.m. Four hours later, it began the long journey northward, up through Wisconsin and into the Upper Peninsula, arriving at Calumet early on the morning of December 16. There, radiating out from the small depot, stood residents of the Keweenaw, thousands in number, many weeping as the train carrying their native son rumbled to a stop. From the baggage car that carried his body, the crowd extended the length of a football field. Stores in Calumet and Laurium closed on Saturday afternoon, December 18, as residents gathered at the Light Guard Armory, the only place in the area big enough to accommodate the expected crowd for Gipp's funeral. Ministers from the churches of Gipp's parents presided over the Protestant service. Teammate Frank Coughlin delivered the eulogy, saying, "George Gipp was perhaps the greatest athlete I have ever known. He was a man among men, brilliant and unassuming, and has endeared himself to the heart of every Notre Dame student by his athletic prowess, magnetic personality, keen mind, and his great love for the old school." Then, Coughlin and his teammate pallbearers, minus boots and coats, lifted the casket onto a horse-drawn sled for the final trip: six miles through snow and cold to the Calumet cemetery. There, Gipp's father Mathew said a few final words, and the 24-year-old was laid to rest.

Back on College Street in South Bend, Knute Rockne replayed what was the roller coaster of the past few months. From the frantic days of sending Dorais to Detroit to talk Gipp into returning to Notre Dame for his final season, to watching his reticent star put on a display of football at West Point that had left observers shaking their heads in wonder. Yes, Gipp had taxed the coach's patience on numerous occasions. There were the missed practices, followed by the surprise appearances a day or two before a big game. "Hello Gipper," Rock would chortle. "Got the asthma today?" But it seemed as though the sense of drama and performance helped bond the two together. As Rockne later wrote, "The boy was really a master showman, with a mind alert to catch every effective detail of a show. Secretly, although he gave no outward sign, he loved the dramatic....The lad had brilliance, a sense of dramatic opportuneness, of doing the right unpreconceived thing at exactly the right, unpreconceived moment that made me wonder, at times, what self-dramatizing leaders of men must have been among his forebears."

It was hard for the coach to reconcile the natural athletic prowess of an individual who had thought of himself as only talented enough to play baseball. Rockne had never been able to answer the question of how someone could kick a ball such a distance without toiling at daily practice. Rockne recalled his initial thoughts of Gipp being a flash-in-the pan, and then the coach smiled as he contemplated the years he had spent nurturing and coaching this incredible individual talent. Still, Rockne also acknowledged Gipp's role as teacher. It would have been foolish to tamper with Gipp's ability; rather, Rockne had learned, it was better to trust Gipp's instincts. "I wonder what kind of player he would have been had he ever been aroused," Rockne said. Was it a curse or a blessing—or both—to have all that talent wrapped in one body?

But Rockne knew only one direction—forward. He would grieve, yes, as he had done for those who had lost their lives in the Great War. But there were the holidays to prepare for, and the joy he wished to see in the faces of young Billy and Junior. And the birth of Mary Jeanne last May added even more life and activity to the Rockne house. Before long, classes would start again, and track meets, and spring football. Always, there was football. Rockne certainly recognized he had coached a once-in-a-lifetime talent in Gipp. He honored that opportunity, and did the best he could to guide an unconventional character. But, as he confided to a friend, he would be satisfied if he never had another player approaching Gipp's greatness, but rather a multitude of dedicated, hard-working students of the game whom he could mold into a successful team. For he felt, as never before, his calling as a teacher—of the fundamentals of the game, the specific strategies of his system, and moreover, the discipline, teamwork, and perseverance needed for success.

The 1920s have been called the most transformative and most exciting decade in American history. So much changed—culture, lifestyles, the economy—it was if a whole new world had been born. Before 1920, a person's lifestyle was largely defined by their income. But the exploding stock market changed all that. One day you could be an elevator operator; the next day a millionaire. In the first decades of the century, women were second-class citizens, denied the right to vote and largely confined to careers as wife and mother. The 19th Amendment to the Constitution, ratified on August 18, 1920, completed a movement started in 1848 in Seneca Falls, New York by Elizabeth Cady Stanton and Lucretia Mott. With their voting rights established, women set new standards in fashion and behavior almost overnight. Shorts skirts and "bobbed" haircuts replaced ankle-length hems and pinned-up long hair.

Sports were not immune to the changing times. Before 1920, baseball was considered America's pastime. By the end of the decade, college football was on equal footing. So too were tennis, golf, and boxing. It was referred to as the Golden Age of Sports, a time when America and the world wanted to put the memory of the Great War behind them. The economic boom times, automobiles that allowed the freedom to travel, and other modern devices meant people had more money, transportation, and time. And with this leisure time, they turned their attention to sports. It was the decade to watch Jack Dempsey, Babe Ruth and Lou Gehrig, Bobby Jones, even the horse Man o' War, and an incredible college football team from a Catholic university in South Bend coached by a Protestant Norwegian.

During the initial decades of college football, the game was played mostly in front of students, some faculty, and recent alumni. As the broader public discovered the game and flocked to it, many universities considered building large, permanent stadiums to house the spectacle of a college game. College football was one of the significant beneficiaries of America's growing interest in higher education, providing a broader population base of potential athletes and ticket-buying fans, quickly outstripping the limited seating capabilities in the existing stadia. After the Great War, the country's enthusiasm for sports and leisure, while casting off the last vestiges of its restrictive Victorian principles, became a driving force in the escalation of college football's popularity. For a nation recently victorious in the Great War, football provided an opportunity to peacefully experience the adrenaline found from engaging in warfare.

By 1920, life for the Big Three on the gridiron had become a struggle. Yale fielded an average team in 1919, but that did nothing to lessen the shock and outrage among the alumni when Boston College beat the Bulldogs, 5-3. In 1920 Boston College repeated the feat (under Frank Cavanaugh), which caused Yale to drop the Bostonians from its schedule. Princeton followers were similarly shocked in 1919, when the Tigers lost 25-0 to West Virginia. The *New York Times* reported, "The husky mountaineers were so decisive that not a shadow of doubt remained as to which was the better team....(The loss) served to indicate that the old order is giving place to a new." Writer Donald Grant Herring attended the Princeton debacle in the company of Walter Camp and later commented, "Walter, with his historical perspective...must have had an inkling then of what so great a victory for a minor team foreshadowed, the beginning of the end of the reign of the Big Three." But perhaps no upset signaled a crack in the Big Three more than the 6-0 win by Centre College of Kentucky over Harvard.

There were now quality, established coaches patrolling the sidelines at numerous schools outside the Eastern flank—Stagg, Yost, and Rockne, of course, along with Bob Zuppke at Illinois, Howard Jones at Iowa, Bill Alexander at Georgia Tech, and Pop Warner at Pittsburgh. The war years also allowed universities in the Midwest and on the West Coast, soon to be joined by schools in the South, to close the gap in technical playing skills. The shift in power, demonstrated by the results of intersectional games and the diversifying All-American teams, illustrated the nationalization of the game. The Notre Dame series at West Point was a well-established intersectional rivalry, and the 1920 season brought a number of other games involving long-distance travel: Michigan versus Tulane, Georgia Tech playing Pitt, Dartmouth traveling to Seattle, and Nebraska taking on Penn State, Washington State, and Rutgers. The Nebraska-Rutgers game played at the Polo Grounds on November 2, 1920 was a signal that big-city promoters were ready to stage college football games in neutral, non-campus ballparks.

The 1920 season also ushered in the "wonder team" of the University of California. In the Rose Bowl on January 1, 1921, Cal whipped an excellent Ohio State team, 28-0. Football fans around the country marveled at the newspaper accounts of the beautiful scenery, the pageantry of the Tournament of Roses, and especially the wide-open Cal attack, led by All-American Brick Muller. The *Los Angeles Times* wrote: "Until this battle, the rest of the nation had looked down a collective nose at Western football. (This game) truly ushered in the Golden Age of Sports in the West." In Atlanta, John Heisman turned Georgia Tech into the "colossus of the South" in much the way Stagg's Chicago had dominated the Midwest. From 1905 through 1919, Heisman's Engineers went 96-25-6, while playing nearly all its games at home. His final five teams went 37-4-2. It was a significant triumph for Notre Dame to have Tech agree to games starting in 1922.

As the 1921 season approached, fans were excited about several intersectional games. Dartmouth was to play Tennessee and Georgia; Penn State scheduled Georgia Tech in New York City, and then would go to Seattle to play Washington; and Harvard had games with Indiana and Georgia. Rockne, too, had added an unusual twist to Notre Dame's slate of games. After the annual clash at West Point on Saturday, November 5, the Fighting Irish would play in New York City for the first time ever, in a game against Rutgers on Tuesday, November 8.

The Fighting Irish opened the 1921 season by routing Kalamazoo, 56-0. The next week, the visitor to Cartier Field was DePauw University of Greencastle, Indiana. It was DePauw's first appearance on Notre Dame's football schedule since 1905, when the Irish whipped the Tigers, 71-0. In six meetings from 1897 through 1905, Notre Dame shut out DePauw all six times, with a 195-0 edge in points. Yet, there was something that put Coach Rockne on edge the week of the game. He took his student publicity assistant Frank Wallace aside, and detailed the reasons the Irish should be concerned. First and foremost, DePauw's new coach was Fred "Mysterious" Walker. Rockne knew that Walker had been a three-sport star at Hyde Park High, then for Stagg at Chicago, where Walker played halfback for the Maroons from 1904 to 1906. His best sport was baseball, though, and he reached the majors with five different clubs, earning his nickname by pitching under an assumed name for the San Francisco Seals of the Pacific Coast League in 1910. In between seasons in the majors and minors, he began a career of coaching college football, basketball, and baseball at a litany of schools. DePauw was the seventh college at which Walker coached football, including two, one-year stints back in Chicago assisting Stagg.

Because freshmen were eligible to play varsity football at DePauw, Rockne figured there was no telling what kind of group Walker might have assembled in Greencastle, lying in wait and ready to pounce on an overconfident Irish squad. Rockne also noted DePauw was bringing its own drinking water to South Bend. And then what appeared to be the final straw: DePauw canceled its first game, not wanting Notre Dame to scout its personnel or strategy. Rockne's apprehension might have served to motivate his team, or simply to sell more tickets. Both seemed to work. A respectable crowd of 8,000 came out, and DePauw played a tough first half before Notre Dame broke loose for a 57-10 victory, running its winning streak to an even 20 games over the past three seasons under Rockne's mentoring.

All the talk around town at Hullie and Mike's, Jimmy and Goat's, and the other gathering spots centered on how good the team looked and how few barriers there might be to another unbeaten season. Especially, the downtown quarterbacks figured, since the Nebraska game was finally to be played at Cartier Field, as the homecoming game on October 22. But first up was a trip to Iowa City for Notre Dame's first-ever meeting with the University of Iowa. The Hawkeyes, under Howard Jones, were developing into a consistently strong club. Jones sported an impressive pedigree, having played on three undefeated national championship teams at Yale, before becoming the first full-time head coach at Syracuse. He coached Yale two seasons, and Ohio State one, before taking over at Iowa in 1916.

Jones had three superlative players: veteran All-Western quarterback Aubrey Devine, whose favorite target was brother Glenn; speedy halfback Gordon Locke; and huge tackle Fred "Duke" Slater, one of the first blacks to play in the Western Conference. Slater played high school football in Clinton, Iowa, against his father's wishes. Clinton players were required to provide their own shoes and helmets, and Slater's father couldn't afford either. So began his years of helmetless play, which was but one of many distinguishing aspects to his play. Walter Eckersall wrote, "Slater is so powerful that one man cannot handle him and opposing elevens have found it necessary to send two men against him every time a play was sent off his side of the line." Notre Dame's line, it was said, "must prepare to withstand the assaults of the mighty negro, and the backfield must learn to place passes where they cannot be touched by either member of the famous combination—Devine and Devine."

The Irish enjoyed a rare daylight train trip to Iowa City and were greeted as heroes by local football fans. Youngsters wanted to know which was quarterback Mohardt, and which player was Hunk Anderson. Frank Wallace, in addition to his publicity role, was entrusted by fellow students with $125 in small bills to place wagers on the Irish. He found few takers among the Hawkeye faithful, who felt their squad had little chance against mighty Notre Dame. On game day, Wallace observed that the players had seemed more nervous heading into the DePauw game a week earlier. All of Iowa City was primed for Notre Dame's visit. One report noted, "Not even the annual games with Wisconsin and Illinois are being anticipated with more eagerness than the fray with Notre Dame." Thousands of Notre Dame alumni throughout the Dakotas and Minnesota, who seldom had a chance of seeing the team, planned to attend. Additional bleachers were erected to handle the anticipated record crowd.

From the opening kickoff, Notre Dame knew it was in for a battle. Led by Slater's blocking, the Hawkeyes made one push after another through the Irish line, until Locke went over for a touchdown. Still in the first quarter, Aubrey Devine intercepted a pass, and after a pair of Irish penalties, Devine booted a 42-yard field goal for a 10-0 Iowa lead. The Irish cut it to 10-7 on a long pass from Mohardt to Kiley, but for the rest of the day failed on several other trips inside the Iowa 10. The fourth quarter was played almost entirely in Iowa's end, but Notre Dame was thwarted each time. Kiley blocked a punt and had an open field ahead of him, but was brought up short. Notre Dame outgained Iowa handily, but a penalty at a key moment or one of Belding's interceptions would end the threat. A long pass from Mohardt to Castner had the Irish challenging again as the final whistle blew, but Iowa's 10-7 margin held up.

After the game, a disappointed Irish team sat in silence in the locker room, some in tears. Rockne came in and said, "There will be no alibis." He went from player to player, checking for injuries, consoling with a few quiet words. He gave a short speech in which he credited Iowa with superior mental poise. He didn't say whether Notre Dame's deficit was the players' or his. On Sunday, waiting to depart Iowa City, Rockne sat in the smoking car with young Wallace and shared several thoughts. He seemed to be depressed, and was not sure he could continue in all his roles—athletic director, football coach, trainer, business manager, track coach. Things would have to be different, he said. He would need help. One loss after 20 straight wins brought his whole operation into a different focus.

The train rumbled across Iowa and Illinois, headed for arrival in South Bend late Sunday night. The coach was tired and wanted nothing more than to get home to Bonnie and the children. But as the train approached the New York Central depot, distinct sounds of cheering—the Notre Dame "skyrocket" cheer—could be heard. Much like the raucous response in 1914 after the shellacking at Yale, Notre Dame men were out to show support for their team. Somewhere around a thousand students and townspeople jammed around the train. Rockne's first instinct was to fight his way through the mob and exit quickly. But the coach accepted their pleas for a speech. "It was the hardest fight we ever made," the coach screamed above the noisy crowd. "We went into that game with everything favoring us, and lost in spite of our hardest efforts. We can only yield to the winning team in a battle that will be history. Iowa played a marvelous game." Added the *News-Times* report: "The rest of his words were drowned in the tumult of cheering that the speech of the coach inspired." Wallace reported that the emotional support of the crowd moved the coach to tears. "After this, I will never leave Notre Dame, as long as they want me," he said.

What followed was a week of grim determination. "We're starting all over again this week," Rockne said. A local columnist, Tex Kelly, praised the way the coach handled defeat. "With no words of contempt for his successful rivals, with no bitterness or malice toward any officials, the Notre Dame coach concedes his excruciating loss as a part of the great man's game." Kelly went on to commend Rockne for choosing not to have Castner attempt a tying field goal in the late stages of the game. "Rockne is the gamest of the game. He went to Iowa to win or to lose. He wanted no halfway score. Notre Dame has lost none of its prestige. As the game is rehashed, she will gain more. Her team always brings honor to the school. Rockne has brought honor to both." That spirit was unleashed against Purdue on October 15, with the Irish steamrolling to a 30-0 halftime lead and a 33-0 victory. Hunk Anderson had a lineman's dream afternoon, scoring two touchdowns after blocking punts.

The next week, Notre Dame alums from far and wide streamed into South Bend, filling every hotel to overflowing and causing private residences to open up to visitors. Nothing like the visit of Nebraska had ever occurred. When the Huskers arrived Friday night, some 10,000 students and townsfolk gave the team a tremendous welcome, packing Main Street and Washington Avenue near the Oliver Hotel, where the Huskers spoke from the balcony. "Deafening cheers greeted the visitors as they basked in the glare of a spotlight" and listened to their leaders speak to the crowd. "Do you know," asked Capt. Clarence Swanson, "that we Nebraskans would not consider our schedule complete unless it included Notre Dame? This is the game that every man on our team has been living for ever since it was arranged last fall. It is the game of games."

On a perfectly sun-dappled October afternoon, before a Homecoming crowd of 14,000, the largest yet to see a game at Cartier Field, the blue and gold took on the mammoth challenge. Nebraska outweighed Rockne's players by an average of 20 pounds per man, with several linemen topping out at 210 to 220 pounds. Hunk Anderson gave away 28 pounds to the behemoth across from him, John Pucelik. But as one observer noted, Hunk "is the most powerful being for his size that has ever lived." And Rockne's emphasis on quickness and preparedness offset the great deficit in size. The Irish had much the better of play and squeezed out a 7-0 victory, totally shutting down the Huskers attack.

Rockne was able to develop great depth by taking the time to work with individuals ostensibly on technique, but often just as much on mental acuity and confidence. At numerous positions, he wouldn't hesitate to play the man who was generally the understudy. At guard, Ed DeGree and Jim Dooley were interchangeable; at center, either Harry Mehre or Ojay Larson could be counted on; and Glen Carberry was more than capable of spelling Roger Kiley. In the backfield, Frank Thomas and Chet Grant could both handle quarterback duties, and there was a plethora of reliable halfbacks, starting with Johnny Mohardt, but also including Danny Coughlin, Paul Castner, and the great hurdler Gus Desch. Rockne was developing the same men who had often been spectators a year earlier—watching Gipp's individual heroics—into outstanding team contributors.

The Irish, backed by about 800 students who boarded special trains for their annual away-game trip, rolled into Indianapolis and pounded Indiana, 28-7; a much different result than the tight games of the previous two years between the in-state rivals. As the Irish prepared for the trip to West Point, the South Bend press reported that "Knute K. Rockne is wearing a smile with his left thumb tucked under the armlet of his vest. He is assuring Notre Dame admirers that the Army can be beat, will be beat and must be beat by the 'Fightingest Irish' he has ever scowled and scolded about...If Notre Dame can whip West Point and three days later subdue Rutgers, then the whole sport world will be willing to admit that despite the Iowan defeat, the Rockers have assembled one of the sweetest little teams that have ever stepped onto the gridiron."

The Eastern press still wasn't sold on Notre Dame. The consensus was that "the great Army team, composed entirely of veterans and numbering among its men several prospective All-Americans, will crush the light Rockmen." Eastern scribes pointed out that Notre Dame had not developed a reliable passing combination. Even Grantland Rice, the esteemed nationally syndicated writer and an admirer of Rockne and his system, predicted a 17-14 Cadet victory. Controversy began even before the kickoff, as Army coach Charlie Daly and his staff registered their vigorous opposition to the Notre Dame shift. Over the past few years, some observers felt that Notre Dame backs were "beating the ball," essentially being in motion when the ball was snapped. Rockne had coached with such precision that, technically, both feet of each man were planted on the ground at the center snap—but "the synchronized swing of the bodies and the split-second timing of the pass was calculated so that the momentum of movement was never lost." Opposing teams were caught off-balance, often jumping offsides, and were generally unprepared for whatever play followed. The 1921 college rules committee deemed the maneuver legal, but that did little to quiet Rockne's critics. In this case, veteran referee Ed Thorp assuaged Army's angst by agreeing to call the strictest interpretation of the "feet on the ground" rule. That allowed the game to proceed, but it wasn't long before Daly was protesting loudly, running onto the field several times claiming Notre Dame was in motion. The Irish simply did what they did best, and used a dizzying array of plays to forge a 14-0 halftime lead. As Thorp walked off the field to rest at the half, Daly and assistant "Pot" Graves intercepted Thorp and the argument escalated, with the coaches even threatening to end the game.

"Forget it," Rockne said, realizing an Army forfeit would benefit nobody. "We won't use the shift in the second half." He walked over to quarterback Thomas and instructed him to run all plays from short punt formation. It didn't halt the Irish attack, as they added two more scores for a resounding 28-0 victory. Moreover, Rockne's decision to stand down had helped ease tensions, and a few days later, when a newspaper report questioned whether the series was to continue, Rockne was quick to support Army's contention that no such break was planned. The game was more popular than ever, with crowds up from New York City taxing the Cullum Field stands to their limit.

Among the visitors to West Point that day was the entire Rutgers team. They were hoping to gain a line on Notre Dame's style of play, but the probable effect was a lowering of team morale as they watched the Irish romp. Tuesday, November 8 was Election Day, a holiday in New York, and 12,000 paying customers came out to the Polo Grounds to witness a 48-0 Irish victory. Buck Shaw continued his amazing streak at kicking the goal after touchdown, with his 20th straight successful boot, giving him 34 of 35 on the season. On November 12, Notre Dame played its third game in eight days, against the Haskell Indians. Rockne put the team in the hands of assistant coach Walter Halas and headed to Milwaukee to scout Marquette in its game against North Dakota. Halas started the second unit and by the third quarter had the third-stringers in, as Notre Dame rolled to a 42-7 win. Rockne's scouting then paid off in a 21-7 victory at Marquette, and the Irish closed out a 10-1 season by pummeling Michigan Agricultural, 48-0.

After the season's success, a campus sports editor described Rockne's coaching philosophy and style that was now coming into focus:

> Rockne is what the psycho-analysts might call a 'football complex,' a bundle of instincts and conscious states governed by a predominant idea of turning out football players and football teams. He lives and thinks football in terms of his everyday life and applies the smallest lessons of his experience to his football theory. He knows psychology and he uses it in his theory and practice. He had a healthy interest in a great number of subjects not concerned with athletics, but he extracts from these extrinsic pursuits, germs of human action and tendency and applies them to his athletic theory. He has a natural drive and a dynamic personality that is ideally adapted to handling a squad of athletes…Rockne loves his boys and he labors to turn them out as men. He believes that athletics are a valuable preparation for future life.…He is strong, courageous and determined; he is also lovable, delightful, and witty. He is stern but is considerate. When a game is on, he 'creacks 'em;' when it is over he binds their injuries. The whole school is behind Rock.

Rockne may have been swept up in an emotional wave when he told the crowd after the Iowa loss that he would never leave Notre Dame. And there were few on campus in the administration who doubted his authoritarian figure. In the midst of fund-raising, Father Burns and his staff knew the importance of athletic receipts—and the value of the Rockne name—to the future of the university. After the undefeated 1919 season, the administration boosted Rockne's salary to $5,000 plus an additional

$1,000 bonus if he won all of his games; a feat accomplished in 1920. Perhaps it was the one loss to Iowa and the lack of a bonus that nagged at Rockne as the 1921 season ended. Or maybe it was the realization that as the primary wage earner for a family with three children, money was becoming a bigger part of any professional career decision. It may even have been that his friends Byron Kanaley and Angus McDonald, one a Chicago mortgage and bond broker and the latter a Notre Dame alumnus and New York stockbroker, were earning amazing salaries. Whatever the reason, by early December Rockne was weighing an official offer to take over as coach at Northwestern.

Kanaley, a 1904 Notre Dame alumnus and four-year baseball monogram winner, wrote to Father Burns on December 7, 1921 urging Burns to consider what an invaluable asset Rockne was to the university and what a loss it would be to see him go. Kanaley wrote that the public relations value of a winning football program was incalculable. Money could not buy the advertising generated from the football team, but moreover, the qualities displayed by Rockne's teams reflected "such tremendous credit on our school." Kanaley believed the best way to keep Rockne at Notre Dame would be to offer him a five-year contract with a salary increase and to eliminate a bonus based on an undefeated system. Burns concurred and met with Rockne the day after Christmas. The two came to terms easily. The coach promised Burns that he would "stay at Notre Dame permanently as long as he was in the coaching business." It was a promise made to Burns and Burns only—something to be remembered as Father Matthew Walsh assumed the presidency in 1922.


Rockne's earlier forays into semi-pro football as an occasional player and coach did not endear him to the pro game. Pro or semi-pro ball, he felt, kept men from their appointed professions and turned them into "football tramps." How could they be considered for respectable jobs if they were forever slipping off to knock heads on a potato patch for a few bucks a match? Rockne, who never lost sight of his training that stressed the Greek principle of strengthening the mind and body, believed in the educated, well-rounded man. He had been one himself at Notre Dame, serious about school and involved in many activities. From early on as a head coach, he worked to place his graduated players into coaching positions on college campuses, where they could further their education, go into a profession, or prepare for business, without the uncertainty of the nascent pro game.

After Notre Dame's strong 1921 season, though, a few of the Irish were tempted to dip their toes into the play-for-pay version. In two coal-mining towns in central Illinois—Carlinville and Taylorville—football fever was raging. On Thanksgiving Day 1920, Carlinville defeated their archrivals 10-7 in a game that made numerous Taylorville supporters a few dollars poorer than when the day began. As the 1921 season unfolded, excitement for the teams' annual battle, set for November 27, the Sunday after Thanksgiving grew. There were whispers around Carlinville that the team would be sporting something of a "new look" this time around and that it might be advisable to go a little deeper into one's savings to put money down on the local eleven.

Rumors spread that "the Notre Dame team" was going to show up and play for Carlinville. A lad who had grown up and played high school ball in Carlinville, Frank "Si" Seyfrit, was a backup end for the Irish. As the excitement in Carlinville grew, more and more folks found the money to wager on the game. Eventually, word spread to Taylorville about Carlinville's planned imports, and before long, a representative of Taylorville had made contact with several University of Illinois players to counter. So, residents of Taylorville also began emptying their wallets to place bets on the local squad. By game day, an estimated $100,000 was in play. Taylorville took a 7-0-halftime lead. It then flooded the Illinois players into their line and stretched three long drives into a 16-0 final.

Back at Notre Dame, there were a few snickers and sideways glances at the men who had "lost to Illinois." Holy Cross Father William Carey, head of the Faculty Athletic Board, wanted to take as strong a stand as possible against the growing allurement of pro ball. Notre Dame was in the middle of an effort to increase its academic standards and dispel charges from other schools that it was becoming a football factory. The Taylorville game finally bubbled up to the Chicago papers, and Father Carey said that the university had been conducting a thorough investigation since the rumors first began to spread that Notre Dame men played in the game. On January 30, eight Notre Dame athletes confessed to playing in the game. They were immediately disqualified from further athletic competition at Notre Dame.

In announcing the discipline, Father Carey said, "We will stand for no taint or hint of professionalism here. Not even if it wrecks our teams forever. We don't permit a man to play on any team unless he is well up in his studies, and we won't permit any other rule to be broken." Shortly after the Taylorville scandal broke, Notre Dame suffered another black eye when the newspaper headline "Johnny Mohardt Admits Playing in 'Pro' Football Game" appeared. After being cleared of playing at Taylorville, Mohardt had come before Father Carey and admitted that he had played in a December 4 game in Milwaukee between Curly Lambeau's Green Bay Packers and the Racine Legion. However, no action was taken in the case, as Mohardt had finished his course of study.

In the days that followed, several prominent Western Conference and other Middle West college athletes faced similar charges of professionalism. Notre Dame leaders were quick to call for a "clean up" of college athletics. The school's investigation of the football scandal discovered that "emissaries from promoters of professional football frequently visit universities to tempt their athletic stars." Father Carey said, "The only salvation for the colleges is to meet the threat of professional football fairly and squarely."

In early February, he presented a six-point plan for his fellow college administrators: It would organize alumni and letter men to combat professionalism; solicit pledges from every graduating athlete not to play in pro games in which men still in college are used; solicit a pledge from each man in college eligible for athletics not to play pro games while still in college, and expel violators; publish each fall the name, hometown, and high school of each high school athletic prospect entering college; disqualify men playing contests after leaving high school and before entering college; and remove the belief that it is unfriendly for one college to notify another concerning its players.

Father Carey advised high school and college athletes to "stop, look, and listen" when faced with the lure of professionalism. "I have never known a young man who chose wrongly to whom the inevitable regret did not come," he said. "When the temptation comes he will do well to hesitate and ask himself, 'Is it worth while?' "

Dave Hayes was one of the lesser-known Notre Dame football players from the group that won 28 of its 29 games from 1919 through 1921. As a Catholic youngster in Manchester, Connecticut, he had dreamed of attending Notre Dame someday. In 1916, he followed that dream, hitching a ride on a freight train and arriving in South Bend penniless, but with a burning ambition to be part of Notre Dame. He came to campus, worked on every available job to put himself through school, and tried out for football, eventually making the varsity. Hayes was always ready, and when his opportunity came to play in the 1917 Army game, he delivered some big plays in the 7-2 victory. He then went off to fight in the Great War and came back with an injured leg, but that did not stop him from being part of the team. He worked his way up the ranks until becoming a capable reserve behind Roger Kiley and Eddie Anderson. Hayes managed to earn his degree with a few dollars to spare. Upon graduation, he met with Father Burns and handed him $250 for the building fund. "I came here broke, on a freight, Father," Hayes said. "I'm leaving the same way." He said he would never forget how the university took him in and helped him become a man, a true Notre Dame man.

Father Burns was deeply touched that a new graduate would give his accumulated savings to his alma mater. It represented the type of spirit the school needed to raise an endowment for Notre Dame. Although middle and working class Catholics were generous with visible projects that touched their lives, such as parish schools in their community, fundraising efforts among immigrant populations was often difficult. While Father Burns was not the first president of Notre Dame to realize the importance of an endowment for the university, he was the first to take the steps necessary to obtain one. This new world of fund-raising led Burns to reach out and form a board of lay trustees who would be tasked with overseeing the establishment of the endowment funds. Burns had accompanied Father Cavanaugh on a trip to New York in 1917 in which the two met with the General Education Board (GEB), later to be known as the Rockefeller Foundation. Because the GEB had little interaction with financial requests from Catholic institutions, the formation of a Notre Dame lay board was imperative. By 1920 the Notre Dame Board of Trustees was established and in 1921 Albert R. Erskine of the Studebaker Corporation was appointed as president of the Board and as chairman of the three-person finance committee. The timing coincided with the General Education Board announcement that John D. Rockefeller had made an extraordinary gift of over $50 million for the specific purpose of assisting private colleges and universities to raise faculty salaries. The GEB announced on February 21, 1921 it had awarded Notre Dame $250,000 for building a lay faculty salary endowment; the caveats included that the university be free of debt and match the funds in order to receive the grant.

The debt-free requirement meant Burns could not borrow funds to construct the much-needed resident halls or classroom facilities. Updates to or replacement of Cartier Field were no longer suggested. Burns began a years-long impassioned fund-raising drive that would take him across the country in search of money. It was in his appeal to the alumni and South Bend communities that netted Burns his biggest financial rewards. Erskine became a trusted partner focused on doing everything he could to make it happen. Erskine took tremendous satisfaction from working for Notre Dame and from the publicity he derived as head of the fund-raising efforts. Erskine strongly believed that raising funds for a salary endowment and new building was a socially desirable activity and that responsible industrial leaders should undertake such civic-minded endeavors. Studebaker dealers from Baton Rouge to Boston contributed to the fund-raiser, and he personally solicited donations from other South Bend business and professional communities. By October 1922, ahead of schedule, Notre Dame had reached its fund-raising drive of $200,000.

Burns realized the long-term nature of fund-raising and the impact it would have on all future presidents. By the spring of 1922, the task had taken its toll on this Holy Cross priest, and he announced his resignation. The official report of the meeting with his superiors simply stated Burns "gave many good reasons for his request." As Burns departed, he had contributed two notable accomplishments. He had left the university on stronger financial footing, and he had assured that Rockne would lead the football team into the 1920s.

# 19

## Birth of a Backfield

At the same time that the university sought to expand and strengthen its academic profile and position among American Catholics, the Notre Dame football coach was settling into a pattern of stability and success. Rockne had survived the uncertainty and upheaval of 1918; managed to tiptoe around the distractions brought by his sometimes wayward star Gipp; and escaped the embarrassment brought on by the "Carlinville Eight." Down to the smallest detail, he knew what he wanted from his players, and demanded it. Football, he said, came down to the three Ds—dirt, drudgery, and discipline. A player had to be willing to get down into the dirt and work out the details of every play, every situation. That would take tremendous effort, which Rockne reminded his men would have benefits beyond the football field. "If you want your head and shoulders towering above the horde in your chosen field," he would tell them, "then you must be willing to sacrifice. That means rising early each morning, rolling up your sleeves a little higher, and working harder than the other guy if you hope to catch him, let alone surpass him."

The mere manner in which he approached the practice field spoke of Rockne's focus on helping his men improve. At 3:40 each afternoon, a team manager swung open a gate in the green-painted board fence that surrounded Cartier Field, and Rockne strode through, quickly and confidently, as he headed to the center of the field. There was power in the set of his shoulders, in his erect bearing, in his purposeful stride. His eyes took in all that was going on around him, as players informally did their work. Without stopping, he pointed with an outstretched arm and offered correction.

To a back, he said, "Joe, you're telegraphing your play. The purpose of a good offense is to deceive. Regardless of intent, keep your eyes glued on one spot on all plays." Then, the biting humor. "If you're going to give away a play, it'd be much better to send your opponent a postcard." To a nearby end, working on blocking: "You're nose-diving, Tom. Keep your eyes up and your stern down, so your drive is concentrated and at the same time you can see where your opponents in maneuvering." If the correction was followed, praise would too. "That's marvelous guard play, Noble," he said to Noble Kizer. "You're greatly improved over yesterday. In pulling out you're more decisive. Now, you're able to get out of there ahead of the ball carrier rather than have him crawl up your back."

Sometimes it was the quality of his voice that made an impression, more than the message that was being conveyed. Rockne's voice, slightly nasally, sometimes raspy, starting with a staccato delivery that blended into an inflection stretching the final syllables, as if to underscore the point, carried a spirit of force, power, and magnetism. One just had to listen.

His vision of football, especially of his now-famous Notre Dame shift, was one of coordination, teamwork, and effortless rhythm. It meant knowing not just one's own role and responsibilities, but teammates' as well. And the better you could know everyone's duties, the greater chance there was for success as a unit. "There never were two football players exactly alike," Rockne told his men. "You've got to learn each other's characteristics. You've got to accommodate yourself to the other fellow's strong and weak points. That's the only way to get smoothness." Just for kicks, a group of linemen took up a position behind the regular backfield practicing the shift, hopping and sidestepping to the "Hip, one, two, three, hip" signal. The linemen mimicked their movements, though quite ineffectively, creating a disorganized, humorous mess. Rockne walked by and barked, "You big muscle and feed fellows had better confine your activities to line play. That is where you are needed. But since you insist on knowing this stuff, let me show you how to work the backfield shift." Inwardly, though, he was delighted that one group wanted to know the workings of the next. He proceeded to give the linemen a crash course in the shift. "Keep on the balls of your feet," he told tackle Joe Bach. "Then you'll look like something neat." Rockne would use that kind of language. "That's lovely," he could compliment in a low voice. "That's marvelous." "That's sweet." Football didn't have to sound like war. It could be a well-choreographed performance, and be just as successful.

Drudgery aside, there could be moments of utter fun. One of his innovations, the annual spring game, begun in 1922, was eventually played in front of a paying crowd, raising funds for one cause or another. That first game matched the fellows expected to form the varsity the coming fall against a team of alumni, many of them the graduating seniors. The coach anointed himself starting quarterback for the alumni team. There stood Rockne, barking signals in his penetrating voice, just the way he wanted his quarterbacks to do it. The center snapped the ball—and suddenly all eleven varsity players had a clean line to Rockne, as his 10 teammates had conspired to neatly step out of the way of the charging defenders. Swarmed under, Rockne came up glaring, and sputtered, "Wise guys." He called another play, this one a pass, Mohardt to Rockne, and the old left end snared it perfectly for a nice gain. He retired to the sidelines, preferring to go out on top.

Starting practice in September 1922, Rockne knew he had some work to do to create his team. Gone were 14 of the 22 lettermen who excelled the year before, including all 11 regular starters. Competition for playing time would be wide open, and no spots were assured. It was the type of challenge Rockne relished—working with men at all different stages of their football development, drilling and instructing to bring out the best in each. For as one player noted, "He could talk his players into being twice as big, twice as fast and twice as good as they thought they were."

Among the best of the returnees was fullback Paul Castner, a third year player on the varsity and veteran of two battles with Army, one as a surprise starter. The 6-0, 190-pound Castner had developed self-discipline and a strong work ethic at St. Thomas Military Academy in St Paul, Minnesota, and it carried him through a hectic schedule at Notre Dame. In addition to football and studies, he was the star pitcher of the Irish baseball team and player-coach of the school's hockey team. From his earliest days skating on White Bear Lake near his Minnesota home, Castner was a superb skater. As hockey coach, Castner invited fellow athletes from the North Country to join the team. From the Upper Peninsula of Michigan there were Percy Wilcox, a skilled puck-handler, and defenseman Hunk Anderson, who Castner called "a bruising competitor who knocked down opponents like pins in a bowling alley. He was reckless…He swept the ice clear with what resembled a giant fir from the north country. He slam-banged around the rink." One day, Rockne was walking past the rink—the Badin bog—and stopped to watch practice. Castner, proud of his squad, skated over and asked, "Well, coach, what do you think?"

"Hockey is all right," Rockne answered, "but it's too rough."

"Football isn't exactly an old maid's game," Castner replied. "Players have been known to get a bloody lip there, too."

"Yes, football is rough," Rockne admitted. "But it can't compare with hockey. Any game where Hunk Anderson carries a club is rough!"

Castner made it through another hockey season relatively unscathed, and he was ready for football. So too were a handful of veterans. Frank Thomas returned with some experience at quarterback; Ed DeGree had seen plenty of work at guard; and Gene "Kentuck" Oberst, well familiar to Rockne as a budding star in track, stood out at tackle. Team captain Glen Carberry, from Ames, Iowa, patrolled one end position and had come a long way since that day when he first heard Coach Rockne chortle, "Carberry, you keep playing like that and you'll spend more time on the bench than any judge in history." From that day forward, he was "Judge" Carberry.

The freshmen from 1921 had done little to distinguish themselves, losing badly to Lake Forest Academy and the Michigan Aggie frosh. Of the lot, the most promising to make the jump to varsity, Rockne said later, was a little quarterback, Harry Stuhldreher. Not yet 150 pounds, "he sounded like a leader on the field. He was a good and fearless blocker and as he gained in football knowledge he showed signs of smartness in emergencies." Stuhldreher hailed from football-mad Massillon, Ohio, where he and Rockne had first met. While assistant coach to Jesse Harper at Notre Dame, Rockne—along with his good pal Gus Dorais—suited up for the Massillon pro team for two games in 1915, and another pair in 1916 against archrival Canton, featuring the great Jim Thorpe. An adoring young local football player, Stuhldreher, a slight lad of about 14, would occasionally help carry Rockne's football gear into the stadium. This experience planted the youngster's dream of his own football glory.

In the fall of 1915, Stuhldreher witnessed one of the most memorable Massillon-Canton tussles of all time. The teams played a pair of games two weeks apart, with Rockne, Dorais, and Massillon taking a 16-0 victory on November 15 at home. The return match November 29 at Canton stands as one of the strangest, most controversial games in football history. More than 8,000 viewers, most with money riding on the game, crowded the field in Canton, which was without police or security of any kind. Massillon trailed Canton in the fourth quarter, 6-0, when, from Canton's 11-yard-line, Dorais lofted a perfect pass to his halfback Briggs, who sprinted for the Canton goal line. As he approached the goal line, the crowd surged onto the field and Briggs dove into the mass of bodies, across the goal line with the ball securely tucked under his arm, for an apparent touchdown. But while Briggs was buried in the crowd, someone kicked the ball out of his arms, and a Canton player emerged with the ball. The fans stormed onto the field while the argument went on.

Both the umpire and head linesman said the last time they saw the ball it was in the possession of Massillon and that the Tigers had scored a legal touchdown. The referee, Conners, failed to keep control of the situation, and allowed the argument to go on at length until it became too dark to play. He finally called the game with eight minutes remaining, and said he would make a decision later, when he was alone with the officials. That Sunday evening, at the Courtland Hotel in Canton, Conners gave the game to Canton 6 to 0 in a sealed envelope, overruling the other two officials, even though he did not see the end of the touchdown play. Conners left specific instructions that the sealed envelope could not be opened until 12:30 p.m. the next day, after he had left town.

Young Harry Stuhldreher developed a great love for the game while growing up near the center of Massillon, just around the corner from the imposing double spires of St. Mary's Catholic Church, where he began playing ball. Harry's dad ran a small grocery store, and his older brother Walter, not gifted athletically, was a strong student. Walter, to his mother's great joy, went off to attend Notre Dame. He served in Notre Dame's SATC until the Armistice was signed in November 1918. Harry played football for local sandlot teams, but he would be regularly teased for his slight stature. That only made Harry more focused on developing his speed, quickness, and deception. At Washington High, he entered his senior year as a 138-pound backup halfback, but when the regular quarterback suffered a broken leg, Harry's chance as signal-caller came. Stuhldreher's own injured arm, however, kept him out of the big Massillon-Canton high school battle his senior year. After high school, the diminutive Stuhldreher spent a year at Kiski Prep outside of Pittsburgh, to prepare for college academically and athletically. At one point he thought he might be headed to Princeton, before deciding to follow brother Walter to South Bend.

Another football hotbed, the area of northeastern Wisconsin near Green Bay, had already produced one Rockne protégé, fullback Earl Lambeau from the 1918 team. Lambeau had left Notre Dame after one semester to return to Green Bay and do what he did best—organize football teams. When he convinced his employer, the Indian Packing Company, to advertise by spending $500 for the team's uniforms, the Green Bay Packers were born, starting play in the American Football Professional Association. But Lambeau's primary job was that of head football coach at his alma mater, East High School, which was now consistently turning out top stars. One of them who Lambeau helped direct to Notre Dame was Jim Crowley, now a sophomore in 1922.

Crowley was born in Chicago, but when his father Jeremiah developed consumption the family moved to Colorado to take advantage of its clean air and facilities for treating the ailment. After Jeremiah died, Agnes Crowley moved her two sons back into her mother's home in Green Bay. There, Jim excelled in sports, became adept with a pool cue, and delighted friends and strangers alike with his witty banter. One classmate described him this way: "He never works, and never worries, seldom flunks, and never hurries." He rejected an offer to play baseball for the Cincinnati Reds in order to attend Notre Dame. On the practice field, Crowley's drowsy demeanor and quick comebacks quickly made him stand out. "Crowley," Rockne roared, "You look like a tester in an alarm-clock factory," forever stamping Crowley with the nickname "Sleepy Jim."

Elmer Layden, a sprinter from Davenport, Iowa, was another promising sophomore. He had already faced his most severe challenge at Notre Dame—a desperate bout of homesickness as a freshman, despite being reunited with his former high school coach Walter Halas, now Rockne's assistant. Early in the fall of Layden's freshman year, Halas invited Layden and a cousin of his who also attended Notre Dame over to his house for dinner. Then Elmer asked to use the phone, called his father collect, and said he was thinking of coming home and calling it quits on the idea of college. "Well, sleep on it first," Tom Layden advised his son. "Call me again in the morning and tell me your decision. Give the school a chance." Almost on cue, there was a knock on the door, and Coach Rockne appeared. Layden and Rockne started talking and the subject of Layden's homesickness came up.

"Son, we've never lost a freshman from our team yet," the coach boasted, fibbing just a bit.

Layden thought to himself, "Mr. Rockne, your record is about to be broken."

Rockne went on to talk about his own path in life, suggesting how lucky Layden was to be able to start college at age 18 and not 22. The coach gave his philosophy on the different types of personalities and made it clear he preferred the "up-and-at-'em, the go-get-'em type." Layden, intrigued by the talk, asked Rockne what made the Notre Dame team special.

"I'd rather have 11 men," Rockne said, "who are willing to follow orders than the most brilliant collection of individual stars on earth." And what, Elmer also wanted to know, was the outstanding characteristic of a Notre Dame player?

"Courage," came the reply. "At Notre Dame there are no quitters."

Elsewhere among the backfield candidates were the two youngest Miller brothers from Defiance, Ohio, Gerry and Don. The line of Millers began with Harry "Red" Miller, 1908 captain and star of the 1909 upset of Michigan. Gerry was two years older than Don, but had missed quite a bit of school—one year was lost due to typhoid fever, the other was spent working. A tiny scatback, he amazed teammates with his darting, change-of-direction running style. Gerry has been poised for a big senior year at Defiance High when he was disqualified due to his age. Don then picked up the mantle and led his team to a string of victories. They graduated together and headed to Notre Dame, where most of the attention was fixed on Gerry, the flashy halfback. In September 1921, Don was disheartened when the football togs were distributed and he received mere scraps. He spent the next three weeks offering up his daily communion to help him deal with the disappointment. Gerry, meanwhile, became the star of the freshmen team. His dizzying moves resulted in three touchdowns in victories over Culver Academy and Great Lakes. Despite his 145-pound frame, he was set to take his place as the next great Miller when he opened the 1922 season as a varsity halfback. Don simply went to work to become the best football player he possibly could be. In a few weeks' time, the brothers' football fortunes would undergo another stark reversal. In the second game of the season, a 26-0 win over St. Louis, Gerry suffered a season-ending leg injury. Don, meanwhile, saw more playing time and became the first of the 1922 sophomores to start regularly, supplanting another speedster, Red Maher, at right half.

Crowley was next to assume a starter's role and opened Rockne's eyes with breakout performances in wins over Purdue, 20-0, and DePauw, 34-7. "Crowley astonished Purdue a great deal," Rockne later observed, "and me a great deal more with the liveliest exhibition of cutting, jumping, side-stepping, change of pace and determined ball-toting that I had seen in many a day." Wrote Frank Wallace of Crowley's entrance on the big stage:

> Watch him stand in the backfield, seemingly asleep—his eyelids add to the illusion. Listen to the quarterback call signals—no sign from Jimmy. The backfield heps into the first step of the shift—Jimmy reluctantly moves with them. The ball is snapped—whiz! The emotional switch has been pulled. Off around end quicker than you thought. When a tackle hit—Jimmy hits too—and let the tackle worry. When a man obstructs his pathway—Jimmy plows into him and does a swan dive through space for a touchdown, if the play is within five yards of the goal. He just has

football instinct. He has a fearless drive, an angelic courage…
Three more years of Rockne and a gang of kids like this—getting better every day!

The Rockmen's next game would be their first venture into Dixie for an October 28 scrap with Georgia Tech in Atlanta, home base of the virulently anti-Catholic Ku Klux Klan. Atlanta remained the citadel of Klan power from the time William Simmons organized a Klan revival at Stone Mountain, Georgia in 1915. By late summer 1921, nation-wide Klan participation and financial contributions from its members were steadily climbing. Simmons banked upwards of 20 percent of the national money and managed to acquire an ostentatious home in an Atlanta suburb that he dubbed Klan Krest. By 1922, the Georgia Knights gloried in the election of their fellow Klansman, Clifford Walker, as governor. Walker would serve two terms and had additional Klan support with other elected state legislators and several other members that he appointed to his administration. In 1924 Walker's celebrity status was highlighted when he spoke at a national Klan convention in Kansas City, Missouri. He rallied supporters when he said a "gang of Roman Catholic priests" controlled the Democratic National Convention.

The Klan had taken on a vigilante role in Georgia. Parades in Columbus marched against anyone who was "loafing, thieving, and prowling." Immigrants from Syria and Lebanon were ordered to leave Marietta, and members of the Atlanta Board of Education were let go for protesting the firing of all Roman Catholic teachers. Atlanta Superior Court Judge Paul Etheridge, a noted Klan member, also served as Fulton county commissioner in 1921. In Macon, a city 75 miles south of Atlanta, police clashed with Klan knight-riders in 1923 as they set out on what was described as an epidemic of floggings. Georgia was not an isolated state. In Gainesville, Florida, in February 1924, the Klan, dressed in full regalia, kidnapped Reverend John Conoley. He was beaten severely, castrated, and left near death on the steps of a church in a nearby town. When he recovered, he identified his attackers as Mayor George Waldo and Chief of Police Lewis Fennell.

While preparing his squad for the trip, Rockne made no reference to the Klan. He was more concerned about the "Rebel Yell" the Tech fans were likely to unleash whenever the Irish were calling signals. Plus, he had other concerns. As dazzling as his new backs had been, the line was showing signs of wear. Fod Cotton and Ed DeGree had already missed games due to injury, and Tom Lieb, the great trackman and versatile football lineman, was through for the year with a broken leg suffered in the first quarter of the Purdue game. Meanwhile, Bob Reagan, a 6-foot-2, 153-pound beanpole at center, had avoided injury so far, as had Harvey Brown, at 5-foot-9, 165 pounds—the first of Rockne's famed "watch charm guards," named for their small stature after the tiny ornaments that dangled from a man's watch chain. As the team was about to leave the South Bend station for an arduous trip over four different rail lines, Lieb was there to see them off, on crutches and wearing plain clothes—corduroys and a flannel shirt—while the traveling squad dressed in their usual natty suits. But minutes before the train pulled out, Rockne leaned out and called to Lieb, "Come on, Tom, you're going!" Rockne was clearly trying to boost team morale, for Lieb was popular and well-respected by his teammates. The *Scholastic* noted, "Many a proud tear glittered in the eyes of the assembled crowd which cheered and marveled at this proud, defiant display of the undying Notre Dame spirit."

Before the game at Grant Field, Rockne entered the locker room with a fistful of telegrams received from Notre Dame alums and other supporters from around the country. He read a few, then finished with one that was "signed" by his son Billy, not yet seven years old. It told of being in the hospital with a serious illness, and closed by saying, "I want my Daddy's team to win." It was later learned that a friend of the Rockne family—as something of a prank—sent the wire. But some witnesses swore Rockne presented it as real, and actual tears ran down his cheeks. Whether he had been fooled or simply went along with an improbable scenario to motivate his team is up for debate.

The young Irish team took the field as a record crowd estimated at 20,000 roared the Rebel Yell. Rockne's men reported that, after the game's first few minutes, it sounded just like regular crowd noise and had little effect on the game. They played nearly perfect football for a 13-3 victory, with Stuhldreher passing to Castner for one touchdown and running for the other. There was one potentially significant error—on a drive that reached Tech's 5-yard line, Stuhldreher passed on second down over the goal-line incomplete, resulting in a touchback and Tech's ball. "Never again did Stuhldreher make a tactical error while running the team at quarterback," Rockne said.

The *Atlanta Constitution* described the inaugural meeting of the two teams in glowing terms:

> Epic is the word. For the 20,000 people who jammed those stands Saturday afternoon will never blot from memory the sixty hair-raising minutes of ripping and tearing, doing and daring performed by the two teams who had foregathered to do each other battle. It was one of those struggles that cause sane people to write books, an event that was shot to the core with romance and drama. It was one of those reasons small boys believe the dime novels, for it proves nothing colorful is impossible to red-blooded men.

The return trip was full of celebration for Notre Dame's traveling party. On the way down, the Irish had befriended a porter whom they nicknamed "Siki" after Battling Siki, the charismatic native of Senegal who had defeated Georges Carptentier for the light-heavyweight world's title a month earlier. Now, "Siki" had become so much part of the traveling party that at a 3 a.m. stop in Danville, Kentucky, he bragged to a station employee that his train carried the famous Notre Dame football team, conquerors of Georgia Tech's Golden Tornado. The man replied, "We got the team right here in Danville, Centre College."

"Centre College? Who ever heard of that," responded Siki.

"Harvard did. We beat Harvard. We've got Bo McMillan," came the reply, and it was true, the Prayin' Colonels had traveled to Cambridge exactly one year earlier and upset the Crimson, 6-0.

"Okay," Siki said, "You go get your team. I'll get my team up, and we'll play right here."

Some 1,500 students greeted the team upon its arrival back in South Bend on Sunday. Before Rockne could attempt a retreat, they carried him for a block on their shoulders, for they knew that it was his mastery that had taken virtually all-new material and molded a team such as this 1922 squad. Over the next several days, as preparations were laid for the greatest of all Homecomings, pride swelled in the accomplishments of the

Irish. F. Henry Wurzer, president of the Notre Dame alumni, wrote as part of his greeting, which appeared in the *News-Times*:

> All hail! To you men of Notre Dame, who have come from far and wide to answer the roll of her loyal sons, to make a holiday in her honor, and to sense again the wondrous thrills of our college days…Upon this brief but happy sojourn we may run the whole gamut of the wholesome joys of youth. We shall live over again the tender memories of the olden days, replete with finest sentiments of life…and then we shall turn to the mighty present, and glory in the splendid progress, the outstanding growth and development of the University itself; and last, but not least, we shall strut about with boyish glee and gusto to vent our swaggering militant pride in the superior prowess and skill of our athletes. Notre Dame—after all it is Notre Dame—and to us who know, that tells it all.

Unprecedented numbers of alumni arrived in South Bend. And many of those who were unable to attend were a large contingent of graduates who would be busy on November 4—coaching their own college football teams. Among them were Jim Phelan, Purdue; Charlie Bachman, Kansas Aggies; Charles Dorais, Gonzaga; Tom Martin, Penn State; Jim Dooley, Catholic University; Buck Shaw, University of Nevada; Dutch Bergman, New Mexico; Allen Elward, Coe College; Harry Baujan, Dayton; Ed Dugan, Franklin College; Biff Lee, Penn of Iowa; Slip Madigan, St. Mary's of California; and assistant coaches Freeman Fitzgerald of Marquette and George Trafton of Northwestern.

A record capacity crowd of 22,000 crammed Cartier Field, filling the newly erected bleachers and thousands of temporary seats for the Homecoming battle with Indiana. The game also represented Notre Dame's entry into the radio age; the new 100-watt South Bend station WGAZ broadcast the game. Its call letters stood for "World's Greatest Automotive Zone" in honor of the massive Studebaker plant located in South Bend. The broadcast consisted of *Tribune* sports editor Eugene Kessler's description of each play, phoned to the newsroom, and connected to outgoing "broadcasting apparatus." It had been less than two years since Pittsburgh's KDKA radio first went on the air in November 1920, but the number of radio stations across the United States had grown significantly, along with the number of radio sets.

The huge crowd witnessed one of the greatest individual displays of football in Notre Dame's history, as Paul Castner accounted for all the points in a 27-0 victory, with three touchdowns, three points-after and two field goals in his final appearance at Cartier Field. For Rockne, the Indiana game offered several moments of pause. The season provided him the chance to work with Father Hugh O'Donnell, his friend and fellow player from 1915 who had entered the priesthood and was now a Holy Cross father. The pair created a football atmosphere on campus unlike any other. O'Donnell had been a huge contributor to Rockne's efforts, and Rockne was grateful for the support. Albert Feeney, the centerman from the great Dorais-Rockne team of 1913 had returned for this game. Rockne was humbled by the tip of the hat to the past, and yet he wondered what lay ahead with the group he had assembled.


When Notre Dame had named Knute Rockne its head football coach in 1918, some people in the college football establishment had questioned the choice. Just turned 30, he was far younger than the "expert" mentors in the land. He did not come from a long-standing football tradition such as Yale, Harvard, Princeton, Chicago, or Michigan. He had been a good, but not great, player. And, his experience was limited to playing for and assisting Harper at Notre Dame, a team still far from the headliners who marked the top echelon of the sport. Now, well into his fifth season as coach, that perception had been thoroughly debunked. Rockne showed not just an eagerness to teach athletics, but wisdom in how best to impart its principles. He never lost the zest for learning he had shown as a youngster at Brentano Elementary, or as a collegian in Father Nieuwland's chemistry courses. And, through the years, as an academic instructor himself, and on the football field and track grounds, Rockne burned with the energy of one called to teach others. Simply knowing a formula, a technique, a strategy, was not enough. It had to be shared with others, so they too could test it, refine it, and use it to their betterment.

In the hours after the 1921 Army game, at which the Cadet coach Capt. Charlie Daly had protested so bitterly Notre Dame's use of the

274

shift, the two men shut themselves off for a lengthy period and discussed the theory and practice of the maneuver. This was the great Daly, who quarterbacked Harvard, belonged to the Hasty Pudding Club, and earned a Harvard degree in 1901; who had gone on to West Point, where he was quarterback, and won another degree in 1905; who had coached the Cadets since 1913; and who served ably in a number of roles in the Great War, with a rank as high as temporary colonel. On that day, after tempers had cooled, Daly was an earnest, curious student for the teacher Rockne. For the rest of that season, Daly tinkered with the shift, and came up with a modified version, in which his backfield would shift from a short punt formation to the box. For Rockne, the session was merely the natural thing to do. There was no sense of aiding and abetting "the enemy." And, very likely, it was that post-game meeting with Daly that coalesced a vision for Rockne of sharing what he knew about the game of football—its strategies for sure, but also its lessons—with as wide an audience as possible. If he could teach as experienced and respected veteran coach as Daly, imagine the hundreds or thousands of other, younger coaches across the land who could benefit from his tutoring.

The next match with Daly would come on Notre Dame's 1922 trip to West Point with both squads undefeated. Daly had Army working out of the shift and an unbalanced line, creating plenty of free-wheeling versatility. Rockne had the Fighting Irish playing with confidence, and more than one player of quality manned most positions. In fact, it was becoming more difficult each trip for Rockne to select a traveling squad. After he posted the list for the Army trip, a dejected sophomore fullback, Bernie Livergood, who had made the trip to Atlanta two weeks earlier, walked past Rockne's office in the Main Building. Rockne called him in and asked Livergood if he was feeling badly because of being left off the list. Livergood said no, but Rockne clearly saw his disappointment; he told Bernie to go pack his equipment and be at the train that evening. Rockne's heart was always with the hard worker, the earnest student, and Livergood was certainly that.

When the train pulled out that night, it carried not just the team but also several members of the "old guard" of supporters: Mike Calnon, Doc Powers, and Ideal Crockett. Phil Pidgeon and Cheerio Gleason were seen climbing aboard the Pullman. And Slim Lannard and Linus Glotzbach were along, on the basis of their outstanding work on behalf of the school's endowment drive. Walter Noveski of Corby Hall was the lucky winner of a drawing at Hullie and Mike's to join the trip to West Point. On Saturday, November 11, four years after the Armistice Day, fans jammed Cullum Hall Field awaiting the ninth battle of the rivals, with a crowd estimated as high as 25,000. A bulletin reported that next year's game most likely would be played at the Polo Grounds in New York City, as "the game has become such an intersectional attraction that the small field here at the Point cannot accommodate the thousands who wish to see the struggle." There was something of a circus atmosphere on the Plains, as "movie cameramen had a busy hour shooting the crowd as airplanes did stunts in the sky."

The game did not disappoint. Each team parried and attacked with slashing force, only to fall short of the goal. Layden got loose for a 35-yard run, but Castner's attempted drop kick was blocked. Crowley slipped through a hole for 12 yards, but fumbled two plays later when charging into "the human maelstrom" at the Army goal line. Army's Garbisch attempted a field goal from 44 yards, and the ball booted straight and sailed end-over-end until it fell one foot short of the crossbar. In the final minute, another try by Garbisch was blocked by a swarming Irish line, and the game ended in a grueling 0-0 tie.

That night, the team and thousands of its Eastern followers enjoyed an evening of entertainment in New York City organized by Joe Byrne Sr. and Jr., Angus McDonald, and Rupe Mills. At one point, from the open upper level of a two-tiered bus, Crowley gave a humorous oration to the Times Square crowd below, promising the repeal of Prohibition if his "party" were elected. The traveling party attended the Ziegfield Follies show, where Will Rogers "discoursed at length upon the Notre Dame team." Gallapher and Sheen composed a special verse of song predicting a Notre Dame win over Nebraska. And a skit written by Ring Lardner won over the audience when an actor appeared in a "good old ND monogram sweater."

Rogers was always on the go, whether making whistle stops across the country on his popular lecture tours or trekking his way across Asia or South America. He circled the globe three times, performing everywhere from a one horse saloon stage in Butte, Montana to New York's Carnegie

Hall. He used his vaudeville appearances on the stage of the Ziegfeld Follies to try out his story-telling and political jokes. By 1920, newspaper editors across the country recognized the national calling card that Rogers' humor possessed, and the Newspaper Enterprise Association had Rogers cover his first political convention. Rogers' appeal to the common man spoke perfectly to Rockne, the hale fellow, well met. They formed an easy friendship, and appreciated each other's style in reaching large audiences. To Rockne, Will's ease in connecting with any type of crowd was a marvel, and something to be emulated. They had first met when Rockne attended his show after the Notre Dame-Army game of 1921. In great theatrical flair that night, Rogers lassoed Rockne in the audience and brought him up on stage for conversation and laughs.

On the train ride home Sunday, though, entertainment was far from Rockne's mind, as he quietly sulked; to him, a tie was equal to a loss. He expected his charges to follow suit, to "do penance" in reflecting on how they might have avoided their fate. At one point, as he walked quietly down the aisle, he heard a group of players harmonizing in song. He came to them and sat down, waiting for them to finish the song. They looked at one another with worried glances, half-expecting a dressing-down for their enthusiasm. Instead, he said, "I don't know that one. Let's sing 'Darling Nellie Gray.'"

A large number of South Bend area residents were expected to travel by automobile to the next week's game against Butler at Indianapolis. Newspapers printed detailed directions for making the trip, recording the numerous turns required to navigate through Plymouth, Rochester, Peru, Kokomo, and finally Indianapolis. A crowd of 12,000 jammed Irwin Park and the Irish ran wild in a 31-3 victory. Castner was everywhere, with dashing runs, completed passes and effective kicking—until a severe blow in the third quarter knocked him out of the game. He was taken to St. Vincent's hospital, where he would stay for more than a week, his playing days in college ended.

Rockne studied his options at fullback. He could go with one of the reserve fullbacks—Livergood or Bill Cerney—as each had the size and strength required for the job. But he had another thought: What about Layden, the sprinter? Only 162 pounds, he could be a different kind of fullback, sleek and swift, able to gain yardage on quick opening plays, and more versatile as a kicker, passer and receiver. At the Claypool Hotel after the Butler game, Rockne approached Layden and asked how he would like to play fullback. Layden, who was frustrated at times jockeying for position with Crowley at left half, said "I don't care where I play, as long as I play." He did question whether his size made him right for the position, but Rockne assured him not to worry. Preparing for a trip to Pittsburgh to meet Carnegie Tech, Rockne and Layden had dinners together during the week so the coach could explain the position's intricacies.

Carnegie Tech, which had cancelled its game with St. Bonaventure the prior week, owing to a number of injuries suffered against Penn State, was lying in wait, backed by a Forbes Field crowd of 30,000—the largest to see a Notre Dame football game to date. Rockne started his Shock Troops, and when Stuhldreher, Crowley, Miller, and Layden all entered the game, they were staring at Carnegie's goal line. Stuhldreher called the signal, the backfield shifted, and the center snap caught Layden unprepared. The ball bounced off his knee and landed near the goal line, where Irish end George Vergara pounced on it for a touchdown. The backfield foursome's first play was successful, if in a roundabout way. Taking turns running, passing, and receiving, they went on to blank the Scots, 19-0.

Five days later, on Thanksgiving afternoon in Lincoln, Nebraska, they dropped a hard-fought battle to the heavier, more experienced Huskers, 14-6. On a critical play late in the game, a huge Nebraska tackle had smothered the 150-pound Stuhldreher for a key loss. At a banquet honoring the team that evening, Crowley noted, "We need a thermometer more than a feed."

But a backfield of Rockne's dreams had been built.

# 20

## Football Machine

The meteoric rise of football paralleled the presidency of Father Matthew Walsh. Football allowed Walsh to adopt the philosophy that Notre Dame would build with the money it had in hand as opposed to undertaking massive fundraising to build everything at once. And build the campus he did. During Walsh's tenure (1922-1928) student enrollment increased 66 percent. To accommodate the growth, Howard Hall (1925), Morrissey Hall (1926), and Lyons Hall (1927) were built at a combined cost of nearly $800,000. An extension had been added to Science Hall and to the gymnasium as well. Walsh pushed for construction of a dining hall, which he told the provincials would be "cared for out of current receipts of the University"—meaning football. No one could be sure how much football would grow or how long the prosperity would last, but the money generated from newfound fame on the gridiron seemed like a gift from above. It also proved to be a more certain and steady source of income than asking people for donations, as Father Burns, Walsh's predecessor, had done.

Father Walsh found himself walking the same fine line of modernism as did Father Burns as he took Notre Dame into the next decade, one of the most robust economic times of the new century. That included dealing with the pressure from Rome for more orthodoxy while realizing the need for more lay faculty and the means to pay them. Father Walsh tackled the challenges of continued campus growth and found himself taxed with how best to build the souls and educational experiences of the young men in his charge while at the same time dealing with the financial reality of building more classrooms and residential halls. Born in Chicago in 1881, Walsh entered the priesthood at age 15. He attended the preparatory school on the Notre Dame campus and graduated from the university in 1903. A former vice president of the university, Walsh had left to serve as a chaplain in the Great War. His first-hand witnessing of the death and destruction in the European battlefields deeply impacted him upon his return. The fragility of life and the conviction that no one individual was indispensable would be part of his governing philosophy.

In addition to all the matters of fund-raising, endowments, and building projects that occupied Father Walsh's time, athletic issues demanded his attention. After the overcrowded conditions at the 1922 Army game at West Point, numerous East Coast alumni wrote Walsh supporting the already circulating idea that the 1923 game might be played in New York City. Keeping the game at West Point would create challenges of travel and accommodation, they argued. Walsh agreed, but went a step further, suggesting that it might be a time for a break in the series with Army.

He urged a home-and-home series with Dartmouth, noting, "There is so much similarity between the spirit of Dartmouth and Notre Dame I believe they would be ideal rivals." In late November 1922, Rockne had written Army Coach Charley Daly to say that, it was reported, "under no condition" would Notre Dame make another trip to West Point. The report concluded, "The future of the West Point-Notre Dame game is contingent on the Army's ability to come to New York next season." Army officials, initially opposed to moving the game from West Point, backed down and agreed to the move to New York rather than risk losing the Notre Dame series altogether. The 1923 game would be played at the Polo Grounds, home to baseball's Giants of the National League.

But Army aside, Father Walsh still wanted Notre Dame to take on the eastern football aristocracy, something that hadn't been attempted since the 1914 debacle at Yale. He finally succeeded, accepting a $5,000 guarantee, but no split of the gate, for the Irish to play at Princeton the week after the Army game. Several selectors had acclaimed the undefeated Tigers as national champions in 1922. Meeting Princeton, one of football's original Big Three and a bedrock of the Ivy League and Protestant establishment, would be a major boon to Notre Dame's prestige, Walsh figured. For his part, Rockne was enthusiastic about moving the Army game to the city, with all the newspaper coverage it would attract. But he was still irked that few major opponents would consider a trip to play at Notre Dame. Whenever possible, he spoke in favor of a new modern stadium; university officials kept mostly quiet about it, but in early 1923 the City of South Bend formed an exploratory committee.

There was also increasing pressure from West Coast alums to schedule a game with the University of Southern California at the new Los Angeles Coliseum. Rockne loved this idea as well, but the faculty athletics board argued such a game constituted too much travel for Rockne's squad, especially with the East Coast trips on the schedule. Some of the school's fund-raisers, including Father McGinn, believed that a West Coast game could help raise endowment funds, but Father Walsh countered that he felt it would be difficult for anyone to "talk endowment or building fund with everybody's head filled with football." Employing football success to open alumni wallets was an idea not yet ready for fruition. Coach Rockne met any schedule upgrade with resounding enthusiasm. The opportunity to take on Princeton was a perfect match for his ambition and fearlessness. He would be able to match wits with one of the greats in coaching, Bill Roper. A star end for the Tigers from 1898 to 1902, Roper took over as their head coach just four years later, in 1906, at age 26. After three seasons (1906-08), he left for one year to coach Missouri in 1909, but returned and coached Princeton in 1910 and 1911 before President Wilson appointed him appraiser of merchandise at the Port of Philadelphia in 1912. Despite the prestigious position, Roper eventually drifted back into coaching, leading nearby Swarthmore in 1915 and 1916. And in 1919, he began his third stint at Princeton; his '22 team was the fourth at Nassau to receive recognition as national champions.

Rockne respected his other major 1923 opponents—Army, Georgia Tech, and Nebraska. But, from spring practice on, he made it clear Princeton was the game to win. Rockne was certainly one of the first coaches to understand that football could not be taught entirely on the practice field; classroom work was necessary for a player to understand its nuances and challenges. The coach developed a unique approach: every day during football season and spring practice, he conducted a half-hour lecture in a classroom in the Main Building. The players would give up part of their lunchtime, and their attendance was expected. Rockne approached the lecture as he would one in chemistry—serious about its structure and intent. Though, as in most any situation, he would use humor when he thought it was needed, directing his one-liners to "characters" such as his star Jim Crowley. Repetition was a key in Rockne's lectures. The first time he covered the material, his expectations weren't high. He would repeat it and look for improved comprehension. Then he would repeat it again, and anybody who still did not understand would have cause for concern. Using chalk on a blackboard, he would present diagrammed plays in great detail, down to the precise work that would be done on the practice field later the same afternoon. At 4 p.m., when practice officially began after the 20-minute warm-up period, players were expected to know exactly what would be done in the next 90-minutes, as they had seen it described at lunchtime.

Whenever he made a point about a tactical issue, the opponent was Princeton. One week, he decided to guide his players through a play-by-play game with the Tigers, describing the conditions: who had the ball and where, the down, yards to go, the wind conditions, time left to play, what type of defense was shown. He would ask someone in the class to call the play. The coach would then decide the result of the play, based on whether or not he agreed with the call. In this way, he kept every team member sharp with an outlook on all the aspects that played into the game. Rockne knew enough of Princeton's system, players, and tendencies that he was using the exercise to prepare the Irish for what they were likely to face in late October at Palmer Stadium.

That week, each day's lecture covered one quarter of the "game" against Princeton. The first day, the usual crowd of players was present. The next day, all the reserves were on hand. By the "third quarter," word of the "game" had spread around campus, and athletes from other sports inched their way into the lecture room. When the "fourth quarter" began, students crowded the hallway outside the classroom, straining to hear each play. Rockne, in true dramatic fashion, left the game tied until the final minute. Then, the coordinated effort of all eleven Irish players pulled out the glorious victory, to the cheers of all those assembled. One observer, student publicity aide Frank Wallace, noted that Rockne "said it would have been bad psychology for us to have lost. He wanted to have the boys go away with the idea that they could beat Princeton—but only after a terrific struggle, with tremendous concentration on every detail." It was that focus on "every detail" that set Rockne apart. His mind conceived of every possibility, and he built it into his preparation and his presentation. Rockne's full genius was on display. He was quick-thinking as he laid out the conditions and judged the responses. Challenging his charges to come along with him on an imaginary journey through a football game of the future. Inspiring their vision to see all that was happening about them. In this scene, he took his knowledge of the game, developed by Walter Camp and passed on through Stagg to men like Eckersall and Jesse Harper, and made it his own, imbued with his unique brand of energy, humor, imagination. He was coach, yes, but so much more—teacher, communicator, entertainer, psychologist, salesman.

More and more often, he was being asked to speak to groups of football coaches and others. At the start, many of these gatherings were rather informal. If he were traveling to a particular area, he might be asked to stop at the local college and talk football with a few coaches, managers, and captains. In the summer of 1923, Rockne was invited to spend two weeks teaching football as part of the summer school program of a little-known college in Provo, Utah: Brigham Young University. The school, known primarily as a religious seminary for the Mormon Church, was not officially recognized as a university by any accreditation organization. Its recently named president, Franklin Harris, was the first BYU president with a doctoral degree, and he was intent on improving the academic standing of the university. Football was new at BYU, the school having just fielded its first team in 1922. Physical education director Eugene L. Roberts, taking his lead from President Harris, wanted to make major strides to quickly expand BYU's profile in athletics. Adding a football course to the summer school program—and inviting coaches from high schools, preparatory schools, and colleges—would help. To attract them, he wanted a "name" coach on the faculty, and Rockne fit the bill. In order to pay Rockne for his services, BYU hired him as a professor for spring term. So, for a short time, Rockne, the Norwegian Lutheran coaching at a prominent Catholic university, was actually an adjunct faculty member at Mormon BYU.

For someone who crossed the Atlantic Ocean at age 5, the trek across America's prairie lands was a snap. It isn't hard to imagine Rockne, on the long train ride out to the salt desert of Utah, shaking his head at the unusual confluence of religious traditions, melded by athletics. It was indicative of his adventuresome spirit, his openness to experience new places, people, and projects. At BYU, Rockne's football students were earnest and serious, soaking up everything they could from their highly respected teacher. Rockne later wrote Professor Roberts, asking him to "remember me to the good people there…I had a wonderful time out in Utah and am very grateful to you for your wonderful hospitality." Rockne also noted that he had not had time to grade the final papers and suggested to Roberts that "if you are in a hurry for grades, (you may) do that yourself using your own judgment, but I do not believe that we should flunk anybody."

From Provo, Rockne returned to South Bend for a short time before setting out via automobile eastward to Springfield, Massachusetts. There, he was to join an esteemed faculty for the Physical Education and Athletic Coaching summer school at the International Young Men's Christian Association College. Thirty years earlier, Amos Alonzo Stagg introduced football to the school as its first official coach. In the ensuing years, the college carved out a very substantial specialized role in instructing those studying to become physical educators at schools, colleges, YMCAs, and other organizations across the nation. Among the subjects one could take at the summer school were: Anatomy, Anthropometry, Biology, Physiology, Physical Diagnosis, Psychology of Physical Education, Hygienic Gymnastics, Physical Directorship, and Physical Department Methods. The school lasted for all of July; Rockne was hired for the first two weeks, July 2-17, to give courses in football and track and field. Other coaches led courses in baseball, basketball, and swimming. In the summer school's catalog, the School of Coaching was described as offering, "Practical courses in the theory and practice of coaching the major sports, designed to aid coaches who wish more training and to assist teachers in high schools and academies who also coach some sport. The presence of Knute Rockne of

Notre Dame for football and track assured the high caliber of the work in these sports." No other coach apparently merited such a mention in the school's materials.

An emblem depicted in the brochure showed ancient Greeks engaged in athletic competition with the caption "The Joy of Effort." It was in this spirit that Rockne and his cohorts carried out the instruction. Yes, they taught technical and practical skills in all the various disciplines, but their efforts were aimed at making physical education and athletics part of moral development. In that respect, they were carrying forward the notions espoused by men like William Rainey Harper and Stagg years earlier. While engaged at Springfield, Rockne was the featured guest at a dinner given by the Notre Dame Club of New England at the Hotel Nonotuck in Holyoke, Massachusetts. The toastmaster was the Honorable John F. Shea, president of the club, former baseball captain, and co-composer of the Notre Dame Victory March. Among the other former Notre Dame athletes at the banquet was Dave Hayes of Hartford, Connecticut, he who a year earlier had given nearly his entire wealth to the school fund drive. Hayes was now well on his way toward using his Notre Dame education to become a great business success. On July 17, after the Springfield stay, in which Rockne made a number of new friends, he noted, "I have had a fine bunch here." The coach then began a 10-day automobile trip back to South Bend.

Upon his return to South Bend, Rockne prepared to host his first football-coaching course at Notre Dame. He kept a handwritten list of those expected, crossing out and adding names as needed. They were mostly from high schools or combined college/prep schools in states across the Midwest. The program was essentially an expanded version of how he taught his Notre Dame men: classroom presentation and discussion in the morning followed by work on the practice field in the afternoon. He enlisted a handful of varsity players to demonstrate his concepts on the field. Rockne's coaching schools included from the beginning plenty of opportunity for everyone involved to talk informally and kick around football questions and ideas, which often led to conversation about athletics in general. Education and maybe even current events were also discussed. The coach never made a grand entrance or quick getaway at any coaching school; he was there for endless rounds of hallway banter or late-night discussion sessions. He understood that the interaction with others in informal discussion resonated with those eager to learn. And Rockne would count himself among the learners.

For all his ease as a traveler, Rockne was glad to return home to Bonnie, Billy, Junior, and Jeannie. And now, it was a homecoming to their comfortable new home on St. Vincent Street, just south of campus. The substantial home and the one next door to it were built by the well-established South Bend contracting firm of Thos. L Hickey Builder. Its principal, Thomas L. Hickey, at 37 just two years Rockne's senior, occupied the home next door, along with his wife Kate and their six young children, ranging in age from Tom Jr., 10, to John, a toddler of 14 months. In 1916, Thomas Hickey purchased three lots from the University of Notre Dame on the northwest corner of St. Vincent Street and Frances Street for $1,250. His construction company completed the new dwelling for his family, a colonial revival with four upstairs bedrooms, and the family moved into their new home in February 1917. In the years that followed, the firm built the house next door that in 1923 became the Rockne home. The Hickeys warmly welcomed the coach and athletic director and his family to the neighborhood, now fairly teeming with active children.

The Hickeys represented an established Catholic family in South Bend with deep connections to the history of the area and that of Notre Dame. Tom's grandfather, Louis Etier, was a trusted friend of Father Sorin. Etier was born in 1829 in St-Roch-de-l'Achigan, about 32 miles northwest of Quebec. At age 20, young Louis began a two-week journey to South Bend, arriving on All Soul's Day, November 2, 1849. For his first two weeks in the area, he stayed in the log cabin of fellow Frenchman Pierre Navarre, one of the area's pioneer European settlers. Navarre had arrived in the South Bend area around 1820 as a fur trader for the American Fur Company, the business that made a fortune for its owner, John Jacob Astor. Pierre built his log cabin along the river. Alexis Coquillard, born in Detroit in 1785, arrived in South Bend around 1823 and bought out Pierre Navarre's fur business the next year.

In moving to South Bend, Louis Etier was following in the footsteps of another French-Canadian from his hometown, Joseph Archambault, who arrived in South Bend around 1840. Archambault may have let others back home in Quebec know about the opportunities in South Bend; more likely communication between South Bend and Quebec would have involved the French Holy Cross priests at Notre Dame writing to the priests at the parish in St-Roch-de-l'Achigan, who then passed the information on to young men such as Louis Etier. Some have surmised Louis Etier was personally recruited by Father Sorin to come and help build Notre Dame. Louis was one of four families who purchased land from Father Sorin to build their lodgings. Father Sorin dabbled in real estate by selling land to help create living quarters for Catholic workers. Knowing that they could obtain year-round work at Notre Dame where laborers were always needed, Father Sorin provided the land for those desiring to secure work, land of their own, and good education for their children. When Louis arrived he found a tight-knit French Canadian community in the area surrounding Notre Dame. In Clay Township, which included Notre Dame and the adjacent area north, there were numerous households with Anglicized names; Louis Etier would follow suit, and became Louis Hickey, considered the closest Irish surname to Etier.

Louis Hickey became an early employee of Notre Dame and handled a number of jobs, including wood chopping, brick making, wood and lumber hauling, corn husking, and water hauling. Lewis engaged in brick making for a substantial amount of his Notre Dame employment. The distinctive yellow bricks were made on the school grounds using marl from beds of the two lakes on campus. Notre Dame built many buildings using these bricks, which can still be distinguished by the yellow hue of the walls. It is entirely like that, due to his brick-making and other construction skills, Louis Hickey played a part in the rapid reconstruction of the Main Building after the fire of 1879.

In 1888, Louis helped to install the huge bell in the tower of Sacred Heart Church, just prior to its dedication on August 15, 1888. It is known that Louis Etier Hickey made a contribution of $10 for the purchase of a tabernacle for the new church in 1873, and, family lore holds, Louis' name is engraved on the inside of that tabernacle. When Louis Etier Hickey, the friend of Sorin and great pioneer settler, died in 1912, the bell he helped install in Sacred Heart Church tolled out of respect—the first time the bell had done so since the death of Pope Leo XIII in 1903. Louis Hickey was laid to rest in Cedar Grove cemetery. In the ensuing decades, his descendants successfully operated Thos. L. Hickey, Inc., contracting to construct 45 buildings, additions, and projects on the campus of Notre Dame and nearby St. Mary's College.

Knute Rockne and Tom Hickey struck up a close friendship; the "back fence" conversation was easy and sincere as the two talked football and families. And when the conversations ended, the two would often engage in a relaxed game of horseshoes in the Hickeys' yard. Tom Hickey recalled he never saw Rockne with a sports book or magazine. More likely, Rockne would be reading about chemistry or history. Tom had been a loyal fan of Notre Dame football since the turn of the century, when as a teenager he and a group of East Side lads would awake early, cram a sandwich in their pockets, and head for the campus. The objective was to sneak into Cartier Field before the ticket sellers arrived. The sandwich was for lunch, eaten during the long wait for kickoff. Now, as a close Rockne friend and confidant, Tom began accompanying the Irish team on its road trips. The two would pass the journeys in conversation and card playing in the club car.

The new home and neighbors on St. Vincent Street provided the perfect setting for the families' children to play together. The two homes were a beehive of activity, with kids coming and going, playing games, and keeping busy. It wouldn't be unusual to find the head coach coming home and enjoying a ground-level impromptu "football game" with the Hickey lads and his own boys. Bonnie enjoyed the company of Kate; the two often enjoyed card games on road trips they would take with their husbands. Because of the proximity to campus, Notre Dame football players would make frequent visits to the Rockne home, hoping to find some of Bonnie's cooking or baking available.

With a successful first summer of coaching schools concluded, Rockne turned his attention back to his own squad. Prospects were strong for another excellent season, but as usual, he took nothing for granted. The challenge of traveling to play defending national champion Princeton cast a strong shadow over the 1923 Irish schedule. As he had done every season since taking over as head coach, Rockne personally wrote every man on his roster, reminding them of the start of another season and inviting their presence on campus. It didn't matter if the man had received All-America mention the previous season or was a deep reserve;

the coach found something encouraging to say about the player's role on the team and the need for him to prepare himself for the upcoming season. The missive was particularly important at positions, which had been depleted by graduation, injury, or players not expected back.

Such was the case for Chuck Collins of Oak Park, Illinois. He began the 1922 season as the third man at left end, Rockne's old position, behind team captain Glen Carberry and backup Paul McNulty. Carberry had graduated and McNulty had suffered an injury, which knocked him out of football. So Rockne wrote Collins in August 1923:

My dear Chuck,

> Just a line to remind you to report on the opening day of practice. As we play the Army and Princeton so early it is very necessary that we get in shape early. We are playing the hardest schedule ever so get on your mark. I am relying on you at end as Paul is out for good. I know you can come thru [sic] so put some thought on your responsibility and start doing some work at once. You ought to report in fair shape.

> Trusting you are well after a good Summer, I am

> Sincerely, K. K. Rockne

In late September, Rockne wrote another type of letter, this one concerning the handling of football tickets, and had copies mailed to all alumni. The *Alumnus* described it thusly:

> There has been considerable worry, inconvenience and disappointment within the past few years because someone unintentionally and unfortunately forgot that football games at Notre Dame attract 20,000 people when they only attracted 2,000 when that someone lived gloriously under the rule of night pers [sic] and demerits. And when he applied for tickets at Homecoming the noon of the day of the game, discovered that the choice seats on the fifty-yard line were sold. We regretted his disappointment and we often tried to help him. We were able to do it just through a happy break of luck. But those days are gone.

> It is the belief of all concerned at the University that the system Mr. Rockne had adopted is the only logical one. He can

obtain any number of tickets for you at any game, either at home or away, when cash or check accompanies your order. One thousand tickets were secured for the Army, Princeton and Carnegie Tech games and the location of the seats covered by the tickets are of the best. The sale of tickets for all games on Cartier field opened October 7, and all orders are filled immediately upon receipt of order. If preference in location is desired, it is strongly advised that you take immediate action.

The days of ticket director Rockne dispensing ducats from a roll in his coat pocket or a cigar box in his messy office were gone. Among 1923's home games, the ticket crush would be a big factor for the mid-season clashes with Georgia Tech on October 27 and the Homecoming tilt with Purdue the following Saturday. Crowds of 10,000 and 8,000—which would have been considered enormous five years earlier—came out to watch the Irish defeat Kalamazoo, 74-0, and Lombard, 14-0, in the first two weeks of the season. When the 1923 football season started, all that was certain about the October 13 Army-Notre Dame game was that it would not be played at West Point, though the actual site remained in question. The World Series between the Giants and the Yankees meant that both the Polo Grounds and the new Yankee Stadium would be in use. The Brooklyn Robins offered their stadium, Ebbets Field, and representatives of both schools agreed. The day Notre Dame was to leave for New York, members of the team were gathered at Sacred Heart Church with Father O'Hara. One of the eastern press had written in jest that the star of Broadway musicals and comedies, Elsie Janis, also known as the "Sweetheart of the A.E.F." in the Great War, would be kicking off for Army. Father O'Hara responded, "Joan of Arc will kick off for Notre Dame." As was his custom before big games, he had given each member of the squad a Joan of Arc medal.

Unlike Notre Dame's other visits to West Point, which earned the school a guarantee that had risen from $1,000 in 1913 to $5,000 in 1922, the game in Brooklyn carried much more financial risk. West Point was on the hook for the stadium rental, and Notre Dame had all of its travel expenses at stake. Any worry was a waste of time. Well before kickoff, a capacity crowd of 35,000 packed the stadium, with thousands more mobbed outside hoping to gain admission. The great crowd slowed the march of the Corps of Cadets from Prospect Park Plaza to Ebbets Field. When the Army team, which outweighed their counterparts by an average of 15 pounds per man, took the field, "they looked like giants compared with the Rockmen," said one observer. On this day, it would be the guile of Irish quarterback Harry Stuhldreher and his mates that would confuse Army and dazzle the spectators.

Early in the second quarter, Stuhldreher stepped back to pass, eyeing Crowley and Miller to one side. Army defenders converged on the pair, and suddenly Stuhldreher pivoted, spotted Layden alone on the other side, and hit him for a score. It was the first touchdown of the season Army had allowed, after shutting out Tennessee (41-0) and Florida (20-0). Army threatened late in the half, but was stopped when Layden intercepted a pass at the Notre Dame 30. The half ended 7-0, Notre Dame. The crowd, buzzing at halftime, marveled over the play of the four Notre Dame backs. Their shiftiness, speed, deception, and daring were all displayed as advertised. Up in the lines, it had been a brutal matchup, with several players from each side laid out on the turf.

The game's grueling style continued in the second half, with several more stoppages for injuries, and Army penalized 15 yards at one point for slugging. Each team looked for the field advantage with punts on any down, and the Irish ran with some success after faking kicks. Midway through the final quarter, Crowley intercepted a pass and, slipping past several Cadets, raced to the Army 24. Sleepy Jim added 17 yards from scrimmage on the next play, setting up the Irish at the Army 7. Don Miller took the next snap and faded into pass formation. He executed the fake perfectly, and once West Point's defense was diffused, he whirled and dodged his way into the end zone. The Irish held off Army's final charge and won, 13-0.

Just four days later, the Notre Dame traveling squad headed off for the monumental battle with mighty Princeton. There had been virtually no talk of keeping the team out East, as the prevailing powers of Notre Dame were committed to requiring four days of classwork on campus from members of the football team. A few young alums had spent the week between games nearby. Former manager Morris Starrett, far from his home in Port Townsend, Washington, and former student publicity aide Frank Wallace were housed at the Newark Athletic Club, courtesy of the ever-thoughtful alumni boss Joe Byrne. In Princeton, Notre Dame was taking on true football royalty. In going undefeated in 1922, Roper's men had pulled off one of the greatest triumphs in Nassau's history. Princeton had made headlines simply by agreeing to make its first journey—to play Stagg's Chicago Maroons. The Tigers were unbeaten, despite being considered the underdog in most of its games, and were not expected to defeat the Chicago juggernaut.

A crowd of 32,000 jammed Stagg Field, and Coach Stagg, then in his 32nd season as head coach of the Maroons, had another undefeated powerhouse. Three touchdowns by Chicago's All-American fullback John Thomas gave the Maroons an 18-7 fourth quarter lead. Minutes later, the Tigers' hopes appeared to fade as John Cleaves lined up to punt from the back of his own end zone. But he faked the kick, and lofted a pass that brought Princeton to midfield. Then Chicago fumbled a punt, and Princeton scored to close within four points.

The fighting Tigers, inspired by Roper's typical never-say-die attitude, stiffened on defense, got the ball back and drove down the field with the clock ticking down. On fourth-and-goal from the three, Harry Crum wrestled his way out of the grasp of Chicago's defense and scored. Princeton converted and led, 21-18. Stagg's Maroons, stunned by the reversal, took to the air and made a desperate attempt to pull out the victory they thought should be theirs. Down the field they drove to the Princeton one-yard-line. Only seconds remained. John Thomas, as expected, would get the ball and a chance for his fourth touchdown of the day. But the orange and black line, anchored by All-American tackle Herb Treat, rose up as one, smothered Thomas and left him a foot shy of the goal line. Princeton won, 21-18. Roper was hailed as a genius coach, not for his strategy or technique, but rather for his ability to instill a fighting spirit into his players, which fueled the heroic upset victory.

On Friday, October 19, a steady downpour was making a quagmire of Palmer Stadium and would surely slow down Notre Dame's quartet of backfield magicians. From their rooms at the Colman House in Asbury Park, New Jersey, the Irish mood was anything but bright. However, Saturday morning brought a break in the weather, and by the afternoon, a bright sky greeted the teams, and 32,000 attendees, at Palmer. The Irish dressed in the old Princeton Fieldhouse and charged onto the field with a "sure-to-win" look in their eyes. Aside from an Irish punt blocked into their own end zone for a safety, the day belonged to Rockne's men. Don Miller and Crowley, in particular, ran wild, and Layden returned an interception 45 yards. The outcome was never in doubt, and Notre Dame's 25-2 victory was called "one of the worst trouncings in the history of Nassau." One report noted, "Roper sent man after man into the line hoping to solve the mystery attack that marched down the field with all the majesty of an Atlantic liner and speed of the Century...Never had a Princeton team been so completely routed...Notre Dame rolled on with her straight football tactics, disdaining to take the aerial route for two or three other touchdowns that might have been had for the asking."

New York and Philadelphia writers were effusive with their praise for Rockne's team:

—"Six touchdowns for 38 points against the Army and Princeton on successive Saturdays has been one of the leading football triumphs of many seasons."

—"Rockne's wizards attack relentlessly...they were thorough, superb."

—"It seems to be a strange device composed of eleven steel prongs that move only forward—forward—forward, eternally forward in great, swift moving strides."

—"Miller, Layden, Crowley and Stuhldreher comprise the finest backfield that has been seen in a decade in the east."

—"The brainiest, fastest, fightingest football outfit throughout the length and breadth of these United States."

—"On the sidelines, tense and fidgety, sat Knute Rockne, a special of football 'master-mind,' master-minding with exquisite intelligence and victorious effect."

—"We want to pay tribute to the clean playing of the Notre Dame eleven, no member of which forgot the code of the game in the heat of the conflict. The glory of victory is fleeting, but good sportsmanship leaves an indelible mark on the pages of time."

The Irish came home to demolish Georgia Tech, 35-7, and Purdue, 34-7, taking a 6-0 mark and plenty of confidence to Lincoln, Nebraska. They were greeted by a bold newspaper headline that read, "The Horrible Hibernians Arrive Today." Anti-Catholic and anti-Irish taunts were everywhere. Also waiting was a tough, talented Husker team. In front of 30,000 full-throated backers, on an afternoon in which nothing seemed to work for the Irish, the Huskers prevailed, 14-7, with Notre Dame's only score coming in the final seconds. Walter Eckersall reported, "It simply was a case of one team being alert and on its toes while the other did not show any of the dash or drive which featured its play in the Princeton and Army games."

In the late going, Rockne dropped to one knee desperately searching for any spark that might ignite his charges, when reserve back Max Hauser approached him, wearing his completely clean uniform. "Put me in, Rock," Hauser demanded. "It's all right, Max," Rockne replied, "I'm saving you for the junior prom." But moments later he relented and sent Hauser in. Stuhldreher was the only regular back in at the time, directing Hauser, Bill Cerney, and Red Maher, instead of Crowley, Miller, and Layden. The Huskers didn't miss a beat in taunting Hauser. "Don't strut, handsome—if you were any good you'd have been in here long ago." A late scoring pass from Stuhldreher to Cerney only made the final margin look closer than the game actually had been.

With the drive for an undefeated season ended, the Irish could have collapsed. But Rockne insisted on focus and determination the rest of the way, and the team responded by trouncing Butler, 34-7, Carnegie Tech, 26-0, and St. Louis, 13-0. A 9-1 record brought plenty of season-ending accolades. "The team possesses large gobs of real football ability, individually and collectively, plus combined team speed that blinds opposition, and a wall of interference that protects runners most effectively... the backfield collectively is the fastest and smoothest working thing I have seen in action," noted Jemison in the *Atlanta Constitution*. There was talk, which Rockne strongly supported, of a possible trip to the West Coast for a postseason game. But for all the modernization occurring in American life and at the university, there was little doubt that the major decision-makers at Notre Dame were still the Holy Cross fathers. President Father Walsh, struggling to raise funds to add more lay faculty to the staff, emphatically refused the proposal for a western postseason trip. The game, which had been highly recommended by the school's lay athletic board and even by Walsh's vice president, Father Thomas Irving, was a line too far for Father Walsh.

At the same time Father Walsh nixed the postseason game, Rockne found another batch of job offers arriving from other schools. Rumors of a departure for Carnegie Tech never found much traction, but the offers from Iowa were solid. Iowa Coach Howard Jones had left to take over at Trinity in North Carolina, and Iowa officials dangled a three-year contract at $8,000 per year in front of the Notre Dame coach. Enter Angus McDonald, the New York stockbroker who had helped keep Rockne at Notre Dame when the Northwestern offer emerged after the 1921 season. McDonald persuaded Father Walsh to consider what McDonald thought were reasonable requests from Rockne. In addition to a salary increase, McDonald suggested hiring a full-time business manager for the athletic department and giving Rockne a stronger role in shaping the new constitution for the Faculty Board in Control of Athletics.

Father Walsh was amiable to the salary increase and staff hiring; he knew athletic revenue would pay for those. Father Walsh went far beyond the Iowa offer, presenting Rockne with a new 10-year contract and a salary of $10,00 a year for ten months' work, which would allow him two months in the summer to pursue his schedule of coaching schools. It was a staggering salary for any Notre Dame employee in 1924. Rockne quickly accepted and once again professed his desire to say in South Bend for the rest of his professional career. But issues with the new Athletic Board constitution and Rockne's role in it were another matter. Holy Cross priests simply would not tolerate lay interference in high-level administrative decision. No such role was granted.

# 21

## Defending The Faith

Neither the Notre Dame administration nor the Fighting Irish football team could escape the anti-Catholicism sentiment, fueled by the Ku Klux Klan that was growing throughout the country. The football team had already encountered Klan influences when it traveled to Atlanta—national Klan headquarters—to take on Georgia Tech in 1923. By 1924, Klan roots had taken hold across the nation, as Catholics, more so than other immigrant populations were widely dispersed. In Missouri, Iowa, Ohio, North Carolina, New Jersey, Rhode Island, and Maine, the support of the Protestant clergy as part of the Fundamentalist movement was indispensable to Klan growth. In Spokane, Washington the Klan was heralded as "the return of the Puritans in this corrupt and jazz-mad age." And the Klan was proclaimed to be "a Clearing House for the cause of Protestantism." In 1922, H.L. Mencken said: "Heave an egg out of a Pullman window and you will hit a Fundamentalist almost everywhere in the United States." Approximately 40,000 Protestant ministers joined the Klan, preaching pro-Klan messages from their pulpits. Churches were turned over to the Klan to hold meetings while Protestant ministers spoke at Klan rallies. Although fundamentalism would make a controversial and often divisive contribution to religion in the 20th century, without it, the Klan would never have achieved its fantastic membership numbers nor have wielded its remarkable power in the 1920s.

By the 1920s, elementary schools had become a critical function of the typical Catholic parish, confirming the Fundamentalists' fear that the Protestant way of life was being threatened. Irish Americans in Chicago, led by Patrick O'Donnell, formed the Unity League to fight back. Their publication *Tolerance* often published lists of Klan members in pamphlets entitled "Is Your Neighbor A Kluxer." In January 1923, when the Unity League opened its office in South Bend, the city Chamber of Commerce held a meeting after a wrong list of names was published. Protestant ministers attended, demanding apologies. Notre Dame president emeritus Father John W. Cavanaugh showed up as well, who then lectured the ministers:

> Reverend Clergy: You are six months too late (for criticism). For six months the libelous and cowardly magazine of the Klan, 'The Fiery Cross,' has circulated among you without let or hindrance. For six months, this sheet has been before your eyes and before the eyes of your congregations. And not once have you said anything to prevent the spread of that spirit of hatred of Catholics which fills the pages of The Fiery Cross.

David Curtis Stephenson, a transplanted Hoosier who would develop into one of the Klan's most powerful leaders in the 1920s, became synonymous with the rise of the Klan in Indiana. Once described as "the most talented psychopath ever to tread the banks of the Wabash," Stephenson took advantage of the Hoosiers' penchant for joining clubs and attending all-day meetings and used the Klan paper the *Fiery Cross* to spread the Klan's messages and play on the fears of the populace. Stephenson's influence with the Indiana Klan also affected state politics. From Kokomo to Indianapolis, Stephenson's Klan-back supporters actively campaigned for Republican politicians, eventually leading to the election of Ed Jackson as Indiana governor in 1924. Klan political influence extended all the way to Washington, D.C. Republican President Warren Harding, elected in 1920, was said to have been sworn into Klan membership in the Green Room of the White House by a five-man Imperial induction team headed by Imperial Wizard William Simmons.

Stephenson was a man with a flair for the spoken word and who possessed the skills of a successful salesman. He dazzled Indiana crowds and used the telephone as a new marketing tool to disseminate misinformation of American Catholic doctrine. When Stephenson took control of the *Fiery Cross*, the weekly Klan newspaper based in Indianapolis in late 1923, he had a built-in audience of 500,000 in Indiana and neighboring states whom he could urge to work for "pure Americanism to triumph in America." South Bend and Mishawaka, however, proved to be almost impenetrable cities for the Indiana Klan. Three critical factors stemmed the Klan's tide there: the presence of Notre Dame, the large Catholic immigrant populations of the two cities, and the strong anti-Klan position taken by the *South Bend Tribune*. The 1924 state political scene offered Stephenson what he viewed as an opportunity to make inroads in an area in which Klan organization was weak. Stephenson and other Klan leaders decided something needed to be done in order to persuade state Republican convention delegates to accept the anticipated primary election victories of Klan-endorsed candidates as politically correct and irrevocable. Stephenson's solution was to stage an incident during the two-week interval in May between Indiana's primary election on May 6 and the opening of the Indiana Republican Convention in Indianapolis on May 21. He hoped that such an event would provide evidence of Catholic aggression and would solidify the hold of Klan-endorsed candidates for state office. The message from the Klan was clear: Proudly show the hooded robes of the Klan, but do nothing to incite the local populace. South Bend proved to be the likely setting for such a confrontation, and when local Klansmen agreed to host a tri-state meeting in South Bend for Klan members and their families on Saturday May 17, 1924, the stage was set.

Rockne, from his days as secretary of the Woodrow Wilson Club in 1916, took an active interest in the political climate of his day. He was well aware of the activities going on in South Bend, and he kept abreast of the Klan activities through newspaper accounts and discussions with Father Walsh. Rockne, as well as the Notre Dame administration, staff, and students all felt the uneasiness in the air in the spring of 1924. But despite the Klan activities, preparation for the upcoming track season could not

298

be ignored. Rockne's obligations as head track coach belonged in particular with Gene Oberst, his football lineman and javelin thrower. Rockne needed to keep the senior focused on his final collegiate meets with De Pauw, the Michigan Aggies, and the Indiana state meet at the end of May. Even more so, Rockne knew Oberst stood an excellent chance to make the United States track team for the 1924 Olympic Games to be held in Paris. For all of his love of the gridiron, Rockne would never shake his passion for track and its individual nature. "Don't judge him too soon," Rockne would often tell Eddie Hogan, a former track star and current program helper, about any member of the track team. "Let's see how they develop." Rockne's ability to encourage and cultivate the potential within was applied to both the star and the sub equally. Oberst would indeed take home a bronze medal from the 1924 games in July with a javelin throw of 58.35 meters. In the spring of 1924 Rockne advised Tom Lieb as well, Oberst's Notre Dame football teammate, who also made the 1924 U.S. Olympic team. Lieb won the collegiate discus title in 1922 and 1923 and the AAU title in 1923 and 1924. His discus throw of 44.83 meters captured the Olympic bronze medal.

Father Walsh and Holy Cross Father J. Hugh O'Donnell, prefect of discipline at the university and center on the 1914-15 football teams, remained solely fixated with local officials preparing for the Klan march. The two promised to do what they could to keep students on campus, but the large number of students living off-campus at the time proved to be a force that the university could not easily control—further motivation for Walsh to accelerate the building of additional residence halls.

Trouble began early the morning of Saturday, May 17 in the South Bend business district. The Klan claimed 25,000 visiting members in South Bend that day, although police estimates were lower. No matter the number, hooded Klansmen began appearing on downtown South Bend streets and soon afterward, "young men, identified by reporters for the South Bend Tribune as Notre Dame students, traversed the main thoroughfares of the business district. At the same time, bands of young men showing intense hostility to the Klansmen showed up on foot and began surrounding the masked men wherever they could find them. Some of those bands were identified as being composed of Notre Dame students. Others were made up of West Side Polish and Hungarian ethnics. Within an hour, robes and masks had been torn from about a half a dozen Klansmen and several of them had been very roughly handled."

By early afternoon, a large crowd of anti-Klan demonstrators had congregated in front of the local Klan headquarters at Michigan and Wayne Streets, and once again a riotous atmosphere prevailed. Mounted policemen broke up the crowd into smaller groups, but the confrontation continued, including one small group who hurled potatoes at the local Klan headquarters. A mid-afternoon meeting between Notre Dame student leaders and Klan officials at the Klan's headquarters resulted in a truce of sorts. Local officials had denied Klansmen a parade permit, meaning that any Klan march would be breaking the law. By 3:30 p.m. the crowd had dispersed to a large pool room at the corner of Washington Avenue and Michigan Street, where about 500 students heard one student leader plead for vigilance and restraint. The crowd was asked to disperse and return to the Jefferson Boulevard bridge at 6:30 p.m. to prevent Klansmen from coming into the city center from the east to participate in an illegal parade—an event that never occurred. Stephenson, who had come by car from Indianapolis to South Bend that morning, decided not to push for any more Klan activity or a parade without a permit. In Stephenson's eye, his goal had been accomplished: Peaceful Klansmen had been attacked by Catholic students from Notre Dame and by ethnic ruffians. The Klansmen had been denied their constitutional right to peacefully assemble. No Protestant voter in Indiana need know more than that.

Sunday morning accounts in the *South Bend Tribune* proved embarrassing for Fathers Walsh and O'Donnell. They had been unable to control the student body, and Notre Dame students had failed to respect authority or to generally comport themselves as Notre Dame men were expected. Even worse, the fathers were helpless to prevent another occurrence. Walsh and O'Donnell's fears were validated within 48 hours. Local Klansmen reinstalled the fiery electrical cross that had been damaged earlier outside of Klan headquarters. By 7 p.m. on Monday, May 19, reports filtered out from a Klan meeting that a payback to Notre Dame students was being planned. Word spread via telephone to the Notre Dame dormitories of a Klan meeting in progress and of Notre Dame students under attack at Michigan and Wayne. As night fell, nearly 500 students raced onto Michigan Street, where they began marching toward the intersection of Michigan and Wayne—right into the Klan "ambush." The *South Bend Tribune* reported that the Klansmen had dispersed to nearby strategic locations to await the students. Also awaiting the students were local police, who were on the scene in force. Together they surprised the anti-Klan forces as they neared the intersection of Wayne and Michigan streets. Bottles, stones, clubs, and many other objects were thrown about at random. Police charged the scene and injuries resulted among the demonstrators, Klan participants, police and bystanders. Some were even taken to local hospitals.

By 10 p.m. Fathers Walsh and O'Donnell arrived on the scene and were appalled and frightened by what they saw. Walsh, who climbed atop a ledge on the Civil War Memorial outside the courthouse, addressed the students within earshot. By midnight most students were back on campus. The past few days' events had strained relations between the university and city officials. For the rest of May and most of June, campus security was beefed up to include volunteer night patrols by faculty and priests. Father Walsh also met with Rockne and implored the coach to speak to the student body in Washington Hall on the importance of law-abiding conduct. Rockne talked of the importance of avoiding confrontation, playing by the rules, and respecting themselves and their religion. Following the Washington Hall talk, students were asked to sign a pledge, similar to a Temperance pledge students took promising to avoid use of alcohol. In this pledge, the students promised to abstain from Klan confrontations in South Bend.

An uneasy calm engulfed the campus and the city from that point. The Klan moved on to the state Republican convention and focused its work on securing the nomination of its members for state offices. Summer months offered students, administration, and city leaders a time of respite. After Labor Day would come the state and national election campaigns, the start of a new school year at Notre Dame with record enrollment, and the excitement of a promising football season scheduled to begin in early October.

By the start of the 1924 football season, the city of South Bend and the university were quietly trying to move past the tumultuous spring and the "riot" between Notre Dame students and the Ku Klux Klan. The Klan had disseminated an excellent promotional campaign since May that portrayed privileged Irish Catholic students assaulting innocent American Protestant patriots. Father John O'Hara, Notre Dame's prefect of religion, was entertaining ideas on how to counteract the perception now held by many through the country that Notre Dame students were a bunch of hooligans. O'Hara had not forgotten the editorial that had appeared in the *New York Times* in December 1923, months before the May incident. The *Times* tried to inject "humor" into a less than humorous situation: "There is in Indiana a militant Catholic organization...engaged in secret drills. They make long cross-country raiding expeditions...worst of all, they lately fought and defeated a detachment of the United States Army. Yet we have not heard of the Indiana Klansmen rising up to exterminate the Notre Dame football team."

Even earlier, in October 1923, one New York writer penned the following after Notre Dame's pivotal 25-2 win over Princeton: "In every branch of the sport Knute Rockne's pupils gave the easterners a lesson in how this game is played and tonight with the Orange buried deep under the Green, it looks as if it is up to the klan to do something about these happenings." Father O'Hara and other university officials were keenly aware of the enormous public relations value the university could garner if Rockne's team had another outstanding football season. Winning—and winning in the style of Notre Dame men–could show the American public and anyone who professed to be a reader of the Klan's Fiery Cross what Catholics and Catholic education was all about. For O'Hara, the 1924 season became something of a spiritual crusade.

As prefect of religion, many students regarded O'Hara as father-confessor, someone to whom they could confide anything and everything without fearing retribution from the university. His door in Sorin Hall was always open, and the students would bring to O'Hara their problems of the heart, their problems of the pocketbook, and their problems with their studies. He never failed to provide an answer. Father O'Hara also founded the *Religious Bulletin* in 1921, a one-page paper packed with messages and statistics to keep Notre Dame men focused on "clean living." The same year he launched the Religious Survey, which tapped into his deep respect for scientific research, statistical analysis, and data. The survey consisted of a number of student-directed questions to be answered anonymously. Additionally, he helped to usher in chapels in each of the residence halls.

Working to keep young male students living a high moral life was a constant challenge for Father Burns in an evolving post-war world. In the first years of the new century, social and technological change traveled at lightning speed, but by 1920, it roared even faster and louder. The 1920s heralded the large-scale use of automobiles, telephones, motion pictures, and electricity. Those who survived the Great War and the influenza epidemic of 1918 thrust themselves into a sometimes-raucous lifestyle of music, dancing, and illegal alcohol. The decade ushered in a rich period of American writing, distinguished by the works of such authors as Sinclair Lewis, Willa Cather, William Faulkner, F. Scott Fitzgerald, Carl Sandburg, and Ernest Hemingway. Father O'Hara and Father John Talbot Smith, a Catholic novelist and essayist, kept close watch over what was appropriate reading for students on campus and encouraged unofficial bans on "condemned" books such as those by Norwegian dramatist Henrik Ibsen and George Bernard Shaw.

O'Hara, who had often been the "answer man" for so many of the young students, now looked to Rockne to provide a piece of the response to the Klan dilemma. The 1924 football team and season could provide the opportunity to restore pride and dignity to Our Lady's University. And Rockne stood ready to assist.


Rockne knew the tremendous versatility and teamwork displayed by his backfield players offered great hope for an outstanding year. But it was Rockne's ability to also understand public relations that also appealed to Father O'Hara. More than most football coaches, Rockne keenly understood the value of publicity, especially in major news centers such as Chicago and New York, two areas that provided key support to Notre Dame. With so few Notre Dame home games against big-name teams, the big-name sports writers rarely ventured to South Bend. But over the years, Rockne made it his business to get to know and be known by the major scribes, whose stories and columns ran in papers across the country. The giants of journalism—Grantland Rice, Damon Runyon, Westbrook Pegler—all knew that Rockne was a good source of copy. By 1924, Rockne had actually joined their ranks, in a way, as he, Pop Warner, and Tad Jones of Yale were hired by the Christy Walsh Syndicate to write a series of columns.

Rockne's connections throughout the college football world—through former Notre Dame players now coaching, other coaches he worked with in putting on summer coaching schools, and writers of all types—put him in an excellent position to dispense the latest information and to comment broadly on the world of college football. Rockne had pioneered a novel approach to dispensing the day-to-day news coming out of his football camp. Each season, he would hire one Notre Dame student to serve as his publicity aide and be the official source of news regarding his team. The student writer would have access to Rockne and the team, travel to away games, and pen articles for either or both of the South Bend newspapers—the *News-Times* and the *Tribune*—and for several out-of-town papers.

Arch Ward, a bright, eager student from Irwin, Illinois was the first student publicity assistant. Ward transferred to Notre Dame after starting college at St. Joseph's in Dubuque, Iowa, where he gained the attention of athletic director and football coach Gus Dorais. Ward held the job for the 1919 and 1920 football seasons, after which he graduated and went on to start his sports writing career in Chicago. During the 1920 season, with Ward writing exclusively for the *Tribune*, another aspiring Notre Dame journalist arrived on the scene. J. Francis "Frank" Wallace, an energetic, earnest philosophy major from Bellaire, Ohio, in coal country on the West Virginia border, was hired by the *News-Times* to cover campus sports. Over the next couple of years, Wallace expanded the role. In addition to covering the team for one or the other local paper, he began sending out press releases to various papers, paying for the postage himself. He also wrote for the *Scholastic* and the *Dome*. After graduation, Wallace went directly to New York, where he began working as an editor for the Associated Press and continued as an unofficial press agent for all things Notre Dame. Part of that role was conveying information back to Rockne, especially about the two big eastern opponents, Army and Princeton.

Writing Rockne in the summer of 1924, Wallace lamented moving on from the fall afternoons spent in Rockne's office, soaking in the wit and wisdom of the coach. Now, in the fall of 1924, the job belonged to George Strickler, a local fellow in his second year at the university. Strickler had been around Notre Dame all his life. His father was the butcher in the slaughterhouse on the university farm and ran their threshing crew in the summer. A knee injury ended Strickler's football playing days, but Rockne, a family friend, hired him to be his student publicity aide starting in September 1924. Strickler provided daily reports for the *Tribune* and sold stories to out-of-town papers as he could. Neither could envision what the 1924 season would hold in terms of newspaper reporting on the four-backfield members of this year's squad.

The summer of 1924 was winding down as Rockne boarded the train in Williamsburg, Virginia on Saturday, September 13, after concluding the last of his summer coaching schools at the College of William and Mary. It had been a fulfilling two weeks, visiting another part of the country and getting to know and teach young coaches. He had made another round of friends with whom he could discuss football, athletics, and life. Now, as the locomotive belched and the coach lurched through the Appalachians, Rockne turned his attention to the 1924 Fighting Irish. In two days, he would greet 130 candidates for the varsity on Cartier Field.

Back in South Bend, the newspaper headline laid out the challenge: "Line is Chief Worry of Notre Dame." The returning backs—Stuhldreher, Don Miller, Crowley, Layden and their backups—were proven, experienced, and ready for their final year. On the line, meanwhile, graduation had left some significant holes. Gone was left guard Warren Brown, who had captained the 1923 squad to its 9-1 record. George Vergara, the primary right guard from last year was on the field, but his role had switched from player to assistant coach. Vergara was originally scheduled to be part of the 1924 team until it was learned that he played one half of one game for Fordham three years earlier before coming out from the Bronx to Notre Dame. The school declared him ineligible when the news was discovered, but Vergara then joined Rockne's coaching staff and completed his coursework at Notre Dame. And at right tackle, Rockne searched for someone to take over for giant Gene Oberst, 6-foot-4 and 200-plus pounds, and now the proud bearer of a bronze medal from the

1924 Olympics.

Fortunately, Rockne had one known quantity on which to build his line: senior center and captain Adam Walsh. At 6 feet tall and 190 pounds, the handsome, sandy-haired Walsh felt very much at home on the Notre Dame campus. Earlier that summer, he made a cross-country journey with younger brother Charles, nicknamed Chile. The pair had driven a Ford Model T from their home in Hollywood, California some 2,400 miles to the Notre Dame campus in time to enroll for the summer term. Across the deserts of California and Arizona, up through the Rocky Mountains, past Denver and out onto the plains, to the great crossroads of Chicago, the Walsh brothers traversed one series of rutted dirt and gravel roads after another. By their estimation, they had encountered barely 100 miles of paved highway on the entire route. The car, after numerous dings, flat tires, and other maladies, now resided in an off-campus garage. As a freshman in 1921, Walsh impressed Rockne as a young man willing to do the work needed to be a star player. By the start of the 1924 season, Walsh had become a mature man with a well-honed work ethic and a tremendous sense of self-reliance. Walsh's engaging personality made him a magnet for other students on the team and the campus, as well as the logical choice as 1924 Irish football captain.

Besides Walsh at center, the main returnee was Joe Bach at left tackle. Short of injury, it would be unlikely for anyone to wrest the spot from Bach. Born and raised on the rugged Mesabi Iron Range of northern Minnesota, Bach came from a family and a town steeped in iron ore mining. His parents settled in the Shenango location, one of the many mining camps outside of Chisholm. Despite austere conditions in a miner's home, Chisholm's schools were a different story. Heavily funded by the tax base of the mining companies, they were far advanced, with well-furnished classrooms, excellent instructors, a "college prep" curriculum, and extensive activities. Chisholm kids heard early and often that their goal should be to gain an education—and preferably a college one. Sports were an outlet for an active, sometimes rambunctious young Joe Bach. He led the high school basketball team to the state tournament, held at Carleton College in Northfield, Minnesota, where his physical play impressed football coach Cub Buck. Bach began college at Carleton as a halfback, and his play in a hard-fought battle with rival St. Thomas College in St.

Paul caught the eye of the St. Thomas coach, former Notre Dame quarterback Joe Brandy. He and others convinced Bach he could excel on a larger stage, and after one semester at Carleton, Bach—the son of an immigrant miner—reached a pinnacle few back in Chisholm could have imagined when he transferred to Notre Dame.

On the second day of practice, Rockne turned his attention to the tackles and guards. He spent an hour explaining his system of blocking to more than 40 men evenly divided for both positions. Once drills began, several linemen from the 1923 freshman squad made their presence known. John McManmon, a big farm boy from Dracut, Massachusetts, was already 190 pounds as a sophomore. Dick Hanousek, from Antigo in northern Wisconsin, was a standout at guard. But the man making the strongest bid to play tackle opposite Bach was senior Edgar "Rip" Miller, the fellow from Canton, Ohio who had gone up against Stuhldreher when Miller played at McKinley High School. Miller's boyish looks belied his toughness, and toughness would be needed, as Rip was five inches shorter and 25 pounds lighter than Oberst, the man he was trying to replace.

At the guard position, the early favorites were a pair of monogram men, seniors John Weibel and Noble Kizer. Neither was exceptionally big for the position, both about 5 foot 9, 165 pounds. Weibel, a studious, serious son of a physician from Erie, Pennsylvania, took the lead to replace Harry Brown at left guard. In 1924, Weibel balanced football with a rigorous academic schedule set to prepare him for entrance to medical school. Kizer, who came to Notre Dame primarily as a basketball player from nearby Plymouth, Indiana, had split time with Vergara at right guard and seemed a natural to take over that spot. Though he was active playing and coaching basketball at the South Bend YMCA, Kizer had never played football because Plymouth High School did not have a team at the time. At Plymouth, Kizer had already shown leadership and initiative. He coached the track team and helped coach the basketball team. He dropped out in 1918 to join the Marines and was sent to Quantico, Virginia. After the armistice was signed in November 1918, Kizer came back to Plymouth and graduated high school in 1919. He began working at the South Bend YMCA to earn money for college. Rockne saw him working out at the Notre Dame gym and was impressed enough to ask Kizer to come out for football.

At the end positions, Rockne only had to replace right end Gene Mayl. Senior Chuck Collins returned on the left side, while Clem Crowe and Ed Hunsinger were backups with experience. Crowe also came from a strong Indiana basketball family from Lafayette. Hunsinger, from St. Mary's High School in Chillicothe, Ohio, shared a similar football experience with Kizer in that St. Mary's did not play high school football. Hunsinger's football experience came through playing in Notre Dame's inter-hall league. Rockne counted on Collins, from St. Ignatius High School in Chicago, for the grit needed to play through the tough '24 schedule. Collins showed his mettle when his younger brother fell through the ice of the Des Plaines River, and Chuck led a daring rescue to save him. And, he played despite missing an index finger, amputated after it became infected from a football injury.

Rockne had some quality help in coaching the line. Hunk Anderson arrived on campus September 22 and Rockne immediately put him to work with the guards in one corner of the field, while Tom Lieb, back from his proud Olympic showing, handled the tackles. Rockne drilled all the other positions. Rockne made something of a surprise announcement September 25: there would be no official cut of the roster. He would let attrition take its course and work with everyone who remained. "The boys who feel themselves outclassed withdraw after an honest try, and retire to the sidelines where they become more intelligent observers and sympathetic critics," the *Tribune* explained. "Rockne always allows every man to judge his own courage and capabilities."

One reason the coach didn't mind carrying a larger than usual squad was the quantity and quality of the senior class—22 members of the Class of 1925 were among the top 50 or so prospects for the team, and Rockne wanted as good a look as possible at their potential replacements. In order to handle the size of the squad, Rockne also announced a different approach. Rather than simply having varsity units scrimmage repeatedly against the freshman team, he divided the varsity, putting about 30 players directly under Lieb's supervision. Lieb was instructed to develop an offensive scheme for his unit, which would differ from the main varsity. The two groups would be pitted against each other in daily scrimmages. In building a line, Rockne would stress to his players that blocking, far from being routine, should be a source of great satisfaction. He felt it was a special man who worked to become an excellent blocker. "Love to block," Rockne would say, "and let them know that you like it. If all teams could do just that thing, they would always be winning."

Rockne sensed this 1924 group had extraordinary potential. He had gathered a group that typified what he cherished most: loyalty, respect for the game, spirit, and unselfish service. He could see it in all of them starting with his anchor and captain Adam Walsh, whom Rockne felt would solidify the line. Rockne reflected on his four senior backs – Miller, Layden, Stuhldreher and Crowley. Their athletic talent was unquestionable, and their unbridled enthusiasm was waiting to be unleashed. Rockne smiled as the season started. He was pleased. He had instilled in this group his most trusted idea: "Work, work hard, prepare and then go."

Less than a week into practice, Rockne guided the team through its first full scrimmage. George Strickler described it in the *Tribune*:

"Sun rays, clear white from sheer intensity, beat down on Cartier Field yesterday afternoon like a driving rain of molten lava. In the stands a cluster of curious onlookers gazed in wonder at some 250 athletes, playing and sweating on the long stretch of green before them.

> A man, bareheaded and clothed in a uniform symbolic of no particular profession, but strangely different from that worn by other persons in the enclosure, was shouting commands and inspiring these athletes, while other elements seemed to be undermining their morale and ordering a halt.

> In the scale with which he was measuring the ability of the individuals at their every turn, time had no specific value for him, just as his goal was neither far nor near. Now he was on his knee studying some particular chap, who had solicited his plaudits a moment before with a startling achievement, not uncommon throughout the afternoon. Now he was racing toward a group of men who had failed in their attempt to execute his commands. Spectators shifted their eyes from him only when some extraordinary event was being enacted in another section of the field. There was something picturesque about him, and worth remembering.

He was, without shouting or advertising the fact, Coach K. K. Rockne, Czar of football at Notre Dame and premier grid specialist of the day. His assignment for the afternoon, as selected by himself, was the directing of the first scrimmage in the Irish camp. Unmoved by the weather or other conditions embarrassing to his charges, he drilled them hard and long. Long after the large stands had been clothed in the blood of the dying sun and the last enthusiastic bleacherite had forsaken his post along the sideline for a more popular position in the university dining room, Rockne was picking flaws in a substitute offensive unit. At the close of the afternoon's activities, the famous mentor voiced satisfaction over the outcome of the mix-up, declaring his primary objective had been accomplished.

There was considerable excitement on campus and in South Bend anticipating the October 4 season opener against Lombard College of Galesburg, Illinois. Coach Harry Bell's squad, led by quarterback Roy Lamb, remembered well playing the Irish tough in 1923. Over the past three seasons, Bell's team had amassed a stunning scoring margin of 987 to 103. In addition to victories over Illinois rivals, Lombard had beaten teams as notable as the University of Detroit's Titans. So it was not mere hyperbole when the *Tribune*'s October 1 headline read: "Lombard Regarded as Mighty Foe in Notre Dame Camp." But this Notre Dame team was simply too much for the visitors to handle. Pulling away from a 14-0 halftime lead, the Rockmen rolled to a 40-0 victory.

The visit of Wabash College's "Little Giants" for the second game of the season Saturday, October 11 at Cartier Field would bring one of the great characters in Notre Dame football history back to campus. Robert E. "Pete" Vaughan was born in Lafayette, Indiana and raised in an Irish-Catholic family in Crawfordsville, home of Wabash. He was a star football and basketball player for Crawfordsville High before enrolling at Notre Dame in the fall of 1908 as a 6-foot, 190-pound fullback. The next season, Vaughan scored the decisive touchdown in Notre Dame's historic 11-3 upset of Michigan at Ferry Field in Ann Arbor. A legend had developed that Vaughan smashed through the Michigan line with such force that his head broke the wooden goal post. In the 15 years since, he argued that it must have been his shoulder that drove into the post. But that didn't stop the story of how Pete Vaughan broke the Michigan goal post from being repeated on countless occasions—even by university president Father Walsh.

In 1910, Vaughan had an opportunity to attend Princeton, where he starred for the Tigers, played semi-pro football, helped coach the freshman team and even played some pro basketball. After brief stints as line coach at Purdue and California, Pete was sent to Europe during the Great War and coached football teams of Camp Shelby and the 38th Division of the 152nd Infantry. After the armistice, he continued with the Army in Europe, and on a tour of Belgium explained the game to an interested spectator: King Leopold.

Following his discharge, Vaughan returned to Crawfordsville and began coaching Wabash in both football and basketball. The Little Giants, representing a school of a few hundred students, regularly took on much larger institutions. 1924 was no exception, with games set against Purdue, Notre Dame, and Indiana. Similar to the Lombard game, Notre Dame started slowly and led, 14-0, at the half, but put the Little Giants away in the fourth quarter with three touchdowns to win, 34-0.

Much of the Midwest's focus on Saturday, October 18 would be on the big Western Conference matchup between Michigan and Illinois at Champaign, where the mammoth new Memorial Stadium would be dedicated. Built with two large decks of seating on both sides of the field, the stadium was being hailed as the gem of the region. Seating for more than 67,000 was expected to be filled to capacity when Michigan came to town. Notre Dame, however, had its eyes on the trip east for the battle with Army at the Polo Grounds.

# 22

## Outlined Against

As Notre Dame prepared to head to New York City to play Army at the Polo Grounds, football fans across the country grew eager with anticipation for the intersectional battle of the year. Under Rockne's leadership, Notre Dame had moved past an intriguing interloper stealing the thunder from the more established names in the sport; it was becoming the standard against which all other teams were compared. Those doing the comparing included the nation's most prominent writer of sports, Grantland Rice. At the *New York Herald Tribune*, Rice's columns were a feature of the running New York newspaper wars. But his audience was truly national, as his syndicated column *The Sportlight* ran in more than 100 newspapers nationwide with an estimated audience of 10 million readers. Rice had also authored numerous books and written for many popular magazines, including *Colliers, American Magazine, McClure's, Outing, Literary Digest* and *Country Life*, his poems, odes, and flowery speech entertaining readers. He made a consistent effort to liven his subjects with a clever turn of the phrase. The Tennessee native majored in Greek and Latin at Vanderbilt, where he also starred on the baseball team at shortstop, played football despite numerous injuries, and ran track.

He was also attracted to the glamour of the foot soldier after habitual reading of Rudyard Kipling, in which war was romanticized and shown as adventuresome. He enlisted for service in the Great War in December 1917. Private Rice displayed superior skill and talent and was quickly promoted to Second Lieutenant. He eventually saw duty in the European campaign, although he never learned how to load artillery; instead, he put his talents to work writing for *Stars and Stripes,* the eight-page weekly which reached a peak of 526,000 readers during the war. He also dabbled in poetry while in Europe, though he failed to dazzle critics.

In September 1924, Rice looked ahead with excitement to October 18, when in addition to the Notre Dame-Army game, Dartmouth would meet Yale and Michigan would travel to Illinois. He considered them three of the best games of the year. "We have an earnest desire to look upon all three contests, and yet so far have discovered no answer to the complication," Rice wrote. He went on to note, "Rockne rarely leaves the east without his annual supply of scalps. But the odds are he will have a better Army team to overthrow than he has faced for some time. Wilson alone is half a team." Rice may have had in interest in watching the other two games, but he would be at the Polo Grounds, as he had been at Ebbets Field the previous year to watch Notre Dame and Army. He attended that game with Brink Thorne, Yale's outstanding 1895 captain. They had sideline passes only, and Rice recalled nearly being run over by the Irish backfield on one particular end run. "It's worse than a cavalry charge," Rice said to Brink as he scrambled back to his feet. "They're like a wild horse stampede."

Rice first met Rockne when Notre Dame played at West Point in 1920. He went with fellow New York writer Ring Lardner, who grew up in Niles, Michigan, just miles from Notre Dame, and was aware of its budding football fame before most in the East. Rockne made an immediate and lasting impression, and the two became great friends. "Rockne was a man of great force, deep charm, and an amazing personality," Rice would later write. "I have never known anyone quite his equal in this respect... Whenever there was a gathering of coaches in any city, there was usually just one question. 'Where's Rock staying?' That's where they all gathered. There have been so many fine coaches, but Rockne was the greatest of all in the way of human appeal."

Rice thought back to one of Rockne's earliest trips to the city. Rice suggested the pair attend a late-afternoon cocktail party hosted by Vincent Bendix, an automotive and aviation inventor and industrialist, at Bendix's midtown apartment. Rockne was hesitant, but Rice assured Rockne that seeing magician Nate Leipsic, who was providing the afternoon's entertainment, was worth the trip. Rice was correct; the magician's skill astonished Rockne. Leipsic made rubber balls "disappear." He showed again and again how much faster the hand is than the eye. Rockne asked to see some tricks repeated. He came away inspired. "I've learned a lot today about deception in handling a ball," Rockne told Rice. "This matter of handling and facing with the ball is one of the biggest things in football, and I aim to make it bigger." From that point on, his Notre Dame quarterbacks were excellent at faking with the ball. None was better than his current signal-caller, little Harry Stuhldreher. In 1923, Rice invited Rockne to his apartment for a Sunday brunch the morning after the Ebbets Field game. Rockne brought Stuhldreher, and Rice and his wife Kit marveled at this seemingly miniature football genius, whom they called "Rockne's brain" on the field. It was the beginning of an enduring friendship between Rice and Stuhldreher.

In New York, Rockne's old pal and Notre Dame alum Joe Byrne, Jr. had worked hard promoting the 1924 Army game and selling tickets for it, and a large crowd was expected at the Polo Grounds. New Yorkers of all stripes were lining up to see Rockne's "wonder team." And across the country, those who followed sports—especially readers of Grantland Rice—wondered whether Rockne would again prevail against the Army. The Notre Dame following extended far beyond alumni now scattered about the country. Catholics nationwide had a unifying representative in the Fighting Irish. First- and second-generation immigrants saw themselves embodied in some of Notre Dame's players—and certainly in Rockne. These fans brought another wave of support.

There were still others—school and college coaches who had learned from and met Rockne at coaching schools in Springfield, Massachusetts; Williamsburg, Virginia; Corvallis, Oregon; and Notre Dame, Indiana—who could point to Rice's columns and other coverage of Notre Dame and say with pride, "I know Rockne! I've met him and talked with him, and consider him my friend." By extension, the young men playing football for these coaches quickly turned into followers and fans of the team from northern Indiana.

The travel to New York meant a short week of practice, so Rockne called for a Monday marathon session to prepare. Rice was correct to highlight Harry Wilson's strength. The flashy back from Penn State was representative of one huge advantage West Point had over all other teams: the ability to enroll superlative football players who had completed their normal athletic eligibility at their original school. Another backfield star was Tiny Hewitt, formerly of Pitt. Centering the line was the most veteran player on this or any other college football squad, 24-year-old Ed Garbisch, the captain of the corps of cadets as well as the football team. A product of Washington, Pennsylvania, he played four years for his hometown university, Washington & Jefferson, from 1917 through 1920. He was now in his fourth and final year playing for Army, his eighth campaign overall. This would be his fifth time facing Notre Dame, the first being Notre Dame's 3-0 victory over Washington & Jefferson in 1917, in Jesse Harper's final game as coach. Going up against Garbisch would be a challenge for an opposing center on any day. Adam Walsh would carry a handicap with him into this game, as he had suffered a broken bone in his right hand during the Wabash game. Stuhldreher was fine, but Walsh's injury, which Rockne had carefully kept hidden, was sure to be a major hindrance.

Wednesday evening, the day before the squad headed for New York, several of the players walked from their halls to Washington Hall, where Notre Dame Brother Cyprian would occasionally show second-run movies. The bill this evening featured *The Four Horseman of the Apocalypse*, a drama starring Rudolph Valentino. The film was based on the novel of the same name, written by Vicente Blasco Ibanez, and it propelled Valentino to stardom. Valentino played Julio, the hero of a story based on greed, self-indulgence, love, and war set in Argentina and France before the Great War. In the movie's climactic scene, Julio encounters a prophet known as the "stranger" who foresees the end of the world and calls out the Four Horsemen of the Apocalypse from the Book of Revelation. They charge out of the clouds on horseback: the helmeted Conquest, the hideous War, then Pestilence, and finally Death. Among those watching Wednesday night's showing was George Strickler, Rockne's young publicist and student newspaper writer who had become a great fan of the movie.

Thursday, October 16 a squad of 33 Notre Dame players, along with their coaches, manager Leo Sutliffe, and cheer leader Eddie Luther boarded a train at South Bend's New York Central station. After years of preparing for this moment—as a player, as an assistant coach, as a head coach facing the challenges of a war-shortened season, a star that went his own way, and players stealing away to pro games—everything was finally in place. Rockne described Stuhldreher, Crowley, Miller, and Layden as "four young men so eminently qualified by temperament, physique, and instinctive pacing to complement one another perfectly and thus produce the best coordinated and most picturesque backfield in the recent history of football."

For Notre Dame students, Saturday began as usual, with classes until noon. An hour before game time, the entire student body would pack the dirt-floored Fieldhouse, just east of Washington Hall. They would come to "view" the game on the grid-graph, an innovation first used for major away games in 1922, provided by the Student Activities Committee. A large rectangular glass-like screen was marked off with the lines of a football field. A student would hold a flashlight behind the screen to indicate the progress of the ball. Student runners would receive updates on the game at the Western Union telegraph office, on the ground floor of the Main Building, and race what seemed to be the length of a football field to the Fieldhouse and give the details to the "light man." The university band would play before the game and during breaks, and the atmosphere was lively and loud. Admission was 25 cents. Across town, the Palais Royale was also charging 25 cents admission for its grid-graph showing of the game.

The train carrying Notre Dame pulled into the New York Central station about mid-morning Friday, and the team had breakfast at the Belmont Hotel before being ferried by automobiles through the Bronx and up the Boston Post Road to their headquarters at the Westchester-Biltmore Hotel at Rye, New York. The pastoral setting was to Rockne's liking since it lacked the noise and distractions of the big city. New York was bustling with activity, in which monumental achievements were nearly routine. Earlier in the week, officials of the "Highway under the Hudson" announced a major milestone in building a tunnel expected to double the amount of traffic carried between New York and New Jersey. At Grand Central Palace at Lexington Avenue and 46th street, the New York Edison Company was sponsoring the Electrical and Industrial Exposition, where electric trucks, electric elevators, electric refrigerators, and "a wide variety of household applications" would be on display. A highlight of the two-day show was the appearance of the great inventor, Thomas Edison. The gigantic Gimbel's Department Store was celebrating Founders Day, in honor of Adam Gimbel, who opened his first Gimbel trading post in 1842 in Vincennes, Indiana—the same year Father Sorin left Vincennes to found Notre Dame.

The biggest buzz of all in the great city was over the arrival of the German-made dirigible ZR-3, which commanded front-page headlines tracking its epic maiden voyage from Friedrichshafen, Germany to Lakehurst, New Jersey. "Z" stood for lighter than air. "R" stood for rigid construction, and the 3 indicated the model type. Captained by Dr. Hugo Eckener, the ZR-3 represented the height of technological advancements and the hope of future air travel, as the dirigible averaged a speed of 55 miles per hour. Citizens tracked the ZR-3's daily progress and The *New York Herald Tribune* screamed headlines of its nearing arrival and confirmed radio contact on October 14. Other papers carried editorials stating that if the ZR-3 landed safely, it would hail the dirigible as having made a significant step forward in the development of regular transoceanic air service. Not to be overlooked was the fate of the British-built ZR-2, which blew up over Hull, England with the loss of 62 lives, or the airship Roma, a dirigible acquired by the United States from Italy that crashed near Hampton Roads, Virginia, killing 35 people.

Tickets for the big game were disappearing fast. Close to 60,000 people were expected, more than the capacity for baseball, though less than the record-setting crowd of more than 82,000 who a year earlier attended the world heavyweight title fight in which Jack Dempsey defended his championship with a second-round knockout of Luis Firpo, who had gained fame as the "Wild Bull of the Pampas." Fans unable to attend the game were making plans to listen to the game on either of the two New York radio stations providing live coverage. On WEAF, Graham McNamee would be announcing; on WJZ, J. Andrew White would have the call. Many of those nestled in front of their radio sets would be families of Irish Catholic descent. Immigration and the rise of Catholicism in New York City had gone hand-in-hand during the last part of the 19th century. By 1924, the Archdiocese of New York City boasted more than 1.3 million Catholics, the largest ethnic groups being Irish and Italian. Close-knit Catholic communities, anchored by the local parishes and the nuns who taught in parish schools, dotted the city's landscape from lower Manhattan and East Harlem to the Bronx and Staten Island. Being Catholic and "American" was a source of pride for the immigrant wave and their first generation

On Friday evening, Notre Dame spirit was riding high at a meeting hosted by the New York City Notre Dame club at the Inter-Fraternity building at Madison Avenue and 38th Street. The highlight came when Rockne addressed the gathering, giving his assessment of both upcoming games against Army and Princeton, giving the opponents proper respect while proclaiming the Irish ready to give their best.

Saturday, October 18 dawned sunny and pleasant in New York City. The Irish bused into the city from Rye for Mass, followed by breakfast at the Belmont Hotel. Conversation was minimal. The task was at hand. By late morning, the subway lines came alive with the bustling activity generated by the arrival of college football fans. Some fans arrived by exiting the subway station at 155th Street; others approached the stadium from atop the bluff along the Harlem River Speedway, descending a series of ramps that brought them to the ticket booths. Another set of ramps led fans down to the lower seating levels. Fans came across the Hudson River from the Bronx via the elevated trains of the Macombs Dam Bridge and the Putnam Bridge. Many entered on the Eighth Avenue side.

Fans carried pennants, lunch boxes, and jackets. Throngs arrived from a distance and appeared as columns of determined ants converging on the great stadium from several directions. Fans who hadn't availed themselves of the advance sale jammed the ticket booths. Spread below was the green grass and grandstands of the Polo Grounds. It was almost as though the Emerald Isle was smiling on the Irish. But the crowd would be composed of a variety of people. Some, like the Irish-Americans eager to see Notre

Dame, were true partisans. Others were drawn by the prospect of seeing two powerful gridiron elevens match wits, strategy, and strength. And still others looked forward to the great spectacle and pageantry of the day, highlighted by the entrance of 1,200 marching cadets greeted by loud, sustained cheering.

Rockne's squad hit the field with full force, with three full elevens breaking off a series of dummy plays in perfect formation. Every ten yards, the men would set themselves, await the signal, then erupt in motion for another first down. The capacity crowd loved the show. It was Rockne at his entertaining best. Referee Ed Thorp blew his whistle and called the captains together at midfield. Adam Walsh, right hand in a cast, greeted Ed Garbisch with a left-handed handshake. The two had great respect for each other. As referee, Thorp too commanded great respect. At more than six feet and 200 pounds, he was a towering presence, and his intricate knowledge of rules and sense of fair play made him among the most respected of football officials.

Both teams started cautiously, like a great pair of heavyweights parrying and thrusting, each seeking the opponent's strategy. Depending on field position, they might run only one play from scrimmage before punting, in the hopes of pinning the opponent deep in its own end. Every play was a fierce skirmish; every yard was hard-won. On one of the first plays of the game, Walsh went to block Garbisch, but the wily cadet jumped like a rabbit to avoid the hit. When he came down, one foot landed squarely on Walsh's left hand, Garbisch's cleats carrying his full 180 pounds. Walsh felt a searing pain radiating from his hand. *This can't be happening,* he thought to himself. The game meant everything to him and his fellow seniors. The pain wasn't subsiding, but it had to be overcome. Somehow, he willed himself to continue. Rockne's faith in him as captain and leader of the Irish was being rewarded in a big way. Notre Dame, using its shift, deception, and teamwork, put together several sustained drives, one of which culminated in Layden's short burst for a touchdown. At halftime, the Irish led, 6-0.

Up in the wooden press box, newspapermen were marveling at the precision and skill shown by Notre Dame in the second quarter. Rice held court with one group of sportswriters that included some of the biggest names in the business. There was Damon Runyon, who was called by

William Randolph Hearst "the best reporter in the world," and gained fame covering baseball and boxing for Hearst's *New York American*; Gene Fowler, serving as backup to Runyan; Jack Kofoed, who had started his newspaper career in Philadelphia as an 18-year-old in 1912 and was now with the *New York Post*; Paul Gallico of the *Daily News*, at 27 already one of the most powerful sportswriters in the city; Davis Walsh, lead football writer for the United Press; and Notre Dame alum Frank Wallace, reporting for the Associated Press. Into this conclave strolled young George Strickler, Rockne's publicist and *South Bend Tribune* correspondent. Part of his assignment from Rockne was to keep an ear open for analysis from the "big guys" in the newspaper business. Rockne always wanted to know, "What were they saying about us?" The conversation revolved around the exceptional work of the Notre Dame backfield in thwarting Army at every turn. "Yeah, just like the Four Horsemen," Strickler piped up, recalling Wednesday's movie. No reaction was noted from among the professional scribes. The confab eventually broke up as folks settled into place for the second half.

Notre Dame again started rolling, and the crowd was buzzing at the tremendous coordination and sophistication of the Irish attack. Notre Dame, lining up quickly, going into the shift and snapping off plays in rapid succession, seemed to be catching the Cadets flat on their feet. Midway through the quarter, Layden intercepted an Army pass, a big play typical for the senior, and lifted his teammates. The Irish neared the Army goal line, and Crowley made an amazing run, juking and stiff-arming Cadet opponents till he snuck into the corner of the end zone. Notre Dame led, 13-0.

The fourth quarter saw tremendous action as possession bounced back and forth between the two squads, each giving every bit of possible effort. Army cut the lead to 13-7 and was threatening again when Walsh, playing through excruciating pain, made a leaping interception to seal the soldiers' fate. The Irish had prevailed, sending its followers—at the Polo Grounds, back in South Bend, and listening via the radio—into wild celebration. Both captains, the centers, had given their all. Garbisch wanted to enter the Notre Dame locker room to congratulate Walsh, but Rockne intercepted him. Thanks for the thought, the coach told him, but Walsh was in no shape to see anyone but a doctor. Walsh was taken to Roosevelt

Hospital on 10th Avenue where an X-ray showed two small broken bones in his left hand to go with the three he already had in his right hand. Doctors urged Walsh to remain in New York for treatment, but he insisted on returning home with his team.

The crowd of 1,200 who packed the Palais Royale in South Bend for the *News-Times'* grid-graph whooped, clapped, and sang along with the Lucky Seven as the combo played the Victory March over and over. It had been a raucous afternoon, and the experiment was dubbed a huge success. Fans didn't have to stand outside straining to hear an announcer from a megaphone; they had a complete description of the game, lots of lively music, and like-minded Notre Dame fans with whom to cheer. The newspaper enthused: "Had Captain Adam Walsh and his ... fighting gridders heard the cheers that went up for them here, who knows but that the Notre Dame score might have mounted."

On campus, the students who packed the gym had shouted themselves hoarse in the excitement. The Notre Dame band kept playing. Spilling out of the gym, students cheered and shrieked in a celebration that lasted into the night. It was reported, "echoes reverberated over the university buildings as the student body in true Notre Dame fashion celebrated the impressive victory of the Fighting Irish." The students, led by the band, paraded across campus, hailing their heroes. The march culminated at the Main Building, where President Father Matthew Walsh addressed the crowd. Standing atop the building's steps, it was an entirely different feeling than that of five months earlier, addressing students from atop the Civil War statue downtown during the Klan incident. As was his custom, in hailing today's heroes, Father Walsh recounted the famous 1909 Michigan game and Pete Vaughan's reputed smashing of the goal post to claim an Irish victory. After the demonstration, plans were made for a welcoming ceremony to greet the team on its arrival back in South Bend Sunday afternoon.

At newspaper offices around New York and across the country, columns of coverage of the big college games were being prepared for the Sunday papers. It had been a monumental day for the sport. In Urbana, Illinois, "a flashing, red haired youngster, running and dodging with the speed of a deer, gave 67,000 spectators jammed into the new $1,700,000 Illinois Memorial stadium, the thrill of their lives when Illinois vanquished

Michigan 39 to 14 in what probably will be the outstanding game of the 1924 gridiron season in the west." Harold "Red" Grange had taken the opening kickoff and raced 95 yards for a touchdown to christen the new building. He then broke loose for touchdown runs of 65, 55 and 45 yards—all before the first quarter ended. Grange finished the day with five touchdowns and 402 total yards. His feat was "declared by gridiron experts to be one of the most phenomenal in the history of the game." Newspapers scrambled to find pictures and sketches of the Illinois star to run with their game coverage. In addition to the 67,000 at Illinois and 60,000 in the Polo Grounds, 50,000 gathered in Cambridge to see Harvard defeat Holy Cross, 12-6, and crowds of 45,000 were tallied for both the Yale-Dartmouth and Penn-Columbia games.

Reporters covering the Army-Notre Dame batted out stories that covered a variety of elements of the big game. The *New York Times*, in addition to expansive game coverage, went into great detail on the arrival of the West Point band and corps of cadets, the pageantry and atmosphere of the contest. Westbrook Pegler, whose account was dispatched to a number of papers nationwide, commented on the makeup of the 60,000: "It was a strange crowd which filled the permanent stands and bleachers because Notre Dame had brought only a few non-combatants along to kick up a noise, and the Army's cadets filled only a pocket of the capacious stadium. It was largely a non-partisan crowd, come to see a good game of football."

Damon Runyon, writing for the *New York American* and the Hearst syndicate, took a different approach, opting to focus on the Army mule mascot and the blanket that draped the mule. He thought Notre Dame fans would emulate the tradition shown by victorious Navy fans, who would charge from the stands after defeating the Cadets and snatch the mule's blanket. Although the enthusiastic Notre Dame fans never approached the mule, Runyon stuck with his idea for the lead. Young Frank Wallace was torn between his allegiance to Notre Dame and the need to write a lead for the Associated Press that would appeal to a diverse reader base. He managed to do both when he wrote: "The brilliant Notre Dame backfield dazzled the Army line today and romped away with a 13 to 7 victory in one of the hardest-fought of the intersectional series between the two teams. More than 50,000 people saw the game."

Grantland Rice, in the evening twilight and gathering chill, sat at his typewriter in the Polo Grounds press box and pondered his opening. Something about Strickler's halftime comment and the imagery of horses stuck in Rice's mind when he reflected on the Notre Dame backfield. He recalled the 1923 game at Ebbets Field, when an out-of-bounds play brought to mind the possibility of being trampled by a runaway team of horses. It all clicked. His fingers hit the typewriter keys:

> Outlined against a blue-gray October sky, the Four Horsemen rode again. In dramatic lore they are known as Famine, Pestilence, Destruction and Death. These are only aliases. Their real names are Stuhldreher, Miller, Crowley and Layden. They formed the crest of the South Bend cyclone before which another fighting Army football team was swept over the precipice at the Polo Grounds yesterday afternoon as 55,000 spectators peered down on the bewildering panorama spread on the green plain below.
>
> A cyclone can't be snared. It may be surrounded, but somewhere it breaks through to keep on going. When the cyclone starts from South Bend, where the candle lights still gleam through the Indiana sycamores, those in the way must take to storm cellars at top speed. Yesterday the cyclone struck again, as Notre Dame beat the Army, 13 to 7, with a set of backfield stars that ripped and crashed through a strong Army defense with more speed and power than the warring cadets could meet.

From there, Rice described "the driving power of one of the greatest backfields that ever churned up the turf of any gridiron in any football age." He noted the following on the second quarter scoring drives: "the unwavering power of the Western attack that hammered relentlessly and remorselessly without easing up for a second's breath." Rice paid particular homage to the speed of the Irish attack, the precision with which it worked, and the consistently effective blocking it used to advance the ball on the ground.

Rice also had high praise for Notre Dame's defensive play. "When a back such as Harry Wilson finds few chances to get started you can figure upon the defensive strength that is barricading the road. Wilson is one of the hardest backs in the game to suppress, but he found few chances yesterday to show his broken field ability. You can't run through a broken field until you get there." He concluded by stating "we doubt that any team in the country could have beaten Rockne's array yesterday afternoon, East or West. It was a great football team brilliantly directed, a team of speed, power and team play. The Army has no cause for gloom over its showing. It played first class football against more speed than it could match. Those who have tackled a cyclone can understand."

The editors at the *Herald Tribune* felt the quality of Rice's piece and the significance of the game merited front-page play, and so the story ran on the front of Sunday's paper—page one, column one at the top left-hand corner. Rice was not totally alone in developing the equine theme. Heywood Broun, a fine wordsmith writing in the New York World, wrote that Notre Dame "defeated the West Pointers with sweeping cavalry charges around the ends...They were light horsemen, these running backs of Notre Dame, but they swung against the Army ends with speed and numbers. The players were run wide and again and again, some unfortunate soldier sentinel would race all the way across the gridiron and over the sidelines without ever getting contact with any one but one of the interfering outposts."

Before boarding the train home, Strickler stopped at a newsstand and grabbed copies of the "bulldog" early editions of the Sunday papers. Reading Rice's lead, he could barely believe his eyes. According to Strickler, he sent a wire to his father back in South Bend, advising Mr. Strickler to round up four horses for a publicity photo he wanted to have taken. In the coming days and weeks, the notion of Notre Dame having not only a "wonder team" but a backfield of biblical proportions would sweep across the country. Rice's phraseology would gradually make its way into other sports writers' descriptions. William F. "Bill" Fox, Jr., a 1920 Notre Dame graduate, joined the sports staff of the *Indianapolis News* as a reporter. He saw the 1924 team, as long as it continued to perform at a high level, as a major national sports story. Fox strongly encouraged Strickler to take advantage of the opportunity Rice's story presented and offered to help in any way he could.

During the week of practice before the Princeton game, Strickler enlisted his father, who had more experience around animals because of his job on the university farm, to help with a publicity photo shoot. His assignment was to round up four riding horses for the famous backfield to mount. Instead, he came up with four well-worn workhorses, of different sizes and condition. Strickler arrived at the practice field, explained the stunt to the guard, and brought the horses onto the field. The commercial photographer Strickler hired for the shoot, Mr. Christman, was already there. The four players were summoned, and they began to look askance at one another. Except for Stuhldreher, who had handled horses while delivering groceries for his father's store, the four had little equine expertise. But more than that, each knew that being thrown from a horse could cause an injury that would, in an instant, put an end to their participation in a magical season. All that risk just for a photograph? With the players anxious, and Rockne not wanting his practice interrupted any more than necessary, it was a quick photo shoot. A couple of shots were taken, the players were on their way, and Strickler guided the horses off the field.

Once the prints became available, Strickler went to work distributing the photo. His first sale was to *Pacific & Atlantic*, a national news photo agency. Every time P&A syndicated the photo in another newspaper, Strickler received a royalty. One by one, the major newspapers in the country ran the photo. The nickname and photo became vehicles for the sporting public to connect a personal story to the feats of a team, which was picking up admirers by the thousands. The efforts of Rice, Strickler, Fox, and others aside, a rapidly growing fan base, especially one of Irish-Americans, was eager to embrace the story of the college boys representing the school in South Bend. Rockne was delighted to see this particular group, which had worked so hard for four football seasons, reap the rewards of their efforts.

The new-found fame seemed to have little direct impact on the Irish players. There were injuries to heal, exams for which to study, and daily activities that demanded their attention. The fellows also possessed a natural modesty of a group of down-to-earth players who simply loved the game of football. After returning from the Army game, Layden wrote his romantic interest, Evelyn Byrne, back home that "against the Army, I played a few minutes, and was fortunate enough to score a touchdown." As for the upcoming Princeton game, Layden wrote, "I hope I am again fortunate enough to make the trip."

Layden, indeed, made the trip back East just four days after returning from New York. Though banged up from the battle with Army, all of the Irish, except Walsh, would be able to play against Princeton. That included Stuhldreher, whose throwing arm had been giving him problems the past several weeks. Before the Army game, Rockne told him there was a doctor in New York who had prepared a new liniment meant to "limber dead nerves" like nothing else. "Before the game," Stuhldreher noted, "they worked on my arm, massaging the liniment well into the skin so that its healing oils penetrated the muscles, and put a hot pad on it." In the game, Stuhldreher was able to use his arm as if there were nothing wrong with it. The same procedure was used for the Princeton game, and Stuhldreher again felt fine. Only after did Rockne tell him "that this wonderful liniment was none other than the one they used all the time at Notre Dame. He had put it into a different bottle so that I would think it different."

In the area of beaches, boardwalks, and golf clubs along the northern New Jersey shore, Joe Byrne had set up Rockne and the Irish with the desired level of quietude before the Princeton game. Friday, the team practiced on the polo field at the Deal Golf Club. Before that, Rockne planned another brief stop. Just outside the Deal Club stood a grain scale, and Rockne took several of his players, most notably his star backfield, and met members of the New York sporting press at the scale. Some newspapermen had questioned whether the Irish backfield was really as light as advertised. Rockne had Grantland Rice call each of the backs, one-by-one, up to the scale in dramatic fashion. The results matched the reported weights of the players: Layden was the heaviest at 161 pounds, Crowley and Don Miller were both close to 157 pounds, and Stuhldreher came up a few ounces short of 152 pounds.

The next afternoon against Roper's Tigers, the Irish won 12-0, with one touchdown called back, and other drives ending deep in Princeton territory. They racked up 374 total yards to just 97 for the Tigers and had an 18-4 advantage in first downs. "Never in my life have I spent such a frustrating afternoon," Princeton back Charlie Caldwell later wrote. "The final score could have been 28-0 or possibly higher. I felt as if we were being toyed with. I would get set to drop the ball-carrier in his tracks and someone could give me a nudge, just enough to throw me off balance, just enough pressure to make me miss. There was no getting around it, I had been sold by Rockne football."

Caldwell and his teammates had experienced Rockne football in full flower—a blend of science with art, with overwhelming results. Frank Wallace described it this way: "The new thing Rockne had created…the refinement of the game until all brutish elements seemed removed, leaving speed, imagination, grace – wrapped in such a flawless performance that it…looked like a well-rehearsed, finished motion picture in color. The Horsemen needed and utilized space; they swept wide, passed overhead; wasted little of their energy on interior body-to-body smashups. But when the defense spread to contain Crowley and Miller, Layden would find daylight for jet-darts down the middle. Ahead of the speed and guile of the Horsemen was the offensive blocking of the Mules. Guiding it all was the artisan Rockne—and at the controls his little master mechanic, Stuhldreher."

Rockne enjoyed a moment's levity at halftime of the game; he felt comfortable in his ability to chide Sleepy Jim Crowley. In the opening half, Crowley broke loose for a long run, but was caught from behind by Jack Slagle. In the locker room Crowley said to Rockne, "I made a mistake. I didn't know Slagle was that fast. I should have cut back."

"That wasn't the mistake you made," said Rockne. "That wasn't it."

"Yes, it was," Crowley protested. "I admit it. A mistake."

"No," the coach replied. "Slagle didn't know who you were. If you had shown him those New York clippings you've been saving, telling how good you were, he wouldn't have dared come near you." Crowley, the jokester, laughed harder than anyone at the coach's punch line.

Rockne had developed near-perfect rapport with his 1924 players; it wasn't just Crowley he knew how to handle. Although it was heavily dominated by seniors, there were juniors and sophomores sprinkled in. Rock knew exactly how to interact with each. Junior Wilbur Eaton, out of Creighton Prep in Omaha, was one of the Shock Troops, and played with such intensity that Rockne would remind Eaton not to close his eyes when making a tackle. One day, the coach on the practice field sang to the tune of child's song, doing a little dance and holding out the sides of his pants:

> Wilbur closed his eyes
> Wilbur closed his eyes
> Heigh-ho the derrio,
> Wilbur closed his eyes.

Another player might have been embarrassed and angered. For Wilbur, the tactic worked, and he never forgot the lesson, both as a player and later as a coach.

The Princeton victory put Rockne and his fellows in a celebratory mood. Saturday night back in New York City, they had a theatre party, attending the Ziegfield Follies show at the Amsterdam Theatre on West 42nd street. Rogers, now a great friend of the coach, came out on the stage wearing a blue Notre Dame sweater with the interlocking ND monogram. The crowd went crazy. Another member of the cast shouted from the wings, "What's going on out there?"

"I don't know," Rogers said, trying to act befuddled. "Unless they're cheering my North Dakota sweater." The crowd ate it up.

# 23

## Run For The Roses

O n Monday afternoon, October 27, 1924, Notre Dame's triumphant football team returned home to the cheers of students and citizens gathered at the train station. Back in New York City, Coach Percy Haughton was directing his Columbia University team's practice at Baker Field. The Lions were coming off a 27-3 victory over Williams College. They were 4-1 on the season and looking forward to their "game of the year" in five days at Cornell. Haughton, 48, complained of feeling ill, and was taken by taxicab to St. Luke's Hospital in Manhattan. He died a few minutes after arrival of what was called "acute indigestion." Haughton was considered one of the giants in college football coaching, right there with Stagg, Warner, Yost, and now Rockne as well. A former Harvard lineman, Haughton had taken the reigns at his alma mater in 1908 and lifted Crimson fortunes to unprecedented heights, including national championships in 1910, 1912, and 1913. He came out of football retirement in 1923 to coach Columbia, which was still on a slow climb back to respectability after fielding no team from 1906 through 1914. "He was something more than a great coach," wrote Grantland Rice, who had watched Haughton coach his last game against

Williams. "He was an inspiration such as few may ever chance to know. He did something more than give his teams winning plays—he gave them morale beyond any leader we have ever known." For Rockne, Haughton's death was a personal loss of a friend and fellow member of the often tight-knit coaching fraternity.

Rockne was fueled by the feedback, questions, and camaraderie of other coaches, whether he was in front of 100 or more students at one of his coaching schools, or on his own practice field. His 1924 Notre Dame staff looked far different than it did six years earlier, when Rockne was the "one-man band" doing everything from handing out equipment, to fixing injuries, to selling tickets. By 1924, his staff included Tom Lieb and Hunk Anderson—two superlative assistants to coach the linemen. George Keogan, already established as a leading college basketball coach, helped immensely in football by guiding the freshman team. George Vergara, lineman from New York who had exhausted his eligibility, but wanted to do what he could to help while he finished school, assisted Keogan. Rockne had implemented a competitive student manager system, for which Leo Sutliffe was now serving as senior member.

One other individual served a vital role as a trainer looking after the day-to-day health of the players. Verly Smith, who had spent time working in various boxing camps, including Jack Dempsey's, brought valuable experience as he cared for the players' bumps and bruises. And, he was the lone black associated with the football team, long before any black student attended Notre Dame or represented it on the playing field. Rockne embraced Smith and praised his role, apparently without any undue consequences. In that way, he was following history in South Bend. St. Joseph County had a rich history of supporting the underground railroad before the Civil War, with residents offering their homes, barns, and businesses as safe places in which runaway slaves could eat and rest as they made their way north. By the turn of the century, more black families headed to South Bend with the promise of employment from the city's strong manufacturing base; however, the overall black population remained small. By 1924, The Olivet African Methodist Episcopal Church at 310 W. Monroe Street and Pilgrim Baptist Church, established in 1890, at 116 N. Birdsell Street provided houses of worship for a growing black community. South Bend, in its small way, was something of a safe haven for blacks while

Indiana, especially in rural areas, was still heavily Klan-dominated.

After back-to-backs trips and two grueling victories, Rockne excused the regulars from scrimmages Monday and Tuesday before the next Saturday's clash. In Georgia Tech, the team would be facing one of the South's consistently strong teams. Bill Alexander, who graduated from Tech in 1912, had taken over as head coach from John Heisman in 1920, after a 16-year stint in which Heisman and Tech rolled up a 102-29-7 record, including four undefeated teams. Since then, Alexander had built an imposing 29-7-5 record. On Friday, October 31, the South Bend *News-Times* proclaimed, "Notre Dame and South Bend are ready to welcome the crowds of alumni and their families who will attend the greatest Homecoming in the history of the university." ND monograms and blue and gold streamers could be seen at nearly every downtown business. Storefronts were decorated with the school colors of both Notre Dame and Georgia Tech. Eddie Luther revved up the students at a Wednesday pep rally and bonfire. Thursday evening several hundred students and townspeople watched an elimination-boxing tournament at the gymnasium with 13 bouts of 3 two-minute rounds. Verly Smith served as a judge.

Dispatches from Chicago indicated that hundreds of football fans from the Chicago area were passing up the Purdue-Chicago game at Stagg Field and the Indiana-Northwestern tussle in Evanston to come to South Bend. Easily the largest crowd in the history of Cartier Field was expected. All but a few reserved-seat tickets were sold out by Thursday. Al Ryan, director of ticket sales, said that 4,000 general admission tickets would be sold Saturday starting at 1 p.m. On Thursday, a crew hastily constructed temporary bleachers at the south end of the stadium to seat an additional 1,500 fans. Though this was just Notre Dame's fifth Homecoming, the sense of family—the bond between alumni and current students, between alumni and alma mater—had been a vital part of the university since the school's founding. Father Sorin's vision of a great university was one that carried the benefits of Catholic higher education across America and around the world, creating an ever-widening circle of influence. As educated men went out into the world, they would always remain warmly embraced by Notre Dame. An 1897 graduate active with the Alumni Association put it this way:

"I have been back to Notre Dame (several) times in a period of twenty-five years. These visits have been delightful, and why?....New faces are observed. You meet the present generation and when these men are told you were at Notre Dame years back, your hand is grasped in genuine friendship and the old boy feels that he's sure enough back again with his own folks. The longer the time is away from Notre Dame, the more keenly will one appreciate the sterling worth of the men of Holy Cross and the splendid spirit that permeates every individual of the Congregation. Their welcome is real and genuine…The analogy of a college and a mother of a family is right here thrown out in strong lights. The love of a real mother is never divided—her son who succeeds is loved by her but not more or less than the son who fails. When it comes to loyalty, first, hand it to the old college and men of Holy Cross—they are the salt of the earth. Win, lose or draw—they are behind you to a man, and that's loyalty."

Thousands of Notre Dame alumni, fans, families of current students, and Georgia Tech supporters streamed into South Bend all day Friday, October 31. Student volunteers met visitors at each of the train stations and hotels and manned information booths all day. The major hotels—the Oliver, the LaSalle, the Jefferson—were full, and townspeople once again opened up their homes to handle the overflow. At 7 p.m. sharp Notre Dame students gathered behind the band for the Halloween homecoming torchlight parade through campus. Alumni and fans entered campus under a welcome arch of electric lights, courtesy of engineering students, who also designed an ingenious display of electric lights on their classroom building. The assembled masses, now including hundreds of alumni, stood in front of a temporary stage just south of the gymnasium.

Georgia Tech's Alexander addressed the crowd. "We consider it a great honor down south to be included on the Notre Dame football schedule, and we will try to give your team a game tomorrow that will be worthy of your Homecoming." The crowd, now numbering in the thousands, was treated to a vaudeville-style variety show put on by the entertainment committee of the Blue Circle Club. The highlight of the evening was the presentation of several members of Notre Dame's first football team, from 1887. It was the first effort to bring these pioneers of Notre Dame football back to campus as a group in the 36 years since they had donned a set of unpadded canvas football suits and, after a brief scrimmage against a team of "scrubs" outfitted in their civilian clothes, took on Michigan. "We had one football, three rule books and no coach," recalled Dr. H. B. Luhn in preparing for the reunion. "But we did the best we could, and after all, it was the start from which the great Notre Dame teams of later years are the results."

At 11 a.m. on a glorious November 1 Saturday, the lunchroom staff from O.A. Clark began serving a barbecue dinner in the field next to the gym. Fans were treated to an unusual sight as they packed the wooden stands. Slowly rolling onto Cartier Field was a brand new Studebaker Bix Six sedan, the top-of-the-line model, driven by George F. Hull of Hullie & Mike's. When the auto pulled up near the Irish bench, Frank Shaughnessy of the Chicago Notre Dame Club made a quick presentation—the car was a gift of the alumni to coach and athletic director Knute Rockne in appreciation of his years of work in putting Notre Dame on the nation's athletic map and, indeed, the world. The players were not overlooked, as Notre Dame monogram blankets were presented to 33 varsity players.

The Irish players received their final instructions, which included a simple refrain—"Watch Wycoff." The junior fullback presented a triple threat of running, passing, and kicking unlike nearly anyone else Notre Dame had faced. Wycoff had some early gains and a field goal to put Tech ahead, 3-0. But after that, Notre Dame rolled to a 34-3 victory. Three Saturdays, three intersectional victories—it was an unheard of feat. Notre Dame was winning over fans and the press from coast to coast. And behind the scenes—unbeknownst to most Fighting Irish fans, and even the team—conversations were underway to extend the season with a West Coast spectacular. With a 5-0 start, Father O'Hara's hopes to showcase the university were becoming reality.

Next up was a trip to Wisconsin, which was the official student trip for 1924, and in a sense a "second homecoming." Notre Dame alums and fans from across the Midwest—and those simply wanting to see the "Four Horsemen" and their mates—made plans to travel to Wisconsin's capital city for the first meeting between the two schools since 1917. For weeks, ticket requests had been pouring into the Wisconsin athletic department for the November 8 game. It was the deepest foray into the West on the Irish schedule and the best chance to see the team that had wowed the East. "That the crowd at the Notre Dame game will be more evenly divided in support of the two teams than usual is the prediction of Paul F. Hunter, director of ticket sales," noted a Madison paper. Notre Dame was expected to fill the entire south half of the east stand with more than 5,000 seats in one block. In addition to the 5,000 tickets sent under registered mail to Notre Dame, several thousands more were sold to Irish followers from the Madison ticket office. Additional bleachers were being constructed, and a record crowd was expected.

While preparing his team for Wisconsin, Rockne also kept an eye on the rest of the college football landscape. The first six weeks of the season had weeded out several contenders for top honors. In the East, Yale and Pennsylvania drew the most interest. In the far West, California, Leland Stanford, and Southern California had risen to the top. Notre Dame had put itself into strong consideration with its 5-0 record. Yet, in the past few years, the Irish and their fans had read and heard about several possible invitations to postseason games that either never materialized or were declined by the school for a variety of reasons. Early in the week before the Wisconsin game, reports surfaced that Notre Dame would be invited to play in the annual Tournament of Roses game at Pasadena, California. Rockne was quick to tamp down the rumors. "If any such game is being arranged between Notre Dame and a western team, it is news to me," he averred, adding that the report sounded "like the annual bunk." In the next several days, though, the headlines blared: "Fighting Irish Play in California New Year's Day."

On Wednesday night, Gwynn Wilson, graduate manager of the University of Southern California team, announced to the press that his team would meet Notre Dame in the annual Pasadena classic. The announcement followed long distance telephone conversations between Wilson and Rockne. By noon Thursday, Notre Dame's faculty board of athletics met and ratified negotiations for the game. Southern Cal already had one "postseason" game scheduled, against Syracuse in Los Angeles on December 6. Scheduling Notre Dame, one report noted, "means the opening of athletic relations with Notre Dame that will see a return contest in 1926 or 1927 either at South Bend or at the Grant Park stadium, Chicago." On the practice field, there was a new bounce in the Irish's step, as described in the *News-Times*: "Thirty-six years of football prestige at the school of the Fighting Irish is now preparing to stand validation in one of the greatest football classics of all time. The announcement came with joyous suddenness, but the hugeness and importance of it all is too much for many of the players and students who are still groping through the mist of happy anxiety, hardly daring to trust their senses of sight and hearing and not quite able to reconcile themselves to the fact that the 'wonder team' will be the feature attraction at the Tournament of the Roses."

At 8:30 Friday morning, the Irish players boarded their train in South Bend. The first stop was Beloit, Wisconsin, at the Illinois border. After arriving at 3 p.m., Rockne's men went through a signal drill with the Beloit College varsity, coached by Tom Mills, who had attended one of Rockne's coaching schools. Beloit was also the hometown of Irish back Ward "Doc" Connell. Connell's family lived in Beloit, next door to the St. Thomas parish rectory and was actively involved with the church. Saturday began with team Mass at St. Thomas, followed by the resumption of the train trip, directly to the gates of Camp Randall stadium by 11:00 a.m. The Notre Dame students and thousands of Notre Dame fans that had gathered for the game saw an Irish attack perform as advertised. The Horsemen dazzled the crowd with a variety of big-gaining plays. Several of the Notre Dame regulars went to shower, and it was said Crowley spent part of the fourth quarter in the stands with his mother, who had made the trip with a large contingent of fans from Green Bay anxious to watch their native son.

After the final 38-3 score was posted, the Notre Dame band led the students on a march down the field and through the goalposts, where "hats were tossed up and over in token of the conquest." A final chorus of the Victory March reverberated among the emptying stands. Then the parade continued toward downtown, where traffic was again stopped and car horns blared triumphantly. Saturday night, the Crystal Room of the Loraine Hotel was packed for a banquet sponsored by the Knights of Columbus to honor Rockne and his team. Tributes came from Judge "Ikey" Karel, former Wisconsin football star; Badger basketball coach Doc Meanwell, a good friend of Rockne's; and Notre Dame alums such as Warren Cartier and Willie "Red" Maher, the former Madison high school star who was an Irish teammate of the current players in 1922 and

1923. Rockne and Adam Walsh thanked the local Knights of Columbus Council and praised Wisconsin's sportsmanship.

In attendance at the Notre Dame-Wisconsin game were Nebraska Coach Fred T. Dawson and several of his key players, since the Cornhuskers were idle that day. Upon returning to Lincoln, Coach Dawson was diplomatic in his comments to a Nebraska paper. "Notre Dame has everything," he said. "They are fast—every man—and work like a well-oiled machine." Huskers captain Ed Weir was more direct: "Notre Dame has a great team, but Nebraska can and will beat them next Saturday," said Weir. If Weir's comments made it back to South Bend, they could add little to the fervor the Fighting Irish felt about this game. Ever since the 1924 schedule was released, Rockne's players were intensely focused on November 15 and the chance for revenge with their prime nemesis of the past two years. The Irish lockers were adorned with all manner of signs such as:

"Get the Cornhuskers."
"Remember the last two defeats."
"This year, we ought to beat 'em, got to beat 'em, WILL beat 'em"

In the lobby of the Oliver Hotel, up and down the cigar shops and haberdasheries that lined Michigan and Washington avenues, in every barber shop in town, the talk was the same: Can the Irish beat Nebraska this time? The sting of the two losses at Lincoln hung heavily over the town and campus. Wrote one observer, "The memories of these two games will live long with the score of men whose college football careers end at the Tournament of Roses on New Year's Day." A third consecutive loss to the Huskers—before an expected record crowd at Cartier Field—with this team of seniors was unthinkable. Preparations began to take on the air of a "second homecoming," as thousands were expected to pour into South Bend on special trains and by automobile. Football games at Notre Dame were becoming an event. In the midst of Nebraska preparation, it might have been easy for the locals to miss an important development coming out of Chicago on Monday. Officials at Northwestern University, Notre Dame's next opponent on November 22, announced that the game had been moved from the school's field in Evanston and would be played in the mammoth new stadium at Grant Park in Chicago, which could accommodate 55,000 fans.

Rockne ran his usual Monday and Tuesday practices but kept a Tuesday appointment to address 150 members of the Lions clubs of South Bend, Mishawaka, Elkhart, Gary, and Hammond at the LaSalle Hotel. "The things a coach expects from his men are no more than the qualities an employer expects from an employee, that the world expects from those who endeavor to succeed," the coach said. "First of these is brains. A successful player must be able to analyze; he must be resourceful." The coach went on to describe the other key attributes he sought in players—ambition, energy, and dependability: "The price of success on the gridiron is effort, self-denial, and perseverance."

Perseverance could also describe the football fans attempting to gain entry to Saturday's big game. According to reports, the few ticket-holders willing to part with their passes were asking $7.50 to $15 apiece; in Chicago, choice seats were changing hands for as much as $32.50 each—more than 10 times face value. The *News-Times* also reported, "Coach Rockne has been flooded with applications for press reservations. Additional facilities to take care of the small army of newspaper men have been provided, the second time that the press coop has been enlarged this season." Station WGN of Chicago requested and received permission to broadcast its first game ever from Cartier Field.

The Cornhuskers pulled into the New York Central station a little after 7 p.m. Friday, and the Nebraska contingent noticed the lineup of automobiles decked out in the colors of both schools. To the cheers of onlookers, the Huskers were escorted to the vehicles, which were operated by Notre Dame's Villagers Club. The caravan, with horns blaring, wound through downtown and brought the Huskers to the Notre Dame campus, where a huge pep fest was waiting to honor the visitors.

Eddie Luther, Notre Dame cheer leader, introduced the Nebraska coach and players amid a greeting of the wildest cheering that ever resounded in the Notre Dame gymnasium. Coach Dawson, appearing first in the gallery, was greeted with a full three minutes of din and noise that brought forth unstinted praise from the coach whose mission here was to defend the famous jinx of the Notre Dame-Nebraska game. What Coach Dawson said to the huge assembly, which awaited him, bespoke the greatest of feeling for the Notre Dame team and its enviable record. He made no predictions and voiced no claims, but after eulogizing the merits of both elevens, he concluded with the hope that the best team might win. More than a thousand guests were registered at the Oliver, another 500 or more at the LaSalle and 350 at the Jefferson. Friday afternoon, a long distance telephone call from Detroit came in for Rockne. It was Edsel Ford, son of the famous auto manufacturer, looking for tickets to the game. "I'd like to fix you up," came the reply, "but the only thing I've got left is my place on the coaching bench and I'd give you that only I'm afraid the boys might not like it if I walked off on them right at this time."

Saturday morning, South Bend was inundated with train traffic. Four specials from Chicago came over the New York Central line. One from Detroit arrived on the New Jersey tracks. A special from Indianapolis on the Pennsylvania line brought nearly 200 fans. And the regular New York Central run from the east carried three extra coaches carrying fans from Cleveland. Al Feeney, Rockne's teammate from 1910-13 and now an Indianapolis businessman, arranged for 13 Pullman coaches to bring fans from downstate. Up in the Cartier Field "press coop," the great crush of newspapermen jockeyed for spots from which to cover the game. One Nebraska paper, it was reported, "is sending an aeroplane here to return with photos for their Sunday paper." Chicago's WGN spent $650 to lay a wire for its radio broadcast.

As it had the two previous meetings, Nebraska scored first, and led 6-0 after one quarter. But Stuhldreher and Miller scored touchdowns early in the second quarter and the Irish were on their way. Everything they tried seem to baffle the Huskers; the noise from the Notre Dame fans was ear-splitting. Two years of pent-up frustration was being loosed upon the outgunned Huskers. One Nebraska writer described it succinctly: "At will, literally at will, Rockne's hordes drove, hammered, decoyed their adversaries back, back and back....Rockne hasn't only a marvelous backfield, the smoothest, most beautifully functioning quartet ever assembled, but he has just such an entire first eleven." Now, one by one, each received their curtain call, taken out to loud ovations. Connell replaced Don Miller, Crowe went in for Collins, Eggert replaced Weibel. On this afternoon, there had been touchdowns scored by three fourths of the famous quartet—Stuhldreher, Miller, and Crowley. Now it was the fourth member's moment. On a final drive, Elmer Layden carried the ball six straight times, his low profile shooting into openings for four yards, seven yards, five yards. His final burst was a three-yard touchdown that made the final score 34-6. Hats and banners flew into the darkening skies. A din lofted from the wooden grandstands. Tired. Relieved. Vindicated. The greatest team in Irish history trotted happily to their dressing room. There, an eerie silence prevailed. "When the fellows entered the dressing room," one of the star backs explained, "they couldn't talk, they were so happy over the victory."

Following the Nebraska game, Notre Dame was the subject of recognition and adulation, including one visiting scribe from Nebraska who wrote: "Notre Dame stands where Notre Dame deserves to stand, where it had stood all this season, as the greatest football team in the republic, possibly the greatest football eleven of all time." Illinois' claim to being the best eleven in the middle west was tarnished by virtue of its 21-21 tie with Chicago on November 8. In one of the most stunning upsets in recent Western Conference history, the Illini ventured to Minneapolis and were spanked, 21-7, by Minnesota at its new Memorial Stadium. The Gophers knocked Red Grange out of the game.

In the far west, a season of controversy and intrigue was unfolding, putting into doubt Notre Dame's opponent for the game at Pasadena on New Year's Day. Late in October, a major rift over player eligibility pitted the University of Southern California on one side and the Bay Area schools—the University of California and Leland Stanford—on the other. On Monday, November 3, the controversy took another shocking turn when Southern Cal announced its executive committee had voted unanimously to cancel the game with Stanford and gave $50,000 in ticket sales to the Palo Alto school to avoid the threat of a lawsuit. Both teams scrambled to find replacements who could show up to play in five days. Stanford brought in the University of Utah and scored an easy 30-0 victory to improve to 6-0 on the season. Southern Cal figured to do the same against St. Mary's from Oakland, coached by former Notre Dame star Edward "Slip" Madigan. But, as one report noted, "debacle succeeded disaster," and St. Mary's stunned the Trojans and 27,000 fans at the Coliseum, 14-10. Southern Cal had the ball at St. Mary's 1-yard line on third down when the final gun sounded. The Trojans, who just days earlier had announced they were to play in the Tournament of Roses, now found themselves with back-to-back losses, broken relations with the two north-ern California schools, and the loss of a major payday from the sale of tickets for the Cal game. The Los Angeles City Council made a last-ditch attempt to keep Southern Cal headed to Pasadena, but the plea went no-where. Stanford had all the momentum in the battle for the Pacific coast slot vs. the Irish.

In the Notre Dame administrative offices, the bid to Pasadena and the convincing victories over Wisconsin and Nebraska led to a whirlwind of activity. Memories of the South Bend KKK rally from May still burned within Father O'Hara. While President Walsh clearly understood the fi-nancial benefits a postseason trip might provide, it was Father O'Hara who recognized the huge potential public relations opportunity the trip held. O'Hara's deep devotion to the Blessed Sacrament and daily commu-nion helped him see a connection between Catholic religious practice and the success of the Irish football team. Under his watch, daily communion had become an integral part of life for Notre Dame athletes, and now those athletes were winning accolades and friends across the country. The trip to Pasadena provided a singular chance to make the school and its Catholic affiliation even more visible. O'Hara's popularity on campus and his abounding energy and enthusiasm made him a natural to take the lead in planning the preparation for the trip to Pasadena. The trip, O'Hara de-cided, would showcase Catholic pride and achievement to alumni, alumni clubs, local Knights of Columbus councils, and football fans in the South, Middle West, and West.

The team still had two remaining contests, the first against North-western on November 22 in the game switched to the new Grant Park stadium. It seemed to some that every Chicagoan who called himself a football fan was planning to head to the lakefront Saturday. True, some 32,000 would pack Stagg Field to watch the Maroons attempt to clinch the Big Ten title against Wisconsin. But by now Rockne had begun to sup-plant Stagg as the mastermind of the game, and fans sensed the change. One columnist noted about the tickets: "Northwestern hasn't got 'em. Notre Dame hasn't got 'em. South Park Board hasn't got 'em. Where in....ARE the tickets?" Those unable to score a ducat had the next best thing. WGN was continuing its series of college football broadcasts and made the Northwestern-Notre Dame tussle their game for November 22.

Northwestern's movable bleachers were installed at the north and south ends of the gridiron, adding several thousand seats. Officials decided several thousand more could be admitted to standing room areas. Workmen also thickly dressed down the field with hay to protect the turf.

On game day, though, the new field showed the effects of the recent snow and rain and was in poor condition. Players slipped and slid in pre-game warm-ups, while the heavily bundled crowd, many arriving at the stadium for the first time, struggled to find their seats. The muddy field was the first thing in weeks to slow down the Irish attack. They clung to a 7-6 lead into the fourth quarter, when the Wildcats were driving. Pass after pass threatened the Notre Dame defense. Then, timing his move perfectly, Layden stepped in front of an aerial at the 45 and sprinted untouched into the end zone. In an instant, the Northwestern charge was repelled, and the Irish led, 13-6. A huge portion of the 45,000 fans stood and cheered wildly as Layden was mobbed by his teammates. Even a missed extra point didn't dim their enthusiasm. In the dark and mud, the Irish held on.

While the Irish were in their tussle with Northwestern, a tremendous battle for the Pacific coast crown was waged at Berkeley, California. A throng of 76,000 filled the stadium with another 24,000 crowding Tight Wad Hill for a vantage that offered a clear view down onto the gridiron. Pundits described the gathering of 90,000 as the "largest sporting event in the history of the West" and said that the colorful enthusiasm of the fans surpassed any such previous contest in memory. Stanford's star running back Ernie Nevers was sidelined with a broken ankle, causing the game between the two great rivals to be deemed a toss-up. In what Walter Camp described as "one of the most exciting games I've seen in any part of the country" the teams traded scores all afternoon, with Stanford rallying late for a touchdown and kick after for a 20-20 tie. On Monday, November 24, reports began filtering out of Los Angeles that it would be Stanford and not Southern Cal selected as the Pacific coast representative to face the Irish in the Tournament of Roses football classic. Yet intense local lobbying on behalf of the Trojans kept the decision up in the air, and no official announcement was made. Rockne spent the day in Chicago, visiting friends and family and preparing for a speech that evening to the Chicago City club, entitled "Football as Shown in the Present Season."

At 7:07 p.m. on Wednesday, November 26, a group of 33 Notre Dame gridders and their coaches pulled out of the Pennsylvania station in South Bend, bound for Pittsburgh. The venture would allow another entire region to get a look at the "four horsemen" and their teammates. With the Thanksgiving holiday weekend, few would be coming from South Bend or the East Coast, but the whole football-mad region of western Pennsylvania and eastern Ohio would be tempted to make the trip and see the imminent national champions. One Ohio resident making the trip was William J. Stuhldreher, Harry's father. He had never seen his son play football during Harry's high school, prep, or college years. As Saturday was the busiest day in the grocery trade, William was never able to leave the store to see a game. This time, he made arrangements and joined a group of about 100 other Massillon residents who traveled to Pittsburgh for Harry's last game. As Notre Dame worked out Friday at Forbes Field, various coaches and visitors milled about. "Other coaches of smaller achievements insist upon secret workouts," noted one local columnist, "Rockne's eleven probably was scouted more thoroughly than any contemporary team." In addition to the famous backfield, the Notre Dame line had achieved its own fame. On one trip, Adam Walsh heard a knock on his door. The visitor inquired if this room was where he would find the four horsemen. Walsh replied, "Nah, we're just the seven mules." The name stuck. A running gag among the fellows was the question of which unit was more important to the team's success. A "vote" was taken and the mules won, 7-4.

A crowd estimated at between 30,000 and 40,000 made its way through the streets of the Forbes neighborhood and into the home ballpark of baseball's Pirates for the 2 p.m. kickoff. Carnegie played many of its games down the boulevard at its Tartan Field in front of crowds as thin as 6,000. But this game was big-league in all respects. Because many other college teams had completed their schedules, the sidelines were packed with coaches. Among the mentors in attendance were Sutherland of Pittsburgh, Spears of West Virginia, Stagg of Chicago, Phelan of Purdue, Spaulding of Minnesota, and Bezdek of Penn State. Stuhldreher's prep coach Marks was there, and scouting for Leland Stanford was assistant coach Andy Kerr.

A trick play near the end of the first half allowed Carnegie to tie the game at 13. A sideline scribe noticed Rockne's "troubled brow" as the trick play snookered the Irish and "a mood of troubled expectancy fell upon thousands of Notre Dame shouters as the two clubs walked off the field...There were many close students of the game who seemed to sense the South Bend machine would start to hum in the last half, but fears for the worst were held by many." One half of football stood between the Fighting Irish and an undefeated nine-game schedule. They had traveled thousands of miles, and they had faced some of the nation's top teams. Now, they would have to dig into their reserve of effort, spirit, and perseverance to finish what they had started. Rockne made one personnel change to begin the second half. He split the chore of replacing Layden by putting in Bernie Livergood for Cerney. With the game in the balance, Livergood eagerly took his spot on the field. And early in the half, Stuhldreher barked the signals, took the snap, faked a handoff and found Livergood open over the middle. Livergood corralled the ball and raced past the safety for a touchdown. Notre Dame added three more scores to win convincingly, 40-19.

From Pittsburgh, Rockne and Stuhldreher said goodbye to the rest of the team and took a train to New York City, where they were honored Monday evening at a dinner given by the Notre Dame alumni of New York. Speaker after speaker paid homage to the coach and his team. They quoted sports columnists from around the country who were proclaiming the Fighting Irish as national football champions for 1924. "For the first time these many years," wrote Davis Walsh, sports editor of the International News Service, "we have an unchallenged national champion of collegiate football and Notre Dame is it...Notre Dame rates the national championship without a dissenting vote." And from the Associated Press: "Comparing countrywide performances, critics generally pick Knute Rockne's flashy Notre Dame eleven which blazed a conquering path through opposing teams from the east, south and middle west, as the greatest combination of the season." Rockne would not be drawn into the discussion. "Picking or claiming championship teams is not part of a coach's or player's duty," he told the gathering. "Let the critics do that. Our job is to play football and when the schedule is completed, our work is done." The coach offered praise for his 1924 club, calling it the greatest he had ever coached. "I do not mean that it was the most brilliant team of individuals, but I never had a team in which the spirit of co-operation and team play was so fully developed. They all played together and that made them the great team they turned out to be."

As he was finishing his remarks, Rockne was asked about the impending meeting with Stanford, who eventually won the nod to play at the Tournament of Roses, and whether he would continue his practice of starting his Shock Troops. "They tell me Pop Warner has a great team," he replied with a wink. "Maybe the first team will not be good enough." Three days later in Philadelphia, the Irish received an historic honor when the Veteran Athletes Association of Philadelphia voted unanimously to award its new national football championship trophy—the Bonniwell Cup, named for Judge E. C. Bonniwell, president of the association—to Notre Dame. The group, which for several years had awarded a cup to the team it judged to be Eastern champion, said it would honor Notre Dame January 24 at the Veteran Athletes Association banquet.

Back in South Bend, a banquet presented by local businessmen to honor Rockne and the team became the hottest ticket in town. The December 10 event was scheduled for the dining room at Studebaker Corporation headquarters. Organizers estimated the room could seat 350 guests. Meanwhile, alumni and student leaders were planning a celebration at the Notre Dame gymnasium three nights later, on December 13. Byron Kanaley, a Chicago broker and Notre Dame alum who had been instrumental in keeping Rockne at Notre Dame in 1921, was putting together a program that featured several prominent alumni speakers. The *News-Times* speculated, "It is also very likely that the time is not far distant when Notre Dame will have a stadium of comfortable dimensions in which to accommodate the mammoth crowds that turn out to see Rockne's phenomenal football teams perform." The paper offered several editorials proposing a new civic stadium, noting: "Notre Dame has no facilities for meeting the demand of the football fans of the nation who have shown a very real interest in men trained by Rockne. There is needed, at once, a stadium large enough to accommodate the visitors who will inevitably be drawn here next season to witness the games."

In just one season, Notre Dame had blown away all its previous attendance records. A preliminary count showed that some 265,000 fans had seen the Fighting Irish in its nine-game campaign, far exceeding the previous high of 197,000. In fact, the season total had increased nearly five-fold from that of just five years earlier. The notion of fans streaming in from out-of-town for a game other than Homecoming, as they had in setting the Cartier Field record crowd for the Nebraska game, had leaders dreaming of joining the ranks of those schools with new concrete stadiums.

Early December was also the time of year for the nation's leading sports writers to name their all-America teams. One of the first, picked by Billy Evans, had Stuhldreher and Crowley on the first team and Adam Walsh on the second. Davis Walsh of the Independent News Service loaded his team with Irish stars—Stuhldreher, Crowley, and Layden comprised three fourths of his first-team backfield, joined by Grange of Illinois. Adam Walsh made his second team, and Don Miller and Joe Bach the third. Walter Eckersall's squad included the same four men as Walsh's on his first two teams. *Liberty* Magazine put Stuhldreher and Layden on its first team. Walter Camp, probably the most respected expert, placed Stuhldreher on his first team, Crowley on the second, and Walsh on the third.

On Wednesday evening, December 10, the players finished practice, cleaned up, and donned suits and ties for the Studebaker banquet. Local businessman Rome C. Stephenson served as toastmaster and welcomed the guests of honor: not just Rockne and his team, but two fellow coaches who had traveled from each coast to honor their friend. Army coach Major John J. McEwan arrived from West Point, and Paul Schissler, the former Lombard coach now guiding the Oregon Aggies, made the long trek from Corvallis, Oregon. Two prominent Notre Dame presidents, past and present—Rev. Matthew Walsh and Rev. John Cavanaugh—were also at the head table.

"Rockne makes football a means to an end and not an end in itself," said toastmaster and local physician Dr. C. A. Lippincott. "And that end is a man in all his fullness, with the proper mental, moral and physical qualities. For this reason we respect him and are gathered here tonight to pay tribute to him and his football team." Rockne was then asked to speak, and he deflected attention away from himself and toward his players. "If anyone were to ask me the reason for the success of the past season, I would say it was because each player on the team likes his fellow player and any one would give his right arm for the other. Team results rather than individual results were their aim and ambition and this united spirit carried them through to a successful close."

On Saturday, it was time for the big event at the Notre Dame gym. More than 2,000 students, alumni and fans packed the place and sent its timbers shaking with the reverberations of their chants and cheers. Programs cut into the shape of a cartoon football player included the order of speakers as well as the yells and songs. Rev. Hugh O'Donnell complimented the Irish players for not just their victories, but also for the way the team represented the Christian ideals of the university. A wish of success from the Western Conference was carried by Avery Brundage of the University of Illinois, the former Olympian in decathlon and pentathlon and holder of the United States' all-around title. Brundage, an athlete who had competed in numerous countries across the globe, called Notre Dame the "center of the athletic world." Angus McDonald, now vice president of the Southern Pacific railroad and assisting Father O'Hara with travel plans, was introduced as one of the school's greatest all-around athletes. The Glee Club performed several songs, and a takeoff written by band director Joseph Casasanta, to the tune of Al Jolson's current hit song "California, Here I Come," was a howling success:

"Leland Stanford, here we come
Way down here to have our fun
With horsemen and Rockmen ready to run
We'll crash you and smash you
To make the fun for everyone.
Leland Stanford, we can't wait
To make that score that you'll relate
Open up for Notre Dame
We will win this final game."

On Thursday, December 18, nearly two dozen Irish seniors completed their final practice on Cartier Field. Hopes had been high when September practices started, but had any of them dreamed this season would play out as it did? Lose any one of the games that followed Army, and the foursome would have just been a good backfield with a fancy nickname. Boredom, overconfidence, lack of concentration—anything could have derailed the perfect season. It had happened plenty to senior-laden teams.

But the Horsemen and Mules had worked too hard, and felt pride in their effort, to let up. And Rockne, the master psychologist, wouldn't let it happen, wouldn't settle for less than their best. The players felt a personal debt to the coach to play at a high level. Four years of effort, self-sacrifice, and discipline had brought them national fame and adulation. Now it was time to travel together one last time.

Father O'Hara and McDonald had sketched out a southern route, which would bring the team to Chicago, Memphis, New Orleans, Houston, El Paso, Tucson, and finally Los Angeles. At 10:17 on Saturday morning, December 20, from a campus nearly deserted by students headed home for the holidays, the Fighting Irish, with their head coach and his wife, started their journey, heading first to Chicago. Almost on cue, a winter storm slammed into South Bend. Rockne's support of the long trip out looked wise. At 8:15 Saturday evening the team, cheered by several hundred Notre Dame fans that had gathered, left Chicago on the Illinois Central bound for New Orleans. The first stop, at 8:50 Sunday morning, was Memphis, where a group of Notre Dame alums and Knights of Columbus met the Notre Dame party and escorted them to St. Peter's Church for Mass. The entire stop lasted an hour and a half. Hugh Magevney of Memphis, a star pitcher with the Notre Dame baseball team, accompanied the football squad as far as his hometown.

Sunday afternoon in New Orleans, the temperature dipped below freezing and for a few moments, snow flurries fell for the first time in a decade. Despite the chill, more than 600 people gathered outside the Union Station long before the approach of the Notre Dame football train, anxious to get a look at the famous team. Among the crowd were Notre Dame alumni as well as students from Holy Cross College, which like Notre Dame was operated by the Congregation of the Holy Cross. The school was founded in 1849—just seven years after Notre Dame— when five Holy Cross priests and brothers traveled to New Orleans from South Bend. In 1879, when Notre Dame's Main Building burned to the ground and seriously threatened the continued existence of the school, the Holy Cross school of New Orleans sold a piece of its property for $10,000 and sent the money north to help Notre Dame rebuild.

From the station, the squad was ferried by auto to the Roosevelt Hotel, where they were mobbed by well-wishers in the lobby. A "carnival crowd" pushed as they tried to get near the players; Stuhldreher had a large group offering congratulations. Rockne exchanged greetings with an old Notre Dame classmate, former New Orleans district attorney Tom Craven. Before departing for Houston on the Sunset Limited just after noon Tuesday, Rockne thanked New Orleans for its gracious reception, but added that once in Houston, the social calendar would be cleared out and the players would get down to work in preparation for the big game. He also changed the team's itinerary, skipping the stopover at El Paso in order to arrive more quickly in Tucson, where he felt the team could establish a base of operation more conducive to working up to game readiness.

Houston was under a mantle of ice from a storm that dropped temperatures to 22 degrees, the city's lowest reading in years. So far, the idea of acclimating the team to warm southern weather was not working out. Pulling into Houston late Tuesday night, they were greeted by the local Knights of Columbus and taken to the Bender Hotel. A noon banquet on Wednesday, December 24, honored the team, after which a practice at the Rice Institute field elicited more pessimism from Rockne. The team looked soft and slow, he told reporters, due to too many rich meals at banquets and not enough physical exertion. On Christmas Eve, Father O'Hara tried to lighten the mood by playing Santa Claus for the fellows, giving them each a token of the school's admiration of them. For most of the players, it was the first Christmas away from home.

When Knute Rockne stepped off the train in Tucson, he looked up at a bright blue sky and broke into a wide grin, rubbing his hands together in anticipation. Finally, they had encountered the mild weather he had hoped for. Minutes later, after a member of the welcoming committee gave him the schedule of receptions, dinners, and banquets, his mood darkened. Rockne thought that his club was already showing the physical and psychological effects of too many feasts on the trip and that the players needed a different regimen. His hosts explained that special care was being taken to feed his players healthy food and allow them plenty of rest, and he again smiled and gave his approval. The stop in Tucson was originally scheduled for December 29 and 30, but with El Paso off the itinerary, the team spent four days in the Arizona city. On the Tucson gridiron, under clear skies, with the air crisp and the field dry and fast, the

Irish started to look like themselves again. The hundreds of onlookers marveled at the team's speed as it ran through rapid-fire signal drills.


In Glenn Scobey "Pop" Warner of Stanford, the Irish would face one of the most experienced, accomplished and innovative coaches in college football history. The wily veteran had seen almost everything in his 30 years as a college coach—and much he had developed, as well. The spiral pass, the spiral punt, numbered plays, the dummy scrimmage, the double-wing formation, the unbalanced line were all the creative work of Warner. At Pennsylvania's Carlisle Indian School and now at Stanford, he was a giant in the sport. And in fullback Ernie Nevers, Warner had one of the greatest talents in the game. Warner's offense was designed to hand the ball to Nevers on nearly every play. He was almost unstoppable as a bruising running back, accomplished as a passer and punter, and ferocious on defense.

Warner prepared for the Irish with every bit of information available. Former Princeton all-American Franklin B. Morse, writing in a San Francisco paper, put it this way: "Never before did a coach have as much information about a team as has Warner. The intelligence section of the United States expeditionary force during the World war...was a mere amateur compared to Warner's volunteer informants." Warner had numerous photos of the Irish, some taken from the sidelines, others from grandstand roofs. All showed action immediately after the snap of the ball, as plays and blocking schemes developed. Warner consulted with coaches of Irish opponents; it was said Coach Roper of Princeton gave detailed description of Notre Dame's strategy. He also had some moving pictures of the Notre Dame system to use in his planning. Rockne's reconnaissance on Stanford consisted of reports from two former Irish stars now coaching in the west—Slip Madigan at St. Mary's of California and Bob Matthews at Idaho. Madigan spent some time at Tucson drilling the Irish players on what to expect from the Cardinal. Madigan stressed Stanford's use of plays that kept Cardinal backs wide in the backfield for a pass, then upfield once they had the ball.

For millions of fans across the country, the game would enter their homes via radio, with four stations providing coverage. A direct wire from the field in Pasadena to the WGN studios in Chicago was to be relayed to WCBS in New York, resulting in the first time in radio history that Eastern stations directly broadcast a Pacific coast event. Two California stations, KPO in San Francisco and KHJ in Los Angeles, would also broadcast the game, KPO via a direct wire from the stadium and KHJ from its microphones at the event. Across the Midwest, telegraph offices in countless towns and cities planned to remain open on the holiday to receive reports from Pasadena. By all accounts, the game would be the most widely followed in the history of football.

A huge crowd greeted the Irish upon their arrival in Los Angeles, including world heavyweight champion Jack Dempsey. The players were hustled into waiting autos for the ride to their headquarters at the Maryland Hotel. There, another rousing reception awaited the squad, and people crowded the lobby day and night hoping to see any of the lads in person. Walter Eckersall, in his dispatches back to Chicago, noted that "never before in the history of football along the Pacific seaboard has so much interest been shown in a pending gridiron struggle." A capacity crowd of 53,000 was expected, and Eckersall noted, "If the stadium was larger, double that number of tickets could have been sold."

January 1, 1925 began in customary fashion in Pasadena with the annual Tournament of Roses parade, a colorful assemblage of pageantry attracting tens of thousands of viewers to the city's streets. Throughways were clogged with traffic for hours after the last of the floats finished the route. Despite that, the 53,000 seats of the stadium in the Arroyo Seco valley were filled by 1:45 p.m., a half hour before the scheduled kickoff. When Jack Dempsey and his date, actress Estelle Taylor, arrived, they caused a stir no different than as if he were arriving for one his prizefights. In the hills surrounding the valley, thousands more onlookers took their spots alongside the eucalyptus trees. In the distance, the snow-capped San Gabriel Mountains stood sentinel over the scene. Down below, the Rose Bowl's grass field gleamed in the brilliant sunshine. The soft breeze created perfect comfort. Rockne had been vague about who he planned to start, but the answer came soon enough when the Shock Troops ran out into kickoff formation. Harry O'Boyle, the son of a coal miner and the first in his family to attend college, was about to kick off in the most-anticipated football game in history. He started in the backfield with Scherer,

Hearden, and Cerney. Maxwell was at center, flanked by guards Hanousek and Glueckert. Boland and McManmon were the tackles, with Crowe and Eaton at the ends. The Shock Troops held Stanford to a missed field goal try, and now it was time for the regulars.

The crowd roared as they saw the "four horsemen" and "seven mules" take the field. After a Stanford field goal, the Irish drove and went ahead, 6-3, on a dive by Layden. Minutes later, everything old "Pop" tried seemed to be working. On a third-and-five from deep in Irish territory, Ernie Nevers faded and attempted a cross-field pass. Elmer Layden anticipated this play and perfectly timed a leap between two Cardinal targets. The ball hit his shoulder and bounced a few feet over his head. But Layden kept his eye on the ball, snared it in his arms and continued running. With his sprinter's speed, Layden dashed into an open field. Within seconds, there was only a blue-jerseyed horseman accompanying him. Layden waltzed into the end zone to complete a 78-yard play. Frenzied Notre Dame backers jumped and hugged. Crowley made the kick and the Irish led, 13-3. Another huge Stanford miscue—a bobbled punt returned 20 yards for a touchdown by Irish end Ed Hunsinger—resulted in Notre Dame's 20-3 lead. Warner's warriors felt they were getting the better of Rockne's men and that it was only a matter of time before they broke through for a touchdown. But they needed to hang onto the football; two interceptions and a fumble in one half were unacceptable. Stanford scored to cut the lead to 20-10, but could get no closer; Layden picked off another pass in the fourth quarter and returned it 63 yards for a score. The Irish only needed one touchdown from their offense to defeat the Cardinal, 27-10, to the delight of their fans across the nation.

The Notre Dame locker room in the Rose Bowl was a mob scene after the game, with numerous well-wishers desiring to greet the victorious players. There was more urgent business, though. Three players needed immediate medical attention. Harry Stuhldreher had suffered a broken bone in his right foot and was taken to Pasadena Hospital; Joe Bach had a badly strained back; and Bill Cerney had two broken ribs. The team as a whole was terribly battered from the tremendous pounding at the hands of the larger Stanford players. That evening, as hundreds of fans swarmed the Hotel Maryland for the team's celebratory dinner-dance, many Irish players were not up for the party—an ice pack and a soft bed sounded much more enticing. Elmer Layden said his jaw was so sore he could barely eat and that Nevers and Lawson hit him harder than he had ever been hit.

The consensus among most observers was that in a game of mistakes, Notre Dame made far fewer of them and deserved the victory. Wrote Ed R. Hughes, who covered Stanford the entire season for the *San Francisco Chronicle*: "Stanford grads tried to make me say that the best team lost yesterday. I don't think so. Notre Dame won by taking advantage of Stanford's mistakes and that is a mighty important factor of football." Hughes went on to praise the Irish as "a modest lot of young men who are a credit to their university. Their behavior is perfect. Rockne will stand for no foolishness and the boys know it." Walter Eckersall sent a similar dispatch to Chicago: "It is true Notre Dame got the breaks but the players were smart enough to take advantage of them. Their ability to snare the ball on Stanford's attempted forward passes was due to the happy facility of being in the neighborhood of the oval." He said Stanford also came in for its share of credit, and that "the heroes of the battle were Elmer Layden and Ernie Nevers and the supporters of both teams are loud in their praise for both warriors."

"We never beheld a team so completely exhausted as were the Rockne champions after the game," wrote columnist Otto Floto in the *Denver Post*. "Their eyes were hollow, they breathed heavily and all were in the grip of that tired feeling which tells you a man is all in—physically. Only a super team under the leadership and direction of a super coach could have landed the victory at Pasadena. Notre Dame is all of the above and that's why they won. In the final quarter, the Catholic boys played on their nerve. Their fighting instinct is what kept them going." It was a fighting instinct that had become second-nature, modeled after that of their coach. Rockne's fearlessness, daring, and dogged persistence had played out in supreme fashion, and a group of some two dozen Notre Dame seniors finishing their football careers would never forget it.

# 24

## After The Horsemen

On Friday, January 2, the Notre Dame traveling party enjoyed a tour of Hollywood and the motion picture studios. The Irish players, sore from the terrific battle, were able to smile through the festivities; all day, cameras clicked as the players met movie stars, who signed studio publicity photos for the players. The highlight was the meeting between the greatest of all movie stars, Rudolph Valentino, and Knute Rockne, the newly crowned king of college football. Each resplendent in their finery, they chatted and posed for a photo. Rockne's easy manner made for pleasant exchange, though it was unlikely "The Sheik" had watched much football in 1924, or any other season for that matter. Still, the fact that one of his motion pictures now had its name attached to Rockne's star backfield made the few moments the two spent together a perfect finale to the 1924 season.

That evening, Leo Ward and the Notre Dame Club of Los Angeles hosted a dinner-dance at the Hotel Biltmore, providing the players with their first real chance to celebrate. No expense was spared, and the players enjoyed what one called "one of the outstanding events of the trip." By 7:30 the next morning, they were aboard the Daylight Limited headed to their next stop, San Francisco. But Knute and Bonnie Rockne stayed behind in southern California, for several days of relaxation. Angus McDonald had paved the way for the Rocknes' stay, writing Father Walsh in mid-December that Rockne would need a break after the long, grueling season "for the sake of his own and his wife's health." McDonald noted that the coach was in a "highly nervous condition...I fear that unless he takes a rest he will break down." Few alumni could address Walsh as McDonald did, suggesting the president "should let Rockne know that his absence from the university will not seriously interfere with anything, and thereby relieve his mind." Walsh offered no resistance, and the layover was planned.

What neither Walsh nor McDonald counted on was a meeting the Rocknes had with officials at the University of Southern California. The school's football team was coming off a season filled with embarrassments: a fifth consecutive loss to the University of California; broken athletic relations with both Cal and Stanford over allegations of Southern Cal using ineligible players; and, following the cancellation of the Stanford game, the loss to Slip Madigan and little St. Mary's. Over six seasons, "Gloomy Gus" Henderson had a 45-7 record, but he twice had perfect season bids upset with losses to Cal. Officials were ready for a change—especially if they could nab the hottest coach in football. Bonnie Rockne had already fallen in love with southern California. The sunny days, soft breezes, comfortable nights, open spaces, and orange groves all spoke to a more relaxing existence than back in cold, snowy, sometimes stark South Bend. Here, the kids could easily play outdoors year-round, with plenty of activities from which to choose. For Knute, now a celebrity in his own right, the idea of mingling with movie stars and other notables had some appeal. And when they were taken on a tour of the recently constructed Coliseum, with columns and arches that mimicked its Roman namesake and its huge field surrounded by nearly 76,000 bleacher seats, the Rocknes were sold. No longer would Rockne have to dream of the far-off day when the authorities at Notre Dame and in South Bend could become perfectly aligned and the coffers full enough to build a proper stadium. Here, he envisioned year-round use of the magnificent structure for not just football games, but track meets, athletic festivals, and coaching schools.

Southern Cal was willing to meet a number of conditions and make Rockne a relatively wealthy man. Their offer was vastly different from the other schools that had approached him. Northwestern, Iowa, Carnegie Tech—most of these were trial balloons being floated by school officials hoping to get a read on Rockne's willingness to leave South Bend. As recently as December, a prominent Wisconsin alumnus approached Rockne about taking over as football coach and athletic director. Rockne chose not to pursue the lead, in deference to his great friend, Badger basketball coach Doc Meanwell, who was himself a candidate for athletic director. But the Southern California offer, from a land with so much to offer, was different. Big plans and big ideas took on an even brighter hue in the Southern California sunshine. Rockne's pledge that he would never leave Notre Dame seemed long ago and far away, even after winning a national championship.

The Rocknes wrapped up their stay, said goodbye to the palm trees and sweet smells of jasmine, and headed back to snowy South Bend. On January 15, 1925, the Southern Cal comptroller wired Rockne that all of his conditions had been met. But the agreement soon took an awkward course. News of the offer made the Los Angeles papers, and then other papers across the country, before Rockne could meet with Father Walsh to discuss ending his long-term Notre Dame contract. Walsh, like many others, heard about the offer from newspaper reports, and threatened legal action if the deal proceeded. Southern Cal officials apologized for the leaked story, but reiterated its desire to sign Rockne. In the end, though, Walsh's bluff worked to scuttle the deal. Rockne feared legal action, and told Southern Cal he regretted the whole incident, since it might have put him in a negative light with important Notre Dame alumni. In the end, Southern Cal didn't get its man, instead turning to former Iowa coach Howard Jones, victor over the Irish in 1921 at Iowa City, to take over its football fortunes. One positive result of the back-and-forth over Rockne's services was an agreement between the two private institutional powers to begin a football series in 1926.

The intrigue over Rockne's future wasn't the only drama that played out in the post-Rose Bowl days. Shortly after assistant coach Tom Lieb and the Irish left for San Francisco, Jim Crowley was walking toward his train berth when he collapsed in the aisle and was carried to his bunk by Father O'Hara and teammate Charlie Glueckert. For the next half hour, they said, he appeared to be at times delirious and at others stiff and still. Before the train's noon stop at San Luis Obispo, the conductor summoned a physician to attend to Crowley. With their teammate who was normally the life of the entourage lying quiet and pale during the afternoon, the other players mostly tried to sleep, not wanting to disturb Jim. Finally, Crowley was able to eat some toast and have a cup of tea, and his teammates' mood brightened. Upon arrival in San Francisco, he was placed in a wheelchair and taken to St. Francis Hospital. His condition was reported as exhaustion, but it was later suspected he might have had a reaction to the lobster dinner served at Friday's banquet. With Harry Stuhldreher on crutches (his foot in a cast) and with Crowley in the hospital, the "horsemen" were not whole for the visit. But led by Lieb, the team enjoyed their time by the Bay. Nearly 2,000 people turned out for their arrival, and a large banquet at the Palace Hotel awaited them. Sunday morning, the team received a blessing from Archbishop Edward J. Hanna, who had been part of Notre Dame's silver jubilee celebration in 1915, during a special mass at St. Mary's Cathedral. After a sightseeing tour, automobiles chauffeured the team to Villa Montalvo, the ranch of former San Francisco mayor and U.S. Senator James D. Phelan, for an afternoon of sun and relaxation.

Father O'Hara smiled as he read the report from one San Francisco writer, who commented: "Knute Rockne's boys impressed all who met them as clean-cut, well-mannered young men. Their football record speaks for itself, and the boys don't try to help it out in any way. On the contrary, they take their honors modestly and their trips to every corner of the United States seemingly have in no way changed their outlook from that of any other collegians." San Francisco was the last California stop before the cross-country trek back to Chicago and South Bend; the team and entourage loaded it with a lifetime of memories. Crowley stayed behind, still hospitalized. Salt Lake City provided a brief stop as the team drove through the city, listened to an organ recital given by Ed Kimball at the Mormon Tabernacle, toured the University of Utah, and enjoyed a dinner hosted by the Chamber of Commerce. The evening before the team's arrival, the first Notre Dame Club of Utah was formed, largely to organize the welcome for the team. In an editorial entitled "The Wonder Eleven," the local paper opined: "A clean-cut, upstanding company, these Notre Dame football players—the highest type of American young manhood... Foregathering for even a brief few hours with these healthy, clear-eyed, broad-shouldered young men, is a privilege. Contemplating them...one feels that the future of the United States in indeed in safe and strong hands."

At noon on Wednesday, January 7, the team's stop in Cheyenne, Wyoming was met by a delegation that included cowboys on their mounts, an old stagecoach, six-gallon hats, and a military band. The traveling party continued over the Rio Grande tracks to Denver, arriving in the late afternoon at the mammoth Union Station. It was said that in Denver's history, the welcome it gave the Fighting Irish was equal to any it had ever given presidents or kings. Thousands strained against a traffic cordon. Leading the alumni delegation was Will McPhee, known as "Skinny Willy" when he was an honorary member of the first Notre Dame football team in 1887. The players were inundated with requests for handshakes and photographs. Next was a parade of Packard automobiles up 17th Street, through the financial district, where more crowds welcomed the honored visitors.

A final stop completed the trip's circle for the 22 Notre Dame seniors who had begun their playing careers with two difficult defeats in 1922 and 1923. On Friday, January 9, the Irish pulled into Lincoln, Nebraska. There, they were honored at a dinner attended only by members of the Nebraska and Notre Dame teams, Nebraska's university officials, a limited number of faculty members, and a few newspapermen. To be hosted by an opposing team—especially one with whom such fierce battles had been fought—reminded everyone that sportsmanship was the highest calling for those privileged to play college football. "Notre Dame played its best game against Nebraska," noted Coach Lieb. "The team was pointed for that game and gave all it had." Back on the train, they rolled into Chicago, a three-week odyssey concluded. For the entire season, the team logged approximately 15,000 miles on trains. They had become the first football squad to play in front of sold-out stadiums in New York, Chicago, and Los Angeles all in the same year.

Once back in South Bend, Father O'Hara beamed with pride. The ugly clash with the Klan in May had opened an opportunity to promote Notre Dame and a Catholic ideal to people across the country. And the men who achieved the task were the Fighting Irish football players. Not only had they gone unbeaten and brought national attention to the school as never before, they had proven themselves to be upstanding citizens, model Christians, and true gentlemen. He could have asked for little more than that.

Rockne, now coach of the national champions, was in high demand. Requests for speaking engagements at athletic banquets, schools and colleges, civic clubs, alumni groups, and business gatherings, flooded his office. Fortunately, Ruth Faulkner had been hired as Rockne's personal secretary, a role she would fill with poise and skill for the next several years. The athletic staff was growing side-by-side with the additional lay faculty being added by Father Walsh. Faulkner would have her hands full managing what appeared to be the never-ending requests for Rockne's time.

The addition of Faulkner was a true gift. As organized as he was on the field, Rockne's off-field administrative skills sometimes fell a tad short. In his office, which was never locked, there was an ancient roll-top desk rumored to be old enough to have been Father Sorin's. A table against the wall was piled high with a leaning tower of correspondence, which occasionally reached heights that forced it to tumble. It was not hard to figure out why the coach would sometimes find himself booked for three engagements on the same day. When that occurred, he would attend one, send an assistant coach to the other, and personally write his regrets to the third. It was the banter with people that defined his space in the Main Building. People were in-and-out all day; with few chairs in the office, business was typically conducted in short order. A small closet in the back of the room housed the boxes of records that constituted Notre Dame athletic history.

And Rockne the football icon and athletic director was still Rockne the head track coach, with indoor and outdoor meets to be scheduled and run. Spring held a full slate with the Ohio Relays in Columbus and the

Penn and Drake Relays all in April. And the first day of spring football practice saw the arrival of more than 200 "horsemen and mule hopefuls." Replacing the talent from 1924 was no surprise task to anyone. Rockne greeted the candidates with an outline of his 21-part lecture series in which training in fundamentals and groundwork would be stressed before fall practice began. His serious tone enumerated some of the innate qualities the football candidates must possess if success was to be attained in any measure. He sought players, he said, who wanted to be part of a team and "not just in the picture." And true to his belief in the mental prowess of the game, he reminded the group, "Your size will make no difference to me if you can produce when called upon."

That restless spirit that had begun as a young lad in Voss was clearly evident in 1925, when Rockne's schedule and activities filled his days and weeks. As athletic director, he was charged with assembling the 1925 football schedule. Plans were underway to write his first book, simply entitled *Coaching.* And, Rockne busied himself preparing for a full summer of football coaching schools. There were numerous letters and telegrams and constant correspondence with schools across the country; as with speeches, he had far more offers to give coaching schools than time in which to give them. Coaching schools also allowed him to reconnect with old acquaintances and establish new friendships. With Rockne, it was always a priority to connect with people, to share ideas and camaraderie with his peers. And, thanks to train travel, it was now possible to move from Massachusetts to Oregon in shorter time than ever before. For his established friends at the International YMCA College, he could now only commit to one week. When it was all said and done, he had arranged an aggressive schedule of six such schools, which had him crisscrossing the country:

June 10-17, College of William & Mary, Williamsburg, Virginia

June 22-July 5, Oregon Agricultural College, Corvallis, Oregon

July 6-22, Culver Academy, Culver, Indiana

July 24-31, International YMCA College, Springfield, Massachusetts

August 1-15, St. Edward's College, Austin, Texas

August 17-Sept. 1, Notre Dame

His plan was to allow some family time before the final coaching school and the start of football practice in mid-September. But one man just wouldn't take no for an answer as he sought to engage Rockne's services for that time. Fred "Mysterious" Walker, the former major league pitcher who, it seemed, showed up coaching a different college nearly every fall, was now the football coach at little Drury College in Springfield, Missouri. Since leading DePauw against Rockne and the Irish in 1921, Walker had spent several years coaching basketball and baseball at Michigan Agricultural. But now, a man who had once been head football coach at Carnegie Tech, Utah Agricultural, and Williams College, with two stints assisting Stagg, was wondering how and when he could get back to a coaching position with more pay and prestige. Walker thought he had come up with the answer—if he could get Rockne to come down and give a coaching school at Drury, surely, he thought, his stock would rise immensely. Rockne politely declined his friend's request, as he had to many other coaching friends and acquaintances. His 1925 summer schedule was set. But Walker persisted. "It would permit me to get established here as nothing else (not even a winning team) would do," Walker wrote Rockne in a long handwritten letter.

> Your presence here would make the whole thing a success and for that reason I will give you anything at all you want, 50, 60%, 75%, 90% of the tuition. What I need, Rock, is you; this money proposition isn't nearly as important to me...as my success in putting this thing over. Your presence here, if only for a few days, will ensure my success in this. I need this badly. You're at the top of the world now, I'm trying to climb back...Everyone down here wants to come if you are here.

The pitch from a man a little down his luck hit Rockne in the soft spot of his heart, and he finally agreed to come to Drury for five days from September 2 through 7.

In mid-March, a number of the "old guard" in college football gathered at the Football Rules Committee annual meeting in New York. Included were Bill Roper of Princeton, Edward Hall of Dartmouth, William

Langford of Trinity, Fred Moore of Harvard, Stagg himself—and Walter Camp, at age 65, the oldest man at the meeting. Camp, just returned from a long football-watching tour of western states, showed his old zest at the meeting. Others remarked on how well he looked. On the evening of March 13, with the committee's work largely finished, the group had dinner, then Camp's peers bid him goodnight. When he did not appear at the next morning's session, his hotel room had to be jarred open. Walter Camp had died peacefully in his sleep, in the middle of doing what he most enjoyed: crafting the game of football.

Camp had created the center and the quarterback positions, debarred the graduate student from playing on college teams, and still later helped to banish mass plays and excessive injuries. How fitting that the inventor and guardian of modern American football died with football on his mind. Men die, but institutions continue; Camp had lived to see football become an institution. It was said that there was something almost Greek in his love of the lithe grace, the supple skill, the hard clean strength of the human body, and in his admiration of those qualities of character that reveal themselves in the fine achievement of college sport. Camp had spoken these words to players of the game, great and small:

> I wish I could impress indelibly upon your minds that with you rests the standard of amateur sport. With no disrespect to any other class or condition, I say that the collegian's standard of purity in sports should be the highest. The very fact that he has leisure to devote four years to a higher education should be taken to involve the duty of acquiring a keener perception of right and wrong in matters where right and wrong depend upon delicacy of honor. Gentlemen do not cheat, nor do they deceive themselves as to what cheating is…It is your duty to know that every one of your men is straight and square. I know what I am talking about when I say that a college captain can, in ninety-nine cases out of hundred, know the exact truth about every man he thinks of trying. In investigating and in legislating, remember that what a gentleman wants is fair play, and the best man to win.

Camp summarized his vision of football, which had been embraced by Rockne, this way: "The great lesson of the game may be put into a single line: It teaches that brains will always win over muscle."

As Rockne traversed the nation from Virginia to Oregon, he kept up with correspondence to friends, former players, and coaches looking for their next opportunity. He always had his ear to the ground for which schools were looking for someone new to guide their athletic programs, and he was always suggesting to his legion of fellow coaches where they might apply. Enduring the summer's blistering heat, Rockne also kept abreast of major events of the day. At every train stop, on the street corners of every city, Rockne encountered the newspaper hawkers screaming out the headlines that captivated the country: "'Monkey Trial' Grips Nation!" As a student and teacher of science, Rockne was mesmerized by the story.

In the sweltering July Tennessee heat, science teacher and part-time football coach John T. Scopes stood trial in the tiny town of Dayton for violating state law because he included evolution theories as part of his classroom curriculum. In January 1925, Tennessee Governor Austin Peay signed anti-evolution legislation into law as part of a sweeping education reform bill and stated, "Nobody believes that it is going to be an active statute." He was apparently unaware of Arthur Garfield Hays and the newly formed American Civil Liberties Union. By the mid-1920s, Hays had carved his legacy with the ACLU because of his personal commitment to direct action to defend free speech. Now, defending labor was a key priority for the ACLU, and Hays stated, "The cause we now serve is labor and labor includes public school teachers."

The epic trial pitted Clarence Darrow, defending Scopes, against William Jennings Bryan, arguing for the state. Darrow stood at the height of his powers as America's greatest criminal defense lawyer. Bryan, who had been a three-time Democratic nominee for president and was dubbed the "Boy Orator of the Platte," had become the leader of the Fundamentalist crusade against teaching evolution in public schools. Charles Darwin's evolutionary theory, first published in 1859, did not suddenly appear in high school education in 1925; it had been incorporated into leading textbooks during the last part of the 19th century. Textbooks, however, became more Darwinian in the 20th century when the newly organized field of biology began to replace separate courses on botany and zoology in the high school curriculum. In addition, the number of pupils enrolled in American high schools leapt from 200,000 in 1890 to nearly two million in 1920. In Tennessee, for example, less than 10,000 students were enrolled in 1910; by the time of the Scopes trial the number stood at 50,000. This increase resulted in part from tougher Progressive-era school attendance laws and also from greater access to secondary education as the number of public high schools rose dramatically during the early part of the century. These new schools inevitably included Darwinian concepts in the biological classes.

Darrow had gained his reputation as the "attorney for the damned" for his defense of unpopular causes, murderers, and anarchists. He entered the Scopes Trial on the heels of successfully arguing against the death penalty in the (Richard) Leopold-(Nathan) Loeb trial that had fascinated the nation the year before. His days-long closing arguments delivered without notes won miraculous reprieves for men doomed to hang for their senseless murder of 14-year-old Bobby Franks. The Scopes Trial ended in a prolific debate between the two iconic orators that was moved to the porch of the Dayton courthouse because of the throngs that had gathered—and the oppressive heat inside the courtroom. The crowd swelled to an estimated 3,000 people sprawled across the lawn, nearly twice the town's normal population. "The spectators, however, instead of being only men, were men, women, and children, and among them here and there a negro," the *New York Times* reported. The *Nashville Banner* added, "Then began an examination which has few, if any, parallels in court history. In reality, it was a debate between Darrow and Bryan on Biblical history, on agnosticism and belief in revealed religion."

Eventually the jury conferred for only nine minutes before returning a verdict of guilty. Although the anti-evolution crusade began as a legitimate national movement, it became, for the most part, a regional phenomenon after the Scopes trial. And as the summer heat faded and the country moved on, attention turned backed to the change of season, a new school year, and America's love of college football.

Rockne returned home to St. Vincent Street on August 16 exhausted from more than two months of coaching schools, yet pleased at the number of young men he had the opportunity to influence. Horseshoe pitching and croquet with the Tom Hickey family was the perfect antidote for Rockne. It felt good to relax and watch the children playing in the open lots behind the houses and swinging from the trees that lined those lots. The next two weeks, with his camp at Notre Dame, offered Rockne respite and a workable routine. A number of current and former Irish players were also on hand to help out. The thought of going out for one more coaching school, even for an old friend, seemed overwhelming. He wired Walker at Drury that, for the sake of his health, he need to take a few days' break before the start of the football season. There was also one item on his mind completely unrelated to football. After years of employment at one of America's leading Catholic universities, interactions with Holy Cross priests, watching his players attend Mass and take daily communion, and getting to know a bedrock Catholic family such as the next-door Hickeys, Rockne had begun religious instruction from Father Vince Mooney in preparation for joining the Catholic faith. He asked Tom Hickey to be his godfather when Rockne was finally received into the church. The flirtation with Southern Cal and interest from others schools had receded into the background. Notre Dame, with its emphasis on faith and spirit, was the place he ultimately decided he wanted to be. And to be fully at Notre Dame meant being Catholic.

As he had articulated at spring football, his 1925 Irish team would look dramatically different from the national champions of 1924. None of 1924's eleven regulars was on hand to assist their successors. As testament to their football proficiency and Rockne's overwhelming national reach, all were on other college campuses coaching the sport, including three as head coaches of Catholic schools. Harry Stuhldreher, the wily field general, was leading the troops at Villanova outside Philadelphia; rugged captain Adam Walsh was now the head man at Jesuit-run Santa Clara back in his home state of California; and Elmer Layden moved on to be head coach at Columbia College in Dubuque, Iowa, not far from his Davenport home. Layden was the third former Irish star to coach Columbia in the last decade, following Gus Dorais (1914-17) and Eddie Anderson (1922-24). Anderson had moved to DePaul in Chicago. Layden's backfield mates Jim Crowley and Don Miller were now backfield coaches at Georgia and Georgia Tech, respectively. "Mules" Rip Miller and Noble

Kizer didn't have to leave the state to catch on as line coaches, Miller at Indiana and Kizer at Purdue. Joe Bach was line coach at Syracuse, Chuck Collins was an assistant at Tennessee, while John Weibel entered medical school at Vanderbilt and caught on as an assistant there. Ed Hunsinger joined Stuhldreher at Villanova, serving as his assistant.

During days of grueling workouts to form essentially a completely new team, Rockne's coaching acumen would be tested as never before. Who could he ride mercilessly, who could he chide gently to mold the type of leaders needed to infuse their teammates with the familiar Notre Dame spirit? Fortunately, Tom Lieb and Hunk Anderson were back for their second seasons as primary assistant coaches. Rockne was ahead of most of his peers in organizing his team's coaching. For the most part, he did not instruct his squad as a whole, but he broke it down into its parts, position by position. As Stuhldreher noted, Rockne always painstakingly trained each group in the rudiments of its position. For this, the assistants were invaluable. Lieb would concentrate on the tackles and ends, Hunk the guards and centers, leaving Rockne to work primarily with the backs. And even beyond positional groups, Rockne had a way of coaching each individual differently. Stuhldreher described his mentor's approach: "Each man must be studied, he felt; his characteristics noted, and the best manner of handling him worked out…He realized you can't take a whole team and bawl the life out of them, pat them on the back, ridicule them, or ignore them. But there were individuals on this team to whom you can apply these methods. If he could find out who they were and what their reactions were, he could get each man to working as a unit."

Using his unique understanding of psychology, Rockne could give one player hearty praise without instilling too lofty a self-image; to the next man, he could give a tongue-lashing, yet not see the player get down on himself; and to yet another, he could ignore, but have the player remain engaged and ready to help the team. Rockne, it was said, was able to study the character of each player and surmise exactly what he needed to succeed. He saw the practice field as a laboratory, and like any good scientist he took note of the results of his experiments. But, despite his psychological mastery, years of success, and stability in his coaching staff, the 1925 season appeared to be a steep uphill climb. "We don't have much material," he confided to a friend before the season. "I can see only a handful of games we really have a chance." It would be a typical Rockne exaggeration, yet there remained a nugget of truth. For all the work done to develop a deep squad, the 1925 team provided precious little experience to build on. Fans far and near expected a consistent winner, of course. The golden glow of 1924's magical ride resonated with Notre Dame backers. Why couldn't it be repeated? Rockne wanted to tamp down their expectations. It was around this time he started using one of his signature lines: "A loss now and then is good for the soul. Too many losses are bad for the coach."

For the 1925 opener, Rockne set up a different challenge from previous seasons. Small regional opponents such as Kalamazoo, Lombard, or Wabash typically served as easy foes. This year it would be the Baylor Bears, the pride of Waco, Texas, invading Cartier Field. Baylor was only the second intersectional foe, after Georgia Tech in 1923 and 1924, to visit South Bend. Baylor had been playing football since 1899, but it was only since 1914 that they were known as the Bears. In 1914, an alumnus offered a $5 gold piece to the winning student in a contest to name the team. Doyle Thrailkill took home the prize, defeating other entries that included Antelopes, Buffaloes, Ferrets, and Frogs. Coach Frank Bridges brought the Bears into 1925 with a stellar five-year record of 32-13-4, including Southwest Conference championships in 1922 and 1924. The team arrived in South Bend as honored visitors, much like Georgia Tech and Nebraska had in 1924. The Bears ventured before a crowd of 13,000 opening day spectators who watched in a steady rain; but they were not the only Texans making their Cartier Field debut.

Notre Dame's retooled backfield featured Christie Flanagan at one of the halfback spots. Flanagan had graduated from Port Arthur High School on the Texas gulf coast in 1923. He had played two seasons of high school football at Port Arthur, and while he wasn't an All-State selection in the already football-rich Texas, he was considered a fine player. During high school, Flanagan spent two summers attending camp at Culver Military Academy, just 50 miles down the road from South Bend. There, one of his officers, a Notre Dame alum, suggested he consider coming north for college. He did, though in 1923 he limited himself to interhall football, feeling he was too slight for varsity ball. When he came out in 1924, he excelled in a drill that matched him against some of the Horsemen. Rockne was impressed. But with such depth on the team, Rockne kept Flanagan out of games, working him in practice daily against the rigors of facing the horsemen and mules. Rockne, in effect, presaged the practice of redshirting, keeping Flanagan eligible for three seasons starting in 1925. Joining Flanagan at halfback were Harry O'Boyle and Red Hearden, who followed Jim Crowley from Green Bay's East High to Notre Dame. Hearden scored two touchdowns, and Flanagan and O'Boyle one each, as the Irish rolled to a resounding 41-0 thrashing of shell-shocked Baylor.

The following week, Lombard College from Galesburg, Illinois, made its third visit in as many years to Cartier. And where they had proven hardy opposition in 1923 and 1924, this one was no contest from start to finish. Rockne played some 60 men in a 69-0 whitewash, one headline proclaiming: "Rockne Makes Changes So Fast, Fans are Groggy." October 10 brought the season's second newcomer to Cartier Field—Beloit College from Wisconsin. Rockne had established a close friendship with Beloit coach Tommy Mills, who made his school's facilities available to the Irish on their trip to defeat Wisconsin a year earlier. A game against Notre Dame was Rockne's way of repaying his friend. And Beloit proved to be worthy opponent, holding Rock's men to just a 19-3 decision.

Now, with a 3-0 record, it was off to meet Army. Notre Dame fans were thinking: Has he done it again? Has the magic man Rockne, like he did in 1922, fashioned a team bereft of all its starters into another unstoppable unit? Will the current 16-game winning streak extend through another championship season? An answer would come in front of the largest crowd yet to see the Irish play—65,000 turned out at Yankee Stadium, as the game now found its natural home in New York City, the massive, modern "house that Ruth built." Rockne and Notre Dame now commanded the biggest venues possible. This time, though, the experience of Harry "Light Horse" Wilson and his fellow Cadets proved just too much for the Rockne's green troops. The Irish, despite using four different quarterbacks, could get nothing going on offense. The 27-0 defeat was the worst ever tasted by one of Rockne's squads. On the train ride back to South Bend, gloom hung over the team. "Nobody talked, we ached all over, and were a badly beaten bunch," Flanagan recalled. Rockne sensed the team's mood, gathered his men together on the train, and said: "You've taken a good physical beating. You're beginning to grow up. I want everybody that played in the ball game to join hands in a firm resolution not to let anything come between you and the rest of your fellow members of the team, from now until next November 13, when we go back to Yankee Stadium to play the Army again. Keep up your grades, don't get out of shape all through the coming months—and we're gonna come back here next season and kick the hell out of 'em!"

Rockne's words lifted the team's spirits, as did the reception that awaited them in South Bend, which resembled so many other homecomings of Notre Dame teams returning from great victories. Notre Dame and South Bend wanted Rockne's men to know they were with them, and looked forward to better days ahead. It was a fired-up Irish team that made its first trip to Minneapolis the next week, defeating Doc Spears' Gophers before 49,000 at the magnificent new, red-brick Memorial Stadium. The Irish again looked strong in defeating Georgia Tech at Atlanta the next week, 13-0. Then it was off to Penn State. And it was there that the human side of Rockne had one of its most profound moments.

The pressures from travel for football and speaking engagement, the stress to meet deadlines for the increasing number of national magazine articles he was authoring, and the strain of finding time for a family life crystallized in one instant. In his pre-game talk, the steady voice, the focused mind failed, and he broke down in tears. The team, stunned by the display, ended up playing to a scoreless tie. Afterward, Rockne confided to his friend Joe Byrne and wondered aloud, "What must you think of me?" "We think you're human, like the rest of us." Byrne replied. "And you'd better start to think so, too." On the trip back from Penn State, the team was at a layover in Tyrone, Pennsylvania, and visited a fair with a shooting gallery. Rockne, still shaky, took a shot and missed all the arcade ducks, but hit a supporting column instead. All the ducks came loose. "What a shot," he laughed, and just that simply, came out of his gloom. Rockne's mood, and his team's, stayed gleeful when the Irish rolled over Carnegie Tech, 26-0, in their Homecoming game.


Knute Rockne's conversion to Catholicism was a deeply personal matter and, similar to many other things personal, Rockne kept the discussion about why he converted mostly to himself. Rockne was raised as a Norwegian Lutheran, and was a member of the Scottish Rite of Masons until he joined the Catholic faith. He spent most of his adult life surrounded by Holy Cross fathers at an institution that was steeped in Catholic tradition. It was impossible for Rockne to escape Catholicism as he walked the campus and interacted with others on and off the football field. Whether discussing chemical formulae with Father Nieuwland or travel plans with Father O'Hara, Rockne saw the Holy Cross priests as they lived their lives of faith. Rockne would follow his team into the little Catholic church across from Grand Central Station when they went to New York to play Army. He would see his boys get up early on the morning of a game and head for a church. Bonnie, who had converted before their marriage, exemplified her Catholic faith around their children.

Neighbors and friends Tom and Kate Hickey, and their family, demonstrated the faith in action. All were undeniably influences on him. So too was his friendship with Father Vince Mooney, the priest at Notre Dame, who, after having instructed Rockne in the Catholic faith, baptized him on Friday, November 20, 1925 in the Old Log Chapel on campus. Mooney administered Rockne's First Communion the next day—the same day as Rockne's son Knute, Jr. received his first communion—in St. Edward's Hall. No one knew that Rockne was under instruction except Bonnie, Father Mooney, and Tom and Kate Hickey, Rockne's sponsors. It was an eventful weekend even before the scheduled clash with Northwestern.

Father Mooney said Rockne learned his religion by knowing football—he had the Seven Sacraments for a line and a backfield consisting of Faith, Hope, Charity, and the All-American quarterback Justice. And as any good coach knows, it's the quarterback that directs the team, and social justice was at the heart of theology for the immigrant church taking shape by the second decade of the 20th century. Father John A. Ryan authored the Bishops' Program for Social Reconstruction, which advocated for measures such as a living wage, public housing, and a national employment service. Ryan had witnessed firsthand some of the deplorable working conditions which greeted many of the Irish Catholic immigrants to American shores, and saw the church as an advocate for social justice.

Rockne inquired of Mooney more about the Fundamentalist movement that was sweeping the country. An avid reader, Rockne knew of their role with the Klan and how Fundamentalism helped to spread Klan bigotry against Catholics. An immigrant and a gentled-natured soul, Rockne found it difficult to understand how religion and the Klan mixed. He also discussed modernism with Mooney and engaged Father O'Hara in discussions about the *Religious Bulletin* O'Hara had founded years before. Bishop William T. Manning of New York later recounted the psychology of sport and religion after Rockne's conversion when he said, "Human contact and fellowship are the soul of religion and the spirit of sacrifice for the team, and the devotion and loyalty that are given in sport develop spiritual qualities that religion seeks to develop."

Any calm Rockne felt by entering the faith dissipated at Cartier Field the following day. The Irish appeared listless in the first half against Northwestern and trudged back to the locker room trailing, 10-0. In silence, they waited for what they expected would be a detailed critique of their play, and how it could be corrected in the second half. They waited, and waited. Finally, Rockne burst through the door, "his eyes almost popping, the cords in his thick neck standing out." He proceeded to rail: "Hah! Fighting Irish, are you? You look more like peaceful Swedes to me! You can have the honor of telling your grandchildren that you played on the first team that ever quit at Notre Dame! I'm through with you! I'm going to sit in the stands for the second half." And out of the room he hurried. The Irish came out charged up and scored immediately, pummeling the Wildcats with a series of hard-driving charges, quickly going ahead, 13-10. And there was Rockne, not in the stands, of course, but hidden among the substitutes on the Irish sideline, twirling his cigar in his hand, the faintest sign of a grin on his face.

The season of highs and lows ended on Thanksgiving Day in Lincoln, Nebraska, where the Irish were again subject to heavily anti-Catholic chants. This sentiment came as somewhat of a surprise to university officials who assumed the verbal abuse and harassment would wane after Notre Dame's warm reception in Lincoln following the 1925 Rose Bowl win. When the Notre Dame team and fans arrived in Lincoln, they were genuinely shocked by public displays of animosity against them. Anti-Catholic, anti-Irish epithets were reported from every corner of the stadium. And at halftime, a group of Nebraska students pulled a stunt that desecrated the celebrated Four Horsemen and Irish Americans in general. Four Nebraska students, each carrying a brick-mason's hood and riding ersatz horses, galloped around the field to the delight of the partisan crowd. Their message was clear: Notre Dame football players were better suited as menial laborers than college students, and Irish Americans were similarly meant for the lowest rung of society. The stunt was stunning in its tastelessness, and it caused more of a reaction than the Huskers' 17-0 victory that day.

Notre Dame officials were incensed over the depiction, figuring that someone in the Nebraska administration must have approved the stunt. When the team returned to South Bend, Dean James McCarthy advised President Walsh that members of the athletic board believed Nebraska should be dropped from the schedule and the series ended. Although Nebraska football coach Ernest Bearg blamed the decision to drop the series on "disgruntled gamblers in South Bend" who were tired of losing their money, Notre Dame officials decided the ethnic halftime insult could not and would not be forgiven. The game scheduled for 1926 was dropped, and all negotiations for future games ended. Rockne strongly opposed canceling the series and distanced himself personally from the board's decision both in public relations releases and in private correspondence. However, the decision was final. Rockne was furious that the decision to end the Nebraska series was made without asking his opinion. He would have suggested attempting to ease tensions and finding a way to maintain the rivalry. Angry and frustrated over the whole situation, Rockne headed off to post-season coaches meetings in New York City. When his ire seethed, Rockne was never at his best; he often veered from his usual focus and clear-thinking. He wondered, did coaches at other schools have it easier than he did with the constant approval process that always ran through the priests at Notre Dame? Was there a less complicated place to coach than at Notre Dame? The Nebraska cancellation cut to the bone.

While in New York, he met with James R. Knapp, an unpaid representative of the Columbia University athletic department. Since Percy Haughton's death a little over a year earlier, Columbia had hired as its head coach a Notre Dame man, Charlie Crowley, who played under Rockne on the 1918 and 1919 teams. Crowley had guided the Lions to a

6-3-1 record in 1925, but the opportunity to lure as big a name as Rockne to the Columbia campus was too much to pass up. To Rockne, New York meant the big-time just as surely as California would have. The chance to mix with his friends, from writers Grantland Rice and Ring Lardner to politicians such as Jimmy Walker and entertainers Will Rogers and Flo Ziegfield, held much appeal. He loved being around people, and where better to do that than the big city? As for Columbia football, Rockne saw it as a sleeping giant, able to challenge the Big Three of Yale, Princeton, and Harvard with some concentrated direction.

Money was no object to Columbia. The school offered Rockne a three-year contract for $20,000 and Rockne signed, asking only that the matter remain private until he returned to South Bend to obtain a release from his contract from Father Walsh. The similarity to the beginning of 1925 was unmistakable. This time, however, the conflict between school and administration was so strong that Rockne believed a release was probable. But Rockne had planned a stop in Philadelphia before returning to South Bend, and in the meantime, someone at Columbia leaked the story to the press. That set about several days of chaos and acrimony between the two universities and their representatives. Deliberations tried to wind back the offer, amid drama and secret meetings. Both schools had a public relations mess on their hands, and various attempts to smooth it were awkward, at best. In one release, Columbia made the dubious claim that it never would have offered Rockne a contract if it knew he was still under contract to Notre Dame. Father Walsh made an equally incredulous statement, after he already had received assurances that the coach was staying, that the decision to stay or go was completely up to Rockne.

In the end, Rockne's impetuous decision to engage with Columbia brought nothing but trouble for the reputations of Notre Dame, Columbia, and himself. Following on the Southern Cal hubbub to start the year, Rockne took time to reflect, and his impulses to listen to tempting offers. By the end of 1925, Rockne knew Notre Dame would remain his home base. He would return to South Bend and embrace the challenges there. But as 1926 dawned, it was time for a temporary change of scenery.

# 25

## Traveling Man

On January 26, 1926, Knute Rockne began his first venture across the Atlantic since he had come to the United States as a five-year-old in 1893. He joined good friends Joe and Marie Byrne aboard the ocean liner S.S. *DeGrasse* for a European vacation. Byrne asked Rockne where his trunk was, and the coach replied, "Who needs a trunk?" Rockne preferred to travel light; he carried a suitcase with a dinner jacket, an extra business suit, and just enough of anything else he would need on the trip. He was focused on relaxing from the stress of another football season that included twin episodes of possible coaching changes. But sports were always on his mind, and when he found out that Helen Wills, the three-time U.S. Open tennis champion, was on board headed to European competitions, Rockne quickly became a fan.

If Rockne had planned to quietly submerge himself in European crowds, he was in for a surprise. In Paris, the locals were intrigued that he was associated with Notre Dame, and there were plenty of Americans abroad to keep him engaged in witty banter. "He was king among the Americans," noted Byrne. "Very big around Harry's Bar. As usual, he was available to all comers." Rockne tried to use as much French as he could squeeze out of a guidebook and tried to order his meals using the language. He would engage the French in simple conversation—he knew he could always make a reference to Epinard, the great French racehorse. At Harry's, he made friends with several members of the house band, and when he found out that two of them were from Nebraska, he shared plenty of anecdotes from the many great battles in the now-ended rivalry. The vacation continued in London, where even more people knew about his American football fame. He found himself laughing and joking with fellow travelers, and the return voyage passed in pleasant fashion. The Byrnes bid him goodbye in New York, and Joe Byrne later said, "There were tears in his eyes when he took the train for home. He said, 'You don't know what this has done for me.' He was rested, ready to explode again. I think what really pleased him was the realization that he was an international celebrity. He needed that for his morale at that time." For all his success, Rockne was occasionally beset with bouts of insecurity.

Rockne's good friend Will Rogers also took a European trip in 1926 that boosted his steady rise as America's most widely read and eminently trusted source of political and social commentary. On July 26, 1926 Rogers was on the cover of *Time* magazine, capping a steady climb in his popularity since the McNaught newspaper syndicate hired him to write a weekly column in 1922, launching a national following. Rogers, throughout the 1920s, proved to be as much of a hit on the radio and the phonograph as he was on the stage, screen, and in newspapers. With audiences now numbering in the millions, he gave his readers and listeners a surprisingly sophisticated and penetrating analysis of the prevailing issues of the day. Amid this serious business he also made people laugh. He once said: "Ancient Rome declined because it had a Senate; now what's going to happen to us with both a Senate and a House?"

It wasn't difficult to understand how Rockne, an immigrant's son, found much to like in a part-Cherokee entertainer with little formal education. It was said Rogers loved his fellow man and when he said he never met a man he didn't like, he meant it. Rogers and Rockne were two of the nation's leading syndicated columnists and both were tapping into the growing audiences using radio for information and entertainment. Rogers wrote in a personal and casual style as if he were talking face-to-face with his readers; Rockne's rapport with his players, newspapermen, and fellow coaches was built on face-to-face interactions. And both were comfortable interacting with either the common man or the millionaire. Rockne was invited to a fishing trip at the estate of railroad tycoon E.H. Harriman in the Ramapo Highlands near Tuxedo, New York. His host, William Averell Harriman, was a venture capitalist who was active in New York state's Democratic Party. Rogers became great friends with billionaire John D. Rockefeller. In February 1927, Rockefeller invited Rogers to his Ormond Beach, Florida estate after hearing Rogers was in town. The two spent hours talking and playing golf and would engage each other in conversation when their schedules allowed. It was said Rogers was as at ease roping calves as he was performing at Carnegie Hall.

In both his writings and lectures Rogers explored complex, controversial political issues, and frequently made backhanded swipes at the commercialism of the 1920s. Rogers wrote in the *Saturday Evening Post*: "Our children are delivered to schools in automobiles. But whether that adds to their grades is doubtful. There hasn't been a Thomas Jefferson produced in this country since we formed our first Trust…There hasn't been a Patrick Henry showed up since business men quit eating lunch with their families, joined a club and have indigestion from amateur Oratory." It would be easy to understand how Rockne, a coach dedicated to making his players disciplined men ready to take their place in society, would concur with Rogers when he said: "The trouble with football is, you can't carry your cheerleaders with you through life."

The coach and the humorist also shared another love—aviation. Rogers was an advocate for more American involvement in the air industry, and he eventually made at least 25 crossings of the continent by airplane and logged over a half million air miles before the end of the decade. Rarely did a week pass without Rogers campaigning for the latest navigation and airport facilities, safer planes, more training for aircrews, and direct government subsidies to spur commercial aviation.

The Rockne family became complete on April 14, 1926, with the birth of John Vincent, his middle name honoring Father Mooney, who brought Knute into the Catholic faith just months earlier. The youngster was known as Jackie, joining Billy, Junior, and Mary Jeanne. In reflecting on family times, Bonnie Rockne recalled, "Knute was never happier than when sharing the amusements, the games and the noisy delights of our children. Indeed, he was always interested in the little ones and always very kind to them. He used to get a particular thrill out of the bright sayings…he was acutely interested in watching them develop in anything they took up."

With such a demanding schedule, Coach Rockne prized the time in between his commitments, when he could be with his family. Laughter and love were evident in the Rockne home whether in South Bend or at their summer home perched on a rise overlooking Lake Michigan. There, on the sandy beach, the family enjoyed warm summer days and dips in the cool water. The kids would run races along the beach, with Rockne, ever the track coach, ready to award a sandwich or bottle of soda pop as a prize. Rockne also loved to take the entire family to the movies where, typically, young Jackie would last through about half the picture before falling asleep in his father's arms. When the family vacationed in Florida, Rockne would drive up and down the streets to search out movies the entire family could enjoy. A story told in an educational way was always a winner.

As Rockne's only daughter, Mary Jeanne had a special place in his heart. He would hint about purchasing "something for your neck" and her thoughts conjured a nice necklace. That started a routine in which the coach, calling home while traveling, would always ask his young daughter if she had rigorously washed her neck that day. The boys became a blur of activity. Once, Knute demanded of one of the boys to report his age. "Seven," came the reply. "Impossible," the coach said. "No young man could possibly get so dirty in just seven years."

Music was never far away at home. In an attempt to soothe a squealing baby, Knute would take out his flute and after just a few notes, the coach said, the infant stopped its wailing. The child, Rockne said, had "undoubtedly forgotten the old torment in the presence of an even greater one!" At bedtime, Knute the entertainer took over, meeting the kids' demands for one more story or song before bedtime. It could be a nursery rhyme, a campground story about bears, or a raucous chorus of an old standard:

There is a boarding house, far, far, away.

Where they serve ham and eggs three times a day.

Woe, woe! The boarders yell
When they hear the dinner bell
For they know the eggs will smell far, far away.

Music was a constant outlet and source of relaxation for Rockne. He was justifiably proud of his ability on his trusty flute, which made its way with Rockne on numerous trips, football and otherwise. As a musician, while mostly a virtuoso in whistling out some tunes in his hotel room, Rockne followed the same philosophy reflected in athletics—dedication through continual practice and repetition yields superior results. And, Rockne saw how a musician flawlessly playing his part in an orchestra related to a football player taking care of his responsibility in a perfectly executed play. The whole became greater than the sum of its parts, as long as each part was handled as directed by the conductor.

Rockne favored bandleaders such as Paul Whiteman and Isham Jones, whose orchestras rang out from the nation's ballrooms and radio stations. In his early years as Notre Dame coach, Rockne would stop by manager Frank Doriot's room in the Gymnasium and enjoy dance tunes on his hand-cranked Victrola. Every so often, Doriot said, "he would exclaim 'Just a minute, I'll tell you just who that sax player or trombone player is.' And he would invariably be right." By the mid-1920s, Rockne had developed an acquaintance with Whiteman, known across the nation as the "King of Jazz." Born to a musical family in Denver in 1890, Whiteman played viola with the Denver Symphony as a teenager and built on his classical training to lead a jazz-influenced dance band in San Francisco. His commercial career took off when he moved to New York and started recording for the Victor Talking Machine Company. Whiteman became known for his blending of symphonic music and jazz, as typified by his 1924 debut of George Gershwin's jazz-influenced "Rhapsody In Blue."

Over the years, Whiteman, referred to as "Pops," sought out and encouraged musicians, vocalists, composers, arrangers, and entertainers who looked promising, either hiring them for his orchestra or directing them to other openings. Whiteman hired many of the best jazz musicians for his band, including Bix Beiderbecke, Frankie Trumbauer, Joe Venuti, Jack Teagarden, and Bunny Berigan. He also encouraged aspiring black musical talents and crossed racial lines behind-the-scenes, hiring black arrangers like Fletcher Henderson and helping black combos with recording sessions and scheduling tours. Whiteman also helped launch the career of one of the most popular entertainers of the 20th century in 1926, when he hired a young graduate of Gonzaga University named Harry Lillis "Bing" Crosby as one of The Rhythm Boys, a three-man act that went on tour with Whiteman's orchestra. The crowds Whiteman attracted from coast to coast were young, active men and women ready to throw off the stodgier melodies of their parents.

The changing roles of women, especially young working women, could now be seen in the nightclubs of many major cities in America. Flappers—as they were called—were mostly northern, urban, single, young, middle-class women. Many held steady jobs in the changing American economy. The clerking jobs that blossomed in the Gilded Age were more numerous than ever. More phone usage required more switchboard operators. In the consumer-oriented economy of the 1920s, women were needed on the sales floor of department stores to relate to the most precious customers—other women. By night, flappers engaged in the active city nightlife, frequenting jazz clubs and vaudeville shows. With the political field leveled by the 19th Amendment, which granted women the right to vote, women sought to eliminate societal double standards.

From a football standpoint, women were also becoming a larger part of the crowds attending games in the giant new concrete and brick stadiums. There was now much more of a social element in attending the games, as couples could meet and mingle with other couples at social events connected to the athletic contests. The "old days" of nearly all-male crowds weathering the cold and peering into the mass of bodies slugging it out a yard at a time was giving way to the wide-open game that Rockne advocated, in which any play might yield a large gain. Fans throughout the stadium could more easily follow the action, especially if the ball were passed. They also huddled around their radios on Saturdays to listen to the ever-increasing number of games being broadcast.

Anne Butschle, a young working girl and Catholic daughter of German immigrants in Milwaukee, planned her fall Saturdays around the Notre Dame football broadcasts. She would tell her friends that she waited all week to hear what Rockne's teams would do. Anne was like many listeners of the day: awaiting not just details of the game, but descriptions of the event. The crowds, the bands, the card sections, the cheer leaders—the spirit of the college game—were crucial to the game's appeal. It was the announcer's job to figure out the accurate description of a game being played far from his watch and in uniforms with small numbers, as well as to try to capture the experience. Rockne saw first-hand the entry of women more stridently into the football world. His nearly annual summer trip to Springfield, Massachusetts to teach on the faculty of the International YMCA College summer program would now include lectures about football to women. His lectures were now tailored to an audience more interested in general knowledge about the sport than in coaching.

As Rockne prepared for another summer of coaching clinics around the country, he was continually tweaking his material, which he carried in typewritten form, page after page of highly detailed pointers on a great many areas. His course outline at times would include: 1) Equipment, 2) Training, Diet & Injuries, 3) Use of Mechanical Appliances, 4) Fundamentals, 5) Offense, 6) Tactics, Strategy, Generalship, 7) Defense, 8) Each Individual Position, 9) Signals, 10) Scouting, 11) Shifts, 12) Forward Pass, 13) Written Quiz

A section he added on punting included eight pages of notes. Detailed preparation applied not just to the game, Rockne felt, but also to the teaching of the game. And yet, when giving a lecture or a chalk talk, he was not bound by the typewritten words on a page. His delivery was free flowing, and full of anecdotes and jokes. As Harry Stuhldreher observed, "He could translate the intricacies of the plays into simple language that his boys could understand. He could argue with them with the greatest heat, and chat with them with the greatest ease." As thoroughly prepared as Rockne was for every session in his summer coaching schools, he did not demand any kind of introduction or grand entrance. He often was available to chat informally with the attendees as they gathered. Stuhldreher told of one coaching school, at which Rockne's arrival was a day or two late due to his demanding travel schedule. As the coaches attending the school prepared to start another day, they heard that Rockne had arrived, and hurried over to the classroom building. There they found the great coach, sitting in the morning sun on the steps of the building, casually tossing peanut shells over his shoulder as he enjoyed a morning snack. "Hi ya fellas," he said. "Ready to get started?"

Ever since he was a young boy playing in the woods and waters around

Voss, Norway, Rockne held a fondness for the great outdoors. Although, owing to his nearly non-stop travel for speaking engagements and coaching clinics, he often found limited opportunity to enjoy much more than a sniff of natural wonders. But it was that basic urge, still strong in his late 30s that drove another of his growing network of interests—Camp Rockne. For years, the coach had envisioned a place, preferably in the North Woods, which would offer a personal respite from his fast-pace life and serve as a base of operations for instructing football. He envisioned a multi-purpose camp that could host gatherings of fellow coaches; instruct schoolboys in the ways of athletics; and possibly even serve as a pre-season training camp for his Notre Dame players.

Rockne partnered with Frank Hayes, Notre Dame alum and executive with the Union Bank of Chicago, to develop plans for the camp. In 1924, Hayes found a possible location, in the woods of Sawyer County in northwestern Wisconsin, seven miles north of the town of Winter. There, a former logging camp with 85 heavily wooded acres on the shore of Hunter Lake, a widening of the Chippewa River, was for sale. Hayes took the lead on purchasing the land and turning it into a summer camp for athletics. He hired a local woodsman to clear a patch of land—larger than an actual football field—to create a level, wide-open athletic field, as well as to construct benches, tables, and barracks.

Hayes and Rockne enlisted Northwestern University track coach Frank Hill to operate the summer boys' camp, with Notre Dame assistant coach Tom Lieb in charge of the recreational program. In the spring of 1925, Hayes wrote Rockne to report that he had been up to Camp Rockne and things were progressing, but then shared a concern he had heard from several people by then. "They say that on account of your signing up for all these coaches schools you would not be able to give any time to the camp…You see, a great many of these boys are expecting you to be there and if you do not spend some little time they may feel they have been slighted and will not return the following year." Rockne understood the concern, and agreed that he could be at the camp for about one third of its summer schedule.

The camp suffered a setback in its first summer of operation, when camper Ralph Loveland of Santa Fe drowned. "It was a sad event for me particularly, as he was my personal protégé and Mrs. Hill and I had come to look upon almost as a son," Hill wrote Rockne. But the camp moved forward and set up an eight-week session for the summer of 1926, with "expert instruction in swimming, canoeing, baseball, football, basketball, volleyball, tennis, and track; and woodcraft and nature work taught by an experienced woodsman while on canoe trips and hikes."

Coaching clinics, summer camps, travel, and family time—all demanded Rockne's time and attention. So too did the 1926 schedule, which included three games with Big Ten opponents—Minnesota, Northwestern, and Indiana—the most in a single season since 1921.

It had been more than 15 years since the famous feud between Michigan and Notre Dame began over a game canceled during the 1910 season. And in early 1926, a new Notre Dame president, Father Walsh, decided it was time to take a fresh look at approaching the Big Ten about joining the conference. It had been a banner year for both Notre Dame and the Big Ten in 1924. Red Grange dazzled crowds, while the Four Horsemen and Rockne won hearts nationwide with their perfect season and Rose Bowl victory. Notre Dame had also spent much of 1926 addressing concerns of the Carnegie Commission, which was evaluating the role of athletics within academic environments nationally. Each president since Father Sorin had painstakingly made efforts to bring Notre Dame up to the scholarly standards of the premier public and private institutions. Father Walsh, aware of rumors of Big Ten conference expansion, felt the time was right, and he planned carefully for it.

Father Walsh began by instructing Rockne to make a goodwill tour of conference member schools to speak with coaches and athletic directors. That was to be followed up shortly afterward by a visit from faculty representative and secretary of the Notre Dame athletic board Dean McCarthy, who would discuss matters with faculty members and athletic boards of the conference schools. Rockne reported back that all the visits had gone well, except for one—his visit to Ann Arbor and the University of Michigan. Time had not healed old wounds. Michigan football coach Fielding Yost, known for his anti-Catholic sentiment, still harbored hostilities toward Notre Dame. In short, Rockne and Yost agreed to disagree on just about everything concerning football and athletics. McCarthy reported back in with even less optimism. He believed that Big Ten animosity and jealousy of Rockne were the principal obstacles.

By May, Walsh decided to switch strategies. Instead of submitting a formal application, Walsh asked the conference members to appoint a committee to visit Notre Dame and to investigate all matters academic and athletic at the university. Walsh said that Notre Dame would abide by the findings of this committee as to whether or not to submit an application in December for admittance. The majority of Big Ten schools said no, and the Big Ten voted 6-4 against any expansion. Walsh was deeply disappointed and tried to resolve the matter by meeting with the presidents of the Universities of Chicago and Michigan, the main opponents of Notre Dame's application. After he visited them, he came away with a clear understanding of how deep the hostility of Yost and Stagg was toward Rockne and the Catholic school. Walsh, however, went through with the December application at the Big Ten meetings. The application was denied. Privately, Rockne attributed the rejection to Yost's undisguised anti-Catholicism, calling Yost a "hillbilly" who was forever grinding a religious ax against Notre Dame.


While Walsh was working behind the scenes for Big Ten conference admission, Rockne faced the start of the 1926 season with a team made up largely of juniors who had gone 7-2-1 as sophomores in 1925. Some began to speculate whether the possibility for another of Rockne's "wonder teams" even existed. The team sparked some hope after winning its opener, 77-0, against Beloit, a team it had beaten only 19-3 the previous year. But the first big test was in Minneapolis against Doc Spears' Gophers. The game started ominously as left tackle Joe Boland, trying to block a punt, suffered a broken leg when a teammate fell on him. On the very next play, fullback Fred Collins had his jaw broken in three places. They shared an ambulance ride while Minnesota took a 7-6 halftime lead. The pair managed to send a telephone message to Rockne, saying, "We're all through. All we can do is get the score when the game is over." On the first play of the second half, Christie Flanagan scooted 68 yards for a score, and the Irish prevailed, 20-7.

What followed was one of the most impressive stretches of defensive football in Notre Dame history: six consecutive shutouts, of Penn State, Northwestern, Georgia Tech, Indiana, Army, and Drake.

Only two games were even close—the 6-0 win at Northwestern in which the Irish scored on a crossing pattern pass from Art Parisien to Butch Niemiec, and the 7-0 triumph over Army at Yankee Stadium when perfect blocking allowed Flanagan to scamper 62 yards for a score. Said Paul Castner of Notre Dame's defensive play, "Men who knew football never overlooked the fact that every team Rockne coached was remarkably well drilled in that basic principle of good football, deadly tackling. At times the team may have lacked a good kicker or a triple-threat backfield star, but every Rockne team was deadly in tackling." None more so than this squad, who had the look of invincibility. The 8-0 Irish had two games remaining, at Carnegie Tech in Pittsburgh, and at Southern Cal.

Rockne frequently worked to combat overconfidence among his players. "A sucker," he said, "is one who lets notoriety go to his head and throw him off balance." He added, "It's a good thing to be confident. I wouldn't give much for the boy who wasn't...but any time you're inclined to slow up, or get filled with your own importance, take out your watch and remember that when that second hand moves from 60 to 60, that minute is gone. If you have wasted it, it will do you no good, because it is gone, never to come back. But, if you've taken advantage of it, you can say, 'I've made the best of my time.'"

On Thanksgiving weekend in Chicago, the Big Ten schools met and set schedules for the next year, and Rockne of course desired more opportunities to face conference opponents. Father Walsh was also still working on the conference application, to be submitted the following month. On Saturday, November 27, Army and Navy were to play for the first time anywhere but the eastern seaboard, meeting at Chicago's Soldier Field. Rockne wished to scout both teams, as he would face both service academies in 1927. So, as Jesse Harper had done a decade earlier when he went to Chicago and sent assistant coach Rockne on with the squad to Nebraska, Rockne put Hunk Anderson in charge of the team on its journey to face Carnegie. That was all a wily old veteran like Judge Wally Steffen needed to know.

Ironically, Steffen spent very little time with his Carnegie squad. As a judge, he presided over court in Chicago during the week and caught up with the team each Saturday. On this Saturday, he carefully selected his words to inspire his team about their upcoming match with Notre Dame, Rockne's absence, and the disrespect for Carnegie. Steffen's approach worked as the Tartans dismantled the Irish, and their perfect season, 19-0. "Tech got stronger as the game went on," said Niemiec. "They sensed the upset, and were relentless." Rockne took the loss, and attendant criticism, in stride. In a phone conversation after the game, he absolved Anderson of any blame. The team, set to leave for Southern Cal on Monday, had a rare Sunday practice, at which Rockne told the players: "It was my fault. No blame is to be attached to Hunk or Tommy (Mills). Let's be glad we have a chance to redeem ourselves against Southern Cal."

In front of 75,000 screaming onlookers at the Coliseum, the Irish trailed 12-7 in the closing minutes, staring at the prospect of a two-game losing streak, which no Rockne team had ever suffered. The ball was on the Southern Cal 24, with only 30 seconds left. Backup quarterback Parisien faded back, and looked for his prime receiver—who had been knocked to the ground. "It seemed like I was on the ground for an hour," Niemiec said. "But I got up and took off for where I was supposed to be...I caught the ball on the five-yard-line and stumbled over the goal." Final: Notre Dame 13, Southern Cal 12.

A season, a year of drama, excitement, heartbreak, exhilaration, was over. Rockne again felt exhaustion, but had an escape. While the team returned home, he and Bonnie stayed in California and sailed to the territory of Hawaii. There, Rockne spoke to several groups and was the honored guest at a game between the universities of Hawaii and Utah. As Rockne sailed the miles between Hawaii and Los Angeles on his return trip, he enjoyed banter with his shipmates. But in a quiet moment, he still felt sting of his error in missing the Carnegie Tech game and what it had cost the team and fans. But he tried to live by the message he always gave his players: "Get up. Get back at it. Move forward."

# 26
## High Flying

To call Knute Rockne a rambler was certainly an apt description. If he wasn't on a train headed somewhere, he was thinking about his next trip. The 1926 ocean voyages to Europe and Hawaii were quite satisfying; he called Hawaii "the finest place I have visited yet for vacation." He had crossed the oceans on either side of America, once as a small boy and once as an accomplished adult. It was the true Norse spirit at work. In the short term, between coaching track and spring football in 1927, his schedule was the usual whirlwind of dashing off to speak at one athletic banquet or another, talking to civic groups, and attending coaches' gatherings.

In many ways, he typified the American spirit of being "on the go," which was changing with new technologies. Since the Wright brothers' first flight more than 20 years earlier, aviation had taken off, although continental passenger air travel was still in its infancy. For Americans and Europeans, the race to see who could be the first to fly solo across the Atlantic Ocean was especially captivating. On the tails of Richard E. Byrd's solo flight over the North Pole in 1926, a solo trans-Atlantic flight was imminent. Pride and innovation—as well as the prize money that awaited

385

the winning pilot—fueled the drive to be first. As early as 1919, French businessman Raymond Orteig put up $25,000 to the first aviator to fly non-stop from Paris to New York—or New York to Paris. The offer was good for five years, during which time nobody successfully attempted the feat. He extended the offer in 1926 for another five years. Now, in 1927, technology had advanced to such a point where some believed it might actually be possible.

It wasn't just prize money and daring pilots that dominated air travel development; as practical a task as delivering the mail drove aviation expansion in the United States. As a young Chicago postal clerk, Knute Rockne had memorized train schedules in order to ensure sacks of mail for transport to their destinations across the country. But by the end of the Great War, airmail routes connected New York City, Philadelphia, and Washington. Otto Prager, the hard driving assistant postmaster general, directed steady improvements to the air system, which delivered millions of letters and packages each year by the mid-1920s. Similar to what passenger transcontinental travel looked like in the early days, mail transcontinental service consisted of loading mail onto railroad cars by night and then onto planes for travel during the day, guided by visible landmarks. In 1923, the postal system made a critical breakthrough by introducing rotating beacons that offered illumination for a 50-mile radius. In the following year, on July 1, 1924, night flights began, which promised to cut the time for cross country deliveries to less than 33 hours.

Daring airmail pilots followed the "iron compass" routes—the railroad tracks that guided them to their destination. These pilots were still considered members of a "suicide club." They cultivated a dash of bravado, of fatalistic flyboys who scorned death. One such airman based in St. Louis, Charles Lindbergh, would write letters to his buddies and mention crashes and near misses with a chilling casualness. Eventually the U.S. Postal Service knit together more than 2,600 miles of linked service, the longest continuous air route in the world. By 1925, with the Kelly Air-mail Act, Congress turned over the entire system to private companies, providing them with an expensive aviation infrastructure complete with airfields, established routes, and a half million dollars in night flying equipment. America attracted some of the world's foremost airplane manufacturers by the 1920s, including the Italian-born expert Giuseppe M. Bellanca;

Igor Sikorsky, who fled Russia after their Revolution in 1917; and the Dutch-born designer Anthony Fokker, who had directed German aircraft design and production during the Great War.

Byrd's solo flight in 1926 occurred in a Fokker tri-motor plane, but debates continued as to whether single-motor or multi-motor planes had the best aviation design. Fokker's multi-engine paradigm had been favored for its redundancy, which gave it greater power, but the extra weight came at a great price. The crashes of multi-engine planes in the 1920s recalled the words of the *Scientific American* writer more than a decade before who lamented, "This machine which does so much and falls so treacherously... Monuments have been erected over the graves of young men who have thought the air was conquered."

On March 14, 1925 Second Lieutenant U.S. Air Reserve Charles Lindbergh graduated at the head of his aviation class, yet the question his mother had continued to ask still haunted him: "Has the occupation of pilot any future?" With the United States disinterested in building an air defense in peacetime and with American commercial aviation dormant, highly trained pilots were not in high demand. Lindbergh, who had been fascinated by the changes in air travel since he was a child in Little Falls, Minnesota, was hired by the Robertson Aircraft Corporation in 1925 to fly the mail between St. Louis and Chicago. St. Louis, which had lost out to Chicago as a hub for the railroad industry, was anxious to make its mark as the primary center for aviation. Chamber of Commerce president Harold Bixby enthusiastically promoted local ambitions, and he was a primary force behind St. Louis securing an airmail franchise.

Lindbergh, who lived at a boarding house near St. Louis' Lambert Field, tapped into this civic energy and went looking for money and backers to support his attempt to fly solo over the Atlantic. Lindbergh was not a part of the Byrd team in 1926, and had considered the Fokker tri-motor as one plane design option. However, he felt a single-engine plane was better suited for the flight; Lindbergh was informed Fokker would never consider a single-engine model. Lindbergh then turned to the Ryan Aeronautical Company of San Diego to manufacture a single-motor special plane, which he helped design and later named *The Spirit of St. Louis*. Lindbergh's strategy, built around endurance and efficiency, was to load a stripped-down ship with enough fuel to fly across the ocean. The design ignored comfort, sleep, food, emergency equipment, and communication devices, skipping the navigator, cutting down on the motors, and doing everything to save on weight, including tearing the margins off the maps. By May 10, 1927, the plane was ready. Lindbergh tested it by flying from San Diego to New York City, with an overnight stop in St. Louis. The flight took 20 hours, 21 minutes, a transcontinental record. As Lindbergh prepared to leave San Diego, he received news that two French pilots, also vying for the $25,000 in prize money, had attempted the flight from Paris to New York on May 8. After takeoff, the two were never seen again.

Raw nerves, courage, determination, and a spirit of imaginative experimentation came together on Friday, May 20, 1927. Was Lindbergh crazy, or was the *Spirit of St. Louis* the true embodiment of a spectacular feat of individual daring and collective technological accomplishment? Lloyd's of London, insurers of almost every conceivable risk, refused to quote a price on Lindbergh's chances. After a night of heavy rain, the weather cleared slightly, and Lindbergh made the decision to go. At 7:52 a.m. he took off from Long Island, New York. A crowd of 500 spectators cheered him on as he lifted off. He carried only a compass, a sextant, his maps, and several fuel tanks. He had even replaced the pilot's chair with a lightweight wicker seat. Several storms awaited him in the North Atlantic.

That night 40,000 fans gathered in Yankee Stadium to watch a heavyweight championship fight between Jack Sharkey and Tom Maloney. The announcer, Joe Humphrey, delivered a message to the crowd: "I want you to rise to your feet and think about a boy up there tonight who is carrying the hopes of all true-blooded Americans. Say a little prayer for Charles Lindbergh." The humorist Will Rogers began his piece for the next day's *Los Angeles Times*, "No jokes today. An odd, tall, slim, smiling bashful boy is somewhere out there over the middle of the ocean, where no lone human being has ever been before...If he is lost, it will be the most universally regretted single loss we ever had. But this kid ain't going to fail." The *New York Times* received 10,000 calls inquiring about his progress.

When darkness fell and exhaustion set in, Lindbergh brought the plane up to a higher elevation so that he could see the stars to keep himself oriented. He thought of every creative way to stay awake, including stamping his feet and singing aloud. After flying through the night and the following day, Lindbergh finally spotted fishing boats and Ireland's rugged coastline. He had made it to Europe. At 10:24 p.m. on May 21, 1927, he landed at Le Bourget Airport in Paris. His tanks had a reserve of 85 gallons—enough for another 1,040 miles. His senses were frozen. Pinpoints of lights had confused him as he first approached Le Bourget. The dots were in fact headlights of thousands of automobiles, part of the estimated 150,000 people waiting to celebrate his remarkable accomplishment. The poet Harry Crosby described the scene by saying, "It was as if all the hands in the world were trying to touch the new Christ." The German newspaper *Vossiche Zeitung* wrote: "Such men mark the path of humanity; they are the peacemakers of technical progress; they set the pace for their eras" making it possible for lesser men "to reach the highest mountains without climbing."

Lindbergh's flight inaugurated America's Air Age, propelling a nation where trade, travel, and transportation had been conveyed by rail and road into the modern aviation era. The late 1920s brought a dizzying array of activity in the air industry, as it adapted its technology for mass passenger travel. A complex series of mergers and stock market takeovers created an ever-changing lineup of companies and individuals in the industry. For someone such as Anthony Fokker, developing new models was a financial stretch; he could not match the latest designs of other companies without major new investment. Eventually, his F-10 tri-motor drew the attention of Dillard Hamilton, an inspector for National Parks Airways. Hamilton wrote a letter to Gilbert Budwig, director of air regulation for the Department of Commerce, expressing concerns about not being able to inspect the internal structure of the Fokker wings because they were bonded together with glue. Checking the wing spars and the internal bracing would involve removing the plywood covering of the wing, thus damaging it. Subsequently, the U.S. Navy tested the F-10A, found it unstable and rejected it for naval use.

Americans were abuzz over Lindbergh's feat, and what it might mean for the future of air travel. The aviator was greeted with ticker-tape parades upon his return to the United States, and everywhere people gathered, his flight was the center of conversation. People hummed along to Nat

Shilkeret and The Victor Orchestra's version of "Lucky Lindy." It was no different when Rockne convened his coaching schools in the summer of 1927. Attendees asked one another, "When do you think you'll fly in a plane?" For now, though, the coaches used trains and automobiles to travel to Rockne schools at Bucknell University in Lewisburg, Pennsylvania; Utah Agricultural College in Ogden, Utah; and at Notre Dame.

At each school, Rockne's personal network of football friends extended further across the land. He was anxious to welcome previous attendees and to meet new ones. Each school became a new adventure. At Superior State Teachers College in the summer of 1926, Rockne expected to see Danny Coughlin, now coaching high school football in Duluth, Minnesota, across the St. Louis River. Coughlin, an Irish back in the early 1920s, said to his star player, Ted Twomey, "There's a coaching school being held over at Superior. Knute Rockne is going to be there. Why don't you and your dad go over and meet him." When Twomey and his father arrived at the school, Rockne was busy in a conference with other coaches. But when word reached him that he had visitors, he excused himself from the group and came out to the lobby. "I was simply electrified by the way he greeted us, the nice things he said he had heard about me, and an invitation to come to Notre Dame." There were no fancy promises, nor high pressure pitches. "We sure would love to have you at Notre Dame if you can see your way clear to come," Rockne simply said. And with that, his sphere of influence increased by one more man.

One of Rockne's coaching students at Superior was Walt Hunting, a native of Iron Mountain, Michigan, who played football at Lawrence College in Appleton, Wisconsin. Hunting, an aspiring high school coach, was influenced by Rockne to change from his T-formation offense. He did so with great success, in a hall-of-fame career coaching Denfeld High School in Duluth. His teams were called Hunting's Hunters, which gave the school its teams' official nickname. Rockne, it was said, was particularly kind to young coaches; anyone who wanted to spend time mentoring youth was a stand-up guy to him. "It was my pleasure to have known him during my years of coaching at Georgetown," said Lou Little, who later took the job at Columbia that might have been Rockne's. "He was of great help to me and also gave me great inspiration."

Once they met Rockne at one of his schools, other coaches could—

and would—call and correspond with him throughout the year over all sorts of questions and issues, some related to strategy, but many others simply on the operation of their football program. Their letters often began, "You may not remember me, but..." and Rockne would respond that he did, often referring back to some particular in their interaction. Common was a message such as this from a young coach in Texas: "I haven't words in my vocabulary to express how highly we appreciated your course and most of all your Friendship for it was a great treat to talk to you at the Hotel and to eat with you."

With his extensive network of contacts including athletic directors, newspapermen, and business and civic leaders in countless areas, Rockne held a unique position when it came to knowing which colleges and schools had openings for coaches and athletic directors. He used that knowledge to connect candidates to open positions, suggesting they be in touch with this or that official at a school looking to fill a spot. Coaches were always asking Rockne for recommendations or for direction as to where to apply. Rockne made a strong impression with coaches who attended his summer schools. One such fellow was Leonard "Stub" Allison, a colorful figure who became a good friend. A Minnesota native, Allison played football at Carleton College in Northfield, Minnesota, then entered the Army in 1917. Two years later, his college coach, Claude Hunt, was hired as head coach at the University of Washington, so Allison moved to Seattle and became his assistant.

When Hunt abruptly quit in 1920, Allison was suddenly head coach at a major university. A bit overwhelmed, his Huskies went 1-5 and he was out of a job. In 1922, he landed at the University of South Dakota and spent much of his four years there writing long, colorful letters to Rockne asking for his help in getting back into "the big time." Exaggerating about playing on a cow pasture with a half-dozen worn-down footballs, he would address letters to "Mr. K.K. Rockne, Chief of Bone and Grissle (sic) Dept." at Notre Dame. Rockne told Stub, "I hope you can come down this summer as the old coaching school wouldn't be complete without you and I think I have some ideas that might help the cause along." Finally, in May of 1927, Rockne's efforts were successful, as Allison was hired as an assistant at Wisconsin. "Congratulations...I am very glad to hear it," Rockne wrote. "At Wisconsin you will find (Glenn) Thistlewaite and (Tom) Lieb great fellows to work with and I look for Wisconsin to come along in great shape next fall."

As for Rockne's former Notre Dame players, they were like sons to him. His coaching never ended with their graduation. He fully expected them to come to him with their personal or business problems, and he offered behind-the-scenes help in any way he could. For the many who became football coaches themselves, Rockne became their lifelong companion on the field, no matter where it might be located. By the late 1920s, an impressive array of former Notre Dame players coached at schools large and small across the nation. There was a particular concentration of former Irish stars at the major schools of the South, including Frank Thomas at Chattanooga and then Alabama; Charlie Bachman at Florida; Chuck Collins at North Carolina; Harry Mehre at Georgia; and Chet Wynne at Auburn. Later, Rex Enright would guide South Carolina, Tom Lieb would take over at Florida, and Wynne moved on to lead Kentucky. Many would keep in touch regularly, none more so than Bachman, who sent long, typed letters detailing questions of training and strategy, with plays diagrammed by hand in the margins, with a notion such as, "What do you think of this one, Rock?" It was as if the coaching schools had continued year-round.


Summer brought a new season at Camp Rockne in the Wisconsin north woods. Rev. J.J. O'Boyle from Pio Nono High School in Milwaukee had taken on an administrative role, promoting the camp among the Catholic schools of Chicago and Milwaukee. O'Boyle met Rockne when the coach came to give a talk at the high school. In thanking Rockne, O'Boyle wrote, "You cannot appreciate how grateful we felt for that visit and how delighted the boys were in seeing you and hearing your splendid talk." Regarding Camp Rockne, Father O'Boyle noted, "It is a great delight to me to know that you are going to spend some time in camp, my only regret is that it will not be longer." The coaching school schedule would again be a challenge for Rockne, but he had added incentive to make it up to the camp: sons Billy, 12, and Knute Jr., 9. were going to be campers.

In promotional material, Rockne wrote that "the Boys Camp is at a spot far enough removed from civilization so that the boy will forget everything for a period of eight weeks except the activities of the camp and correspondence home....We have a beautiful spot at Hunter Lake... which is as beautiful and as woody a spot as I have seen in that wonderful state....We will have every form of camp activity...the four day canoe trip and hike will be one of the features of the camp. We aim to make an atmosphere about the camp which will make for cheerfulness, character, and we will chase old man grouch the second or third night after our arrival in camp." With an eight-week session, campers were thrilled to have Rockne on hand for even a few days. And Rockne enjoyed the time away from his hectic schedule and the ability to spend time on the dock watching the youngsters enjoy the best of outdoor life. And the rest of the time, the campers enjoyed the activities as directed by Tom Lieb and guided by college-age athletes from Notre Dame, Northwestern, and Wisconsin.

A typical camper was 10-year-old Laddie Helland, from Wisconsin Dells, Wisconsin. Laddie developed a fascination with Notre Dame and Rockne almost from the time he was old enough to hear stories being told by those around him. He would scour the newspapers for any mention of his favorite school. Helland's family was in the tourism business in the area of the Dells, where great stone cliffs overlook the rushing waters of the Wisconsin River. His father, Oliver "O.P." Helland, was the son of a Norwegian immigrant and one of the first local rivermen to organize sightseeing boat tours along the Wisconsin River, when he founded the Riverview Boat Line in 1921. As a respected businessman and civic leader, O.P. Helland helped transform the local economy by recognizing the area's potential to attract tourists, drawn by the scenic beauty of the Dells. The Riverview Boat Line expanded its holdings by acquiring land along the Wisconsin River and developing retail shops, a restaurant and tavern, a gas station, and a hotel. Hotel Helland was built across from the busy local train station and served tourists and businesspeople alike as they traveled through the area.

Laddie Helland's campmates included youngsters between the ages of 8 and 18, most from Midwestern families, with a few others from further away. Rockne, after one visit earlier in the summer, had hoped to return to Camp Rockne for a few days in August. However, he had to have his tonsils removed and stayed in South Bend to rest. Father O'Boyle wrote, "We were all keenly disappointed to learn from Tom that it would be impossible for you to come (back) to camp…I know that it is a disappointment to you as well." Replied the coach, "I think your Camp is a dandy and I certainly want to congratulate you on the wonderful success you have had—you have done some very fine work." Rockne later wrote, "I feel like a million dollars since I had my tonsils out. I certainly enjoyed my short stay at the Camp and if it is agreeable to you next summer I will make it a full week." O'Boyle wrote that "monumental Irish gall" prompted him to ask for a block of 12 tickets to the Southern Cal game, so he and Father Felsecker could chaperone a group of campers and their parents. Rockne, perhaps feeling sheepish over his paucity of trips to the camp named for him, agreed to the request, at a time when he had to turn down many others. Camper John Coyle, whose father M.E. Coyle was an executive with Chevrolet Motor Company in Detroit, and Peter Brennan of Winnetka, Illinois, won coveted tickets to the November 26 Notre Dame game against Southern Cal at Soldier Field, the first time the Irish would be hosting the Trojans.

The 1927 Irish roared to another 5-0 start, which included a 20-0 win against Gus Dorais and his University of Detroit team, and a 19-6 victory in the first-ever game with Navy, in Baltimore on October 15. Rockne was proud to now be playing both service academies—truly national teams similar to his own. A tough Minnesota squad led by the incomparable Bronko Nagurski made its first visit to Cartier Field on November 5, and 25,000 onlookers felt they were watching a classic. The team battled over inches for 58 minutes, with the Irish leading 7-0. But a botched snap on a punt from deep in Notre Dame territory sent the ball bounding free, and Nagurski jumped on it. On fourth down, the Gophers completed a touchdown toss and came away with a 7-7 tie. Rockne's Irish normally came away from a loss—and this one felt like a loss—with a superior effort, and a victory, the next week. But this team, even wearing green jerseys in front of a frenzied crowd at Yankee Stadium, couldn't keep up with a loaded Army team, and lost 18-0 to the Cadets. "Army played heads-up football and deserved to win," Rockne said. "We fired our best at them, but Army fired back just a little harder. They were alert and took advantage of our errors. That's good football."

Notre Dame gained some consolation by drilling Drake, 32-0, on a frozen field at Des Moines, setting up the big finale: Southern Cal's first visit to the Midwest. In a year of firsts and superlatives—from the Lindbergh flight to Babe Ruth's record 60 home runs to a huge crowd at Soldier Field for the Tunney-Dempsey "long count" title fight on September 22—the Notre Dame-Southern Cal game promised to be another spectacular. Ticket demand was unprecedented. At Notre Dame, Rockne had Ruth Faulkner sending out polite but definite turn-downs to many late ticket requests. One description of the crowd noted, "Not all of the boxes were occupied by notables and society folk, for the gangsters and detectives called off their shootings until after the game and were out in almost full force except a few, who didn't have tickets and were left in jail, but all the 'big shot hoodlums' were there, behaving just like gentlemen."

An estimated 120,000 packed Soldier Field on November 26. Notre Dame's athletic business manager Herbert Jones said, "Some doubt this figure and it is an estimate, but I believe there were that many. Unfortunately, all of them did not pay to get in. I believe that the Chicago 'boys in the know' took us 'country boys' for a ride. Many friends of those working the gates were passed in. Also, Rock had invited all of the Big Ten teams (who had finished play a week earlier). Those teams saw the game from the top of the colonnades on both sides. It was a mob."

They watched an epic struggle, which Notre Dame led, 7-6, in the closing minutes. Notre Dame's Charlie Riley attempted to field a punt near his own goal line, juggling the ball as he crossed into the end zone. The officials ruled a touchback; Southern Cal claimed it should have been a safety, which would have likely given the Trojans an 8-7 victory. A wild argument ensued, but the ruling stood, and the Irish won, 7-6. It was a positive finish to a season with some bumps—and, freeloaders notwithstanding, a huge payday for the university.

Football attendance continued its surge in 1927, led by the University of Michigan's newly built stadium, which replaced Ferry Field and was designed to seat 80,000. Michigan coach Fielding Yost had lobbied for a stadium to seat 150,000, but the Osborne Construction Company of Cleveland, limited by financial construction funding, designed the stadium to expand to accommodate seating for 100,000. Although fans still flocked to football games, by October 1927 another form of entertainment was vying for their attention: the talkies. When silent movie star Al Jolson said, "Wait a minute, wait a minute, you ain't heard nothin' yet," he spoke the first words in motion picture film history. The movie premiered at the Warner Theater in New York City on October 6, 1927 and became a national phenomenon even though only 200 theaters nationwide were equipped with Vitaphone's sound-on-disc technology, where a 16-inch disc was synchronized with standard 35m projection equipment. In less than two years, some 8,000 theaters were "wired for sound," and the silent picture was virtually dead.

And as had been the case on the campus of Notre Dame, change continued to mark the year 1927. President Father Mathew Walsh was bound by canon law requirements to leave office by 1928. He had dutifully served the university and the Holy Cross order, and he was ready to relinquish leadership to Father Charles L. O'Donnell, an energetic and engaging priest who would be tasked with leading Notre Dame during the enormous financial crisis that was affecting every avenue of American life. O'Donnell, like his predecessors, was the son of Irish immigrants, born in Greenfield, Indiana in 1884. He entered the seminary at the age of 16, and he graduated from Notre Dame in 1906. He was said to have extraordinary gifts of sharp wit and sarcasm that he displayed with embarrassing regularity. During his teaching days at the university, he provided English instruction to young Knute Rockne and had been a rector when the now-head coach had been a resident at Corby Hall. O'Donnell chose as his vice president Father Michael A. Mulcaire, whom O'Donnell would also place as chairman of the athletic board. Mulcaire, born in Ireland in 1894 and graduated from Notre Dame in 1917, looked forward to the challenge. Described as aggressive, direct, sometimes coarse, and aware of it, Mulcaire attempted to manage Rockne and bring the athletic department under closer supervision. Mulcaire would later tell Hunk Anderson that the Holy Cross fathers very much wanted to regain control over a situation they felt needed correction.

Near the end of Father Walsh's tenure, he had mellowed to the idea of a new football stadium. From the time he arrived in 1922, Walsh had resisted attempts to build a new stadium, even during the stadia-building craze of 1924. But at the end of November 1927, Walsh agreed to establish a special committee of trustees to inquire into the feasibility of a stadium project. Spring of 1928 brought a new 10-year contract for Rockne and committee recommendation for a new stadium. With retirement so close, Walsh left the decision-making to the new president.

But for all the talk of football and stadium building, the biggest hit on campus was the new student dining facility, which opened for the 1927 fall semester. Its Gothic arches and towering spires stood in testament to how far the university had come since the days when Father Sorin first arrived. The simple fare shared by few in the winter of 1842 had grown to provide a bounty for the growing number of students and guests who came to Notre Dame. The farms around the university that had supplied the food, and the Sisters of the Holy Cross who had cooked the meals, were fading into memory. The dining hall served nearly 2,000 students daily and had rooms on the east and west wings of the building. At breakfast more than 4,000 of the famous "Notre Dame Buns" and 20 sacks of potatoes were consumed. Sunday lunch saw 600 chickens and 560 heads of celery eaten. The cafeteria also contained a soda fountain and a cigar and cigarette counter.

And visitors for home football games were finding the new dining hall to their liking as well. From noon to 2 p.m. before the big game with Minnesota, it was necessary to open the east and west wings of the building to accommodate nearly 1,500 more diners than usual. V.C. Stephens, manager of the soda fountain in the cafeteria, reported a record 25 gallons of milk and 30 gallons of ice cream consumed in that time span. In the dining halls and cafeteria, 440 pounds of butter were used, along with 225 pounds of coffee, 75 bushels of potatoes and 10,000 rolls. Some visitors wondered aloud if any other campus in the country could feed so many so well in such a short time.

Feeding students daily onsite also provided its own revenue for the university and with football profits increasing at a steady pace, a November 15th meeting of the Board of Lay Trustees appointed a stadium committee consisting of Father James Burns, past president of Notre Dame, current president Matthew Walsh, and Chicago businessman and Rockne friend Byron V. Kanaley. What seemed like an endless wait to build a fitting stadium at Notre Dame could nearly be over.

# 27

## The Decade Roars On

"Everybody up."

Coach Rockne's standard command brought the mass of Notre Dame football players in a tight circle around him, all eyes and ears at attention. "Let's look sharp today, boys. The talkies are here taking some moving pictures." So much had changed in the decade since Knute Rockne became Notre Dame's head coach—on the campus, in the nation, across the world. An "extension" phone for homes was becoming commonplace. Automobiles and radios were omnipresent. Americans flocked to watch films with sound. Regular travel through the air seemed just within reach.

Rockne was now a bona fide celebrity, sometimes earning as much as $500 for giving a single speech. He had friends across the spectrum of sports, entertainment, business, radio, and newspapers. His columns and magazine articles reached millions. He often wrote about the important role of football within the academic setting as the debate over college football continued after the resolutions resulting from the 1905 meeting of college football coaches and President Teddy Roosevelt. By the early 1920s, as commercialism intensified, there were renewed calls for oversight of intercollegiate athletics. Edgar Fauver, former athletic director at Wesleyan, suggested that a large foundation, such as the Rockefeller Foundation or Carnegie Foundation, conduct a thorough study of intercollegiate athletics. Fauver served with the NCAA, which was formed in 1906 shortly after the Roosevelt meetings. Fauver wanted facts, not sentiment, on which future college athletics could be conducted.

In January 1926, the Carnegie Foundation for the Advancement of Teaching announced that it would carry out the study. A team, led by Howard J. Savage, visited more than 100 U.S. and Canadian schools, including 72 private and 40 public colleges, among them Notre Dame. Father Walsh welcomed the members when they arrived and worked hard to illustrate the huge steps Notre Dame had made in scholastic advancements and strict eligibility of its athletes. Ultimately Savage authored a 350-page report, published on October 24, 1929, that attacked practices in intercollegiate athletics. It criticized recruiting and subsidization, the hiring of professional coaches, the abandonment of amateurism, and the lack of student involvement in decision-making. More than anything it condemned the rampant commercialism in intercollegiate athletics. Nevertheless, the Carnegie Report did little to change the direction taken by intercollegiate athletics.

In his writings, Rockne strongly advocated for the place of athletics in the academic setting. His newspaper columns were written for the Christy Walsh Syndicate; Walsh sold them primarily to the Hearst newspaper chain. Typically, Rockne's pieces would appear in the Friday and Saturday editions, once the baseball season ended. He also wrote pieces for national general-interest magazines, including *Colliers*, with whom he agreed to develop a series of articles in 1930 on his life story. In an article for *Rotary* magazine, and reprinted in The Notre Dame *Alumnus*, entitled "Football or Hand Grenades," Rockne espoused the value of athletics as he saw them:

> Sportsmanship is simply a corollary of the Golden Rule. You want to play your best; hence, you take no advantage that will prevent the other fellow from doing the same. You respect him, as you want him to respect you. You give and take on a fifty-fifty basis. You play the game. And when it is over, there are no

whines nor excuses. You have both done your best...We need sportsmanship everywhere and every day...As the fine spirit of sportsmanship develops in athletic competition, men bring it into their other relationships. They introduce it into domestic situations. They apply it in meetings of boards of directors, where unfair advantages could be taken. They are beginning to use it in national politics. May we hope it will some day be extended to the field of international relations...what the world most needs today is a spirit of sportsmanship among nations.

In one of his magazine articles, he related athletics to Plato's directive to "know thyself:"

Every year hundreds of thousands of young men receive their diplomas from their colleges and go out to face the world. I wonder just how many of these lads know themselves...We are swinging away from the old fashioned ideas of education. The three words which are seldom mentioned in educational circles are courage, competition, and personality...The graduate needs, above all, courage to face the tough problems of life. All life is competition, and yet many of our young men have been taught by teachers who shun competition. Only the boys who have worked their way through school, have competed in athletic contests, political contests on the campus, or have competed on various scholastic journals, understand fully the meaning of the word. And as for personality, that goes along with confidence. I wonder just how many of these young men have had experiences of the kind that build up confidence?

Rockne celebrated the football player who "learns to take his hard knocks without squawking, without kicking, without knocking, and without becoming cynical. He learns to take them as a matter of course. He learns how to play his game with the proper value...trying to win just as hard as he can and if he does, not bragging. And should he lose, he learns no alibi. Nothing destroys character more than constant alibi-ing over failure. He learns to take his sports as a means to an end, not an end in itself...He learns how to take care of himself and how to curb his baser

400

emotions such as hatred, fear, passion, anger, and so on. And last but most important of all he imbibes the spirit of co-operation."

In 1928 Rockne agreed to headline a tour to the Olympic Games in London, with stops in several other European cities, marketed as "Knute Rockne's Olympic Tour." For $750, participants would receive first-cabin passage to Europe aboard the *Carmania*, admission to the Olympic Games for a week, rooms and meals, sightseeing trips, railroad travel on the continent, admission to museums and other places of interest, and first-class return aboard the *Transylvania*.

To operate the football program, Rockne now had a team of managers, assistants, trainers, business managers, and ticket sellers working at his side. This allowed him the freedom to pursue a variety of interests, including writing his national columns and magazine articles, delivering lectures, operating his coaching schools, and keeping tabs on his coaching brethren, many of whom he had assisted in landing their jobs. Hunk Anderson was one such example, as Rockne helped Anderson land his first head coaching position at St. Louis University in 1928. There, with Chile Walsh as an assistant, Anderson was thrilled that 52 players came out for spring football. "Chile and I are very much pleased right now, to think that we have that many men to work up," he wrote Rockne. "We had to arrange all the lockers and equipment and give them all out ourselves. Just like you did back in 1918."

Before sailing for Europe on July 20, Rockne had time to squeeze in three coaching schools at Southern Methodist, Oregon Agricultural, and Hastings College in Nebraska. A young coach in his Dallas school was 24-year-old Mark Raymond Berry, who had just started coaching at Breckenridge High School, about 90 miles west of Fort Worth. Berry was from a farm family of seven children, whose father died when he was five years old. His mother somehow kept the family going, and Raymond, as he was known, was able to attend Trinity University in Waxahachie, Texas, where he played football and studied to be a math teacher. From Rockne, Berry said he learned the importance of teaching fundamentals, the value of repetition and execution, and developing players who could think for themselves in the heat of competition.

Just a week into the Southern Methodist school, Rockne received word that John "Divvy" Devine, the fellow Chicago track star who was so instrumental in guiding Rockne to attend Notre Dame, had died June 10 in an automobile accident in Burlington, Wisconsin. Devine, always full of energy, always on the go, was gone. Rockne couldn't travel from Dallas to Chicago for the funeral, so he mourned his friend quietly while continuing to teach the game of football.

Rockne couldn't avoid reading of the deaths of numerous aviators, many of whom died flying stunts for the moving pictures. One report from Hollywood noted that "daring stunt men, particularly fool hardy aviators who make a precarious living here risking their lives so film fans may get a thrill while viewing the pictorial testimony to their bravery, continue to pay the price which fate demands of those who tempt her too often." Clement Phillips, a 25-year-old from Madison, Wisconsin, one of Hollywood's best-known daredevils, tumbled to his death when his motor stalled at a low altitude near Oakland, California. Actor-aviator Ben Lyon crashed upside down in the dry bed of the Los Angeles River while flying for a moving picture. Howard Hughes was injured when an old British warplane he was piloting crash-landed.

The night before the Olympic tour embarked for Europe, the travelers had an evening free in New York, and many attended a Broadway performance of the popular musical *Good News*. It was rumored Rockne was expected to appear on stage during the performance—he would likely be called up to take a bow, they figured. But during the play, when the professional actor playing a football coach had delivered a halftime address to his players, he stopped them and said, "Just a minute, boys. I want you to meet a friend of mine, Knute Rockne of Notre Dame." Rockne strolled onto the stage to huge applause from the audience. Perhaps that was all the show had expected from him. But the great showman wasn't about to waste this opportunity. A reporter described the scene:

"Using Notre Dame traditions and names, he started slowly, using short staccato sentences, then he began to pace, to get madder and louder, asking them 'what would Pete Vaughan think of the way you played that first half—Pete Vaughan who broke the goal post at Michigan in 1909 with his charge through the line for the winning score?' He went on, bringing in other incidents and other players, then he went into his finish:

'Never mind the breaks—make your own breaks—feet spread out, seats low—charge, charge, charge.'"

The power and emotion Rockne put into the speech was far superior to that of the actor portraying a coach. The actors playing football players appeared ready to charge. And a veteran football official who happened to be in the audience remarked: "I have been in football all my life, but that was one of the most thrilling experiences of my career. I tingled from the top of my head to my toes. It was positively electrifying."

The Olympic tour proceeded in a less electrifying fashion, with Rockne content to banter with the cruisers about football, travel, the Olympics, and history. It was said he took to the role of authoritative tour guide, as he had studied the various landmarks and high points, and could anticipate them before they were visible.

The 1928 Notre Dame football team returned just one starter from the 1927 squad, captain and left tackle Fred Miller, of the Miller Brewing family in Milwaukee. It would be the 6-foot, 195-pound Miller's third year starting. Backing him up was a tested sophomore from the little town of Winner, South Dakota, named Frank Leahy. Several hearty Irishmen looked to take over spots on the starting line, including center Tim Moynihan and right guard John Law. Moynihan was Irish through and through, the son of a Chicago fireman. And in John Law, Notre Dame had the kind of Irish pride that defined the school, and its football team. Charles Law was born in Ballymacaldrick, Dunloy in County Antrim, Northern Ireland, one of 10 children of farmers John and Mary Law. Not interested in farming, Charles apprenticed to become a bricklayer with a local construction company, run by the McAlonans of Dunloy. In 1898, Charles and his brother John left Ireland to look for work in America, living first in Philadelphia, then Brooklyn. Finding work in the construction trades, Charles established himself in the new land, then returned to Ireland in early 1904 to marry Jennie McAlonan and bring her to America. On February 13, 1905, their first son John was born. The Laws settled in Yonkers, just north of Manhattan, where Charles and his brother built a three-story, three-flat home. Charles, Jenny, and young John lived on one flat and rented out the other two. Later, they bought land on the next block, and the Law brothers built a row of one-story commercial buildings they rented to local businesses for additional income. Charles became a master mason and did decorative and specialty chimney and smokestack work for the James O'Brien Construction Company. His work was evident around Yonkers, a major center for factories, including those making carpeting and Otis elevators. Because of the valleys, the smokestacks were built extremely tall. Throughout the Northeast stood smokestacks bearing the work of Charles Law. At home, Jenny had her hands full with a family that eventually included six children.

From an early age, young John Law showed promise as a student and an athlete. In 1921, he entered Yonkers High School, where for two years he played basketball, football, and baseball, excelling in each. He then transferred to Hamilton Institute, where "his ability gained him immediate prominence on the teams and his personal popularity won to him so many friends that he was chosen captain in the three major sports." He led an undefeated football team, and at graduation was awarded a medal as the most versatile athlete and high honor student at Hamilton. At the same time, he captained an undefeated gridiron squad for the La Rabida Knights of Columbus, where he also participated in boxing. In football, he played halfback but also some guard, despite being just 5-foot-9, 170 pounds. The Hamilton and LaRabida teams played across the city, including Baker Field at Columbia and Von Cortland Park, and Law's reputation grew. Contemporaries predicted that "we will hear of John Law in college...the qualities of sterling character, uprightness of purpose, frankness of method, modesty and manner...make John a man strong of body, strong mind and strong of heart." Yonkers mayor Bill Walsh, who quarterbacked Notre Dame in 1895 in its first decade of football, suggested Notre Dame for young Law. And so began the path from an immigrant bricklayer's son to the a student at the nation's best-known Catholic university as Law boarded the train for South Bend in 1926.

Perhaps no one individual signified how far immigrants—in particular, Irish Catholic immigrants—had progressed in the first quarter of the 20th century than did Al Smith. The New York Governor and 1928 Democratic presidential candidate formed his identity from his Irish ancestry—

and the streets of the lower East Side of Manhattan. He was first elected governor in 1918, and although he lost the 1920 election, he ran successfully again in 1922, 1924, and 1926. He considered his work with funding public education as one of his major accomplishments. By 1926 he had increased state spending to $70 million, a nearly tenfold increase in less than 10 years. Smith represented the new emerging immigrant generation who were redefining what it meant to be Irish in America. Proudly Catholic, they strongly protested the bigotry they encountered because of their religion. Smith's rise personified the Irish success story that was taking place as increasing numbers of American-born Irish moved into the middle class. By 1928, Smith had climbed the New York social ladder from lower east side tenements to an apartment on Fifth Avenue, where his neighbors were the Vanderbilts and the Rockefellers.

Smith won his party's 1928 endorsement for president on the first ballot—a stark contrast to four years earlier, at the 1924 convention in New York City when John W. Davis finally won the nomination on a record 103rd ballot. At the July 1924 Democratic National Convention, held in New York City, Franklin Roosevelt tossed Smith's name into the ring as candidate for president. Smith, dubbed the Happy Warrior, looked as though he had a legitimate chance of winning the nomination. However, the Klan-backed faction within the party pushed hard to defeat the Democrats' anti-Klan amendment—which failed by one vote—and even staged cross burnings at rallies. They would never support a Catholic for president. The convention turned into a weeks-long slog of nomination ballots that continued in deadlock until a compromise candidate, Davis, finally won.

In 1928, Smith made repeal of the Volstead Act his top priority, but it was his religion that haunted him during the campaign. In an April 1927 article in the *Atlantic Monthly*, prominent Episcopalian New York lawyer Charles C. Marshall penned an "Open Letter To The Honorable Alfred E Smith," in which he argued that a Catholic president represented a conflict between Rome and American constitutional law. After praising Smith's accomplishments that included his advocacy of progressive social and economic ideals, Marshall wrote:

> ...and yet—through all this tribute there is a note of doubt, a

sinister accent of interrogation, not as to intentional rectitude and moral purpose, but as to certain conceptions which your fellow citizens attribute to you as a loyal and conscientious Roman Catholic, which in their minds are irreconcilable with that Constitution which as President you must support and defend, and with the principles of civil and religious liberty on which American institutions are based.

The article quoted numerous papal encyclicals and concluded with: "Nothing will be of greater satisfaction to those of your fellow citizens who hesitate in their endorsement of your candidacy because of the religious issues involved than such a disclaimer by you of the convictions here imputed, or such an exposition by others of the questions here presented, as may justly turn public opinion in your favor."

It was reported that after hearing of the article, Smith's first comment was: "What the hell is an encyclical?" But he did respond in the May issue of *The Atlantic* with an article entitled: "Catholic and Patriot: Governor Smith Replies," in which he went point-by-point to counter all the arguments. He concluded by saying:

I summarize my creed as an American Catholic. I believe in the worship of God according to the faith and practice of the Roman Catholic Church. I recognize no power in the institutions of my Church to interfere with the operations of the Constitution of the United States or the enforcement of the law of the land. I believe in absolute freedom of conscience for all men and in equality of all churches, all sects, and all beliefs before the law as a matter of right and not as a matter of favor. I believe in the absolute separation of Church and State and in the strict enforcement of the provisions of the Constitution that Congress shall make no law respecting an establishment of religion or prohibiting the free exercise thereof. I believe that no tribunal of any church has any power to make any decree of any force in the law of the land, other than to establish the status of its own communicants within its own church. I believe in the support of the public school as one of the cornerstones of American liberty. I believe in the right of every parent to choose whether his child shall be educated in the public school or in a religious school supported by those of his own faith. I believe in the principled noninterference by this country in the internal affairs of other nations and that we should stand steadfastly against any such interference by whomsoever it may be urged. And I believe in the common brotherhood of man under the common fatherhood of God.

Religious persecution dogged Smith throughout the campaign, including Klan cross burnings along his campaign train route near the end of the campaign trail in Oklahoma City that included a crowd of 70,000 well wishers. Smith addressed the crowd and the issue of anti-Catholicism, stating that such hatred was "so out of line with the spirit of America. I do not want any Catholic to vote for me…because I am a Catholic. But on the other hand I have the right to say that any citizen of this country who votes against me because of my religion, he is not a real, pure, genuine American."

Will Rogers, who supported Smith to the point where some called Rogers a proxy candidate, wrote: "What do we care about a man's religion? We don't want to be saved spiritually, we want to be dragged out of the hole financially. He has been three times Governor of New York. The Jews elected him. Now if they can trust him to run the biggest state in the world…and trust a Catholic over a Protestant…What do we care about a President's religion?" On the other side, firebrand evangelical preacher Billy Sunday labeled Smith's supporters as "the damnable whiskey politicians, the bootleggers, crooks, pimps, and businessmen who deal with them."

It was no surprise that the 1928 election generated much attention on the Notre Dame campus. By October, students were competing for $1,000 prize money for writing the best essay as to "Why Alfred E. Smith Should Be Elected President of the United States." Mrs. James W. Gerard, wife of the former U.S. ambassador to Germany, sponsored the national competition. Weekly notices from many Notre Dame clubs told of active involvement by alumni working to elect a Catholic president. Father O'Donnell, who would later describe himself as a "nonpartisan Democrat," was obviously sympathetic to Smith's campaign. But, the university president realized Smith's campaign would most likely fail. O'Donnell concentrated more behind the scenes, assisting *Commonweal*, a Catholic-focused magazine founded in 1924, on how best to handle the Catholic issue.

But the endorsement Smith sought most—from the country's most successful and well-known football coach—never came. Both political parties realized the incredible power of a Rockne endorsement, but the Notre Dame coach turned down both invitations. The Republican request came from Major John Griffith, commissioner of the Big Ten and longtime business associate of Rockne's. Rockne, like O'Donnell, believed Smith could not win and took a neutral stance. Rockne conferred with O'Donnell on a course of action and the two confirmed that it would not be well for Rockne to identify himself or Notre Dame with either candidate.

In addition to Catholicism, it was also Smith's campaign promise to repeal Prohibition that contributed to his defeat. The Methodist church, through its Board of Temperance, Prohibition and Public Morals, led a nationwide fight to defeat Smith. Deets Pickett, Research Secretary for *The Voice*, a monthly organ of the Methodist Board, planned more than 40 Methodist conferences before Election Day to speak of what might befall the nation if Smith were elected. And one of the most prominent speakers at many of those conferences was Mabel Walker Willenbrandt, named by President Warren G. Harding to enforce the 18th Amendment. Willenbrandt, who was the highest-ranking woman in the federal government, actively called for the election of Herbert Hoover. Her zealous campaign against Al Smith gained national headlines. She urged Prohibitionist Protestant ministers to try to convince the nation that Smith was a threat to the U.S. Constitution.

Between dry anti-Catholic Protestants and evangelical fundamentalists, Smith was doomed. Republican Herbert Hoover won a landslide victory, garnering more than 6 million more popular votes and winning with an Electoral College margin of 444-87.

Rockne told a friend before the 1928 season that "we don't look so hot" and that senior halfback John "Butch" Niemiec "will make or break us."

The early going proved him right. In the opener against Loyola of New Orleans, Niemiec reinjured his knee and the Irish struggled. Niemiec returned to the game during the closing minutes and helped pull out a much too difficult 12-6 victory. The Irish then went to Madison and were decisively beaten, 22-6, by Wisconsin. Rockne's former aide Tom Lieb and his coaching-school pal Stub Allison, now both Badger assistants, did no crowing. Notre Dame was in some trouble. Rockne abandoned the idea of using Shock Troops; he had a difficult enough time finding a healthy and reliable starting eleven. Against Navy before another huge throng at Soldier Field, a still-hobbling Niemiec pulled out a 7-0 win with a late pass to John Colrick. Against Georgia Tech, Rockne turned to an untested fullback, Joe Savoldi, the somewhat wild son of Italian immigrants who lived in Three Oaks, Michigan. Tech tested Savoldi's defensive skill and found it wanting, topping Notre Dame, 12-0. More than ever, Rockne and his men needed to heed the words of the signs hanging in the Irish locker room:

"A winner never quits and a quitter never wins."

"Success depends on what the team does – not on how you look."

"A good interferer always gets his man."

"A team that won't be beaten can't be beaten."

"Keep trying—you've got a break coming."

A 32-6 pasting of Drake helped some. That win was followed by a 9-0 victory over Penn State on a soggy Franklin Field in Philadelphia. At 4-2, hope remained high that the Irish could finish strong, but the three most imposing opponents—Army, Carnegie Tech, and Southern Cal—awaited. Notre Dame needed one win in those games to avoid ignominy: its first losing record in a full season of football in its entire history. In front of the largest crowd yet to see a Notre Dame-Army game, more than 78,000 crowded Yankee Stadium. One New York writer, in describing the atmosphere of the rivalry noted, "it has the Big Town in something approaching a mild hysteria. It's bigger than the World Series, the heavyweight championship fights." He attributed a lot of the attention to Rockne, "the sort of fellow the Big Town goes for: an individualist, a leader, a showman."

That day, in a cramped dressing room in the bowels of Yankee Stadium, Rockne the showman was at his best. Looking around at the faces of his underdog team, he invoked the spirit of the greatest Irish star ever, George Gipp, saying that, one day, when the team most needed it, he should ask them to win a big game for Gipp. From there, his squad went out and played over their heads against an experienced, superior Army eleven. Late in the fourth quarter, the game was tied, 6-6, and appeared destined to end that way.

A botched snap had left the Irish with 4th-and-16 from its own 32-yard-line. Rockne called timeout and huddled with his troops. With play ready to resume, Johnny O'Brien, a lanky sophomore end from Los Angeles who had not been in the scrum all afternoon, entered the game. By rule, a player entering the game could not say anything in the huddle. But O'Brien didn't have to. Sophomore quarterback Frank Carideo knew the play. Johnny "Butch" Niemiec, the pride of Bellaire, Ohio, whom Rockne called "tape and guts" due to his two injured knees and endless courage, rolled out with the ball, saw he had enough time, pulled up, and lofted a long, arching pass—deep, deep, and finally into the waiting arms of Johnny O'Brien. His clean jersey visible through the gloaming, dark day, O'Brien juggled the ball for a second, nearly lost his balance, but carried it into the end zone for the winning touchdown. Notre Dame took a 12-6 lead on the most unlikely play imaginable. But it wasn't over. Army's star Chris Cagle returned the kickoff a mile, and Army drove to the shadow of Notre Dame's goal line before the final whistle blew.

Frank Wallace's story in the Monday, November 12 *New York Daily News* was headlined: Gipp's Ghost Beat Army; Irish Hero's Deathbed Request Inspired Notre Dame." It quoted Rockne as saying, "On his deathbed George Gipp told me that someday, when the time came, he wanted me to ask a Notre Dame team to beat the Army for him." Wallace added: "It was not a trick. George Gipp asked it. When Notre Dame's need was greatest, it called on its beloved 'Gipper' again." Wallace said that what was thought to be Notre Dame's weakest team in 15 years "overcame physical strength, pure form, theory and bad breaks. They played as few teams have ever played. They were underdogs and that helped. They had Rockne and he helped. Football people knew that Rockne would fire up his boys in his speech before the game."

That evening, Rockne appeared drained, but pleased. He smiled quietly, knowing that, with a banged-up, less-than-stellar team, he had pulled off a huge victory, and assured a winning season in this, the most challenging of years. The next morning, he was energized, reading the New York papers in his hotel suite, including Paul Gallico's stirring description. "As this is written, the spell of Collins and Niemiec and Chevigny and Cagle is still on this mundane spot and one regrets that they have gone and that they are not still charging over the turf and flinging their bodies like living scythes through the air. I'm glad Notre Dame won the way they did...It would've been heartbreaking to see them lose after so much gallant effort."

After such a thoroughly emotional, draining game, a letdown was perhaps inevitable. As badly as Rockne wanted to defeat Carnegie Tech for the heartbreak it caused two years earlier, his Irish had nothing left, and lost to the Scots, 27-7, in what would be the final game ever played at Cartier Field. It ended a streak that included 89 victories and three ties on Notre Dame's home field over 23 years. Not since the 5-0 loss to Wabash in 1905 had Notre Dame tasted defeat at Cartier. Rockne confided to a friend that "our football team was all in Saturday from the Army game and we probably couldn't have beaten anybody. We probably had too much of a schedule—seven hard games in a row is just too much." It was much the same the following week in Los Angeles, when Southern Cal marched to a 27-14 victory. For the first time, a Rockne team had lost consecutive games. And for the first time, it had been outscored on the season, 107-99. The four losses equaled the number of games lost in the previous four seasons combined. Only the Army victory saved the season from being considered a disaster.

A trying season in the books, Rockne focused his attention on what seemed like a never-ending battle to build a new stadium. His frustration at the slow and cautious decision-making process of the Holy Cross fathers who ran Notre Dame grew. There certainly was enough cash on hand, due in large part to his thriving football program, but Rockne was seeing other buildings—such as Lyons Hall—erected while the stadium plans lagged. Rockne had traveled to Ann Arbor, studying the new stadium there, and developed detailed plans for a smaller but similar stadium for Notre Dame. There was widespread support among the business community in South Bend. Yet progress was stalled.

At Columbus, Ohio, the Buckeyes' athletic director, Lynn St. John, was looking for a new football coach. Dr. Jack Wilce, the former Wisconsin star who had guided Ohio State football since 1913, was retiring to practice medicine full-time. St. John took a phone call from Major John Griffith, the Big Ten commissioner, who said he had a candidate for the job sitting in his Chicago office. It was Rockne. They agreed to discuss the job at the upcoming coaches meeting in New Orleans, and Rockne indicated he was interested. Unspoken was his desire to take on Yost at Michigan and Zuppke at Illinois, neither of whom would play him as long as he was at Notre Dame. Rockne's demands included a $10,000 salary, full professorship, ability to run coaching schools and continue his writing, and the power to name his own assistants. Ohio State agreed. Then came the all-too-familiar qualifier: no publicity until Rockne had a chance to talk to Notre Dame officials. The deal would have to remain tentative until then. But news of the talks leaked from the New Orleans meetings, and Ohio State called off the deal. There was speculation that Studebaker had put pressure on Rockne to remain in South Bend.

Earlier in 1928, Paul Castner, the former great Irish back, now a Studebaker executive, went to vice-president Paul Hoffman and suggested hiring Rockne to speak to company sales meetings. "You're letting one of the greatest, most inspirational speakers in America get away," Castner warned Hoffman, stressing that Rockne could travel the country addressing Studebaker dealer luncheons. Hoffman agreed, and on May 1, 1928, Rockne signed his first Studebaker contract, for $5,000, to address more than 20 sales meetings from January through March 1929. The timing was ideal—Studebaker would be gearing up for its national sales campaign during those months, and Rockne would be between the football regular season and spring football. And, more than anything, it appealed to Rockne's desire to travel. Notre Dame alumni and other followers would often surround Rockne whenever his train arrived for a Studebaker meeting. The throng would usually rush off with Rockne for a talk to a school, college, or civic group. He would arrive at the Studebaker meeting later in the afternoon. The dealer meetings began around 8:30 a.m., with attendees eagerly awaiting Rockne's speech. But the company would hold Rock back until around 4 p.m., thus assuring the dealers would be in attendance for the entire day's business schedule.

Rockne's first speech for Studebaker was a talk to the National Automobile Chamber of Commerce convention at the Commodore Hotel in New York City. Rockne, somewhat nervous, asked Castner to go along with him. During the train trip east, Rockne repeatedly asked Paul, "But what am I going to talk to them about?" Don't worry, Castner told him, "You'll think of something." It was a black-tie, formal luncheon, with all the biggest names in the automobile industry in attendance, starting with Henry Ford, and Alfred Sloane, Jr., president of General Motors. Rockne performed magnificently, ad-libbing his way through 40 minutes of inspiration, and closing with his traditional "Go, go, go," exhortation. Castner said Rockne had "that normally placid Ivy League crowd on its feet and cheering like college sophomores at a Harvard-Yale game. Even Mr. Ford and Mr. Sloane came up off their chairs. Few out-of-town speakers have ever aroused a sophisticated New York audience as much."

As 1929 began, Knute, Bonnie, and the four children had something else to anticipate. Work had begun on their new home in the new Sunnymede Addition east of downtown. In the 1870s, brothers Jacob and John Studebaker bought much of the land in the area and built country estates for their families. In 1909, Clement Studebaker Jr. built a lavish, Beaux-Arts residence that was later owned by Vincent Bendix, founder of the Bendix Corporation. The partnership of Leslie Whitcomb and Fred Keller began developing Sunnymede in 1925, attracting professionals to a part of the city that had already become an exclusive enclave for the more prosperous members of the community. Purchase agreements specifying lot sizes and minimum construction costs created a neighborhood of impressive houses, including the handsome new Rockne home on East Wayne Street. Built in an English Tudor style, it featured stucco and brick construction, finely detailed stonework framing the living and dining rooms, and four upstairs bedrooms.

Rockne had passed up opportunities to coach and live in sunny southern California and bustling New York City. He was determined to give his family the best that South Bend, Indiana had to offer.

# 28

## Rockne's Ramblers

In his nationally syndicated column, Rockne's friend Will Rogers wrote, "Just passed through Chicago. It's not a boast, it's an achievement. The snow was so deep today, the crooks could only shoot a tall man." From the city's frontier days through fierce labor disputes in the 1890s to the "muckraking" era of the early 20th century, bribery and violence were part of the fabric of Chicago. One London observer claimed, "Other places hide their blackness out of sight; Chicago treasures it in the heart of the business quarter and gives it a veneer." Or as George Kibbe Turner wrote in *McClure's* in 1907, "Chicago, in the mind of the country, stands notorious for violent crime." By 1929, Prohibition merely added another layer to the story. Liquor robberies and hijackings had begun to occur within the first hours of the Volstead Act taking effect, and by 1929 thousands of "speakeasies"—establishments where one could illegally obtain an alcoholic beverage—dotted the city and its suburbs. Al Smith, the 1928 Democratic candidate for president, had promised during his campaign to repeal Prohibition. With his defeat, the 18th Amendment remained firmly in place. The bloody beer wars of Chicago, which had raged since the beginning of Prohibition, would continue, and would now make famous Al Capone, whose name became synonymous with Chicago's violent existence.

Capone, the son of immigrant parents, was born on January 17, 1899 in Brooklyn, New York. He became involved with gang activity at a young age after being expelled from school when he was 14. In his early 20s, he moved to Chicago to take advantage of a new opportunity to make money smuggling illegal alcoholic beverages into the city. Capone's name became associated with the 1924 shooting of gang leader Dion O'Banion in his North Side flower shop, the 1926 machine-gunning of Hymie Weiss on the steps of Holy Name Cathedral, and, perhaps most famously of all, the 1929 St. Valentine's Day Massacre of seven men in a garage at 2122 North Clark Street, which had targeted George "Bugs" Moran. Moran and his North Side gang remained the largest obstacle to the Capone organization's power in Chicago, with their constant hijacking of Capone's liquor shipments. On February 13, Moran received a call from one such hijacker who had intercepted a truckload of whiskey from Detroit. The driver was told to deliver it to the Clark Street garage the next morning, which dawned with freezing temperatures and bone-chilling winds.

Six men sat around a table in the garage, their hats and coats still on to guard against the cold, while a coffee pot percolated on an electric plate. The men included James Clark, alias Albert Kashelleek, a convicted robber and burglar and Moran's brother-in-law; Frank and Peter Gusenberg, gunmen for the Moran gang; Reinhardt Schwimmer, an optometrist and known companion of the Moran gang; John Snyder, alias Adam Hyers, a convicted robber; and Albert Weinshank, a strong-arm agent of Chicago's cleaning and dyeing industry and a known Moran henchman. John May, an auto mechanic and safe-cracker before joining the Moran gang, worked on a truck in the garage, his German shepherd tied by a leash to the axle of the truck. That morning, a black Cadillac touring car with a police gong on the running board headed toward the garage-warehouse. Fastened to the back of the driver's seat was a gun rack similar to those carried by police squad cars. The driver wore a policeman's uniform, complete with blue cap and brass star. So too did the man beside him. Three men in the back seat were in civilian clothes. Mrs. Max Landesman, a second-floor resident of the rooming house next door, assumed it was another police raid and took little notice. Moran, arriving late to join the other men, took one look and retreated quickly as the apparent police car arrived.

The noise inside the garage was like the chatter of a pneumatic drill. It lasted but a few moments after the five men entered, and it was followed by two single blasts like a car backfiring. As a dog began to howl, Mrs. Landesman moved back to the window. She saw two men come out with their hands raised. Two men behind them, wearing the police uniforms, held pistols to their backs and prodded them toward the car. A police raid and an arrest, the woman concluded. The fifth man, she assumed, must have been a plainclothes detective. As the dog kept howling, Mrs. Landesman became uneasy. She finally urged one of her lodgers to check out the scene. Moments later he came out yelling, "They're all dead." The blood bath horrified the city. The seven had been lined up facing the wall and shot execution-style. Police recovered 70 empty .45-caliber machine gun cartridges and 14 spent bullets of the same caliber. However, with Capone at his winter home in Miami at the time of the shooting, it became impossible to convict him of any direct involvement.

Though the St. Valentine's Day Massacre marked the end of any significant gang opposition to Capone's rule in Chicago, it also marked the beginning of his downfall. Determined to prove that police were not responsible for the malicious act, Police Commissioner William F. Russell led an intensive investigation that led to one conviction. "It's a war to the finish," Russell said. "I've never known of a challenge like this—the killers posing as policemen—but now the challenge has been made, it's accepted. We're going to make this the knell of gangdom in Chicago."

The University of Notre Dame, situated just 90 miles east of Chicago and with a sizeable Chicago enrollment, was always attuned to the latest news from the larger city. But in the spring of 1929, after years of behind-the-scenes battles—though not of the bloody Chicago type—an important decision in the history of Notre Dame and South Bend came to fruition that would link the university and the metropolis closer together.

At a special meeting in April, university officials approved plans for a new athletic stadium that would seat between 50,000 and 60,000, situated south of Cartier Field. The next month, the university signed a contract

416

with the Osborne Construction Company of Cleveland, builders of the stadiums at Michigan and Minnesota, for construction of a 54,000-seat stadium that would be ready for the 1930 season. The sod from Cartier, considered some of the best playing turf in the country, would be transported to the new stadium. The project costs totaled $900,000, to be financed from cash on hand, as well as a subscription program in which 240 six-person groups would commit to 10 years of purchasing prime-location box seats. Rockne's long-awaited dream of a modern stadium that could attract and host big-name opponents was finally within sight.

But in order to build the team's new home, the entirety of the 1929 football season would have to played away from South Bend. Of the nine-game schedule, three games would be played at Soldier Field in Chicago—against Wisconsin, Drake, and Southern Cal. The Navy game would be played in Baltimore and the yearly Army clash would be fought in New York City. Four true road games included contests at Indiana, Carnegie Tech, Georgia Tech, and Northwestern. The schedule would inevitably allow the team to make an impression on large population centers: four games in Chicago and environs, and one each in Baltimore, New York, Pittsburgh, and Atlanta. Only the season opener at Bloomington, Indiana, would be played outside the glare of major newspapers and big-city crowds. By the time the 1929 football season would end, a record number of 551,000 would see Rockne's Ramblers play in person. That was a 10-fold increase in a decade. The ironic element was that Rockne himself would only attend four games, as a severe attack of phlebitis in his right leg prevented walking, much less travel.

On the 1929 commencement weekend, however, the mood remained optimistic about the future. But Notre Dame was a school keenly aware of its history and a most unusual track meet was staged as a farewell that drew more than 2,000 visitors to Cartier Field to use the bleachers for the final time before they would be razed. Three decades of athletic competition at Cartier, including the playing careers of Rockne, Dorais, Gipp, the Four Horsemen, and so many others, were coming to a close. A special dual meet featured Notre Dame taking on Rockne's old track home, the Illinois Athletic Club. The IAC featured athletes such as F. Morgan Taylor, Olympic gold medalist hurdler and former world record holder. But Cartier Field magic triumphed, as two Irish hurdlers prevailed—Johnny

O'Brien edged Taylor in the high hurdles, and Roy Bailey defeated Taylor in the lows. Captain Jack Elder, taking his final Cartier Field bows, beat a strong field in the 100-yard and 220-yard dashes. One feature of the meet was the half-mile, won by Notre Dame freshman Alex Wilson, a member of the 1928 Canadian Olympic team.

The summer coaching circuit took Rockne to Wittenberg University in Springfield, Ohio, located 50 miles east of Columbus. Assisting Rockne with the clinic were Jack Chevigny and Joe Boland. On the trip, the pair stayed in adjoining rooms, with a connecting door. On one of the last nights of the school, a thief made his way through the rooms, wiping the assistants out of all the cash they had on hand. Boland was distraught. He was headed to St. Paul, Minnesota at the conclusion of the clinic to assume head coaching duties at St. Thomas. He wasn't scheduled to receive a paycheck until October 1, so he had transportation and living expenses still to worry about. But as he fretted, Rockne walked into the room. "You lost all the money you had last night, didn't you?" he asked. "Yes," Boland replied. And the coach dropped a thick roll of bills onto Boland's lap. "That should hold you until you get paid, kid." Rockne did the same for Chevigny, who had also fallen victim to the thieves. Rockne did not discuss payback with either. The young coaches were his responsibility while at this clinic, Rockne figured, and he needed to take care of his boys.

The summer of 1929 presented Rockne with the opportunity to instruct his peers as well as refocus his attention on his own coaching staff. Hunk Anderson had accepted the head coaching job at St. Louis University; Chevigny, whom Rockne prized for his quick thinking, would be Anderson's replacement. Rockne's first choice to replace Anderson had been Adam Walsh, the great center and captain from the 1924 national champs, who now had four years experience as head coach at Santa Clara. Rockne and Walsh agreed to contract terms, but two days later Rockne called Walsh with a change of plans. Rockne had just learned of an opening for a line coach at Yale and felt Walsh would make a great candidate. How appropriate, Rockne thought, that one of his students would be heading back to the roots established by Walter Camp. If Walsh took the position, he would break new ground as a non-Yale graduate being hired at the birthplace of the game of football. Yale, one of the original Big Three. The prestige of Notre Dame—and the quality of its player-coaches—

would be greatly enhanced. Walsh, always following his old coach's advice, sought the job and won it. Later in the fall, Walsh earned many accolades, as his line was instrumental in helping Yale garner headlines for upsets over Army and Dartmouth.

The most important coaching hire Rockne made in the spring of 1929 was when he brought Tom Lieb back to South Bend. Lieb, after spending his first three years after graduation from Notre Dame as an Irish assistant, had most recently served for three years as line coach at Wisconsin. Lieb was familiar with Rockne's methods and could follow his psychology. Similar to Rockne, Lieb didn't shy away from challenges and enjoyed additional responsibilities. His people skills were outstanding, and he understood the teamwork needed to make an entire squad successful. 1928 had been a roller-coaster ride for Rockne, and he sought familiarity for the challenges of 1929. Lieb's role immediately took on more than that of a typical assistant coach. Rockne's role with the Studebaker Manu-facturing Company now had him traveling across country to speak to car dealer groups, leaving him with less time for all the demands of being head football coach. Rockne put Lieb in charge of spring practice and the daily noon football classes in the Main Building.

When assessing the prospects for the 1929 season, Rockne said with a deep sigh, "Fair, just fair." But astute observers noted that five years earlier, before the 1924 campaign began, when queried about that team's prospects, Rockne responded, "Not so good, but possibly fair." The ma-jor difference, however, between the two years was the schedule that took the Irish on the road for all of their games.

For 1929, Rockne had 19 returning lettermen, including 14 linemen. The Irish would miss Fred Miller, but Rockne could count on returning linemen such as Tim Moynihan at center, captain John Law, and Jack Can-non. In the backfield, Marty Brill, a Philadelphian who had transferred from Penn showed promise. A sophomore, Marchmont Schwartz, ap-peared capable of backing up Jack Elder at left halfback. At just 5-foot-7 but brimming with confidence, junior quarterback Frank Carideo re-minded some of Gus Dorais. He was always in command, able to size up a situation quickly and made sound decisions. Roy Mills had discov-ered Carideo at Mt. Vernon, New York. Mills, an earlier Mt. Vernon high school star who attended Princeton, played varsity football. Mills was an extraordinary kicker and spent most of his adult life teaching high school and college fellows his skill. He was a wizard at drop-kicking, putting on exhibitions that included curving a kick from the corner of the field, along the goal line, and through the uprights. He taught a brand of punting that stressed kicking away from the receiver and came up with the concept of the "coffin corner"—placing a punt deep in the opponent's territory, near the sideline, where the receiver could be "buried" by the punting team. Mills developed Carideo into one of the greatest corner-kickers of his era.

Carideo did not show early greatness at Notre Dame, but he was a student of the game and an extremely fast learner. Prior to the 1929 season, Rockne had him stop by the house one evening, where the coach presented him "the four basic principles of quarterback play: 1) When in doubt, punt! 2) Know when not to forward pass. 3) Remember what plays are working and what plays aren't working—particularly the former. 4) Look up and see who makes the tackles. It may suggest a play to use." Rockne worked with Carideo, helping him to recognize and out-guess defenses; learn when to hustle play and when to slow it down; when to gamble and when to play it safe; how to conserve energy, saving up for the "goal-line and special scoring plays he kept in his head all the time." It was training meant not just for the quarterback, but to inspire "every player on the team to think along the same lines, so that every one of them could play smart football defensively."

After the Irish dispatched Indiana, 14-0, in the opener, Rockne felt ill and stayed in bed. It had already been a difficult year for him physically; earlier, he had four teeth extracted, after which he suffered a number of ailments. All through the week, there were mixed signals as to whether he would be able to accompany the team to Baltimore for its game with Navy. On Thursday morning, Rockne had a copy of *Gray's Anatomy* on his bed. He called his personal physician, Dr. Sensenich, and said, "Doc, I think I have phlebitis." The scientist Rockne was correct. He suffered from thrombophlebitis, an inflammation of the veins in his legs. Doctors ordered continued bed rest and warned Rockne against excitement—or even activity—that might dislodge a blood clot from his legs and send it through his bloodstream, potentially causing a heart attack or stroke.

Rockne's decision to bring Lieb back on the staff looked prescient.

Every morning and every evening, Lieb came to the Rockne house and sat in the sickroom with the head coach, going over planning and personnel. Lieb then presided over the noon-time football talk and the afternoon practice. The team made the trip to Baltimore without its head coach, where it played before 65,000 fans. In the moments before the game, the regulars were called one by one from the locker room into a small alcove where a telephone had been installed. On the line was Rockne, back in South Bend. He talked to each man about his responsibilities in the game. It was all very calm, not the typical high-pitched pep talk. Finally, Lieb took the phone and the pair finalized the game plan. The atmosphere on the Notre Dame bench reflected the pre-game talk—the Irish were poised and prepared, although their beloved coach was hundreds of miles away. Carideo, the sharp field general, completed a key pass while nearly being tackled, and Notre Dame won, 14-7.

In front of 90,000 spectators in the first of three Soldier Field games, the Irish throttled Wisconsin, 19-0, payback for the 22-6 loss at Madison the previous fall. Next up was Carnegie Tech, the team that always seemed poised to spoil Notre Dame's season. It was only 11 months ago that Wally Steffen's bunch embarrassed the Irish, 27-7, in their final game at Cartier Field. Carnegie had become a thorn in Rockne's side that needed to be extricated. Rockne wanted this one—badly. Rockne ignored his doctors' orders and was on the train with the team as they left for Pittsburgh. On Friday, he lay on a sofa in his room at the Pittsburgh Athletic Club, trading wisecracks and handing out tickets to his coterie of friends and admirers, including a number of newspapermen. In many ways, he was the old Rockne—jovial, witty, full of energy, the center of attention. Friday afternoon, he was wheeled to the gymnasium, where he oversaw the team's drills. That evening, there was quiet in the vicinity of Rockne's room. The coach was not entertaining visitors. It was so unlike the normal hustle and bustle of activity surrounding the night before a big game that rumors began to spread about his condition.

On game day, in the locker room at Forbes Field, where 66,000 fans who packed every nook and cranny awaited the action, Notre Dame's players sat waiting, not sure whether Rockne had even survived the night. Suddenly, the door flung open, and Lieb strode in, carrying Rockne in his arms. He placed him on a table, where Rockne sat with his legs stretched out straight; he looked emotionless, serious, staring straight ahead and saying nothing, seemingly barely conscious of his surroundings. The players fidgeted in the nervous silence. Who was this man masquerading as their coach? They knew him as strong, fierce, animated, and emotional, and now he sat in their midst as an invalid. Was he there merely as a spectator? The moments passed, with the 2 p.m. kickoff now almost upon them. In a corner, team physician Dr. Maurice Kelly said to the man next to him, "If he lets go, and that clot dislodges, to his heart or his brain, he's got an even chance of never leaving this dressing room alive."

Then, as suddenly as a great gust of wind, the coach began to speak, clearly and forcefully. "A lot of water has gone under the bridge since I first came to Notre Dame, but I don't know when I've ever wanted to win a game as badly as this one. I don't care what happens after today. Why do you think I'm taking a chance like this? To see you lose?" His voice, rising now into a shout, went on. "They'll be primed. They'll be tough. They think they have your number. Are you going to let it happen again?" The room went quiet, as Rockne let his words penetrate the players' souls. Then, like a great fighter making a final, valiant charge, he let loose, pouring every ounce of energy into his oration: "Go out there and crack 'em. Crack 'em. Crack 'em. Fight to live. Fight to win. Fight to live. Fight to win, win, WIN!" With a mighty roar, the players exploded from the room toward the field. Rockne collapsed, his eyes closed, his face sweating. The doctor attended to him, wiping his brow. It was no exaggeration to say Rockne had looked death in the face and survived. He wanted his boys to show similar courage—today on the football field, but also some other day, in some other place, when one would be summoned to perform against all odds.

As expected, Carnegie played Notre Dame tough in a fierce, physical battle. Rockne watched the proceedings from his wheelchair, calm now, efficiently grading the results and making adjustments. After a scoreless first half, he expected the Scots to pass; they did, and Notre Dame was ready. The biggest play came when Elder returned a punt to the Carnegie 7-yard line, and from there, the Irish fought their way to the game's only score, a one-yard blast by Savoldi. With their 7-0 victory, the tired and battered Irish, and their ailing coach, made the return trip to South Bend in higher spirits.

Several days after their return, news from the larger world again shook campus. The decade that had started with prosperity unlike any the country had known ended in the stock market crash on October 29, 1929. The nearly 10-year span that saw overvalued stocks, a housing "bubble," and investments based on the unstable basis of margin buying literally ended with a financial jolt. The lead article from the October 30, 1929 *New York Times* said:

> Stock prices virtually collapsed yesterday, swept downward with gigantic losses in the most disastrous trading day in the stock market's history. Billions of dollars in open market values were wiped out as prices crumbled under the pressure of liquidation of securities which had to be sold at any price.
>
> From every point of view, in the extent of losses sustained, in total turnover, in the number of speculators wiped out, the day was the most disastrous in Wall Street's history. Hysteria swept the country and stocks went overboard for just what they would bring at forced sale.
>
> Efforts to estimate yesterday's market losses in dollars are futile because of the vast number of securities quoted over the counter and on out-of-town exchanges on which no calculations are possible. However, it was estimated that 880 issues, on the New York Stock Exchange, lost between $8,000,000,000 and $9,000,000,000 yesterday. Added to that loss is to be reckoned the depreciation on issues on the Curb Market, in the over the counter market and on other exchanges.

Investors bought borrowed money from their brokers, who went to banks for that money. When stocks failed and investors needed to default, the money was permanently lost. Consumer demand for durables such as refrigerators, radios, and automobiles declined. This in turn affected the companies and workers that produced these items, setting a downward spiral in motion. In South Bend, the early years of the decade had been prosperous for the Studebaker Company. By 1923, the South Bend plants, which became one of the major employers in the city, dominated the city's skyline and development. Plant No. 2 included a powerhouse and machine shop with sub assembly buildings. There was the new iron foundry, a forge shop, and a stamping plant adjoining the main building. The car assembly, storage, and shipping buildings occupied adjacent space. Men, many of them first- and second-generation immigrants, flocked to work in the foundries and the assembly plants. Locals made their own fortunes as tool and dye makers, supplying Studebaker with parts. Women worked as office clerks and typists in the company's main building. On January 2, 1927, Albert Erskine led a festive celebration of the company's Diamond Jubilee with more than 1,800 in attendance. But shortly afterward, things would sour for Erskine and Studebaker.

The company introduced a smaller "Erskine 6" model in Paris in the spring of 1927, but it proved to be a disappointment on both sides of the Atlantic. Studebaker also acquired Pierce Arrow in 1928, but despite tweaks in engineering features, sales and profits slumped to their lowest levels since the company had gone public in 1911. Studebaker also incurred a cash drain because Erskine insisted on paying dividends, and went into cash reserves to do so. In 1928 Erskine ordered a 69 percent dividend, and from 1929 on spent more on dividends than the company made in after tax profits. Erskine was adamant about continuing the dividends, firm in his belief that a return to prosperity was "just around the corner."

The stock market crash of 1929 would eventually lead to the Great Depression, which ushered in massive unemployment, a rapid collapse in federal tax collections, a wide distaste for the Republican Party, and the murmurings of a constitutional amendment to repeal Prohibition. Millions of individuals saw their daily lives forever changed. Recent Scandinavian immigrants such as Carla Due, whose family had bought a Nebraska farm just before the crash, saw land values drop to less than half of what it had been. Their farm was no longer worth what they still owed on the land. During those years, Chicago was especially hard-hit. Unemployment was as high as 40 percent in some neighborhoods. In a downtown Chicago office, Les Orear was forced to return home from college after his father lost his job as a newspaperman. "I got the call right after the market crashed and was told I had to come back to Chicago to help support the family," Orear recalled. "I got a job at the stockyards making 37 cents a day." And for the Boyer family, who had grown up in South Bend at the turn of the century, 1929 and 1930 brought personal heartache as well as financial strain. John, who had graduated Notre Dame in 1920 and had obtained his medical degree from the University of Michigan in 1924, died in Detroit at the age of 38 from a staph infection in his blood system in November. He was only a few years into his recently opened medical practice on Grand Boulevard. Gladys made a frantic trip from South Bend to Detroit as a passenger in a two-seat, open-air mail service plane after doctors called and said John was near death. She arrived at the hospital just moments after he died. One of the nurses told her John's last words were, "It's a great day to be alive." His death came less than a year after the family buried sister Helen, who died of tuberculosis. Helen had work in the downtown South Bend millinery shops in the 1910s and married Stephen Kubiak, a Studebaker factory worker.

South Bend residents turned to Notre Dame football for a bit of relief from their troubles and entertainment to brighten their days. And now, like the 1924 and 1926 teams, a string of impressive victories had everyone around town talking about the Irish. With Lieb once again leading the trip in Rockne's absence, the team traveled to Atlanta and ripped Georgia Tech, 26-6, then downed Drake at Soldier Field, 19-7, to bring their record to 6-0. The team had acclimated to a routine in which Rockne arrived at practice on a gurney, often in a hearse provided by the McGann Funeral Home. Managers would carry Rockne up to a wooden tower constructed to overlook the practice field, where he could sit up, his legs wrapped in blankets. There, Rockne's rat-a-tat voice boomed out over the field via a loudspeaker. "Nice going, Savoldi. Big Joe is going to go in there Saturday. Attaboy Savoldi. Big Joe will go." Whoever was in need of a boost, Rockne was there to provide it, now in a most public way.

Despite the stock market crash and the deteriorating economic conditions, ticket demand for the November 16th clash with Southern Cal was insatiable. Southern Cal was making its second trip to Soldier Field, and again more than 112,000 turned out on a brilliant fall afternoon, the largest crowd in Chicago sports history. It was billed as the game of the decade, and notables from the worlds of education, politics, industry, entertainment, religion, and, of course, sports attended. Included were mayors Jimmy Walker of New York and Chicago's William Thompson; Vincent Bendix and Studebaker's Erskine were among the business leaders; former world's heavyweight champ Jack Dempsey was on hand, as was movie actress Anita Page. In the Irish locker room, Rockne was "brought in on a wheel-cot, looking wan and tired." This time it took only a few words to inspire the boys. In the first half, Jack Elder stood out by launching a pass from midfield that Tom Conley secured at the 15-yard line and walked into the end zone. With the score tied 6-6 in the second half, a dive by Savoldi netted the second touchdown, and Carideo added the point for a 13-6 lead. Southern Cal ace Russ Saunders took the ensuing kickoff 95 yards for a touchdown, but the Trojans missed the point-after, and Notre Dame came away with a 13-12 victory.

The next Saturday, it was back to Chicago for a 26-6 victory over Northwestern at Evanston before a crowd of more than 50,000. The Irish were now 8-0, with the season finale against Army at Yankee Stadium the only thing standing in the way of a perfect season. The demand for tickets was again enormous. The *Scholastic* reported this typical exchange in the athletic offices: "We are very sorry, sir, but the ticket sale for the Army game was closed October 3, and at the present time we have no tickets and do not expect to have any." The unhappy fan says, "But I have made a special trip here from Cleveland; I must have tickets. Can't Mr. Rockne help me?" And the reply: "I am sorry, but we can do nothing to help you; Mr. Rockne is ill and has no tickets."

Rockne's health remained a constant concern with scant evidence to indicate a change in his condition. Yet, there was little doubt Rockne would make the trip east with his squad. The importance of the Army game, and the chance to renew acquaintances with eastern writers and good friends from West Point like Colonel Herman J. Koehler, Master of the Sword, was too much for Rockne to pass on the trip. On Friday night, he sat on his bed with a glass in his hand, chatting with visitors. The work on the field once again had fallen to Lieb. Friday practice was held at the Westchester Country Club in Rye, New York, where the team was headquartered. A gallery of onlookers didn't know what to make of it when Lieb himself lofted a series of long passes to "Army's right end" who was crossing over to the left side of the field, with Jack Elder defending. In the second quarter the next day, the answer came, with Army driving deep into Notre Dame territory. Chris Cagle, Army's outstanding back, swept wide to his right, stopped, and launched a pass to the opposite corner of the field; Army receiver Ed Messinger raced toward the spot as the ball spiraled straight and true, for what appeared to be a sure touchdown. But Elder had crossed the field and stepped in front of the receiver, picking off the ball at the 3-yard line. The track star evaded an Army tackler around the 20 and took off along the sideline, keeping his balance on the icy turf while outrunning the rest of the Cadets. The score held up for a 7-0 victory before 79,000 fans, and Notre Dame celebrated a 9-0 season. The Notre Dame band, 83 strong under director Joseph Casasanta and making its first trip to an Army game, serenaded the thousands of Irish faithful in attendance at Yankee Stadium.

The sheer number of rabid fans who had watched Rockne's Ramblers make the road their home established the 1929 season as one for the ages. For the first time since 1924, Notre Dame stood alone at the top of the college football world, as consensus national champions, edging out Jock Sutherland's 9-0 Pittsburgh Panthers. As Grantland Rice noted in his column, "There is no questioning the fact that among the unbeaten teams who were not even tied, Notre Dame fought its way through the hardest field." The road had not always been an easy one for the coach, but there could be no denying the sense of satisfaction. Back on campus, the outline of a modern new stadium was rising, and the man most responsible for its construction needed to focus on his health in order to enjoy fruits of his labor. The decision by the Holy Cross fathers to proceed on the stadium without borrowing money looked wise indeed, given the financial uncertainty that now plagued the nation. And for Knute Rockne, the winds of fate had kept him at Notre Dame while other colleges beckoned. During the 1929 season in particular, it was a comfort to remain at the school that had been his home for nearly two decades.

# 29

## Perfection Again

I n early 1930 at the University of Detroit, head football coach Gus Dorais received a call from his old friend and teammate Knute Rockne, asking if Dorais would be able to go to breakfast. Dorais asked Rockne what brought him to town. "I'm going to give a talk...to the Catholic Ladies Study Guild," came Rockne's reply. Dorais seemed startled, and asked what Rockne's topic would be. "Oh, I don't know what I'll talk about, but it's all right. I was reading the *Atlantic Monthly* on the train." Rockne did, in fact, talk to the Ladies Guild about football, and they loved every minute of it. On his next trip to Detroit, Rockne spoke to a group of automobile dealers, and, Dorais explained, "he told some of the best trained, most capable salesmen in the country how to sell cars, and they loved it, too. He had those salesmen cheering and whistling at the end, more worked up than his own football teams ever got." Dorais would chuckle, thinking back to the Rockne he remembered addressing the Notre Dame football dinner their senior year, 1913. Rockne had been embarrassed, and was fumbling, halting, and red-faced. Just more than a decade later, Rockne's transformation into one of the most sought-after speakers in the nation was truly remarkable. It spoke to Rockne's persistence, to a never-ending quest for self-improvement, and an absolute refusal to rest on his accomplishments. Sometimes, it was a refusal to rest, period.

In January 1930, Rockne and the family vacationed in Miami. On January 16, he sent former player and current University of Florida head coach Charlie Bachman a hand-written note that he "arrived here Tuesday but in bad shape as regards my legs. Will not be able to get around any for a month at least. Did not wire you to meet me at Jacksonville as I could not get out of berth anyway. Is there any chance for you to drop down here, we have a great plan for me to sort of vegetate…Will drive up in our car to your place just as soon as I can travel. Have lots of football I want to go over with you…As ever, Rock."

The vacation was the closest thing to an extended period of rest and recuperation that Rockne had ever attempted. While in Florida, he needed to summon his personal physician Dr. C.J. Barborka to check Rockne for what was reported to be "aethmatic bronchitis." By April, Rockne was on an early train for Rochester, Minnesota for a stay at the Mayo Clinic. He was accompanied by assistant coach Jack Chevigny and Dr. Barborka. From Rochester, Rockne sent a letter to the *Scholastic*, stating, "I hope to be back with you at least by the second week of May." He assured the students and his many friends that he would not leave Rochester until cleared to do so by doctors. "I have had too many upsets to be taking any chances," he wrote. But the *Scholastic*, knowing Rockne well, opined, "Deep down in his heart there is a big urge to get back to the old battleground, see his boys in action once again, and send his voice booming across the gridiron."

Rockne returned to campus by mid-May and immediately sent brief letters to Bachman and a handful of other close coaching associates, informing them, "We are holding a meeting of all the Notre Dame coaches in my office at one o'clock, May 31, to discuss the problem which affects all of us very vitally." It's suspected the hush-hush meeting was called to cover contingencies in case Rockne—or his doctors—determined that his health would not allow him to coach Notre Dame's 1930 squad. Still, Rockne swung back into action with an appearance at the school's commencement exercises at the end of May. The coach also presided over one of the best-attended Monogram Luncheons, held in conjunction with commencement. He introduced more than 75 letter winners, many of them his former players who were now coaches. Among those he welcomed back to campus were the Four Horsemen, Slip Madigan, Chuck Collins, Adam Walsh, Harry Mehre, Chet Wynne, Rodge Kiley, Chile Walsh, Biffy Lee, Jack Meagher, Harry Baujan, Judge Carberry, Hunk Anderson, Red Magevney, Rex Enright, Bill Cerney, Dan Lamont, Wilbur Eaton, John Noppenberger, Noble Kizer, Joe Harmon, John Frederick, and his old comrade Gus Dorais. Older Monogram men on hand included Frank Hering, Red Miller, Walter Miller, Joe Pliska, and Byron Kanaley. It was as if these men, some of the closest to Rockne over the years, knew they needed to be at this event.

When students returned to Notre Dame in September, they were greeted by two impressive new structures representing the university's bold efforts at improvement and expansion. The new stadium and the Law Building culminated years of planning and fund-raising by presidents Cavanaugh, Burns, Walsh, and O'Donnell. The structures announced to the athletic and academic world that Notre Dame was serious about staying among the giants in college football, as well as becoming a prestigious academic institution. Notre Dame's College of Law was established in 1869, making it the oldest Catholic law school in the nation. Now, it would be housed in a most impressive building. "The new Law School Building at Notre Dame, as to its position and architectural character, represents the initiation of a most important change in the physical organism of the University," the Notre Dame *Alumnus* wrote. "The President, Rev. Charles O'Donnell, C.S.C., is persuaded that future building at Notre Dame should be controlled by a most thoughtful regard for the interests of architectural unity and harmony. The Law Building definitely strikes a note of collegiate Gothic which is to be consistently associated with the future building program."

On the football practice field, in the shadow of the new stadium, another innovation was in the works. Rockne, it was reported, would coach the Irish by means of a public address system. "Seated in a specially constructed tower and speaking into a microphone, the noted mentor's caustic remarks will be carried to his team by means of amplifiers which will reach all parts of the practice field," the Notre Dame *Alumnus* reported. "Coach Rockne was ill last season and most of the winter and while his physical condition is said to have greatly improved, he is expected carefully to conserve his strength for the arduous duties that will be his this coming fall in whipping another championship team into shape." Two young South Bend technicians, Albert Kahn and L.R. Burroughs, built the apparatus Rockne would use and marketed it under the name Electro-Voice Manufacturing Co.

Perhaps the most impressive aspect of the stadium was the fact construction was completed essentially in four months. Although work began in September 1929, labor on the foundations did not start until April 1930. On April 19, a battery of mixers and pourers began to lay the foundation, and little more than four months later, the brickwork had been completed, seats had been erected, and the stadium was ready. The seats were made of genuine, almost indestructible California redwood, immune to the effects of the harsh South Bend weather. Some 400 tons of steel made up the framework of the stadium, and 75 rail carloads of cement went into the mixers. The 500 men who worked on the stadium required nearly a ton of food each day, and 500 gallons of water. The sod from 35-year-old Cartier Field, famous for its firm texture, was transferred to the new stadium, first cut into ribbons, then rolled up like carpet, then unfurled at the stadium and tamped into place to form a perfect gridiron. It was a quite practical use of excellent sod, of course, but the gesture also spoke to the spirit of the Notre Dame teams who had won all but a handful of games on the old field.

On October 4, a crowd of just under 15,000 came out to see the first game at the new stadium, something of a dry run, as Notre Dame beat Southern Methodist, 20-14. Ponies coach J. Ray Morrison was a long-time friend of Rockne's, and he had helped host Rockne's coaching school in the summers of 1928 and 1929 in Dallas. The Irish played without their starting right tackle, senior Frank Leahy, who suffered a leg injury in workouts and was lost for the season. His replacement, 6-foot-2 Dick Donoghue, was clipped from behind in the SMU game and tore his Achilles tendon. Rockne, frustrated over the way things had started, was disappointed when Donoghue said he couldn't move. At the team meeting the following Monday, he questioned Donoghue's courage. "To hear my idol, the usually fair-minded Rockne, call me gutless in front of my own team-mates was totally out of character for him." Donoghue insisted on playing the next game—the official stadium dedication to be played against Navy, which would be making its first trip to South Bend.

A celebratory atmosphere engulfed South Bend for Stadium Dedication weekend. On Friday evening, October 10, thousands entered the new edifice for the first time to attend the official dedication. The university band led a student march around campus; as it reached each residence hall, students fell in line. Once at the stadium, amplifiers were set up for all the speakers. First up was Prof. Clarence Manion of the Law School, who opened the ceremonies, and "proved himself a brave man indeed by his stoicism when his first words into the amplifier came echoing back from the distant end of the stadium." Among the honored guests was G. K. Chesterton, the influential British writer and philosopher who was on campus as part of an American speaking tour. He was given "a rousing ovation when he took his place in one of the front row seats." After Rockne and President O'Donnell addressed the crowd, the impressive pageant concluded with "the explosion of multi-colored bombs over the stands."

On Saturday, more than 40,000 exuberant fans—double the previous record attendance at Cartier Field—comprised the largest crowd to watch a game at Notre Dame. The Irish made the occasion memorable, defeating Navy, 26-2, behind three touchdowns by Savoldi. The *Scholastic* noted: "With the new stadium dedicated, Rockne's dream has come true. Maybe he has another dream—maybe he has dreamed that the great Notre Dame teams will make the same glorious record in the new stadium that they did in the old; that future students will talk reverently about the ghosts of another Gipp, or another Four Horsemen, that roam within the walls of Notre Dame Stadium. We wonder."

The next week the Irish hosted Carnegie Tech, which had just hammered Georgia Tech, 31-0. Rockne earnestly promoted the Skibos. "We're scared dizzy of Carnegie. This is sincere. Our team has been coming along as well as expected, but doesn't begin to stack up with Wally Steffen's boys." A crowd of 30,000 watched the Irish take care of Carnegie Tech, 21-6. A trip to Pittsburgh resulted in a 35-19 victory over Pitt, followed by a 27-0 pasting of Indiana. The Irish had started another season

5-0, running their winning streak to 14 games. They were playing with the moxie and creativity Rockne loved. "Rock urged us to be independent out there," Carideo later reflected. "He wanted us to show the courage of our convictions. Whenever I was in doubt I did what I thought best, because I knew that was what Rock wanted. He simply told us to use the knowledge he had implanted in us. We had a large arsenal. If you wanted to put variations on them, we had hundreds of plays in our attack. But Rock always narrowed the selection down each Saturday to fit a particular defense. His credo was, 'Use the best we have against their weakest spots. Be intelligent. When we get the ball, don't just bang away. Ask yourself, what is the best maneuver against a certain defense?'"

Next up was a trip to Philadelphia's Franklin Field to meet the University of Pennsylvania Quakers. It was Notre Dame's first meeting with an Ivy League opponent since its victories over Princeton in 1923 and 1924. A capacity crowd of more than 75,000 filled the massive stadium for a game billed as a homecoming for Marty Brill, the Irish back who had begun college at Penn before a falling out with Quakers coach Ludlow Wray. There were stories rumored—and vehemently denied—that Brill's father was offering him $1,000 for every touchdown he could score that day. For much of the season to date, Brill had distinguished himself by blocking for Savoldi and Marchy Schwartz. On this day, the roles were reversed, and Schwartz repeatedly blocked for his pal. Carideo called more running plays for Brill than on any other Saturday, and Marty responded with three scores in a 60-20 rout. "Marty was brilliant," Schwartz said. "I never saw him run better. He turned in a spectacular all-around performance."

The final home game of 1930 ended with a workmanlike 28-7 victory over Drake. Then, on November 22, the Irish found themselves in an old-time, back-and-forth, scoreless stalemate with undefeated Northwestern in front of 45,000 in Evanston. Dick Hanley, a good friend of Rockne's, had already guided the Wildcats to a share of the Big Ten title with wins over Ohio State, Illinois, Minnesota, Indiana, and Wisconsin. A victory over Notre Dame would complete a perfect season. Late in the fourth quarter, Notre Dame took the ball near midfield, and Carideo looked over to Rockne, who gave him a signal to punt on first down. The move caught the Wildcats by surprise and pushed them back against their goal. On the next four straight possessions, Carideo dropped perfect punts deep in

Northwestern territory. Notre Dame took advantage of the short field to score twice, pulling out a 14-0 victory. Roy Mills, the kicking genius who had guided Carideo over the past few summers, trekked from New York to South Bend the next week at Carideo's invitation and spent an afternoon comparing notes with Rockne. Mills watched the Irish work out and commented, "With that sort of enthusiasm, I don't see how Notre Dame will ever lose again." Replied Carideo, "We owe it all to Rock, his leadership. He's got us believing in ourselves." Mills agreed, "I know. I wasn't with him five minutes before I felt it."

For the first time, the Notre Dame-Army game would not take place in the state of New York. Father O'Donnell had asked the Academy to shift the site of the 1930 game to Soldier Field in Chicago, due to academic considerations. With the Irish's final game scheduled December 6 at Southern Cal, a trip to New York the week before would have put the Irish on the road for too many school days for the faculty's liking. It also allowed Notre Dame to reprise its hugely successful games at the mammoth stadium, as another crowd topping 100,000 braved rain and snow on November 29 to attend the battle. The protective hay and tarpaulin, when removed from the field, uncovered a gridiron glazed with a thin coating of ice.

With just minutes remaining, a quick kick by Carideo traveled 60 yards in the air and pushed the Cadets deep in their zone. The Irish defense held, and after an Army punt, Notre Dame took over at its own 46-yard line. On the next play—out of the shift—Schwartz and Mullins formed the right half of the box. Bert Metzger, the little guard, pulled out and led interference ahead of Carideo, Mullins, and the ball carrier Schwartz. Marty Brill, Joe Kurth, and Tom Conley all provided key blocks, which allowed Schwartz to break loose for 54 yards and a touchdown; Carideo's kick made it 7-0. But in the final minute, with Carideo punting from his own 10, an Army surge blocked the kick and the Cadets recovered, scored, and pulled to within 7-6. Army's Church Broshous stood bareheaded on the 12-yard-line, waiting to drop-kick a ball that the Cadets continued to wipe dry in the sleeting elements. The lines crashed together, and Notre Dame's wall surged upon Broshous; the ball never moved from the ground. Notre Dame won the classic, 7-6, and headed to California still undefeated.

In Southern Cal, Notre Dame faced a squad that had also made headlines across the country. Howard Jones' boys were 8-1, winning six straight games since an early 7-6 loss at Washington State. In their last three games they had outscored Cal, Hawaii, and Washington by a combined 158-0. The Irish were 9-0 largely on the strength of a strong running game, and Rockne saw no need to diversify his attack. So when Carideo and Schwartz began flinging short passes on the floor of the Coliseum, the Trojans and 74,000 spectators were shocked. Some in the Southern Cal camp expected "an overtired team from the East," but Notre Dame possessed great energy, rolling to a remarkable 27-0 upset. Reported the *Scholastic*: "Even the most optimistic supporter of the team lacked the imagination to foresee such a complete slaughter of the Trojans. The overwhelming victory clinched the football championship of the United States. It provided further proof that Rockne is the master mind among coaches…The nation marvels at the deed of Coach Rockne and his band of gridiron warriors."

Rockne's good friend and California resident Will Rogers, in attendance for the game, said afterward:

> There we were all packed in the stadium, really pitying those poor little boys from back there in South Bend and hoping that the California kids wouldn't seriously hurt any of them running over them on the way to the goal posts. Well, on the very first play USC fumbled. From then on it was just too bad. You never saw a team beaten so coolly and deliberate-like. Notre Dame when they came out of the huddle would walk so slow to their places, and that got poor USC's goat….It wasn't the score, it was the deliberate and mechanical way they did it. It was a machine doing things where the others were trying their hands.
>
> And here was a great thing Rock did. As each of his stars were taken out in the last half—and it was their last game for Notre Dame—he would jump up from the bench and go out and meet each boy and hug him; you could just see the affection that he had for each one, and it was conveyed to that whole audience. I will never forget when little Carideo left the field. He had played a whale of a game, had handled his team expertly…I

think Rockne pulled him out just to get him that great ovation as he left the stadium. Well, when old Rock went out and flung his arm around the little Carideo and walked him off the field, it wasn't an ovation; it was a hurricane.

Upon their return on December 10, a crowd of 25,000 greeted the Irish. All business in town was suspended for two hours to allow people to assemble at the Union station. Unlike some of the raucous homecomings of prior years, though, this was a more subdued, mature homage of respect to Rockne's fellows. Beaming faces looked at one another as if to say, "Can you believe it? They've done it again." Among the speakers at the celebration was 1924 captain Adam Walsh, who called the 1930 Irish "marvelous." The team's winning streak stood at 19 games, and the national championship was Notre Dame's third in seven years. The 10-0 Irish were a near-unanimous selection of those choosing a national champion. Alabama, coached by Wallace Wade, also finished 10-0 with a Rose Bowl victory over Washington State and finished second. As in 1929, Notre Dame received the nod due to vanquishing the "suicide schedule" Rockne assembled. No other team could boast of traveling the miles to defeat the teams the Irish had beaten. No fewer than seven Irish stars merited one All-American honor or another—quarterback Frank Carideo, halfbacks Marchy Schwartz and Marty Brill, fullback Joe Savoldi, guard Bert Metzger, end Tom Conley, and tackle Al Culver.

The 42-year-old Rockne had now spent nearly half his life affiliated with Notre Dame since arriving as a 22-year-old freshman in 1910. His 13-year stint as head coach of the Irish had produced an amazing record of 105-12-5. He was in demand as a syndicated newspaper columnist, selector of All-America teams, radio commentator, and motion picture advisor. He also had an expanded role motivating sales executives of South Bend's Studebaker car company. Clearly, the journey had brought him to a pinnacle even he may not have envisioned.

During the 1930 season, as in recent years, offers poured in for Rockne and Notre Dame to play in postseason charity games, in a variety of formats and locations. Groups across the nation looked to raise funds to help those in need during the economic crisis caused by the stock market crash of October 1929. A year after the collapse, the nation's economy was in terrible shape. But university officials remained absolute in their refusal to allow a postseason game. It would be impossible for Notre Dame to accept one game and disappoint so many others.

Unemployment was the stark reality for millions in the fall of 1930, and nowhere were more people out of work than in New York City. Mayor Jimmy Walker began the Mayor's Relief Committee in hopes of providing aid to the unemployed and needy. He strongly urged college and professional teams in several sports to consider staging exhibition games in New York to benefit the fund. Rockne, with his great popularity and deep connections among New York newspaper and radio men, performers, and politicians, often came up in any talk of benefit games. So it was only natural for sportswriter Dan Daniel to approach Rockne during the season with an invitation to bring his Notre Dame team to the big city for an exhibition after the college campaign ended.

Rockne, who never forgot his humble immigrant beginnings, looked at the proposed date—December 14—and knew it would be a stretch, coming just one week after the grueling trip to southern California. He proposed an alternative. He would muster a group of former Notre Dame stars to take on the opponent, professional football's New York Giants. The two sides struck a deal, and in the closing weeks of the Irish season, commitments from various former Irish standouts—including The Four Horsemen and several of the Seven Mules—came into Rockne's office. The game was promoted as the "Notre Dame All Stars" vs. the Giants. When it came time to assemble the team in person, the euphoria of the USC triumph and the legendary backgrounds of the "All-Stars" could only account for so much optimism. In reality, it had been some time since many of the ex-Irish had suited up or been in game condition. But despite the distance in time from their prime playing days, the former Irish stars answered the call from their beloved coach to help benefit others. Rockne described his team's participation as such: "Notre Dame teams consider New York City as their second home. It is now almost ten years since the Army-Notre Dame game outgrew West Point and was moved to New York. Ever since, our players have been received with the warm friendliness that the big town would usually reserve for its own. Consequently, it is our privilege and pleasure to contribute our services in this game to swell Mayor James Walker's Fund for the needy unemployed."

The motley crew gathered in South Bend, and, after a handful of workouts, headed to New York. On the morning of Saturday, December 13, Rockne and the "All-Stars" attended a ceremony at City Hall in which the mayor and other dignitaries honored their participation in the charity game. Next, they made a quick visit to the Polo Grounds for a final practice. The Giants, on the other hand, were a well-honed group of professional athletes battling for a National Football League championship. Led by quarterback Bennie Friedman and tackle Steve Owen, they had reeled off eight straight wins to boost their record to 10-1 by early November, before losing three of their next four games. But they rallied to close the pro season with a pair of victories. By the time kickoff came on Sunday afternoon, December 14, in a chilly Polo Grounds, it was obvious to almost everyone that the two sides were in for a mismatch. When Rockne and Friedman met prior to kickoff, Rockne asked for some concessions from the Giants' leader. "Free substitutions?" Rockne asked. "Fine," said Friedman. "Ten minute quarters?" asked Rockne. "Twelve and a half minutes," said Friedman impishly as they shook hands again. "Anything else?" asked Friedman. "Yes, one thing," said Rockne. "For Pete's sake, take it easy."

The on-field result wasn't pretty for Rockne and his charges. Even when more recent backs such as Carideo, Jack Elder, and Bucky O'Connor replaced the Horsemen, the results were similar. For the game, the Notre Dame "All-Stars" managed just one first down, 34 yards rushing, and never crossed midfield. Friedman, meanwhile, led a strong Giants attack that marched up and down the field en route to a convincing 22-0 win. The greatest victory, though, was the money raised for the unemployed. Gate receipts for the event totaled $115,153.

After Frank Leahy's season-ending injury during the SMU opener, Rockne made Leahy one of his assistants. Each day in practice, Leahy had a chance to observe everything the coach said and did. One day, Rockne called Leahy over and said, "Frank, why in the world are you so downhearted?" Leahy replied, "Rock, because I am not able to be part of this great season." Rockne said, "Well, stop worrying about anything physical, because at the conclusion of the season I am going up to Mayo Clinic, and I am going to take you with me." As promised, Rockne and Leahy headed for Minnesota. Rockne arrived in South Bend after the New York game just as classes were ending for Christmas vacation. On the last day, he sent team manager Danny Halpen to Frank Leahy's room to inform Leahy that he needed to be packed and at the South Bend train station at 8:15 that evening. Rockne's own reasons for heading to Mayo included a need for a thorough examination and rest, and to make sure that the recent twitching in his leg was not a recurrence of phlebitis. Dr. Barborka said Rockne was suffering from fatigue "induced by strain of emotions" to which he was subjected during the football season. "Mr. Rockne looks fine," the doctor said. "Except that he is tired from strain and from making three or four speeches every day. His condition is just what is expected of anyone who has gone through such a strenuous season."

For 14 days, Rockne and Leahy were hospital roommates, and for 14 days, the senior tackle peppered his coach with football questions. "Never once," said Leahy, "did he refuse to try and answer to the best of his ability all that I asked him." Eventually, Rockne suggested that Leahy might want to go into coaching football himself. "And, Frank," he said, "once you arrive you should work your heart out, be very, very thorough, and above all else, be your natural self. Don't ever attempt to emulate, don't ever try to copy anyone's way of speaking or anyone's vocabulary. Be yourself at all times! If you aren't that, the players will soon recognize the fact and won't respect you. Don't be an actor. Your players will never, never be thoroughly fond of actors on a steady basis. They will not respect that type of man. You must be the sort of man that you can be each and every single hour of the day."

Back in South Bend, the *Tribune* reported, "Rumors regarding the possibility that Knute K. Rockne would retire from active coaching and confine his work at Notre Dame to that of athletic director, starting next season, persisted in South Bend today. Persons holding this opinion point out that Rockne has several times in the last few weeks expressed doubt as to whether 'it was worth it all,' and made other utterances which would indicate that possibly he was beginning to tire of the constant glare of publicity and manifold duties that accompany the present position. They also say that Rockne has, like Bobby Jones, 'won about all there is to win.'" Speculation on a replacement centered on Harry Stuhldreher, 37-12-4 in six seasons as head coach of Villanova, possibly assisted by Hunk Anderson. Other names floated included former Irish stars Jimmy Phelan, just finished with his first season at Washington after an eight-year run at Purdue, and Slip Madigan, the charismatic and popular coach at St. Mary's of California.

Dr. Barborka, finding the coach in a state of complete exhaustion, warned that an attack of phlebitis was likely to recur "or a complete breakdown result unless he quits his strenuous mode of living and takes life easy. His outside interests coupled with the strenuous work of coaching are too much for one man." Barborka explained that his findings did not mean that Rockne must quit coaching, but that Rockne should curb his other activities. Barborka also gave a stern warning against Rockne traveling to Los Angeles for another charity postseason game, noting that if the coach "flies to Los Angeles we will refuse to assume responsibility for his future care." Rockne's only comment on the doctor's statement was, "I am here resting and have no definite plans," thus allowing speculation on his coaching future to continue. On December 24, Bonnie and the children arrived from South Bend to spend a Christmas far from home, but together as a family. They spent part of Christmas Day at Dr. Barborka's home in Rochester. Rockne departed Rochester on December 30—but only after fulfilling a speaking engagement at a Knights of Columbus banquet the night before.

As 1931 began, Rockne did not appear to be limiting his schedule. Due to the salary he was receiving from Studebaker, he felt obligated to meet the speaking schedule that came with the position. On January 20, Rockne delivered a major address to the Studebaker annual convention at the Detroit-Leland Hotel. In typical fashion, Rockne allowed, "I don't know anything about selling automobiles; I never sold a car in my life. Perhaps a few remarks here on the psychology that is necessary for success in a football organization might not be out of place, because the same psychology will make for success in any organization, particularly in a selling organization."

Rockne went on to describe the five kinds of athletes he didn't want: the swellhead who rests on his laurels and ceases to make an effort; the chronic complainer; the quitter; the lad who dissipates energy through all types of outside activities; and the man who suffers from an inferiority complex. Regarding the latter, he noted, "If there are any among you who feel that way, forget about it and get a superiority complex. I say to the lads, 'You are just as good as any man out here, and by getting a superiority complex you can show the coach you belong at the top of the 33 men where you think you would like to be.'"

Rockne told of how he talked to his players about ambition. "I say ambition—the right kind of ambition—means that you must have the ability to cooperate with the men around you, men who are working with you; and it is my observation that ability to cooperate is more essential than individual technique. In this day and age of ours, no individual stands alone anymore; he must be able to cooperate in every sense of the word." And the coach added that "there can be no ambition without perseverance…the ability to stick in there and keep giving your best at all times; the ability to stay in there and keep trying when the going is tough and you are behind and everything seems hopeless. There can be no success, no reward, unless every man has the ability to stay in there until the last whistle blows."

Rockne certainly had plenty of material from the recent championship seasons on which to draw. He told several stories of specific games and situations. In one instance, the Irish had pulled out a last-minute victory, but it wasn't the result that mattered. "Winning that game wasn't the most important thing," he said. "The most important thing to me was the fact that this team wouldn't be beaten and proved to me that the team or the individual who wouldn't be beaten couldn't be beaten. This also applies to you men out there on the firing line. You men are facing keen competition this year, perhaps facing more opposition than you ever faced in your lives, but I say to you that this is the sort of challenge you should thrill to. I think your organization—the Studebaker organization—has demonstrated that you can go better when the going is tougher, and I say to you that this year you should thrill to the challenge."

Paul Castner then accompanied Rockne on a trip traversing the Western states. They began at the automobile show in Kansas City on February 9; next was Dallas-Fort Worth. From there they swung up to Minneapolis-St. Paul, then out west to Spokane, Portland, and Seattle, and finally Salt Lake City on the way back to South Bend. At Spokane, Rockne met former Irish star Maurice "Clipper" Smith at the station. Smith had succeeded Dorais as head coach at Gonzaga when Gus went on to the University of Detroit. Smith had been renting a room at the home of the local Cadillac dealer, so he was driving a Cadillac the dealer had loaned him. A press photographer was also on hand to greet Rockne, and posed Smith and Rockne for several pictures, standing in front of the Cadillac. Rockne, trying not to be too obvious, kept positioning himself to block the Cadillac hood emblem from the shot. On the way to Rockne's hotel, Smith asked him, "Why the fuss back there at the station?" Rockne replied, "You don't understand. I'm out here representing Studebaker. I can't be seen riding around in a Cadillac!" He then instructed Smith to take side streets to get him to the hotel.

The next day, Rockne spoke to some 500 Studebaker dealers and others from throughout the Pacific Northwest. Rockne was asked about athletes who became successful after leaving college. He noted, "There have been bankers, lawyers, judges, automobile executives, engineers, doctors, research scientists, and teachers—all with splendid Notre Dame football backgrounds." When asked why, he thought a minute and said: "Well, they learn not to procrastinate but instead do the thing now! They learn how to cooperate in team play, and cooperation is the essence of big business. They learn to keep on trying even though results seem hopeless. How important this is for life I hardly need to say. They learn self-restraint and self-control. They overcome fear and become essentially courageous. And lastly, what is most important of all, they learn fair play and to know themselves."

The coach could just as easily have been describing himself.

# 30

## The Final Ride

In March 1931, the Notre Dame Athletic Board discussed the continuation of the series with the University of Southern California. It was time to renew the agreement, Rockne reported to the board. If Notre Dame didn't approve it soon, the risk of losing the rivalry loomed. University vice president Father Michael Mulcaire, who had recently challenged Rockne and his methods, argued against continuing the series. "The game involves too much train travel," Mulcaire said, implying that football players missed too much school.

"But we go out there only every other year," Rockne replied. "Anyway, in a few years all teams will be giving up trains for air travel."

"Have you lost your senses?" Mulcaire responded, clearly agitated. "We will never allow such a thing!"

"It probably sounds far-fetched now," Rockne allowed, "but I see the day coming when most college teams will be going by air exclusively. As a matter of fact, I'm flying to Los Angeles next week."

"You're out of your mind," Mulcaire sniffed.

For Rockne, the future was to be embraced, not denied. He knew no other way. If there was a new invention to do something quicker, more efficiently, or more thoroughly, he wanted to know more. Rockne had been a student of flight almost since his days as a teenager spent reading of the Wright brothers and their experiments at Kitty Hawk. In the past 20 years, traveling all directions the length and breadth of the country, he had logged countless miles and endless hours on trains, breathing the soot from steam locomotives and being awakened by lurching starts and stops. As much as he enjoyed chatting with fellow passengers, the trips became long and difficult, especially when phlebitis came along. The advantages of traveling by air were almost too obvious. He had already taken several flights, and he looked forward to many more.

Air travel seemed especially appealing to Rockne as he carried out his duties for Studebaker Corp., traveling to speak to sales meetings 20 or more times a year, in locations from coast to coast. Earlier in March, Albert Erskine, president of Studebaker and chairman of the board of lay trustees at Notre Dame, appointed Rockne manager of sales promotion for Studebaker. Erskine was enthusiastic about the plans he approved in 1930 for a new car line named after the coach. Paul Hoffman provided Rockne with his own office at company headquarters, next to that of Jim Cleary, vice president of sales. Just down the hallway, Paul Castner had his office; he was delighted to have the coach nearby, though it was unclear how often Rockne would actually occupy his office. It was also uncertain how the new Studebaker position would affect his "day job" as athletic director and head football coach at Notre Dame. If Father O'Donnell even knew of the promotion, his power to intervene in Rockne's affairs was negligible.

Rockne was also mulling an interesting offer from Universal Pictures in California: $50,000 to appear in a motion picture version of the Broadway musical *Good News*. The feel-good story opened on Broadway in 1927 and wowed audiences with its energy and cheer in telling the story of romance, academics, and football at fictional Tait College. Rockne, in an attempt to gain presidential approval of his role in the project, wrote O'Donnell a letter in which he downplayed his own interest in appearing in the film, but noted that perhaps he could influence Universal to create a movie more directly about Notre Dame. "There might be a chance to put out a picture that might be instructive and educational as regards Notre Dame in every sense of the word." A trip to Los Angeles to discuss the film project would be necessary. Rockne quickly thought of the other business that could be conducted on such a journey.

After signing his new agreement with Studebaker, Rockne left South Bend on Thursday, March 19, flying from Chicago to Miami, to join Bonnie, Mary Jeanne, and Jackie at their rented winter house in Coral Gables for fun and relaxation. On Saturday, March 21, Knute and Bonnie joined Frank and Mary Wallace at the Hialeah Race Track. As was customary, Rockne was the star of the show, with local officials escorting him to the track's executive box, high above the rest of the pari-mutuel bettors below. "He was contentedly relaxed," Wallace observed. "He did not seem to have to prove anything." He was able to just "sit and enjoy it." Smoking his cigar and looking out over the track, Rockne told another writer that his health had improved greatly, and he was looking forward to another football season. When asked about his airplane trips, Rockne said: "I travel often by air. I like it. With a good plane and a good pilot, it's as safe as any other method of travel and much more comfortable."

Leo Ward, close Rockne friend and confidante, was certain that Rockne's coaching days were drawing to a close. He had already had a very serious health scare with the phlebitis, and his doctors continued to warn him that the stress of coaching was taking a further toll on his body. The rub, in Rockne's mind, was the place football had in his life. It challenged him and fulfilled him, kept his faculties sharp and his drive strong. He truly loved to work turning teenage boys into young men through the rigors of athletics. Rockne might grouse about faculty and administration making his life miserable, but in truth he had extremely wide latitude in running the Notre Dame program, while continuing to operate coaching schools, work for Studebaker, and sell books and articles. Now, it seemed, he would have the opportunity to appear in films. He had to ask himself: by stepping away from football, and all the headlines it brought him, would the spotlight quickly fade, and in turn affect his other ventures? But, as was usually the case, Rockne had precious little time for much deep reflection. His schedule was too full. After a few days at the track and on the beach, he returned to South Bend, leaving Bonnie and the younger kids with hugs and kisses. They'd all be back home before too long, he said, after he returned from the West Coast.

His schedule for the Los Angeles trip continued to fill when he agreed to join Will Rogers as speakers for a Los Angeles Junior Chamber of Commerce luncheon on Thursday, April 2. Rockne seldom passed up a chance to join his great pal Rogers, if it was at all possible. This would be a great time to get together, after concluding his business with Universal pictures. On Saturday, March 28, Rockne dashed off a quick letter to Charlie Bachman, to say that he "enjoyed very much our short visit while in Jacksonville" and that "I hope the family stops at least a little while in Gainesville when they come up." As for spring practice, Rockne noted that it was "going along just so-so, but it might be worse."

That evening, in Father O'Donnell's office at the Main Building, another of Rockne's coaching recommendations came to fruition. Bill Jones, about to graduate with a law degree, had been helping coach Notre Dame's freshmen. He was now looking for his first full-time job. Visiting Father O'Donnell was Bishop George Finnigan of Helena, Montana, a former Notre Dame vice president. He was looking for someone to take over as football coach at the diocese's St. Charles College, replacing former Irish lineman Wilbur Eaton, who was moving on after five years. "Rockne says that you're the man for our football job," the bishop said. "My real interest is law," Jones replied. "I'll take the coaching job only if I can get into a law firm." Bishop Finnigan assured Jones he could get him into Walsh and Nagel, the firm responsible for the diocese's legal work.

The next afternoon, on Palm Sunday, the final scrimmage of spring football took place on the old "sophomore field" at Cartier. Jones interrupted Rockne for a moment to tell him about the offer from Bishop Finnigan. "The job includes a salary I can live with, plus room and board in the college dormitory," Jones explained. "It sounds good to me, Jonesy," Rockne said. "You'd better take it." With that, Rockne turned back to the scrimmage. But seconds later, he started after Jones and said, "Wait a minute, Jonesy. Are you planning to get married soon?"

"That's a funny question for you to ask," Jones laughed. "You've always told us that football was our life here at Notre Dame, and studies are our life, and for us not to get involved romantically until we were ready to settle down. Why do you ask?"

"Well," Rockne said, smiling. "I figure it would be a heck of a thing to expect a wife to live in a dormitory."

The spring workouts were important in forming the 1931 Irish team.

With Carideo graduating, Rockne was on the lookout for his next quarterback. There were numerous candidates, led by Chuck Jaskwhich. Others included Emmett Murphy, Laurie Vejar, and Joe Foley. Further down the bench stood Larry O'Neil, whose biggest moment in Notre Dame football to date was trying to tackle Joe Savoldi and ending up in the hospital with a badly injured shoulder. There, he awoke looking into the face of Knute Rockne, who had come to see how O'Neil was doing. "I was pleased as punch to think that he thought enough of me, an unknown freshman, to come to the hospital to see if I was alright," O'Neil later said. "That convinced me that I wanted to play football for him."

It was a cool, rainy afternoon, and O'Neil had spent two hours on the sideline without a parka. He noticed Rockne ready to leave, so O'Neil snuck down the sideline alongside Rockne, hoping to possibly grab the coach's parka if he left. Rockne turned and spotted the quarterback and snapped, "O'Neil, where have you been? Were you late coming out?" "No sir," said O'Neil. "I've been here all the time, waiting for a chance to play." Replied the coach, "Then get in there for Al McGuff. Let's see what you can do." O'Neil reported to Hunk Anderson, directing the scrimmage, and was sent to play safety. Just then, the other team went into punt formation and O'Neil dropped back to receive the kick. He fielded the punt, but soon saw huge tackle George Kozack bearing down on him. *Please, not a replay of the collision with Savoldi*, O'Neil thought.

He faked in one direction, quickly shifted his weight and neatly avoided the charging Kozack. Heading upfield, O'Neil made a return of 35 yards before he was forced out of bounds. The whistle blew, and the scrimmage ended on that play. Rockne came out and gathered the squad together. With O'Neil front and center, the coach began: "Well, O'Neil, you're not strong as an ox and just as smart after all. That was a nifty bit of running." He went on to remind his squad how important intelligence was in winning football. It was O'Neil's quick thinking that turned a possible disaster into a big gain. And with that, Rockne walked off Cartier Field.

That evening, Rockne stopped by his old neighborhood on St. Vincent Street and found Tom and Kate Hickey at home with several of their children. During the visit, Rockne got down on the floor for some impromptu "football" with chunky little three-year-old Joe Hickey. Their roughhousing broke a vase, but the Hickeys didn't flinch. Tom loved seeing his old pal smiling and having fun. "I never saw him in better health or more relaxed," Tom said later. "I never saw Rock in better spirits."

Monday morning at the Studebaker offices, Rockne went into Jim Cleary's office to check on an audio recording he had made for the dealers. The coach didn't have much time to visit, owing to all the details he was trying to wrap up before heading for Los Angeles. Cleary wanted to ask about a young man out for football that spring. Cleary had an uncle in Chicago, whose barber was a Swedish fellow named Nelson. The barber's son, Cleary said, worshipped Rockne and enrolled at Notre Dame for the sole purpose of playing football for him. But the lad was overwhelmed at the size of Notre Dame's roster, and the players' skills, and figured Rockne didn't know who he was. Cleary had asked Rockne if there was anything he could do for young Nelson, and Rockne replied, "I'll take care of it."

Now, Rockne had left the building, but soon was tapping on Cleary's first floor window. "That Swede from Chicago," Rockne said. "I forgot to tell you, I took care of him." The coach then explained how, in a scrimmage, he showed the team a new play, which he was sure would result in touchdowns, as long as the tackle handled his job correctly. "I then looked over and pointed to your pal and said, 'Nelson, come here.' He was so surprised he could hardly move. But I finally got him in position, ran him through the play several times until he understood it, and then congratulated him in front of the entire team. He now knows that I know him, and I think he's happy." With that, Rockne left Studebaker headquarters.

Rockne headed to campus, and ran into Moon Mullins, his graduating fullback from Pasadena. Rockne had recommended Mullins to help coach the backfield at the University of Kansas, where his pal Phog Allen was athletic director and Bill Hargiss football coach. Mullins had just returned from helping out at the Jayhawks spring practice, and Rockne wanted to know all about the time in Kansas. The pair spent the next half-hour talking football and coaching, Mullins much more at ease chatting with Rockne as a coaching peer than in the traditional coach-player relationship. When Rockne got up to leave, they shook hands, and Mullins said, "You know, Coach, I've been going to return something to Mrs. Rockne since the Southern Cal game in December, but I just haven't gotten over to your house yet to give it back to her."

"What's that, Larry?" Rockne inquired. Mullins then told Rockne that, on the way out to California, with his knee troubling him since the Army game, the team stopped in Tucson for some practice and to acclimate to the heat. It was there Bonnie Rockne had given Mullins a medal of the Little Flower, St. Therese, saying, "Larry, with that bum knee you're going to need some extra help in Los Angeles." And there, in his home-town suited up for the final time for Notre Dame, Mullins had to look on helplessly, his injury too serious to allow him to play. Nobody knew he had the Little Flower medal taped to his injured knee. With Notre Dame safely ahead, Rockne put Mullins in for one play, "a wonderful gesture and so typical of him," Moon would say. After the 27-0 victory, his team-mates awarded Mullins the game ball. "To me, that ball symbolized Knute Rockne, sportsmanship, the great game of football—and the true spirit of Notre Dame," Mullins said. Now, it was time to pass the medal on. "Coach," said Mullins, "I want you to have this little medal to protect you on your flight to the coast. I wish I were going with you."

While Mullins and Rockne were chatting, Bill Jones joined the con-versation. Rockne told Jones that he had been giving Mullins some ad-vice, including to "save our Notre Dame stuff for the day when he gets a head coaching job of his own." Then he said, "Now, Jonesy, you've got a head coaching position, so use everything we've taught you here at Notre Dame. But bear in mind one thing, Jonesy. Remember that you're a trained lawyer, and football is only a means to an end. So get yourself acquainted with people in law out in Montana and begin your practice as early as you can. That's what you really want, that's what you should be, and you'll find happiness there. But even more important, both you and Moon are going to soon learn that football coaching is going to become an ever-hazardous career. Twenty years from now there won't be a coach-ing job worth its pay, what with all the aggravation from administration and alumni you'll be expected to tolerate."

As the chat ended, Jones asked Rockne about his upcoming trip. Rockne detailed his itinerary—train to Chicago, train to Kansas City, then airplane to Los Angeles. "But why can't you go by train?" Jones asked. "They're a lot safer."

"No, they're not," Rockne replied. "You don't read your statistics. Anyway, I want to save time. Bonnie and the kids are still down in Florida, and I want to be back home to greet them when they return. Flying to and from California is the only solution to the time problem." Mullins and Jones wished Rockne well, and the coach went on his way.

Rockne took a quick train ride to Chicago, where he visited his mother and sisters. Martha Gjermo Rockne would turn 72 in a few days, while Rockne would be on the West Coast, and the loyal son wished to celebrate with her when he could. Filled with birthday cake and ice cream and caught up on family news, Rockne boarded a night train for Kansas City. He welcomed Tuesday, March 31 with a meeting with his old pal Dr. Nigro. The pair had breakfast at the dining room of the ornate Union Station. A train expected in early morning would be carrying Bill and Junior, headed back from the family's Florida vacation, to resume studies at the Pembroke School. Rockne was anxious to see the boys, but he also knew he'd be back in a couple of weeks, as he was to be main speaker at Pembroke's winter athletic banquet on Sunday, April 12.

Rockne was scheduled to fly out of the Kansas City Municipal Airport, built in 1927 on the Missouri River bottoms next to the rail tracks near the Hannibal Bridge. Since flights were being used in conjunction with rail service to move people across the country, the location was considered ideal. Charles Lindbergh, along with Amelia Earhart, helped dedicate the airport as New Richards Field in 1927. It was three miles north of Union Station. Rock and Doc Nigro checked for the arriving trains every few minutes, and then called the airport. There, Transcontinental & Western Air's Flight 599 was awaiting several sacks of mail prior to its scheduled takeoff at 8:30 a.m. Rockne and Nigro waited until 7:45 a.m., but the boys' train was still not in the station, so they sped off to the airport. There, Rockne told Nigro that he would see him on his return trip through Kansas City in a few days. He was also able to send a telegram to Bonnie. The flight was delayed 45 minutes to await the mail, but at 9:15 a.m. agent R.S. Bridges waved Flight 599 out of the gate area. Minutes later it took off, into an overcast sky with light snow falling, ceiling 400 feet, visibility seven miles, light winds and a temperature of 37 degrees. But it was just 6 degrees at Dodge City; to reach its first stop at Wichita, Flight 599 would have to penetrate a sharp cold front. With the cold air meeting moist, warm air to the east, there were likely to be clouds, fog, ice, and low ceilings.

The plane, a Fokker F-10-A Trimotor, bore a Department of Commerce number NC 999 E. The Fokker Aircraft Company of Teterboro, New Jersey had manufactured the plane, commissioned on October 29, 1929. Valued at $80,000 when new, it now had logged 1,887 hours of flying time. At 14,000 pounds, the F-10-A was heavier than its predecessor, the F-10, and featured a longer, one-piece wing, 79 feet; the fuselage was 50 feet in length. Three 450-horsepower Pratt & Whitney engines with triple-headed propellers powered the craft to a cruising speed of 123 miles per hour. At the controls was Captain Robert Fry, who had been with the airline since June 1929. A native of football-crazy Canton, Ohio, Fry had grown up in Milwaukee and enlisted in the U.S. Army in the Great War. Later, in the early 1920s, before becoming a civilian pilot, Fry had a hitch as a gunnery sergeant and fighter pilot with the U.S. Marines' air service, serving in Guam and China. During one mission in China, his plane was shot, and he was forced to bail out into a rice paddy. On the morning of March 31, Fry had breakfast with his wife Mary and, before leaving for the airport, presented her with a new photo of himself in his captain's uniform. She wished him "a good and safe flight." Such a flight was not always a guarantee. Just months earlier, Mary had buried her sister, well-known flyer Clair Fahy, a star of the 1929 Women's Air Derby, after she crashed in the Nevada desert. Clair's husband, Herbert J. Fahy, was an aeronautical record holder and Lockheed test pilot before he died in a crash, a few months before Clair's death. The Fahys had operated the Battlefield Airport in Gettysburg, Pennsylvania.

Co-pilot Herman Jess Mathias, 30, began flying for Transcontinental Air Transport before its merger with Western Air Express. That morning, Mathias finished a letter to his mother and put it in his navigation kit, planning to send it later from Albuquerque, New Mexico, one of the stops Flight 599 was scheduled to make, the others being Wichita, Kansas; Amarillo, Texas; and Winslow, Arizona. Rockne's fellow passengers included one man he knew, 39-year-old John Happer, a representative for Great Western Sporting Goods in Chicago. Their plans, while in Los Angeles, included some promotional work for the company's football equipment. One other man had a Notre Dame connection. C. A. Robrecht of Wheeling, West Virginia, president of the Robrecht Produce Company, was headed to Amarillo, Texas. His son was a graduate of Notre Dame.

The others were Spencer Goldthwaite, a 25-year-old New York advertising man, who reported the plane he took from Chicago to Kansas City two days earlier was forced to make an emergency landing; W. B. Miller, an insurance man; and H.C. Christen, an interior designer.

Paul Johnson, an airmail pilot flying a faster craft than Fry's, left Kansas City 15 minutes after Fry, but passed Flight 599 over Emporia, about 100 miles from Kansas City. Johnson later reported encountering fog, cloud cover, and icing, forcing him to fly close to the ground. At 10:22 a.m., Jess Mathias radioed the station in Wichita and was told the weather was clear there. But Mathias responded, "The weather here is getting tough. We're going to turn around and go back to Kansas City." Fry was flying low to the ground, under the low ceiling. A few minutes later, the Wichita agent confirmed that weather there was clear, and Mathias and Fry apparently decided to try Wichita after all. If they couldn't make it, Mathias said, perhaps they would turn back and go as far as Olpe, a field sometimes used for refueling emergencies.

In a final transmission at 10:45 a.m., Mathias said, "It's getting tighter. Think we'll come on to Wichita. It looks pretty bad." Flying so close to the ground, with heavy clouds and a hilly terrain, just making a simple 180-degree turn would have been treacherous. By now, the flight had also drifted off course to the west. It was possible Fry and Mathias were navigating via the "Old Iron Compass." Pilots, without instrumentation or radio navigation, would often follow railroad tracks, and the Atchison, Topeka, and Santa Fe Railway connecting Kansas City and Wichita, was several miles west of the flight's original course. Mathias told the Wichita agent he and Fry were "too busy" to talk; they may have both been squinting through rain-slicked windshields, trying to follow the rail tracks just 300 feet or less below them.

On the ground, the rolling Flint Hills of eastern Kansas bore the dull brown of a long winter, with greening still ahead in April. It was said that Zebulon Pike was among the first white settlers to lay eyes on these lands, and for generations, they supported ranchers as pastures for cattle. For as far as the eye could see, the prairie met with open sky, a panorama that could make a man feel small and insignificant. Cattle drives, pushing herds of thousands of head, from Texas to Kansas City, came through this area. Robert Blackburn, a rancher feeding a herd of cattle near the crossroads of Bazaar, heard an airplane overhead, apparently headed south toward Wichita. Edward and Arthur Baker, sons of Seward Baker, who operated a ranch near Matfield Green, were moving cattle when they heard an airplane's engine around 10:30 a.m. They strained their eyes, but the cloud cover and fog prevented them from seeing the craft. They cupped their ears to the skies, and heard sounds that seemed to indicate the plane was increasing speed. Then it began backfiring. Finally, they heard no engines at all—followed by the sounds of a crash.

A few miles away, James Easter Heathman, working on his family's farm, heard the sound of an engine and thought at first that cars were racing on the nearby dirt road. Just a week shy of his 14th birthday, he was interested in all things mechanical. "Let's go see the cars race," he called to his brother. A few minutes later, a neighbor called to say there had been an airplane crash. The Baker brothers rode their horses in the direction of the backfiring and were the first upon the horrific crash scene. The fuselage was badly burned, and the wing lay several hundred yards to the southeast. Bags of mail dotted the landscape. Debris was strewn for nearly as far as the eye could see. And, north of the wreckage, five bodies lay motionless. One, about 20 feet from the plane itself, was Knute Rockne. All eight men had died instantly upon impact.

Within minutes of the crash, the plane's ID number was wired to Kansas City by way of Emporia. Officials quickly confirmed the names of the crew and passengers, including Rockne. Meanwhile, local residents combed over the crash site, before the Bakers' father and the coroner Dr. Titus arrived. The Bakers, at the direction of Dr. Titus, started the process of identifying victims through personal items. Knute Rockne was carrying a card giving him guest privileges at the Kansas City Athletic Club, courtesy of Dr. Nigro. The bodies were soon gathered up and taken to funeral homes in Cottonwood Falls.

In newsrooms across the country, wire copy machines rang and spit out the bulletin:

BY UNITED PRESS

Bazaar, Kansas, March 31 – Knute Rockne, noted Notre Dame football coach, and seven other men were killed in an airplane crash near here today.

Afternoon editions of newspapers, set with news of an earthquake in Managua, Nicaragua that killed 2,000 people, quickly rearranged their front pages, adding huge headlines: "ROCKNE KILLED IN AIR CRASH."

In offices and public places across the nation, the news spread quickly. "Rockne's dead."

At the house in Coral Gables, a handful of Rockne friends had gathered, waiting for Bonnie Rockne, who was at the beach with family friends, Tom O'Neill and his wife. Telegrams were already starting to arrive. The first, though, wasn't sending condolences. It was the wire Knute had sent from Kansas City, simply stating: LEAVING RIGHT NOW STOP WILL BE AT BILTMORE STOP LOVE AND KISSES.

When Bonnie arrived at the house, she appeared calm. Every so often, she would softly say, "I just don't believe it." But finally, she turned to Jackie and said, "Your Daddy has gone away. He loved you so." She began to pack for the trip back to South Bend, filling an old trunk with the initials K.K.R. scrawled inside. As the trunk filled, there was a football that wouldn't fit, and it was suggested she deflate it. "Oh, no," she replied. "Knute blew that up himself." She would keep the ball intact, Knute's breath and all.

On the Notre Dame campus, the first reports around 12:30 p.m. brought lunchtime activity to a halt. Students passed one another with baleful gazes, searching eyes, as if to say, "Have you heard?" and "Can it really be true?" At 1:30 p.m., when the initial reports were confirmed, students streamed to Sacred Heart church. Many stayed all afternoon. Though Good Friday and the Easter vacation was three days away, all classes for the week were canceled immediately. Telephone lines were jammed as students connected with their loved ones back home, confirming the tragic news. Father O'Donnell, it was said, "surveyed the trembling on the campus, knowing that the shock would be felt, not for days or months, but for years. Into the troubled scene he stepped and took command, calm, deliberate, fully poised."

He spoke for the university, saying, "Nothing that has ever happened at Notre Dame has so shocked the faculty and the student body as the tragic news that came at noon Tuesday of the accident which took Mr. Rockne's life. To every person at Notre Dame, this was a personal grief as it would be if a member of his family died. Everybody was proud of

Rockne, everybody admired him; but something far more than that, we loved him. Altogether apart from the unique and deserved success which he achieved as director of athletics and as football coach, he was a great personality with the attributes of genius."

Said Tom Conley, captain of the reigning national champs: "I can't believe it, I'm too broken up to really say anything. Rock died as he had lived—in action." And 1931 captain-elect Tommy Yarr added: "I only hope I will be able to live up to the ideals he left me." Other players, such as Jack Chevigny, could say nothing, leaving the athletic offices in tears.

Nearby in South Bend, Paul Castner was in the middle of moving his wife and infant son from an apartment into their new house. Coming out of the apartment with arms loaded, he saw a neighbor rush to him and call out: "The news on the radio just reported that Rockne has been killed in an airplane crash in Kansas!" With a feeling of shock, and tears in his eyes, Castner ran back into the apartment and called Father O'Donnell. "Yes, Paul," Father O'Donnell said, sadness evident in his tones. "It's frightfully sad but it's true. Our old friend is dead."

In Chicago, Mrs. Martha Rockne heard the news of her son's death over the radio. A woman of great faith, she is said to have calmly remarked, "It's God's will and we must not question it."

In Syracuse, New York, 13-year-old Theodore Hesburgh, a student at Most Holy Rosary School, heard the news and said a silent prayer for the man that schoolchildren across the nation had come to associate with fair play and striving for excellence. In Wisconsin Dells, 14-year-old Laddie Helland had a hard time accepting what he was reading in the *Milwaukee Sentinel*. His idol, his friend was gone. In the coming days, he would collect every newspaper article and photo on Rockne's life and death he could find, and bind them into a scrapbook. In Los Angeles, Tom Lieb heard the news and fell silent. He would not be heading to the airport to greet Coach Rockne's plane. Lieb, head football coach at Loyola Marymount, had so looked forward to hosting his great friend on the visit. He was now numb with pain.

Back in the Flint Hills of Kansas, a handful of reporters made it to the crash site. William L. White, son of the immensely popular journalist William Allen White, editor of the *Emporia Gazette*, described the scene this way:

On a wind-swept promontory of the Flint Hills, out of sight of any vestige of human habitation, lies the twisted wreckage of a giant Fokker, its three motors buried deep in the stony soil, which carried to death Knute Rockne, the Viking of football, two pilots and five other passengers.

Among the first to reach the wreckage was R. Z. Blackburn, who was feeding his cattle in a pasture. He heard the roar of the morning mail plane. It is just as this point in the Flint Hills that the old stage road, marked by furrows in the prairie sod, intersects with the transcontinental air mail line marked by flashing beacon lights, running between Kansas City and Wichita.

The hum of airplane motors was a familiar sound to Blackburn. Today the plane was invisible above the gray clouds which hung a scant one thousand feet above the Flint Hills. After dying away in the fog, the hum returned and attracted his attention. Something apparently was wrong with the regular morning mail plane. He look up from his work in time to see the silver Fokker drop like a plummet from the low-hanging clouds. Behind it fluttered a silver wing.

Its motors still roaring, the Fokker disappeared behind a hill, there was a splintering thud and the motors ceased. Early in the afternoon as the news spread that a mail plane was down and Knute Rockne was dead, airplanes from Wichita zoomed overhead, swooped like great birds curiously inspecting a wounded fellow and settled unsteadily on the neighboring hills.

Khaki-clad pilots were driving away a crowd of excited, overgrown boys who were tearing bits of fabric for souvenirs. Cowboys were viewing the tangled aluminum from their saddles, their ponies stamping nervously at the unfamiliar odor of gasoline, an endless stream of curiosity seekers trudging from their motor cars parked along the road. Miraculously, there had been no fire.

So died the great Viking of football, on a high hill overlooking a prairie, at the crossroads of the old forgotten stage road and the new highway of the air, and at his bier keeping vigil on the hilltop stood, not the Four Horsemen of Notre Dame, but four sun-tanned horsemen of the plains, forcing back from the tangled wreckage a gaping, curious crowd.

Swiftly and painlessly he passed from a land of far horizons into a horizon without bounds."

Across the nation, condolences and tributes flowed to the university, to Bonnie Rockne, and to the South Bend newspapers. President Hoover said in a telegram, "Mr. Rockne so contributed to a cleanness and high purpose and sportsmanship in athletics that his passing is a national loss." Former President Coolidge called Rockne "a great man, an inspiring leader and a profound teacher. He put intellectual and moral value into games. Right living and right thinking went into his victories. His activities had the benefit of publicity but that does not account for his hold on young men."

Personal messages to the family included Gus Dorais: "Please call on me if I can be of the slightest help. God bless you and the children in your terrible loss." And Jack Dempsey wrote: "Please accept my heartfelt sympathy in this your hour of great sorrow."

The five Miller brothers saluted Rockne "with love, admiration and loyalty, and with the same understanding, respect and camaraderie that you gave so unstintedly to every Notre Dame man and to all your friends. We are sad and sorrowful because Notre Dame and we have lost your comradeship and your genius."

Members of the coaching fraternity expressed their grief. "I have lost a true friend," Southern Cal's Howard Jones wrote. "I shall always cherish the memories of the years of our association." Georgia Tech's Bill Alexander expressed "regret and sorrow at the passing of the man whom we all loved and admired." Lou Little of Columbia wrote, "They have taken our leader from our midst, but his work and memories will always be a monument that will carry us on." And from the University of Michigan, Fritz Crisler wrote, "Endeared in the hearts of all his colleagues; our great esteem and admiration for him will endure forever."

An editorial in the *Denver News* noted, "Perhaps no other death could have brought more universal sorrow than this—sorrow among men, women and even little children. Knute Rockne's name was a household word...He had long since o'erleaped the sports page. Persons who seldom followed sports knew Rockne. Boys who could not yet read could tell you about Rockne and his Ramblers."

As the shocking day of March 31, 1931 wound down, nobody summed up the nation's collective emotions better than the coach's great friend, Will Rogers:

"We thought it would take a President or a great public man's death to make a whole nation, regardless of age, race or creed, shake their heads in real, sincere sorrow…Well, that's what this country did today, Knute, for you. You died one of our national heroes. Notre Dame was your address, but every gridiron in America was your home."

# Epilogue

S tudents returning to campus after Easter break read the *Scholastic's* editorial as they confronted the reality of life after Rockne's death:

> It has often been said that time is the great healer of all wounds. Perhaps, but the wound that Notre Dame has suffered by the death of her most-loved man will never be healed completely. Even now, after the nation has partially recovered from the passing of one of its greatest citizens, it is hard to realize what the loss of 'Rock' means to us all.

> Notre Dame without Rockne...the United States without Rockne. What does it mean? We hardly know, yet. The thousands of telegrams and letters received at the University are only partially indicative of the grief felt by the entire nation. It mattered not whether the newsboys in San Francisco or New York or Florida knew 'Rock' personally; he was a friend to everyone and they loved him.

> We at Notre Dame were closer to Rockne than anyone else; his very appearance on the campus made the world look bright-

er; his kind face, his soft smile, his cheery hello gave a thrill to all who spoke to 'Rock.' And no one was ever intentionally snubbed. Rockne was that kind of a man—'a man's man.'

We shall remember Rockne because he wanted us to do the right things in the right way. Always clean, always fair, always fighting for the highest things in life. That was Rockne.

On Thursday, April 9, the students had their moment to honor Rockne, as 2,500 of them filled Sacred Heart to its doors for a solemn requiem High Mass. The following Sunday, the campus began a Novena— nine days starting with a High Mass each day. Numerous student organizations were involved in the ceremonies. Sunday, April 19, was designated a universal Notre Dame communion, with widespread reception of the sacrament in honor of the late coach. Talk turned to a fitting memorial on campus. Two residence halls completed in 1931 bore tributes: Alumni Hall sported a portrait of the coach, holding a canine football mascot; at Dillon Hall, the chapel was dedicated to the Norwegian St. Olaf, honoring Rockne's heritage. Elsewhere, the schoolchildren in a small town in Bastrop County, Texas, were given the opportunity to vote for a new name for their town, and chose Rockne, which it has been ever since.

Plans for a lasting memorial to Rockne at Notre Dame soon led to the creation of the Memorial Association, which settled on raising funds for the construction of a multi-use recreational facility, housing a variety of pools and courts. The Rockne Memorial Building opened in 1937. Its exterior features a series of frescoes depicting athletes in various sports. In its lobby sits a bronze bust of the coach; for generations, students and others have rubbed his nose smooth for good luck.

Campus life at Notre Dame attempted a return to normalcy in May, with concerts, dances and other events continuing as planned. In the Athletic Department, the considerable shoes of Rockne needed to be filled, and officials determined it would require hiring an athletic director and head football coach separately, an expensive proposition. Father O'Donnell's first choice for athletic director was Major John Griffith, commissioner of the Big Ten and friend of the university, but Griffith turned the job down. Officials then turned to Jesse Harper, who agreed to leave the Kansas ranch and come back to Notre Dame in its hour of need. Harper's focus would be nearly entirely on business operations, taking a close look at how dollars were being earned and spent, and leaving coaching to others. The unenviable task of following a legend fell to Hunk Anderson. But in a further nod to the impossibility of truly replacing Rockne, Anderson was given the title of "senior coach" and Jack Chevigny was named "junior coach." That approach only lasted one season. Hunk, after a losing record in 1933, was replaced by Four Horseman Elmer Layden.

Rockne's plane crash had an immediate and lasting affect on the future of aviation. It was said that the industry could not have had worse publicity "had the victim been the president of the United States himself." The Aeronautics Branch of the U.S. Department of Commerce began an investigation immediately after the crash. After previous wrecks, it issued no public statements; this time, with a public clamoring for answers and an airline industry nervous as to its future, the Branch needed to say something, which it did, clumsily. It first incorrectly attributed the crash to a wing severed by overstressing. Then it switched to a theory, also false, that ice thrown from a propeller hub had broken a blade. On May 4, 1931, Col. Clarence M. Young, assistant secretary of commerce, barred all F-10s and F-10As from carrying passengers until they were thoroughly inspected. The probable cause of the crash—rotted wood in the wing's framework of glued wooden joints—was glossed over in favor of stressing improved maintenance and inspection. The warning issued months before the crash, about the inability to inspect the wooden framework of the Fokker's wing, had proven fatally prescient.

The American market for Fokker's wooden-winged aeroplanes was immediately and permanently gone, and Fokker was ousted from the company he had founded. Even the all-metal Ford Trimotors were doomed, due to their resemblance to the "plane that killed Rockne." Later, a former mechanic who inspected the doomed plane just days before the crash, said that "the wing panels were all loose...they were coming loose and it would take them days to fix it, and I said the airplane wasn't fit to fly and I wouldn't sign the log...Nobody was safe in that airplane."

Four years later, Rockne's great friend Will Rogers was hanging around the airport in Burbank, California, where famed aviator Wiley Post was modifying a Lockheed Orion with floats for a trip surveying a mail-and-passenger route from the West Coach to Russia. Rogers thought the voyage could provide material for his newspaper column, and signed on to accompany Post. On August 15, 1935, the plane plunged into a lagoon near Point Barrow, Alaska, killing both men instantly.

Laddie Helland, the youngster who idolized the coach after meeting him at Camp Rockne, became a top student and athlete at Wisconsin Dells High School, and entered Notre Dame in 1939. Among his many talents, Helland excelled at drawing caricatures, and his work enlivened the *Dome* and other campus publications. He, like Rockne and Rogers, was fascinated by flight, and he enlisted in the Army Air Corps. Sadly, he shared their fate. Helland lost his life in a training flight.

The Rockne crash eventually led to the design and manufacture of the Douglas DC-2, the first airliner built using all-metal, stressed-skin construction, and a host of other innovations. It, along with the DC-3, provided the safety and comfort, combined with economy that allowed the swift expansion of the worldwide passenger airline industry as we know it today. The role of government in requiring safer planes also took off. Spurred by the crash of March 31, 1931, the Aeronautics Branch took on greater duties in certifying aircraft and regulating the industry, and in 1934 was renamed the Bureau of Air Commerce to reflect its enhanced status within the Commerce Department. In 1940, it was split into the Civil Aeronautics Administration and the Civil Aeronautics Board; eventually it became today's Federal Aviation Administration.

The legacy of which Knute Rockne would undoubtedly be most proud is the legion of coaches he inspired, who in turn guided young athletes and influenced many of them to become coaches, in schools and colleges located all across the United States. Dozens were his former Notre Dame football players, who in life knew "Rock" as their mentor and friend. Hundreds of others had attended Rockne's summer coaching schools— everywhere from Williamsburg, Virginia to Superior, Wisconsin, to Dallas, Texas, to Corvallis, Oregon. They, too, called the coach "friend" and handed down his message of perseverance, self-sacrifice, teamwork, and sportsmanship to generations of young athletes.

They were men like Coach Mark Raymond Berry, for whom the Physical Education Complex at Paris, Texas, High School is named, who spent

48 years teaching and coaching. Upon his death in 1999 at age 95, it was recalled that Coach Berry said his greatest achievement was his influence on the lives of young people during his years as a coach and teacher.

Around the United States, over many years, countless youngsters found their confidence, their strength, through athletics, guided by coaches who had been influenced by the life, the words, and the example of Coach Knute Rockne...Coach For A Nation.

# APPENDIX A: YEAR BY YEAR RESULTS AND ROSTERS

## 1910 (4-1-1)

| | | Opponent | Score |
|---|---|---|---|
| October 8 | W | Olivet | 48-0 |
| October 22 | W | Butchel (Akron) | 51-0 |
| October 29 | L | at Michigan State | 0-17 |
| November 12 | W | at Rose Poly | 41-3 |
| November 19 | W | Ohio Northern | 47-0 |
| November 24 | T | at Marquette | 5-5 |

| Position | Name |
|---|---|
| LE | Joe Collins |
| LT | George Philbrook |
| LG | Torgus "Turk" Oaas |
| C | Tom Foley |
| RG | John Stansfield |
| RT | Ralph Dimmick |
| RE | Charlie Crowley, Bill Martin, Knute Rockne |
| QB | Charles "Gus" Dorais |
| LH | Walter Clinnen, Dan McGinnis, Pete Dwyer |
| RH | Lee Mathews, Billy Ryan, Alfred "Dutch" Bergman |
| FB | Art Clippinger, Chester McGrath |

## 1911 (6-0-2)

| | | Opponent | Score |
|---|---|---|---|
| October 7 | W | Ohio Northern | 32-6 |
| October 14 | W | St. Viator | 43-0 |
| October 21 | W | Butler | 27-0 |
| October 28 | W | Loyola Chicago | 80-0 |
| November 4 | T | at Pittsburgh | 0-0 |
| November 11 | W | St. Bonaventure | 34-0 |
| November 20 | W | at Wabash | 6-3 |
| November 30 | T | at Marquette | 0-0 |

| Position | Name |
|---|---|
| LE | Knute Rockne, Dan McGinnis |
| LT | George Philbrook, Ralph "Zipper" Lathrop, John Larson |
| LG | Torgus "Turk" Oaas, Walter Yund |
| C | Al Feeney, Glen Smith, Bill O'Neil |
| RG | Paul Harvat, Ray Jones |
| RT | Luke Kelly, Eddie Duggan |
| RE | Charlie Crowley, Bill Dolan |
| QB | Charles "Gus" Dorais, Charles "Sam" Finegan, Jay Lee |
| LH | Alvin "Heine" Berger, Art Smith |
| RH | Alfred "Dutch" Bergman, Joe Pliska |
| FB | Ray Eichenlaub, Bill Kelleher, Keith "Deak" Jones |

## 1912 (7-0-0)

| | | Opponent | Score |
|---|---|---|---|
| October 5 | W | St. Viator | 116-7 |
| October 12 | W | Adrian | 74-7 |
| October 19 | W | Morris Harvey | 39-0 |
| October 26 | W | Wabash | 41-6 |
| November 2 | W | at Pittsburgh | 3-0 |
| November 9 | W | at St. Louis | 47-7 |
| November 28 | W | Marquette at Comiskey Park | 69-0 |

| Position | Name |
|---|---|
| LE | Knute Rockne, Dan McGinnis, Ray Miller |
| LT | Keith "Deak" Jones, Ray Dunphy |
| LG | Freeman "Fitz" Fitzgerald, Ralph "Zipper" Lathrop |
| C | Al Feeney, Tom McLaughlin |
| RG | Walter Yund, Bill Cook |
| RT | Paul Harvat, Emmett Keefe |
| RE | Charlie Crowley, Bill Dolan |
| QB | Charles "Gus" Dorais, Charles "Sam" Finegan |
| LH | Alvin "Heine" Berger, Art "Bunny" Larkin |
| RH | Joe Pliska, Fred "Gus" Gushurst |
| FB | Ray Eichenlaub, Pat Doherty |

## 1913 (7-0-0)

| | | Opponent | Score |
|---|---|---|---|
| October 4 | W | Ohio Northern | 87-0 |
| October 18 | W | South Dakota | 20-7 |
| October 25 | W | Alma | 62-0 |
| November 1 | W | at Army | 35-13 |
| November 7 | W | at Ferris State | 14-7 |
| November 22 | W | Christian Brothers at St. Louis | 20-7 |
| November 27 | W | at Texas | 30-7 |

| Position | Name |
|---|---|
| LE | Knute Rockne, Allen "Mal" Elward, Paul "Curly" Nowers |
| LT | Keith "Deak" Jones, Bill Cook |
| LG | Emmett Keefe, Hollis "Hoot" King |
| C | Al Feeney, Tom McLaughlin, John Voelkers |
| RG | Freeman "Fitz" Fitzgerald |
| RT | Ralph "Zipper" Lathrop, Art Sharp |
| RE | Fred "Gus" Gushurst, Bill Kelleher, Rupert "Rupe" Mills, Harry Baujan |
| QB | Charles "Gus" Dorais, Hardy Bush, Joe Gargan |
| LH | Charles "Sam" Finegan, Art "Bunny" Larkin, Alvin "Heine" Berger |
| RH | Joe Pliska, Alfred "Dutch" Bergman |
| FB | Ray Eichenlaub, Eddie Duggan |

## 1914 (6-2-0)

| | | Opponent | Score |
|---|---|---|---|
| October 3 | W | Alma | 56-0 |
| October 10 | W | Rose Poly | 102-0 |
| October 17 | L | at Yale | 0-28 |
| October 24 | W | South Dakota at Sioux Falls | 33-0 |
| October 31 | W | Haskell | 20-7 |
| November 7 | L | at Army | 7-20 |
| November 14 | W | Carlisle at Comiskey Park | 48-6 |
| November 26 | W | Syracuse | 20-0 |

| Position | Name |
|---|---|
| LE | Allen "Mal' Elward, Hollis "Hoot" King |
| LT | Keith "Deak" Jones, Art Sharp |
| LG | Emmett Keefe, Leo Stephan, Lorenzo Rausch |
| C | Freeman "Fitz" Fitzgerald, Hugh O'Donnell |
| RG | Charlie Bachman, Gilbert "Gillie" Ward |
| RT | Ralph "Zipper" Lathrop, George "Ducky" Holmes |
| RE | Rupert "Rupe" Mills, Harry Baujan |
| QB | Alfred "Dutch" Bergman, Art "Bunny" Larkin |
| LH | Stan Cofall, Charles "Sam" Finegan, Alvin "Heine" Berger |
| RH | Joe Pliska, Bill Kelleher |
| FB | Ray Eichenlaub, Eddie Duggan |

## 1915 (7-1-0)

| | | Opponent | Score |
|---|---|---|---|
| October 2 | W | Alma | 32-0 |
| October 9 | W | Haskell | 34-0 |
| October 23 | L | at Nebraska | 19-20 |
| October 30 | W | South Dakota | 6-0 |
| November 6 | W | at Army | 7-0 |
| November 13 | W | at Creighton | 41-0 |
| November 25 | W | at Texas | 36-7 |
| November 27 | W | at Rice | 55-2 |

| Position | Name |
|---|---|
| LE | Allen "Mal" Elward, Ray Whipple |
| LT | Leo Stephan, Hollis "Hoot" King |
| LG | Emmett Keefe, Jerry Jones |
| C | Hugh O'Donnell, Frank Rydzewski |
| RG | Freeman "Fitz" Fitzgerald, George Frantz |
| RT | Arnold McInerny |
| RE | Henry Baujan, Leslie "Dutch" Yeager |
| QB | Jim Phelan, Joe Dorais |
| LH | Stan Cofall, John Miller |
| RH | Arthur "Dutch" Bergman, Grover Malone |
| FB | Charlie Bachman, Fred "Fritz" Slackford |

## 1916 (8-1-0)

| | | Opponent | Score |
|---|---|---|---|
| September 30 | W | Case Tech | 48-0 |
| October 7 | W | at Western Reserve | 48-0 |
| October 14 | W | Haskell | 26-0 |
| October 28 | W | Wabash | 60-0 |
| November 4 | L | at Army | 10-30 |
| November 11 | W | South Dakota at Sioux Falls | 21-0 |
| November 18 | W | at Michigan State | 14-0 |
| November 25 | W | Alma | 46-0 |
| November 30 | W | at Nebraska | 20-0 |

| Position | Name |
|---|---|
| LE | Harry Baujan, Jack Meagher, Alfred Morales |
| LT | Frank Coughlin, Frank "Bodie" Andrews |
| LG | Charlie Bachman, Pete Ronchetti, George Frantz |
| C | Frank Rydzewski, Edward "Slip" Madigan, Sherwood Dixon |
| RG | Walter "Cy" DeGree, Gilbert "Gillie" Ward |
| RT | Arnold McInerny, Dave Philbin |
| RE | Ray Whipple, Tom King, Leslie "Dutch" Yeager |
| QB | Jim Phelan, Chet Grant, Joe Dorais |
| LH | Stan Cofall, Walter Miller |
| RH | Arthur "Dutch" Bergman, George Fitzpatrick, Grover Malone |
| FB | John Miller, Fred "Fritz" Slackford, Ward Miller |

## 1917 (6-1-1)

| | | Opponent | Score |
|---|---|---|---|
| October 6 | W | Kalamazoo | 55-0 |
| October 13 | T | at Wisconsin | 0-0 |
| October 20 | L | at Nebraska | 0-7 |
| October 27 | W | South Dakota | 40-0 |
| November 3 | W | at Army | 7-2 |
| November 10 | W | at Morningside | 13-0 |
| November 17 | W | Michigan State | 23-0 |
| November 24 | W | at Washington & Jefferson | 3-0 |

| Position | Name |
|---|---|
| LE | Dave Hayes, John Powers, Larry "Red" Morgan |
| LT | Frank "Bodie" Andrews, Bob McGuire |
| LG | Clyde Zoia, Pete Ronchetti |
| C | Frank Rydzewski, Sherwood Dixon, Barry Holton |
| RG | Edward "Slip" Madigan, Basil Stanley, Walter "Cy" DeGree |
| RT | Dave Philbin, Raleigh "Rollo" Stine, John "Thunder" Flanigan |
| RE | Tom King, Tom Spalding, Bill Andres |
| QB | Jim Phelan, Bill "Tex" Allison, Frank "Abbie" Lockard |
| LH | George Gipp, Maurice "Clipper" Smith, Norm Barry |
| RH | Leonard "Pete" Bahan, Joe Brandy, Dudley Pearson |
| FB | Walter Miller, Jim Ryan |

## 1918 (3-1-2)

| | | Opponent | Score |
|---|---|---|---|
| September 28 | W | at Case Tech | 26-6 |
| November 2 | W | at Wabash | 67-7 |
| November 9 | T | Great Lakes | 7-7 |
| November 16 | L | at Michigan State (R) | 7-13 |
| November 23 | W | at Purdue | 26-6 |
| November 28 | T | at Nebraska (S) | 0-0 |

| Position | Name |
|---|---|
| LE | Bernie Kirk, Frank "Rangy" Miles |
| LT | Raleigh "Rollo" Stine, Romanus "Peaches" Nadolney |
| LG | Heartley "Hunk" Anderson, Cy Sanders |
| C | Fred "Ojay" Larson |
| RG | Maurice "Clipper" Smith, Ben Connors |
| RT | Charlie Crowley, Earl Miller |
| RE | Eddie Anderson, George Shanahan |
| QB | Bill Mohn, Frank "Abbie" Lockard |
| LH | George Gipp, Paul Hogan |
| RH | Leonard "Pete" Bahan, Norm Barry, Johnny Mohardt |
| FB | Earl "Curly" Lambeau, Chet Wynne |

## 1919 (9-0-0)

| | | Opponent | Score |
|---|---|---|---|
| October 4 | W | Kalamazoo | 14-0 |
| October 11 | W | Mount Union | 60-7 |
| October 18 | W | at Nebraska | 14-9 |
| October 25 | W | Western Michigan | 53-0 |
| November 1 | W | Indiana (R) at Indianapolis | 16-3 |
| November 8 | W | at Army | 12-9 |
| November 15 | W | Michigan State | 13-0 |
| November 22 | W | at Purdue | 33-13 |
| November 27 | W | at Morningside (S) | 14-6 |

| Position | Name |
|---|---|
| LE | Bernie Kirk, Roger "Rodge" Kiley |
| LT | Frank Coughlin, Lawrence "Buck" Shaw |
| LG | Heartley "Hunk" Anderson, Cy Sanders |
| C | George Trafton, Edward "Slip" Madigan |
| RG | Maurice "Clipper" Smith, Jim Dooley, Ben Connors |
| RT | Walter "Cy" DeGree, Charlie Crowley |
| RE | Eddie Anderson, Dave Hayes |
| QB | Leonard "Pete" Bahan, Joe Brandy, Dudley Pearson |
| LH | George Gipp, Grover Malone, Johnny Mohardt |
| RH | Arthur "Dutch" Bergman, Norm Barry |
| FB | Fred "Fritz" Slackford, Walter Miller, Bob Phelan, Chet Wynne |

## 1920 (9-0-0)

| | | Opponent | Score |
|---|---|---|---|
| October 2 | W | Kalamazoo | 39-0 |
| October 9 | W | Western Michigan | 41-0 |
| October 16 | W | at Nebraska | 16-7 |
| October 23 | W | Valparaiso | 28-3 |
| October 30 | W | at Army | 27-17 |
| November 6 | W | Purdue (HC) | 28-0 |
| November 13 | W | Indiana at Indianapolis | 13-10 |
| November 20 | W | at Northwestern | 33-7 |
| November 25 | W | at Michigan State | 25-0 |

| Position | Name |
|---|---|
| LE | Roger "Rodge" Kiley, Glen "Judge" Carberry |
| LT | Frank Coughlin, Art "Hector" Garvey |
| LG | Heartley "Hunk" Anderson, Jim Dooley |
| C | Harry Mehre, Fred "Ojay" Larson |
| RG | Maurice "Clipper" Smith, Ed DeGree, Forrest "Fod" Cotton |
| RT | Lawrence "Buck" Shaw, Bill Voss |
| RE | Eddie Anderson, Dave Hayes, George Prokop |
| QB | Joe Brandy, Chet Grant, Frank Thomas |
| LH | George Gipp, Johnny Mohardt, Earl Walsh |
| RH | Norm Barry, Danny Coughlin |
| FB | Chet Wynne, Paul Castner, Bob Phelan |

## 1921 (10-1-0)

| | | Opponent | Score |
|---|---|---|---|
| September 24 | W | Kalamazoo | 56-0 |
| October 1 | W | DePauw | 57-10 |
| October 8 | L | at Iowa | 7-10 |
| October 15 | W | at Purdue | 33-0 |
| October 22 | W | Nebraska (HC) | 7-0 |
| October 29 | W | Indiana at Indianapolis (R) | 28-8 |
| November 5 | W | at Army | 28-0 |
| November 8 | W | Rutgers at Polo Grounds (NYC) | 48-0 |
| November 12 | W | Haskell | 42-7 |
| November 19 | W | at Marquette | 21-7 |
| November 24 | W | Michigan State | 48-0 |

| Position | Name |
|---|---|
| LE | Roger "Rodge" Kiley, Glen "Judge" Carberry, Gene Mayl |
| LT | Art "Hector" Garvey, Forrest "Fod" Cotton |
| LG | Heartley "Hunk" Anderson, Harvey Brown |
| C | Harry Mehre, Fred "Ojay" Larson, Bob Reagan |
| RG | Jim Dooley, Ed DeGree |
| RT | Lawrence "Buck" Shaw, Bill Voss, Jack Flynn |
| RE | Eddie Anderson, Frank "Si" Seyfrit |
| QB | Chet Grant, Frank Thomas, Les Logan, Pete "Red" Smith, Frank Reese |
| LH | Johnny Mohardt, Tom Lieb, Earl Walsh, Joe "Dutch" Bergman |
| RH | Danny Coughlin, Paul Castner, Gus Desch, Willie "Red" Maher |
| FB | Chet Wynne, Bob Phelan |

## 1922 (8-1-1)

| | | Opponent | Score |
|---|---|---|---|
| September 30 | W | Kalamazoo | 46-0 |
| October 7 | W | St. Louis | 26-0 |
| October 14 | W | at Purdue | 20-0 |
| October 21 | W | DePauw | 34-7 |
| October 28 | W | at Georgia Tech | 13-3 |
| November 4 | W | Indiana (HC) | 27-0 |
| November 11 | T | at Army | 0-0 |
| November 18 | W | at Butler | 31-3 |
| November 25 | W | at Carnegie Tech | 19-0 |
| November 30 | L | at Nebraska | 6-14 |

| Position | Name |
|---|---|
| LE | Glen "Judge" Carberry, Paul McNulty, Chuck Collins |
| LT | Forrest "Fod" Cotton, Gus Stange, Jack Flynn |
| LG | Harvey Brown, John Weibel, Neil Flinn |
| C | Bob Reagan, Adam Walsh |
| RG | Ed DeGree, Noble Kizer |
| RT | Gene Oberst, Tom Lieb, Edgar "Rip" Miller |
| RE | George Vergara, Gene Mayl, Tim Murphy, Ed Hunsinger |
| QB | Frank Thomas, Harry Stuhldreher, Les Logan |
| LH | Elmer Layden, Jim Crowley, Joe "Dutch" Bergman, Mickey Kane |
| RH | Don Miller, Ward "Doc" Connell, Willie "Red" Maher, Gus Desch |
| FB | Paul Castner, Bill Cerney, Bernie Livergood |

## 1923 (9-1-0)

| | | Opponent | Score |
|---|---|---|---|
| September 29 | W | Kalamazoo | 74-0 |
| October 6 | W | Lombard | 14-0 |
| October 13 | W | Army at Ebbets Field, Brooklyn | 13-0 |
| October 20 | W | at Princeton | 25-2 |
| October 27 | W | Georgia Tech | 35-7 |
| November 3 | W | Purdue (HC) | 34-7 |
| November 10 | L | at Nebraska | 7-14 |
| November 17 | W | Butler | 34-7 |
| November 24 | W | at Carnegie Tech | 26-0 |
| November 29 | W | at St. Louis | 13-0 |

| Position | Name |
|---|---|
| LE | Chuck Collins, Clem Crowe, Tom Farrell |
| LT | Joe Bach, Gus Stange, John Noppenberger |
| LG | Harvey Brown, John Weibel, Charles Glueckert |
| C | Adam Walsh, Bob Reagan, Russ Arndt |
| RG | Noble Kizer, George Vergara, Vince Harrington |
| RT | Gene Oberst, Edgar "Rip" Miller, Frank Milbauer |
| RE | Gene Mayl, Ed Hunsinger, Tim Murphy |
| QB | Harry Stuhldreher, Frank Reese |
| LH | Jim Crowley, Joe "Dutch" Bergman, Max Houser |
| RH | Don Miller, Willie "Red" Maher, Ward "Doc" Connell |
| FB | Elmer Layden, Bill Cerney, Rex Enright, Bernie Livergood |

## 1924 (10-0-0)

| | | Opponent | Score |
|---|---|---|---|
| October 4 | W | Lombard | 40-0 |
| October 11 | W | Wabash | 34-0 |
| October 18 | W | Army at Polo Grounds | 13-7 |
| October 25 | W | at Princeton | 12-0 |
| November 1 | W | Georgia Tech (H) | 34-3 |
| November 8 | W | at Wisconsin | 38-3 |
| November 15 | W | Nebraska | 34-6 |
| November 22 | W | Northwestern at Grant Park | 13-6 |
| November 29 | W | at Carnegie Tech | 40-19 |
| January 1, 1925 | W | Stanford (Rose Bowl) | 27-10 |

| Position | Name |
|---|---|
| LE | Chuck Collins, Clem Crowe, Joe Rigali |
| LT | Joe Bach, Joe Boland, John McMullan |
| LG | John Weibel, Charles Glueckert, Vince Harrington |
| C | Adam Walsh, Joe Harmon, Joe Maxwell |
| RG | Noble Kizer, Dick Hanousek |
| RT | Edgar "Rip" Miller, John Wallace, John McManmon |
| RE | Ed Hunsinger, Wilbur Eaton |
| QB | Harry Stuhldreher, Eddie Scharer, Glen "Red" Edwards, Frank Reese |
| LH | Jim Crowley, Max Houser, Harry O'Boyle |
| RH | Don Miller, Ward "Doc" Connell, Tom Hearden, John Roach |
| FB | Elmer Layden, Bill Cerney, Bernie Livergood |

## 1925 (7-2-1)

| | | Opponent | Score |
|---|---|---|---|
| September 26 | W | Baylor | 41-0 |
| October 3 | W | Lombard | 69-0 |
| October 10 | W | Beloit | 19-3 |
| October 17 | L | Army at Yankee Stadium | 0-27 |
| October 24 | W | at Minnesota | 19-7 |
| October 31 | W | at Georgia Tech | 13-0 |
| November 7 | T | at Penn State | 0-0 |
| November 14 | W | Carnegie Tech (HC) | 26-0 |
| November 21 | W | Northwestern | 13-10 |
| November 26 | L | at Nebraska | 0-17 |

| Position | Name |
|---|---|
| LE | Clem Crowe, John "Ike" Voedisch, Charles "Chile" Walsh |
| LT | Joe Boland, John McMullan |
| LG | Ray Marelli, John "Clipper" Smith |
| C | Joe Maxwell, Art "Bud" Boeringer, John Frederick, George Murrin |
| RG | Frank Mayer, Dick "Red" Smith, Ed Crowe |
| RT | John McManmon, John "Bull" Polisky |
| RE | John Wallace, Joe Rigali, Joe Benda |
| QB | Gene "Red" Edwards, Art Parisien, Eddie Scharer, Vince McNally, Charlie Riley |
| LH | Christy Flanagan, Harry O'Boyle, John Roach |
| RH | Tom Hearden, Francis "Lew" Cody, Joe Prelli, Ray "Bucky" Dahman |
| FB | Rex Enright, Dick Hanousek, Elmer Wynne |

## 1926 (9-1-0)

| | | Opponent | Score |
|---|---|---|---|
| October 2 | W | Beloit | 77-0 |
| October 9 | W | at Minnesota | 20-7 |
| October 16 | W | Penn State | 28-0 |
| October 23 | W | at Northwestern | 6-0 |
| October 30 | W | Georgia Tech | 12-0 |
| November 6 | W | Indiana | 26-0 |
| November 13 | W | Army at Yankee Stadium | 7-0 |
| November 20 | W | Drake (HC) | 21-0 |
| November 27 | L | at Carnegie Tech | 0-19 |
| December 4 | W | at USC | 13-12 |

| Position | Name |
|---|---|
| LE | John "Ike" Voedisch, Charles "Chile" Walsh, Frank Keefe |
| LT | Fred Miller, John Hogan, Joe Boland |
| LG | John "Clipper" Smith, Ray Marelli, George Leppig |
| C | Art "Bud" Boeringer, John Frederick, Tim Moynihan, George Murrin |
| RG | Frank Mayer, Dick "Red" Smith, John Law |
| RT | John McManmon, John "Bull" Polisky, Jerry Ransavage |
| RE | Joe Maxwell, John Wallace, Joe Benda |
| QB | Gene "Red" Edwards, Charlie Riley, Vince McNally, Art Parisien |
| LH | Christy Flanagan, John Niemiec, John Roach |
| RH | Tom Hearden, Ray "Bucky" Dahman, Jack Chevigny |
| FB | Harry O'Boyle, Elmer Wynne, Dick "Red" Smith, Fred Collins |

## 1927 (7-1-1)

| | | Opponent | Score |
|---|---|---|---|
| October 1 | W | Coe | 28-7 |
| October 8 | W | Detroit | 20-0 |
| October 15 | W | Navy at Baltimore | 19-6 |
| October 22 | W | at Indiana | 19-6 |
| October 29 | W | Georgia Tech | 26-7 |
| November 5 | T | Minnesota | 7-7 |
| November 12 | L | Army at Yankee Stadium | 0-18 |
| November 19 | W | at Drake | 32-0 |
| November 26 | W | USC at Soldier Field | 7-6 |

| Position | Name |
|---|---|
| LE | John "Ike" Voedisch, John Colrick, Jim Hulbert |
| LT | Fred Miller, Jerry Ransavage, Dick Donoghue |
| LG | John "Clipper" Smith, Jack Cannon, Gus Bondi |
| C | John Frederick, Tim Moynihan, Joe Nash |
| RG | George Leppig, John Law, George Murrin |
| RT | John "Bull" Poliksy, Jack McGrath, John Doarn |
| RE | Charles "Chile" Walsh, Joe Benda, Manny Vezie |
| QB | Charlie Riley, Jim Brady, Joe Morrissey, Charles McKinney |
| LH | Christy Flanagan, John Niemiec, Jack Elder |
| RH | Ray "Bucky" Dahman, Jack Chevigny, Joe Prelli |
| FB | Elmer Wynne, Fred Collins, Billy Dew, George "Dinny" Shay |

## 1928 (5-4-0)

| | | Opponent | Score |
|---|---|---|---|
| September 29 | W | Loyola (New Orleans) | 12-6 |
| October 6 | L | at Wisconsin | 6-22 |
| October 13 | W | Navy at Soldier Field | 7-0 |
| October 20 | L | at Georgia Tech | 0-13 |
| October 27 | W | Drake | 32-6 |
| November 3 | W | Penn State at Philadelphia | 9-0 |
| November 10 | W | Army at Yankee Stadium | 12-6 |
| November 17 | L | Carnegie Tech | 7-27 |
| December 1 | L | at USC | 14-27 |

| Position | Name |
|---|---|
| LE | Eddie Collins, John Colrick, Johnny "One Play" O'Brien |
| LT | Fred Miller, Jerry Ransavage, Frank Leahy |
| LG | George Leppig, Gus Bondi, Tom Kassis |
| C | Tim Moynihan, Joe Nash |
| RG | John Law, Jack Cannon, Bert Metzger |
| RT | Ted Twomey, Dick Donoghue, Jack McGrath |
| RE | Manny Vezie, Tom Murphy, Tom Conley |
| QB | Jim Brady, Frank Carideo, Joe Morrissey |
| LH | John Niemiec, Jack Elder, Jack Montroy |
| RH | Jack Chevigny, Billy Dew, Jim Bray, Paul "Bucky" O"Connor |
| FB | Fred Collins, Larry "Moon" Mullins, George "Dinny" Shay |

## 1929 (9-0-0)

| | | Opponent | Score |
|---|---|---|---|
| October 5 | W | at Indiana | 14-0 |
| October 12 | W | Navy at Baltimore | 14-7 |
| October 19 | W | Wisconsin at Soldier Field | 19-0 |
| October 26 | W | at Carnegie Tech | 7-0 |
| November 2 | W | at Georgia Tech | 26-6 |
| November 9 | W | Drake at Soldier Field | 19-7 |
| November 16 | W | USC at Soldier Field | 13-12 |
| November 23 | W | at Northwestern | 26-6 |
| November 30 | W | Army at Yankee Stadium | 7-0 |

| Position | Name |
|---|---|
| LE | John Colrick, Eddie Collins, Johnny "One Play" O'Brien |
| LT | Ted Twomey, Al Culver, Regis McNamara |
| LG | Jack Cannon, Tom Kassis, Joe Locke, Bill Cassidy |
| C | Tim Moynihan, Joe Nash, Tommy Yarr |
| RG | John Law, Bert Metzger, Gus Bondi |
| RT | Dick Donoghue, Art McManmon, Frank Leahy, Charles Schwartz |
| RE | Tom Conley, Manny Vezie, George Vik, Tom Murphy, Roy Bailie |
| QB | Frank Carideo, Al "Bud" Gebert, Tommy Kenneally, Norb Christman |
| LH | Jack Elder, Marchy Schwartz, Bernie Leahy |
| RH | Marty Brill, Paul "Bucky" O'Connor, Clarence Kaplan, Carl Cronin |
| FB | Larry "Moon" Mullins, Joe Savoldi, George "Dinny" Shay, Al Howard |

## 1930 (10-0-0)

| Date | | Opponent | Score |
|------|---|----------|-------|
| October 4 | W | SMU | 20-14 |
| October 11 | W | Navy | 26-2 |
| October 18 | W | Carnegie Tech | 21-6 |
| October 25 | W | at Pittsburgh | 35-19 |
| November 1 | W | Indiana | 27-0 |
| November 8 | W | at Pennsylvania | 60-20 |
| November 15 | W | Drake | 28-7 |
| November 22 | W | at Northwestern | 14-0 |
| November 29 | W | Army at Soldier Field | 7-6 |
| December 6 | W | at USC | 27-0 |

| Position | Name |
|----------|------|
| LE | Ed Kosky, Paul Host, Johnny "One Play" O'Brien |
| LT | Al Culver, Frank "Nordy" Hoffman, Regis McNamara |
| LG | Tom Kassis, Jim Harris, Norm Greeney |
| C | Tommy Yarr, Frank Butler, John Rogers |
| RG | Bert Metzger, Bill Pierce, Bob Terlaak |
| RT | Joe Kurth, Art McManmon, Dick Donoghue, Frank Leahy |
| RE | Tom Conley, George Vik, Dick Mahoney |
| QB | Frank Carideo, Chuck Jaskwhich, Carl Cronin |
| LH | Marchy Schwartz, Mike Koken, Nick Lukats, Bernie Leahy |
| RH | Marty Brill, Paul "Bucky" O'Connor, Clarence Kaplan |
| FB | Larry "Moon" Mullins, Joe Savoldi, Al Howard, Dan Hanley |

# APPENDIX B: ROCKNE VS. INDIVIDUAL OPPONENTS

Knute Rockne's record as Notre Dame head coach vs. individual opponents.

| Opponent | Games | W | L | T | PF | PA |
|---|---|---|---|---|---|---|
| Army | 12 | 9 | 2 | 1 | 126 | 90 |
| Baylor | 1 | 1 | 0 | 0 | 41 | 0 |
| Beloit | 2 | 2 | 0 | 0 | 96 | 3 |
| Butler | 2 | 2 | 0 | 0 | 65 | 10 |
| Carnegie Tech | 8 | 6 | 2 | 0 | 146 | 71 |
| Case Tech | 1 | 1 | 0 | 0 | 26 | 6 |
| Coe | 1 | 1 | 0 | 0 | 28 | 7 |
| DePauw | 2 | 2 | 0 | 0 | 91 | 17 |
| Detroit | 1 | 1 | 0 | 0 | 20 | 0 |
| Drake | 5 | 5 | 0 | 0 | 132 | 20 |
| Georgia Tech | 8 | 7 | 1 | 0 | 159 | 39 |
| Great Lakes | 1 | 0 | 0 | 1 | 7 | 7 |
| Haskell | 1 | 1 | 0 | 0 | 42 | 7 |
| Indiana | 8 | 8 | 0 | 0 | 170 | 26 |
| Iowa | 1 | 0 | 1 | 0 | 7 | 10 |
| Kalamazoo | 5 | 5 | 0 | 0 | 229 | 0 |
| Lombard | 3 | 3 | 0 | 0 | 123 | 0 |
| Loyola, Louis. | 1 | 1 | 0 | 0 | 12 | 6 |
| Marquette | 1 | 1 | 0 | 0 | 21 | 7 |
| Michigan State | 4 | 3 | 1 | 0 | 93 | 13 |
| Minnesota | 3 | 2 | 0 | 1 | 46 | 21 |
| Morningside | 1 | 1 | 0 | 0 | 14 | 6 |
| Mount Union | 1 | 1 | 0 | 0 | 60 | 7 |
| Navy | 4 | 4 | 0 | 0 | 66 | 15 |
| Nebraska | 8 | 4 | 3 | 1 | 84 | 67 |
| Northwestern | 6 | 6 | 0 | 0 | 105 | 29 |
| Penn State | 3 | 2 | 0 | 1 | 37 | 0 |
| Pennsylvania | 1 | 1 | 0 | 0 | 60 | 20 |
| Pittsburgh | 1 | 1 | 0 | 0 | 35 | 19 |
| Princeton | 2 | 2 | 0 | 0 | 37 | 2 |
| Purdue | 6 | 6 | 0 | 0 | 174 | 26 |

| Opponent | Games | W | L | T | PF | PA |
|----------|-------|---|---|---|-----|-----|
| Rutgers | 1 | 1 | 0 | 0 | 48 | 0 |
| St. Louis | 2 | 2 | 0 | 0 | 39 | 0 |
| Southern Cal | 5 | 4 | 1 | 0 | 74 | 57 |
| SMU | 1 | 1 | 0 | 0 | 20 | 14 |
| Stanford | 1 | 1 | 0 | 0 | 27 | 10 |
| Valparaiso | 1 | 1 | 0 | 0 | 28 | 3 |
| Wabash | 2 | 2 | 0 | 0 | 101 | 7 |
| Western Mich. | 2 | 2 | 0 | 0 | 94 | 0 |
| Wisconsin | 3 | 2 | 1 | 0 | 63 | 25 |
| | | | | | | |
| Totals | 122 | 105 | 12 | 5 | 2,846 | 667 |

# APPENDIX C: ROCKNE VS. OPPOSING COACHES

| Coach | School(s) | GP | W | L |
|---|---|---|---|---|
| Alexander, Bill | Georgia Tech | 8 | 7 | 1 |
| Ashmore, James | DePauw | 1 | 1 | 0 |
| Barron, Albert | Michigan State | 1 | 1 | 0 |
| Bearg, Ernest | Nebraska | 1 | 0 | 1 |
| Bell, Harry | Lombard | 3 | 3 | 0 |
| Bell, Madison "Matty" | Haskell | 1 | 1 | 0 |
| Bezdek, Hugo | Penn State | 3 | 2 | 0 |
| Bohler, Ray | Beloit | 1 | 1 | 0 |
| Brewer, Chester | Michigan State | 1 | 1 | 0 |
| Bridges, Frank | Baylor | 1 | 1 | 0 |
| Clark, George "Potsy" | Michigan State | 1 | 1 | 0 |
| Daly, Charles | Army | 4 | 3 | 0 |
| Dawson, Fred | Nebraska | 4 | 2 | 2 |
| Dietz, William "Lone Star" | Purdue | 1 | 1 | 0 |
| Dorais, Charles "Gus" | Detroit | 1 | 1 | 0 |
| Eby, Moray | Coe | 1 | 1 | 0 |
| Gauthier, George | Michigan State | 1 | 0 | 1 |
| Hanley, Dick | Northwestern | 2 | 2 | 0 |
| Herron, James P. | Indiana | 1 | 1 | 0 |
| Ingram, Bill | Navy | 4 | 4 | 0 |
| Jones, Biff | Army | 3 | 2 | 1 |
| Jones, Howard | Iowa | 1 | 0 | 1 |
|  | Southern Cal | 5 | 4 | 1 |
|  | *Totals vs. Jones* | *6* | *4* | *2* |
| Keogan, George | Valparaiso | 1 | 1 | 0 |
| Kline, William | Nebraska | 1 | 0 | 0 |
| McDevitt, Elmer | Northwestern | 1 | 1 | 0 |
| McEwan, John | Army | 3 | 2 | 1 |
| McReavy, C.J. | Great Lakes Naval | 1 | 0 | 0 |
| Mills, Tommy | Beloit | 1 | 1 | 0 |
| Morrison, Ray | SMU | 1 | 1 | 0 |
| O'Brien, George | Mount Union | 1 | 1 | 0 |

| | | | | |
|---|---|---|---|---|
| Page, Harlan "Pat" | Butler | 2 | 2 | 0 |
| | Indiana | 4 | 4 | 0 |
| | *Totals vs. Page* | *6* | *6* | *0* |
| O'Rourke, Steve | St. Louis | 1 | 1 | 0 |
| Phelan, James | Purdue | 2 | 2 | 0 |
| Roper, Bill | Princeton | 2 | 2 | 0 |
| Ryan, Jack | Marquette | 1 | 1 | 0 |
| | Wisconsin | 1 | 1 | 0 |
| | *Totals vs. Ryan* | *2* | *2* | *0* |
| Sanford, George F. | Rutgers | 1 | 1 | 0 |
| Sasse, Ralph | Army | 1 | 1 | 0 |
| Saunderson, Jason | Morningside | 1 | 1 | 0 |
| Savage, Dan | St. Louis | 1 | 1 | 0 |
| Scanlon, A. Butch | Purdue | 3 | 3 | 0 |
| Schulte, Henry | Nebraska | 2 | 2 | 0 |
| Shaughnessy, Clark | Loyola, La. | 1 | 1 | 0 |
| Solem, Oscar "Ossie" | Drake | 5 | 5 | 0 |
| Spaulding, William | Western Michigan | 2 | 2 | 0 |
| Spears, Clarence "Doc" | Minnesota | 3 | 2 | 0 |
| Stiehm, Ewald | Indiana | 3 | 3 | 0 |
| Steffen, Wally | Carnegie Tech | 8 | 6 | 2 |
| Street, J. Maynard | Kalamazoo | 1 | 1 | 0 |
| Sutherland, Jock | Pittsburgh | 1 | 1 | 0 |
| Thistlethwaite, Glenn | Northwestern | 3 | 3 | 0 |
| | Wisconsin | 2 | 1 | 1 |
| | *Totals vs. Thistlethwaite* | *5* | *4* | *1* |
| Townsend, J. Russell | Wabash | 1 | 1 | 0 |
| Vaughan, Robert "Pete" | Wabash | 1 | 1 | 0 |
| Walker, Fred | DePauw | 1 | 1 | 0 |
| Warner, Glenn "Pop" | Stanford | 1 | 1 | 0 |
| Wray, Ludlow | Pennsylvania | 1 | 1 | 0 |
| Young, Ralph | Kalamazoo | 4 | 4 | 0 |

# Acknowledgements

*Coach For A Nation: The Life and Times of Knute Rockne* has taken nearly a decade to produce, since the early days of research for our first book, *Loyal Sons: The Story of The Four Horsemen and Notre Dame Football's 1924 Champions*. Many people contributed effort and encouragement to make it happen.

Let me begin by thanking my great friend, author, and journalism professor Samuel G. Freedman, who has now added a book about college football to his world-class body of work with the release of *Breaking the Line: The Season in Black College Football That Transformed the Sport and Changed the Course of Civil Rights*. Sam was an early advocate and steadfast supporter of "going the distance" and writing a comprehensive biography of Rockne, rather than carving out just a slice of his life and work. Another dear friend and football author, Denis Gullickson (*Before They Were the Packers* and *Vagabond Halfback*) has been a constant sounding board, always asking the pertinent question. And, it was my great pleasure to meet Pulitzer Prize winner David Maraniss, whose *When Pride Still Mattered: A Life of Vince Lombardi* is considered by many, including me, as the finest sports biography ever written. That David and I share a heritage as Wisconsin-raised Packer fans and Madison newspaper writers adds to the connection.

Speaking of Wisconsin newspapers, I should mention that it helps tremendously to take on a project like this with the love and support of two long-time friends who are sportswriters-turned-priests, Rev. Jay Poster and Rev. Peter Etzel, S.J. What a treat it was to bring each of them to the Notre Dame campus for a game, so they could absorb some of the mystique, which has captured so many.

Prof. Michael R. Steele of Pacific University in Oregon, a Notre Dame alumnus, provided an excellent road map to the coach's life in *Knute Rockne: A Bio-Bibliography*, as well as personal encouragement and insight. The late Paul Castner, the tremendous multi-sport athlete at Notre Dame in the time of Gipp and the Four Horsemen, had the great foresight and energy in his 70s to climb into a mobile home and travel the country, interviewing dozens of Rockne's players. His volume, written with John D. McCallum, *We Remember Rockne*, is an invaluable resource for our work.

At Notre Dame, Charles Lamb and his excellent staff at the Notre Dame Archives make research a smooth process. Elizabeth Hogan, Kevin Cawley, and Joe Smith can be counted on for their able assistance. In the Athletic

Department, John Heisler and Carol Copley provided moral and material support.

We are delighted to continue our partnership with *Play Like A Champion Today*, an outstanding program improving youth and school sports nation-wide, led by our dear friends, Prof. Clark Power and Kristin Sheehan.

In traveling the country researching the Rockne era of college football, it has been our great pleasure to meet and become friends with interesting people with a passion for the sport, and collections of items to prove it. Some have allowed us to peek into their treasures, especially Captain Gerry Motl, a source of so much related to Navy, Army, and Notre Dame football; and Ken Inadomi, whose focus is the Notre Dame-Southern Cal rivalry.

Our travels and phone calls put us in touch with so many people gener-ous with their information and help. Nils Rockne, grandson of the coach, keeps alive Knute's legacy, and has been a gracious supporter of these ef-forts. An early trip to Dorais Chevrolet in Wabash, Indiana, allowed us to meet Bill Dorais, son of Gus, and grandson David Dorais. Bob Dorais freely shared research, and Mary Kay Dorais provided enthusiastic support. Sue Law Hawes gave an information-packed tour of Yonkers, New York, home of her father, 1929 captain John Law. Margaret Mary Conley and Margaret Mary O'Neill loaded me up with information. Bob Erkkila and Jerry Vairo proved amiable hosts during my trip to Gipp Country. And Bob and Maggie Braun opened up their girls' summer camp, once known as Camp Rockne, to our sleuthing. In South Bend, John Hickey Jr., Karen Hickey, and Ro Hickey provided fascinating local history, especially about the home on East Wayne, which has been occupied by just two families since 1929: the Rocknes and the Hickeys. Other South Benders providing help included Anne Luther, Phil Krause, and Patti Walsh.

The book could not have come together without the excellent work of the staff at Great Day Press, particularly Elizabeth Lefebvre, who served as primary editor. Angela Cox offered essential design assistance. Phillip Veli-kan's dramatic jacket design completed the package.

Finally, we offer our sincere appreciation for the significant support pro-vided by Bob Sullivan, Notre Dame Class of 1976; and the Rockne Heritage Fund at Notre Dame, guided ably by Mary Rattenbury.

For all the time and talents graciously shared by so many—thank you.

# Bibliography

Alexander, June Granatir. *Daily Life In Immigrant America, 1870-1920*. Westport, Connecticut: Greenwood Press, 2007.

Anderson, Heartly "Hunk," and Klosinski, Emil. *Notre Dame, Chicago Bears, and Hunk*. Orlando, Florida: Florida Sun-Gator Publishing, 1976.

Armstrong, James E. *Onward to Victory: A Chronicle of the Alumni of the University of Notre Dame*. Notre Dame, Indiana: University of Notre Dame Press, 1974.

Bachman, Charles W. *The Modern Notre Dame Formation*. Pompano Beach, Florida: Charles W. Bachman, 1969.

Badger, Reid R. *The Great American Fair: The World's Columbian Exposition & American Culture*. Chicago: Nelson Hall, 1979.

Barry, John M. *The Great Influenza*. New York: The Penguin Group, 2004.

Beach, Jim, and Moore, Daniel. *Army vs. Notre Dame: The Big Game, 1913-1947*. New York: Random House, 1948.

Bonsall, Thomas E. *More Than They Promised: The Studebaker Story*. Stanford, California. Stanford University Press, 2000.

Brondfield, Jerry. *Rockne: The Coach, the Man, the Legend*. Lincoln: University of Nebraska Press, 1976.

Brown, Dorothy M. *Mabel Walker Willebrandt: A Study of Power, Loyalty, and Law*. Knoxville: The University of Tennessee Press. 1984.

Brown, Gene. *The Complete Book of Track and Field*. Indianapolis: The Bobbs-Merril Company, 1980.

Buford, Kate. *Native American Son: The Life and Sporting Legend of Jim Thorpe*. New York: Alfred A. Knopf, 2010.

Burns, Jeffrey M., Skerrett, Ellen and White, Joseph M. *Keeping Faith: European and Asian Catholic Immigrants*. Maryknoll, New York: Orbis Books, 2000.

Burns, Robert E. *Being Catholic Being American: The Notre Dame Story, 1842-1934*. Notre Dame, Indiana: University of Notre Dame Press, 1999.

Carlson, Stan W. *Dr. Henry L. Williams: A Football Biography*. Minneapolis: Stan Carlson Publisher, 1938.

Cavanaugh, Jack. *The Gipper: George Gipp, Knute Rockne, and the Dramatic Rise of Notre Dame Football*. New York: Skyhorse, 2010.

Chalmers, David M. *Hooded Americanism: The History of the Ku Klux Klan*. Durham, N.C.: Duke University Press, 1987.

Chelland, Patrick. *One for The Gipper: George Gipp, Knute Rockne, and Notre Dame*. Chicago: Henry Regnery Co., 1973.

Coan, Peter M. *Toward A Better Life: America's New Immigrants in Their Own Words From Ellis Island To The Present*. Amherst, New York: Prometheus Books, 2011.

Cooper, John Milton, Jr. *Pivotal Decades: The United States, 1900-1920*. New York: W.W. Norton & Co, 1990.

Corle, Edwin. *John Studebaker: An American Dream*. New York: E.P. Dutton & Co., 1948.

Crouch, Tom D. and Jakab, Peter L. *The Wright Brothers And The Invention of The Aerial Age*. Washington, DC: Smithsonian Institution, 2003.

Danzig, Allison. *Oh, How They Played the Game: The Early Days of Football and the Heroes Who Made It Great.* New York: Macmillan, 1971.

Davies, John. *The Legend of Hobey Baker.* Boston: Little, Brown and Company, 1966.

Dierikx, Marc. *Fokker: A Transatlantic Biography.* Washington, DC: Smithsonian Institution Press, 1997.

Dinnerstein, Leonard and Reimers, David M. *Ethnic Americans: A History of Immigration.* New York: Columbia University Press, 2009.

Dohn, Norman. *The History of the Anti-Saloon League.* Columbus, Ohio: Ohio State University Press, 1959

Dolan, Jay P. *The Irish Americans: A History.* New York: Bloomsbury Press, 2008.

Emery, Edwin. *The Press and America: An Interpretative History of the Mass Media.* Englewood Cliffs, New Jersey: Prentice-Hall, 1972.

Erskine, Albert Russell. *History of the Studebaker Corporation.* South Bend, Indiana: The Studebaker Corporation, 1924.

Farnsworth, Marjorie. *The Ziegfeld Follies* New York: Crown Publishers, 1961.

Fokker, Anthony H. and Gould, Bruce. *Flying Dutchman: The Life of Anthony Fokker.* New York: Arno Press, 1931.Goddard, S

Fountain, Charles. *Sportswriter: The Life and Times of Grantland Rice.* New York: Oxford Univ. Press, 1993.

Francis, David W., and Francis, Diane D. *Cedar Point: The Queen of American Watering Places.* Fairview Park, Ohio: Amusement Park Books, Inc., 1995.

Gekas, George. *Gipper: The Life & Times of George Gipp.* South Bend, Indiana: And Books, 1987.

Goddard, Stephen B. *Getting There: The Epic Struggle Between Road and Rail In The American Century.* New York: HaperCollins, 1994.

Goodspeed, Thomas Wakefield. *A History of The University of Chicago: The First Quarter Century.* Chicago: The University of Chicago Press, 1916.

Goodspeed, Thomas Wakefield. *William Rainey Harper: First President of the University of Chicago.* Chicago: The University of Chicago Press, 1928.

Grant, Chet. *Before Rockne at Notre Dame.* South Bend, Indiana: Icarus Press, 1978.

Gullickson, Denis, and Hanson, Carl. *Before They Were the Packers: Green Bay's Town Team Days.* Black Earth, Wisconsin: Trails Books, 2004.

Gullifor, Paul F. *The Fighting Irish on the Air: The History of Notre Dame Football Broadcasting.* South Bend, Indiana: Diamond Communications, Inc., 2001.

Harper, William A. *How You Played The Game: The Life of Grantland Rice.* Columbia, Missouri: University of Missouri Press, 1999.

Hatch, Anthony P. *Tinder Box:The Iroquois Theater Disaster 1903.*Academy Chicago Publishers, 2003.

Heaps, Willard A. *The Story of Ellis Island.* New York: The Seabury Press, 1967.

Holzman, Jerome. *No Cheering in the Press Box.* New York: Holt, Rinehart and Winston, 1973.

Hope, Arthur J., CSC. *The Story of Notre Dame.* University of Notre Dame Press, 1999.

Howard, Timothy: *A History of St. Joseph County, Indiana, Volume 1.* The Lewis Publishing Company.

Heffelfinger, W.W., *This Was Football.* New York: A. S. Barnes & Co., 1954.

Kaye, Ivan N. *Good Clean Violence: A History of College Football.* Philadelphia: J.B. Lippincott, 1973.

Kessner, Thomas. *The Flight Of The Century: Charles Lindbergh And The Rise Of American Aviation.* New York: Oxford University Press, 2010.

Klapper, Melissa R. *Small Strangers: The Experiences of Immigrant Children in America, 1880-1925.* Chicago: Ivan R. Dee, 2007.

Klosinski, Emil. *Pro Football In The Days Of Rockne.* Los Angeles: Panoply Publications, 2006.

Klosinski, Emil. *Gipp At Notre Dame: The Untold Story.* Baltimore: Publish America, 2003.

Kobler, John. *Capone. The Life and World of Al Capone.* Cambridge, Massachusetts: DaCapo Press, 1971.

Langford, Jeremy and Langford, Jim. *The Spirit of Notre Dame: Legends, Traditions, and Inspiration from One of America's Most Beloved Universities.* New York: Doubleday, 2005.

Larson, Edward J. *Summer for the Gods: The Scopes Trial and America's Continuing Debate Over Science and Religion.* New York: Basic Books, 1997.

Layden, Elmer, and Snyder, Ed. *It Was A Different Game: The Elmer Layden Story.* Englewood Cliffs, NJ: Prentice-Hall, Inc., 1969.

Leaman, Paul. *Fokker Aircraft of World War One.* Ramsbury, Marlborough Wiltshire: Crowood Press, 2001.

Lefebvre, Jim. *Loyal Sons: The Story of the Four Horsemen and Notre Dame Football's 1924 Champions.* Minneapolis: Great Day Press, 2008.

Lester, Robin. *Stagg's University: The Rise, Decline, and Fall of Big-Time Football at Chicago.* Urbana, Illinois: University of Illinois Press, 1995.

Lovoll, Odd S. *A Century of Urban Life: The Norwegians in Chicago Before 1930.* Urbana, Ill.: The University of Illinois Press, 1988

MacCambridge, Michael. *ESPN College Football Encyclopedia: The Complete History of the Game.* New York: ESPN Books Hyperion, 2005.

Maggio, Frank. *Notre Dame And The Game That Changed Football.* New York: Carroll & Graf, 2007.

McCallum, John D., and Castner Paul. *We Remember Rockne.* Huntington, Indiana: Our Sunday Visitor, Inc., 1975.

McRae, Donald. *The Great Trials of Clarence Darrow: The Landmark Cases of Leopold and Loeb, John T. Scopes, and Ossian Sweet.* New York: HaperCollins, 2009.

Meanwell, Walter E. and Rockne, Knute K. *Training, Conditioning and the Care of Injuries.* Madison, Wisconsin, 1931.

Miller, Donald L. *City of the Century: The Epic of Chicago and the Making of America.* New York: Simon & Schuster Paperbacks, 1996.

Miller, Ross. *The Great Chicago Fire.* Urbana, Illinois: University of Illinois Press, 1990.

Mortimer, Gavin. *Chasing Icarus: The Seventeen Days In 1910 That Forever Changed American Aviation.* New York: Walker Publishing, 2009.

Moore, Edmund A. *A Catholic Runs For President: The Campaign of 1928.* Gloucester, Massachusetts: The Ronald Press Company, 1956.

Morris, James McGrath. *Pulitzer: A Life In Politics, Print, and Power.* New York: HarperCollins, 2010.

Mordden, Ethan. *Ziegfeld: The Man Who Invented Show Business.* New York: St. Martin's Press, 2008.

Newton, Michel. *The Ku Klux Klan: History, Organization, Language, Influence and Activities of America's Most Notorious Secret Society.* Jefferson, North Carolina: McFarland & Company, 2007.

O'Connell, Marvin R. *Edward Sorin.* Notre Dame, Indiana: University of Notre Dame Press, 2001.

Okrent, Daniel. *Last Call: The Rise and Fall of Prohibition.* New York: Scribner, 2010.

Oriard, Michael. *King Football: Sport & Spectacle in the Golden Age of Radio & Newsreels, Movies & Magazines, The Weekly & The Daily Press.* Chapel Hill, NC: The University of North Carolina Press, 2001.

Oriard, Michael. *Reading Football: How the Popular Press Created an American Spectacle.* Chapel Hill, North Carolina: The University of North Carolina Press, 1993.

Poole, Gary Andrew. *The Galloping Ghost: Red Grange.* New York: Houghton Mifflin, 2008.

Powell, Harford, Jr. *Walter Camp: The Father of American Football: An Authorized Biography.* Freeport, New York: Books for Libraries Press, 1926.

Pridmore, Jay and Hurd, Jim. *Schwinn Bicycles.* St. Paul, Minnesota: MBI Publishing 2001.

Rice, Grantland. *The Tumult and the Shouting: My Life in Sport.* New York: A.S. Barnes & Co., 1954.

Robins, David. *The Birth of American Film* New York: Columbia University Press, 1996.

Robinson, Ray. *American Original: A Life of Will Rogers.* New York: Oxford University Press. 1996.

Rockne, Knute. *Rockne's Football Problems.* South Bend, Indiana: University of Notre Dame. 1927.

Samuelson, Rube. *The Rose Bowl Game.* New York: Doubleday, 1951.

Slayton, Robert A. *Empire Statesman* New York: Simon & Schuster. 2001.

Smith, Red. *Strawberries in the Wintertime: The Sporting World of Red Smith.* New York: Crown, 1974.

Sperber, Murray. *Shake Down the Thunder: The Creation of Notre Dame Football.* New York Henry Holt & Co., 1993.

Steele, Michael R. *Knute Rockne: A Bio-Bibliography.* Westport, Connecticut: Greenwood Press, 1983.

Sterling, Bryan B. and Sterling, Frances N. *Will Rogers' World: America's Foremost Political Humorist Comments on the 20s and 30s – and 80s and 90s.* New York: M. Evans and Company, 1989.

Stross, Randall E. *The Wizard of Menlo Park: How Thomas Alva Edison Invented The Modern World.* New York: Crown Publishers, 2007.

Stuhldreher, Harry A. *Knute Rockne: Man Builder.* New York: Grosset & Dunlap, 1931.

Teachout, Terry. *The Skeptic: A Life of H.L. Mencken.* New York: HarperCollins, 2002.

Thornbrough, Emma Lou. *Indiana Blacks in the Twentieth Century.* Indiana University Press, 2001.

Thurner, Arthur W. *Rebels on the Range: The Michigan Copper Miners' Strike of 1913-1914.* Hancock, Michigan: Book Concern Printers, 1984.

Thurner, Arther W. *Strangers and Sojourners: A History of Michigan's Keweenaw Peninsula.* Detroit: Wayne State University Press, 1994.

Valenzi, Kathleen D. and Hopps, Michael W. *Champion of Sport: The Life of Walter Camp 1859-1925.* Charlottesville, Virginia: Howell Press, Inc., 1990.

Wade, Wyn Craig. *The Fiery Cross: The Ku Klux Klan in America.* New York: Oxford University Press, 1987.

Wallace, Dave. *Capital of the World: A Portrait of New York City in the Roaring Twenties.* Guilford, Connecticut: Lyons Press, 2011.

Wallace, Francis. *Knute Rockne: The story of the greatest football coach who ever lived.* Garden City, New York: Doubleday & Company, 1960.

Watterson, John Sayre. *College Football: History, Spectacle, Controversy.* Baltimore: Johns Hopkins University Press, 2000.

Watts, Steven. *The People's Tycoon: Henry Ford and the American Century.* New York: Random House, 2005.

Weyand, Alexander M. *Football Immortals.* New York: The Macmillian Company, 1962.

White, Richard D. *Will Rogers: A Political Life.* Lubbock, Texas: Texas Tech University Press. 2011.

Whyte, Kenneth. *The Uncrowned King: The Sensational Rise of William Randolph Hearst.* Berkeley, California: Counterpoint Press, 2009.

Young, Eugene J. *With Rockne at Notre Dame.* New York: G.P. Putnam's Sons, 1951.

# Notes

## Chapter 1

*Holy Saturday, April:* Descriptions of Coach Rockne's funeral, and the days leading up to it, are drawn from multiple sources, including newspaper articles in the *South Bend Tribune* and *South Bend News-Times*, April 1-5, 1931; and the May, 1931 issue of the Notre Dame *Alumnus*.

4. *For three days:* Tributes to Rockne, from personal telegrams to the family to widely-read newspaper editorials, could fill a volume. For a sample compilation, please visit www.CoachForANation.com.

7. *There would be:* In the Roman Catholic tradition, Mass is not celebrated between Holy Thursday night and the Easter vigil mass on Holy Saturday night.

9. *Two hours before:* Rockne was buried at Highland Cemetery, in northwest South Bend, rather than Cedar Grove at the entrance to Notre Dame, because the family was offered plots there from the McGann Funeral Home before the coach's death.

## Chapter 2

11. *The Roknes of:* Rockne, Knute K., *The Autobiography of Knute K. Rockne,* p. 26-27.

12. *Lars' skills in:* Rockne, p. 26, 29. Years later, Lars' brother George, Knute's uncle, became the first Voss resident to purchase an automobile.

14. *The significant numbers:* Dinnerstein, Leonard and Reimers, David M. *Ethnic Americans: A History of Immigration,* p. 63.

14. *Castle Garden, an:* Heaps, Willard A. *The Story of Ellis Island,* p. 1.

15. *Medical examiners inspected:* Ibid.

16. *Lars Rokne and:* Alexander, June Granatir. *Daily Life In Immigrant America,* 1870-1920, p. 63, p. 141.

16. *Irish immigration helped:* Dolan, Jay P. *The Irish Americans: A History,* p. 233.

17. *Not unlike other:* Burns, Jeffrey M., Skerrett, Ellen *Keeping Faith: European and Asian Catholic Immigrants,* p. 87.

19. *Sorin and the:* O'Connell, Marvin R. *Edward Sorin,* p. 103.

19. *'The site of:* Ibid., p. 114.

20. *Sorin was a:* Ibid., p. 183. Sorin's successful bid for a Post Office is why, to this day, it is accurate to state the university is location not in South Bend, but Notre Dame, Indiana.

21. *A day off:* Ibid., p. 650.

22. *Malfunctioning water tanks:* Notre Dame *Scholastic,* April 26, 1879,

22. *"...those who followed:* O'Connell, p. 652.

23. *'The final adoption:* Sorin to Corby, May 13, 1879 AIP.

23. *Nothing would dampen:* O'Connell, p. 656.

24. *Classes resumed in:* Ibid., p. 658.

25. *The May celebration:* Ibid., p. 701.

25. *The August celebration:* Ibid., p. 706-7.

## Chapter 3

27. *The Chicago that:* By 1900 there were 41,551 Norwegian residents in Chicago, of these 63 percent lived in the Norwegian neighborhoods on the Northwest Side. These were the golden years of Chicago's "Little Norway," the third-largest Norwegian population in the world, after Oslo and Bergen.

28. *In 1836 a:* George Powell ran an inn where Milwaukee and Armitage intersect today, and the story goes that he promised the surveying crew wine, whiskey, and a good dinner if the road came his way. Later when street signs were erected, Kimball was posted as Kimball. Henderson, Harold, "It Started With A Farm," *Chicago Reader,* Aug. 10, 2007.

28. *The Logan Square:* Ibid.

29. *It was only:* Miller, Ross. *The Great Chicago Fire,* p. 13; Cook, Frederick Francis, *Bygone Days in Chicago.*

29. *From 1837 to:* Miller, p. 32

30. *Fires were a:* www.GreatChicagoFire.org.

30. *The county coroner:* Miller, Donald L. *City of the Century: The Epic of Chicago and the Making of America,* p. 159-66; Miller, R., p. 12. Miller, R., p. 106.

32. *Railroad development in:* Miller, D., p. 180-1.

33. *To live in:* Ibid., p. 181, p. 90.

33. *By 1893, Chicago:* Lester, Robin. *Stagg's University: The Rise, Decline, and Fall of Big-Time Football at Chicago,* p. xviii.

34. *Queen Victoria opened:* Badger, Reid R. *The Great American Fair: The World's Columbian Exposition & American Culture, p. 19-20.*

34. *At the closing:* Ibid., p. 29, 38-39.

35. *The success of:* Ibid., p. 44, 48-49.

36. *A Chicago lobbyist:* Miller, D., p. 379.

38. *The Court of:* Ibid., p. 206; "The Making of the White City," *Scribner's* Magazine, Oct. 12, 1892.

## Chapter 4

39. *In early May:* Rockne, p. 30; Ship manifests, www.ellisisland.org.

40. *That was not:* "Outbreak of Cholera and Quarantine at New York Harbor," *Harpers Weekly Journal of Civilization,* September 17, 1892.

40. *For Martha Rokne:* Family lore also included a tale about little Knute wandering off and climbing the ship's crow's nest to try to be the first to spot the new land. "How my mother," Rockne, p. 58-59.

41. *The World's Columbian:* Miller, R., p. 488. Larson, Erik, *The Devil in the White City,* p. 235-6.

42. *Greeting the fairgoers:* www.hydeparkhistory.org.
42. *Footsore sightseers could:* Miller, R., p. 491-.495.
43. *On March 18:* The original Ferris Wheel remained on the Midway until 1895, when it was dismantled and moved to North Clark Street. It operated there until 1903 when it was moved to St. Louis for the Louisiana Purchase Exposition of 1904 before it was eventually dynamited and sold for scrap in 1906. www.hydeparkhistory.org.
45. *Strolling to the:* World's Columbian Exposition, 1893, Official Catalogue, at www.archive.org.
47. *The Columbian Exposition:* Larson, p. 373-374, Quote from Octave Chanute on the opening of the Aviation Conference at the World's Columbian Exposition, Aug. 1, 1893. Chanute was chairman of the committee, which sponsored and organized the conference. Notre Dame Prof. Albert F. Zahm first conceived of holding an aeronautical conference at the fair. Zahm had a tremendous influence on the history of aerospace research in the U.S.
48. *For millions of:* Miller, D., p. 488.
48. *One of the:* Miller, R., p. 220-1.

**Chapter 5**

50. *Princeton won the:* Kaye, Ivan N. *Good Clean Violence: A History of College Football,* p. 22.
52. *American football began:* Oriard, Michael. *Reading Football: How the Popular Press Created an American: Spectacle,* p. 139-40.
52. *Football's formative years:* Powell, Harford, Jr. *Walter Camp: The Father of American Football: An Authorized Biography,* p. 6.
53. *No one was:* Emery, Edwin. *The Press and America: An Interpretative History of the Mass Media,* p. 318.
54. *As college football:* Oriard, p. 57-60.
55. *It was like:* New York Journal, Nov. 4, 1895.
55. *Davis' account of:* Whyte, Kenneth. *The Uncrowned King: The Sensational Rise of William Randolph Hearst,* p. 279.
56. *In the early:* Lester, p. 1-4.
57. *As mercurial as:* Ibid. p. 7-8.
58. *Pitching was Stagg's:* p. 9-12. Stagg's teammates included Gifford Pinchot, who would go on to become governor of Pennsylvania and a national conservation leader, and Frederick Remington, an artist whose depictions of the old American West brought him widespread fame.
59. *At the newly:* Lester, p. 13-14.
60. *It soon became:* Ibid., p. 18-20.
60. *University of Chicago:* Ibid., p. 24-26.
62. *The Maroons experienced:* Ibid., p. 28-31. Hering left Chicago to coach Bucknell in 1895, and then arrived at Notre Dame in 1896, where he was player-coach. He was mostly associated with Notre Dame from then on, coming back to speak at numerous occasions, including the banquet honoring the 1924 national champions.

**Chapter 6**

63. *The Emerald Necklace:* The Encyclopedia of Chicago.
64. *The northwest corner:* Lovoll, Odd S. *A Century of Urban Life: The Norwegians in Chicago Before 1930,* p. 238-40.
65. *After the Fair:* Ibid., p. 176, 101.
65. *By 1870 Skandinaven:* Ibid., p. 176
67. *Half-way around the:* New York Times, April 6, 1896.
68. *The Stadium has:* New York Times, April 7, 1896.
70. *Without any involvement:* Rockne, p. 60-61.
71. *Four children in:* Ibid., p. 61-63.
71. *At a critical:* Ibid., p. 62-63.
72. *On October 31:* Chicago Daily Tribune, Nov. 1, 1897.
72. *In view of:* "Revolt Against Football," *Chicago Daily Tribune,* Nov. 22, 1897.
72. *At the conclusion:* "Eight Players Killed," *Chicago Daily Tribune,* Nov. 25, 1897.
73. *Fatalities and serious:* "Regulating the Game of Football," *Chicago Daily Tribune,* Dec. 6, 1894.
73. *Against that background:* Lester, p. 74, 103.
74. *Another survey in:* Watterson, John Sayre. *College Football: History, Spectacle, Controversy.*
74. *Further Rules Changes:* Pierre de Coubertin borrowed the phrase "Citius, Altius, Fortius," first used by Rev. Henri Didon a French Dominican writer, educator, and preacher, who used it at a Paris youth conference in 1891.

**Chapter 7**

76. *Of the millions:* Chicago Daily Tribune, Sept. 18, 1891.
77. *Judge Elliott Anthony:* Chicago Daily Tribune, Sept. 21, 1891. *Chicago Daily Tribune,* Jan. 1 and May 28, 1893.
77. *A typical classroom:* Chicago Daily Tribune, June 30, 1894 and Aug. 31, 1895.
78. *For all the:* Chicago Daily Tribune, April 26, 1896
79. *Enrolled at the:* Rockne, p. 32-33.
79. *As much as:* Int John Aaberg; Norlie, O.M., ed. Norsk Lutherske Menigheter i Amerika, 1843-1916; Rockne, p. 33, 36. Hans Nielsen Hauge lived from 1771 to 1824; in a total of 18 years, he published 33 books. Estimates are that 100,000 Norwegians read one or more of them, at a time when the population was 900,000 more-or-less literate individuals. He had a profound influence on both secular and religious history in Norway; his defiance of religious and secular establishment gave voice to ordinary people, paving much of the way for the liberal and democratic tradition in Norway and the entire Nordic region.
80. *Although Knute's happiest:* Rockne, p. 34-35
80. *Knute finished eighth:* Ibid., p. 35-36.
81. *Bicycling increased mobility:* Pridmore, Jay and Hurd, Jim. *Schwinn Bicycles, p. 18.*
82. *Bicycling may have:* Lester, p. 40.

83. *It was ironic:* Ibid., p. 42-46.

83. *Still, in May:* Ibid., P. 46-47.

84. *The proposal also:* Ibid., p. 47-48.

85. *Coach Stagg played:* Chicago Daily Tribune, Dec. 5, 1902.

85. *Hyde Park was:* Touchdowns were worth five points at the time; a 6-5 score indicates that one team converted a point-after, the other didn't. *Chicago Daily Tribune,* Dec. 1, 5, 1902.

85. *Hype Park alumni: Chicago Daily Tribune,* Nov. 29, Dec. 1, 3, 5, 1902.

86. *Preparations in Chicago: Chicago Daily Tribune,* Dec. 5, 1902; Rockne, p. 55. *Chicago Daily Tribune,* Dec. 5, 7, 1902.

86. *Mesmerized by the:* Rockne, p. 55-56. *Chicago Daily Tribune,* Dec. 7, 1902; Rockne, p. 56.

**Chapter 8**

88. *By 1904, Knute:* Rockne, p. 65.

89. *Rockne, anxious to:* Chicago Daily Tribune, Sept. 18, 1904.

89. *So Rockne's only:* Chicago Daily Tribune, Nov. 20, 1904; Rockne, p. 65. Luther Pollard's younger brother Fritz starred at Lane Tech, the former North Division High, through 1912, and went on to lead Brown University to the 1916 Rose Bowl, and become the first black on Walter Camp's All-America team. He played for several pro teams, and was inducted into both the College and Pro Football halls of fame. Chicago Daily Tribune, Dec. 11, 1904.

90. *The uncertainty and:* Ibid. Rockne, p. 66.

90. *Trained in the:* Steele, Michael R., *Knute Rockne: A Bio-Bibliography,* p. 59.

90. *One fine spring:* Rockne, p. 37. In later years, Tuley High, the former Northwest High, produced novelist Saul Bellow, actor Mike Todd, and entertainer Allie Sherman.

91. *For Rockne, who:* Rockne, p. 37-38.

91. *The game was:* Lester, p. 68-72.

92. *Knute spent most:* Wallace, Francis. *Knute Rockne: The story of the greatest football coach who ever lived,* p. 26; Rockne, p. 38. Teddy Roosevelt, who would oversee the reformation of college football, brokered peace ending the Russian-Japanese War, winning the Nobel Peace Prize in 1906.

93. *"Most of the:* Rockne, p. 69, 39-40.

93. *The transportation revolution:* Goddard, Stephen B. Getting There: *The Epic Struggle Between Road and Rail In The American Century,* p. 71-72.

94. *In Chicago, the:* Ibid., p. 72-73. Opposition to the streetcar company came in the form of the People's Traction League organized by Harold Ickes.

94. *Growing as fast:* Ibid., p. 77-78.

94. *Indianapolis had 13:* Ibid., p. 78.

95. *Henry Ford's Model:* Watts, Steven. *The People's Tycoon: Henry Ford and the American Century,* p. 54, 112.

95. *By 1910 nearly:* Goddard, p. 57.

95. *It seemed to:* Crouch, Tom D. and Jakab, Peter L. *The Wright Brothers And The Invention of The Aerial Age,* p. 68.

96. *Orville sat in* Ibid., p. 70.

96. *Aeronautics and aviation:* Kessner, Thomas. *The Flight Of The Century: Charles Lindbergh,* p. 22-23.

97. *Rockne read of:* Mortimer, Gavin. *Chasing Icarus: The Seventeen Days In 1910 That Forever Changed American Aviation,* p. 6-8.

97. *Chicago native John:* Ibid., p. 81. Moisant is honored today as the MOI signifying the New Orleans International Airport; Roland Garros is remembered by the French, who named the site of the French Open tennis tournament after him.

98. *"I am experimenting:* Stross, Randall E. *The Wizard of Menlo Park: How Thomas Alva Edison Invented The Modern World.*

99. *Nickelodeon operators charged: The Encyclopedia of Chicago.*

100. *For Knute Rockne:* Rockne, 38, 40, 67.

100. *In his earlier: Chicago Daily Tribune,* May 14 1905; April 17, 1907; Feb. 26, 1909.

**Chapter 9**

102. *A fellow Chicago:* Brundage would go on to serve as president of the International Olympic Committee from 1952 to 1972, the only American to hold the position.

103. *Rockne couldn't help:* Rockne, p. 70-71.

104. *After a hasty:* Rockne, p. 71; Wallace, p. 29.

105. *The change from:* On Jan. 17, 1992, Pope John Paul II elevated the Church of the Sacred Heart to the status of Basilica.

105. *Another Chicagoan to:* Int. Mary Margaret Conley.

106. *It didn't take:* Notre Dame Scholastic, Oct., 1930; Steele, p. 66.

106. *"Never on any:* Rockne, p. 73.

107. *Rockne's pals only:* Advertisement from Elks Official Souvenir Brochure, Indiana State Association B.P.O.E., 1910.

107. *Approximately one quarter:* Bonsall, Thomas E. More Than They Promised: The Studebaker Story, p. 77.

108. *The downtown Oliver: South Bend Tribune,* Feb. 4, 2008.

108. *"Since the founding: A History of St. Joseph County, Vol. 1.*

109. *Fraternal societies, service: South Bend Tribune,* Feb. 4, 2008.

110. *Errand boys rode:* Int. Gladys Boyer Zylka.

111. *Cavanaugh believed Catholic:* Burns, Robert E. *Being Catholic Being American: The Notre Dame Story, 1842-1934,* p. 70.

111. *College life! How:* Notre Dame Scholastic, Aug., 1910.

114. *The controversy underscored:* The Intercollegiate Athletic Association became the National Collegiate Athletic Association, the NCAA, in 1906.

115. *On January 21, 1911:* Notre Dame Scholastic, Jan. 28, 1911. Rockne, not yet well-known on campus, was almost always

referred to as "Rochne" in the Scholastic during his freshman year. Martin, in 1911, earned the title of "world's fastest human." He coached track at Harvard, and eventually returned to coach at Whitman College. The track stadium is named for him.

**Chapter 10**

116. *John L. "Jack":* Rockne, p. 75-76.

117. *The Scholastic welcomed:* Notre Dame *Scholastic*, Sept. 23, Oct. 7, 1911. An editorial said, "If students knew the advantages to be derived from military tactics, there wouldn't be a civilian around the place from five to six."

118. *Gus grew up:* Int. Robert Dorais.

118. *Although school life:* Int. Robert Dorais.

118. *My Dear Mr.:* Letter from Fr. Cavanaugh to Coach Longman, ND Archives UPWC 180/9.

119. *Gus followed the:* Arch Ward in *Chicago Tribune*, Jan. 5, 1954. Ward was a Notre Dame alum, former Rockne student publicity aide, and Chicago sports writer and editor.

119. *At Notre Dame:* Notre Dame *Scholastic*, Sept. 23, 1911. Rose Fitzgerald was the future Mrs. Joseph Kennedy, mother of President John F. Kennedy.

119. *Alfred "Dutch" Bergman:* Notre Dame *Scholastic*, Oct. 7, 1911. Rockne, p. 77-78.

120. *And Marks saw:* Notre Dame *Scholastic*, Sept. 30, Oct. 7, 1911.

121. *At noon on:* Notre Dame *Scholastic*, Oct. 7, 1911.

121. *October 7 dawned:* Notre Dame *Scholastic*, Oct. 14, 1911. Rockne, p. 80

122. *The following week's:* Notre Dame *Scholastic*, Oct. 21, 1911. Two prominent clergymen, Bishop Fulton Sheen and Bishop Bernard Sheil, were St. Viator graduates. The college operated until 1939, when Olivet Nazarene College purchased the campus. Now Olivet Nazarene University, it has been the Chicago Bears' training camp home since 2002. Notre Dame *Scholastic*, Oct. 28, 1911. Touchdowns were still worth five points.

122. *With a 3-0:* Notre Dame *Scholastic*, Oct. 28, 1911. Columbia was run by the Holy Cross order since 1902, serving as a prep school and junior college for two decades. It became today's University of Portland. Notre Dame *Scholastic*, Oct. 28, 1911.

123. *The result: "The:* Notre Dame *Scholastic*, Nov. 4, 1911. Art Smith's time at Notre Dame ended later in the season when it was discovered that, the previous summer, he had secretly married the 16-year-old daughter of the Minneapolis City Council president. He was immediately expelled from Notre Dame.

124. *A crowd of:* Notre Dame *Scholastic*, Nov. 4, 1911. Rockne, p. 83.

125. *A star for:* Notre Dame Scholastic, Nov. 11, 1911. Rockne, p. 82-83.

126. *Notre Dame was:* Notre Dame *Scholastic*, Nov. 18, 1911.

127. *Jesse Claire Harper:* Maggio, Frank. *Notre Dame And The Game That Changed Football*, p. 64-66.

127. *Jesse Harper did:* Maggio, p. 65-67.

127. *In 1910, Harper:* Maggio, p. 76-77.

128. *Harper's task in:* Notre Dame *Scholastic*, Nov. 25, 1911.

128. *In the third:* Notre Dame *Scholastic*, Nov. 25, 1911. Rockne, p. 85. Among the 1912 rules changes, passes traveling further than 20 yards beyond the line of scrimmage were made legal.

129. *"Playing with fierceness:* Chicago Daily Tribune, Dec. 1, 1911.

129. *Notre Dame had:* Notre Dame *Scholastic*, Dec. 2, 1911. Rockne, p. 75.

**Chapter 11**

132. *It was then:* Rockne, p. 79

132. *Rockne, similar to:* Buford, Kate. *Native American Son: The Life and Sporting Legend of Jim Thorpe*, p. 120.

133. *The buzz of:* Ibid., p. 115

133. *The pentathlon, which:* Ibid., p. 127-28.

133. *Pacing himself for:* Ibid., p. 131. Thorpe was stripped of his Olympic titles after it was found he was paid for playing two seasons of semi-professional baseball before competing in the Olympics. In 1983, 30 years after his death, the IOC restored his Olympic medals.

134. *In the fall:* ND *Scholastic*, Oct. 19, 1912. Cooper, John Milton, Jr. *Pivotal* Decades: The United States, 1900-1920, p. 167.

135. *With changing roles:* Ladies Home Journal, Jan. 10, 1910.

135. *Also gaining strength:* Norman Dohn, *The History of the Anti-Saloon League*, p. 94.

*Evangelist William "Billy:"* Okrent, Daniel. *Last Call: The Rise and Fall of Prohibition*, p. 97.

136. *The Notre Dame:* Notre Dame *Scholastic*, Nov. 11, 1912.

137. *In the east:* Davies, John. *The Legend of Hobey Baker*, p. 31. Since 1981, the Hobey Baker Award has been presented annually to the top college hockey player in the United States.

137. *The United States:* Comiskey was a friend of Notre Dame; he came to campus to visit a nephew who was a student.

138. *Prospects for the:* Notre Dame *Scholastic*, Oct. 5, 1912.

139. *"I know it,:"* Rockne, p. 78. Versions of this story have been told featuring various teams.

139. *Later that afternoon:* Notre Dame *Scholastic* Oct. 19. 1912.

139. *October 19 brought:* Morris Harvey is now known as the University of Charleston. In 1915, outfielder Shelton had an eight-day career as a major leaguer, played in 10 games for the New York Yankees. He had just one hit in 40 at-bats, for a .025 lifetime batting average, the worst in major league history for players who had at least one base hit in their career. His lone hit came off Yankee pitcher Harry Coveleski, whose brother Stan, a Hall of Famer, was a long-time resident of South Bend, where the minor league baseball stadium bears his name.

140. *"Bruised, bleeding, battered:* Indianapolis Star, Oct. 27, 1912.

140. *Although proud of:* Notre Dame *Scholastic*, Nov. 2, 1912.

141. *A fluke in:* Notre Dame *Scholastic*, Nov. 30, 1912.

142. *"With the exception:* Notre Dame *Scholastic,* Dec. 7, 1912.
142. *Tuesday, December 10:…the football field:* All from Notre Dame *Scholastic,* Dec. 14, 1912.
145. *"It is easy:* Notre Dame *Dome,* 1913.

**Chapter 12**

147. *It was known:* Francis, David W., and Francis, Diane D. *Cedar Point: The Queen of American Watering Places,* p. 40-41.
148. *So when Knute:* Rockne, p. 85-86.
149. *As a senior:* Rockne, p. 43.
150. *But student life:* Ibid., p. 45-46. Wallace, p. 45. Joe Gargan served in France during the Great War, and later married into the Kennedy family; he was brother-in-law to Joseph P. Kennedy, and uncle to President John F. Kennedy.
150. *Above all, though:* Wallace, p. 46.
151. *Football workouts in:* Notre Dame *Scholastic,* Oct. 11, 1913.
151. *South Dakota, next:* Notre Dame *Scholastic,* Oct. 18, 1913. *Chicago Daily Tribune,* Oct. 19, 1913. Gene Vidal's fame as a football player and coach were later eclipsed by that of his son, writer Gore Vidal.
151. *Next up was:* Notre Dame *Scholastic,* Nov. 1, 1913.
152. *In practice the:* South Bend Tribune, Oct. 29, 1913. *South Bend News-Times,* Oct. 30, 1913.
152. *Shortly after noon:* South Bend News-Times, Oct. 30, 1913.
152. *Nearly the entire:* Rockne, p. 87-88. South Bend News-Times, Oct. 31, 1913.
*153. "Our attack had:* Rockne, p. 89-90
154. *But the game:* New York Times, 1913. Rockne, p. 90.
155. *"Pandemonium broke loose:* South Bend News-Times, Nov. 2, 1913.
156. *"The Catholic team:* Chicago Daily Tribune, Nov. 2, 1913.
156. *Rockne himself later:* Rockne, p. 91.
157. *But there was:* South Bend Tribune, Nov. 4, 1913.Nov. 8, 1913.
157. *Much of the:* Chicago Daily Tribune, Nov. 7, 1913.
*158. With the open:* South Bend Tribune, Nov. 14, 1913.
159. *"A giant hunchback:* Rockne, p. 94-95.

**Chapter 13**

161. *The spring of:* Bachman, Charles W., *The Modern Notre Dame Formation,* p. 63.
162. *In an instant:* Ibid., p. 63.
162. *Bachman felt privileged:* Notre Dame *Scholastic,* Feb. 14, 1914
163. *Rockne didn't have:* Bachman, p. 64.
163. *"Bill," Rockne said:* Ibid., p. 64-65.
165. *For Dorais and:* Dubuque College later became Columbia College, and is today's Loras University. Dorais was the first of several former Notre Dame players to coach there.
165. *Around the same:* Int. Robert Dorais. A story that Rockne and Dorais flipped a coin to determine who would get the Dubuque job "was made up for the newspapers," according to Dorais family historians.
166. *Rockne was also:* Rockne, p. 12, 50-51.
167. *Everyone within earshot:* Rockne, p. 105-6.
168. *In the previous:* Weyand, Alexander M. Football Immortals, p. 4.
168. *Notre Dame opened:* Rockne, p. 199-200. *Chicago Daily Tribune,* Oct. 18, 1914. Heffelfinger, W.W., *This Was Football,* p. 108.
169. *Harper, Rockne and:* Chicago Daily Tribune, Oct. 16, 17, 1914.
169. *A short distance:* The Yale Bowl was the model for big American football stadiums in the following years, including Michigan Stadium, the Los Angeles Coliseum and the Rose Bowl.
170. *With 12,000 looking:* Chicago Daily Tribune, Oct. 18, 1914.
170. *In the third:* Chicago Daily Tribune, Oct. 19, 1914.
170. *In the third:* Yale paid a price for the victory. It gave Harvard weeks to prepare for the lateral-passing attack, and when they met, the Crimson were ready, and rolled to a 36-0 victory in the opening of the Yale Bowl. Hinkey never recovered, and was replaced before the Princeton game of 1915.
171. *On the train:* Heffelfinger, p. 109. Rockne, p. 200. Notre Dame *Scholastic,* Oct. 24, 1914.
172. *Harper and Rockne:* Rockne, "To Shift or Not to Shift," *Colliers* magazine, Nov. 29, 1930.
172. *The backbone of:* Stuhldreher, Harry A. *Knute Rockne: Man Builder,* p. 143-44.
173. *South Bend teams…for all concerned."* Klosinski, Emil. *Pro Football In The Days Of Rockne.*
175. *The Fighting Irish:* Beach, Jim, and Moore, Daniel. *Army vs. Notre Dame: The Big Game, 1913-1947,* p. 10-15. Neyland became a coaching legend at Tennessee; Bradley had a future as an Army general, joining Dwight Eisenhower, an Army football reserve.

**Chapter 14**

180. *The possibility of:* Cooper, p. 227.
181. *Although the Preparedness:* Kessner, p. 24-25.
181. *The main cause:* Leaman, Paul *Fokker Aircraft of World War One,* p. 64, 73
182. *In 1915, the:* Notre Dame *Scholastic,* June 1, 1915.
183. *War or not:* Burns, R., p. 86. The building served as the principal library of the entire campus from its construction until the Hesburgh Memorial Library was constructed in 1964. The building today is Bond Hall, which houses the School of Architecture, and hosts the Notre Dame Band's pre-game concerts.
184. *"How gratifying this:* Notre Dame *Scholastic,* June, 1917.
184. *After Mass, an:* Ibid.

184. *Father Cavanaugh also:* Bonsall, p. 101-2, 112.

185. *Erskine, a true:* Ibid., p. 93-94, 116.

186. *Around 1912, a:* Wade, Wyn Craig. *The Fiery Cross: The Ku Klux Klan in America,* p. 81, 168. Chalmers, David M. *Hooded Americanism: The History of the Ku Klux Klan,* p. 31.

186. *To the Klan:* Wade, p. 179.

187. *However, the reality:* Ibid., p. 219.

189. *In the early:* Thurner, Arthur W. *Rebels on the Range: The Michigan Copper Miners' Strike of 1913-1914,* p. 52.

190. *The hot summer:* Ibid., p. 151.

## Chapter 15

193. *During one stretch:* Gekas, George. *Gipper: The Life & Times of George Gipp, p. 30.* Dolly Gray was the name of a popular song at the time, so there were many individuals, a lot of them baseball players, known as "Dolly Gray." Proctor became a staunch defender of Notre Dame and the Catholic Church, fighting back against the Klan during the height of its activity in Indiana.

193. *Antoine Gipp was:* Gekas, p. 18-20, 21-23.

194. *As a 13-year-old:* Ibid., p. 23-24

194. *Gipp played YMCA:* Ibid., p. 28.

195. *However, Gipper, it:* Ibid., p. 27.

195. *By the summer:* Ibid., p. 29; Int. Bob Erkkila.

196. *'I'm too old:* Gekas, p. 30.

196. *George Gipp arrived:* Ibid., p. 35-37

196. *Assistant coach Rockne:* Ibid., p. 37-38

197. *When they finished: …passing and kicking:* Rockne, p. 217-19. Curious about Gipp not being with any team before Rockne spotted him, Rockne learned that Gipp had gone out for the Brownson Hall team, as would be expected of a freshman, but had quit the team after a few days.

197. *Despite the absence:* Wallace, p. 58-59

198. *That same day: …his player's brashness:* Ibid., p. 38.

199. *The next day:* Notre Dame *Scholastic,* Nov. 11, 1916.

200. *Though Gipp's feat:* Rockne, p. 220-21. *South Bend News-Times,* Nov. 26, 1916.

200. *The Irish had:* Notre Dame *Scholastic,* Dec. 2, 1916.

201. *Rockne's role was:* Sperber, p. 59.

201. *So, when the:* Notre Dame *Scholastic,* Dec. 16, 1916.

202. *After the fall:* Gekas, p. 43-45.

204. *But once war:* Burns, R., p. 97.

204. *Gipp may have:* Gekas, p. 46.

205. *Notre Dame clobbered:* Ibid., p. 47-48.

205. *The next week:* Ibid., p. 50.

205. *Notre Dame celebrated:* Klosinski, p. 84-87.

207. *'Rockne seems to:* Notre Dame *Scholastic,* March 2, 1918.

207. *It was almost:* Notre Dame *Scholastic,* Dec. 18, 1917; Jan. 19, 1918.

## Chapter 16

209. *By early 1918:* Cooper, p. 293-94.

209. *His former passing:* Notre Dame *Scholastic,* Jan. 26, 1918.

210. *Although the departure:* Notre Dame *Scholastic,* Dec. 18, 1917, Jan. 12, 1918.

211. *"College men are:* Notre Dame *Scholastic,* Jan. 26, 1918.

211. *By commencement in …the country's call.:"* Notre Dame *Scholastic,* Feb. 23, 1918.

212. *Stan Cofall, the…pack of 'Faborites:'"* Notre Dame *Scholastic,* June 8, 1918.

213. *"This world war…store for you.:* Notre Dame *Scholastic,* June 8, 1918.

214. *Summer brought a:* Steele, p. 80.

215. *Anderson protested that:* Anderson, Heartly "Hunk," and Klosinski, Emil. *Notre Dame, Chicago Bears, and Hunk,* p. 20-21.

216. *The thought of:* David Condon in *Chicago Tribune,* Dec. 11, 1976.

216. *Gipp and Larson…'em down again:"* Anderson and Klosinski, p. 22-23.

217. *The next day:* Ibid., p. 23-24.

218. *Without a line:* Ibid., p. 24. Lambeau came from the North Side of Green Bay, Wisconsin, one of the heaviest concentration of Belgians in the nation. Many of his neighbors, named Moreau, Duchateau, Delvaux, Lefebvre, Deprey, Frisque, Parmentier, Jossart and Joannes, attended Sts. Peter and Paul church, where Masses were held in the Walloon language of their homeland.

219. *As if player:* South Bend News-Times, Sept. 20, 1918. Gekas, p. 55.

219. *But any momentum:* South Bend News-Times, Oct. 4, 1918.

219. *The football schedule:* South Bend News-Times, Oct. 1, 1918.

220. *Throughout 1918, a:* Barry, John M. *The Great Influenza, p. 93.*

220. *By October 1918:* Burns, R., p. 100.

221. *On Thursday, October:* South Bend News-Times, Oct. 8, 10, 1918.

222. *"At the present:* Notre Dame *Scholastic,* Oct. 23, 1918.

222. *One report in:* South Bend News-Times, Oct. 16, 17, 1918. *South Bend News-Times,* Nov. 1, 1918.

223. *Next up was:* South Bend News-Times, Nov. 7, 1918. *South Bend Tribune,* Nov. 11, 1918.

223. *And the following:* South Bend Tribune, Nov. 19. 1918.

**Chapter 17**

225. *In South Bend: South Bend Tribune*, Dec. 14, 1918.
225. *"Though classes have:* Notre Dame *Scholastic,* Jan. 11, 1919. Burns, R., p. 134.
226. *James Aloysius Burns:* Ibid., p. 108-110.
226. *Burns, the oldest:* Ibid., p. 106, 124, 141.
227. *Prohibition advocates painted:* Okrent, p. 99.
228. *Golden D. "Goldie":* Chelland, Patrick. *One for The Gipper: George Gipp, Knute Rockne, and Notre Dame,* p. 103-107.
229. *Gipp, flush with:* Ibid., p. 109-110. It was said that Gipp would wager, and lose, as much as $300 on a single roll of the dice.
230. *In the final:* Ibid., p. 111.
230. *Rockne was gearing:* Notre Dame *Scholastic,* Jan. 11, 1919.
231. *"Some native principle:* Rockne, p. 228.
232. *By Friday night:* Notre Dame *Scholastic,* Oct. 25, 1919.
233. *The 5-0 record:* Beach, p. 47. Chelland, p. 124.
233. *Back on campus:* Notre Dame *Scholastic,* Nov. 15, 1919.
233. *George Gipp—perhaps:* Chelland, p. 124-125.
234. *With a 7-0:* Notre Dame's lack of membership in the Western Conference would not prevent it, or any other school, theoretically, from claiming the "Western" championship if it had the strongest record in the region. Oregon went on to play in the Tournament of Roses game, losing to Harvard, 7-6.
234. *Four days later…a single vote:* Chelland, p. 128.
235. *As the spring:* Chelland, p. 131-132. Burns, R., p. 102.
236. *It did little:* Burns, R., p. 206. Chelland, p. 150.
236. *Rockne, too, needed:* Burns, R., p. 206-213.
237. *Just before heading:* Chelland, p. 153.
237. *Ojay Larson, financial:* Ibid., p. 155-156.
238. *The next week:* Gekas, p. 144-147.
239. *The October 30:* Chelland, p. 159.
240. *"George Gipp is:* Ibid., p. 171
241. *With only minutes:* Rockne, p. 232.
241. *Saturday evening, back…me," Gipp responded:* Chelland, p. 180.
242. *Notre Dame's Alumni…on the turf.:* Ibid., p. 182.
243. *Gipp's condition far:* Ibid., p. 185-186.
243. *Through the first:* Ibid., p. 191-192.

**Chapter 18**

244. *The snow began:* Chelland, p. 196-197.
245. *"When the first: South Bend Tribune,* Dec. 16, 1920.
245. *In Chicago, a:* Chelland, p. 198-199. Gipp was said to have been interred with his Cubs contract in his coffin.
246. *Back on College:* Rockne, p. 225.
246. *It was hard:* Stuhldreher, p. 206-213.
247. *Sports were not:* Wallace, Dave. *Capital of the World: A Portrait of New York City in the Roaring Twenties,* ix-xi.
248. *During the initial:* Oriard, p. 41.
248. *By 1920, life:* Schmidt, Raymond. *Shaping College Football: The Transformation of an American Sport, 1919-1930,* p. 10-11.
248. *There were now:* Ibid., p. 27.
250. *Because freshmen were:* Wallace, F., p. 92-93.
251. *Jones had three: South Bend News-Times,* Oct. 6, 1921.
251. *The Irish enjoyed:* Wallace, F., 93-94. *South Bend News-Times,* Oct. 5, 1921.
252. *From the opening:* Notre Dame *Scholastic,* Oct. 15, 1921. Iowa went on to win the Western Conference championship.
252. *After the game:* Wallace, F., p. 94, 97-98. Rockne, p. 111.
252. *The train rumbled:* Wallace, F., p. 98. *South Bend News-Times,* Oct. 10, 1921.
253. *What followed was: South Bend News-Times,* Oct. 12, 1921.
253. *The next week: South Bend News-Times,* Oct. 22, 1921.
254. *The Irish, back: South Bend News-Times,* Nov. 3, 1921.
254. *The Eastern press: South Bend News-Times,* Nov. 3, 1921. Beach, p. 61.
255. *"Forget it," Rockne:* Beach, p. 64-65.
256. *Rockne may have…presidency in 1922.:* Burns, R., p. 182-184.
260. *Dave Hayes was:* Wallace, F., p. 107.
260. *Father Burns was:* Burns, p. 142-144.
261. *The debt-free:* Ibid., p. 148.

**Chapter 19**

262. *At the same:* McCallum, John D., and Castner Paul. *We Remember Rockne,* p. 68, 99.
262. *The mere manner:* Stuhldreher, p. 11-12.
263. *His vision of:* Ibid., p. 13-14.
264. *Drudgery aside, there:* Wallace, F., 108-109.
264. *Among the best…club is rough!":* McCallum and Castner, p. 24.
265. *The freshmen from:* Rockne, p. 133.

269. *"Watch him stand:* Wallace, F., p. 114-115.
270. *The Rockmen's next:* Chalmers, p. 15, 203.
270. *While preparing his:* Wallace, F., p. 115-117. Ibid., p. 116. Notre Dame *Scholastic,* 1922 Football Review.
271. *Before the game:* Wallace, F., p. 117.
271. *The young Irish:* Rockne, p. 134-135.
272. *"Epic is the:* Atlanta Constitution, Oct. 29, 1922.
272. *The return trip…through five games:* Wallace, F., p. 117-118.
273. *"All hail! To:* South Bend News-Times, Nov. 4, 1922.
274. *The huge crowd:* Notre Dame *Scholastic,* Nov. 11, 1922.
274. *In the hours:* Beach, p. 69.
275. *The next match:* Wallace, F., p. 120.
275. *When the train:* South Bend News-Times, Nov. 10, 12, 1922.
276. *The game did:* Beach, p. 71-76.
277. *On the train:* Wallace, F., p. 123.

**Chapter 20**

279. *The meteoric rise:* Burns, R., p. 331.
279. *Father Walsh found:* Ibid., p. 226.
280. *In addition to:* New York Evening World, Nov. 28, 1922.
282. *Whenever he made…entertainer, psychologist, salesman.:* Wallace, F., 136-139.
284. *For someone who:* Ltr. Rockne to Eugene Roberts.
284. *From Provo, Rockne:* 1923 Summer School Brochure, International YMCA College, in Springfield College Archives.
285. *An emblem depicted:* Notre Dame Alumnus, Oct., 1923.
286. *For all his…or baking available.:* Int. and family history, John P. Hickey, Jr.
289. *My dear Chuck:* McCallum and Castner, p. 54.
289. *"There has been:* Notre Dame Alumnus, Oct., 1923.
290. *The days of:* Wallace, F., p. 144.
291. *The game's grueling:* Notre Dame Alumnus, Nov., 1923.
291. *Just four days:* Wallace, F., p. 146.
292. *On Friday, October:* Ibid.
293. *New York and…K.K. Rockne:* Ibid.
294. *The Irish came:* Wallace, F., p. 147-151.
294. *With the drive:* Notre Dame Alumnus, Nov., 1923.
295. *At the same:* Burns, R., p. 182-184.

**Chapter 21**

296. *Neither the Notre:* Wade, p. 170-176.
297. *By the 1920s, :* Dolan, p. 237.
297. *"Reverend Clergy: You:* Hope, Arthur J., Notre Dame: One Hundred Years, p. 372-373.
297. *David Curtis Stephenson:* Wade, p. 221.
Remainder adapted from Lefebvre, Jim, *Loyal Sons: The Story of The Four Horsemen and Notre Dame Football's 1924 Champions.*

**Chapter 22**

312. *He was also:* Harper, William A. *How You Played The Game: The Life of Grantland Rice,* p. 233-239.
313. *In September 1924:* Rice, Grantland. *The Tumult and the Shouting: My Life in Sport,* p. 178.
313. *Rice first met:* Ibid., p. 185-186.
313. *Rice thought back:* Ibid., p. 185, 189-190.
Remainder adapted from Lefebvre, Jim, *Loyal Sons: The Story of The Four Horsemen and Notre Dame Football's 1924 Champions.*

**Chapter 23**

Adapted from Lefebvre, Jim, Loyal Sons: *The Story of The Four Horsemen and Notre Dame Football's 1924 Champions.*

**Chapter 24**

353. *That evening, Leo:* Burns, R., p. 442.
354. *What neither Walsh.:* Ibid., p. 442-443. Howard Jones had left Iowa after the 1923 season in a dispute over his request for new contract that would require him to live in Iowa City only during football season, as his wife was not fond of Iowa City. He resigned and in 1924 coached Trinity College, today's Duke University.
358. *Rockne, now coach:* Wallace, F., p. 139-140.
358. *And Rockne the:* Notre Dame Scholastic, March, 1925.
359. *His plan was…2 through 7. :* Correspondence with Fred Walker, Drury College.
*In mid-March:* Powell, p. 183-190.
361. *"I wish I:* Ibid., p. 203-204.
362. *In the sweltering:* Larson, Edward J. *Summer for the Gods: The Scopes Trial,* p. 58, 65.
362. *The epic trial:* Ibid., p. 23.
363. *Darrow had gained:* Ibid., p. 187.
363. *Rockne returned home:* Int. John P. Hickey, Jr.
365. *During days of:* Stuhldreher, p. 16.
366. *For the 1925:* Int. Christy Flanagan.

367. *Now, with a:* McCallum and Castner, p. 114.

370. *Rockne inquired of:* Notre Dame Alumnus, Jan., 1926. Wallace, F., p. 176.

370. *The season of:* Burns, R., p. 444.

371. *Notre Dame officials…up to Rockne.:* Burns, R., pp. 445-446.

**Chapter 25**

373. *On January 26:* Wallace, F., p. 182-183.

373. *If Rockne had:* Ibid., p. 183.

374. *Rockne's good friend:* White, Richard D. Will Rogers: A Political Life, p. 51, 104.

375. *The coach and:* Ibid., p. 129.

376. *Rockne favored bandleaders:* Wallace, F., p. 70-71.

377. *From a football:* Oriard, Michael. King Football: Sport & Spectacle in the Golden Age of Radio & Newsreels, Movies & Magazines, The Weekly & The Daily Press, p. 44-45.

379. *A section he:* Stuhldreher, p. 54.

379. *Rockne partnered with…trips and hikes.":* Correspondence between Rockne and Frank Hayes. Advertisement and brochure, Camp Rockne, 1926, 1927.

381. *Father Walsh began:* Burns, R., p. 450.

382. *While Walsh was:* Wallace, F., p. 196.

382. *What followed was:* The most notable play of the Indiana game came when a Notre Dame player tackled Indiana's ball-carrier near the sideline, and the ensuing pileup crashed into Rockne, injuring his leg. In the weeks that followed, it continued to bother him.

382. *Only two games:* Stuhldreher, p. 178-179.

**Chapter 26**

385. *In many ways:* Kessner, p. 37.

386. *It wasn't just:* Ibid., p. 39-40.

387. *Lindbergh, who lived:* Ibid., p. 70.

389. *Lindbergh's flight inaugurated:* Komons, Nick A., *Bonfires to Beacons: Federal Civil Aviation Policy Under the Air Commerce Act, 1926-1938*, p. 185.

390. *At each school:* McCallum and Castner, p. 200.

390. *One of Rockne's:* Ltr. From L. "Dusty" Boggess, Waco HS, Feb., 1926.

391. *With his extensive:* Correspondence between Rockne and Stub Allison.

392. *Summer brought a:* Ltr. from Rev. John J. O'Boyle, April 23, 1927.

393. *A typical camper:* Ints. Pete Helland, Eric Helland.

394. *The 1927 Irish:* Beach, p. 105-112.

395. *Notre Dame gained:* Wallace, F., p. 203-204.

396. *And as bad:* Burns, R., p. 461, 464.

396. *Near the end:* Ibid., p. 458-460.

396. *But for all:* Notre Dame *Scholastic*, Sept. 23, 1927. Notre Dame *Alumnus*, Nov. 1927.

**Chapter 27**

399. *"Sportsmanship is simply:* Rockne, Knute, "Footballs or Hand Grenades," The Notre Dame *Alumnus*, Nov., 1930.

400. *In one of:* Rockne, Knute, "The Modern Trend of Football," in *Knute Rockne on Football*.

400. *Rockne celebrated the:* Rockne, Knute, "The Spirit of Co-operation," in *Knute Rockne on Football*.

401. *To operate the:* Ltr. from Hunk Anderson to Rockne, April, 1928.

401. *Before sailing for:* Berry went on to a Hall of Fame career coaching at Corpus Christi and then Paris, Texas. His son, Raymond Emmett Berry, earned a spot in the Pro Football Hall of Fame as a receiver for the Baltimore Colts. Int Raymond E. Berry.

402. *Rockne couldn't avoid:* Wisconsin State Journal, Oct. 7, 1928.

402. *The night before…was positively electrifying.":* Wallace, F., p. 209-210.

403. *The 1928 Notre…Bend in 1926:* Int. Sue Law Hawes. Family history.

*Perhaps no one:* Slayton, Robert A. *Empire Statesman: The Rise and Redemption of Al Smith*, p. 169-171.

405. *In 1928, Smith…in your favor.":* The *Atlantic*, April, 1927.

406. *It was reported:* Dolan, p. 213.

406. *"I summarize my:* The *Atlantic*, May, 1927.

407. *Religious persecution dogged:* Slayton, p. xiv.

407. *Will Rogers, who:* New York Times, March 8, 1928.

407. *It was no:* Notre Dame *Scholastic*, Oct. 12, 1928.

408. *But the endorsement:* Burns, R., p. 478-479.

409. *A 32-6 pasting:* Only the 1888 squad, second in school history, had a losing mark, 1-2, with the losses occurring to Michigan in a pair of demonstration games in April that year, a month after Rockne was born.

410. *Frank Wallace's story:* Wallace, F., p. 217. Johnny would wear the nickname "One Play" for the rest of his career.

410. *That evening, Rockne:* Ibid., p. 216-218.

411. *A trying season:* Ibid., p. 221-222.

412. *Earlier in 1928:* McCallum and Castner, p. 172-173.

412. *Rockne's first speech:* Ibid., p. 173-174.

413. *As 1929 began:* A Guidebook For South Bend Indiana's East Wayne Street Local Historic District, publication of the Historic Preservation Commission of South Bend and Saint Joseph County, p. 1-2, 14.

**Chapter 28**

414. *In one of: Encyclopedia of Chicago.*
415. *Six men sat: New York Times,* Feb. 14, 1929. Kobler, John. *Capone. The Life and World of Al Capone,* p. 240.
416. *Though the St.: New York Times,* Feb. 14, 1929. Kobler, p. 245.
417. *On the 1929:* Notre Dame *Alumnus,* June, 1929.
*418. The summer coaching:* Wallace, F., p. 222-223.
418. *The summer of:* Ibid., p. 222. Notre *Dame Scholastic,* Nov. 22, 1929.
419. *The most important:* Ibid., p. 223.
419. *For 1929, Rockne:* Notre Dame *Scholastic,* Sept. 20, 1929. McCallum and Castner, p. 148-149.
420. *After the Irish:* Wallace, F., p. 223.
421. *Rockne's decision to:* Ibid., p. 224-225.
421. *In front of:* Ibid., p. 226.
421. *On game day:* Ibid., p. 226-227.
422. *Then, as suddenly:* Ibid., p. 227-228.
423. *"Stock prices virtually:* New York Times,* Oct. 30, 1929.
423. *Investors bought borrowed:* Bonsall, p. 135.
*424. The company introduced: Ibid., p. 160*
424. *The stock market:* Okrent, p. 328.
425. *South Bend residents:* Wallace, F., p. 225.
425. *Despite the stock:* Burns, R., p. 492. Notre Dame *Scholastic,* Nov. 22, 1929.
426. *The next Saturday:* Notre Dame Scholastic, Nov. 29, 1929.
426. *Rockne's health remained:* Notre Dame *Scholastic,* Dec. 6, 1929.

**Chapter 29**
428. *In January 1930:* Ltr to Charles Bachman, Jan. 16, 1930.
429. *The vacation was:* Notre Dame *Scholastic,* May 2, 1930.
429. *Rockne returned to:* Ltr to Charles Bachman, May 16, 1930. Notre Dame *Alumnus,* June, 1930.
430. *When students returned:* Notre Dame *Alumnus,* Sept., 1930.
430. *On the football:* Ibid.
431. *Perhaps the most:* Notre Dame *Alumnus,* Oct., 1930.
431. *On October 4:* McCallum and Castner, p. 165.
432. *A celebratory atmosphere:* Notre Dame *Scholastic,* Oct. 17, 1930.
432. *On Saturday, more:* Ibid.
432. *The next week:* McCallum and Castner, p. 154.
433. *Next up was:* Ibid., p. 160-161.
*433. The final home:* Ibid., p. 155156.
434. *With just minutes:* Beach, p. 131-132.
435. *In Southern Cal:* Notre Dame *Scholastic,* Dec. 12, 1930.
435. *"There we were:* McCallum and Castner, p. 146-147.
436. *Upon their return:* Notre Dame *Scholastic,* Dec. 12, 1930.
438. *After Frank Leahy's:* McCallum and Castner, p. 141-142. *Associated Press,* Dec. 18, 1930.
439. *For 14 days:* McCallum and Castner, p. 142.
439. *Back in South:* South Bend Tribune, Dec. 18, 1930.
440. *Dr. Barborka, finding: Associated Press,* Dec. 23, 24, 1930
440. *As 1931 began:* McCallum and Castner, p. 176-178.
441. *Rockne told of:* Ibid., p. 179, 182.
441. *Rockne certainly had:* Ibid., p. 184.

**Chapter 30**
445. *After signing his:* Wallace, F., p. 253-254.
445. *Leo Ward, close:* Ibid., p. 52-253.
445. *His schedule for:* McCallum and Castner, p. 210.
446. *That evening, in:* Ibid., p. 212-213.
446. *The next afternoon...in a dormitory.* Ibid., p. 213
447. *It was a:* Ibid., p. 215-216.
447. *That evening, Rockne:* Ibid., p. 210, Int. Joseph Hickey.
448. *Monday morning at...left Studebaker headquarters:* Ibid., p. 216-217.
448. *"What's that, Larry?"....on his way.* Ibid., p. 211-214.
450. *Rockne was scheduled...in Cottonwood Falls.* Narrative relies on a variety of newspaper accounts from March 31, 1931 and April 1, 1931; and subsequent articles, including Friedman, Herbert M. and Friedman, Ada Kera, "The Legacy of the Rockne Crash," *Aeroplane* Magazine, May, 2001.
454. *At the house:* Wallace, F., 256-257.
455. *Nearby in South:* McCallum and Castner, p. 219.
455. *In Syracuse, New:* Ints. Rev. Ted Hesburgh, Peter Helland, Eric Helland.
455. *Back in the: Emporia Gazette,* April 1, 1931.
457. *Across the nation...was your home.* Notre Dame *Alumnus,* May, 1931.

# Index

Addams, Jane, 33, 135
Ade, George, 48
Alexander, Bill, 6, 249, 331-33, 457
Allerdice, Dave, 158
Allison, Leonard "Stub," 391-2, 409
Allouez, Rev. Claude, 10, 19
Altgeld, Gov. John, 33
Anderson, Eddie, 5, 231, 241
Anderson, Edward "Goat," 228
Anderson, Gilbert, 100
Anderson, Heartley "Hunk," 1, 2, 215-18, 231, 244, 253, 265, 365, 383, 401, 418
Anderson, John, 65-66
Anderson, Magnus, 42
Anderson, William, 215-16
Anson, Cap, 103
Anthony, Elliott, 77
Armour, Philip, 32-33, 35-36, 46
Army—see United States Military Academy
Astor, John Jacob, 19, 286
Aubut, Oscar, 86

Bach, James Henry, 165
Bach, Joe, 306, 345, 351
Bachman, Charlie, 5, 158, 161-2, 167, 169, 175, 179, 210, 223, 429, 446
Badin, Rev. Stephen , 19
Bahan, Leonard "Pete", 224, 237
Baker, Arthur, 452-53
Baker, Edward, 452-53
Baker, Hobart "Hobey," 137, 160
Balzarina, Marie, 166
Barborka, Dr. C.J., 429, 440
Barry, Christopher, 105
Barry, Norman, 5, 105, 110, 224, 237-38, 242, 244
Bartelme, Philip, 114
Baum, L. Frank, 47
Beiderbecke, Bix, 376
Bell, Madison A. "Matty"
Bendix, Vincent, 314, 413, 426
Benson, William S., 183
Berger, Alvin "Heinie," 120, 124, 141, 151
Bergman, Alfred, 117, 119, 122, 169-71, 175, 178-9

Bergman, Arthur, 120
Bergman, Joe, 120
Berigan, Bunny, 376
Bernts, Olaf, 4
Berry, Raymond, 401
Bezdek, Hugo, 342
Bible, D.X., 6
Blatz, Valentin, 227
Boland, Joe, 382, 418
Bolstad, Nils, 13
Bonniwell, Judge E.C., 344
Borkowski, Lot, 174
Bow, Clara, 377
Boyer, Gladys, 110
Boyer, Helen, 110
Boyer, Henry, 110
Boyer, John, 110, 221
Boyer, Winifred, 110
Bradley, Omar, 175
Brandy, Joe, 205, 237, 244, 307
Brentano, Lorenz, 76-77
Brickley, Charles, 160
Brill, Marty, 6, 419, 433
Brother Cyprian, 315
Broun, Heywood, 324
Brown, Harvey, 271
Brown, Mordecai "Three-Finger," 70
Brown, Warren, 6
Brundage, Avery, 102-3, 133, 346
Bryan, William Jennings, 227, 362
Bullard, Robert Lee
Buck, Cub, 306
Burke, Thomas, 68
Burnham, Daniel, 31, 37-38, 83
Burns, Rev. James, 185, 226, 235, 256-7, 260-61
Butler, Michael "Dad," 100
Byrd, Richard, 385
Byrne, Joe, 5, 140, 155, 210, 292, 314, 326, 368, 373-74
Bystolen, Magne, 13

Cagle, Chris, 427
Call, Charles, 213-14
Callicrate, Dominic, 123

Calnon, Mike, 5, 152, 228
Camp, Walter, 51-53, 58-59, 74, 83, 92, 166, 168, 243, 283, 360-61
Cannon, Jack, 10, 419
Capone, Al, 415-16
Carberry, Glen "Judge," 254, 265
Carey, Rev. William, 258-9
Carideo, Frank, 5, 6, 410, 419-21
Carnegie Foundation, 399
Cartier, Warren, 6, 335
Caruso, Enrico, 209
Casasanta, Joseph, 346
Castner, Paul, 5, 252, 254, 264-5, 274, 277, 412-13, 441, 444, 455
Catholicism
And Immigration, 16-19
Cavanaugh, Rev. John, 104, 111, 118-9, 142-5, 182-3, 203-4, 217, 221-22, 226, 260, 297, 345
Cather, Willa, 303
Cerney, Bill, 343, 430
Chambaerlin, Guy, 176-7
Clark, Dennison, 92
Clark, O.A., 5
Chamberlin, Guy
Chanute, Octave, 47
Chaplin, Charlie, 100
Chautauqua Assembly, 59
Chesterton, G.K., 432
Chevigny, Jack, 2, 7, 10, 418
Chrysler, Walter, 48
Chicago
    Fire of 1871, 30-31; reconstruction, 31-34; World's Fair of 1893 (see World's Columbian Exposition); park districts, 63-64;
Chicago, University of, 56-62, 82-84
Christen, H.C., 452
Clay, Sen., Henry, 20-21
Cleary, Jim, 448
Clements, Walter, 5
Cleveland, Grover, 33, 41, 50
Clinnen, Walter, 117
Clippenger, Art, 117
Cobb, Henry Ives, 49
Cobb, Ty, 209
Cochems, Eddie, 149
Cofall, Stan, 171, 174-5, 179, 197, 212
Cole, J.O., 120
Collins, Chuck, 289, 308

Collins, Joe, 106, 117, 164
Colrick, John, 409
Columbia University, 50, 74
Columbus, Chistopher, 36
Comiskey, Charles, 141
Conley, Tom, 6, 426
Connell, Ward "Doc," 335
Coolidge, Calvin, 457
Coquillard, Alexis, 19, 23, 286
Corbett, James, 55
Corby, Rev. William, 21-23, 25
Corcoran, Jimmy, 6
Cornell University, 51
Coughlin, Danny, 254, 390
Coughlin, Frank, 3, 244-46
Crisler, Fritz, 457
Crosby, Bing, 376
Crowe, Clem, 308
Crowley, Agnes Sweeney
Crowley, Charlie, 138, 142, 371-72
Crowley, Jim, 5, 267-70, 282, 291, 293, 320, 327, 335, 338, 345, 356
Crumley, Rev. Thomas, 145
Curtiss, Glenn, 96-97

Daly, Charlie, 177, 255, 275, 280
Dana, Charles A., 36
Daniels, Josephus, 182
Darrow, Clarence, 33, 362-63
Dartmouth College, 58
Davis, Henry, 99
Davis, John W., 405
Davis, Richard H., 54-55
Dawson, Fred T., 336-38
Debs, Eugene V., 32, 134-5, 203
deCoubertin, Pierre, 67, 75
DeGree, Ed, 254
De la Hailandiere, Bishop Celestin G., 18
Delaney, Martin, 100
Dempsey, Jack, 248, 317, 330, 350, 426, 457
Desch, Gus, 254
Detroit, University of, 18
Devine, Aubrey, 251-52
Devine, John "Divy," 101, 103-104, 114, 121, 124, 149, 162, 402
Dewey, John, 57
Dickson, Wm. K.L., 98
Dimmick, Ralph, 113-4, 117, 122-3, 148
Disney, Elias, 47-48

Disney, Roy, 48
Disney, Walt, 48
Dobie, Gil, 4
Dolan, Sam "Rosey," 148, 164
Dorais, Charles "Gus," 5, 114, 117-9, 121-2, 129, 138-144, 148-154, 157-160, 162-166, 206, 230-31, 236-37, 266, 304, 394, 428, 457
Dorais, Flora, 118
Dorais, Malvina, 118
Doriot, Frank, 376
Dreiser, Theodore, 33
Driscoll, John "Paddy," 223
Ducote, Richard "Moon"
Duke of Veragua, 41
Duncan, Isadora, 135

Earhart, Amelia, 450
Eaton, Wilbur, 327-28
Eckersall, Walter, 85-88, 91, 127, 129, 141, 144, 156, 251, 350
Ecklund, Con, 223, 345
Edbrooke, Willoughby J., 23
Edison, Thomas, 37, 94, 96-97, 317
Edwards, Howard "Cap," 2
Eichenlaub, Ray, 5, 120, 151, 154, 160, 169, 171
Eisenhower, Dwight D.
Elder, Jack, 418-19, 426-27
Elward, Mal, 5, 159, 169
Erikson, Leif, 13, 42
Erskine, Albert, 3, 4, 184-5, 225, 236, 260-61, 424, 426, 444
Evinrude, Ole, 14

Fairbanks, Charles W., 140
Fairbanks, Douglas, 209
Farley, Rev. John "Pop," 162-3
Faulkner, Ruth, 358
Faulkner, William, 303
Feeney, Al, 5, 338
Ferdinand, Archduke, 180
Ferris, George W.G., 43
Ferris, Woodbridge, 190
Ferry, Charles A., 170
Field, Marshall, 33, 36, 46, 53, 60
Fine, John, 74
Finegan, Charles "Sam." 141
Finno, Andrew, 13
Firpo, Luis, 317

Fitzgerald, F. Scott, 303
Fitzgerald, Freeman "Fitz," 5, 152, 154, 175
Fitzgerald, John F., 119
Fitzgerald, Mary, 119
Fitzgerald, Rose, 119
Flanagan, Christie, 366-67
Fletcher, Forrest, 115, 134
Floto, Otto, 352
Fokker, Anthony, 181-2, 387, 389
Foley, Tom, 117
Ford, Edsel, 338
Ford, Henry, 47, 95, 184
Fowler, Gene, 320
Fox, William F., 324
Francis, H.H., 2
Franks, Bobby, 363
French, Daniel Chester, 42
Fry, Robert, 451-52

Gage, Lyman J., 36
Gallico, Paul, 320, 411
Garbisch, Ed, 315, 319
Gargan, Joe, 150, 210, 212
Garrett, Robert, 68
Garvey, Art "Hec"
Gehrig, Lou, 248
Georgetown University, 73
Gibbons, Cardinal James, 25, 183
Gibson, Charles Dana, 54
Gilderhus, Nils, 13
Gill, George, 57
Gimbel, Adam, 317
Gipp, Antoine, 193-94
Gipp, George, 194-205, 215, 247, 410
Godcharles, F.D., 125
Goetz, Charles L., 108, 143
Goldsmith, Rev. C.F.X., 118
Goldthwaite, Spencer, 451
Gould, Jay, 43
Grange, Harold "Red," 322, 339
Grant, Chet, 210
Grant, Ulysses S., 46
Gray, William "Dolly", 193, 196
Gregori, Luigi, 24
Griffith, John L., 6, 408, 412
Grzegorek, Tommy, 174
Gushurst, Fred, 5, 141, 160

Haggerty, Rev. Pat, 243
Halas, George, 223
Halas, Walter, 256
Hamilton, Don, 165
Hammond, LeGrande, 221
Hanna, Edward J., 183, 356
Hanley, Dick, 4, 433
Hanousek, Dick, 307
Happer, John, 451
Harding, Warren, 297, 408
Harper, Jesse, 5, 6, 126-8, 139, 145-6, 151, 156, 158, 163, 168-172, 177-9, 200-201, 206-7, 283, 383
Harper, William Rainey, 48-49, 56-62, 82-83, 285
Harriman, E.H., 375
Harriman, William Averell, 375
Harrison, Benjamin, 36, 48
Harrison, Carter, 41-42, 82
Harvard University, 50-51, 74
Harvat, Paul, 119
Hauge, Hans Nielsen, 79
Haughton, Percy, 329-30, 371
Hauser, Max, 294
Hayes, Dave, 199, 260, 285
Hayes, Frank, 379
Hayes, Rutherford B., 46
Hays, Arthur Garfield, 362
Hearden, Thomas "Red," 367
Hearst, William Randolph, 53-55, 320
Heathman, Easter, 453
Heffelfinger, Wm. "Pudge,' 58
Heisman, John, 249, 331
Helland, Laddie, 393, 455
Hemingway, Ernest, 303
Henderson, Fletcher, 376
Henry, Charles L., 94-95
Hering, Frank, 3, 6, 62
Hershberger, Clarence, 83
Hesburgh, Theodore M., 455
Hickey, Joseph, 447
Hickey, Kate, 288, 369, 447
Hickey, Louis (Etier), 286-88
Hickey, Tom, 5, 286, 363-64, 369, 447
Hildebrand, Arthur, 74
Hill, Frank, 380
Hill, James J., 53
Himle, Odd, 13
Hinkey, Frank, 168

Hinkle, W.R., 3
Hoffman, Paul, 5, 412, 444
Hoffmann, Frank "Nordy"
Hogan, Paul, 193
Hogenson, William, 101
Hogsett, Robert, 160
Hoover, Herbert, 62, 408, 457
Howard, Judge Timothy, 143
Hull, George F. "Hullie," 5, 152, 228-9, 333
Hunsinger, Ed, 308, 351
Hutchinson, Charles L., 36

Ibanez, Vicente Blasco, 315
Ibsen, Henrik, 303
Immigration, 13-16
Ingersoll, Fred, 147
Ireland, Archbishop John, 25
International YMCA College, 59, 284

Jeffrey, Edward T., 36
Joliet, Louis, 29
Jolson, Al, 209, 346, 395
Jones, Bobby, 248
Jones, Herbert, 395
Jones, Howard, 5, 168, 249, 251, 295, 355, 457
Jones, Isham, 376
Jones, Keith "Deak", 206, 223
Jones, Lawrence M. "Biff"
Jones, Mother, 190
Jones, Tad, 304
Jones, William, 446, 449

Kanaley, Byron, 6, 257
Keefe, Emmett, 175, 223
Kelleher, Bill, 163-4
Kelley, Florence, 33
Kelly, Albert "Red," 138, 165
Kelly, Emmett, 120
Kelly, Luke, 119, 125, 158, 165
Keogan, George, 5, 238, 330
Kiley, Roger, 5, 237, 239, 254
Kimball, Ed, 356
Kimbell, Martin, 28
King George I, 68
King Gustav V, 132-4
King Haakon VII of Norway, 4
King Olav, 11
King, Phil, 85
Kirk, Bernie, 237

Kizer, Noble, 263, 307
Klosinski, Johnny, 174
Knapp, James, R., 371
Koehler, Col. Herman, 426
Kofoed, Jack, 320
Koshkonong Prairie, 13
Krajeski, Mike, 110
Kurth, Joe, 434

LaFollette Robert, 202
Lahey, Thomas A., 111
Lamb, Roy, 310
Lambeau, Earl "Curly," 218-19, 241, 259, 267
Lambert, Kent "Skeets." 128
Lambert, Ward "Piggy"
Lardner, Ring, 4, 179, 276, 313
Larkin, Bunny, 5
Larson, Fred "Ojay," 215-16, 231, 241, 244
Lathrop, Julia, 135
Lathrop, Ralph, 5, 163-4
Law, John, 10, 403-4, 419
Layden, Clarence "Irish"
Layden, Elmer, 5, 268, 277-8, 293, 319, 320, 325-6, 338, 341, 345
Leahy, Frank, 403, 431, 438-39
Leeper, Kitty, 149
LeGore, Harry, 170
Lehn, Hakon, 67
Leinenkugel, Jacob, 118
Leopold, Nathan, 363
Leslie, Harry, 4
Lewis, Sinclair, 303
Lieb, Tom, 271, 308, 357, 365, 380, 409, 418, 421-22, 426-27, 455
Lightbody, James D., 81, 101
Lincoln, Abraham, 46
Lincoln, Mary, 46
Lindbergh, Charles, 386-89, 450
Lippincott, Dr. C.A., 345
Little, Lou, 390, 457
Livergood, Bernie, 343
Locke, Gordon, 251
Loeb, Richard, 363
Logan, Gen. John A.
Logan Square, 27-29
Longman, Frank "Shorty," 106, 116-9, 198
Loras College, 18
Louis, Spryidon, 68
Loyola of Chicago, 18

Luhn, Dr. H.B., 333
Luther, Eddie, 316, 331, 337

MacArthur, Douglas, 235, 354
Madigan, Ed "Slip." 5, 339, 349, 354
Mageveny, Hugh, 347
Mahan, Eddie, 160
Maher, Marty, 178
Maher, Willie "Red," 335
Malone, Grover, 209, 242
Mann, Golden "Goldie," 228
Maris, Bertrand, 115, 124
Marks, John L "Jack," 116, 121-4, 139, 141, 145
Marquette, Rev. Jacques, 10, 19, 29
Martin, Bill, 115
Mathews, Lee, 117, 164
Mathias, Herman "Jess," 451-52
Matthews, Bob, 349
Mathys, Charles, 241
McCormick, Cyrus, 36, 46
McDonald, Angus, 257, 295, 346-47
McEwan, John, 152, 178, 345
McGann Funeral Home, 3
McGill University, 51
McKeever, Francis, 118
McManmon, John, 307
McNamee, Graham, 318
McPhee, Will, 357
McReavy, Lieut. C.J.
Meanwell, Walter "Doc," 6, 335, 355
Medill, Joseph, 31, 36
Meehan, Chick, 4
Meehan, Ed, 208
Mehre, Harry, 254
Meli, Giovanni, 24
Mencken, H.L., 296
Merrilat, Louis, 152, 160, 175
Metzger, Bert, 434
Michigan, University of, 51, 60-61, 91-92, 103, 113
Miller, Don, 5, 268-9, 291, 293, 338, 345
Miller, Edgar "Rip," 307
Miller, Fred, 403
Miller, Frederick, 226
Miller, Harry "Red," 148, 164
Miller, Ray, 211-12
Miller, W.B., 452
Mills, Roy, 420, 434
Mills, Rupe, 210

Mills, Tommy, 335, 367
Mohardt, John, 239, 242, 252, 254, 259
Moisant, John B., 97-98
Moody, Dwight L., 59
Mooney, Rev. Vince, 364, 369-70
Moore, Annie, 15
Moran, George C. "Bugs," 415
Moreau, Rev. Basil, 18-20
Morgan, J. Pierpont, 45
Morris Harvey College, 139
Morrisey, Rev. Andrew J., 183, 203
Morse, Franklin, 349
Mott, Lucretia, 247
Moynihan, Tim, 403
Mulcaire, Rev. Michael, 2, 7, 396, 443
Mullins, Larry "Moon." 5, 6, 449-50
Mundelein, George W., 183
Murphy, John P., 121, 124
Murphy, Rev. William F., 166
Muskingum College, 56

Nadolney, Romanus, 218
Nagurski, Bronko, 394
Naismith, James, 59
Navarre, Pierre, 286
Nebraska, University of, 176-7
Nelson, Knute, 14
Nevers, Ernie, 351
Nichols, Edward, 74
Niemiec, John "Butch," 382, 408-10
Nieuwland, Rev. Julius, 112-3, 149-50
Nigro, Dr. D.M., 2, 5, 7, 10, 112, 450, 453
Nolan, James, 121
Noll, Bishop John F., 7
Notre Dame, University of
Founding, 18-21; rebuilding after fire, 2126;
Northwestern University, 60-61

Oaas, Torgus "Turk," 121
Oberst, Gene, 265, 299, 305
O'Boyle, Harry, 350
O'Boyle, Rev. John J., 392, 394
O'Brien, Johnny, 410
O'Donnell, Rev. Charles, 3, 8-9, 10, 396, 407-8, 430, 434, 446, 454-55
O'Donnell, Rev. J. Hugh, 175, 178, 274, 299-301, 346
O'Donnell, Leo, 112
O'Hara, Rev. John, 3, 243, 290, 302-3, 340, 346,

346-48, 356, 358, 369
Oliphant, Elmer "Ollie," 126, 146, 175, 178-9, 199
Oliver Chilled Plow Works, 108
Oliver, James, 108
Oliver, Joseph D., 143
Olmstead, Frederick Law, 31, 37
O'Neil, Larry, 447
O'Neill, Tom, 454
Owens, Leo, 230
Owsley, John, 74
Oyen, Tom, 79

Pabst, August, 227
Palmer, Potter, 36
Parisien, Art, 5, 382, 384
Parker, Gerald, 85
Patton, W. Blaine, 140
Paulhan, Louis, 97
Peay, Austin, 362
Peck, Ferdinand W., 36
Pegler, Westbrook, 304, 322
Pelham, Louis D., 78
Pembroke School, 2
Pennsylvania, University of, 72, 83
Phelan, Jimmy, 5, 175, 201-2, 342
Phelan, James, D., 356
Philbrook, George, 113-4, 134, 163
Phillips-Exeter Academy, 57
Pickford, Mary, 209
Pihlfeldt, Thomas, 29
Plant, John, 5, 101, 103-4, 107, 114, 129, 162
Pliska, Joe, 120, 125, 128, 141, 151-4, 210
Pollard, Luther, 89
Pope Leo XIII, 17
Porter, Cole, 120
Princeton University, 50, 54-55, 74
Proctor, Robert E., 192-3
Pulitzer, Joseph, 41, 53
Pullman, George, 32-33, 36

Quackenbush, Irving, 78
Quantrall, Ernest, 90
Queen Victoria, 34

Reagan, Bob, 271
Reed, Bill, 74
Reihnoltzen, Anton, 64

Rice, Grantland, 255, 303, 312-14, 319, 323-4, 326, 427
Robinson, Bradbury, 148-9
Robrecht, C.A., 451
Rockefeller, John D., 33, 56, 74, 261, 375
Rockne, Anna, 11-12, 39, 131
Rockne, Bonnie Skiles, 3-4, 6-7, 10, 149, 166, 240, 286, 288, 354, 369, 384, 413, 445, 454, 457
Rockne, Florence, 131
Rockne, John V. "Jack," 3, 6, 444, 454
Rockne, Knute Jr., 2, 6, 286
Rockne, Lars (Rokne), 11-14, 27-28, 34, 38, 46, 65-66, 72, 76, 91, 130-1
Rockne, Knute Kenneth
    childhood in Norway, 11-13;
    immigrating to America, 39-41;
    childhood in Chicago, 47, 66-72, 79-82;
    at Northwest High School, 84-91;
    working at Chicago Post Office, 92-93, 99-101;
    student at Notre Dame, 102-107, 112-132, 138-144, 148-164;
    assistant football coach and head coach, track, 165-72, 175-9, 196-202;
    coaching semi-pro teams, 172-5;
    becoming head coach, 206-8;
    military service, 214,
    as Notre Dame head football coach, 218-24, 230-247, 250-7, 262-78, 290-5, 303-53, 364-71, 394-7, 408-11, 418-23, 425-27, 430-6;
    noon football lectures, 282-3;
    summer coaching schools, 283-6, 305, 359-60, 378-80, 390-2, 418;
    home life, 286-8, 363-4, 413;
    job offers from other colleges, 295, 354-5, 371-2, 411-12;
    conversion to Catholicism, 368-70;
    offshore travel, 374-5, 384, 401-3;
    Camp Rockne, 379-80, 392-4;
    writing, 398-401,
    speaking engagements, 412-3, 428-9, 440-2;
    final trip, 450-458;
    visitation, funeral, and burial, 1-10.
Rockne, Knute, Jr., 2, 240, 286, 369, 450
Rockne (Rokne), Knute Knutson, 12
Rockne (Rokne), Knute L., 12
Rockne, Louise, 131-2
Rockne, Martha Gjermo (Rokne), 3, 11, 39-40, 72, 131, 450, 455

Rockne, Martha, 12, 39,131-2
Rockne, Mary Jeanne, 3, 6, 286, 445
Rockne, William "Billy," 2, 6, 179, 214, 271, 450
Rogers, Will, 276-7, 328, 374-75, 388, 407, 435-36, 445, 458
Roper, Bill, 281, 360
Roosevelt, Theodore, 74, 134, 180, 198, 225, 398
Root, Elihu, 74, 180
Root, John W., 31
Rose, Ralph, 101
Runyon, Damon, 303, 319, 322
Rutgers University, 50
Ruth, Babe, 209, 248
Ruud, Helga, 29
Ryan, Rev. John A., 17-18
Rydzewski, Frank, 229

St. John, Lynn, 411
St Louis University, 18
St. Mary's Collee, 21
Salmon, Louis "Red"
Sandburg, Carl, 303
Sanger, Margaret, 135
Savoldi, Joe, 409
Schissler, Paul, 6, 345
Schlitz, Joseph, 227
Schmitt, Bill, 123
Schneider, Jac, 149
Scopes, John T, 362-63
Schwartz, Marchy, 5, 6, 433-34
Schwinn, Ignaz, 81
Selig, William, 99
Seyfrit, Frank "Si," 258
Shaughnessy, Frank "Shag," 164
Shaw, George Bernard, 303
Shaw, Lawrence "Buck," 256
Shea, John, 285
Shea, John Gilmary, 24
Shelton, A.K. "Skeeter," 139
Sheridan, M.J., 81
Shillington, John H., 182
Siki, "Battling," 272
Skiles, Bonnie (see Bonnie Rockne)
Slater, Duke, 251-52
Smith, Al, 404-08, 414
Smith, Art, 120, 124
Smith, Joseph A., 210

Smith, Maurice "Clipper," 442
Smith, Verly, 330-31
Smogor, John, 174
Smyser, W.D., 78-79
Sobieralski, Paster, 174
Sokolowski, Lodge, 174
Sorin, Rev. Edward, 18-26, 104-5, 111, 287
Spalding, Albert G., 73
Spalding, Tom, 210
Spaulding, W.H. "Doc," 232, 342
Spears, Dr. Clarence "Doc," 342, 368
Speik, Frederick, 90
Spoor, George, 100
Stagg, Amos Alonzo, 55, 57-62, 73-74, 82-86, 103, 127, 166, 171, 207, 284-5, 292, 342, 360
Stanford University, 61-62
Stanley, Basil, 211
Stansfield, John, 117
Stanton, Elizabeth, 247
Stappas, Angelo, 195, 202
Starrett, Morris, 292
Steers, Fred, 107, 162
Steffen, Wally, 5, 89, 383
Steffens, Lincoln, 74
Stephenson, D.C., 297-98
Stephenson, Rome C., 345
Stiehm , Ewald O. "Jumbo," 176
Stimson, Henry, 180
Strickler, George, 305, 309, 315, 320, 324-5
Studebaker, Clement, 45, 413
Studebaker Company, 45, 107-9, 413, 424
Studebaker, Henry Jr., 45
Stuhldreher, Harry, 5, 265-7, 291, 293, 338, 343, 345, 351, 366
Stuhldreher, William J., 342
Sutherland, Dr. John B. "Jock," 342
Sullivan, James E., 133
Sullivan, Louis H., 31, 44
Sunday, William "Billy," 136
Sutliffe, Leo, 316
Swetish, Joe, 195

Teagarden, Jack, 376
Taft, William H., 107, 134
Tarbell, Ida, 74
Taylor, Marshall W., 81
Thomas, Frank, 199, 254
Thorp, Ed, 255, 319

Thorpe, Jim, 133-4
Tonti, 10
Tripper, Iris, 235
Trumbauer, Frankie, 376
Tsar Nicholas II, 133
Tuthill, Harry, 178
Twombley, Henry D., 73
Twomey, Ted, 390

United States Military Academy, 137-8, 177-9, 198-200, 254-5, 274-7, 280-1, 290-1, 312-324, 409-11, 426-7,

Valentino, Rudolph, 315, 353
Vanderbilt, Cornelius, 45, 53
Vaughan, Robert "Pete," 103, 164, 310-11
Veblen, Thorstein, 33, 57
Venuti, Joe, 376
Vergara, George, 278, 305
Vidal, Gene, 151, 199
Voll, Bernard, 5
VonGammon, Richard, 72
VonRichthofen, R.M., 181
Voss, Norway, 11-14

Wabash College, 127-8
Waddell, Rube, 69-70
Wagner, Hube, 125
Walker, Fred "Mysterious," 250, 360
Walker, Jimmy, 6, 437
Wallace, Frank, 6, 304, 320, 410
Walsh, Adam, 1-2, 306, 309, 319, 320, 345, 418
Walsh, Charles "Chile," 306
Walsh, Christy, 304, 399
Walsh, Davis. 320, 343
Walsh, Rev. Matthew, 203, 226, 279-80, 295, 299-301, 345, 354-55, 271-72, 380-82, 396
Walstead, Rev. John N., 79, 131, 321
Ward, Arch, 157, 304
Ward, Leo "Red," 6, 353
Warner, Glenn "Pop," 4, 138, 168, 235, 249, 304, 349
Weibel, John, 307
Wells, Ida B., 33
Westerstraat, George B., 101
White, Alma, 186
White, J. Andrew, 51, 318

White, William A., 455
White, William, L., 455-57
Whiteman, Paul, 376-77
Whitney, Caspar, 52
Wieslander, 133
Wilce, John, 412
Wilcox, Percy, 231, 244, 265
Willard, Frances, 136
Willenbrandt, Mabel-Walker, 408
Williams, Cy, 117
Williams, Dr. Henry L., 59, 118, 137, 172
Wilson, Gwynn, 334
Wilson, Harry "Light Horse," 315, 367
Wilson, Ralph "Sap," 127-8
Wilson, Woodrow, 134-5, 179-80, 198
Wisconsin, University of, 148
Wood, Gen. Leonard, 155, 180
Woodruff, George, 59

Woodruff, Harvey, 6
World's Columbian Exposition, 12, 34-38, 41-49
Wright, Orville, 47, 95-96
Wright, Wilbur, 47, 95-96
Wright, Frank Lloyd, 47
Wyatt, Jay, 6
Wynne, Chet, 5, 237, 239

Yale University, 50-56, 58-59, 74, 169-171
Yarr, Tommy, 6
Yost, Fielding, 91, 103, 113-4, 235, 381-2, 395

Zahm, Rev. James, 226
Ziegfeld, Carl, 30
Ziegfeld, Florenz Jr., 30, 43
Ziegfeld, Florenz Sr., 30
Zuppke, Bob, 249

# About The Author

Jim Lefebvre is an award-winning journalist, author, speaker, and sports historian. His first book, *Loyal Sons: The Story of The Four Horsemen and Notre Dame Football's 1924 Champions,* reeived three national honors for excellence. Both *Loyal Sons* and *Coach For A Nation* were awarded bronze medals from the *Independent Publisher* Book Awards (IPPYs). Jim writes at *Forever Irish*, www.NDFootballHistory.com.

Jim is the proud father of two University of Notre Dame graduates—daughters Kerry (B.A., 2007) and Elizabeth (B.A., 2009).

Jim speaks to groups around the country, including Notre Dame alumni and friends, coaches clinics, historical societies, and business and civic organizations. To schedule Jim for a speaking engagement, please email info@CoachForANation.com